W9-ARZ-099

THEOLOGICAL INVESTIGATIONS

Volume XV

THEOLOGICAL INVESTIGATIONS

VOLUME XV
PENANCE IN THE EARLY CHURCH

by
KARL RAHNER

Translated by Lionel Swain

CROSSROAD · NEW YORK

1982

The Crossroad Publishing Company
575 Lexington Avenue, New York, NY 10022

A translation of
SCHRIFTEN ZUR THEOLOGIE, XI
Frühe Bussgeschichte in Einzeluntersuchungen

First published 1982

Library of Congress Catalog Card Number: 82-71546
ISBN: 0-8245-0025-3

Printed in the U.S.A.

CONTENTS

Preface vii

Abbreviations x

PART ONE *Introduction* 1

1 The History of Penance 3
2 Sin as Loss of Grace in Early Church Literature 23

PART TWO *The Roman Tradition* 55

3 The Penitential Teaching of the Shepherd of Hermas 57
4 The Post-baptismal Forgiveness of Sins in the Regula Fidei of Irenaeus 114

PART THREE *The African Tradition* 123

5 Tertullian's Theology of Penance 125
6 The Penitential Teaching of Cyprian of Carthage 152

PART FOUR *The Tradition of the East* 223

7 Penitential Teaching and Practice According to the Didascalia Apostolorum 225
8 The Penitential Teaching of Origen 246

Notes 329

Bibliography 433

Index 447

PREFACE

In this book the reader will find gathered together the studies which I have made on the history of the practice and of the theology of penance in the early Church. It is true that these essays hail from an earlier period of my theological work; but I do not think that they have been outdated. For, on the one hand, historical work on the questions considered in this volume has hardly made any progress in the last two decades. (It is remarkable, for instance, that J. Grotz's major study, which appeared in 1955, has not been anywhere critically examined on the matter of its theses which represent a radical challenge to the notion of the history of penance which has become traditional since Poschmann.) On the other hand, the essays in their present form have been thoroughly revised, and the reader is made conversant with the literature which has appeared up to today on the history of penance. The essays in this book are on the *history* of penance. Systematic studies on the theology of penance are not included here, especially since a large number of them have already appeared in previous volumes of *Theological Investigations* (cf. 'Forgotten Truths Concerning the Sacrament of Penance', II, 135–74; 'Guilt and Its Remission: The Borderland between Theology and Psychotherapy', II, 265–81; 'The Meaning of Frequent Confession of Devotion', III, 177–89; 'Problems concerning Confession', III, 190–206; 'Guilt—Responsibility—Punishment Within the View of Catholic Theology', VI, 197–217; 'Justified and Sinner at the Same Time', VI, 218–30; 'Penance as an Additional Act of Reconciliation within the Church', X, 125–41—to mention but a few of the studies which deal with these questions directly and explicitly) or are easily accessible in my other works (for example, in *Sendung und Gnade: Handbuch der*

Pastoraltheologie, etc.). This fifteenth volume of *Theological Investigations* obviously differs very basically, therefore, from the previous volumes: whereas the previous volumes contained explicitly only systematic studies, this fifteenth volume contains only studies on the history of dogma and of theology. Nevertheless, I think that it is justified to present these historical researches together as a volume of *Theological Investigations,* because all the volumes of these writings are collections of my brief researches on specific points and they all bear a sub-title which marks them off from one another and thus makes each individual volume into a self-contained unit. I consider, therefore, that this collection of individual studies, *Penance in the Early Church,* can form a volume in the whole series.

The introduction of the volume into this series has, however—I must 'confess'—yet another reason. I am suspected by many people of being only a speculative theologian who works without reference to history and who, in some circumstances, attempts to dispel difficulties which arise in understanding statements of the Church's magisterium by the merely speculative interpretation of such statements. I am absolutely convinced that genuine Catholic theology must always proceed on the basis both of exegesis and of the history of dogmas and theology, even if it must be the free choice of the individual theologian whether, in a study of a particular point, he wishes to work 'speculatively' or 'historically'. It is possible, therefore, that the present volume will dispel the suspicion that I have no appreciation of historical theology.

In fact the themes of this volume show that today's theory and practice of church penance will not make any progress without a continually new confrontation with their own history. For example, questions concerning the nature of the mortal sins which must necessarily be submitted to the sacrament of penance in the form of a detailed confession, concerning the ecclesial aspect of penance and the sacrament of penance, concerning the nature of the so-called penitential service, etc. (cf., for example, my essay *'Bussandacht und Einzelbeichte'*: StdZ 190 (1972) 363–72), cannot be answered without a thorough study of the history of church penance. It is for this reason that the patristic studies in this volume are preceded by a brief survey of the history of penance as a whole. This context serves to clarify the significance and the distinctiveness of the view of each of the Fathers considered.

The revision of these essays is due to the necessary previous help of several friends and pupils. I wish to name expressly here: Herrn Dr Leo Karrer (Münster), Frau Dr Helga Modesto (München) and Fraulein Marlies Mugge (Hannover). My special obligation to P. K.-H. Neufeld is evident from the title of the book. Finally, I wish also to thank most sincerely Herrn Professor Dr Paul Mikat, who, as director of the Görres-Gesellschaft, energetically expedited the publication of this volume.

Karl Rahner

ABBREVIATIONS

Antonianum	*Antonianum*. Rome 1926 ff.
Bijdragen	*Bijdragen. Tijdschrift voor Filosofie en Theologie*. Nijmegen 1938 ff.
CCHL	*Corpus Christianorum seu nova Patrum collectio*. Turnhout/Paris 1953 ff.
CSL	*Corpus scriptorum ecclesiasticorum latinorum*. Vienna 1866 ff.
D	H. Denziger, *Enchiridion Symbolorum, Definitionum et Declarationum de rebus fidei et morum*. Freiburg/Br. [30]1955.
DACL	*Dictionnaire d'archéologie chrétienne et de liturgie*, ed. F. Chabrol and H. Leclercq. Paris 1924–53.
DS	H. Denziger and A. Schönmetzer, *Enchiridion Symbolorum, Definitionum et Declarationum de rebus fidei et morum*. Freiburg/Br. [34]1967.
DThC	*Dictionnaire de théologie catholique*, ed. A. Vacant and E. Mangenot, cont. by E. Amann. Paris 1903 ff.
Duchesne LP	*Liber Pontificalis*, ed. L. Duchesne. 2 vol. Paris 1886–92. Reprinted Paris 1955. Vol. 3, ed. C. Vogel, Paris, 1957.
EThL	*Ephemerides Theologicae Lovanienses*. Bruges 1924 ff.
Fischer	J. A. Fischer, *Die Apostolischen Väter*. Munich 1956.
FlorPatr	*Florilegium Patristicum*, ed. J. Zellinger and B. Geyer. Bonn 1904 ff.
FStud	*Frankiskanische Studien (Münster)*. Werl 1914 ff.
GCS	*Die Griechischen christlichen Schrifsteller der ersten drei Jahrhunderte*. Leipzig (since the Second World War, Berlin) 1897 ff.
Gr	*Gregorianum*. Rome 1920 ff.
GuL	*Geist und Leben*. (See ZAM.)
HDG	*Handbuch der Dogmengeschichte*, ed. M. Schmaus, J. Geiselmann, A. Grillmeier. Freiburg/Br. 1951 ff.
HdKG	*Handbuch der Kirchengeschichte*, ed. H. Jedin. 6 vols. Freiburg/Br., Basel, Vienna 1962 ff.
Hennecke	*Neutestamentliche Apokryphen in deutscher Übersetzung*, ed. E. Hennecke. Tübingen [2]1924.
HPTh	*Handbuch der Pastoraltheologie*, ed. Fr X. Arnold, K. Rahner, V. Schurr, L. M. Weber. 5 vols. Freiburg/Br. 1964–72.
HThG	*Handbuch theologischer Grundbegriffe*, ed. H. Fries. 2 vols. Munich 1962–3.
IER	*The Irish Ecclesiastical Record*. Dublin 1864 ff.
JThS	*The Journal of Theological Studies*. London 1899 ff.

König W	*Religionswissenschaftliches Wörterbuch,* ed. Fr König. Freiburg/Br. 1956.
LThK	*Lexicon für Theologie und Kirche.* 2nd fully rev. edn ed. J. Höfer, K. Rahner. 10 vols. Freiburg/Br. 1957–67.
Mansi	J. D. Mansi, *Sacrorum conciliorum nova et amplissima collectio.* 31 vols. Florence/Venice 1757–98. Reprinted and ed. L. Petit, J.-B. Martin. 60 vols. Paris 1899–1927.
Meyers Kom.	*Kritisch-exegetischer Kommentar über das Neue Testament,* founded by H. A. W. Meyer. 16 vols. Göttingen 1832 ff. (several edns).
MThZ	*Münchener Theologische Zeitschrift.* Munich 1950 ff.
NTD	*Das Neue Testament Deutsch.* ed. P. Althaus, J. Behm (Neues Göttinger Bibelwerk), Göttingen, 1932 ff. (several edns).
PG	*Patrologia Graeca,* ed. J.-P. Migne. 161 vols. Paris 1857–66
PL	*Patrologia Latina,* ed. J.-P. Migne. 217 vols. and 4 vols. index. Paris 1844–55
QD	*Quaestiones Disputatae,* ed. K. Rahner, H. Schlier. Freiburg/Br. 1958 ff.
QS	J. Maier, *Die Texte vom Toten Meer.* 2 vols. Munich/Basel 1960.
RAC	*Reallexicon für Antike und Christentum,* ed. T. Klauser. Stuttgart 1941, 1950 ff.
RBén	*Revue bénédictine.* Maredsous 1884 ff.
RET	*Revista Española de teologia.* Madrid 1941 ff.
RHE	*Revue d'histoire ecclésiastique.* Lyon 1900 ff.
RHLR	*Revue d'histoire et de littérature religieuse.* Paris 1896–1907, 1910 ff.
RHR	*Revue de l'histoire des religions.* Paris 1880 ff.
RNT	*Regensburger Neues Testament,* ed. A. Wikenhauser, O. Kuss. 10 vols. Regensburg 1938 ff.
RQH	*Revue de questions historiques.* Paris 1866 ff.
RSR	*Recherches de science religieuse.* Paris 1910 ff.
RThAM	*Recherches de Théologie ancienne et médiévale.* Louvain 1929 ff.
Sacramentum Mundi	*Sacramentum Mundi. Theologisches Lexicon für die Praxis,* ed. K. Rahner, A. Darlap et al. 4 vols. Freiburg/Br. 1967–9.
SC	*Sources Chretiennes,* ed. H. de Lubac and J. Daniélou. Paris/Lyon 1941 ff.
Scholastik	*Scholastik.* Freiburg/Br. 1926 ff. (Since 1966 *Theologie und Philosophie* = ThPh.)
Strack-Billerbeck	H. L. Strack and P. Billerbeck, *Kommentar zum Neuen Testament aus Talmud und Midrasch,* I–IV. Munich 1922–8, reprinted 1956. V (*Rabbinischer Index*), ed. J. Jeremias, K. Adolph. Munich 1956.
ThGl	*Theologie und Glaube.* Paderborn 1909 ff.
ThPh	*Theologie und Philosophie.* (See Scholastik.)
ThQ	*Theologische Quartalschrift.* Tübingen 1819 ff., Stuttgart 1946 ff.
ThRv	*Theologische Revue.* Münster 1902 ff.
ThSt	*Theological Studies.* Baltimore 1940 ff.
ThW	*Theologisches Wörterbuch zum Neuen Testament,* ed. N. G. Kittel, cont. by G. Friedrich. Stuttgart 1933 ff.
TU	*Teste und Untersuchungen zur Geschichte der altchristlichen Literatur. Archiv für die griechisch-christlichen Schriftsteller der ersten drei Jahrhunderte.* Lepzig/Berlin 1882 ff.

VS	*Verbum Salutis. Commentaire du Nouveau Testament,* ed. J. Huby, S. Lyonnet. Paris 1924 ff. (several edns).
WA	M. Luther, *Werke. Kritische Gesamtausgabe* (*'Weimarer Ausgabe'*). 1883 ff.
Wasserschleben	H. Wasserschleben, *Die Bussordnungen der abendländischen Kirche*. Halle 1851 (reprinted Graz 1947).
ZAM	*Zeitschrift für Aszese und Mystik* (Innsbruck, Munich). Würzburg 1926 ff. (Since 1947 *Geist und Leben* = GuL.)
ZKG	*Zeitschrift für Kirchengeschichte* (Gotha). Stuttgart 1876 ff.
ZKTh	*Zeitschrift für Katholische Theologie* (Innsbruck). Vienna 1877 ff.
ZNW	*Zeitschrift für die neutestamentliche Wissenschaft und die Kunde der älteren Kirche*. Giessen 1900 ff., Berlin 1934 ff.

PART ONE

Introduction

1

THE HISTORY OF PENANCE

At first sight, the notion of the 'history of penance' appears to be clear and comprehensible. Upon closer examination, however, its meaning becomes increasingly complicated. This is because penance itself, and when it is properly considered, is always essentially a historical phenomenon, since it implies alteration and change. Although there are other kinds of penance, the one with which we are concerned here is the Christian penance which we have frequently attempted to survey in contributions to various dictionaries.[1] For this reason it is obvious that very little new material is offered here. Indeed it would be useful and desirable for the reader of the present volume to have ready access to such a comprehensive treatment. It is only in the wider theological and historical context that the meaning of these studies will be fully understood and that they will be able to produce an impact far beyond that of a particular theme of the history of dogma, capable of interesting only a small number of specialists.

I. EXPLANATION OF THE NOTION AND OUTLINE OF THE PROBLEM

Penance is primarily and generally speaking man's moral and religious attitude in reaction to sin, given by Christ's grace. It is conversion to God and aversion from sin. Its specific and central act is sorrow, but, in addition, in its various forms it includes essentially absolutely all the interior and exterior attitudes of the Christian towards what is called sin. It is evident, therefore, that a more precise notion of penance will correspond to the notion of sin and the nature of justification. In the Christian view both sin and justification presuppose the effective revealing word of God himself. For his part, man must respond to his word with a zeal both for the fear of God and for his own authentic existence, despite all 'suppression'. This zeal, in its turn, is due to previous grace. It is only in this way that man can have the right attitude towards his past and with a willingness which is itself a gratuitous gift allow God's revealing word to destroy in him pharisaic self-righteousness and convince him of sin. As for the future, this experience produces the decision to renounce the permanent menace of sin and the determination to fight against it with the biblical means of prayer, fasting, almsgiving, etc.[2] In the effort to change his ways man places his confidence in God's grace which proves itself victorious in human weakness but is opposed by the desire and the world that is concupiscence. All this is naturally accompanied by the readiness to receive the sacrament of the forgiveness of sins as well as to suffer the consequences of sin. Likewise, it calls for cooperation in the fight against sin in the Church and the world, sharing in the burden of sin as it becomes manifest in misfortune and need and the intention to make satisfaction and expiation.

As all other Christian activity, this response to God's revealing word derives from God's unmerited grace and it is a tangible accomplishment of justifying faith and a participation in Christ's cross. The fact that, in the Christian view, sin is a *free* act of man and is guilt before *God* and that, conversely, penance is also man's freely undertaken aversion from his guilty act is not altered by the dependance of penance upon grace. Precisely because penance is necessary for salvation—it is the way in which God's free mercy grants salvation to the free creature[3]—its notion includes the freedom of the saving act; penance is the act of man which, nevertheless, clearly shows that it is God's action upon us that forgives sins and not sorrow, in so far as this sorrow on our part can and must be distinguished from God's activity.

In the Bible this attitude and its many expressions are covered by the notion of 'metanoia', the change of attitude, which is expressed and explained in tangible acts. For Christians this is first and foremost the radical decision which is expressed in baptism. Although, in this case, the notion may be less explicit there is here an act of penance which, nevertheless, both according to the Church's tradition and of its very nature happens only once. This uniqueness is peculiar to the attitude of penance which is expressed in baptism. And this gives rise to the problem of relating the continuing, permanent attitude of Christian penance with the unique, definitive character of baptism. For there can be no doubt that when Scripture refers to penance it is always a matter of tangible, expressed acts and never exclusively of a purely interior attitude which would not be expressed exteriorly. Moreover, there is no reason to deny that even after baptism radical sins can be committed which can be countered only by a correspondingly radical act of penance. But this raises the question of the possibility of such an act of penance after baptism. If our view is correct, this possibility did exist at the time of the New Testament,[4] and it is here that the foundations of the Church's public treatment of this question lie. For it is reflected precisely in the New Testament in the form of a clear distinction between the universal exhortation to repentance and the proclamation that all sins are forgiven by God. Both are connected, however, since the whole being and activity of the Church is a denial of sin. The Church comes into its own as the judging and forgiving presence of Christ in a world of sin by the ministry of reconciliation, by exhorting men to allow themselves to be reconciled with God by God himself.[5] For man this entails a movement towards a new life, beginning with his conviction as a sinner in a variety of ways: in baptism as the basic sacrament of forgiveness,[6] in the celebration of the Eucharist as the memorial and proclamation of the Lord's death for the forgiveness of guilt,[7] in the Church's own confession of guilt,[8] in penance with prayer and fasting,[9] in concern for the concrete situation of the individual by prayer for the sinner,[10] in fraternal correction,[11] in the 'ostracization of the sinner' by an official,[12] if the fraternal exhortation has no effect, by an official reprimand[13] and, finally, by the act of the Church which is its strongest judging or, more properly, forgiving reaction to sin: the binding and the loosing of the sinner.

Just as, therefore, according to Scripture there are sins of the baptized—although it has not yet been considered how these sins are precisely described and classified—so according to the New Testament and the early Church there is a forgiveness of these sins. The idea that there is only one definitive forgiveness of guilt in baptism and that every subsequent sin is either unforgivable or simply already forgiven by baptism in anticipation is entirely foreign to the New Testament. Just as sin or, more precisely, *sinning* can exist after baptism as something which need not and should not have happened, so there is also a forgiveness of sins *after* baptism. This is a new occurrence of God's grace, distinct from baptism, which, although it was promised in baptism, is still a *grace* and, therefore, cannot be derived from baptism with mechanical certainty but remains a new occurrence. Despite its high esteem of baptism, the New Testament recognizes that Christians do commit sins—from the every-day faults due to our weakness to scandals which do not occur even among pagans, including the perversion of the truth of the gospel and the reversion to paganism or Judaism.

II. THE HISTORY OF CHRISTIAN PENANCE

1. The Teaching of Scripture

But what is the basis for the Church's official attitude towards sin? For Catholic theology this relationship originates in an official authorization of the leaders of the community by Jesus which represents a specific and new expression of the effective proclamation of forgiveness to baptized Christians and which, therefore, according to Catholic understanding, provides the basis of specific sacrament independent of baptism.

In order to establish this teaching, the Council of Trent appealed principally to John 20 as the classical text for the institution of the sacrament of penance.[14] In my opinion, however, John's witness becomes much clearer and more enlightening in the setting of the life of the earliest community if Matthew 16 and 18 are taken as the starting-point. Moreover, this approach rejoins an old tradition; for, from the penitential controversies in Tertullian's day to the high Middle Ages, Matthew 16 and 18 were more frequently and explicitly adduced as the basis of the power of the keys in the sacrament of penance than was John 20. Indeed in the tradition the power of the keys was considered to be the power to forgive sins.

Furthermore, this practice has antecedents in the practice of imposing a ban found in the synagogues and in the 'Rule of the Sect'[15] of Qumran, although its proper nature in the Christian setting can be determined only by the self-consciousness of the 'church' of Jesus, given by the Lord and its unity with him, precisely because of the institution of this new covenant. Because the Church is holy it must react with the ban against a member's sin which is incompatible with its own nature.[16]

Admission into the Church through baptism and reconciliation with it is the expression of reconciliation with God. Now, both in theory and in practice such a power for binding and loosing in the Church must be expected from the beginning. It is, therefore, irrelevant to ask how far the direct statements in Matthew 16 and 18 are influenced by the 'theology of the community'.

In fact, according to Matthew 16 and 18, the apostles and Peter, as those authorized by Jesus to be leaders of the Church, possess the power so 'to bind and to loose' that a corresponding act has validity also in 'heaven'. The idea that the sentence of an earthly judge has an effect in the other world in God's eyes was widespread at that time.[17] In this regard, the demonological background—in the original and generally accepted sense of this term—should not be overlooked.[18] Nevertheless, Matthew 18 shows very clearly that it is a matter of the power to impose or to lift a ban with regard to a brother who, by his behaviour, radically and obstinately opposes the nature of Jesus' community or who, conversely, wishes to be reconciled with it again. It is the authority to impose an exclusion which has real meaning before God and which places the guilty person outside the community of salvation that is the Church. Conversely, it is the authority to allow readmission into the Church which has meaning before God and which delivers man from the damning power of the devil. Thus the saving power of loosing has in fact the effect of forgiving the sins on account of which the ban was imposed. From the very nature of the case, this authority in the community can belong only to the authorized leaders of the Church, although their exercise of it is the act of the Church.[19] Provided that the notion of an effective, revelatory, that is, sacramental word, according to which what is said to a person happens to him, is not totally eliminated from the theology of the New Testament, the effect of this authority for man's salvation presents no more difficulties than the word of baptism or that of the eucharistic celebration.

What is said in Matthew in more archaic expressions recurs in John 20:19–23 in a more familiar formulation. This latter coincides perfectly with Jesus' manner of speaking and is not at all specifically 'Johannine'. In order to continue Jesus' mission the apostles, and they alone, are endowed with the authority either to forgive[20] or to retain the sins of individuals (τινων τὰς ἁμαρτίας). Both of these actions do not merely express an already presupposed fact but have as a consequence that it really *is* before God as the apostles say. This authority to decide between two possible courses of action, each having its own effect, cannot be identified either with the commission to preach the gospel of reconciliation to all men or the authority to baptize.[21] It must, therefore, here be a matter of what the text says: the authority exercised in a judicial decision either to forgive a member of the Church his sins so effectively that they are thereby also forgiven in God's eyes or to allow them to become effective as the cause of the ban. If the Church is not merely an external religious organization but the body of Christ[22] alive with the Spirit, then the loss of grace through sin entails necessarily also a change in the (continuing) relationship of the sinner to the Church. This change is 'confirmed' by the ban in the form of an exclusion from the Eucharist in every case of mortal sin.

2. *The Teaching of the Fathers of the Church*

The second century marks the end of the apostolic age.[23] It is in Hermas that we have the first theological reflection on this practice, although couched in obscure imagery. As long as the Church of this time is still developing, the person who, as a sinner, has alienated himself from it is able to be reinçorporated into it and so find salvation.[24] In view of the imminent end of the world Hermas proclaims just one further possible penance, but he is by no means the first to open up this possibility, as if it did not exist previously. Hermas' once and for all penance[25] was subsequently detached from its original basis and became a principle of penitential practice, in the West for the whole of the patristic age,[26] although in the East only in Alexandria.[27] It did not, however, become a dogmatic principle. This tenet was later justified as a rule against a certain laxity within the Church, but without thereby depriving the sinner who falls again of the possibility of salvation. Neither in Hermas[28] nor elsewhere[29] are schismatics, heretics or fornicators who are truly contrite excluded from reconciliation with the Church. There is no indication of capital sins which are fundamentally unforgivable. If one wished to introduce into the practice and theory of Christian penance in the second century the distinction between a forgiveness which is granted by God and one which is refused by the Church for its own legal reasons this would be purely arbitrary. Where the Church recognizes that God forgives, there it also recognizes its own right to grant full church forgiveness. And the view that God always forgives the person who is repentant is in evidence everywhere. This does not exclude the fact that, in the question of reconciliation or its refusal, individual Churches proceeded exceptionally according their own norm whereby they maintained that the proof of subjective repentance is seldom reached very quickly and brought to bear aspects of church discipline which, according to the contemporary view, made readmission into the Church appear to be impossible, even given previous repentance. This explains why individual Churches[30] well into the fourth century refuse reconciliation to certain sinners in particular instances, even when this is not clearly demanded by the subjective unrepentance of the sinner. Nevertheless, the dogmatic question appeared only when the Church's *right* to reconcile those guilty of capital sins was contested as a matter of *principle*. In general, the refusal of one (first and final) reconciliation even on the death-bed[31] was tantamount to the cruelty associated with the Novatianists. Nevertheless, even the case of Cerdon[32] does not prove that the West recognized the possibility of several reconciliations.

The third century is marked by the two Western heresies on the subject of penance: Tertullian's Montanism and Novatianism. Neither of these is to be seen as the defence of an old radical rigorism against a gradual erosion of the unforgivable nature of capital sins (impurity, murder, apostasy). Rather, Tertullian invents the theory which elevates the old possibility of a practical-disciplinary rigorism to the absolute dogmatic obligation to exclude permanently those guilty of capital sins. In reaction to this, the Catholics appeal to the parallel with baptism,[33] to ancient practice and to the authorization by Christ according to Matthew 18.[34] They define their ancient practice in dogmatic-deliberated declarations as in a decree of the metropolitan of Carthage and in the conclusions of the synods of Carthage[35] and Rome about the middle of the third century.[36] Apart from being a defence against Novatian, the lengthy and detailed synodal legislation in Cyprian's Africa is concerned not with the question of a fundamental possibility of reconciliation for apostates but with the practical administration of penance in different cases, as with the length of the period of penance, speedy reconciliation in danger of death, before martyrdom, etc. In the controversy between Hippolytus and Pope Callistus there seems only to have been a question of Callistus readmitting schismatic Christians to the Church without further performance of penance, while not enquiring whether they had committed other sins when they were in schism.[37] Moreover, the liturgy of Hippolytus recognizes that the bishop, in virtue of Christ's authorization of his apostles, can loosen *every* bond of evil.[38]

At this time also the *form of penance* is the penance of excommunication. The Church establishes that a person is a sinner and that he has, therefore, placed himself in opposition to the Church. Thus he is at least excluded from the Eucharist. If he confesses his sins privately before a bishop—which may be simply a way of inquiring whether his sins are really mortal sins and, therefore, have to be submitted to the penance of the Church[39]—and if he is truly sorry, then he is admitted to church penance proper. This access is already a sign of the Church's favour, but it is not yet reconciliation with the Church. The penitent is singled out by his dress, by his particular place in the celebration of the liturgy and by penitential obligations, such as fasting, etc. After some time he is reconciled with the Church by an imposition of hands on the part of the bishop (and of the clergy), accompanied by prayer and in the East sometimes even by an anointing which later evokes the idea of a repetition of confirmation. The performance of penance lasts different lengths of time: sometimes it comes to an end only on the death-bed,[40] but it could last only two weeks. In the latter case it would probably be preceded by a period of personal reform.[41] The necessity of a long-lasting personal penance was based on the not very clear idea that only baptism which is received once and for all is pure remission by grace (ἄφεσις) and that, therefore, later sins 'cannot be *forgiven* in the Church'[42] in this sense. Rather, such sins are to be expiated by the performance of personal penance (μετάνοια) before God.[43]

There is a clear awareness of the *sacramental nature* of church penance, in so far as the necessity of public church penance is stressed,[44] reconciliation with the official Church is considered necessary for salvation,[45] even for martyrs, and the renewed bestowal of the Holy Spirit is ascribed to the rite of reconciliation and not to subjective penance.[46] The access to the reconciliation with the Church, which itself reconciles men with God, is brought about by the bishop.[47] The intercession of confessors supports the sinners' personal penance and may, therefore, help to expedite reconciliation, but—given the definite episcopal structure of the Church at this time—it could not deprive the bishop of the last word. There is no trace of a 'private' sacramental penance. But the degree to which the official penance is made public may vary according to the circumstances. The effectiveness of reconciliation before God is explained with reference either to the infallibly efficacious prayer of the Church[48] or to the Church's authorization by Christ,[49] without a precise definition as to whether it is a matter either of the forgiveness of sins or of the communication of the Spirit. Sinners who are clerics are treated at this time still as other sinners. In theory it is recognized that all sins which destroy the grace of baptism should be submitted to church penance.[50] In practice, however, because of the difficulty of church penance and the view that it cannot be repeated, it is especially capital sins that require penance in this sense, although these sins are taken very broadly. Thus it is not only a question of apostasy, murder and adultery.[51]

In the following high patristic age it is above all the great legislative activity of synods, bishops (especially in the East) and popes in questions of penitential discipline that should be underlined. In the East are elaborated stages of penance, that is, a gradual exclusion or, conversely, readmission with regard to the liturgy and the Eucharist.[52] In the West there are also elaborated lasting consequences for the period after reconciliation, for example, the prohibition of marital intercourse, the interdiction of occupations which present a danger to morals, the impossibility of becoming a cleric.[53] Thus the duration of the actual period of penance becomes irrelevant and in the West it seems to be blended with Lent when, perhaps after a successful conversion, the actual church, liturgical celebration of penance was incorporated into the beginning of Lent.[54]

Nevertheless, the external form of the penitential discipline is, as previously, the penance of excommunication. There is no form of a truly private sacramental kind either in the *correptio secreta* (= the dispensing with public liturgical reprimand, while it remains unclear whether church penance itself is abandoned because it is not practicable or whether the usual *paenitentia publica* is carried out without this reprimand)[55] or in other practices which are only adaptations of the one *paenitentia publica* to particular circumstances.[56] In any case, these practices do not appear to be sacramental. The sins which are subject to this penance are the same as before. In particular, the penitential legislation of the East makes it clear that the notion of capital sins should not be taken too narrowly but means everything that even today would normally be considered subjectively serious sin.

The West maintains even more radically that there is only a single possibility of church penance.[57] Here and there this principle is toned down by the clever use of casuistry in borderline cases.[58] In practice penance is more and more postponed to the death-bed and this practice is even approved;[59] synods[60] warn against undertaking church penance before a mature age, since this—because of the once and for all nature and the lasting consequences of church penance—would be bound to lead to insoluble conflicts.

Gradually special forms of penance are elaborated, such as penance for clerics, which consists of deposition from office (without a further performance of penance) and admission to the community of the laity,[61] or particular ways of reconciling heretics who, having been such from their birth, are reconciled by an imposition of hands without a further performance of penance.[62] Although here generally there is no explicit mention that a sacrament is involved, this is clearly attested with regard to penance. The Church is able to reconcile *all* contrite sinners; since Nicea[63] Novatianism is clearly tantamount to heresy and is explicitly attacked by the Fathers. In this controversy Christ's authorization of the Church to forgive is underlined and confirmed by the parallel with baptism.[64] Penance and reconciliation remit sins.[65] There is an awareness that both the public and the secret destroying of the relationship to the Church by sin is a forfeiting of salvation. Thus there is often an anxious effort to achieve reconciliation with the Church just before death.[66] In so far as the Church's activity is explained not only with reference to Christ's commission, the *pax cum ecclesia* is considered the means of reconciliation with God. Reconciliation always means reconciliation with the Church and, therefore, the 'deprecatory formula of absolution' is to be regarded rather as the Church's support of subjective penance by its prayer.[67] The act of the bishop, in his official capacity, reincorporates the penitent fully into the Church, where he receives the Holy Spirit, in so far as it is the Church of the *sancti spirituales*.[68] This applies even when the official is without the Spirit and, therefore, cannot himself give the Spirit. Occasionally[69] there may appear a purely declaratory view of the Church's activity, although in such texts it is not simply the subjective penance that is stressed as the necessary precondition of effective reconciliation.

With the end of the patristic age the transition to the new system of repeated 'auricular confession' becomes increasingly evident. In theory even now the ancient 'public' penance of excommunication remains in force. It is upheld, for instance, by the synod of Toledo in A.D. 589. But it is imposed by the Church, so long as the sinner is healthy, only in cases of public scandal. Generally it is received on the death-bed as penance of the sick. From the sixth century this then becomes the custom, indeed the legal obligation,[70] for all Christians, including the saints.[71] This death-bed penance loses its defamatory character, even though it is really only a secondary form of public penance. Where this public penance still takes place, the form, duration and obligations are the same as previously. Nevertheless, from the middle of the fifth century exceptional cases are made to perform penance in special groups after the fashion of the Eastern penitential stages.[72] At this time excommunication appears in some cases as a mere ecclesiastical penalty, separate from the whole of church penance, to be imposed and lifted independently without the involvement of actual church penance. This church penance remains to be performed on the death-bed after the excommunication has been lifted.[73] In the seventh century Spanish councils still refer to lasting consequences to which those who have undertaken penance are committed. Only when penance has been undertaken without necessity (that is, not in danger of death) can such a 'penitent' still become a cleric.[74]

From the sixth century in the islands of the Irish-Anglo-Saxon region, and from the beginning with the knowledge that this was different from the continental practice, church penance is not practised once and for all.[75] This fact has not yet been fully explained with regard to its causes (the impracticability of the lasting consequences, the influence of monastic confession, etc.), but as a datum it is indisputable. Once given this practice, it was, on the one hand, impossible to impose a penance which had life-long consequences while, on the other hand, it was possible to subject less serious sins to church penance. It may very well be that these considerations actually gave rise to the practice.

In any case it was in this way that the performance of penance was able to be effective in life itself and not only on the death-bed. The sacrament could, therefore, again be productive in life itself without the necessity to change much of the ancient practice or theory. There was an awareness of the connection with the old form of church penance, all the more so as the early Church's legislation on the times for doing penance, on the duties, etc., were applied to the new form. The only innovation was that the repeated absolution was granted in a simple form by the priest and not in the solemn form by the bishop. Moreover, it was possible on any day and no longer only on Shrove Tuesday. In this sense also it was no longer 'public'. The frequency of confession and the variety of sins which were mentioned in confession necessitated a modification of the obligations which were imposed in penance. The old times for doing penance and the demands made upon the penitents had to be commuted and given substitutes, and thus originated the new kind of book used in the celebration of penance. In the seventh century, with the Irish-Scottish mission, the new system of penance came to the Continent.[76] In any event, the penitential of Columban[77] shows that it was there. Since the old form was practised almost only as penance of the dying, the new form had hardly any opposition. The penance books show that in the eighth century the new practice had spread all over the Continent.

3. The Theology of the Sacrament of Penance in Theologians Since the Twelfth Century

For the further development it is obvious that only a few basic trends and themes can be suggested.

Since the time when the currently accepted notion of the sacrament gave rise to the teaching that there were only seven sacraments, that is, about the middle of the twelfth century, penance also belongs to their number. Alger of Lüttich[78] already cites penance under *his* notion of sacrament; Robert Pullus[79] attempts an explicit proof of its sacramental nature. Where the contemporary notion of sacrament is present—in the *Sententiae divinitatis,* in Simon Magister and the glossators of Gratian's Decree—penance is expressly taught as a sacrament. In local synods of the first decades of the thirteenth century the teaching is already presupposed as self-evident.[80] Never a doubt, capable of disturbing the practice, arose over the teaching received from the ancient tradition that this sacrament was absolutely *necessary* for those guilty of mortal sins, although this necessity was understood in different ways.[81] This remains true even in spite of certain expressions of the synod of Chalon-sur-Saône[82] which will later be quoted by canonists like Burchard of Worms and Gratian.[83] These expressions refer either to the questionable necessity of private confession, so long as the older form of penance still existed, or to the view that forgiveness was already obtained by sorrow before the still necessary sacrament was received. Nevertheless, individual canonists of the twelfth century questioned whether the *paenitentia solemnis* alone was an actual sacrament. The undisputed acceptance of the sacramental nature of penance did not, however, prevent scholastic theology up to the middle of the thirteenth century (up to Thomas Aquinas) from contesting that the priestly absolution effectively influenced the forgiveness of guilt as such (the *reatus culpae*). All the theologians of the twelfth century are above all convinced that true sorrow obtains the forgiveness of sins before confession.[84] In the period of High Scholasticism, until Thomas Aquinas inclusive, it was, therefore, considered normal, indeed obligatory, that a person should be justified already before the actual reception of the sacrament. This view gave rise to various insufficient theories on the effect of priestly absolution. The declaratory theory[85] teaches: the priestly absolution is the authoritative expression of the forgiveness which has already been given by God alone. Another theory[86] tries to find an effect of absolution in the other world: the Church does not indeed forgive guilt, but remits the eternal punishment[87] or changes God's conditional forgiveness of guilt into an absolute forgiveness.[88] It is first William of Auvergne, Hugo of St-Cher, William of Melitona, Bonaventure, Thomas[89] and subsequently theology in general who allow the forgiveness of sins to be an effect of the sacrament as such. At first they argued from the long-recognized influence which absolution had on sorrow. Now, however, they no longer considered it from this psychological angle. Rather, they saw it as a sacramental cause of grace and thus having an effect on forgiveness, without, however, excluding or neglecting sorrow itself as a cause. The question was further complicated by the different theories (physical-dispositive, intentional-dispositive, effective) of sacramental teaching in general on the effect of the sacraments on grace. Thus until Thomas inclusive the personal and the sacramental events still remain interrelated (grace *for* sorrow). It is only in J. Duns Scotus that absolution effects the 'infusion' of justifying grace when there is present a sufficient sorrow (*attritio*), this being considered a mere moral *pre*condition. In this case the justifying grace is no longer communicated and received by an act which corresponds to its nature (genuine contrition). The theological progress attained in the thirteenth century is, therefore, quite clear and established for the future, although this was at the cost of a proper appreciation of the role of the person in the theology of grace and the sacraments. Following in the footsteps of Thomas Aquinas, theology today ought to rediscover this appreciation.

For Thomas from the beginning, as for an even earlier tradition, the sacramental sign consists of the acts of the penitent, considered as the matter, and the absolution, considered as the form of penance. It is only in the Summa theologica III q. 84 a. I–3; q. 86 a. 6 that he ascribes within this whole an effect of the matter upon grace. *Res et sacramentum* is the *paenitentia interior.*[90] The penitent has to produce such a sorrow[91] that he approaches the reception of the sacrament already justified. If he is lacking this sorrow *bona fide,* although he seriously turns away from sin, then—provided that sin poses no obstacle—his attitude is perfected by the justifying grace given by the sacrament and changed to *contritio: ex attritio fit contritus.*[92] The justifying sorrow must, however, be sustained by the corresponding grace and even consists of the existential acceptance of the infused grace. This grace is communicated by the act of acceptance, and therefore the instrumental causality of the sacramental sign—if it is correctly understood—refers not to an *ornatus animae*[93] but only to the justifying grace itself. Thus the place remains open for *res et sacramentum* in Thomas' terms: either it does not exist as a distinct entity or it must be something other than the *paenitentia interior.* This also fits in well with the fact that in the Summa Thomas seems to have abandoned the dispositive view of the effect of the sacraments on grace in favor of an instrumental-effective view.[94]

In the Patristic period since Tertullian ceremonial confession was already increasingly stressed as a necessary presupposition of the celebration of church penance. Even here, however, there is a development both in theory and in practice. Since the Fathers of the Church considered confession to be rather the natural presupposition for the undertaking of church penance—being the expression of attentiveness and the occasion of exhortation[95]—with the introduction of more frequent penance it becomes noticeable for light and secret sins as well as for the more serious and public ones. Thus confession itself becomes, as it were, an actual penitential work with expiatory value, to such an extent that a further confession is considered to be a penitential obligation. The shame involved in making the confession effects reconciliation for the penitent. Whereas in the early period satisfaction was the basic theme of penance, from the eighth century this becomes the confession; this remains the case, but at the time of the Reformation it received particular emphasis. Penance becomes 'confession'.[96] For a long time the obligation to confess lacked a solid basis and was by no means always justified by the *ex institutione sacramenti* of the Council of Trent.[97] From the twelfth century onwards it is sorrow and its relationship with absolution that becomes the main theme of the scientific-theological study of penance.

It remains to be noted that the whole of early and high scholasticism handed on the teaching of the patristic period, according to which one effect of the sacrament is reconciliation with the Church. This is universally verifiable for the eleventh and the twelfth centuries.[98] This idea is still found in Bonaventure,[99] in Hugo Ripelius' *Compendium theologicae veritatis* and in Thomas,[100] although it later disappears. The doctrine, levelled at Wycliffe and Hus, that the sinner still belongs to the Church, because it was an unqualified generalization, must have obscured this insight. But even Luther was still aware both of the ecclesial aspect of sin and its forgiveness[101] and of its connection with the strictly theological aspect of these realities. Today this idea is clearly becoming increasingly accepted (B. Xiberta, B. Poschmann, M. de la Taille, H. de Lubac, M. Schmaus, et al.) and has been endorsed by Vatican II.[102]

This survey explains the meaning and the significance of the studies contained in this volume. They present, as it were, cross-sections of the institution of penance and of its theology which, at the same time, show in the sources discussed a certain corresponding theoretical and practical position on the attitude towards sin. This result is no substitute for either the systematic or the pastoral-theological and pastoral consideration of penance; for this consideration the reader is here referred to the relevant text-books and manuals. Nevertheless, we consider that research into the history of dogma is not irrelevant to contemporary objective and practical questions in connection with penance. Although this point cannot be developed properly here, it should not be overlooked.

III. RESEARCH INTO THE HISTORY OF PENANCE

Finally, something must be said about a part of the research into the history of dogma; this is because our studies belong to a context which perhaps today is no longer very well known. Moreover, the individual studies originated, more or less, in the discussion with other views,[103] to which we ourselves owe a great deal, both where we have agreed and where we have differed. Every scholar knows that, roughly speaking, about the turn of the century the question of penance belonged to those themes which were most contested in apologetics and theological controversy. Indeed, the institution of penance was taken, not entirely without justification—although this view would need to be modified today—as the key to understanding the Catholic view of the Church, as the basis for the differences in the consideration and the understanding of God's saving work, of man's vocation and freedom, etc., in the not infrequently passionate discussions between Catholic and Protestant theologians. Whereas other questions remained in the background and, in any case, received only occasionally a detailed treatment with the new means of historical research, from the beginning the theme of penance was the centre of attraction. One has to see clearly the role which A. von Harnack, for instance, ascribes to penance, penitential discipline and the sacrament of penance for the development of the Catholic view of the Church and of dogma in *History of Dogma*. Thus it is not surprising if this question held a dominant position in theology up to the end of the First World War. Our bibliography alone should be a sufficient proof of this fact.

It was only in the years between the two World Wars, however, that Catholic theology found, in a certain detachment from immediate controversy, the opportunity for those fundamental studies[104] with which our essays are immediately connected. First of all, B. Poschmann's *Paenitentia secunda*[105] must be mentioned here. This is a huge study in the history of dogma, objective, precise, with a scientific analysis of the individual texts and a creative dependence on previous literature. The preparations began before the First World War. Thus it is a question of a slowly maturing work. Because of this growth, the eventual result was, already in 1940—the year of its publication—not surprisingly new. In the main lines of his development Poschmann adheres to the notion already expounded by Esser, Stufler, d'Alès and Galtier. This involves the clear rejection of the theory that there was ever a time in the Church as a whole when certain sins were totally excluded from the celebration of church penance. Neither Hermas' penitential teaching[106] nor the bishop's decree in Tertullian or the moderation in Cyprian should, therefore, be construed as fundamental alterations with regard to the earlier penitential teaching. The same applies even with regard to the earlier penitential practice. Poschmann, however, examines this view again with reference to the texts and defends it convincingly against recent divergent interpretations of the history of penance (especially by H. Koch). In several secondary questions of the history of dogma Poschmann has been widely accepted by Catholic scholars. Thus today the *episcopus episcoporum* of Tertullian is no longer simply identified with the bishop of Rome, nor is the effort made to discover at this time a sacramental penance which was not *paenitentia publica*. Poschmann also took up Xiberta's insight that the *pax cum ecclesia* is the *res et sacramentum* of divine forgiveness and the means of grace. He has developed this idea with greater historical precision and has shown that, on this assumption, many historical difficulties can be resolved easily and in a way that is dogmatically unobjectionable. Nevertheless, we believe that, by having recourse to Matthew 16 and 18, we have reached a better basis than Poschmann and Xiberta, by which it is also possible to eliminate a certain vague terminology[107] which is found in Poschmann. For the sake of this clarity, one ought not, even in a historical work, simply to refrain from detailed dogmatic references,[108] such as we have made here repeatedly in this survey, without, however, wishing to enter into an actual systematic exposition of penance. In our opinion there is also lacking in Poschmann the clear emphasis on the fact that Christian penance developed primarily and exclusively as *paenitentia publica* with all its external and juridical character. He does not explain either why it took so long to realize which sins cause a loss of the Spirit (of grace) in the individual.[109] It is by reflecting on this question that it becomes understandable how, when the number of such sins was originally so small, the institution of penance assumed a form which, when the number of those sins which were subject to penance increased, could no longer be maintained and therefore had to be changed.

Because of the unfavourable time at which it appeared, Poschmann's work was unable to produce an immediate effect. The shift in emphasis in theological work in general after the war from the historical approach to the more speculative approach prevented two further studies by Poschmann from entering the limelight. Nevertheless, they complete the work of this exponent of the history of penance in the early Church and in the early Middle Ages, and they mark a stage in the research for Catholic theology which even today must still be considered fundamental. In 1948 appeared *Der Ablass im Licht der Bussgeschichte*[110] and three years later *Busse und Letzte Ölung* in the *Handbuch der Dogmengeschichte*.[111] A few appropriate remarks are made here on both of these publications. In the first-mentioned study it is obvious that only the ideas on the history of penance are of interest here, while the application to the history of indulgences lies outside the scope of our present discussions.[112]

In this work Poschmann presents first of all the elements of the early Church's teaching on penance: the necessity of subjective repentance for sins committed after baptism as a factor in the remission of sins, with no distinction made between guilt and punishment; the support of this subjective repentance by the cooperation of the Church (community, martyrs, charismatics, etc.) and, especially, by the intercessory prayer of the priests which must be distinguished from the proper act of reconciliation with the Church and thereby with God, and which should not be construed as absolution with the deprecative formula in the modern sense. Next are considered in detail the nature, the forms and the effects of 'absolutions' in the early Middle Ages, both outside and inside the sacrament of penance. These 'absolutions' are the authentic continuation of the priestly intercession for the sinner and, despite the repeated appeal to apostolic authority and the power of the keys which they contain, they are to be interpreted as an intercessory prayer, albeit authoritative, of the Church for complete forgiveness of the sins of the penitent which includes the remission of the *punishment* of sins, but not as the infallible act of jurisdiction granting freedom from the temporal punishment of sin.

This interpretation is based on the occurrence of these 'absolutions' (even quite early) outside the sacrament (especially even in the case of 'general absolutions'), on their style and their involved clauses, as well as on the early scholastic theories concerning the nature and the range of priestly activity in the sacrament of penance. Poschmann takes this opportunity to bring out the historical and theoretical factors which have contributed to the change in the institution of penance from public to private penance with the anticipation of reconciliation before the performance of church penance. This leads to the formal distinction between the actual guilt of sin and the punishment due to it, so that now the subjective penance is more clearly related to the remission of the temporal *punishment* due to sin, and the absolutions are considered as the Church's assistance in the remission of these *punishments*. The absolution is the successor of the early Church's priestly penitential intercession. It is essentially intercessory and ought not to be identified simply and formally with actual reconciliation. For Poschmann even here it is the *pax cum ecclesia* that is the *res et sacramentum* of the forgiveness of guilt before God. Thus the intercessory formula in no way formally represents the act of reconciliation as such. Poschmann, however, saw in this teaching of the early Church only an obsolete theory which is useful for the explanation of ancient penitential practices from the point of view of the history of dogma but which cannot command an important place in contemporary theology. Thus Poschmann's otherwise important studies have had only an indirect influence on Vatican II's re-valuation of this teaching for our time.[113] Nevertheless, it is obvious that the parallel—if temporally distinct—development of the institution of penance and indulgences from the viewpoint of the history of dogma, as far as their basis in Scripture, the notion of a juridical act, etc. are concerned, can help to renew and contribute to a further explanation of church penance. In this sense the results of Poschmann's study of the history of indulgences from the viewpoint of the history of dogma, although they are sometimes superficial, still today represent a good starting-point for further studies.

Poschmann himself set the pace in this field with his sketch of the theology of penance in the history of dogma which in an admirable way presents very succinctly the state of research as it was at the beginning of the fifties. This work comprises a vast amount of fact, detail of sources and literature, and personal scholarship. Its main lines have already been developed above, and they have been widely accepted. Since its appearance this survey has obviously become obsolete on individual points here and there,[114] for instance, on the point that the position of Thomas Aquinas in the question of penance was not that of a complete innovator, as it was understood for a long time. But this does not alter at all the over-all value of Poschmann's work: it is even today still the best comprehensive presentation of the whole of the history of penance.

As far as older studies are concerned, the readers are here referred to book reviews.[115] The discussion with J. Grotz, *Die Entwicklung des Bußstufenwesens in der vornicänischen Kirche* is in our essay, 'The Penitential Teaching of the Shepherd of Hermas'. Research on individual points has obviously progressed until the present day and, despite the revision of the present essays, it has not everywhere received the attention which it perhaps might have deserved. Moreover, we did not think it appropriate to deprive these studies of the character which they have from their origin.

Useful editions of texts, like the collection of H. Karpp,[116] and increasing scientific collaboration even on this question[117] make it clear that there is a new interest in the history of penance. Moreover, pastoral and pastoral-theological demands and many actual serious discussions in this field evince a readiness in the life of the Church to reach new forms. If these new forms are to bring a real deepening of appreciation and new vitality, then one cannot dispense with a serious awareness of what the history of penance is and of its importance.

2

SIN AS LOSS OF GRACE IN EARLY CHURCH LITERATURE

Every Catholic treatise of dogma considers in the section on grace or in the section on sin the loss of sanctifying grace as the consequence of actual serious sin and the essence of habitual sin. Fundamental to all the considerations of this question is the affirmation that there are sins which deprive the justified person of the interior personal grace, received at the moment of justification. However this assertion may be formulated, it is at the basis of the Catholic notion of the essence of serious sin. The personally culpable loss of sanctifying grace is the specific mark of serious sin which the justified person commits. This study[1] is an attempt to cast a little light on the historical beginning of this teaching of faith. It is intended as a contribution to the history of dogma, which has previously had little to say about this teaching,[2] at least as far as the explicit and directly posed question is concerned. It is also a contribution to the method of presenting this teaching in Catholic dogmatic treatises which in this question content themselves in general with very flimsy arguments from Scripture and the Fathers of the Church.[3]

I. THE QUESTION

Already according to the New Testament the Christian, by his baptism, has left the kingdom of this world, the kingdom of darkness. He has died to sin and has become a child of knowledge and freedom, who must lead a new life, who must and can allow the holiness given to him in baptism to become effective in a morally perfect way of life. Nevertheless, however great and good this new life of grace given by baptism and confirmation may be, however radically and far it separates the sanctified person from sin, it still remains threatened by sin. Even the Christian, the 'saint', can sin. The New Testament is acutely aware of the irreducible opposition between this new life and sin, and stresses it so strongly that one almost receives the impression that for the person in grace sin has become completely impossible (cf. 1 John 3:9). Nevertheless, it is just as keenly aware of the danger of sin which still threatens even the saint. It mentions sins and vices which occur among Christians. It exhorts, warns and continually threatens in order to preserve the saints, body, soul and spirit, from sins. All this inevitably raises the question of God's attitude towards the Christian's sin, towards the sinful Christian or—in other words—of the effects of the Christian's sin.

In order to see clearly by means of a historical approach what the New Testament and the Fathers of the Church teach about the Christian's sin, one ought not to consider the effects of sin without any differentiation and simply as a whole, as still happens in the textbooks of dogmatic theology on this question. This is the case when statements to the effect that sin begets death, that the sinner does not have life, that he has been rejected, that he will not inherit the kingdom of God or that he has lost righteousness are simply taken as expressions of one and the same truth: serious sin entails the lost of sanctifying grace. The undifferentiated use of all these phrases as a proof of the truth in question already, at first sight, appears questionable. If one wishes to trace the history of this truth in the available literature, then one must consider the different effects of sin separately.

Both from the nature of the case and from the historical data there are three different ways of considering the effects of sin. The first is the juridical-ethical or moral approach. In it sin is considered a transgression of the divine law, by which man becomes morally inferior and bad, antagonizes God and provokes his anger, offends against God's holiness and justice, causes a scandal both for his fellow Christians and for non-Christians, burdens himself with guilt before God, etc. These and similar ways of speaking about sin have this in common that they all, in one way or another, pin-point the juridical and ethical side of sin in the different relationships of this sin to God, to other men and to the sinner himself. Without wishing to deny the real differences of meaning between these various expressions one can say that they represent a juridical-ethical or moral approach to sin and its consequences.

The second approach we would call the end-of-time or eschatological approach. The person who sins incurs God's judgement; he renders himself liable to eternal death and does not arrive at the final resurrection. He will not inherit the kingdom of God and will be punished with hell-fire. He will not obtain salvation, etc. These and similar expressions attempt to explain the nature and the consequences of sin with reference to man's final destiny. Thus they can be grouped together to represent the eschatological approach.

The third approach is from the point of view of grace. The person who sins destroys the life which he has received in baptism; he expels the Spirit from his innermost being and destroys the seal which he received in baptism. He is already dead. Such expressions describe the immediate consequences of sin for the Christian's life of grace, for his own interior grace. It is in this sense that we speak of an approach to the consequences of sin from the viewpoint of grace.

There are two conclusions to be drawn from this simple distinction. In the first place, these different approaches are really closely linked together. All three correspond necessarily to the very nature of sin. For this reason it is naturally sometimes difficult to assign a particular expression describing the consequences of sin clearly and surely to one of the approaches. In practice these approaches often overlap one another. When, for instance, 'death' is mentioned as a consequence of sin it is not always easy to say whether 'eternal death' means damnation (the eschatological viewpoint) or the death of friendship with God (the juridical-ethical/moral viewpoint) or spiritual death as the loss of interior grace (the grace viewpoint). One can justifiably assign such an expression to the third approach (from the point of view of grace), this being the least evident, only when one has already clearly verified the occurrence of such expressions in this sense in the author in question.

Secondly, once the inner connection of these three groups of expressions is presupposed in dogmatic theology, all of them have the same value in practice for a dogmatic proof in a particular question, and one can take the place of the others. When in the Bible, for instance, the consequence of a sin is described in one of the three ways, then this description can be used as a proof that in the case in question it is a matter of serious sin according to the Bible. Similarly, from one group one can deduce the others. Nevertheless, from the point of view of the present essay, it is important to distinguish these three groups clearly.

Although for speculative dogmatic theology this distinction may have only little value, for the establishment of the historical course taken by the teaching of the consequences of sin it is inevitable and of the greatest importance. The real and objective connection between the different consequences of sin is one thing; the knowledge of this connection quite another. The knowledge of one particular consequence can be more explicit in the consciousness of the faithful than the knowledge of another consequence. The awareness of the connection between the three consequences can itself be obscured, and it is possible that, for various reasons, only one particular consequence is continually stressed and the others not even mentioned. Also, as far as this objective awareness is concerned, it is easy to think of the juridical-ethical and the eschatological approaches as being connected. The approach from the point of view of grace, on the contrary, stands out clearly from the two others and can even recede into the background before them.

These apparently purely *a priori* distinctions and possibilities have, however, had a concrete historical form. In the course of the period of time which we are here considering, i.e. from the New Testament until the middle of the third century, we can observe a real shift in the use of the three kinds of expressions. More precisely, the approach from the point of view of grace—together with its associated expressions—is, at first, scarcely present. It then receives attention, is more clearly formulated and, finally, forms the starting-point for new theological reflections. This is always the clearest sign that a truth has become both clearly grasped conceptually and a sure, undisputed and generally recognized fact. The course and the causes of this development must now be expounded in greater detail.

II. THE NEW TESTAMENT

The teaching of the New Testament on the consequences of serious sin can be resumed briefly as follows: the juridical-ethical and the eschatological consequences are clearly and strongly stressed, whereas the meaning of sin for the interior state of grace acquired by faith and baptism is hardly touched upon or—if it is—receives no emphasis and is mentioned only in passing.

1. The Juridical-Ethical and the Eschatological Approaches

Jesus' teaching on judgment and hell as the punishment for sin[4] is stressed remarkably strongly and emphatically by the synoptics. The Lord refers repeatedly to these consequences of sin. Because the teaching on grace receives very little emphasis in these Gospels it is not surprising that this view on the consequences of sin does not envisage Christians who are in a state of grace. Nevertheless, the early Christian literature, immediately following the New Testament, shows how powerfully effective the idea instigated by Jesus' teaching was that God's judgement and eternal damnation are terrifying punishments even for the sins of Christians. Already in Jesus' discourses on the judgement his return, the day of judgement and the damnation of the wicked are intimately connected. This triad represents the last things also in the teaching of the Apostle's letters and in the Johannine writings. Here, too, God's judgement, damnation and eternal death are taught as the fruit of sin.[5] Likewise, the consequences of sin are viewed eschatologically in Paul's catalogues of vices.[6] Sin is not explained as being incompatible with grace, but it is stated: *ϑεοῦ βασιλείαν οὐ κληρονομήσουσιν*.[7]

2. The Approach from the Point of View of Grace

Besides the texts which present juridical-ethical or eschatological perspectives for considering the consequences of sin, there are here and there in the New Testament passages in which the loss of grace appears to be suggested as a consequence of sin. Expressions like *ἐκπίπτειν τῆς χάριτος, ὑστερεῖν ἀπὸ τῆς χάριτος, ἐνυβρίζειν τὸ πνεῦμα πῆς χάριτος, ἀδύνατον πάλιν ἀνακαινίζειν*, etc., describe the effects of sin and seem to be understandable in this sense. Upon closer examination, however, it becomes evident that, because of the conciseness and vagueness of the expressions, such an interpretation remains questionable. These ideas could also be assigned to the other two approaches. Perhaps they mean to convey no more than a general falling away from God, a departure from the kingdom of his benevolence and contempt for his saving works. In any case, they do not have to refer definitely, explicitly and directly to the interior grace which is the personal possession of the individual Christian. Even if one or other of these expressions is understood in the sense of the loss of interior grace, they are all still so brief and stand in a context which draws the attention in another direction. For the teaching of the loss of grace by sin to be believed consciously, clearly and explicitly at least a further impulse from outside was still necessary.

A closer examination of the relevant texts will make this point clearer.

A) PAUL

In Romans 11:16–24 it is first of all a question of the 'excision' of the Jews from the olive tree, and then of the danger that the same thing could happen to the Christians of Gentile origin. The section should be interpreted with regard to the situation of the whole letter. Thus its theme is not that the individual man can lose his interior grace. The olive tree is Judaism or the messianic kingdom issuing from it while remaining linked with the Patriarchs. The Gentiles have been received into this kingdom, although, because of their origin, they do not have a right to it as do the Jews. The latter are the children of the Patriarchs, the first-born, but by their unbelief they have been excluded and 'excised' from this kingdom. This can also happen to the Gentile Christians.[8] This comes near to saying[9] that a loss of interior grace is possible. But this idea is not yet directly expressed, because here it is a question of the relationship of the whole Jewish people to the messianic kingdom. Thus the individual Gentile Christian cannot stand in contrast to the Jewish people.

When Paul in 1 Corinthians 9:27 expresses his fear that he himself, through his own fault, could become ἀδόκιμος, and when in 1 Corinthians 10:12 he envisages the possibility of a 'fall' for Christians, he has not yet relinquished the ethical-moral approach. It remains unclear how this 'disqualification' (ἀδόκιμος) and this 'fall' effect the interior grace. The same applies to expression like ἀπόλυσθαι (John 3:16; 10:28; Rom. 2:12; 14:15; 1 Cor. 1:18; 8:11;

2 Cor. 2:15; 4:3; 2 Thess. 2:10; 2 Pet. 3:9, etc.) and *φθείρεσθαι* (1 Cor. 3:17; 2 Cor. 7:2; 11:3; 2 Pet. 2:12). Here either the purely eschatological sense predominates or these expressions speak very vaguely of an ethical catastrophe.[10]

In 2 Corinthians 6:1 we read: *παρακαλοῦμεν μὴ εἰς κενὸν τὴν χάριν τοῦ θεοῦ δέξασθαι ὑμᾶς*. Even if here *χάρις* were to mean the interior grace,[11] the sentence is still only an exhortation to take care by our ethical life that the reception of grace does not remain vain and useless. What happens to this grace when our ethical behaviour does not correspond to it is not said.

Galations 5:4 remains to be mentioned: *κατηργήθητε ἀπὸ Χριστοῦ οἵτινες ἐν νόμῳ δικαιοῦσθε, τῆς χάριτος ἐξεπέσατε*. This passage means: the person who hopes for *δικαιοσύνη* from the observance of the law 'has no more to do with Christ';[12] he is separated from Christ and has 'fallen out of grace'. *Χάρις* here does not mean simply interior sanctifying grace, since then one could not say: man falls out of grace. Rather it is the whole economy of salvation of the New Testament that is meant. Only if this is the case can *Χάρις* be construed as 'kingdom', as an 'area' out of which the Judaizer steps to fall back into the slavery of the law.

B) THE LETTER TO THE HEBREWS

The following texts from the Letter to the Hebrews come quite near to an approach to the consequences of sin from the point of view of grace. Hebrews 6:4–6 describes interior grace sufficiently clearly with the expressions *φωτίζεσθαι, γεύεσθαι τῆς δωρεᾶς τῆς ἐπουρανίου, μετόχους γίνεσθαι πνεύματος ἁγίου*. All of these expressions refer to an inner state of man. Sin is characterized primarily as a *παραπίπτειν* (*α.λ.* in the NT), as a falling away and an aberration. *Παραπίπτειν* means simply: (by falling away from faith) 'to sin'.[13] By this expression alone, therefore, nothing is yet said about the consequences of sin. Of those who 'have fallen away' we read: *ἀδύνατον πάλιν ἀνακαινίζειν εἰς μετάνοιαν*. This phrase presupposes that such *ἀνακαινίζειν εἰς μετάνοιαν* has already taken place, and that this *ἀνακαίνωσις εἰς μετάνοιαν* has subsequently been lost. Thus in theory a second *ἀνακαίνωσις* would be necessary. Now if one observes only the *ἀνακαινίζειν τινά* (therefore here *τοὺς φωτισθέντας*, etc.), then the meaning of the phrase would be: it is impossible to renew again such apostates and to return them to the state which has just been described.[14] In this way it would without a doubt be presupposed that this *ἀνακαίνωσις* had already taken place once. Thus it is identified with the enlightenment, the tasting of the heavenly gifts, the participation in the Holy Spirit, in fine, interior grace. And it is precisely this grace that has been lost. Since, however, the text does not run *ἀδύνατον ἀνακαινίζειν τοὺς φωτισθέντας*, etc., but *ἀνακαινίζειν εἰς μετάνοιαν*, it cannot be explicitly a question of the renewal of the interior grace of the baptized but the renewal of the attitude of *μετάνοια* in these Christians. The object of the eventual renovation is, therefore, the *μετάνοια* which, as the active form *ἀνακαινίζειν* indicates, is considered as being performed by the preacher (apostle).[15] If, however, the *ἀνακαίνωσις* is referred directly to the interior grace, then neither the active of *ἀνακαινίζειν*[16] nor the preposition *εἰς μετάνοιαν* is explained. This *εἰς* makes it clear that the *μετάνοια* is the object of the *renovatio*. If the renewal referred immediately to the interior state of grace, then the *μετάνοια* would not be its object but the presupposed means of the renewal of the interior state of grace. In this case the *εἰς* would have to be translated by 'through' or 'in the place of' (Estius) or *accedentes, en les amenant* inserted between *ἀνακαινίζειν* and *εἰς μετάνοιαν* (Estius, Crampon).[17] The illumination, the tasting of the heavenly gifts, etc. are, therefore, to be construed as indications which explain the impossibility of a renewed access to *μετάνοια*. How can the person who has experienced these things and then apostasized be brought to change his attitude? It is nowhere stated, therefore, how the *παραπίπτειν* effects the interior grace itself.

In Hebrews 10:29 sin appears as a spurning of God's Son, as contempt for his blood of the covenant which sanctifies us and, above all, as *τὸ πνεῦμα τῆς χάριτος ἐνυβρίζειν*. This expression is possibly an allusion to Zechariah 12:10, where it is said of the Spirit of grace that it is 'poured out' on us. Thus this expression could evoke the interior grace. '*Ενυβρίζειν* means 'to behave improperly', 'to behave proudly and impudently', 'to abuse a person', 'to inflict an injury on someone'.[18] Generally this verb is used absolutely or with reference to the person against whom the insult is directed. In so far as the *πνεῦμα τῆς χάριτος* is considered as a person,[19] the expression here means: to behave insolently and proudly towards this person of the *πνεῦμα*. Sin is, therefore, characterized only in its immoral nature. That this insult against the Pneuma brings about the loss of the Father's gift of grace is by no means explicitly stated.

Finally, we read in Hebrews 12:15 that the Christian must take care that he does not ὑστερῶν ἀπὸ τῆς χάριτος τοῦ θεοῦ. Ecclestiastes 6:9 and Hermas, *Mand.* IX 4 should be compared with this expression. It always has the meaning of 'to lack', 'not to obtain', 'to be excluded because of one's own hesitation' or also, as in Hebrews 4:1, 'to delay', 'to arrive too late', therefore: 'through one's own fault to arrive too late to receive something'.[20] But the expression never has the meaning of 'to lose . Thus here it cannot be primarily and explicitly a question of the loss of something which was already once possessed. Moreover, χάρις is so general and vague that it can be taken quite justifiably here in the wide sense of 'benevolence' or 'salvation'. Thus the whole sentence ought to be translated along these lines: 'Be careful that no one fails to receive God's salvation, that he does not obtain God's favor.' There is no mention, therefore, of a loss of grace.

C) DEATH AS THE CONSEQUENCE OF SIN

The death which results from a committed sin (Jas. 1:14–15) is, in the first place, the eternal death which is opposed to eternal life.[21] An indication of this is James 2:14 ff., where, as if in opposition to 1:14 f., it is said that faith and works save man for eternal happiness. These passages should be compared with James 5:20, where θάνατος is clearly used metaphorically of the eternal damnation of hell.

The New Testament speaks often about 'death'. It is certain that in the following passages spiritual death is meant in the eschatological sense: Rom. 1:32; 6:16, 21, 23; 7:5; (8:2); 2 Cor. 2:16; (2 Tim. 1:10); (Heb. 2:14b); Rev. 2:11; 20:6, 14; 21:8.[22] Also for the possibility of the spiritual death of grace, here and now, which entails eternal death the following passages may be adduced: John 5:24; 8:51; Rom. 7:10, 13, 24; 2 Cor. 3:7; Jas. 1:15; 5:20; 1 John 3:14; 5:16. But even if 'death' in these passages is not to be construed purely eschatologically and also concerns this present life, what is its precise meaning? Does it mean loss of grace or, at least explicitly and directly, only 'death of the moral life', 'death of sinlessness' or 'death of relationship and friendship with God'? In the later Fathers of the Church death certainly means 'death of grace'. But this is by no means clear with regard to the New Testament. In John 5:24 it is possibly mainly a question of 'moral death', with the further implication of bodily death considered as the counterpart to the final resurrection of the body. This reference to the resurrection, together with the parallel with the judgement (5:22), calls for an eschatological interpretation. It is possible to grasp the profound nature of this death, opposed as it is to 'life', only by taking the whole Gospel into consideration. Only in this way could it perhaps be shown that the Johannine notion of death includes, as a secondary meaning, the idea of 'death by the loss of grace'. In John 8:51 'death' ought certainly to be understood eschatologically,[23] while in Rom. 7:10, 13 it is only a question of moral death through sin.[24] Nevertheless, Paul's notion of the nature of death can be derived only from his theology as a whole. In Romans 8:6 the eschatological meaning is obvious. *Φρόνημα* means the 'thinking and effort' directed to a goal and then, metonymically, this goal itself.[25] *Θάνατος* is, therefore, the last goal and the end of sinful activity and thus is meant eschatologically. 2 Corinthians 3:7 has an ethical-moral meaning; 2 Corinthians 7:10 refers to eternal death,[26] while 1 John 3:14 envisages a death which is already present. Nevertheless, it is only in the light of the whole of Johannine theology that it can be established that this death consists essentially of the loss of grace and, as far as the present life is concerned, is not to be understood merely as the punishment of a fault which entails eternal death but concerns the loss of a personal life of grace. In 1 John 5:16 *θάνατος* means the complete falling away from faith and the total denial of Jesus[27] but not the loss of grace which is associated with a serious sin. By way of conclusion, it remains true to say that *θάνατος* can mean 'moral, spiritual death'. A consideration of the theology of the whole of the New Testament can eventually point to the loss of grace as the inner nature of this death; but this is never directly and explicitly expressed.

In 1 John 3:8–10 sin and righteousness are explained with regard to man's true character. In their effects they are the revelation (*ἐν τούτῳ φανερά*) that one is either a child of God or a child of the devil. Nevertheless, it is not stated that a person who became a child of God through grace becomes a child of the devil through sin and so loses grace. The *οὐ δύναται ἁμαρτάνειν ὅτι ἐκ τοῦ θεοῦ γεγέννηται* seems rather to suggest another meaning. In the light of this passage and seen in its own context the meaning of the observation in 1 John 3:15 is clear. The 'murderer' who hates his brother does not have 'life dwelling' in him and must, therefore—precisely because of this—hate those brothers who, being different from him, do possess this life. It is for this reason that we should not be surprised at the hatred of the world (1 John 3:13). Nevertheless, there is no mention of the fact here that a person loses the 'life dwelling in him', which he once already possessed, when he begins to hate his brothers. According to 1 John 3:8 ff. hatred of the brothers is rather an indication that the 'murderer' never possessed life. What is more, the phrase *οὐκ ἔχει ζωὴν αἰώνιον ἐν αὐτῷ μένουσαν* does not have the same sense as *ἡ ζωὴ αἰώνιος οὐ μένει ἐν αὐτῷ*.

D) IMAGES AND PARABLES

In theological tradition biblical parables have been repeatedly applied to the interior state of grace and its loss. Nevertheless, these parables are far too vague to be able to support on their own such a precise theological notion. Pride of place, in this connection, is usually given to the prodigal son who, upon his return, receives a new garment and a new ring (Luke 15:22); this signifies God's loving acceptance of the sinner. The application of the garment to sanctifying grace, however, goes far beyond the literal meaning of the text.[28] Similarly treated is the man who appears at the royal wedding banquet without a festal robe (Matt. 22:12) and is, therefore, turned away from the table. This seems to be saying[29] that everyone must strive to acquire a wedding garment by leading a life in conformity with the demands of the gospel. The participation in the meal of eternal life is, therefore, connected with the fulfilment of certain conditions. But it is not said that these conditions are tantamount to the preservation of the interior state of grace. Rather, they ought to be interpreted in the light of Matthew 7:21 f. A third image which is adduced here is the destruction of God's temple in which the divine Spirit dwells (1 Cor. 3:16 f.; cf. also 1 Cor. 6:19). According to the whole context, however, *ναὸς θεοῦ* must here mean not the individual Christian but the community and the individual Church,[30] in much the same way as Ephesians 2:21 f. and 2 Corinthians 6:16 refer to the universal Church. The *φθείρειν* is the disintegration of the community by false teachers. The *φθείρεσθαι* which threatens the false teacher is to be understood eschatologically, being the *φθορά* which, as in Galatians 6:8, is opposed to *ζωὴ αἰώνιος*. In 1 Corinthians 6:19, however, it is a question of individuals considered as God's temple. Nevertheless, what effects the sins of the flesh have upon the temple of God remain unclear.

John 15:6 seems to be the best New Testament candidate for a consideration of the consequences of sin from the point of view of grace. 'To remain in Christ' is the activity of the disciples themselves. It is also primarily meant as a moral relationship, and therefore 'not to remain in Christ' belongs to the juridical-moral approach. The images of separation, rejection[31] and burning can be construed eschatologically.

We can sum up this rapid survey of a few important New Testament passages in this way: the juridical-ethical and eschatological consequences of sin are well known and are strongly emphasized. On the other hand, the consideration of the consequences of sin from the point of view of grace and, therefore, the teaching of the loss of sanctifying grace through sin appears only indirectly. In any event, this idea is not prominent in the New Testament.

The reasons for this phenomenon are not hard to find. In the first place, baptism, the simple fact of becoming a Christian, was considered such a decisive and definitive break with sin that the immediate consequence of a further serious sin could hardly be envisaged. Among Christians, at least in general, intense moral effort was taken for granted. Moreover, the approach to the consequences of sin in the Old Testament and in the synoptics, that is, in the original tradition concerning Jesus' message, succeeded in fixing the attention of the other New Testament writings more on the moral and eschatological consequences than on the effects of sin upon the state of grace. The return of the Lord, the day of Christ and the imminent judgement are part and parcel of the living expectation of Christians in the early community. This is why they were warned against sin with reference to these ideas. In this context there was no pastoral necessity as yet to refer to the loss of grace. All the relevant biblical texts warn against sins which have not yet been committed. The approach to the consequences of sin from the point of view of grace, however, must necessarily be concerned rather with sins which have actually been committed.

III. THE APOSTOLIC FATHERS

As far as the question of the effects of sin in the writings of the 'Apostolic Fathers' is concerned, these writings may be divided into two groups. The first group would contain those witnesses which were certainly composed at the beginning of our period, that is, in the first half of the second century: the First Letter of Clement, the Letters of Ignatius of Antioch, the Didache, the Letter of Barnabas and the Letter of Polycarp. The second group of the Apostolic Fathers comprises the writings of the middle or the second half of the second century: the Second Letter of Clement and the Shepherd of Hermas. The Martyrdom of Polycarp and the Letter of Diognetus have no relevance for our question. This chronological division coincides with an objective difference of content, as we shall now show.

1. The Early Apostolic Fathers

The witnesses of this group consider the consequences of sin in more or less the same way as does the New Testament. The juridical-ethical and eschatological approaches predominate almost exclusively. This observation can be confirmed by expressions culled from these writings. Thus it is said that idolatry destroys the covenant with God,[32] that sin relegates man again among the pagans,[33] that it makes him a slave of the devil.[34] Consequently God is unfavourable towards the sinner and becomes his enemy,[35] because he hates sin[36] and curses it.[37] Sin entails misfortunes and dangers.[38] It is the object of a curse,[39] since God will not be mocked,[40] and peace and righteousness are far from the sinner.[41]

The eschatological viewpoint is especially evident in the following expressions: sin is a road leading to death, that is, to eternal damnation, a road of darkness and a death-trap.[42] It leads man to death.[43] Thus sin is threatened by the judgement of God and of Christ.[44] Warning against sin often contains a reference to the end of time.[45] At the judgement the sinner will receive a just punishment,[46] damnation[47] and hell.[48] Quite often Paul is cited verbatim.[49]

Naturally even in these early Apostolic Fathers there are some texts which one could be tempted to interpret in the sense of an approach from the point of view of grace. Quite a few of these passages seem to reflect this approach—those, for instance, which present death as already having been introduced by sin. Thus we are inclined spontaneously to interpret them immediately with regard to grace. If, however, the principle of interpretation is maintained, according to which general and vague phrases can justifiably be understood in a precise sense only if the idea in question occurs clearly in at least one other place in the same author, then these passages cannot be understood in the precise, unambiguous sense of the loss of interior grace. This idea is found nowhere unambiguously in the early Apostolic Fathers. Thus there is no foundation for a precise interpretation of more general expressions in the sense of a loss of grace.

Nevertheless, a series of these texts should still be considered more closely in order to explain and to justify the point which has just been made with reference to the expressions themselves. It is stated in the Didache 16,1:[50] *γρηγορεῖτε ὑπὲρ τῆς ζωῆς ὑμῶν*. This phrase suggests the possibility of the loss of grace, the loss of 'life'. Nevertheless, because the vigilance in question is based upon our ignorance of the moment of the Lord's coming, it is obvious that the life over which we should keep watch should be understood eschatologically as eternal life.

In the First Letter of Clement (57,2)[51] it is stated that it is better to be found *ἐλλόγιμος* and *μικρός* than by pride *ἐκριφῆναι ἐκ τῆς ἐλπίδος αὐτοῦ* (sc. Χρισροῦ). A similar image and a similar idea are found in Barnabas 2:10 and already in Galatians 5:4. Thus the expression here could also be rendered: 'by pride be deprived of the hope (of eternal life)'. In Ignatius 5,2.3[52] the *ὑστερεῖν τοῦ ἄρτου τοῦ θεοῦ* and the *ἑαυτὸν διακρίνειν* signifies separation from Christ in the wide sense for the person who does not stay in communion with the bishop. There is no mention of a loss of interior grace in this passage.

Expressions like *οὐκ εἶναι τοῦ θεοῦ*,[53] *διαφθείρεσθαι*,[54] *τῆς ἐλπίδος* [= Χριστοῦ] *ἐκτρέπεσθαι*,[55] after conversion *θεοῦ εἶναι*,[56] *νεκροφόρος*[57] (describing the person who denies Christ) are too vague to evince with certainty the approach from the point of view of grace, in addition to the evident juridical-moral approach.

There are, however, passages in Ignatius which speak of a death caused by sin. Thus false teaching is a θανάσιμον φάρμακον,[58] of which a person dies. Of those people who do not participate in the Eucharist, it is stated: ἀντιλέγοντες τῇ δωρεᾷ τοῦ θεοῦ συνζητοῦντες ἀποθνήσκουσιν.[59] About the proud Ignatius says: ἀπώλετο,[60] and about the person who elevates himself above the bishop: ἔφθαρται.[61] The ἀποθνήσκειν of Smyrn. 7,1 can certainly be understood eschatologically, because in the same place Ignatius continues: συνέφερεν αὐτοῖς ἀγαπᾶν (i.e. to celebrate the agape-Eucharist), ἵνα καὶ ἀναστῶσιν. Now this resurrection can hardly be understood as other than eschatological. The same applies to Ephesians 20:2,[62] where the Eucharist is praised as φάρμακον ἀθανασίας, and the term 'resurrection' is certainly understood to include eternal life. Similarly, false teaching described as φάρμακον θανάσιμον is to be understood eschatologically. Ad Polyc. 5,2 does indeed refer to a direct consequence of sin, but it does not explain further the nature of the ruin which has already been experienced. The expression of Trall. 11,1[63] comes near to the approach from the point of view of grace. Similarly to Ad Polyc. 5,2, there is a mention of an immediate (παρ' αὐτά) death. In the light of this passage, Smyrn. 7,1 could also be understood in this sense. Nevertheless, in Trall. 11,1 this immediate death is not explained in any detail. There is no explicit reference of this death to the life of grace.

When, in the exhortation to harmony within the community and to subordination to the bishop, it is stated in Philad. 8,1:[64] οὗ δὲ μερισμός ἐστιν καί ὀργή, θεὸς οὐ κατοικεῖ, this must apply here to the community as such. God does not live in a disunited community. This passage is, therefore, not relevant to our present purpose. Obviously the texts which we have just considered and quite a few others already contain the clear foundations for the teaching of the loss of grace as a consequence of sin. These foundations can be developed further as soon as an external factor demands a greater emphasis on the relationship between morality and grace as well as a more explicit formulation of this relationship. But this is not yet the case here. The teaching itself appears as such only later, although it can easily be related with the foundations which we have just seen.

As far as the writings of the early Apostolic Fathers are concerned, the juridical-moral and the eschatological approaches to the consequences of sin predominate. The reasons for this are undoubtedly the same as those given for the case of the New Testament.

2. *The Later Apostolic Fathers*

As we have already said,[65] it is especially the so-called Second Letter of Clement and the Shepherd of Hermas that have any importance for our question. In these writings the approach to the consequences of sin from the point of view of grace appears very clearly. In comparison with the witnesses of the earlier period, it is noticeable that there is here a change of interest in a new direction and a further development in the formulation of the idea. The two other approaches are still in evidence, but the view with which we are presently concerned is so prominent that we are now able to concentrate exclusively on it.

In the Second Letter of Clement it is stated: *ἡμεῖς ἐὰν μὴ τηρήσωμεν τὸ βάπτισμα ἁγνὸν καὶ ἀμίαντον, ποίᾳ πεποιθήσει εἰσελευσόμεθα εἰς τὸ βασίλειον τοῦ θεοῦ*,[66] and in another place:[67] *τῶν γὰρ μὴ τηρησάντων . . . τὴν σφραγῖδα ὁ σκώληξ αὐτῶν οὐ τελευτήσει καὶ τὸ πῦρ αὐτῶν οὐ σβεσθήσεται*. And in the next chapter:[68] *τηρήσατε τὴν σάρκα ἁγνὴν καὶ τὴν σφραγῖδα ἄσπιλον, ἵνα τὴν αἰώνιον ζωὴν ἀπολάβωμεν*. First and foremost, the preacher warns against sin with reference to its eschatological consequences. But—and this is what is new—between sin and what it finally entails—hell—an immediate effect of sin is mentioned: the loss of baptismal grace for the Christian. For its part, the punishment of hell follows from this immediate consequence of sin. The person who sins does not 'keep' the 'seal', does not preserve baptism safe and sound.

In the Shepherd of Hermas we find the same kind of expression. In Sim. VIII 6,3[69] it is stated of the Christians: *εἰληφότες τὴν σφραγῖδα καὶ τεθλακότες αὐτὴν καὶ μὴ τηρήσαντες ὑγιῆ*. And Hermas means that they will receive the *σφραγίς* back if they do penance. This term here means the baptismal grace, the life which is received in baptism, as, for example, Sim. IX 16,3.4[70] clearly shows. Many Christians have broken this seal and have not preserved it in innocence. But they can recover it by penance.[71] This passage teaches unambiguously the loss of baptismal grace which is so decisive for man's eternal destiny. Just how important the possession of this baptismal grace is for Hermas can be seen from his assumption that the righteous men of the Old Testament—in the underworld, as they are—must receive this seal by baptism through the apostles if they are to be able to enter into the kingdom of God.[72] The expression: 'breaking' (ϑλάω) of the seal through sin and the fact that the penitents, according to Hermas, recover it from the angle of penance (*μετανοήσωσιν λαβόντες ὑπὸ σοῦ σφραγῖδα*)[73] show that it is a question of an actual loss of the seal which here means baptismal grace. The other more imaginative expressions, such as the sullying of the seal or of baptism can, therefore, justifiably be understood in the same sense as the loss of baptismal grace. Because of the close relationship between the Shepherd of Hermas and the Second Letter of Clement, this observation is valid for both writings. In Sim. IX 17,4.5[74] many people having received the *σφραγίς* have sullied it again. Thus they have fallen back into their previous state (before baptism) or into a worse state still.

Although, up to this point, the Shepherd of Hermas and the Second Letter of Clement agree in their way of speaking, yet another expression for the loss of grace after baptism is found in Hermas. This is not so clearly discernible in the Second Letter of Clement. Here it is a question of *πνεῦμα ἅγιον* being used instead of, but clearly synonymously with, *σφραγίς*. The person who sins 'sullies' the Spirit.[75] Sin 'expels' the Spirit which dwells within man.[76] It 'injures' the Holy Spirit[77] and brings it about that it 'abandons' man.[78]

This teaching of the loss of grace through sin is developed still further in Hermas in a direction which is quite peculiar to him. Since this point is without great importance, a brief reference to it will suffice for our present purpose. The expressions used by Hermas suggest a kind of physical activity, when, for instance, he speaks of the soul as a container which has a certain capacity. This is filled either with the Holy Spirit or with the wicked spirit. If the latter forces himself into the soul, then the good Spirit becomes 'compressed' and finally leaves man completely.[79]

The following expressions can be understood unhesitatingly in the sense of the loss of grace as a consequence of sin: *λύπην ἐπάγειν τῷ πνεύματι τῷ σεμνῷ καὶ ἀληθῆ*,[80] *λυπεῖν τὸ πνεῦμα τὸ ἅγιον*[81] or *πονηρὰν συνείδησιν μετὰ τοῦ πνεύματος τῆς ἀληθείας μὴ κατοικεῖν*.[82] Similarly, Hermas speaks of the Spirit becoming old, diminishing and becoming powerless.[83] On the other hand, the recovery of the Spirit is *ἀνακαινίζειν τὸ πνεῦμα*.[84] The exhortation to avoid sin is now expressed in this way: *reddite ei Spiritum integrum, sicut accepistis*.[85] At least by way of allusion, the image of the 'robe of grace',[86] which will become so frequent later, is already found in Hermas. Thus we read:[87]

> *Si sic igitur tu doles de vestimento tuo et quereris, quod non illud integrum recipias, quid putas dominum tibi facturum qui spiritum integrum tibi dedit, et tu eum totum inutilem redegisti, ita ut in nullo usu esse possit domino suo? Inutilis enim esse coepit usus eius cum sit corruptus a te. Nonne igitur dominus spiritus eius propter hoc factum tuum (morte te) adficiat?*

Now, once the teaching of the loss of grace as the consequence of sin has been established—as we have seen it to be in the above-mentioned passages—then phrases which speak about the denial of life,[88] of 'to inflict death on oneself'[89] or, conversely, about the renewal of life[90] may also be interpreted in the same sense.

It is a reasonable assumption that the cause of the development which we have discerned in the teaching on the loss of grace through sin, together with its clear formulation, is a reaction to a fundamentally different way of thinking. Only such a reaction could explain the explicit and clear expressions which we have seen. Now the anti-Gnostic character of the Second Letter of Clement and the Shepherd of Hermas is abundantly clear.[91] This tendency is discernible in what could be called the 'teaching on grace' in both of these writings. The Gnostic teachings on the pneuma, on the divine 'seed', on the particle of the 'Father' and on the pleroma could be understood as the opposing 'teaching on grace'.[92] This teaching is fundamentally amoral, and neither in encratistic nor in actually immoral Gnosticism is this Gnostic 'grace' designed to sanctify and to enlighten the whole man. This is because man's material and psychic part, being the fall-out of a pre-human 'original sin', can have nothing at all to do with the pneuma. On the other hand, according to this view, man's immoral behaviour cannot do any harm to this Gnostic 'grace'. Thus we can justifiably assume that the Second Letter of Clement and the Shepherd of Hermas considered themselves called upon—in reaction against this teaching—to declare that the grace received in baptism is lost by sin. This explains how the approach to the consequences of sin from the point of view of grace came in to complement the traditional juridical-moral and eschatological approaches. This assumption is confirmed by the fact that some occurrences of the new formulations appear in sections where there is a direct polemic[93] against Gnosticism. Furthermore, the notion of σφραγίς as a description of the gift of grace received in baptism was a favourite term among the Gnostics.[94] Thus the expression that the σφραγίς is lost through sin would have naturally suggested itself.

The approach from the point of view of grace was fully developed, therefore, in the struggle against Gnostic notions of grace. The Shepherd of Hermas, however, had other opponents with whom he had to enter into the lists on essential aspects of our question. In the penitential controversies Hermas played an important role, in so far as he was the first person to pose explicitly the question[95] of the fate of a fallen Christian who had lost the grace which had been given to him in baptism. One of the most important questions for Hermas is whether there is a further conversion, a second μετάνοια for such an unfortunate person and under which conditions it is possible. In the second and third centuries this question provoked a whole series of theological controversies and led to schisms and heresies. The most notorious of these are Tertullian's penitential rigorism, inspired by his Montanism, the schism of Hippolytus in Rome, the differences of opinion on the celebration of penance at the time of Cyprian of Carthage and his adversaries Novatian, Felicissimus and Fortunatus and, finally, the Novatian schism in Rome. Generally, these controversies are considered solely from the point of view of the Church's increasingly emphasized conviction that it has the authority to forgive sins and of the practical and lenient exercise of this authority in the face of a rigorism which is heretical at least in practice, if not in theory. It is obvious that in these controversies the teaching of the loss of grace through sin had to be recognized ever more explicitly and clearly. It is from this point of view that we must now consider the penitential controversies further, albeit very briefly.[96]

IV. THE RIGORISM OF MONTANISM

The Apologists of the second century may be passed over, since their own interests provide little opportunity for them to speak about the loss of grace as the consequence of sin. Even the intention of Irenaeus of Lyons in his Adversus Haereses is so peculiar to him that we can hardly expect him to provide details on our theme.

Nevertheless, the idea itself is clearly expressed by him: *διὰ τῆς πίστεως καὶ τῆς ἁγνῆς ἀναστροφῆς συντηρεῖν τὸ Πνεῦμα τοῦ θεοῦ, ἵνα μὴ ἄμοιροι τοῦ θείου Πνεύματος γενόμενοι ἀποτύχωμεν τῆς βασιλείας τῶν οὐρανῶν*[97]. In this passage the loss of grace as the consequence of sin is clearly inserted between the sin and the eschatological loss of the kingdom of God. Similarly, we read elsewhere: *ut non amittentes eum, qui nos possidet Spiritum amittamus vitam.*[98] Of the Gnostics Irenaeus says: *propter suam incredulitatem aut luxuriam non adipiscuntur divinum spiritum et variis characteribus eiiciunt se vivificans Verbum.*[99] Thus the heretics are *in mortem demergunt sibi credentes*[100] . . . *letaliter vulnerantes.*[101] In Irenaeus, therefore, the connection between sin, the loss of grace and exclusion from the kingdom of God is clearly expressed.[102] Apart from this, the few passages in Irenaeus which touch on the question of the practice and the theology of penance in the early Church offer little help for the problem with which we are presently concerned.[103]

Although the idea that grace could be lost was already clearly expressed before Tertullian, in the witnesses which we have questioned so far this was rather indirectly and in contexts where the main emphasis was on exhortation, even though they included a sharp attack on the heretical notions on grace. In the discussions about the Church's power to forgive sins which break out so acutely towards the end of the second century with Tertullian there begins the actual theological consideration of this question. The attempt is now made to prove the idea from the Bible and to establish more precisely which sins have this effect and which consequences this loss of grace itself further entails, etc. Thus this problem becomes an object of 'theology', i.e. one of the explicit and direct truths of the faith.

The attention which has been given to Tertullian's position regarding the possibility of a forgiveness of sins after baptism has perhaps led to a certain neglect of the theological presuppositions which underlie Tertullian's teaching on penance itself. We will here outline one of these presuppositions, since it is relevant to our question. After a general consideration this notion of Tertullian will be examined further in more detail.

In his Montanist period in order to justify and to promote theologically his penitential rigorism Tertullian had to explain, first of all, why certain sins cannot be forgiven after baptism. And to do this he had to touch, at least briefly, on the idea of a loss of baptismal grace. Only after he had done this was Tertullian able to conclude with his trenchant dialectic:[104] what baptism has given to a man, namely the Spirit, grace, is lost again through sin. Now a man is able to receive baptism only once. Through serious sin after baptism, therefore, there occurs a loss which cannot be made good again. The one and only way remaining to do this is the other baptism which God still gives, the baptism of blood in martyrdom. Otherwise, all that remains is the uncertain prospect that God will perhaps still be gracious towards a life-long penitent. In any case, for such sins there is no forgiveness by means of a precise ritual, analogous to baptism,[105] which would restore baptismal grace to the sinner. This would mean the introduction of a second baptism.

It is possible today to underestimate the force of this argument in Tertullian. Thanks to the sacrament of penance, the possibility of a second bestowal of grace has become accepted, and the nature and effects of penance are considered in such a way that the definitive character and the uniqueness of baptism are not thereby neglected. In Tertullian's day, however, this view was by no means quite so clear. Tertullian could be quite justified, therefore, in thinking that he had a decisive argument for his thesis that certain sins were unforgivable. He reasoned as follows: either the baptized person does not lose the baptismal grace through sin or—if he has lost it—he cannot recover it and is for ever dead. The first solution was not acceptable, being recognized as Gnostic and considered false. Against the second solution was the witness of the teaching of the Bible and the Church's self-awareness which was expressed in its practice and, to a greater or lesser extent, in its teaching. How are both of these truths to be reconciled without detriment to the decisive significane of baptism—a point on which all were profoundly agreed?[106]

As often happens elsewhere, the Church's awareness of its faith here appears to contain two contradictory truths. And there is a temptation to sacrifice one truth in order to save the other. Nevertheless, in his De paen. the reconciliation of these two truths does not yet appear to have presented any difficulties to Tertullian; thus it is not here that we should look for the basis of his erroneous teaching on penance. In his De pud., however, he later saw the problem clearly and there solved it in a false sense on the basis of practical rigorism supported by his rigid dialectic. The Church's answer to this question in Tertullian's time consisted simply in maintaining these two apparently contradictory truths. It was only at a later period that the Church succeeded in showing how these two truths were not mutually exclusive. In the Fathers of the Church there are only the first elements of the distinction which has to be made in order to resolve the question.[107] Apart from Origen, however, these witnesses hail from a century after Tertullian. As in other cases, theological progress in this question was made possible by the clear distinction between the recognition of a truth of the faith, on the one hand, and the speculative justification of this truth, together with its integration into the body of all the truths of the faith, on the other. This process is demanded by the very nature of revealed truth.

Although, in this essay, we are not concerned with the penitential controversy as such, Tertullian's way of arguing is still of some importance. It shows how the teaching on the loss of baptismal grace is already a presupposition for Tertullian from which other views can be derived. We have already been able to trace the historical development of this teaching up to its explicit formulation. For his part, Tertullian now considers its consequences and how it is connected and compatible with the other truths of the faith. This is surely an indication of how clearly at this point of time the teaching of the loss of baptismal grace was already recognized.

On yet another question Tertullian's view of penance proved to be important. If, with his teaching that serious sins are unforgivable, he wished to take any account of the daily life of Christians he had to restrict the number of these sins as much as possible.[108] He could not make such strict moral demands that would include the majority of Christians among those sinners who were excluded from the Church. Thus he had to compensate the exaggeration in his view of the consequences of sin with an excessive leniency in his judgement of the gravity of the sins themselves. Only a few sins, therefore, entail the loss of baptismal grace. In this way he arrived at his teaching on capital sins,[109] which, as a special group, are sharply distinguished from other sins. Only the former are 'serious' or mortal sins in today's sense. Although even the distinction which Tertullian drew between serious and light sins was a false one, this view still remains the first attempt we know of to make a distinction between serious and venial faults, in the sense of essentially different categories, especially in reference to their effect on grace. We must now examine these main lines of Tertullian's teaching in greater detail.

1. *The Loss of Grace in General*

Tertullian's teaching on the possibility of the loss of grace in general did not change when he passed over to Montanism. Thus there is no need to make any distinction here between his writings from his Catholic period and those from his Montanist period. He certainly does not waste many words on this question. The Shepherd of Hermas and Irenaeus of Lyons, both of whom he knew and used, had a clear position on this question. At the same time, Christian experience, the practice of the Church and the teaching of the Bible pointed clearly in the same direction. Thus the question no longer called for explicit treatment. Tertullian merely reiterates it clearly and succinctly.

We are *templum Dei illato in nos et consecrato Spiritu Sancto* and must beware *ne Deus ille qui inhabitat inquinatam sedem offensus derelinquat.*[110] Without the virtue of patience, which 'safeguards the Spirit', the Spirit cannot stay long in man. If this virtue is lacking the Spirit of God cannot withstand the assaults of the enemy and, therefore, will not remain in us.[111] The confessors are admonished by Tertullian not to sadden the Holy Spirit (cf. Eph. 4:20): *et ideo date operam, ut (Spiritus Sanctus) illic vobiscum perseveret.*[112] Tertullian presupposes, therefore, that the Spirit of God, who previously helped the confessors to bear imprisonment, can be lost. He recognizes, therefore, that it is possible to lose the Spirit.[113] Indeed, in another passage he teaches clearly that the Spirit received in baptism is in fact lost, along with all his gifts, through several sins. This is how Tertullian describes the gifts of grace which the Christian receives as his mysterious fortune (*substantia*) and as his inheritance as the child of God: *remissio delictorum, absolutio mortis, regeneratio hominis, consecutio Spiritus Sancti.*[114] In baptism we receive the Holy Spirit[115] and are enlightened by him;[116] we put on Christ.[117] Thus baptism is a *regeneratio caelestis,*[118] a *nova nativitas.*[119] In baptism we receive the image and likeness of God and the Spirit with all his heavenly gifts (*bona caelestia*), in other words, everything which

Adam lost in paradise.[120] Tertullian is talking, therefore, about the reception of interior gifts, about the Spirit and grace which are bestowed on the soul in baptism. However, the Christian loses these gifts completely if he commits a serious sin after baptism. Penance before baptism prepares in man a pure dwelling for the Holy Spirit, *quo se ille (Spiritus Sanctus) cum caelestibus bonis libens inferat.*[121] If a person does not take seriously the conversion which is required for baptism he must reckon with Tertullian's warning that what God is about to give in baptism can be lost again after baptism: *Non enim multi postea excidunt? Non a multis donum illud aufertur?*[122] To lack true seriousness when receiving baptism is to run the risk of losing the baptismal grace, the *donum* again, supposing that it is received in the first place. Similarly, in De paen.[123] Tertullian presupposes the loss of baptismal grace when he says to the sinner faced with the second penance: *Amisisti quod acceperas* (that is, in baptism). This is even more clearly expressed in De pud.: the person guilty of impurity is completely dead.[124] There are sins, therefore, which are mortal.[125] The sinner is a lost son who has lost and squandered completely the property which he has received in baptism from God his father (*substantia baptismatis*).[126] It is precisely here that Tertullian describes particularly clearly the nature of this lost baptismal gift: it is the *indumentum Spiritus Sancti,* the *signaculum lavacri,* the *substantia utique baptismatis, utique Spiritus Sancti.*[127] The person who has sinned seriously no longer has any wedding garment, he is *spoliatus, exutus bonis mentis.*[128] The person guilty of impurity expels the Lord from his body instead of glorifying him and bearing him in his body.[129] The sinful flesh kills the Spirit: *spiritum elidit.*[130] In De pud. 9 Tertullian says that, in baptism, the pagan receives *vestem pristinam, statum scilicet quem Adam transgressus amiserat.*[131] Moreover, in the same chapter it is stated that, according to the Catholics, the repentant apostate will receive back the *vestis prior.*[132] Thus both Tertullian and the Catholics presuppose that an apostate has lost the *vestis prior,* i.e., the position which Adam had in Paradise.[133] Tertullian frequently explains the nature of this *status* of Adam. Even in De paen. already the sinner is the lost son[134] who, after squandering his father's goods, returns naked. Taking part in idolatrous shows is a *signaculum rescindere,*[135] this being Tertullian's translation of Hermas' ϑλᾶν τὴν σφραγῖδα.[136]

2. *The Consequences of the Teaching of the Loss of Grace*

Tertullian uses this teaching of the loss of grace to arrive at further theological conclusions. In his Montanistic period he derives from this teaching the idea that certain sins are unforgivable, and it is in this connection that he draws a distinction between sins which entail the loss of grace and those which do not have this effect. The latter point is of special importance for our present purpose.

Along with other considerations, Tertullian derives his view that some sins, which he calls capital sins, are unforgivable from the fact that these sins destroy the baptismal grace. Although this is not the only and the most important reason for his view, it is still very clear. According to Tertullian, man is redeemed by Christ's unrepeatable suffering on the cross. This redemptive offering is appropriated by man at baptism which, however, he is able to receive only once. If a man has lost the gift of baptism, he has no further means—at least, no sacramental means of the institutional Church—of regaining the baptismal grace. *Homo cum inquinatur, occiditur.*[137] The sinner is not only 'lost' or 'wayward', he is 'dead'.[138] Baptism has been lost.[139] Thus the sinner has ceased to have God as the source of his existence.[140] The incestuous person is *mortuus, devoratus,*[141] as Tertullian puts it. And this consequence, this loss of the baptismal grace is caused by the serious sins. They are *delicta ad mortem.*[142] Of the sins which Paul enumerates in 1 Corinthians 6:9 f. Tertullian observes: *delicta ista . . . post lavacrum irremissibilia constituit* (*scl. Paulus*), *siquidem denuo ablui non licet.*[143] But this means only that a baptism through which these sins would be able to be remitted is no longer possible, i.e. these sins cannot be forgiven. Tertullian does not develop this idea any further. Nevertheless there can be no doubt that he bases the fact that these sins cannot be forgiven on the impossibility of repeating baptism. Thus Tertullian must presuppose that only those sins which he describes as unforgivable destroy the baptismal grace totally. What, according to him even in his Montanistic period, can be forgiven[144] by the Church cannot, therefore, have this totally destructive effect. If these sins, too, caused the total loss of the baptismal grace, then the same would apply to these *leviora delicta: irremissibilia siquidem denuo ablui non licet.* But Tertullian in fact declares that sins other than capital sins do not annihilate the baptismal grace. The person who frequents the circus or the dubious theatre, who tries to compromise himself with ambiguous formulas when making his confession of faith, who provides objects for the worship of idols, etc., is aberrant and a *vivens adhuc peccator.*[145] His faults are *sordes,* but not irremissible *maculae.*[146] Even those sins of which Paul disapproves in Corinth—apart from incest—do not, according to Tertullian, bring it about that a sinner is lost totally. Rather, he remains a *salvus.*[147]

As a proof that some sins are unforgivable we read in Tertullian: *quis enim timebit prodigere* (*scl. substantiam utique baptismatis, utique Spiritus Sancti, et exinde spei aeternae*)[148] *quod habebit postea recuperare.* This presupposes, however, that in the case of sins which can be forgiven by the Church there is no loss of the baptismal grace. Otherwise, it should also be said of these sins: *Quis timebit prodigere, quod habebit postea recuperare, quis curabit perpetuo conservare quod non perpetuo poterit amittere.*[149] Elsewhere also Tertullian's train of thought presupposes this idea. Thus, in his view, for some sins there is only the penance of baptism. The pagan sinner is a *semel diluendus per gratiam Christi semel pro peccatis nostris morte functi.*[150] Thus Tertullian argues from the unrepeatable character of Christ's death on the cross to the unrepeatable character of baptism, considered as the application of Christ's offering to men, and then to the conclusion that capital sins are unforgivable.[151] These sins are indeed forgiven at baptism but if they are committed afterwards they annul the effects of baptism. This is not the case with those sins which Tertullian considers forgivable. The same conclusion follows from Tertullian's idea that there is only one way that such sins committed after baptism can be forgiven: the baptism of blood.[152] Thus it is *martyrium . . . quod solum omni substantia prodacta restituere filium poterit.*[153] There are *crimina non nisi proprio martyrio diluenda.* This is because martyrdom is an *aliud baptisma.*[154] Already, in earlier writings, Tertullian had called martyrdom *secunda regeneratio, secunda intinctio, secundum lavacrum.*[155] Against this background the statement that some sins, by which the whole property of the son is squandered, can be forgiven only by the second baptism—itself only possible once—that is, by martyrdom, has a meaning only if the sins which can be forgiven by the Church have not dissipated the whole baptismal gift and, therefore, have not made a second baptism necessary.

Let us now resume the whole of Tertullian's train of thought as we have traced it in our interpretation. He expressed its premisses, albeit in a different sense, already in his Catholic period. In De bapt. he says:[156] *semel ergo lavacrum inimus, semel delicta diluuntur, quia ea iterari non oportet.* Here already he speaks of the baptism of blood in exactly the same way as later in De pud: *hic est baptismus qui lavacrum . . . perditum reddit.*[157] How is this to be understood in Tertullian's Catholic period? It has been taken to mean[158] that according to Tertullian penance has indeed the power to forgive sins but does not bring about readmission into the community of the Church. Since this distinction is totally alien to Tertullian, such a view is patently false. In De paen. he teaches clearly that there is a readmission into the Church.[159] Moreover, other Fathers of the Church use the same expressions and they also recognize a readmission into the Church. Indeed, as a Montanist, Tertullian understood the whole relationship between God's forgiveness, which we receive already in this life, and the *pax* of the Church in a sense which is exactly the reverse to that suggested by the above-mentioned view. *Satis denegavit (Spiritus Sanctus) veniam eorum quorum custodiam elegit . . . Hinc est quod neque . . . pax ab ecclesiis redditur.*[160] Because God, therefore, does not forgive sinners, neither do they receive a *pax.* Otherwise these sinners receive no *pax,* even though God gives them forgiveness. During his Catholic period Tertullian recognized a complete divine and church forgiveness for all sins committed after baptism. In this case, what is the meaning of the passage in De bapt.: *semel delicta diluuntur, quia ea iterari non oportet?* The attempt has been made to explain the view expressed in these words with reference to later Fathers of the Church.[161] But it always remains unsatisfactory to have recourse for an explanation to expressions which arise a hundred or a hundred and fifty years later. Certainly the sentence could be a paraphrase of the *semel lavacrum inimus,* which would mean that the uniqueness of baptism were stressed without, however, a penance which has partly the same effects as baptism being at all contested. Nevertheless, what is the reason for such a stress on the uniqueness of baptism? Certainly the second penance—especially in the practice of that time—was the more onerous. But this difference ought not to be exaggerated. A change in moral behaviour was also demanded of candidates for baptism, as is evidenced both by Tertullian with his exhortations in

De paen. and the numerous formulas of renunciation demanded before baptism. It is possible that the reason for a stress on the uniqueness of baptism is the existence of false teachings which recognized repeated baptism.[162]

But what are the reasons for the stress on the *semel dilui peccata,* in particular, and what did Tertullian as a Catholic understand by this phrase? It is, after all, somewhat vague and ambiguous. At that time there was no clear idea either of its meaning or of its compatibility with the possibility of a further penance after baptism. Tertullian was able to understand the phrase in De bapt. quite correctly, while some twenty years later he could give it a precise but false meaning from which he was able to derive a new penitential teaching. Nevertheless, the expression which is already found in De bapt. does not provide a definite key to Tertullian's view in De pud. In the latter text he was able to define the meaning of phrases in a way which previously one would not even have suspected. Nevertheless, the new teaching could receive a basis which the original and previous meaning of the formulas could not provide. Against this explanation it may be objected that Tertullian afterwards in De pud. recognizes a penance for sins[163] which can only be interpreted as venial, i.e. do not entail the loss of baptismal grace. But this admission does not seem possible. Nevertheless, this contradiction concerns not only the explanation which is offered here: it has its basis in Tertullian himself. Moreover, it is not the only case of contradiction in De pud. This case, however, can be explained without great difficulties. Tertullian wished to prove the unforgivable character of capital sins. To do this he uses the line of argument which we have explained. On the other hand, he is aware of the church institution of penance which he cannot simply explain as false and reprehensible. He simply ascribes to it, therefore, the treatment of the other sins, without considering further whether the institution of penance was actually superfluous for these sins alone, since now it is a question only of 'venial' sins.[164] Despite his restricting the number of actual serious sins, there still remained faults which were in fact sufficiently 'serious' for the institution of penance. The idea that capital sins are the only actual serious sins was not completely outlandish at that time. This is borne out by the fact that even later only those sins count as *materia confessionis* which are hardly less grave than Tertullian's capital sins.[165]

It is not necessary to inquire here, in particular, which sins according to Tertullian belong to the mortal sins which cannot be forgiven. Even the principles governing such a distinction are not of importance here. Basically, sins against God are not to be forgiven, whereas faults against men can receive forgiveness. In any case, this principle works when applied with reference to Tertullian's capital sins.[166] In some passages he has attempted to define these sins in detail with the help of biblical expressions.[167] As far as the number of these faults is concerned, a certain oscillation is noticeable. In De pud. idolatry, impurity and murder are usually mentioned, although accompanied by seven or more such sins.[168]

For Tertullian, therefore, the *delicta irremissibilia* are not only sins which, because of their gravity, God does not forgive. Rather, they form a group of faults by which the baptismal grace is destroyed, i.e. mortal sins.[169] There is really no difference between what we call mortal sin and Tertullian's *delictum irremissibile.* Tertullian's *delictum ad mortem* has the same effect on baptismal grace. Thus he can say: . . . *aut neges moechiam et fornicationem mortalia esse delicta aut irremissibilia fatearis.*[170] The deadly effect of these sins demands that they should be unforgivable. Tertullian speaks of these sins above all with reference to 1 John 5:16, according to which one should not pray for the *delicta ad mortem.* Nevertheless, all the explanations given refer to the understanding of mortal sin in today's sense.[171]

Tertullian attempts, therefore, an explicit definition of the difference between light and serious sins precisely with regard to their effect. It is here that we meet this distinction explicitly for the first time, although—from the very nature of the case—it was already clear to the conscience. Serious sins destroy grace, light sins, according to Tertullian, let it remain, at least essentially. Further, he begins to establish in detail which sins in fact belong to each group. This attempt, as far as it was carried out, was a failure. The statement that for mortal sins, in the sense outlined, there is no forgiveness is even false. Nevertheless, a certain progress in the knowledge of the nature of different kinds of sins was achieved.

V. THE BASIS OF FURTHER DEVELOPMENT

What follows in the further course of the penitential controversies and in the development of penitential teaching during the first half of the third century is, as far as our question is concerned, rather a continuation of these positions than an elaboration of truly new aspects. The Montanist errors died out. There remains the clearly expressed doctrine that man loses baptismal grace through serious sins. The distinction is maintained between the two main groups of sins, a difference based on their nature and their effects on grace. A few random and by no means complete references will serve to illustrate this, by way of a conclusion.[172]

The loss of grace through sin is clearly expressed by Cyprian of Carthage. Just as in Tertullian, so in him we read that by baptism we have become the temple of God and must now take care, *ne quid immundum et profanum templo Dei inferatur, ne offensus sedem quam inhabitat derelinquat*.[173] The *lapsi* are dead,[174] the sinner has lost his wedding garment, he is naked and mortally wounded,[175] spiritually dead he carries his own corpse around with him.[176] The baptized person loses grace if he does not preserve his innocence.[177] By this 'grace' is certainly meant interior grace, since according to Epist. 70,2[178] the baptized has *in se gratiam Christi,* and according to Epist. 64,3[179] the 'grace' of baptism is the Holy Spirit. The sinner loses this 'grace of the life-bestowing bath'.[180] Even children who with their parents are involved in apostasy lose what they received immediately after their birth.[181] Nevertheless, the two groups of sins do not appear as clearly distinct with regard to their effects on grace in Cyprian as they do in Tertullian. Nevertheless, the further development in this regard in Tertullian is not proper to him. It has already been noted that according to Cyprian there are sins which destroy grace. He even knows already the notion of *mortale crimen*[182] which is used for sins such as *adulterium, fraus* and *homicidium*. This expression already means at this time the 'sin causing the death of the life of grace' and not simply the sin which finally entails the death of hell. Moreover, Cyprian knows the group of unforgivable sins against God[183] mentioned by Tertullian which certainly denote the death of grace. Besides these he also knows other sins to which he is clearly unwilling to ascribe such deadly effects for the life of grace. According to him no one is completely without sins and faults.[184] We all fail daily[185] and are never quite without a wounded conscience, even if we are *sancti*.[186] The Our Father reminds us of daily sin[187] and so, even after the *gratia baptismi,* we are still often burdened with sin.[188] It can certainly be assumed, therefore, that the bishop of

Carthage was clearly aware of the distinction between sins which annihilate the life of grace and those which allow the radical grace to remain.

This idea is also found in Origen. The soul is alive when no *mortale peccatum* lies on it; otherwise it is dead. Christ does not then come to it.[189] The person who 'sins to death' does not preserve the baptism of the Holy Spirit.[190] Every mortal sin (*peccatum ad mortem*) means death.[191] The person who commits mortal sin loses the Holy Spirit, since Origen says that the penitent recovers the Holy Spirit, the garment (of grace) and the ring.[192] All this expresses in Origen the loss of inner grace by sin. Whether only these *ἁμαρτήματα θανατήφορα* are mortal sins for him in today's sense or whether still other sins, which he describes as *ἁμαρτήματα μὴ πρὸς θάνατον*, are also to be regarded as such, depends upon the way this distinction in his writing is to be understood. To attempt to give an answer to this question here would lead too far from our present study.[193] But that there are several kinds of sins and that these have different effects on grace is self-evident in Origen.[194]

Similarly the Didascalia Apostolorum, which originates from the first half of the third century, teaches that sin expels from the soul the Holy Spirit who otherwise dwells permanently in the baptized person, and allows access to the evil spirit.[195] If a person has sinned, then he recovers the baptismal grace, the Holy Spirit, by being reconciled through the imposition of the bishop's hands.[196]

These examples show how the progress in the question considered in this essay, which seems to have presented itself clearly as such only with Tertullian, is to be observed generally. The need to arrive at greater clarity in the penitential questions and discussions pushes the question and its development to the fore. Everywhere the concern is expressed to preserve what man has received in baptism. Everywhere is expressed the Christian conviction that God's free mercy lifts man to the mysterious participation in the divine nature and the divine life. This participation transcends human comprehension. Nevertheless, man has to safeguard it by a way of life which corresponds to his call to share in the life of God.

PART TWO

The Roman Tradition

3

THE PENITENTIAL TEACHING OF THE SHEPHERD OF HERMAS

Anyone who has been at all interested in the history of the practice and the teaching of penance in the early Church knows the important role which the 'Shepherd of Hermas'[1] with his teaching plays in this question. There is a vast amount of literature on this subject.[2] Nevertheless, after the penetrating study of this teaching by B. Poschmann[3] one would be tempted to think that the last word had been said on the correct understanding of it. This is so in so far as Poschmann has proved convincingly that the Shepherd of Hermas cannot be adduced as evidence for the view that it was only in the second century that there was opened up a further possibility of penance after baptism, whereas previously the Church, considering itself sinless, had precluded a further possibility of forgiveness after baptism. According to this view, it is only in the Shepherd of Hermas that a new, previously unheard-of, jubilee of a second penance was announced through a new revelation.

I. THE STATE OF THE RESEARCH

More recently, however, since Poschmann's major study, a quite new situation has arisen with regard to the interpretation of Hermas' penitential teaching, in so far as it has been taken as the starting-point in a very important attempt to place the penitential teaching of the early Church on an entirely new basis. What is referred to here is the important study of Joseph Grotz.[4] It is neither our task nor our intention here to expound the content of this book and to adopt a critical stance with regard to the theses which are defended therein. In the present instance, rather, the penitential teaching in the Shepherd of Hermas will be explained in its own right without much polemic or discussion with other views on the subject. This approach[5] (which was already completed some time before the appearance of Grotz's study) receives a further justification from the study just mentioned, although—at least incidentally—there must be some discussion with the interpretation which the penitential teaching in the Shepherd of Hermas receives at Grotz's hands.

It is for this reason that, by way of an introduction, a few observations on Grotz's study in general cannot be avoided. As for his interpretation of Hermas, this will be considered in the course of the exposition of the penitential teaching of Hermas itself.

What were the main lines of the previous interpretation of the penitential teaching of the early Church? Certainly there was a difference of opinion among Catholic historians of dogma on the question as to whether besides the *poenitentia publica* which generally, for some decades, was considered the normal basic form of the ancient penitential discipline, there also existed a 'private' sacramental penance, and from which point in time such a penance was in evidence. But, apart from this disagreement, it was fairly unanimously accepted that public penance, which could be designated as penance of excommunication, was also the normal basic form of the ancient penance, that it was concluded at the end of the whole process with the reconciliation of the sinner with the Church and with God in one act,[6] and that the 'excommunication', the 'binding', was the natural expression of the fact that the sinner (and precisely because of all the sins which are subjected to this penance) has placed himself in contradiction to the Church, and thus this 'excommunication' represents an essential aspect of this whole penitential process.

Against this view Grotz now defends the following basic thesis: The actual essential form of sacramental church penance, from the very beginning, has had nothing to do with such an excommunication. This excommunication was introduced only in the second century before the actual penitential process, and then only in certain, specially determined cases; it is not an essential element of the actual sacramental penance but an external measure of church discipline. It is not lifted at the time of reconciliation, at the end of the whole period of penance, but earlier so that the readmission into the community of the Church and the bestowal of divine peace are not only in reality but also temporally two distinct acts of the Church which have no intrinsic relationship the one to the other. From this period of excommunication, which was inserted before the penitential period proper, there arose, through a refinement of the procedure by the Church's discipline, the ancient grades of church penance, which are to be found both in the East and in the West. This more original form of penance, which Grotz is reluctant to style private (because it also represents the second phase of 'public penance'), occurs, precisely because it is the more original, not only within public penance for specially determined cases but also, during the whole of the patristic period, outside public penance and, indeed, for other serious sins. It became so frequently practised that Grotz even suggests that it could explain the great number of priests (beside the bishop) in many Churches.

Already, from this brief exposition of Grotz's basic thesis, it is clear that he is attempting to make a frontal attack on the thesis which is generally accepted today by Catholic historians of dogma. He maintains that there is not only (as Galtier and others hold), alongside the public form, a private form of sacramental penance which, apart from the main institution of penance, has its own distinct existence, but this private form (even if it is not called such) is precisely, from the beginning, the basic form which continues in public penance. It is only for want of close examination that this form could not be discerned within public penance. And it is for the same reason that B. Poschmann, K. Rahner and others could not see that this form of sacramental penance, completely unconnected with excommunication, was clearly practised besides public penance. Grotz begins his study of the history of penance prior to the Council of Nicea with the Shepherd of Hermas. It is here that he attempts to establish for the first time the presence of a church penance without the process of excommunication and which will be the principal norm of church penance.

As already stated, it is not our intention here to give a critical appraisal of the whole of Grotz's study, otherwise we would have to examine carefully his interpretation of penance in Cyprian, Origen and others—all of whom are important for the development of his thesis. Nevertheless, a few more basic and general remarks on Grotz's work are called for, in order to avoid overloading either the actual exposition of Hermas's teaching or the assessment of Grotz's views on this particular topic.

Grotz's thesis presents the whole of the history of penance in Christian antiquity as a unilinear development. This approach meets what the modern dogmatic theologian considers to be his needs. Whereas previously the development of penance in the early Church often appeared to the dogmatic theologian to have been somewhat tortuous, he is now able, starting from what (for him) are the all-important dogmatic theses, to explain this development easily and confidently as follows: what is today recognized and practised as the essence of the sacrament of penance was also previously and on its own the *essence of this sacrament,* and everything else which may have been involved with it, even in the early Church, is a subsequent addition on the part of church discipline having nothing at all to do with the sacrament as such—and this already at that time. But is this reconstruction correct? Only a precise examination of Grotz's argumentation would yield an answer to this question. This argumentation, however, represents such a massive and complicated construction of indirect arguments that such a precise examination would be a mammoth task, requiring as much space as the work of Grotz itself. Nevertheless, it is still possible to submit certain weighty objections which, for their part, need very exact and as direct as possible arguments to be confuted.

In the first place, he has to confine himself to very subtle, indirect arguments. Wherever he pretends that his thesis is to any extent directly attested, it is always a question of texts which have been widely quoted in previous literature. Both the defenders of a private penance existing alongside a public penance and their adversaries used these texts to support their own view. I must say quite frankly that Grotz's interpretation of these texts offers me no more light than that of Galtier and others who defend a private church penance. As far as the numerous other more indirect arguments are concerned, it seems that the texts in question are evidence of the view expressed only for the person who is already convinced of the correctness of the thesis.

In so far as the precise proof for this observation has to go beyond the Shepherd of Hermas, it cannot be given within the limits of this essay.

What appears more important to me is that no dogmatic theologian can doubt that every serious sin also involves the relationship of the sinner to the Church (and not only to God). One may view this change of relationship to the Church, as one wishes, in order to accommodate it with the teaching that the sinner, even as sinner, still remains a member of the Church. But the only person who can doubt that this relationship does change, in so far as the Church is holy, is the person who sees the Church in a nestorian, external and naturalistic way as a purely social entity and construction and who does not recognize in it the body of Christ enlivened by the Holy Spirit. Now this comprehensive and, especially, pneumatic view of the Church was current in the early Church and, indeed, to a greater extent than was the case later after the aberration of Donatism, Wyclif, Hus and the Reformers: the Church is the *holy* Church. To accept this one does not have to share the exaggerations of Windisch.[7] If this is the case, then one ought to expect that when serious sins committed after baptism are remitted the ecclesial aspect should be in evidence. But one can only think along these lines in so far as the Church expressly adverts to this aspect of sin in the celebration of penance and reacts accordingly, that is, regards the sinner as such (irrespective of which sins are involved) as in some sense 'excommunicated'. Such an 'excommunication' is obviously quite different from the excommunication of modern church law where it is only a disciplinary measure against certain sins. On the contrary, in the early Church excommunication followed from the nature of sin and was, as it were, made explicit by the church community; it is, therefore, the confirmation and the response, on the Church's part, to the sinner's change of relationship to it. This excommunication is just as much present (at least in its theological essence) today as it was in the early Church, even though it is not so apparent. Even today the sinner is excluded from the Eucharist. If one does not consider this as a consequence of sin *iuris divini,* one must recognize this exclusion—because it is *iuris ecclesiastici*—as a kind of excommunication by the Church.

Grotz lacks a precise consideration of what an excommunication is. He implicitly takes as his starting-point the modern notion. Where this notion is not verified, there is, according to him, no excommunication and, therefore, no penance of excommunication. It also follows that excommunication, where it was granted as having been present, is treated as lifted, even though there is still exclusion from the Eucharist. This notion is also modern, but it is certainly not envisaged by the early Church, in which a Christian who was excluded from this central act of the Church and from its holiest part did not count even as a normal Christian but as a sinner who had to be alienated from the church community because he was unworthy of its holiness. From this brief glance at the early Church, it is not to be expected that at that time there was recognized a celebration of penance which had nothing to do with 'excommunication'. This does not mean, however, that this 'excommunication' was not susceptible of various degrees and modifications.[8] Our view that all penance in the early Church was 'penance of excommunication' (and *therefore* was 'public') does not exclude an 'excommunication' which would correspond more to our modern notion. The person who is no longer bothered about his Christian life and who in no way has the intention to do penance and mend his ways was naturally excluded from the Church in a way (as can be clearly seen, for example, in Cyprian) which does not correspond simply and in every respect with that 'exclusion' which is imposed on a repentant sinner who has been admitted to penance and is striving to reform himself. This access to penance was already an important step towards a purification of the relationship between the sinner and the Church and, on the other hand, it represents a specific act of grace on the Church's part which is tied to certain conditions. Nevertheless, one cannot conclude from all this that, in those cases where an excommunication has been imposed, this can already have been lifted in the sense attested in the early Church and that all that had to follow was the non-ecclesial, purely sacramental part of penance, that is a simple reconciliation with God through the Church (not, however, any longer a reconciliation through the Church *with* the Church). In any case, I cannot find sufficient proofs for this theory of Grotz. From the early Church's viewpoint, it seems self-evident that in every case where there is an exclusion from the Eucharist (and not even Grotz can deny that such an exclusion is imposed until the definitive reconciliation with God) there is also a kind of excommunication. This follows from the fact that the Eucharist is precisely the sacrament of full church unity.

Moreover, Grotz appears to have committed a fundamental methodological fault in that he begins his investigation with the Pastor Hermae and not with the New Testament. It is true that everyone can begin his theme where he wishes. One may consider patristic theology while presupposing biblical theology. Nevertheless, if one holds that the penance of excommunication is a subsequent and additional secondary form of an original type of penance, and if this development occurred already before the middle of the second century, then the question poses itself whether this was already the case in the New Testament which, after all, is relatively near this time. Without wishing to give detailed proof, we feel justified in claiming that a close exegesis of Matthew 16 and 18, considered in itself and in the context of the Old Testament, the customs of the synagogue communities at the time of Jesus and the practice of sects and groups at that time, together with a precise understanding of the life of the community, as this is attested in Paul's letters, lead to the conclusion that the original biblical notion of church penance is that of a penance of excommunication. The person who sins seriously, who gravely offends the holiness of the community of those who are called, is 'bound' and he *must* be 'unbound'. The loosening forgiveness of sins is the lifting of this binding on earth by which the loosening in heaven, therefore the forgiveness of guilt before God, becomes effective. If, according to a correct interpretation of the text of Matthew 16 and especially Matthew 18 it must be a question of the power to forgive *sins,* and if here the binding is understood as 'banning' and the loosing as the lifting of this ban and precisely as the forgiveness of sins by the whole Church—if, therefore, these texts attest a penance of excommunication, then it is already totally unlikely that we do not have here the actual and original form of the sacrament of forgiveness which Christ left to his Church. Further, if one observes that this excommunication was applied in the Church of the apostles and the way it was applied, and one notices that, in Paul, the catalogue of sins which exclude people from the kingdom of God (therefore all serious sins) coincides with the list of those sins which require an 'avoidance' of the sinners by the Church until they have mended their ways, then a penance of excommunication for the apostolic Church has such evidence in its favour that there is no longer any place for another kind of church penance. Also in this regard, it is hardly to be expected that such a penance with excommunication should have been a secondary development; on the contrary, the possibility has to be faced that the practice of such a penance of excommunication became more variegated and underwent developments and refinements corresponding to the increasingly complicated conditions of the early Church. But this is something quite different from the subsequent appearance of this penance from (or, in addition to) a form which originally had nothing whatsoever to do with such an excommunication.

For methodical progress in the question under discussion there is, therefore, the basic expectation that church penance is *penance of excommunication,* by which is meant excommunication in the theological and not in the modern church law sense of the term. For this assumption to be rejected it must be clearly proved—in the present case, therefore, for the Shepherd of Hermas—that there is a group of sinners which, on the one hand, according to the notion of the early Church needs an actual sacramental measure of the Church for the remission of its sins and for reconciliation with God, but which, on the other hand, does not have to be reconciled with the Church in any way. In this case, one would not have to see any change in the relationship with the Church, either in the sin or in the reconciliation. If such proof cannot be adduced in respect of the Shepherd of Hermas and if, indeed, the very contrary is indicated in his case for all sinners who certainly need a second metanoia, then at least Hermas is excluded from the witnesses to Grotz's theory. This point will be proven here by a positive exposition of the penitential teaching of the Shepherd of Hermas. It is only accidentally, in the course of this exposition, that a position will be taken with regard to Grotz's interpretation of this teaching.

II. THE SHEPHERD OF HERMAS—THE AUTHOR AND HIS WORK[9]

Without going into the many obscure literary questions which are still posed with regard to the Shepherd of Hermas,[10] we may take the following points as being generally accepted. According to the latest results of research, which are partly hypothetical, the composition of the entire work in its present form is to be placed between *c.* A.D. 75–175[11] (while it is not possible to ascribe it to the time of Clement of Rome). A Roman tradition, based on the Muratorian Canon, identifies the author Hermas as the brother of the Roman bishop Pius I (A.D. 142–55).[12] What Hermas, who undoubtedly hails from a Judaeo-Christian milieu,[13] recounts about himself and his family, especially in the first four visions, is hardly a mere literary fiction.[14] It is difficult to deny that these accounts contain a genuine autobiographical core; but this latter has been considerably elaborated with later reflections and developments.

The most important passages for the penitential question in the Shepherd of Hermas are: Vis. I 1,9 (GCS 48:p. 2,14–17); ibid., 3,2 (GCS 48:pp. 3,16–4,2; here the possibility of penance is already assumed!); Vis. II 2,2–3,4 (GCS 48:pp. 5,18–7,4; the content of the 'booklet' which the Church in the guise of an old lady transmits as the great revelation in a vision); Vis. III 2,4–8,9 (GCS 48:p. 9,14–15,16; the vision of the construction of the Church as a tower: the 'allegory of the tower'); Mand. IV 1,4–3,7 (GCS 48:pp. 26,5–28,19; the instruction on marital purity by the 'Shepherd': the singular character of post-baptismal penance; the relationship between baptism and penance after baptism; the justification and the limits of the view of 'certain teachers' on this point); Sim. VIII (GCS 48:pp. 65,18–76,5; the differentiation of various groups of penitents, their examination by the Shepherd and their respective destiny); Sim. IX (GCS 48:pp. 76,7–105,16; appendix and summary: the second 'allegory of the tower').[15]

The problem posed for the history of dogma by the penitential teaching of the Shepherd of Hermas consists in the fact that a forgiveness of all the sins which have been committed after baptism is announced as being possible only once.

Now is this possibility according to Hermas a new and previously non-existent possibility which, as such, needed to be communicated through a new revelation? Is it, therefore, an extraordinary concession made to those who have been Christians for some time, a kind of 'jubilee' which presupposes that previously both in theory and in practice (or at least in practice) a forgiveness (by the Church) was no longer possible for capital sins committed after baptism? (This view could be called the 'baptismal theory' and is held by Funk,[16] Batiffol, Windisch, Preuschen, Schwartz, H. Koch, Dibelius, Weinel, Puech, Laun, v. Harnack, Loofs, Seeberg, Adam, Rauschen, Hoh, Amann).[17] Or does the Shepherd of Hermas attest the existence of a previous practice and theory of the Church, so that the actual significance of the new revelation lies not in the possibility of the forgiveness of all sins but in the urgency of penance in view of the imminent end of the world, in the personal assurance of actual forgiveness to Hermas and his family and in the exhortation to all sinners to do penance in the assurance that such penance will be effective (thus Stufler, d'Ales, Hunermann, Tixeront, Galtier, Poschmann)?

A third possibility, which would count as a middle course between the two views mentioned above, is that Hermas is countering the rigorists who are unwilling to admit a post-baptismal penance. He would be doing this in view of the imminent end of the world. It is possible that in Rome at the time of 'Hermas', because of a strong rigoristic current, there began to emerge a more definite and more urgent tendency which advocated a post-baptismal penance (cf. R. Joly, pp. 23–7). Perhaps we have here, therefore, the attempt to do justice to both tendencies: on the one hand, the possibility of a penance after baptism is presupposed, while, on the other hand, this possibility is limited and confined practically to a single opportunity. It is obvious that Hermas wishes to avoid a head-on clash with the rigorists.[18]

III. THE LIMITATION OF THE ACCEPTED POSSIBILITY OF PENANCE

First of all, we must prescind from the question of whether and how the Church can be a cause for the remission of sins.[19] In any case, Hermas teaches that all sins (including those which will later be the so-called 'capital sins') can be forgiven by genuine sorrow and repentance. According to him, this possibility for those who are already baptized Christians is not a *new* grace which is merely announced through his revelation as a kind of 'jubilee'. Although it is offered only once for sins committed after baptism, it was still previously recognized by the Christian Church. All that Hermas does is to modify this traditional belief by limiting it eschatologically in view of his conviction that the end of the world is imminent. For him personally the renewal of this ancient truth by the 'old woman Church' and the 'shepherd', as far as it concerns himself, his family and his relatives, represents an urgent exhortation, a consolation and assurance of their own salvation, all rolled into one. It is worthwhile considering each of these points in turn.

1. Forgiveness is Possible

A) ALL SINS ARE FORGIVABLE

Hermas certainly recognizes *a kind of apostasy from faith* for which, he says, there is no question of a metanoia. He describes this apostasy (clearly with reference to Mark 3:29 par.) as a 'blasphemous' offence and as completely deliberate (*ἐκ καρδίας:* Sim. IX 26,5 [GCS 48:p. 95 n.26 f.]). Upon close examination, it becomes clear that what makes these sins irremissible is not the objective gravity of the action itself but the obstinacy and remorselessness associated with them (see, e.g. Sim. VIII 6 [GCS 48:pp. 71,7–72,10]). Thus, for our purpose, it does not matter whether, in the relevant cases (i.e. where the angel of penance makes a distinction between the repentant and the unrepentant), Hermas regards this irremissible character as being only tied to this apostasy in fact, or whether he considers it as following with a moral or absolute necessity from the very nature of the sins in question.[20] In any case, he does not mean that a sin for which a person is sorry and does penance is unforgivable. This is clear by the way he stresses that there has been no sorrow for these sins: despite exhortation, not one of these sinners has done penance (Sim. VIII 6,4 [GCS 48:pp. 71,21–72,1]), they have fallen away definitively (Sim. IX 26,3 [GCS 48:p. 95 n.18–21]), they persist in their decision (Sim. VIII 7,3 [GCS 48:pp. 72,17–73,2]) and *therefore* do not receive any penance from God, that is, God does not give them the grace to enable them to answer his call to repentance, since they will only simulate repentance and blaspheme his name still further (Sim. VIII 6,2 [GCS 48:p. 71 n.11–15]). Even in the case of this blasphemous apostasy it is unrepentance that is the reason for the fact that it cannot be forgiven. This point is made clearer by the fact that the same designation of 'those who do not have' penance is applied to sinners who belong to the same class as others who, precisely because of their sorrow, do receive forgiveness (Sim. VIII 8,2 f. [GCS 48:pp. 73,16–74,4]; IX 23,2.4 f. [GCS 48:p. 94, 7–11,14–22]); which means that Hermas (as he himself concedes: Sim. IX 19,3 [GCS 48:p. 92,13–20]) has not been able to distinguish and to categorize sins clearly according to their objective gravity in such a way that it becomes evident why some receive forgiveness while others do not. Such a distinction can express and, to a certain extent, explain only a difference in the spiritual attitude towards penance. It does not represent a difference between what is forgivable and what is unforgivable which is independent of sorrow and repentance or unrepentance. The sin of apostasy does not, therefore, even according to Hermas himself, contravene his general principle: penance for sins entails life, unrepentance entails death (Sim. VI 2,3 [GCS 48:p. 60,2–7]; VIII 6,6 [GCS 48:p. 72,5–10]); the person who repents from the bottom of his heart and so purifies himself from the sins mentioned, to the extent of not committing them again, will receive from the Lord the healing of his earlier sins (Sim. VIII 11,3 [GCS 48:pp. 75,20–76,3]). Following this principle, Hermas promises forgiveness even to the gravest sins: adultery (Mand. IV 1,8 [GCS 48:p. 26,16–20]), falling away from faith (even after a long time: Vis. I 3,2 (GCS 48:pp. 3,16–4,2). In this regard, it is worth noting that Hermas' children had fallen away from the faith and had denounced their parents: Vis. II 2,2–4 (GCS 48:pp. 5,18–6,4); 3,1 (ibid., p. 6,18–23); Sim. IX 21,3–4 (GCS 48:p. 93,14–20); 26,5–6 (GCS 48:p. 95,25–32).[21] Hermas promises forgiveness to false teaching in Sim. IX 19,2 (GCS 48:p. 92,7–13).

In general Hermas sees very clearly that certain sins destroy the grace of baptism, and even for these sins he teaches that there is a forgiveness which restores the baptismal seal (Sim. VIII 6,3 [GCS 48:p. 71,15–21]). He rejects, therefore, the principle by which, from Tertullian onwards, the unforgivable character of capital sins will later be justified: sins which destroy the grace of baptism can be remitted only by a second baptism which (apart from the baptism of blood in martyrdom) does not exist. Already, on the basis of this theological principle, there can be no sinners who, according to Hermas, can be refused the possibility of forgiveness because of the objective seriousness of their faults. Such fundamental gravity must show itself, if anywhere at all, in its detrimental effect on the grace of baptism. But since, according to Hermas, the baptismal seal is restored by penance, on the one hand there can be no unforgiveable sins in his view (granted the presence of penance) and, on the other hand, penance, considered as the remission of sins, is clearly seen as parallel to baptism.

These sinners who, according to Hermas, in general and without exception have a possibilitiy of penance when they are compared with one another evince considerable differences with regard both to the objective seriousness of their sins and to their attitude to penance and their intention to be converted. There is naturally a connection between these two aspects: the more serious the sin the less likely it is (in normal circumstances) that the sinner has the will to repent. Hermas draws the distinction between the different groups of sinners especially in Vis. III (GCS 48:p. 7–19). Grotz has analysed these groups carefully (in our opinion rather too subtly and exactly). There is no need for us to enter any further into these distinctions here. Since, even if Grotz denies that the sinners of some groups are excommunicated, while renouncing the possibility of church reconciliation for other groups (thus, according to him, the stones who are simply rejected in Vis. III 2,7a–5,5 [GCS 48:pp. 926–7; 12,11–17] are not excommunicated, whereas the stones which have been cast far away in Vis. III 2,7c [GCS 48:p. 9,28–9] and 2,9–6,1 and 7,1–3 [GCS 48:pp. 10,3–8; 12,18–22; 13,20–14,6] are, in his view, excommunicated in the fullest sense and can no longer receive a church reconciliation), he nevertheless allows a possibility of salvation for all sinners, at least by means of subjective penance, even if, in this case, the assurance of salvation is not very great.[22] In agreement with Grotz, therefore, we have to make the following observation: there is simply no exclusion from salvation for the sinner who has committed sin after baptism, purely because of the gravity of his fault and quite independently of whether or not he intends to do penance. On this score, at least, even a church reconciliation cannot be impossible.

B) THE LIMIT

That the possibility of penance is in fact only limited is a point often made by the Shepherd of Hermas. In the great and decisive revelation concerning penance in the second vision it is established that for the 'saints' (i.e. for baptized Christians who, although they may be sinners, are still given this name by Hermas) penance 'from the fixed day' on is no longer possible, since the days are fulfilled and Christians can no longer expect salvation from the sins committed from now on (Vis. II 2,4–5 [GCS 48:pp. 5,25–6,8]; similarly Vis. III 5,5 [ibid.,

p. 12,11–17]; 8,8 f. [ibid., p. 15,9–16]; 9,5 [ibid., p. 16,5–8]; Sim. IX 9,4 [ibid., p. 83,26–9]; 19,2 [ibid., p. 92,7–13]; 20,4 [ibid., p. 93,2–6]; 21,4 [ibid., p. 93,17–20]; 26,6 [ibid., p. 95,27–32]; Sim. X 4,4 [ibid., pp. 111,18–112,4]). But in these passages the reason for the limitation is clear: the end of the world is imminent (for Hermas this seems to be announced by the dreaded, near 'tribulation' of a persecution: Vis. II 2,7 [GCS 48:p. 6,10–13]; 3,4 [ibid., p. 7,2–4]) and there is no *τόπος* (Vis. III 5,5 [GCS 48:p. 12,11–17]) for penance. Because the judgement is coming soon and, therefore, the 'tower' is about to be completed, beforehand there is only a *τόπος* for doing good and so for true penance (ibid. 9,5 [GCS 48:p. 16,7–8]). Thus penance must be done 'rapidly' and not delayed (Sim. IX 19,2 [GCS 48:p. 92,7–13] and cf. VIII 9,4 [GCS 48:p. 74,21–5]).

If in Vis. II, 2,5 (GCS 48:p. 6,4–8) the days for penance for the saints are declared as being fulfilled, while the opportunity for (baptismal) penance is still offered to the pagans until the 'last day', the suggested difference between the deadline for the possibility of penance for Christians and that of baptism does not contradict the explanation given above. The Christian must have finished his penance by the last day and cannot begin it only then. If he wishes to complete it he must have begun it quite a while before this day. The critical moment for his penance, therefore, occurs already before the last day and, indeed, is determined by the threatening imminence of the end of the world, whereas for the pagan there is still the possibility of baptism right up to this day. (The idea that the Christian must not merely begin his penance but already have finished it is expressed e.g. in Sim. VIII 7,3 [CGS 48:pp. 72,17–73,2]; 8,3.5 [GCS 48:p. 74,1–10]; 9,4 [ibid., p. 74,21–5]; 10,1.3 [ibid., pp. 74,26–75,3.6–11]; it is even stressed that only after a long penance and after the completion of its conditions will sins be forgiven: Sim. VII 4 [GCS 48:pp. 64,17–65,2]). It might also be asked whether the distinction between a critical deadline for the penance of Christians, on the one hand, and for pagans, on the other, evinces a view which was widespread in Hermas' time, namely that before the actual end of the world and before the judgement there would be a 'reign of a thousand years' in which the pagans would still be able to be baptized, while bad Christians would have no further possibility of penance (since the good Christians would already have begun to reign with the Lord).[23] Moreover, Vis. II 2,5 (GCS 48:p. 6,4–8), translated literally and verbatim, runs: 'The days of penance for the saints are fulfilled; *and* for the pagans, though (δέ) there is penance up to the last day.' Thus the δέ, because of the previous καί, establishes an opposition only between the saints and the pagans[24] but not between the limits of penance themselves; rather, the καί stresses the identity of these two limits. Why, therefore, should Hermas not stress that for the pagans *also* the possibility of baptism ends with the last day? According to his expressed opinion the righteous who have died in pre-Christian times can and must be baptized in the underworld. Thus it can hardly be said that it is impossible that he stresses that from the now imminent day onwards there is no longer any possibility of salvation in the next life and that, therefore, the pagans and the faithful should strive to avail themselves of this last and quickly fading chance of salvation.

The day which in Vis. II is announced as the deadline for the possibility for penance and which here, at least, practically seems to coincide with the day on which this limit is promulgated in the vision to Hermas must not, however, be treated as a rigid and fixed term. In the course of the revelations throughout the book it is repeatedly postponed.[25] Hermas does not understand the exact determination of the term very precisely: it arrives with the completion of the tower, the final construction of which has been interrupted, precisely to allow the possibility of penance (Sim. X 4,4 [GCS 48:pp. 111,18–112,4])!

In any event, in the whole book the limit for penance remains determined by the last day, expected as imminent, and the completion of the tower. If, therefore, because of the imminent end of the world there is for the faithful still a possibility for the remission of faults, but only if they are zealous and do penance immediately, then it is easy to understand that Hermas can deny to those who still have to receive baptism (and for this, at that time, a long preparation was necessary)[26] the possibility of finding the opportunity of further penance after baptism solely because of the nearness of the last day: Mand. IV 3,3 (GCS 48:p. 28,3–7); Vis. II 2,5 (ibid. p. 6,4–8).

The decisive reason for the principle 'Only one, unique remission of sins in baptism' is certainly other than that just mentioned; it is the 'ideal' principle for neophytes and the newly-baptized, which is proposed to them but which does not preclude the possibility of a further penance after baptism.[27]

2. *The Situation before Hermas*

A) THE POSSIBILITY OF A PENANCE FOR ALL SINS

In Vis. II the decisive revelation on penance is given to Hermas in the form of a booklet which he must transcribe and only after a long time be able to decipher (1,1–2,1 [GCS 48:p. 5,3–18]). This revelation concerns Hermas himself and his family (2,2 [ibid., p. 5,18–22]), but also all 'God's elect' (1,3 [ibid., p. 5,7–11]).

According to this vision his family (which has sinned) and 'all the saints' (who are also sinners), together with the church leaders (who also must mend their ways) will be forgiven their sins which they have previously committed (but only these) by God's mercy, provided that they do penance (conversion is taken for granted), change their ways, do not doubt God's readiness to forgive and undergo the 'tribulation' which precedes the end of the world without renouncing their faith (2,2–3,4 [GCS 48:pp. 5,18–7,4]). This is the content of the 'new' revelation.

Now what is the actual meaning of this revelation? Does it mean that previously there was no such possibility for the forgiveness of sins, so that now, for the first time, by means of this new revelation this possibility is offered by God for sins which have been committed after baptism? Or is it merely a question of the promise of the actual conversion of Hermas' family, of the limit for penance and, therefore, of the relative impossibility of being able to do penance later for new sins, both of these circumstances, together with the divine assurance of an actual forgiveness, being the (psychological) reason for the actual conversion of his family?

The second interpretation is the only one possible, and this for the following reasons. In the first place, even before this new revelation Hermas considers it completely self-evident that his children will be inscribed in the book of life along with the saints (Vis. I 3,2 [GCS 48:pp. 3,16–4,2]), if they do penance wholeheartedly, and that only pagans and *unrepentant* apostates (Hermas' children were also apostates) will be really rejected (Vis. I 4,2 [GCS 48:p. 4,18–21]). The possibility of a forgiveness of sins is, therefore, presupposed as self-evident in the first vision, without the murmur of a word to the effect that the promise made is something previously unheard-of. The content of the revelation on penance itself corroborates this observation: if Hermas communicates it as 'the Lord's oath' to his family, it entails the forgiveness of sins because of the change of heart which is thereby elicited (this communication certainly cannot effect anything else; it is obviously not to be considered the reason for the immediate forgiveness itself) (Vis. II 2,4 [GCS 48:pp. 5,25–6,4]). The Lord's oath (2,5.8 [ibid., p. 6,4–8,14–17]), according to the obvious sense of the text, does not have as its subject the first opening of a possibility of penance (there is no mention of this), but the limitation of this possibility for penance. It is easy to see that such a communication can have the announced effect, already mentioned, namely the actual penance and the subsequent forgiveness of the sins of his family. This makes for an increase in the subjective and personal assurance of the forgiveness of sins (which, because of the uncertainty of fulfilling all the conditions necessary for forgiveness, is not absolute), and in turn this certainty becomes a new motive for an effective conversion, in so far as it facilitates the overthrow of doubt and despair (cf. Vis. III 11 [GCS 48:pp. 17,20–18,2]) which otherwise easily have a detrimental effect on the will to do penance.

The content of the revelation is, therefore, not the opening of a new, previously non-existent possibility of penance, but the impossibility of a later penance; and this not simply as a threat but as the effective motive for conversion which is *still* possible 'now', 'in these days'. This interpretation is confirmed by the observation in Mand. IV 3,4–5 (GCS 48:p. 28,7–13) that God, in his providence, has allowed for a penance for the faithful even after baptism because he knew that men, because of their own weakness and the devil's guile, would sin again after baptism.

The fact that Hermas 'has heard from certain teachers[28] that there is no other penance than that by which we descended into the water and received absolution of our earlier sins' (Mand. IV 3,1 [ibid., pp. 27,21–28,2]) cannot be adduced as a proof that the possibility of the forgiveness of post-baptismal sins is opened up for the first time by this revelation. The angel of penance verifies Hermas' grasp of the teachers' thesis (3,2 [ibid., p. 28,2–3]), but the manner in which this is done shows that there must always have been the possibility of penance for sins after baptism. The principle of the 'teachers' is not interpreted as being obsolete, as if it were previously correct but now had been abolished by a new revelation; rather, it is presented as a still valid formulation of the *ideal* prescription (which earlier no less than now excludes the possibility of a second penance): 'You have heard correctly [with this principle of the "teachers"]. It is so. Because the person who has received pardon for his sins must sin no more but must persevere in purity.' The ἔδει in the imperfect implies (as, e.g. in Vis. III 4,3 [GCS 48:p. 11,14–22]; Sim. VI 4,2 [ibid., p. 62,12–13]), as opposed to a δεῖ (Mand. IV 1,8 [ibid., p. 26,16–20]; Sim. VII 1 [ibid., p. 64,2–7]), that the person who was baptized earlier ought not to have sinned, but he has still done so, whereas a present δεῖ simply expresses the strict moral necessity without reference to its being contradicted by the reality. Since this ἔδει is brought in not as an opposition but as the basis for, and as a more precise explanation of, the teachers' principle (γάρ!), this principle, according to the angel of penance (i.e. according to Hermas) is intended to express nothing more than the *prescription* to preserve the grace of baptism.

The rest of the angel's explanation shows that this interpretation is correct, i.e. that it is a question of the compatibility of two axioms ('pardon only by baptism'—'penance for sins after baptism') and not of their mutual exclusion. The angel does not wish to go any further into his explanation (the δηλώσω does not say any more, since the possibility of penance has been known to Hermas for a long time already and, therefore, does not need a new 'revelation'). But, with this explanation, he does not wish to give any opportunity for sinning to either present or future newly-baptized persons. In fact, these newly-baptized persons (the following sentence in Mand. IV 3,3b [ibid., p. 28,5–7] is, as the γάρ indicates, only intended as the justification of the intention not to give a pretext for sin, but not as the content of the announced 'explanation') do not have μετάνοια but the (baptismal-) pardon of their sins; i.e. therefore they must (because they have no pretext for sinning) simply realize that they have to preserve this forgiveness of their sins (3,3b.4 [GCS 48:p. 28,5–7.7–11]).

There now follows the announced further explanation as to why and how there is still a possibility of penance for sins committed after baptism, notwithstanding the ideal axiom of the teachers (3,4–6 [ibid., p. 28,7–16]): those who have been Christians for some time have (and ought to know that they have) a penance for their sins, because God, in his providence, knows men's weakness and the devil's guile and has, therefore, in his great mercy (it is called great and not new!) granted such a possibility for penance. Thus the person who, after baptism (this is the 'great and holy calling'),[29] being tempted by the devil, falls into sin has still one (and only one) possibility for penance and forgiveness. The precise explanation of the meaning and the limits of the teachers' axiom and the justification of the single possibility of penance for those who are already Christians is based not on the fact that an earlier, stricter principle has been replaced by a new, more lenient one—there is no mention of such a change—but on the fact that God, in his mercy, has created such a possibility for forgiveness. Thus this principle of the teachers is more an ideal norm than a principle which does not admit of exceptions in practice.

If it were a question of a 'jubilee' which is to be proclaimed through a new revelation, then the problem of how the opinion of the teachers is to be understood and to be justified as still valid would hardly arise; rather, it could just be said that this axiom has now been abrogated. But then a distinction between 'pardon' in baptism and 'penance' for sins committed after baptism would be completely superfluous; then the possibility of penance for those who are already Christians would not be demonstrable with reasons which are universal, always valid and always known by God; then the inefficacy of a further possibility for penance after the single post-baptismal μετάνοια (Mand. IV 3,6b [ibid., p. 28,14–15]) must appear more clearly and must have its basis in *God* and not in the doubtful state of the human conscience, as it always has according to Hermas.[30]

When Hermas says that, after this explanation of the angel, he 'lives again' (Mand. IV 3,7 [ibid., p. 28,16–19]), this does not mean that he experienced something completely new from the angel; the phrase belongs more to the rhetorical conclusions of a rather clumsy stylist. Hermas was already aware of the possibility of penance (irrespective of how he may have envisaged it). Nevertheless, there was sufficient reason in the angel's explanation for a 'new life'. Even if the fundamental possibility of a remission of sins after baptism was previously recognized and, therefore, presented no purely theoretical problem, the doubt over the effectiveness of post-baptismal penance could, nevertheless, have very well been a practical problem. If one were convinced that a long and tiresome effort was required, that this had to be *metanoia* and not only *aphesis* of sins, then even Hermas could be very unsure about the actual effectiveness of penance (despite the already known theoretical principle). The new explanation of the old possibility must have helped him and his readers to surmount the weakness of their spirit, caused by age and doubt (Vis. III 9,2 [ibid., p. 15,25–7]), and to become sure that their previous sins have really been forgiven, in so far as, from now on, they sin no more (Mand. IV 3,7 [ibid., p. 28,16–19]).

In conclusion we can say, therefore: neither in Vis. II nor in Mand. IV is there any mention of the fact that the announced possibility of penance for sins committed after baptism is a new, previously unheard-of privilege of God's grace. What is new is the eschatological limitation of this possibility of penance and the assurance of its effective success in the present cases.

For the correct assessment of this teaching of Hermas we should keep the following point in mind: as much as this eschatological notion of penance in Hermas with regard to the imminent arrival of the last day is based on subjective and erroneous assumptions,[31] it also contains a nucleus of truth which today is only too easily forgotten: the person who sins after baptism puts himself in a situation which, despite the fundamental possibility for penance and forgiveness, from man's viewpoint contains no guarantee of a new forgiveness. This is because the sinner is deprived of the certainty that he will in fact have again the interior (he has sinned as a believer!) and the exterior (he can always die) possibility of a conversion. If then this possibility is indeed granted to him, it is not simply the mere application of a universal, institutional possibility of forgiveness, but an 'actual', always 'once and for all' grace of God, over which he has no control, which always comes to him as a new miracle, as a 'revelation', and in which there is no guarantee that it will be granted to him ever again if he should squander it. Hermas is more correct than he appears at first sight if, according to our view, he does not announce a 'jubilee'. The sentence directed to the concrete existence of a man, 'Penance is granted to you', must affect the man of today, as it did Hermas then, as an unexpected gift, which one has to doubt when he thinks of the irrational depravity of the man who, while believing, still sins, and when he thinks of his inevitable lack of control over his present existence.

B) BAPTISM AND FURTHER PENANCE

Although this question has already been touched upon briefly, it still needs to be examined separately. This examination will, in its turn, act as a confirmation of the findings of the last section. In Mand. IV 3,3 ([GCS 48:p. 28,3–7]) Hermas makes a distinction between a *metanoia* after baptism and the *aphesis* in baptism. Alongside the general notion of every conversion (cf. Mand. IV 3,1 [ibid., pp. 27,21–28,2]) he knows, therefore, of a narrower, specific kind which applies only to sins committed after baptism. It has already been said that, in connection with Mand. IV 3, such a distinction would be completely superfluous if the post-baptismal forgiveness were simply a matter of a new act of God's grace which was determined only by God's good pleasure. In this case, Hermas would only have to explain that new Christians have no such possibility since it was not granted to those who have been Christians for some time. Indeed, it would be superfluous to explain that new Christians ought not to count on a *metanoia,* but must preserve the *aphesis* (which is obviously meant as the greater and better and, therefore, not to be squandered).

Nevertheless, it is still not yet clear what makes the difference between this *aphesis* and the *metanoia*. This is precisely what is not said. Thus it may be assumed, despite the literary device of an instruction by an angel, that the distinction was already known. And this would be a confirmation of the fact that the possibility of penance after baptism was not an unheard-of novelty. If we wish to explain, at least indirectly, the difference between these two notions, then we could consider that, according to the view of the Shepherd of Hermas, *metanoia* was a difficult and long-lasting operation,[32] a 'humiliation and purification of the soul', emanating from a fresh insight (Mand. IV 2,2 [ibid., p. 27,9–16]), living according to the commandments (2,4 [ibid., p. 27,19–20]), praying for forgiveness Vis. I 1,9 [ibid., p. 2,14–17]), being corrected by others (Vis. I 3,2 [ibid., pp. 3,16–4,2]) and especially by church officials (Vis. II 4,3 [ibid., p. 7,14–18]) who have a right to administer discipline in the community (Vis. III 9,10 [ibid., p. 16,18–21] and Sim. IX 31,5 f. [ibid., pp. 100,11–101,17]) which can extend to excommunication (cf. Mand. IV 1,8.9 [ibid., p. 26,16–23]: if a private relationship with the adulterous wife has already been broken off, then she cannot be tolerated in the community either). To all these would certainly be added fasting (cf. Vis. III 10,6 [ibid., p. 17,7–10]; Sim. V 1 [ibid., p. 52,2–19]), almsgiving (Vis. III 9,4–6 [ibid., p. 16,4–11]; Sim. V 3 [ibid., pp. 54,11–55,13]) and similar works of neighbourly love (Mand. VIII 10 [ibid., pp. 35,21–36,4]; Sim. IX 20 [ibid., pp. 92, 21–93,6]) and finally the patient bearing of the tribulations imposed by God himself (Sim. VI 3,4–6 [ibid., pp. 61,12–62,8]).

It is in such a regulated penance which only slowly (cf. e.g. Sim. VI 4 [ibid., p. 62,9–21]) leads to man's 'healing' and to the 'purification' from sins (healing: Vis. I 1,9 [ibid., p. 2,14–17]; Mand. IV 1,11 [ibid., p. 27,2–5]; purification: Vis. III 2,2 [ibid., p. 9,9–12]; Sim. VII 2 [ibid., p. 64,7–13]) and only in this way to the pardon of sins which Hermas ascribes to *metanoia* (Vis. II 2,4 [ibid., pp. 5,25–6,4]; Mand. IV 4,4 [ibid., pp. 28,27–29,3]; Sim. VII 4 [ibid., pp. 64,17–65,2]; Sim. IX 33,3 [ibid., pp. 104,11–105,15]) that there can be seen a difference from the *aphesis* of baptism in which the forgiveness of sins is obtained more speedily, more surely and with less effort. This is one way of understanding the view of the 'teachers' who know only a single *metanoia* of baptism which leads immediately to a full *aphesis* of sins without the long way of penance.

In this way it also becomes clearer that the angel, despite the possibility of a penance after baptism, does not have to contradict the view of the teachers, since *such* an *aphesis* without penance in the narrow sense of a long-lasting performance of penance is, even according to his message, given only once, and that in baptism. Whether Hermas himself thought exactly along these lines is not easy to prove from the brief reference in Mand. IV 3,3 (GCS 48:28,3–7). Nevertheless, it is a plausible explanation of the difference in question. Also later tradition,[33] beginning with Clement of Alexandria, knows this distinction and explains it in the way we have proposed. If this whole later tradition does not depend upon the brief reference in Hermas, just as it was hardly invented by Hermas himself, then this explanation of his expressions becomes all the more reasonable.

Nevertheless, the difference between the baptismal remission and *metanoia* after baptism should not be exaggerated. As we have said, the early Church knew a very real performance of penance for catechumens, as the successful organization of the institution of the catechumenate in the second century shows. Hermas himself suggests this, since in Mand. IV 3,1 (ibid., pp. 27,21–28,2) the *metanoia*, taken literally, means not baptism itself but 'penance' on the occasion (ὅτε) of baptism.

IV. THE UNREPEATABLE CHARACTER OF THE GRANTING OF PENANCE

The possibility of receiving the forgiveness of all sins committed after baptism is, therefore, according to Hermas, not given for the first time by a new revelation. But it is granted for one occasion only.

1. The Fact of the Unrepeatable Character

In two passages Hermas says that this *metanoia* announced by him is once and for all: Mand. IV 1,8 (ibid., p. 26,16–20); 3,6 (ibid., p. 28,13–16). Here we have the first tangible witness for such an unrepeatable character. Now was Hermas the first to formulate this principle or did he merely take up a previously existing principle? Does this unrepeatable character concern the possibility of a unique granting of *church* penance and reconciliation or does it mean that the sinner can receive the forgiveness of his sins only once from *God*? An answer to this question is possible only (if at all) in so far as the basis of this unrepeatable character in Hermas is clarified.

2. The Basis and Meaning of the Unrepeatable Character of the Granting of Penance

The reasons for the unrepeatable character of penance after baptism according to Hermas are varied. In the first place, the notion of the limitation of penance plays an important role in this connection. Since absolutely every possibility of penance will cease with the imminent end of the world,[34] while the completion of penance requires a certain amount of time, for this practical reason alone Hermas cannot envisage a repeated penance. This idea is many times expressed and, given this assumption, the unrepeatable character of penance is not at all surprising or problematical. This limitation is precisely the decisive point in Hermas' prophecy on penance, even if it is not the unique reason for the unrepeatable character of penance.

Hermas also often emphasizes that a performance of penance which is hesitant, doubtful and does not really come 'from the heart' can only with difficulty hope for forgiveness. The reason why certain sins will not be forgiven is that there is a lack of true repentance. Similarly, Hermas considers a falling back after the first post-baptismal penance as a sign of unrepentance and lack of sincerity in the previous repentance and, because of the hopelessness of the situation, holds a further penance as impossible. In practice, it was always a question, in those days, of a person who had been separated or excommunicated from the Church, who after a long penance had been accepted by the Church again and then, once more, had fallen away from it. Thus it is hardly strange that the decisiveness and seriousness of such a person's penance should have been called into question and that he should have been considered as a 'hopeless case'. We might think of today's practice of the 'refusal of absolution' in the case of a recidivist sinner. In those days one could arrive psychologically more easily at a judgement of unworthiness, arguing from the point of view of admission into the holy community of the Church, than we can from our contemporary viewpoints. Certainly such a judgement had a meaning for God and the Church, but it could, nevertheless, leave the 'hopeless case' to God. If[35] sinners, who sin ὑπὸ χεῖρα, really 'continue' to sin (increasingly) and wish to do penance (Mand. IV 3,6 [GCS 48:p. 28,13–16]), then in this passage the assumed unrepentance of such a sinner is more or less explicitly suggested as the reason for the single meaningful penance after baptism.

Moreover, one could consider that, according to Hermas, this post-baptismal penance stands in a clear parallel to baptism (Mand. IV 3,3 f. [ibid., p. 28,3–11]). It is possible to understand this parallel in such a way that the unrepeatable character of baptism is ascribed to post-baptismal penance. This is at least (and even only) possible in the sense that Hermas, for pastoral-pedagogical reasons—as when he keeps quiet about the possibility of a penance after baptism before neophytes—speaks only of a single possibility of penance to those who have been Christians for some time, in order to give them no pretext for sin and, even in the case of sinful people who have been Christians for some time, to appeal to the 'ideal' principle:

there is only *one metanoia* open to us. These presumed reasons for the unrepeatable character of penance concern the question of the effectiveness of this penance before *God*. They do not allow the conclusion that Hermas thinks that a further *church* penance, which would no longer be performed, is impossible, while it always remains possible to expect the forgiveness of sins before God. Explicitly in the whole of Hermas' treatment of penance it is always a question of whether and in which circumstances the sinner can find forgiveness from God. In any case a further church penance is denied because (and not even though!) there is no longer the certainty that God will still forgive.

Has, therefore, the unrepeatable character of penance nothing to do with church penance? Without going into this question, we should make it clear here that in Hermas this notion, in the final analysis, is not based on church discipline. Nevertheless, there is in fact a connection between this single possibility for penance and the reality of the Church. This is shown already by the parallel with the unrepeatable character of baptism (the great and holy calling; cf. Mand. IV 3,6 [ibid., p. 28,13–16]), therefore, with a tangible and even juridical event which is once and for all and precisely therein ecclesial. If one does not consider the ecclesial character of penance, then one cannot envisage anything further of its "unrepeatable character'. Indeed, what can it mean at all if it is understood merely as an event between the conscience and God? How can an actual forgiveness of sins be conceived, after which a further forgiveness would be meaningless, so that it could be said: from now on, therefore, something is no longer possible? It is precisely the matter-of-fact way with which the principle of the single possibility of penance is introduced which shows that, in Hermas' view, penance in some way (yet to be determined) occurs before the Church and even there receives its clear conclusion.

The above conclusion can be discounted only on the assumption that the unrepeatable character of penance rests on nothing other than the eschatological limitation. Certainly it makes no sense to allow a recidivist access yet again to penance, since this, because of the threatening end of the world, arrives too late. But the limit for this world and the limitation of the possibility of penance do not coincide. In Mand. IV 3 the unrepeatable character is mentioned without reference to the imminent end. It seems there to have as its cause the unrepentance of the sinner, a reason, therefore, which is independent of eschatological considerations. Nevertheless, the single possibility of penance is proposed in such a matter-of-fact way, without an actual justification, that it appears unlikely that Hermas is the first person to have formulated it. Even if he were not the only author of this principle, we ought to assume that it emanated from the same considerations which we can suppose in Hermas' background. But even with this we have not made much progress. It is by no means certain and self-evident (despite the high esteem which the Shepherd of Hermas enjoyed in the early Church) that the later witnesses of the single possibility of penance (already from Clement of Alexandria onwards, where indeed it is understood as *purely ecclesial*) depend solely on Hermas. Would this be sufficient to explain the self-evidence, the universality and the tenacious, long duration of this teaching? On this point there remain questions which do not admit of a complete solution.

What is sure is that in Hermas the single possibility of penance after baptism is discernible for the first time. The reasons which may be supposed for this notion, however, do not prove that this principle could claim to be a universal, always valid and immutable dictate of the divine law. Once, however, this obscure and polyvalent principle was expressed, be this only with the authority of Hermas or with others as well, then it worked even further on its own, independently of the psychological and eschatological ideas which had once determined its origin. From a theological principle (the unrepeatable character of penance before God) it becomes a principle of church law, according to which penance before the Church is possible only once (in Tertullian this passage is fairly easy to discern).[36] It can even (e.g. in Augustine)[37] receive a new justification which almost contradicts the old one; it remains in force because the deviation from such a strict principle always smacks of laxism for an uneducated conscience and, therefore, requires a courage which is not at all common among men. Finally it can be discarded, only because it could die, still without actually being killed.

Nevertheless, there still lives in this principle of Hermas of the single possibility of penance an imperishable nucleus which is usually overlooked. Just as one cannot love truly without excluding in the act of love the thought that it could be revoked and come to an end, so one cannot repent of one's guilt before the unconditioned that is God if this sorrow is not intended as irrevocable and once and for all. Only from the outside and by one who is not involved can it be said that it could happen often.

3. The Fate of Recidivists

On the question of the fate of those who, after the single post-baptismal penance, fall back again, the first point to be noted is that Hermas did not consider cases of this kind very often. The sinners he knew best were those to whom his exhortation to a first penance actually applied. Even in those cases where he has doubts about there being sufficient *metanoia,* he is thinking about unrepentance after baptism and not such an unrepentance after post-baptismal penance.[38]

This could apply especially to the case of Maximus (Vis. II 3,4 [GCS 48:p. 7,2–4]), who belongs to this category in so far as Hermas does not consider the danger of a new fall as excluded for this Christian who has often fallen and been repeatedly received into the Church. It is not surprising that we do not have concrete examples, since the Christian faith at that time hardly provided material advantages, was entirely a matter of personal belief and was menaced throughout the whole world. In this situation it would be unusual to find sinners who, after an official penance (unless it is official it could not be conceived as 'once and for all'), come to the Church after a second, notorious fall and again receive penance.[39]

Thus the men Hermas has in mind are those who, after baptism, have fallen away, become traitors, have alienated themselves from the life of the Church or who otherwise no longer observe the externally tangible obligations of a Christian. He is hardly thinking of men who have already expressed sorrow for such faults in a tangible form (so that they have already done 'penance'), who have fallen again and now wish to rectify their defection. In reality there is no pressing problem of the recidivist, at least as a general phenomenon. Only the latter would lead to a thought-out theory, while previously eventual individual cases were solved—positively or negatively—according to an indefinite norm.

This is also the best explanation of the fact that the whole question of the fate of recidivists is a peripheral one and is 'solved' only vaguely. Thus in Sim. VIII 7,5 (GCS 48:p. 73,6–9) those who have been reinserted into the tower are warned that they will be ejected again and will lose their life if they fall back into their old sin of quarrelsomeness. In this warning there is no assumption that the addressees will do penance once again (either because the will or the possibility is not available for it). But this says nothing about the fate of the recidivist who still *repents*. For this case there remains only Mand. IV 3,6 (ibid., p. 28,3–16),[40] provided that it is here a question of those who fall away after a post-baptismal *metanoia*. Then there would be a reference to those who, in some sense, do penance again (or at least give this impression). Of these Hermas says: Ἀσύμφορόν ἐστι τῷ ἀνθρώπῳ τῷ τοιούτῳ· δυσκόλως γὰρ ζήσεται. The second half of this passage must be understood as the justification, not as the consequence, of the 'uselessness' of such a penance after backslidings (with Poschmann, 169, it is best to relate the ὑπὸ χεῖρα to both the act of sinning and the doing of penance). The person who oscillates between sin and penance in this way can only with difficulty arrive at a complete revival of freedom from sin in this life. Thus such a penance is useless (as Poschmann suggests, the 'life' in question is that of Vis. III 8,3 [GCS 48:p. 15,11–16]; III 11–13 [ibid., pp. 17,20–19,3]; Sim. VIII 7,6 [ibid., p. 73,9–13]; IX 14,3 [ibid., p. 88,13–17]), that is, the present interior life of the person who is genuinely and sincerely repentant). In the Shepherd of Hermas δύσκολος means only 'very difficult'[41] but not 'impossible' (Mand. IX 6 [GCS 48:p. 37, 4–7]; XII 1,2 [ibid., p. 42,21–6]; Sim. VIII 10,2 [ibid., p. 75,3–6]; IX 20,2 [ibid., p. 92,24–9]; 23,3 cp. 23,5 [ibid., p. 94,11–22]). Because of the clear lack of sorrow and repentance envinced in the new fall Hermas considers the recidivists to be in a fairly hopeless situation; thus he rejects the performance of 'church' penance as useless (better: as unfeasible)—and, moreover, he renounces any clear prospect for their further fate.

Hermas holds that the interior, subjective condition of such sinners is vague and, therefore, the forgiveness of their sins by God is uncertain. Thus they cannot be received back into the Church, and in this sense penance after baptism remains necessarily a single possibility. Certainly no definitive judgement can be made about the personal fate of these sinners in the next life. According to Hermas, therefore, no further *metanoia* can be made available to the recidivist sinner *because* it is not known whether he has made himself worthy of the forgiveness of his sins before God by real penance. This view corresponds entirely with the notion that there are sins of such gravity that they do not admit of genuine penance 'from the bottom of the heart', any more than they can be forgiven by God.

Even today, however, it is easy to think of cases in which absolution would inevitably be refused, even though there is no absolute certainty about the unrepentance of the person concerned. Even today, therefore, there is something like a 'once-and-for-all penance' where a person has sorrow 'with difficulty'.

V. CHURCH PENANCE

1. The Church and Salvation

Without a doubt the Church plays an important role in the theology of Hermas. For him it is not only the community of believers, but a transcendent and spiritual reality which was created before all other things and is above all the aim and the meaning of God's creation (Vis. II 4,1 [GCS 48:p. 7.5–10].[42] The fate of all men, that is, their salvation or their perdition, is determined by their belonging or their not belonging to the Church. This is because human destiny is dependent upon both penance in baptism and penance after baptism. The effectiveness of this penance is discernible for Hermas by a man's being integrated into the tower of the Church or his being rejected from it (Vis. II 2,3–8,10 [ibid., pp. 9,12–15,17]; Sim. IX 3,1–10,5 [ibid., pp. 78,8–84,27]; 11,9–33,3 [ibid., pp. 85,28–104,15]; X 4,4 [ibid., pp. 110,20–112,4]). This tower is certainly not simply identical with the actual, visible church community on earth, since it also counts as its members, and even in its first rank, the righteous dead (Sim. IX 15,4 [ibid., p. 89,14–18]; 16,5 [ibid., p. 90,6–11]; 25,2 [ibid., p. 95,6–11]). At the same time, according to Hermas, there are in the earthly Church men who have been ejected from the tower. In quite a few cases one can hardly take it for granted that such men (as apostates) are always separated from the Church (Vis. III 6,4–6 [ibid., p. 13,3–6]; Sim. IX 20,1 f. [ibid., p. 92,21–9]; 21 [ibid., p. 93,7–20]; 22,4 [ibid., pp. 93,30–94,4]).[43]

Nevertheless, this Church of Hermas' visions is not simply a pure ideal being which has nothing to do with the visible earthly Church. This 'ideal' image is rather the empirical Church, which is based on baptism as a tangible event, which needs purification (Sim. IX 18,2 [ibid., p. 91,15–20]), which, being involved in the sins of its members, is old and weak, so that it can be rejuvenated only by their penance (Vis. III 11–13 [ibid., pp. 17,20–19,3]).[44] The Church in Hermas' visions is, therefore, the *earthly Church,* which is entered by baptism (Sim. IX 17,4 [ibid., p. 91,3–9]), which is still being built (Vis. III 5,5 [ibid., p. 12,11–17]; Sim. IX 14,2 [ibid., p. 88,8–13]; X 4,4 [ibid., pp. 110,20–112,4]) and which can be soiled. Nevertheless, it is viewed from God's standpoint; empirically it evinces a clash between the reality and the appearance, without, however, there being two quite independent realities: an ideal and an empirical Church.

Visible belonging to the Church (especially by baptism) is in the first place so necessary for salvation that, according to Hermas, mankind before Christ still needed baptism (Sim. IX 16,5 ff. [ibid., p. 90,6–18]). At the same time, however, mere empirical belonging is still not an absolute guarantee of salvation, since, in some cases, it does not express an inner reality and the men in question—from God's viewpoint—are not actually in the tower. In fact even sinners belong to the Church (at least externally), and therefore the 'holy church' (Vis. I 1,6 [ibid., pp. 1,17–2,3]; 3,4 [ibid., p. 4,7–15]; IV 1,3 [ibid., p. 19,8–12]) cannot consider itself holy in the sense that it has nothing at all to do with sin and sinners.

2. *Church and Penance*

A) PENANCE OF EXCOMMUNICATION

The Church, however, is so 'holy' that it wishes to express in its earthly reality the fact that its sinful members do not actually belong to it, which fact is evident to God. Thus the Church 'excommunicates'[45] sinners, while it remains irrelevant whether, by so doing, it has actual success. In the case of apostates and others who themselves break their external relationship with the Church such a specific act of the Church is obviously superfluous (cf. Sim. IX 26,3 [ibid., p. 95,18–21]). In other cases, however, e.g. in the case of adultery, such an act can be necessary and is even prescribed:

Mand. IV 1,5 (ibid., p. 26,8–11). This passage concerns only the innocent partner who must break up the marriage relationship, but it is unthinkable that, at the same time, both partners should continue their fellowship with each other within the Church.[46] The obligation to separate (1,9 [ibid., p. 26,20–4]) is immediately changed into a fundamental and universal principle ('If a person [masc.!] remains in such works and does not do penance, keep yourself far away from him and do not live together with him, otherwise you share in the guilt of his sin'), so that it is reasonable to suppose that the empirical Church tries—as far as it can—to respond to the sin which separates a man interiorly from itself with institutional measures ('excommunication'), this being considered the natural and prescribed reaction to sin (how this actually took place the text does not say).[47] Precisely because the Church is necessary for salvation and yet belonging to it offers no guarantee of salvation, the attempt is made to resolve the tension between these two points by expressing in the external sphere what has happened within man by sin. If perdition is seen as involving loss of relationship with the Church, the Church itself will appear as holy, salvific and necessary for salvation even in its empirical reality.

Now Grotz is convinced, by his thorough analysis of the text of Hermas, that he has provided the proof that there is mention in Hermas of sinners who have need of sacramental penance and yet are not excommunicated. He thinks that he can recognize a group of such sinners in the people who in Vis. III 2,7a (ibid., p. 9,26 f.); 5,5 (ibid., p. 12,11–17) (Grotz, p. 19) 'therefore have not strayed far away from the tower, because they will be very useful for the building when they have done penance'. These people are certainly different from those who do not lie by the tower but have been expelled far from it (in Grotz the group E: Vis. III 2,9 [ibid., p. 10,3–8]; 7,1–3 [ibid., pp. 13,20–14,6]). But does this mean sinners who are not excommunicated? The answer to this question will naturally depend upon the view that one has of excommunication. If it means that the 'relations with the tower, i.e. with the Church have been broken' (Grotz, ibid.) then obviously this group is not excommunicated. It is readily granted that the relationship of these men to the church community, according to Hermas' image, is radically different from that of the group E. The latter have been driven away from the tower and this—as Grotz rightly stresses—because they have themselves defected from the Church as apostates with a certain definitiveness through their own decision and without having the intention of doing penance in any way. Nevertheless, this in no way proves that the group C2 (Grotz distinguishes this group from C3 and E) cannot be treated as excommunicated. Grotz overlooks the basis for the whole of Hermas' image: all those who have to do penance find themselves outside the place in the tower itself where they were and should be because of their baptism. This applies also to the group C2. One may only unwillingly call this state of being outside the tower 'excommunication'; one may stress that those who are 'cast right out' are in a totally different position from the men of group C2, because they are not influenced at all by the Church's penitential concern, because the Church—at least for the time being—does not bother about them any more and has practically given up hope of their conversion. Nevertheless, one ought not to overlook what is also for Hermas obviously the most important point and what is presupposed by the Church's actual penitential concern, having as its aim the reincorporation into the tower: even these well-disposed sinners near the tower are not in the tower itself. They are not, therefore, merely sinners with a destroyed relationship with God, but they also do not stand in the relationship with the Church to which they were introduced by their baptism. Even their penance is, therefore, not only a reconciliation by the Church, but also a reconciliation with the Church. Such a penance can still be called meaningfully 'penance of excommunication', provided that one is clear that 'excommunication' in this context has a different sense from the one which it has in modern church law.

The above consideration is not weakened by the fact that (as Grotz, e.g. p. 21, stresses) 'excommunication' considered in itself has nothing to do with penance. It can obviously exist in cases where there is no intention, either on the part of the sinner or on the part of the Church, of obtaining the reincorporation into the tower of the Church by penance. But this does not affect Hermas' assumption that, whenever it is a question of penance, the sinner is also outside the tower (whether near or far is irrelevant), and still less does it affect the result of this penance (not its presupposition), namely the actual incorporation into the tower. In Vis. III 5,5 (ibid., p. 12,11–17) we read: 'If they do penance they are fitted for the building.'

Whether the penance of those who are cast far away has several levels (first the appearance before the angel of punishment and then the correction of the angel of penance), what this means in the life of the community and how the effect of the penance of these people might appear, i.e. whether they are inserted into a 'lesser place' or right into the tower again—all these questions do not alter the fact that the Shepherd of Hermas, contrary to Grotz's view, in Vis. III does not know of any men who, on the one hand, are subject to church penance while, on the other hand, are not to be considered in any way 'excommunicated'. And even if Hermas were to know sinners who do penance, i.e. have to mend their ways, without seeing them outside the tower, i.e. without hinting at an excommunication of these sinners, then this would not prove that the penance of such sinners should be understood as sacramental, even if the Church plays a role in it. Not every concern of the Church over the penance of a sinner has to be understood as sacramental, either in Hermas' sense or in the sense of modern theology. According to the Shepherd of Hermas a distinction between a sacramental and another kind of penitential help offered by the Church for the conversion of a sinner (if one wishes to pose the question in this way at all) can be made only by asking whether or not it is a question of the restoration of baptismal grace (of the seal), of the reincorporation into the tower of the Church. If this aim and this necessity are not present, then it is no longer possible to say for certain in what a sacramental act of the Church consists according to Hermas' theology and how it would be distinguished from other exhortations to penance, from the assistance afforded by prayer, etc.

Before considering (e.g. in the conclusion to Vis. III 2,7a–c [ibid., p. 9,26–9] in Grotz p. 19) which of the groups of sinners listed are excommunicated, it is first necessary to clarify what it means for them, in general, to be no longer in the tower. This common characteristic is just as important to Hermas as is the following differentiation according to a greater or lesser proximity to the tower. In explaining this common characteristic (which really presents no difficulty) one could more easily understand that only those sinners who are alienated far away from the tower must be really excommunicated, if among them are found only those who, according to today's theological notion, have placed themselves 'outside the Church' by the kind of sin which they have committed (e.g. heresy or schism). But this is not the case; according to Grotz himself, the adulteress

(p. 30 f.) and especially the obstinate sinners (p. 30, etc.), even when it is not a question of sins against faith, are excommunicated (whether definitively or temporally is irrelevant). If, therefore, even sins which are not against the faith entail excommunication, and if, at the same time, according to Hermas,[48] excommunication is not simply imposed or not imposed at the Church's whim (as it is according to modern church law in the lower levels of excommunication of those who are not *vitandi*),[49] then he must have a principle for excommunication which differs from the modern practice of excommunication. Today, in fact, two kinds of excommunication are recognized: one which involves no actual exclusion from the Church, another which involves an exclusion which the sinner has already brought about objectively, *iure divino,* by his own fault. The point of this observation is that it is methodologically false to read the modern notion of excommunication into the Shepherd of Hermas. Indeed, this notion does not cover the excommunication which even Grotz allows in Hermas. In other words, it should be asked what Hermas himself thinks about the matter. What becomes fundamental then is his idea that all serious sins (of deed) lead men away from the tower. This basic state of affairs may be expressed in this way: since every serious sin causes the loss of the Spirit of the Church, the seal of baptism, every sinner, according to Hermas, is 'excommunicated'—bound, as one would say in biblical terminology.[50]

Thus one can hardly gather from Mand. IV with Grotz that there are sinners who have committed mortal sins and yet are not excommunicated. In Grotz's interpretation in this passage Hermas receives the commission or the concession that a man ought to live with his wife who has committed adultery but afterwards has repented (1,5 [ibid., p. 26,8–11]). From this Grotz (pp. 30–3) concludes (and obviously this can be no more than a conclusion) that the woman could not be excommunicated, since the husband otherwise would not be permitted to live with her. The assumption here (which Poschmann and we ourselves share with Grotz) is that the prohibition of married life together with an adulterous and unrepentant wife (1,9 [ibid., p. 26,20–4]) is based on a measure taken by the Church in the form of an excommunication. Grotz (p. 32) identifies the case of the adulterous but immediately repentant wife with his group C2 of Vis. III and thus places himself in an unfortunate position at the outset. Certainly, the identification itself appears to us to be correct, but precisely the group C2 must be thought of, according to the phraseology of the vision, as being outside the tower (even if, to use Grotz's expression, in its 'forecourt') and is, therefore, to be considered as a group of those who are excommunicated (in the theological sense). This would apply, therefore, also to this adulterous, even if immediately repentant, wife. Indeed, what does Hermas himself say about this? All that we have is: 'But if the husband notices the sin (of his wife) and his wife does not repent (μετανοήσῃ) but persists in her impurity, and the husband (in these circumstances) lives with her, then he will share in the guilt of her sin and take part in her adultery' (1,5). From this it is concluded that in Hermas the husband must leave his wife if she persists in adultery (1,6).

But does all this warrant the conclusion drawn by Grotz? In no way. In the first place, it is certainly clear for Hermas that the husband of an unrepentant adulteress must separate from her. Nevertheless, it is by no means self-evident for him that the separation of the spouses is only the mere effect of a church excommunication. It is rather demanded by the principle that a Christian should not share in the sin of another (by tolerating, condoning, etc.). From the fact that the communal married life has ceased one can conclude that the church fellowship no longer exists either, since two people separated in their private lives for *religious* reasons could not communicate with each other in the Church. But the opposite conclusion does not necessarily follow: where two people are united in their private life their ecclesial relationship (to the Church and to each other within the Church) must also be in order. Even in modern church law not every excommunication causes a secular separation of the person who is excommunicated.[51] Thus it is perfectly conceivable that a man should live with his wife when she, at least by sorrow and renunciation of the adulterous relationship, has abandoned sin, without it being any longer possible to maintain that, by living with her, he shares in the guilt of her sin.

Nevertheless, the question of the relationship of this woman to the Church—whether she is already again 'in the tower' or comes to full reconciliation only after a long penance before the Church—is still not necessarily decided. We have the right, therefore, to say, even according to Grotz: it is here a question of a well-disposed sinner who, in the sense of Vis. III 2,7a (ibid., p. 9,26–7) is truly repentant (5,5) but, as far as the Church is concerned, still belongs to those who have been 'cast away'. For Grotz's conclusion to be absolutely convincing, it would have to be proven first of all that the secular and the ecclesial relationships of two people correspond to each other exactly. But such a presupposition is purely gratuitous. In fact it is a question of a wife who is sorry and who is willing to do penance (however the husband may establish this fact). On the supposition that indeed the performance of church penance is already in progress, but not yet completed—even though, because of the wife's good disposition, it is bound to achieve good results—it is precisely a question of *a* church penance (Mand. IV 1,8 [ibid., p. 26,16–20]). The full reconciliation with the Church and with God is guaranteed, if not yet actually achieved. On these hypothetical suppositions, is the idea impossible that Hermas allows the husband already to live with his wife? And could it not then be concluded, since Hermas has made this concession, that the assumptions which we have just mentioned do not exist, i.e. the wife is not considered as being 'outside the tower'? In my opinion, the person who argues in this way derives from the text points which it will not support and which, moreover, are precluded by the fact that Hermas considers even a repentant sinner as still a stone lying outside the actual tower. It is not only a question of the cessation or the continuation of married life in the strict sense but of whether the household community should be continued or whether the wife—to put it simply—should be turned out of the house. Now Hermas lays it down that a wife who has been ejected from the house should be accepted back if she—albeit only later—repents. What would be the sense of turning her out of the house, if, because of the sorrow she has expressed, it is already established that she can and ought to return to the house? Or should one really believe that all excommunicated sinners either then or later when they do public penance are also, on this account, to be punished with a secular boycott? Where, for example, did Hermas' repentant children live while, as even Grotz does not dispute, they were under a penance of excommunication? It is obvious that they lived with their father so that he shared their affliction.

Grotz has to admit that a wife who is not definitively obdurate in her adultery, but has not immediately repented, is under a 'provisional excommunication', a 'revocable excommunication'. This is because, on the one hand, he must grant that such a wife can still come to a complete penance, while on the other hand he knows that

Hermas still considers her as excommunicated (p. 31 ff.). We should prescind from the problem posed by a 'provisional', 'revocable' excommunication which has no clear basis in the sources and has to be constructed indirectly. This notion appears to be problematical already in Hermas himself, since, from what he says, it is by no means clear that he knows an excommunication which occurs for any other reason than the sinner's unrepentance, even though he is convinced that it is automatically associated with certain sins. But if this is the only reason for the continuation of an excommunication, then every excommunication lasts until penance is done and is temporary.

Nevertheless, we could ask a further question: if Hermas had not considered the act of adultery (as opposed to the mere sin of thought: Mand. IV 1,1–2 [ibid., pp. 25,22–26,3]) as the reason for an excommunication, would he then, as Grotz also stresses, have justified a (provisional) excommunication by the persistence in this adultery? Obstinacy derives its moral value from the evil of the state in which one persists, even if it aggravates this sin. Moreover, Hermas presupposes that the husband of an adulterous wife does not sin by living with her if he knows nothing of his wife's sin (Mand. IV 1,5 [ibid., p. 26,8–11]). This self-evident observation would be meaningless if the husband is only to interrupt his married life when a church excommunication has already taken place. If, however, this is not the case, then the husband can have reasons for interrupting, continuing or recommencing his married life which do not coincide simply with those of the Church for its excommunication or the lifting of this excommunication. If one considers further that Grotz demands that the adulteress who only later comes to her senses must do a long penance and provide visible proof of her conversion (p. 30), then surely the husband who keeps his sinful wife because she is doing penance must demand such a visible and tangible document proving her conversion. Is this not precisely where church penance comes in? The undertaking of this penance can, therefore, be just as well considered as the reason for the husband's obligation to dismiss his wife, as the non-dismissal can count as a proof that there is no excommunication. Even according to Grotz the adultery of the wife who is immediately repentant demands a 'church penance' (p. 33) which obviously must have 'nothing to do with excommunication' (ibid.).

But how does Hermas envisage concretely such a church penance which on the one hand is sacramental, while on the other is not a penance of excommunication? Grotz does not seem to give an answer to this apposite question. In Hermas, wherever there are serious sins of deed to be expiated, there is always found a penance which involves that the sinner, after a long time of penance, is again incorporated into the tower, therefore a 'penance of excommunication'. In the light of these observations the existence of sins in Mand. IV which require church penance without entailing a 'penance of excommunication' must be questionable.

Along with Hoh, Grotz (p. 51 f.; p. 32) also wishes to recognize in Sim. IX sinners who are indeed submitted to church penance without, however, being excommunicated. According to Grotz, the reason for this is that these sinners (certain kinds of stones) still lie beside the tower and are found in a place which belongs to the rock on which the actual tower is raised. But the objection already raised against the interpretation of Vis. III also applies here. It has already been granted that the tower in Sim. IX signifies the empirical Church (p. 47 f.). This Church is built upon the rock which has a door (2,2 [ibid., p. 77,18–21]; 3 [ibid., p. 78,8–23]). The stones for this building are brought to the rock through the door (3,4 [ibid., p. 78,18–21]; 4,1 [ibid., pp. 78,24–79,4]); the tower thus consists of many stones (4,1–8 [ibid., pp. 78,24–80,4]). In this regard, it is noticeable that the stones have the right colour, i.e. the qualification for being inserted into the tower. This insertion is carried out by virgins (the virtues) who carry the stones through the door (4,5–7 [ibid., p. 79,16–26]), which is the Son (12,6–8 [ibid., p. 86, 17–27]).[52] Thus both faith in the Son of God in baptism and virtue are necessary in order to arrive at the tower. Even if only virtue is lacking, the stone remains lying in its black colour beside the tower (4,6 f. [ibid., p. 79,20–26]). If a white stone (i.e. a faithful and virtuous man) is inserted into the tower and then, under the influence of the spirits of the vices (the black-clad women, 13,8 [ibid., pp. 87,27–88,1]), becomes black again and, upon examination by the Lord of the tower, shows his black colour, then he will again be ejected from the tower (6,5 [ibid., p. 81,13–15]; 7,1 [ibid., p. 81,26–8]). If such stones still lie on the rock, this is indeed an indication that they are not considered as having fallen totally from the faith and that they have not been completely abandoned by the Church. But this does not alter the fact that they no longer occupy the place which they held in virtue of their sincere conversion and their baptism. As opposed to the time immediately following their baptism, they now lie *beside* the tower, if even still on the rock of faith and so within the door.

All this expresses that alienation from the Church and by the Church which we have called excommunication in the theological sense and which makes a penance of excommunication necessary. It is only after such a penance that one can be reinserted into the tower. That the still worse stones in this allegory are alienated much further from the tower (7,2 [ibid., pp. 81,29–82,1]; 8,1 [ibid., p. 82,19–21], etc.) does not change this state of affairs radically. It has already been established that, according to the Shepherd of Hermas, there can be grades of the sin of obstinacy and, therefore, of alienation from the Church by excommunication which—at least temporarily—even hold such a sinner back from an actual church penance. But this does not prove that only such sinners are 'excommunicated'. All those concerned in Sim. IX are no longer in the walls of the tower and must first again arrive at the tower. The state of no longer being in the tower is not, in itself, a means of salvation. It cannot be said (p. 55), however, that excommunication is not a means of penance and, therefore, concerns only those sinners who offer no prospect of penance. The condition of no longer being in the tower makes the situation of the sinner as sinner clear. Whether immediately afterwards, later or never, there follows conversion and consequently readmission into the Church depends, according to Hermas, upon the different dispositions of the sinners. On the one hand, all the sinners in Sim. IX are taken out of the walls of the tower, but, on the other hand, they all have the radical possibility of coming back to the tower, since in all the different groups mentioned there is an explicit reference to the possibility of a reinsertion into the tower. Wherever it is presented as being impossible in fact (not actually as *a priori* impossible) it is a question of a lack of disposition (which Hermas obviously assumes to be present here and there somewhat categorically), not, however, of a refusal of forgiveness by God and the Church which is independent of the state of mind of the sinner concerned.

Moreover, it is worth noting that according to Grotz those who, by reason of sins of deed, need church penance enter a special place as penitents but without, according to him, being excommunicated.

This special place beside the tower is thought of primarily for these well-disposed and, therefore, not excommunicated sinners. But in fact, in certain circumstances, other sinners who are already (provisionally) excommunicated come to this place (without the prospect of proceeding further).

But how can one arrive at the idea of a special place for penitents (irrespective of whether this is considered either a symbol of the relationship of sinners to the Church or more materially a special place to be occupied during the celebration of the liturgy), if for these men the idea is fundamentally excluded that a sinner, by his fault and the corresponding reaction of the Church, enters into a different relationship with the Church than the baptized who have not sinned? In Grotz there is no answer to the question of where the 'life setting' or the 'theoretical setting' for the idea and the practice of a special place of penance could be sought. The fact that Hermas' notion of penance (even there where according to Grotz there is no penance of excommunication) is completely determined by the idea that the sinner is rejected from the tower and has a special place for his penance, shows very clearly that his basic idea of penance—in so far as it is church penance—must be of a penance of excommunication. Conversely, it follows from this that wherever Hermas considers an obligatory church penance, sin, of its very nature, is so conceived that, of itself and by the reaction of the Church (so far as this is possible), it leads to a kind of excommunication.

This stress that according to Hermas all serious sins of deed objectively exclude the sinner from the tower and, therefore, in so far as they are known, are met by the Church with an 'excommunication', so that penance is always a penance of excommunication, does not derogate in the least from the wide variety of penitential procedures which exist despite this common denominator in all the individual cases. The useful and meaningful observations of Grotz on this point are to be fully recognized. The treatment of certain groups of sinners by the punishing angel *before* they are handed over to the angel of penance only at a later point of time and after a certain performance of penance at the hands of this angel of punishment, only then to arrive at the place which is fixed for the usual penitents (near the tower itself), can certainly have its counterpart in the treatment of sinners by the Church itself. This may be a way of expressing the grace and favour of the Church in allowing a man who is guilty of particularly serious sins (apostasy, etc.) to have access to actual penance, as well as the prerequisite for this penance, namely another kind of previous penance in which the willingness to do penance and the readiness for a performance of church penance in the strict sense are already expressed (cf. Sim. VI and Grotz, pp. 23–6). We do not, therefore, reject the idea of a graded penance already in Hermas. All that is rejected is the idea that only the group under the punishing angel is to be considered as excommunicated. Even according to Grotz the place to which these sinners come after their treatment by the punishing angel, 'the lesser place' (Vis. III 7,5–6 [ibid., p. 14,7–16]), is in practice identical with the place for the usual penitents (Grotz, pp. 21–3; 26). But also there from the beginning are those who are outside the actual tower and, therefore, ought to be considered as excommunicated, even though they did not have to pass first through the examination of the punishing angel.

B) THE CHURCH FORM OF PENANCE

Hermas' intention is not to describe church penance but to stir the conscience of sinners. He is a preacher of penance, not a dogmatic theologian or a canonist. We cannot expect him to say a great deal, therefore, about the form of penance with which his addressees were familiar or about how or how widely this form was used. The explanations which we have already given, however, suffice to give us some idea of the way in which the penance of a Christian sinner was performed within the Church in those days.

It has already been shown that a church excommunication is discernible in Hermas, at least in so far as he recognizes the obligation to 'avoid' certain sinners. But this must also be worked out in the sphere of the Church, which is obviously possible only if the sinner is in some active form expelled from the community. This does not mean that such an excommunication in fact occurs in the actual Church in all those cases where Hermas exhorts to penance and thereby theoretically presupposes that such a sinner no longer belongs to the tower in God's eyes and, therefore, ought to be treated correspondingly by the Church (cf. all the different sins in Sim. VIII and IX). To this extent, Hoh is right (p. 32) in stressing that, on this supposition, the Church would be 'de-peopled', since even according to Hermas himself there are only a few in the Church who do not belong to one or other of the groups of sinners distinguished by him and urged to penance. For many of them it is practical only to think of the doing of subjective penance. Nevertheless, this does not prove that in these cases it is a question of a 'private' (because it is without an excommunication) but still sacramental penance,[53] since in Hermas there is not the slightest trace of an act on the Church's part which could in these cases clearly be styled sacramental.[54] In these cases, in fact, one can detect a lack of theological consistency in Hermas. For, on the one hand, even for these groups of sinners he presupposes a loss of the baptismal seal, the loss of life, the expulsion from the tower (Sim. VIII 6,3 [ibid., p. 71,15–21]; 7,3.5 [ibid., pp. 72,17–73,9]; 8,3 [ibid., p. 74,1–4]; 9,2.4 [ibid., p. 74,17–25]; 10,1.3 [ibid., pp. 74,26–75,11]; Sim. IX 14,2 [ibid., p. 88,8–13]; 19 [ibid., p. 92,4–20]; 21,1.4 [ibid., p. 93,7–20]; 22,3 f. [ibid., pp. 93,26–94,4]; 23,2 [ibid., p. 94,7–11]; 26,2 [ibid., p. 95,14–18], etc.); on the other hand, because of their great number, it is impossible to think of a church penance in their regard. It would be asking too much to put such theological consistency in practice. Such theological 'inconsistency' can be met even in Augustine, although in his case it has been the subject of some reflection.[55]

Be all this as it may, there is in Hermas an excommunication which is presented as self-evident and in no way as his own invention. Moreover, it is applicable to sins such as adultery, etc. which do not simply, of their very nature (as apostasy), automatically bring about excommunication as a separation from the community. The fact that he does not insist on its application in every case where he presupposes a separation from the Church or from the 'tower' springs from his strict theory of moral theology, which recognizes 'serious sins' (in the modern sense) precisely where he cannot treat them according to his own principles.

It would be false, however, to conclude from this inconsistency that according to Hermas, as a matter of principle, serious sin (which destroys the baptismal grace) is not always and everywhere, as in the case of adultery, to be countered with a church excommunication.

Apart from this, it is possible to discern directly further acts of the Church in the overall performance of penance. The leaders in the community doubtless play an important role in this regard. Thus Hermas receives the commission to transmit his revelation to the presbyters and leaders of the Church (Vis. II 4,3 [ibid., p. 7,14–18]);

the latter must obviously subsequently take the corresponding measures. It appears incumbent on the church leaders, 'God's chosen', to take charge of discipline (παιδεύειν): Vis. III 9,7–10 (ibid., p. 16,11–21). If the sheep stray from the flock through their fault they are answerable for it: Sim. IX 31,5 (ibid., p. 100,11–13). Thus there is clear evidence for the Church's active right to exercise penitential discipline over its members.

It is, however, possible to make further indirect conclusions. Although the angel of penance in Hermas may not be simply a symbol of a church official (say, of the bishop), there is in Hermas an emphasis on the comparison with the 'shepherd' of the empirical Church: '. . . I *also* am a shepherd' (Sim. IX 31,6 [ibid., p. 100,11–13]). This even suggests the idea of the heavenly shepherd of penance 'being called to account' by God over his activity (Sim. IX 31,6 [ibid., p. 100,13–17]; VIII 2,7 [ibid., pp. 67,27–68,4]), which is doubtless a transfer of an earthly reality into the heavenly world. This reflection is the justification for concluding to the existence of other activities of the earthly shepherd which correspond to other aspects of the heavenly angel of penance's activity. This applies particularly to those aspects which cannot be easily understood as the explanations of the general idea of the influence of angelic powers on men's subjective penance. If, therefore, the angel of penance examines sinners and tries as hard as possible to lead them all to penance, if he feels himself responsible for them, drives them from the tower and abandons the obstinately impenitent to their fate, then it becomes difficult to dispute that, in these cases, (especially in Sim. IX) there are transferred to the activity of the angel of penance aspects of the work of church leaders which are obviously presupposed as already existing and not introduced here for the first time.

The same must be said of the activity of the angel of penance when he inserts those people who are repentant but not yet fully healed not yet into the tower itself but into the 'walls', therefore into a 'lesser place' (Vis. III 5,5 [GCS 48:p. 12,11–17]; 7,6 [ibid., p. 14,10–16]; Sim. VIII 2,5 [ibid., p. 67,20–5]; 6,6 [ibid., p. 72,5–20]; 7,3 [ibid., pp. 72,17–73,2]; 8,3 [ibid., p. 74,1–4]) and even in this case only gradually, according to their (relative) worthiness (Sim. VIII 2,5 [ibid., p. 62,20–5]). This 'lesser place', these 'walls' are not in or on the tower itself;[56] it is a question of a place which is distinguished from the actual tower of the Church itself. To this place come sinners who are indeed doing penance, after they have been brought to their senses and to conversion by the external punishments of the angel of punishment (Sim. VI 3 [ibid., pp. 61,4–62,8]; Vis. III 7,6 [ibid., p. 14,10–16]), but who have not yet completed their penance. What is meant, therefore, is a place which explains the situation of a sinner before the completion of his penance, and indeed directly his situation in this world (even if this obviously has its counterpart in the next world, in the event of his penance not being completed before the final construction of the tower). This is because even a person who lives in the 'walls' can certainly move up into the tower and has to remain only temporarily in the walls on account of the long duration of his penance (Sim. VIII 8,3 [ibid., p. 74,1–4]; 6,6 [ibid., p. 72,5–10]). The lesser place outside the tower itself but in the walls which surround it is to be understood, therefore, as a symbol of the situation of those penitents who have indeed begun their penance (and thus are sure of their salvation), but have not yet completed it and so do not yet actually belong again to the tower of the Church. It is impossible to deny that Hermas has here spiritualized a reality existing in the empirical sphere of the Church: the access of repentant sinners to church penance and their relationship to the Church before the definitive and complete readmission into it. Without such a real background it is difficult to find a sufficient explanation for such an elaborate idea. This does not mean that there was in Rome in the middle of the second century already the kind of structured institution of penance which appears fifty years later with Tertullian. It is not only possible but even probable that these two institutions differed from each other in much the same way as the catechumenate in Justin (Apol. 61; 65,1; 66,1) differs from the catechumenate attested in the Paradosis of Hippolytus (17 ff.; Dix p. 28 ff.). (The most that one can think is that Hermas' theology of baptism and penance is closer to the theology of Hippolytus than is that of Justin, in so far as Hermas also ascribes an important role to demonology, considering sin as possession by demons and liberation from sin as their expulsion.) So the structure of penance may have been fairly improvised, according to the cases which occurred. But there certainly was such a structure, since 'excommunication' and the community leaders' right to administer discipline are clearly discernible.[57] Both of these were naturally exercised in certain forms which must have demanded more precise regulations as the Church and the number of sinners and penitents increased.

In this context, after the explanation we have just given of the 'lesser place' for certain penitents, it is necessary to broach the question of whether, according to Hermas, as Grotz maintains, there are also such penitents who are refused definitively and permanently an actual church penance. These would be precisely those people who come only to the lesser place (Vis. III 7,6 [ibid., p. 14,10–16]) and are not inserted into the tower itself. Grotz is of the opinion that this place is identified not formally but practically with the place for penitents (p. 22 f.). If one considers that a certain penance is necessary in order to arrive at the place for penitents i.e. to be allowed access to the official church penance, then the 'meaningless tautology' of Vis. III 7,5.6 (ibid., p. 14,7–16) of which Grotz (p. 22) is afraid and which hinders him from identifying the lesser place simply with the place for penitents is resolved. But, despite this, Grotz only admits that the lesser place is 'practically' identified with the place for penitents (p. 23). He holds that those who are once (definitively) excommunicated go no further beyond this place (pp. 23; 25 f.; 65; 68), that excommunication is definitively absolute and that consequently certain groups of sinners never again become full members of the Church (p. 27). Rather, they must remain permanently in the 'lesser place' which Grotz (p. 68) compares with the 'first walls' (Sim. VIII 6,6 [ibid., p. 72,5–10]; 7,2 f. [ibid., pp. 72,13–73,2]; 8,3 [ibid., p. 74,1–4]), even though he has previously sharply distinguished the 'first walls' from the place for penitents (p. 44 ff.)[58] and sought this mysterious middle position between the outside of excommunication and the inside of the church fellowship principally in the other world (p. 46).

Thus the question poses itself: does the residence of certain repentant sinners in the lesser place, in the first walls, mean the final, impassable point reached by their penitential efforts independently of the intensity of their penance, and this only because they were once (according to Grotz, definitively) excommunicated? We think that this question should be answered in the negative. Naturally this question does not include the group of those who, after a church penance, have again fallen away and who, therefore, according to Hermas' principle, can no longer be allowed access to a further church penance. This case, however, because of the conditions which it supposes, arises only theoretically and peripherally. Leaving aside the radical hope of God's mercy, which is open to all penance, nothing can be concluded, therefore, from the Shepherd of Hermas about this group of sinners or about another form of penance to which they may be allowed access. Nevertheless, these men are not among those who have been fitted into the lesser place, the first walls. Our question concerns those who, having been excommunicated (definitively), do penance for the first time. Are they, as Grotz maintains, radically unable to pass further beyond the lesser place? This question calls for further clarification, since Hermas does in fact assume that there are certain cases, at least in practice, in which some sinners do not pass beyond this stage.[59] It should be noted, however, that in the passages where these cases are mentioned by Hermas the long duration or the late commencement of the penance is given as the reason. Our question does not, therefore, concern the fact that, because they began their penance late or because it lasts a long time, penitents in fact do not complete their penance and, therefore, are taken unawares by this day, being outside the tower although near it, and consequently, according to Hermas, are neither completely lost nor able to share in the happiness of those who are perfect. On Hermas' assumptions this situation needs no further explanation. The question we have raised, therefore, is only whether the Church refuses a full reconciliation to penitents who have once been excommunicated, and for this reason alone, and leaves them permanently on the place for penitents and indeed even if they demonstrate every possible and effective attitude of repentance as well as a clear improvement in their way of life. What precludes this view, in the first place, is the fact that Hermas knows of men who actually come to the tower again from all the classes of sinners, and indeed from the same groups from which others are banished to the outer walls (Sim. VIII 7,2.3 [ibid., pp. 72,13–73,2]; 8,4.5 [ibid., p. 74,4–10]; 9,2 [ibid., p. 74,17–18]; 10,1.4 [ibid., pp. 74,26–75,3.11–13]). The difference of effect seems to have no other reason than the different intensity of penance which the individual performs (even because, for example, he has begun sooner or later with his penance or undertakes it more seriously, etc.).

It can hardly be objected against what we have just said that the tower into which people are incorporated in Sim. VIII refers not to the earthly Church but to the final salvation (p. 35 f.). Even if this were the case,[60] our observation would still be correct, since, even according to Grotz, there is a mere existence in the first walls which, while expressing a reality in the Church of this world, is also a symbol of the final state in the next world. Now irrespective of what may be in the foreground, membership of the tower similarly has its earthly and heavenly counterpart; otherwise it is not possible to see why Hermas claims that some people (he has definite cases in mind) are already inserted into the tower of the next world before they are allowed access to the Church of this world. Thus Hermas recognizes men in all groups of sinners, apart from the apostates in Sim. VIII 6,4 (ibid., pp. 71,21–72,1) (therefore, such sinners who have not simply denied the faith, but as enemies and traitors of the Church have in fact fully, unrepentently and obstinately separated themselves finally from it), who return to the tower. The fate of having to remain in the walls must, therefore, relate to the deficient subjective penance. Grotz's attempt to prove anything different from this rests solely on the fact that in some cases nothing more is said than that these people come into the walls, that is, to the lesser place. But when we read in Vis. III 7,5.6 (ibid., p. 73,6–13) that those who are rejected 'are not able to enter into the tower, but are suitable for a far lesser place and only after they have been tested', then to make this meaningful we should insert the phrase 'not immediately' (come into the tower). From the Church's answer to Hermas' question one can work out the distinction between the penance of those who are rejected and that of those who are lying near the tower. The latter are able, by their penance—under the angel of penance—to be reincorporated immediately into the tower, while the former are only led by the punishing angel to that attitude of, and readiness for, penance, by which they become ready and worthy to assume church penance in the strict sense in the actual place of penitents. That they are later able to proceed further is not excluded by the text. Indeed, such a progress is implied in the prospects which Hermas offers these sinners in Sim. VIII. If in Sim. VI there is mention only of their being handed over to the angel of penance, but not of an eventual end to this time of penance, this is no proof (as Grotz assumes, p. 26) that this time simply has no end.

All that is really excluded by these texts is an 'immediate pardon' (cf. Sim. VII 4 [ibid., pp. 64,17–65,2]). Thus, just as Hermas' children are refused an immediate forgiveness of sin (ibid.), so, in all probability, all that is rejected in Vis. III 7,5.6 (ibid., p. 14,7–16) is an immediate arrival at the tower, and what is taught is an arrival at the outer walls (=the place for penitents, for those arriving to do church penance) as the first, not the definitively last, step on the way of penance. When one considers that it is perfectly reasonable that those sinners who came from far off should first of all do penance in order to be allowed access to church penance, therefore before they are handed over to the angel of penance, and when one considers further that the handing over to the shepherd of penance (Sim. VI 3,6 [ibid., pp. 61,20–62,8]) is, of its very nature, a transfer to a further penance, now conducted by the Church, then one cannot say (cf. p. 26) that the penance of those who were previously remaining near the tower and that of those coming from far off are essentially different and that this is proven by the fact that the second group obtains a confirmation of faith, but otherwise nothing more is said.

Moreover, the point is made about these sinners that, as a result of the discipline under the shepherd of penance, from now on they serve the Lord with a pure heart (Sim. VI 3,6 [ibid., pp. 61,20–62,8]). How is this possible, if not by penance under the leadership of the angel of penance? But why should the aim of the angel of penance, namely the reincorporation into the tower, not be achieved in this instance? In any case the text of Hermas does not exclude this explicitly and clearly. Moreover, if the people (of Grotz's group D) in Vis. III (ibid., pp. 9,29–10,3) are the same as those sinners who, according to Sim. VIII, are inserted into the walls by a long penance (p. 43), and if, still according to Vis. III 2,9 (ibid., p. 10,3–8); 7,1–3 (ibid., pp. 13,20–14,6), they belong to those who are ejected *farther* than the men of the group D but who are still able to return to the tower itself, according to Sim. VIII (e.g. those who err in their faith: Vis. III 7,1 [ibid., p. 13,20–4] and Sim. VIII 6,5.6 [ibid., p. 13,6–16]), then it is impossible to see that for the group D the first walls are the impassable goal of their penance.

Grotz's assumption also implies a distinction beween a definitive excommunication and one which is only temporary, this latter not excluding a full reconciliation with the Church. The sole criterion for such a distinction, even according to Grotz, is obduracy (cf. p. 31 f.; 57 ff.; 66 f.), which is expressed in the refusal of penance.[61] But in this case the only explanation for a permanent excommunication is the sinner's continuing obstinacy.

Now if a person does not go any farther than the place for penitents, not as a mere matter of fact, i.e. because he dies or the Lord arrives before he completes his personal penance, but as a matter of principle, then there would be a permanent excommunication which is not based on the definitive obstinacy of the sinner. But, if this were the case, how can the adulteress, for example, still come to full penance, even if she has been obstinate for a short time? In fact those people who, according to Grotz, have been definitively excommunicated because they have not responded to the first call to penance have done nothing worse than she has done (p. 66 f.)

How can Grotz write: 'When we consider once again in order the groups of sinners to whom, according to Sim. IX, the notion of a *temporary* excommunication applies, it becomes immediately obvious that it is a question of the same sinners who, according to Sim. VIII, arrive, in certain circumstances, at the "first walls" and who are, as we have seen [p. 41 ff.], in turn identical with those of the group D in Vis. III' (p. 67)? A temporary excommunication can still (even according to Grotz) end with a full reconciliation. Must not those, therefore, who (in our view, first) come to the first walls also not be able to proceed further if they were only temporarily excommunicated? Grotz avoids this conclusion with the idea that there are people who belonged to group D but then, because they did not complete their penance quickly enough, have been definitively excommunicated and for this reason, with the help of the penance already undertaken, have only been able to arrive at the walls (p. 68). But a definitive excommunication based solely on the refusal—which is itself understood as necessarily provisional—of penance is a hypothesis which has not the slightest support. In fact, how could a precise deadline be fixed by the Church for the end of the toleration of a temporary obstinacy (as in the case of the adulteress who does not repent immediately)? Why does Hermas say nothing at all about this point? If a person is definitively excommunicated he certainly does not belong any longer to group D.

Finally, it should be emphasized that the idea of a penance which is granted merely once is precisely based on the assumption that the sinner, in this single penance, is really reconciled with the Church and indeed by an act of the Church. This possibility is offered to all sinners without exception or reserve (apart from those sinners who in fact are unrepentant). A reserve must be expressed if it really exists. What would be the point in proclaiming solemnly such a possibility if, from the outset, it remained inaccessible to a whole group of sinners?

This is our conclusion: it is not proven that Hermas recognized an excommunication which, independently of the sinner's definitive obstinacy, excludes him from full communion with the Church, even though he has not yet received the one *metanoia,* and which banishes him as a matter of principle and for ever to a 'lesser place'.

C) CHURCH RECONCILIATION

But is it possible to show that Hermas knew a church reconciliation of sinners? Does the church-regulated penance end with the reacquisition of full church rights, or is it not possible to discern such an act on the Church's part in the Shepherd of Hermas, which of course does not mean that it did not exist or that he did not know such an act? The only passage which speaks explicitly about the 'readmission' of a sinner into the empirical sphere of the Church is Mand. IV 1,8 (ibid., p. 26,16–20.)[62] A sinner who is converted must be received (παραδέχεσθαι), again, and indeed only once, and the husband must treat his adulterous but repentant wife, from whom he had separated himself, accordingly.

It has been claimed[63] that this 'readmission' refers only to the access to church penance, but does not include a church reconciliation. Apart from the fact that, in general, it supposes before Hermas an absolute rigorism in the treatment of sinners which in reality cannot be proven, this opinion is based on the observation that the prerequisite demanded for the readmission is only a μετανοεῖν, but not the previous performance of penance. This reason is certainly not tenable, since, as Poschmann (p. 193) rightly says, μετανοεῖν even in the present can be used of a person 'whose heart is already clean from every evil work' (Sim. VII 5 [ibid., p. 65,2–7]) and thus is already fully healed (p. 4). If, therefore, there is no reason to understand the readmission as only an access to penance, it can be taken to mean a proper, full readmission into the Church. We find the term in Ignatius, Smyrn. 4,1 (Fisher:206,10–14) (only repentent heretics ought to be 'received'), where it is obviously understood of a full church communion.

According to Hermas, the 'readmission' can take place only once, since only one penance is granted to God's servants. Such a readmission can refer only to full church communion, since it presupposes an exclusion which is very difficult to envisage for an access to penance. Otherwise, this exclusion would have to be conceived as a public renunciation of penance before the Church, after which no further access to church penance would be allowed. But there is not the slightest trace of such a refusal to do penance in the early Church. A further penance later was impossible, however, only when a person fell back into sin after the church reconciliation. This did not apply to relapses during the time of penance itself. As the case of the Gnostic Cerdon in Rome at the time of Hermas shows, this was already church practice at that time (Irenaeus, Adv.haer. III 4,3).[64]

Moreover, according to Hermas, the fully completed performance of penance doubtless reopened the possibility of integration into the tower of the Church, at least as an interior community of grace and salvation, and indeed already in this life, before the 'completion' of the tower (cf. e.g., Sim. VIII 6,6 [GCS 48:p. 72,5–10]; 7,3.5 [ibid., pp. 72,17–73,9]; 8,2.3.5 [ibid., pp. 73,16–74,10]; 9,2.4 [ibid., p. 74,17–25]). If this is correct and implies that at least certain sinners were excommunicated by an act of the Church, then it is unthinkable that such a sinner should not be received back into full external fellowship with the Church by an act of the Church, once he has completed the performance of penance. If full *inner* church communion is granted to such a sinner how can the Church still refuse him the external fellowship? Again, if Hermas makes a distinction between a full insertion into the tower and an existence 'beside the tower in a lesser place in the walls round the tower', and if this latter position of the penitent, as we have already seen,[65] reflects his relationship with the empirical Church at least, then the full insertion into the tower must be expressed exteriorly in such a way that, also in this position, such a penitent differs from the one who is only 'by the tower'. He must receive complete reconciliation with the Church. This is all the more proper, in that this belonging to the Church was in no way considered an absolute guarantee of grace, since it was recognized that even those who had lost the seal of baptism still belonged to the external community of the Church. How could one, therefore, have refused this external communion with the Church to a repentant person after a long period of serious penance?

Finally, even Tertullian (to whom this testimony was very inconvenient) had to admit that Hermas was a witness for the reconciliation of adulterers (De pud. 10,12 [CSL 20:p. 241,10–19]; 20,2 [CSL 20:p. 266,20–4]). He stood fairly near to Hermas' time and was not disposed to accepting such a testimony.

If there had been another way of interpreting the evidence Tertullian would not have derived a reconciliation from the Shepherd of Hermas. 'We must have very convincing reasons to ignore Tertullian's judgement on our question' (Poschmann, p. 199). Naturally, we can hardly expect any theories on the meaning which this church reconciliation has for salvation from Hermas. The healing of the sinner takes place through the personal act of penance of the sinner himself; he is accepted into the tower only after he has completed his penance. To this extent, the accent is here entirely on the subjective side. Nevertheless, since the visible Church into which one is received by baptism and—as we can now say, by reconciliation—is necessary for salvation the saving significance of the Church's act is still, in principle, sufficiently guaranteed. In the final analysis, the whole of Hermas' theology of penance revolves around the question of the right relationship of sinful man to the *Church*. Even if this relationship is put in order again principally by the penance of the sinner himself, it is still important for this theology that man's penance directs him to the *Church*. And just as in the case where new Christians are inserted into the tower, the accent is placed on their subjective conversion (Vis. III 7,3.5 [ibid., p. 14,1–6, 7–10]; 6,1 [ibid., p. 14,17–19]: to become a Christian only in appearance; Sim. IX 31,1 f. [ibid., pp. 98,10–100,4]; Mand. IV 3,1 [ibid., pp. 27,21–28,2]: penance *in* baptism), without the sacramental significance of baptism being contested, so something similar ought to be assumed for reconciliation by the Church. If the 'seal', despite penance which is a necessary condition for its reception, is given only by baptism, how can this seal be restored by subjective penance alone?

VI. CONCLUSIONS ON HERMAS' PENITENTIAL TEACHING

We have come to the end of our exposition of Hermas' penitential teaching. In it we have also tried to examine J. Grotz's exposition of this teaching. Our conclusions differ from his on a whole series of points which it is now worthwhile to resume.

It seems historically certain that wherever in Hermas there is a question of an intervention by the Church in the penance of a sinner which can actually be considered a sacramental act, it is always a question of a sinner who is considered 'excommunicated'. In other words, penance as a church-sacramental event and penance of excommunication are identical in the Shepherd of Hermas. He shows no sign of any kind of church penance other than that which considers the sinner alienated from the Church. Hermas' book on penance cannot be taken as a historical witness, therefore, for the view that *before* the actual church penance, and indeed only in certain cases, there preceded a phase of excommunication.

All that can be observed here is that the access to actual church penance, in which the sinner is not yet considered reconciled with the Church, is itself an act of the Church which is only granted after a certain examination of the sinner's genuine repentance and sorrow. This examination will lead to a positive result more or less easily, according to the particular cases presented; i.e. the sinners who, despite their very superficial Christian life, have never lost their close relationship with the community will obviously very easily and without many formalities be given access to actual church penance. Others, on the contrary, who have separated themselves from the community by a very clear and 'secular' defection from the faith or a radically un-Christian way of life will be given access to penance only after a more probing examination.

This difference, however, does not alter the fact that basically all penitents were considered to be, in some sense, 'outside' the Church (which does not mean: without relation to it) and that, consequently, the performance of their penance—considered as the work of the penitent and the act of the Church—is seen precisely and principally from the viewpoint of the Church: the act of the Church is the incorporation into the Church of the penitent who has expiated his sins. It is only by this act that the penitent is assured of his salvation. The act of the penitent is his effort to prove to the Church that he is worthy of such a full reincorporation. This basic structure of Hermas' teaching on penance is exactly what we would expect after our consideration of the teaching and practice of penance attested in the writings of the New Testament.

We cannot here examine critically other sections of Grotz's major study, i.e. especially his explanation of church penance in the writings of Cyprian, Origen, Clement of Alexandria, Tertullian, the Didascalia, etc.[66] This would be possible only in a detailed work which follows, step by step, Grotz's own development. Nevertheless, the result of this examination of his interpretation of Hermas' teaching on penance does not augur well for any of Grotz's further conclusions. The reason for this scepticism is obviously not simply that, in our opinion, his interpretation of the Shepherd of Hermas contains errors. Rather, we consider it entirely improbable that, if from the New Testament and from the first work on penance by a Father of the Church the penance of excommunication is met as the first actual type of sacramental penance in the Church, penance in a different form can present itself at a later time with the claim of representing the pure and original essence of sacramental penance. This observation prescinds from the fact that the dogmatic theologian (even if he is not a historian of dogma) can say: this is not possible because it cannot be possible, since every penance which concerns serious sin sacramentally means something which excludes man *iure divino et iure ecclesiastico* from the Eucharist, the Church's central celebration. It is, therefore, something which establishes him in a broken relationship with the Church and brings it about that the sinner no longer belongs to the Church in the same sense as does the baptized person who is just. (All this applies only if the Church is regarded as more than an external juridical organization.) Thus every sacramental penance and absolution of a serious sin is also a reconciliation with the Church. And this presupposes that the person to be reconciled is actually 'excommunicated'. Every sacramental penance—at least for serious sins—is, therefore, a penance of excommunication. This was recognized not only by the patristic age but also by the whole of the Middle Ages, although it is not so central in modern theological thinking. This strange fact in the first centuries of the Church, that wherever the sacrament of penance appears clearly, it always has the form of a penance of excommunication, is perfectly comprehensible on dogmatic grounds and is to a certain extent to be expected *a priori*. It is also evident that it should be explained in the light of this dogmatic nature and not by a subsequent and slowly developed notion and practice of excommunication springing from church law. If, therefore, the penance of excommunication, which is the essence of sacramental penance, has a dogmatic and still valid nature, and if, the further one goes back in time, one discovers more and more of a process of excommunication in the external and tangible form and practice of penance, then it cannot be false to understand this external, tangible and clear process of excommunication historically as the concrete expression of the nature of penance and not as something which only in the course of time and subsequently is connected with penance.

So it seems to us most likely that the process of development went in the opposite direction to that thought by Grotz. Excommunication in the modern sense of church law has not become connected with penance subsequently and as a purely disciplinary measure. Rather, it gradually became separated from penance and developed into what is today called excommunication. Obviously this is not the place to demonstrate these *a priori* ideas. Nevertheless, from what has been said it appears unlikely that we will be able to discover the older and more original form in later Church Fathers if in Hermas we can only trace a secondary type of the sacrament of penance.

These objections could be countered by the observation that excommunication in the sense envisaged by us is not disputed. At the same time, that other kind of excommunication in the Shepherd of Hermas occurs only for certain groups of sinners but not for all. Thus we are talking at cross-purposes. Now it is agreed that the 'excommunication' which, in our opinion, is (always) in the early Church a hall-mark of every church penance is not explicitly contested by Grotz. But the point is that he appears not to have noticed it even once. And this must be considered as a fundamental defect in a history of penance. In this work the application of a modern notion of excommunication hides the basic structure of the institution of penance in the early Church, as this appears in the sources. This entails that other things too are distorted. Thus, for example, it is indisputable that for the Shepherd of Hermas the place of penitents (the lesser place, the first walls, whether these are formally or only practically identical with the place of penitents) can be reached even by people who come from far away, who therefore, according to Grotz, were excommunicated—at least temporarily. But when they arrive at the place of penitents does the excommunication still continue? If this is not the case, why do they not also come into the tower (at least after further penance)? By what right can one dispute the possibility of explaining such a permanent exclusion from the Church as an excommunication? But if the excommunication persists, then what was previously a temporary excommunication has changed into a permanent one. Thus penance brings only further punishments, without really improving the situation. Moreover, the penitents are no better off than they were before they came to the place of penitents, since even where they were (i.e. disconnected from the community) they could receive pardon for their sin and hope for God's grace. If, therefore, Hermas is convinced that there is a way into the Church, the excommunication must be able to be lifted in principle. But if that is possible, then in those days one did not have to reckon with a definitive and permanent exclusion from the Church for such sinners.

The modern notion of excommunication only leads to constructions which raise new problems not envisaged by Hermas. At the same time, the same problems cannot be applied to the case of those who fall again after *metanoia,* who indeed even in our opinion were refused a further church penance. On the contrary, it is simply to be observed that Hermas (rightly or wrongly is in this context irrelevant) considers these people definitively unrepentant. For him, therefore, the assumption that there are sinners who are excommunicated by an act of the Church and who are no longer allowed access to full church fellowship, although they are recognized as repentant, poses no problem. The same notion of excommunication must then lead further to the attempt to prove later, by a subtle dialectic, that in Cyprian, et al. the lifting of excommunication and the absolution of guilt before God are two different and temporally distinct acts. This, however, does not correspond at all to the data provided by the sources. This view could contain a grain of truth[67] in so far as perhaps those groups of sinners are alienated from the Church not only because of their own serious faults and their own separation from the life of the community but also through an actual and clear act of excommunication on the Church's part, as in the case of those sinners for whom 'excommunication' consists only in the fact that, by their own confessions and their own repentance, they have put themselves in the class of penitents and then have been considered 'excommunicated'. Such an explicit act of excommunication could easily have existed. And perhaps in this sense the Shepherd of Hermas contains the basis of the modern practice of excommunication. Nevertheless, this assumption cannot be sustained on the basis of the text itself. This is not to dispute that, in certain cases, even the early Church could and did excommunicate (e.g. in the case of heretics who were not willing of their own accord to abandon fellowship with the Church) already in the form which the excommunication of church law later acquired. But it remains impossible to say.

Everyone has the right to look for such things in connection with the penitential practice of the early Church and to distinguish them from the actual essence of penance.

What is opposed, however, is the attempt to dispute that the penance of the early Church was, as such, a penance of excommunication. Such an attempt does not only contradict the sources but also incurs the risk either of denying that the penance of the early Church was more than an external event of church discipline (namely a sacrament) or of having to look for the sacrament in another place, where one can find it only because one looks. Or one simply disputes—because no penance can be found which is not a penance of excommunication—that there was a sacrament of penance in the early Church.

4

THE POST-BAPTISMAL FORGIVENESS OF SINS IN THE REGULA FIDEI OF IRENAEUS

There is no doubt that the Regula Fidei, in which Irenaeus of Lyons summarizes the faith which the universal Church recognises as the inheritance which it has received from the apostles and their disciples and which it carefully preserves, belongs to the most important texts of Christian antiquity (Adv. haer. 1,2; edition of W. Harvey I: 90 f.). Certainly it is easy to understand Irenaeus' teaching on penance[1] quite independently of this text; and, in any case, the Regula Fidei offers nothing at all new on the subject. Nevertheless, in interpreting such a rule of faith which presents itself as the clear expression of the belief of the whole Church, it is not without interest to ask whether or not it provides any evidence for the possibility of a penance after baptism.

I. EXPLANATIONS OF THE POSSIBILITY OF PENANCE ACCORDING TO IRENAEUS

If Irenaeus does testify to such a possibility of penance and forgiveness of sins in this context, that is, as part of the Church's universal belief from the beginning, then he certainly cannot count as the last advocate of the old ideal of holiness and as the representative of a rigoristic theory of baptism, as, for example, H. Windisch,[2] H. Koch[3] and G. N. Bonwetsch[4] consider him to be. In fact, several scholars, in their researches into Irenaeus' teaching on penance, have found evidence for a post-baptismal possibility of penance and forgiveness of sins, even in this passage. This is the case of the earlier authors Feuardent (1575)[5] and Grabe (1702),[6] and the more recent Stufler,[7] d'Alès[8] and Hoh.[9] Nevertheless, B. Poschmann,[10] in the excellent exposition of Irenaeus' penitential teaching which forms part of his comprehensive work on church penance in early Christianity up to Cyprian and Origen, has contested this view. It would seem, therefore, that the question of whether or not Irenaeus in fact attests the possibility of a post-baptismal penance in this Regula Fidei merits a re-examination.

For the above-mentioned advocates of a positive answer to this question the text itself appears to be so clear that they do not offer an actual proof for their view. Thus there is no need to consider them further here. Poschmann's negative answer is based on the fact that the two classes, named in the text, of those who reach salvation mean not two classes of men but angels and men. The ones who 'from the beginning' persevered in love are to be understood as the good angels, and the others, who 'by penance' remain in love, are, accordingly, men 'who all, after Adam's fall, can regain it [grace] only by way of penance'. Poschmann sees the proof that these two classes must refer to angels and men in the fact that, in the same context, there is also a mention of the judgement and the rejection of fallen angels and of sinful men. In the case of those, therefore, who, through the judgement, attain happiness, it must be a question of angels and men.

As is usual in confessions of faith, in the Regula Fidei the final phrases of the disputed text refer to eschatology (Adv. haer. I PG 7 10,1). First of all, the belief is here expressed that the Lord Jesus Christ will come again from heaven in the glory of the Father to gather everything together. He will raise up all flesh, the whole of mankind, so that the knee of everyone in heaven, on the earth and under the earth may bend before our Lord and God, the Saviour and King, according to the will of the invisible Father, and that every tongue may praise him. Then the Regula Fidei continues:[11]

> Then he will hold a righteous judgement over all; the wicked spirits and the disobedient angels, who deserted God, and the godless, unrighteous, transgressors and blasphemers among

> men he will commit to everlasting fire. But to the righteous, the pious, those who have followed his commandments and remained in his love—some from the beginning, some by penance—he will grant life as a grace, give immortality and provide eternal glory.

It is, therefore, a question of the judgement which Christ will hold, acting as judge, at the end of time. It is stated *who* will be judged and *what* the content of the verdict (or its effect) will be. Those judged and the corresponding verdict are divided into two classes: the wicked, for whom eternal fire is reserved, and the good, who receive ζωή, ἀφθαρσία and δόξα αἰωνία. The wicked are, for their part, again clearly subdivided into two groups: the wicked angelic powers, who err (παραβεβηκότες) and fall away, and men who, as a sub-group, are more closely characterized by four adjectives: ἀσεβεῖς, ἄδικοι, ἄνομοι, βλάσφημοι.[12] On the other side, the class of the good is similarly described more precisely by four characteristics,[13] and then is still further divided in another sense, so that one part belongs to this class ἀπ' ἀρχῆς and the other belongs to it ἐκ μετανοίας. Now the question is whether, in this class of the good, we have to reckon with angels who have remained faithful, so that those who are good ἀπ' ἀρχῆς means precisely the angels who have remained faithful, and those who are good ἐκ μετανοίας means men who, since Adam's fall, are all in need of a penance. Or is the whole class of the good to be understood only of men, of whom some have persevered in Christ's love 'from the beginning' of their Christian life, while others have done so only after a (second) penance?

II. THE REFERENCE TO MEN

Our view is that only the second possibility does justice to the interpretation of the text itself. First, this view is demanded by the striking fourfold description of the class of the good, which is quite clearly paralleled to the class of wicked men, this class itself being more closely characterized by four types.[14] Second (and this is a point of particular relevance to such a traditional formulation),[15] the idea that *good* angels would be judged by Christ during his judgement at the end of time is totally alien to the tradition before

Irenaeus. Rather, they appear as the judge's companions, as his court, as assistants and executors of his sentence; in no way do they appear as those who are judged.[16] This is all the more striking in that the idea is freely current that the *wicked* angels will be judged at this judgement.[17] Third, according to Poschmann's interpretation, the text would suggest that it is only at the judgement that good angels receive life and eternal glory. And this, again, is an idea which contradicts the world-view of early Christianity, according to which the angels belong from the beginning to the world of the God of the living and appear with Christ at the judgement already in the glory of the Father.[18] Indeed, according to this interpretation, it is only at the judgement that they receive even ἀφθαρσία, a prerogative which is theirs precisely in contrast to man, who is bodily and therefore mortal.[19] Fourth, if by those who remain in Christ's love from penance onwards are meant *all* men (Christians), and by μετάνοια something concrete and specific is to be understood, which, in this instance, can only be baptism, then the text would say that all those—and only those—who have preserved their baptism will be saved. But this view clearly contradicts Irenaeus' teaching (even according to Poschmann's interpretation). In the class of the good, therefore, it is a question only of good men. And it is said of them that they will all be saved, both those who have kept Christ's love from the beginning of their Christian life and those who, after a later penance, have persevered in this love until death.

The terminology in which this situation is expressed cannot be brought to bear against this interpretation. It is neither surprising nor unusual that the beginning of the Christian life should be described simply as ἀπ' ἀρχῆς.[20] For this, one has only to consider, for example, especially 1 John 2:7; 2:24; 3:11; 2 John 5:6; Martyrium Polyc. 17,1; Polyc. Epist. ad Phil. 7,2, apart from Hb 3,14; 5,12; 6,1. It is not in the least surprising,[21] either, that the post-baptismal conversion is described simply as μετάνοια after the Shepherd of Hermas, which Irenaeus considers 'Scripture'.[22] Thus there are in Irenaeus two groups of Christians, just as they are already described repeatedly by Hermas. The one group of believers

> are as innocent children, whose minds are entered by nothing that is evil and who have never learnt what sin is, but who remain always innocent; now these will certainly obtain a dwell-

> ing place in the kingdom of God, because they . . . have persevered all the days of their life in the same innocent attitude of mind (Sim. IX 29,1 f.).

The others all belong to the different categories who have kept the 'seal', only after a second post-baptismal penance.

A further point deserves attention: if—as is easy to see—the whole of Irenaeus' Regula Fidei is loaded with certain anti-Gnostic nuances, then it is already understandable why what appears, at first sight, to be a subtle and far-fetched differentiation for the group of those who are saved at the judgement should be made. Such a differentiation is, in fact, anti-Gnostic in a polemic sense, because it is directed against the Gnostic notion that the Spirit is an inalienable quality of those who have received it just once (either by baptism or already from eternity).[23] The same point is anti-Gnostic in an irenic sense, because it invites recusant Gnostics to penance and conversion to the Church by opening up the possibility of salvation after baptism.[24]

It must be said, therefore: according to Irenaeus, it is part of apostolic faith that even those who have sinned after baptism attain salvation, provided they have returned to the love of Christ by means of a new *metanoia* and have remained in it until Christ's return in judgement. It is not stated explicitly how often such a *metanoia* is possible. But since the main emphasis of the passage is on the fact that man will be saved in so far as, at the judgement of Christ, he is found to be in Christ's love[25] only through *metanoia* (considered as personal conversion), this text precludes the idea that there can be sins which, because of their objective gravity, are unforgivable, even if a man has turned away from them by penance. There is no mention in this text of the once-and-for-all character or of the possibility of repeated *church* penance, least of all of a relationship of this penance to the Church, therefore, of a readmission into the Church. But this can hardly be expected, since these questions do not fit at all into the context given. Nevertheless, on the basis of this text alone, it can be said: If it belongs to the deposit of faith that a man, even after baptism, can return to Christ's love through penance and so will find grace in Christ's judgement, then the Church, even at this time, must have drawn the conclusion from its own conviction, at least in general, and have extended *its own* love again to the man who is in Christ's love (cf. 2 Cor. 2:8),[26] that is restored to him the full church fellowship.

III. THE TEXT

To help the reader, the text of Irenaeus' Regula Fidei is reproduced here in its Latin form, as it is presented by W. Wigan Harvey and in the English translation by A. Roberts and J. Donaldson (eds.) in *The Ante-Nicene Fathers*.[27] For the sake of completion, the English text of the Regula Fidei is also reproduced in the form which this has in the 'Proof of the Apostolic Preaching'.[28] Since these texts are not usually included among the witnesses to the practice and the theology of penance in the early Church, and since our brief remarks refer to them directly, it seems appropriate to reproduce them here. In any case, it should be kept constantly in mind that it is here a question primarily of a confession of faith on the part of the Church which has only been adopted by Irenaeus.

1. W. Wigan Harvey, *Sancti Irenaei* . . . , cap. II

'Ecclesia enim (et quidem) per universum orbem usque ad finem terrae (dis)seminata, et ab Apostolis, et discipulis eorum accepit eam fidem, quae est in unum Deum, Patrem omnipotentem, qui fecit coelum et terram et mare, et omnia quae in eis sunt: et in unum Christum Jesum Filium Dei, incarnatum pro nostra salute: et in Spiritum Sanctum, qui per Prophetas praedicavit dispositiones Dei, et adventum, et eam, quae est ex Virgine generationem, et passionem, et resurrectionem a mortuis, et in carne in coelos ascensionem dilecti Jesu Christi Domini nostri, et de coelis in gloria Patris adventum eius, ad recapitulanda universa, et resuscitandam omnem carnem humani generis, ut Christo Jesu Domino nostro et Deo, et Salvatori, et Regi, secundum placitum Patris invisibilis omne genu curvet coelestium, et terrestrium, et infernorum, et omnis lingua confiteatur ei, et iudicium iustum in omnibus faciat: spiritualia quidem nequitiae, et angelos transgressos, atque apostatas factos, et impios, et iniustos, et iniquos, et blasphemos homines in aeternum ignem mittat: iustis autem et aequis, et praecepta eius servantibus, et in dilectione eius perseverantibus, quibusdam quidem ab initio, quibusdam autem ex poenitentia, vitam donans incorruptelam loco muneris conferat; et claritatem aeternam circumdet.'

2. A. Roberts and J. Donaldson (eds.), *Irenaeus Against Heresies* (The Ante-Nicene Fathers, vol. I) Buffalo 1887, pp. 330–1

'The church, though dispersed throughout the whole world, even to the ends of the earth, has received from the apostles and their disciples this faith: (She believes) in one God, the Father Almighty, Maker of heaven, and earth, and the sea, and all things that are in them; and in one Christ Jesus, the Son of God, who became incarnate for our salvation; and in the Holy Spirit, who proclaimed through the prophets the dispensations of God, and the advents, and the birth from a virgin, and the passion and the resurrection from the dead, and the ascension into heaven in the flesh of the beloved Christ Jesus, our Lord, and His (future) manifestation from heaven in the glory of the Father 'to gather all things in one', and to raise up anew all flesh of the whole human race, in order that to Christ Jesus, our Lord, and God, and Saviour, and King, according to the will of the invisible Father, 'every knee should bow, of things in heaven, and things on earth, and that every tongue should confess' to Him, and that He should execute just judgment towards all; that He may send 'spiritual wickednesses', and the angels who transgressed and became apostates, together with the ungodly, and unrighteous, and wicked, and profane among men, into everlasting fire; but may, in the exercise of His grace, confer immortality on the righteous, and holy, and those who have kept His commandments, and have persevered in His love, some from the beginning (of their Christian course), others from (the date of) their repentance, and may surround them with everlasting glory.'

3. J. P. Smith, *St. Irenaeus, Proof of the Apostolic Preaching* (Ancient Christian Writers, no. 16) Westminster, Md./London 1952, pp. 51–2

'And this is the drawing-up of our faith, the foundation of the building, and the consolidation of a way of life. God, the Father, uncreated, beyond grasp, invisible, one God the maker of all; this is the first and foremost article of our faith. But the second article is the Word of God, the Son of God, Christ Jesus our Lord, who was shown forth by the prophets according to the design of their prophecy and according to the manner in which the Father disposed; and through him were made all things whatsoever. He also, *in the end of times,* for the recapitulation of all things, is become a man among men, visible and tangible, in order to abolish death and bring to light life, and bring about the communion of God and man. And the third article is the Holy Spirit, through whom the prophets prophesied and the patriarchs were taught about God and the just were led in the path of justice, and who *in the end* of times has been poured forth in a new manner upon humanity over all the earth renewing man to God. . . .

. . . for none shall escape immune from his judgement, neither Jew nor Gentile nor sinner among the faithful, nor angel. But those who are now sceptical of His kindness will know His power in the judgement, as the blessed apostle says: 'Knowing not, that the benignity of God leadeth thee to penance, but according to thy hardness and impenitent heart, thou treasurest up for thyself wrath, in the day of wrath, and revelation of the just judgement of God, who will render forth to every man according to his works (Rom. 2:4–6).'

PART THREE

The African Tradition

5

TERTULLIAN'S THEOLOGY OF PENANCE

The role of Tertullian, especially in the theological tradition of North Africa, but also of the whole Western Church, has remained in the background for a long time. This is doubtless due to the fact that, in his later writings, he veered towards Montanism. It is only in recent times that his thinking has been placed in the limelight, even if earlier there were not wanting a few authors who tried to exploit his voluminous and well-authenticated writings with regard to specific thematic questions.[1] These include his teaching on penance, which has received repeated treatment.[2] Nevertheless, we consider that this question has not yet received a detailed consideration in relation to his thought as a whole.

Our intention, however, is to highlight aspects and points which perhaps have been either overlooked or forgotten today. Such a treatment of Tertullian's theology of penance must obviously involve that a great deal of what is already known be presupposed or even repeated.[3] Revising familiar material in this way is never very satisfying. But, perhaps for that very reason, it is all the more necessary to do.

It is obvious that what is found in Tertullian's writings does not, in itself, have any dogmatic binding force. This would be the case, only if one of his statements could be proven to be a unanimous opinion of the Fathers of the Church. Such direct bases of later opinions are, however, not very numerous in Tertullian. His influence is to be seen elsewhere, since he stands at the beginning of a line of theological development in North Africa which leads, via Cyprian of Carthage, to Augustine and from him to the whole medieval theology of the Western Church. Many of his instigations had only a negative effect, but they did have an effect, nevertheless. This ought to become a little clearer in a historical essay on the question of penance, even if, in this context, that probing from the dogmatic viewpoint is hardly possible which can show up the theological significance of many aspects which, though today somewhat forgotten, are very clearly emphasized by Tertullian. In this essay we are concentrating on the actual theology of penance.

In this consideration of Tertullian's teaching on penance, therefore, the whole question of the existence or non-existence of limits to the Church's power to forgive sins in relation to certain (capital) sins, as they could have existed in the teaching and practice of the Church in Tertullian's time, must be precluded at the outset. What could be said about these limits does not come within the ambit of this investigation, which is concerned with Tertullian's theology of penance in the strict sense.

I. THE OBJECT OF PUBLIC PENANCE[4]

In his work *De paenitentia,* where he considers church penance, Tertullian speaks only about serious sins which cause the loss of grace (cf. De paenit. 2,6.7.8 [CSL 76:p. 143,25–36]). But since penance is here conceived as the restoration of the state which was given to the Christian at baptism (7,10 ff. [CSL 76:pp. 159,33–160,45; 8,8 [ibid., pp. 162,27–34]; 12,9 [ibid., pp. 169:34–170,40), he would surely have agreed with the general theological principle that all sins which destroy the grace received in baptism should be submitted to church penance. Obviously, this does not mean that Tertullian concluded from this idea precisely which sins are in fact serious and, therefore, submitted to church penance.[5]

It does mean, however, that, in Tertullian's view, all those sins which he considers as destroying the grace of baptism, entailing death, etc. are, of their very nature, the object of church penance. The only way to see which sins these actually are is to consider his work as a whole. Thus, in the present context, it is not important to discuss which criteria Tertullian uses to distinguish these faults from those others which do not have such an effect and are, therefore, in today's terms, 'venial sins'.

Tertullian did not draw up a systematic, fixed list of serious sins. Certainly, in his view, these sins are not simply identifiable with the three capital sins,[6] in the strict sense of the term. The 'triad' appears first of all in the work De pudicitia 5 (CSL 20:pp. 226,4–228,2)[7] which hails from Tertullian's Montanist period. And here it is one of his polemical devices. The triad is designed to name the sins which are unforgivable. As Poschmann has convincingly shown, even according to De pud., *moechia* at least did not previously count among such sins. At the same time this triad itself, according to De pud. 19 (CSL 20:p. 262,27–30; p. 265,22–5), is in no way an actual exclusive and clearly-defined group of sins; since here it includes: *homicidium, idolatria, fraus, negatio, blasphemia utique et moechia et fornicatio et si qua alia violatio templi dei.* If even here, therefore, the number of unforgivable sins exceeds the three 'capital sins', there can be no question that Tertullian would maintain that the sins which are to be submitted to church penance are identifiable with the three capital sins.

In fact, in his Catholic period, he recognizes that many more sins destroy grace and are, consequently, the object of church penance. In the work De paen. he includes among these: *concupiscentia carnalis, inlecebrae saeculares,* denial of faith out of fear of worldly power, heresy (*perversae traditiones*) (7,9 [CSL 76:p. 159,28–33]), *stuprum, idolothytorum esus, perversa docere, fidere divitiis* (8,1 [CSL 76:p. 160,1–6]). In Apol.2, the following are enumerated as offences forbidden to Christians: *homicidium, adulterium, fraus, perfidia et cetera scelera* (CSL 69:p. 6,2–3). According to Apol. 11, these deserve hell: *impii quique in parentes, et incesti in sorores et maritarum adulteri et virginum raptores et puerorum contaminatores et qui saeviunt et qui occidunt et qui furantur et qui decipiunt* (CSL 69:p. 32,16–19). Tertullian's treatise in moral theology De spectaculis sets out to prove that the offence of *Deo excidere* can exist,[8] even when there is no argument to be drawn from a scriptural commandment aimed directly against this sin, so that, for instance, taking part in circuses and in pagan spectacles, etc. belongs to the sins which separate men from God. Similarly, deceit is counted among the sins which are incompatible with the grace of baptism.[9] Obviously, various occupations associated with pagan worship, such as that of a master of gladiators, a provider of incense, a seller of sacrificial meat, are likewise also considered as being seriously sinful and punished by exclusion from the community (De idol. 11 [CSL 20:p. 41,16–19]). In view of Hippolytus' Pradosis (16, Dix p. 24 ff.), this can hardly be considered as Montanistic rigorism. The same applies to everything that counts as idolatry, such as the fabrication of the images of idols (De idol. 5 [ibid., pp. 34,29–35,2]; cf. De pud. 7,15 f. [ibid., p. 232,21–6]), soothsaying (De idol. 9 [ibid., p. 39,11–14]; cf. De pud. 7,16 [ibid., p. 233]). Thieves, deceivers, robbers also obviously do not enjoy any church fellowship (De idol. 5). Nevertheless, in other cases Tertullian's Montanistic rigorism later explained things as serious sins which are not such according to Catholic teaching, and then also refused church fellowship to such 'sinners' as, for example, those who marry a pagan (Ad uxorem 11, 3; De monogamia 11), or who marry a second time (De pud. 1,20 [CSL 20:p. 222,2–6]). Also, it is clear from De pat. 5 (CSL 47:pp. 8–9) that belonging to the major offences against God are not only idolatry, murder and impurity, but also enmity, avarice, robbery and hatred. Thus, neither in his Catholic nor in his Montanist period does Tertullian acknowledge a fixed and exclusive triad of mortal sins. Rather, in his view, the number of sins, with regard both to the loss of baptismal grace and to exclusion from the Church, is very much greater. Nevertheless, all these sins are submitted to church penance.

Theoretically, Tertullian acknowledges more mortal sins in his Catholic period than later, although even then, for example (cf. De pud. 7 [CSL 20:233]), the person who takes part in pagan games is described as *vivens adhuc peccator*. Later he restricts the number of mortal sins because they cause the loss of baptismal grace and, therefore, are unforgivable. For practical reasons, therefore, he cannot accept too many mortal sins.

It is possible to see which sins he regarded as being remissible by church penance, in his Catholic period, by considering De pud. and, particularly, those faults for which he prescribes church penance in his Montanist period: the *mediocria delicta,* such as taking part in chariot races, gladiator fights, the theatre, pagan feasts, idolatry and astrology (De pud. 7,15 [CSL 20:p. 232,21–6]). He must have considered these sins earlier as mortal sins, since in De pud. 7,15 f.

(CSL 20:pp. 232,26–233,3)[10] he concedes it as quite self-evident that they alienate men from the Church; such sinners are *extra gregem* and *foris*. It is unthinkable, however, that he should consider a sinner in a state of baptismal grace as being separated from the Church or excluded from it by excommunication. Thus these sins are *leviora delicta*[11] only by comparison with the capital sins. They are here presented precisely as the object of church penance and should not be confused with the *delicta cotidianae incursionis* (De pud. 19 [ibid., p. 265,15]), to which all are subjected. But, since Tertullian considers church penance something which actually ought not to exist, it is hardly possible to assume that, in his opinion, all men have to undergo church penance. Christ is intercessor in the event of daily faults (De pud. 19 [ibid., p. 265,21–2]), but this does not mean that he always plays this role in exactly the same way as he does in actual church penance, where he is intercessor in an official act of the Church through the bishop and the community (De paen. 10,6 f. [CSL 76:p. 165,20–7]). The daily faults are not mortal sins and must not, therefore, be confused with the *mediocria delicta* which are serious sins for Tertullian in his Catholic period. For Tertullian in his Montanist period only those sins properly belong to the obligatory object of church penance which, in his opinion, cannot be forgiven by the Church: namely, the frequently mentioned triad of idolatry, impurity and murder (De pud. 5 [CSL 20:p. 227,28–9]).[12] According to De pud. 19,22 (ibid., p. 265,15–20), he counts among the daily faults of all Christians: anger, acts of violence, cursing, white lies, etc., which, in his opinion, can all be remitted without church penance.

This is all that we can say about Tertullian's 'theory' of the obligatory object of public church penance. The field in which this 'theory' could be applied is very wide, especially if one considers that even secret sins are explicitly included (De paen. 10,8 [CSL 76:p. 165,27–9]). Even sins of thought are understood, in some circumstances, to be just as serious as sins of deed, at least in theory (De paen. 3,4 ff. [CSL 76:p. 145,13–24]). The 'practice', however, was quite different. The situation with regard to church penance in those days may have been the same as that of excommunication as a church punishment today: in theory, it is very frequently in order, but it occurs very seldom in practice, because there are sufficient reasons why 'in this particular case' the excommunication is not verified. Tertullian himself observes that very many people not only repeatedly postpone church penance but probably try to 'flee from' (*suffugere*) it (De paen. 10,1 [CSL 76:p. 164,1–5]), that is they find reasons for considering their fault not so serious that it should demand church penance in fact. Thus it must remain doubtful whether the practice of such a church penance extended beyond the publicly known cases of capital sins. In the light of this practice, it is understandable that later, despite the protest of 'theologians', there is a tendency here and there to restrict the number of actual mortal sins which should be submitted to church penance to the three capital sins. Nevertheless, this number almost always includes other sins.

II. THE PERFORMANCE OF PENANCE

1. The Obligation to Do Penance

The obligation to do public church penance for serious sins is emphasized by Tertullian in De paen. 10–12. All false shame is to be set aside; it ought not be repeatedly postponed; the difficulties of penance should not frighten sinners, because it is only penance that liberates them from the 'hell in their hearts'. Without penance, there is no salvation, and this applies even to secret sins: *an melius damnatum latere quam palam absolvi?* (De paen. 10,8 [CSL 76:p. 165,27–9]).

2. The Confession

Penance consists first of all of the confession, the exhomologesis (De paen. 9,5 [ibid., p. 163,18–22]), in the *publicatio sui* (De paen. 10,1 [ibid., p. 164,1–5]). The sin must not be deprived of the *humana notitia* (De paen. 10,7 [CSL 76:p. 165,25–7]). This public confession to which Tertullian exhorts and which he explains as necessary for salvation consists above all of the undertaking of the public penance itself (cf. De paen, 9–10 [CSL 76: pp. 162–5]). The sinner appears before the community dressed as a penitent, implores his fellow-

Christians for their intercession and installs himself in the place for penitents in the church. It is in this way that he 'confesses' that he is a sinner.[13] This public avowal is difficult to do, it is the *actus* which oversteps the limits of the *conscientia* (De paen. 9,1 [ibid., p. 162,1–3]). Thus Tertullian does not mention, in the first place, a detailed confession of sins before either the bishop or the community. This was least of all demanded in cases where the sins were already known and had perhaps even provoked a spontaneous intervention on the part of the church leaders. This intervention could be thought of either as an excommunication or as the imposition of church penance with exclusion from the Eucharist. Nevertheless, according to Tertullian, sinners should also do public penance for secret, serious sins (De paen. 10,8 [ibid., p. 165,27–9]). In this case, was a general avowal, implied in the announcement of public penance, sufficient, or are we to think that, at the beginning of such a penance, we have a detailed confession of the sinner, at least before the bishop? We ought to assume the latter case. Such a confession before the bishop is implied in the request for penance. The *castigatio* does not depend on the judgement of the penitent alone. At least as far as its duration is concerned, penance varied according to the sins in question. This would have been very difficult to justify solely on the basis of the degree of the sinner's sorrow or repentance[14] (although this may have played a role). And this applies to Tertullian's time as it does later. On this presupposition, it is possible to have a clear idea of the significance of the *censura divina,* the *iudicari magno cum pondere* in God's presence until the excommunication (Apol. 39 [CSL 69:p. 92,14–18]) which, according to Tertullian, occurs in the liturgy. Thus, either before or after the liturgy there must have been a *censura divina* by the bishop by which *castigationes,* that is, church penance (besides a mere excommunication),[15] were imposed. A precise determination of this church penance in the case of secret sins, however, presupposes a detailed confession at some point of time before the bishop.[16] This could also have been the occasion already—as it is later attested by Origen—for the sinner to ask whether in fact church penance was really necessary in his particular case. Nevertheless, it is not possible to tell from Tertullian's statements whether a precise confession of sins, even for secret sins, was required to be made publicly before the whole community. Certainly this was not required later. Leo the Great (cf. DS 323) maintains that the strict personal confession of secret sins before the bishop is the unique *apostolica regula.*[17]

3. *Penitential Practices*

Penance also comprises certain penitential practices which, initially, are of a more private nature, such as fasting, the wearing of a special penitential garb and other practices (including abstention from taking a bath) (cf. De paen. 9,4). It would be natural for the sinner to undertake these practices as soon as he comes to his senses, since when, during the liturgy in the church, he begs to be admitted to the Church's official penance he already appears as a penitent.[18] According to Cyprian a person is able to do private penance in this manner for some considerable time before bothering about church penance and only then take on the exhomologesis proper (cf. Epsit. 16,2). This private 'pre-penance' is perfectly understandable. The period of exhomologesis done during the public liturgy may be experienced as particularly humiliating and difficult. A previous private penance, while not alleviating the serious obligation to do penance for sins, makes it possible to shorten the period of public church penance.[19] In any case, these private penitential practices were also continued simultaneously with actual church penance. It is worth noting that Tertullian considers them in De paen. only after his treatment of the exhomologesis. To this private penance are then added specifically ecclesiastical practices: in virtue of his confession the sinner incurs first of all a *censura divina: a communione orationis et conventus et omnis sancti commercii relegatur* (Apol. 39). He is denied the *communicatio ecclesiastica* (De pud. 18), that is, he is 'excommunicated'. Obviously this excommunication in no way coincides with our modern canonical notion of excommunication. Nor did it at that time denote, in every case, the introduction of the performance of church penance.[20] There was naturally an exclusion of unrepentant sinners from the community and from the liturgy. This was considered a purely punitive measure, at least until the sinner's willing conversion. Nevertheless, in this period excommunication belonged to the very essence of church penance. The penitent's aim was, precisely through his penance, to regain peace with the Church and church fellowship. Moreover, in the case of secret sins, it was not a matter of his simply being already 'outside' because of the act in the sense that all that was required was his official reconciliation with the Church. At least in order to have access to the performance of church penance an official act of excommunication is necessary. In the act the bishop doubtless had the decisive word, even if priests and the faithful co-operated in the decision. 'To put a person outside the church' (*extra Ecclesiam dare*) is the duty of the leader (*praesidentis officium*) (De pud. 14,16). The exclusion is clearly expressed. The sinner has to stand at the church doors (*pro foribus ecclesiae;* De pud. 3,5; 4,5), at *limen ecclesiae* (De pud. 1,21; 4,5), where the faithful proceed to 'disown' him (De paen. 10,4). There *in vestibulo* (De paen. 7,10) he begs on bended knee the bishop, the priests and the faithful to receive him back into the community of the Church (De paen. 9,4.6; 10,6; De pud. 1,21; 3,5; 5,14; 13,7). Already at the time of Tertullian church penance appears to have taken place in two stages. In the first place the sinner, dressed in sackcloth and ashes, and standing before the actual church building, asks the community to be admitted to penance.[21] The granting of this prayer is already an opening of the *ianua paenitentiae* (De pud. 6,1). Then follows the actual penance in the church itself. It is carried out almost according to the same rite as the penitential prayer outside the church, that is by a prayer on bended knee both for the community's intercession with God and for full church communion, only it occurs now after an *inducere in ecclesiam* (De pud. 13).[22] Also according to De pud. 18,13 the exhomologesis appears to take place in the church itself.

The penance which took place inside the church, however, was not a single act. It lasted a fairly long time (cf. De paen. 11,4–6). Thus the penitents obviously had to be present for a long time in their penitential garb on Sundays in the liturgy and to address the above-mentioned prayer repeatedly to the community. For such an exhomologesis they obviously needed a great deal of patience (cf. De paen. 15). The *poenitentiae ambitus* (De pud. 18,12) must have varied in length according to the different cases. Nevertheless, Tertullian obviously does not know of a penance which lasts a life-time (in so far, that is, as he recognizes a church forgiveness at all). This is clear from the fact that he considers the king of Babylon's seven-year penance (Dan. 4:33) as already very long (De paen. 12,7).

The fact that liturgical penance does not always terminate only on the death-bed can be derived from the warning that penance is only possible once and that, for this reason, one must beware of a further fall (*iterato beneficio gratus esto, nedum ampliato;* De paen. 7,11).

4. Reconciliation

Normally penance came to an end not only at a particular point of time (De paen. 12,9: *exomologesi . . . restitutus*), but was certainly concluded by an act of church reconciliation. This involves a *restitutio* (De pud. 9), a *venia ab episcopo* (De pud. 18). It is not very easy to visualize how this would occur liturgically. Obviously it followed the sinner's last exhomologesis in the appropriate liturgy. Details of such a ceremony are still discernible in De pud. 13,7 ff., even despite the smokescreen of Tertullian's mockery. The sinner is once more led into the liturgical assembly (or is he brought forward from the place which he has occupied as a penitent at the back of the church?), and on bended knee he begs for the community's intercession and for readmission into the community. The bishop gives a sermon on the gravity of sin and the mercy of God, and then follows the forgiveness. Tertullian does not say how the actual rite of forgiveness appears as the readmission of a penitent to full church fellowship. But since already in Cyprian[23] the imposition of hands accompanied by prayer was used quite naturally for this purpose and the same ritual was practiced generally in the Church,[24] it is reasonable to suppose that it was employed already in Tertullian's time.

However reconciliation may have appeared liturgically, De pud. leaves no doubt about a proper act of forgiveness by the Church. The aim of the whole work is precisely to dispute that the bishop had the ability of an *Ego . . . dimitto* with regard to certain sins and to reject the claim of the *numerus episcoporum* (21) to the *potestas* (3; 21; 22) to forgive sins. At the same time, it is precisely this power that is defended, at least since the polemic against Montanism, with explicit reference to Matthew 16:18 f. (De pud. 21,9 f.).

Already according to De paen., however, the penance described by Tertullian as being demanded for all serious sins committed after baptism had to be concluded by a church reconciliation. This reconciliation is indeed not explicitly mentioned—or, at least, not as explicitly as in De pud. The notions of *absolvere* as an act of the bishop, of *pax, communicatio* and *communicare* do not occur, although later in De pud. they are very common. Also, already in De paen. penance is seen very clearly as the concern of the Church, in so far as it is to be performed before the Church, that is, publicly in the presence of the community, if it is to avail to salvation. Moreover, it must be supported by the intercession of the Church, if it is to find a hearing with God and obtain the forgiveness of sins. This is because the prayer of Christ's body is the infallibly efficacious prayer of the Lord himself (10,6 f.). Nevertheless, there is no mention of an official act of absolution by the bishop. But that such an act must have existed at this time is clearly suggested by other expressions in De paen.

The difference between Tertullian's two works on this point does not appear to be very considerable.[25] In the later period he contested the Church's claim to be able to grant full forgiveness even for sins of impurity. In this context he naturally had to deal explicitly with an official act on the Church's part. Earlier, however, he was concerned only to exhort sinners not to stay away from penance but to accept it willingly. Such a penitential preaching considers naturally the situation of the sinner but not that of the Church.

We need not consider here whether the Catholics (the 'psychics') at that time, either before or after the bishop's edict which Tertullian challenges in De pud., exempted certain ('capital') sins from the Church's absolution. In fact there is no proof that Tertullian as a Catholic did not recognize a church reconciliation in respect of those sins for which he prescribes penance in De paen. Certainly there are indications from this period of Tertullian's life (Apol. 2; De corona 11; De monogamia 15) that the Church punishes certain sins with excommunication and does not tolerate in its midst those who commit them, as long as they are unrepentant. But there are no indications that these sinners are not to be readmitted if they stop sinning and do penance. Moreover, these texts say nothing about a permanent and irrevocable exclusion.[26]

At the same time, there seem to be positive proofs that at the time of De paen. a church reconciliation was possible. Penance is compared with baptism. It is *paenitentia secunda* (7,10.12; 9,1), the other *planca salutis* (12,9). It restores the lost baptismal grace, and this after a precisely measured period of time in this life, so that one can be afraid of losing it again (7,11).

If penance and baptism are compared in this way, at least as far as their internal effect is concerned, that is to say, if there is the awareness that, through penance, a sinner recovers everything that he received in baptism but, as a prodigal son, had squandered (8,8), then it is unthinkable that he remains permanently excluded from full church fellowship. What he receives again is the baptismal grace which previously had established his full church membership. Moreover, Tertullian considers that this *paenitentia secunda* is unrepeatable (7,10 f.), although its effect can be lost again (7,11). But how can this unrepeatable possibility be established, known and determined in relation to a further penance if it is not followed by a church reconciliation? Naturally a penitent can fall again into sin during the period of his penance without this affecting the single opportunity for penance. This is because any further attempt (which is not allowed anyway) at penance would only count as a new penance if it were previously established that the penitent has already in fact recovered the lost baptismal grace and that he has precisely lost it a second time. Tertullian states explicitly that a further penance after the *paenitentia secunda* is impossible precisely because the penitent has already recovered the baptismal grace a second time and, therefore, ought not to lose it again (7,11). Thus the knowledge that reconciliation has been achieved concludes penance and also clearly distinguishes it from a further possibility. But the sinner can have this knowledge only by being readmitted explicitly into the community of the Church. Otherwise, he would have to do penance for the whole of his life. Penance can be unrepeatable only if it has a tangible conclusion, which is conceivable only as an act of the Church. Accordingly, the *palam absolvi* (10,8) also indicates that Tertullian must be thinking of a church reconciliation. Certainly the absolving subject here is God himself or perhaps also the sinner's personal penance (cf. 9,6), the latter, as church exhomologesis, being already public (*palam*). Nevertheless, the forgiveness which God grants to the sinner in view of his penance is not in itself public and man's public penance is not, on its own, a *palam absolvi*. This expression obviously means more than: to deserve an intangible forgiveness by means of public penance. But how can forgiveness itself be tangible, if not by an act of the Church which expresses full fellowship and peace with God, in the same way as the enmity with God caused by serious sin was expressed by excommunication? Finally, Tertullian says that the *ianua ignoscentiae* which was once opened to him in baptism is indeed closed to the baptized person who sins, but that the *secunda paenitentia* is offered to him by God *in vestibulo* as a door which gives the sinner who is knocking free access to the Church (*patefaciat*) (7,10). This image applies directly only to the access of the penitent who is knocking to penance in the church, since he is standing *foris* and desires to be invited in (cf. De pud. 3). Thus it is irrelevant whether this penance is envisaged as a single act or as a long-lasting exhomologesis. The access to penance in the Church signifies already, therefore, an opening of the *ianua paenitentiae* (De pud. 6). Nevertheless, according to Tertullian, it is quite clear that for him, even in his Montanist period, the access to this penance, the opening of the *ianua paenitentiae,* introduces a process which ends with an act of forgiveness by the Church. As a Montanist he refuses those guilty of sins of impurity access even to this penance (De pud. 13).[27] If this penance did not necessarily end with a forgiveness by the Church, which the Montanist Tertullian will not admit with regard to impurity, it would be impossible to see why he refuses this penance, since, in his opinion, penance must certainly be done for these sins. The access to such a penance would in no way affect the divine privilege of the forgiveness of sins, which must be denied to the Church in the case of these sins. Thus the only reason why Tertullian refuses those guilty of sins of impurity access to church penance is that it necessarily, both previously and even according to his Montanist notions, concluded with an act of forgiveness by the Church. At the same time, he does in fact apply to church forgiveness yet other expressions which, in themselves, refer only to access to penance. This actually contradicts the very principles of Montanism, according to which penance and forgiveness by the Church are not necessarily any longer connected. When, for instance, he wishes to say that the Catholics grant church forgiveness to those who are guilty of sins of impurity, he formulates the idea as follows: this is a *fornicationi quoque paenitentiae ianuam expandere* (De pud. 6), a *fornicationem paenitentia donare* (9), a *secundam paenitentiam promittere* (20). In other words, even for Tertullian as Montanist access to actual church penance is so intimately and indissolubly connected with the idea of forgiveness by the Church that he has to deny access when he does not wish to grant forgiveness and when he formulates the refusal of the possibility of forgiveness in terms of the refusal or the possibility of access. In De paen. it is a question of access to actual church penance for all sins. From what we have seen, this must be taken so unconditionally that this penance ends with an act of forgiveness by the Church. The penance in question here is the *paenitentia secunda* which, because of the concluding church forgiveness, stands in clear parallel to baptism, which makes God's own remission 'public' and which is already so symbolically connected with absolution by the Church that it can no longer be granted if this act of reconciliation by the Church is lacking. To this extent the ideas of Tertullian the Montanist represent the Catholics' argument: penance is meaningless, if *venia* is not granted by the Church (De pud. 3). This is a description of the ancient and traditional nature of church penance. Thus all sins for which Tertullian prescribes church penance in De paen. receive church forgiveness after the appropriate period of penance. All the sinners whom he here exhorts to penance ought to hope for *venia,* the *pax* of the Church and *communicatio.* Among the sins in question Tertullian counts the following: *stuprum, idolothytorum esus, docere perversa* (8,1). His exhortation to sinners and his justification of God's readiness to forgive are so general (8; 10,6 f.) that as far as he is concerned at this period in his life it is impossible for there to be sinners who would be totally ineligible for this church penance. His later division of sins in respect to a forgiveness by the Church into *peccata remissibilia* and *irremissibilia* (De pud. 2; 9; 12; 16) was not yet known to him at that time, despite his own reference to a change of opinion on the subject (1,10). It is to all sinners that he directs his instruction to re-enter the Church through the door of penance. This entrance through the *paenitentia secunda* (De paen. 7,10) which opens itself to the person who knocks is the access to forgiveness by the Church.

Finally, it needs to be underlined that the act of reconciliation is performed decisively by the bishop. It is a fact that according to De paen. the intercessory prayer, which as the prayer of Christ is bound to be heard, is the act of the whole Church, and that the bishop is not mentioned as having a special part in it (De paen. 9,4). The *presbyteri,* the *cari Dei* (confessors) and the brethren, who have been asked to make intercession, are all placed on the same level. Since it is here a question of obtaining everyone's intercession (Tertullian wishes to describe what the penitent himself has to do), there is no need to spotlight the bishop's role. Moreover, at that time the African Churches were clearly organized along the lines of a monarchical episcopate. Tertullian himself in his Catholic period unambiguously testifies to the position of the episcopate as that of a church institution which receives its authority in virtue of the apostolic succession[28] and not merely of a function of a democratic community. There can be no doubt, therefore, that already at the time of De paen. the bishop had the decisive word in the reconciliation of the penitent. This is also evident from the fact that penance began with the excommunication of the sinner which was necessarily expressed by the bishop.[29] The reconciliation of a penitent with the Church must, accordingly, be primarily the prerogative of the bishop,[30] in the same way as baptism, considered as reception into the Church. In De pud. the role of the bishop is clear: he is the one who, through his *potestas,* makes church fellowship possible again for the sinner and who 'remits' sins.[31]

But, given this role of the bishop, what is the meaning of the co-operation of the whole community, as this is attested not only in De paen. but also in De pud.? Naturally the whole community intercedes with God on the sinner's behalf: for the Church *ad remedium conlaboret necesse est* and indeed through its intercession (De paen. 10,5). This act of intercession, which is considered the act of Christ himself, is the work of the Church as such, even if it is expressed in the activity of a particular community and in the prayer of individual Christians. When one considers that in Origen and still in Augustine[32] the Church as a holy community has a genuine part to play in the forgiveness of sins, and this without impugning the bishop's unique authority, even though this is no longer (or not so clearly) expressed 'liturgically', then one might well ask whether this intercessory prayer of the community represents a function of the Church which is even more fundamental than this intercession itself and can still operate even when this prayer is no longer present. It is because the whole Church as such has a significance for the forgiveness of the guilt of the individual sinner that it prays for him. This significance for the sinner's recovery of holiness, therefore, does not reside merely in the fact that the Church prays for him. This significance of the universal Church, representing Christ in the world (*ecclesia vero Christus:* De paen. 10,6) does not necessarily mean that the members of the community share in the sacramental and special power of the bishop (and even less that they have transmitted it to him). Even though he has received it as a special power through the apostolic succession, that is, from Christ through the apostles, he can exercise it nevertheless as a power within the Church, that is, as an authority which is only at all thinkable and meaningful because the holy community of the redeemed exists in Christ. Thus the application of this power involves a participation in that Spirit which is the essential life of the Church and which cannot be received apart from the Church. In this sense it can be said: the Church forgives as a whole. Naturally this is to be understood not in the terms of an active competence which resided initially with the whole Church and was only subsequently transmitted to the bishops by the faithful, but rather as a permanent ability to sanctify. When this is applied to a sinner by a representative of the Church deputed by Christ for this task, then it is communicated to him as the sanctifying reality of the Church. There is an analogy in the Eucharist: only the priest has the power to offer the Eucharist. Nevertheless, he offers it only as the offering of the Church. The community shares in the offering, therefore, and needs to express that it really is a question of its own offering. Similarly, when the bishop forgives in virtue of his unique power the Spirit of the Church is again communicated to the sinner. But in order to express that this Spirit is the Spirit of the Church which from the incarnation onwards and in Christ's crucifixion has bound itself indissolubly with the Church[33] the whole community prays together with the bishop for the forgiveness of sins. The customary form of the sacrament of penance today would correspond to a priest's private mass,[34] that is to say, the co-operation of the whole Church in the celebration of this sacrament is no longer discernible liturgically. But even today, during the mass and on other occasions, the whole Church prays for the forgiveness of its faithful's guilt and thus expresses the fact that all forgiveness is a gift of its own Holy Spirit. This reflection cannot be based on Tertullian's writings. But it does provide a plausible explanation as to why one meets everywhere in these writings the idea that the forgiveness of sins by the bishop and the readmission of a sinner into the Church is connected liturgically with such a prayer by the community. These elements of a reconciliation liturgy are not something which even today's dogmatic theology can treat lightly. The dogmatic theologian ought to be able to see something more beyond the doubtless correct observation that the exclusive power of bishops and priests in the celebration of the sacrament of penance even in the sense in which this sacrament was understood in Tertullian's time was not contested. Without wishing simply to revive the ancient penitential liturgy with its community prayer, he will recognize in this liturgy a reality which still belongs to this sacrament today and which deserves to be brought to the attention of Christians: that he finds reconciliation with God only because he receives in and from the Church that Spirit which lives there in all its holy members.

There is no basis in Tertullian for the idea that a sacramental absolution from sins was granted either before reconciliation with the Church or apart from it. To hold this would be a purely gratuitous assumption. It is with one and the same act that the bishop, at the conclusion of the performance of penance, lifts both the excommunication and the sins. This excommunication is by no means a mere act of discipline on the part of an external church organization. It is the expression of the relationship which exists between the sinner and the mystical but visible body of Christ (*non posse corpus unius membri vexatione laetum agere;* De paen. 10,5).

III. THE EFFECT OF PAENITENTIA

When Tertullian speaks about the effects of penance he is referring to penance as a whole, that is, comprising all the parts which we have just described. There is no justification, from either the dogmatic or the historical viewpoint, for separating these elements and ascribing the effects of penance to just one of them while considering the others mere conditions or unnecessary elaborations. Certainly in De paen. the penitent's subjective penance is emphasized. The *ianua ignoscentiae* of baptism, that is, of simple ἄφεσις (as one may say with some caution)[35] is closed, and the sinner has, therefore, to expiate his further sins through intensive penance: he must *pro delictis supplicare* (11,2), *mitigare* God (9,2), *reconciliare* (11,3), *aeterna supplicia expungere* by means of his *temporalis afflictio* (9,5). All this must not only take place interiorly, within the individual's conscience. It must also issue in an actual performance of penance (9,1). This penance is essentially church penance. Thus it would be futile and meaningless to wish to do it only privately and without exhomologesis in the Church. According to Tertullian, subjective penance itself only has a meaning as church penance. It is true that the *publicatio sui* is also an external penance, but this in itself does not explain why sins can only be expiated by the performance of church penance. Tertullian does not give any reason for it; he just takes it for granted. It could be that only the effective intercessory prayer of the Church makes personal penance fruitful (10,6); but the mere support of the individual's prayer for forgiveness could hardly explain why penance must always be in the Church. Or perhaps penance is only effective because of the subsequent reconciliation with the Church. Both of these reasons reflect the same idea and are hardly distinguishable in Tertullian's way of looking at penance. In any case, according to him subjective penance is effective only in the Church and only public exhomologesis extinguishes hell (12,1). Thus one can neither separate these two aspects of penance nor play one off against the other.

This observation receives further confirmation from Tertullian's theology of the Church in his Catholic period.[36] The Church is the 'mother' of our life (cf. De orat. 2; Ad mart. 1; De praesr. 42). It is the ark of salvation (De bapt. 6) and its judgement is, therefore, a *summum futuri iudicii praeiudicium* (Apol. 39). What then are the effects of this unrepeatable penance?

1. The Pax with the Church

From the mere fact that excommunication belongs to the performance of penance it can be deduced that the first effect is renewed access to the fellowship of the Church. This is what the penitent prays for at the doors of the Church (De pud. 1,21; 3,5). The performance of penance ends with the *recipere in communicationem* (De pud. 15,5), with the *communicare Ecclesiae* (De pud. 3), *concorporari Ecclesiae* (De pud. 15,6) and is an *in castra Ecclesiae reverti* (De pud. 14), with the consequence that the penitent becomes a Christian again in the fullest sense (De pud. 10). It is a question, therefore, of a restoration of peace with the Church: *pax ab ecclesiis redditur* (De pud. 12,11).

2. Reconciliation with God

The parallel with baptism already implies that penance also means the remission of sins before God. It is, therefore, the second plank of salvation, alongside baptism (De paen. 12,9), the *secunda paenitentia* after the original admission into the Christian community (De paen. 7,10). Already in Tertullian it amounts to a *secunda post naufragium tabula,* as Jerome later will call it (Epist. 130,9). Thus penance effects an *absolvi* before God (De paen. 10,8), a *venia* (De pud. 2; 3; 4; 10; 12) and a *reconciliari* (De paen. 7,14). By his sin the Christian has lost the baptismal grace;[37] by penance he has recovered it. Like the prodigal son he returns naked to his father, but he is welcomed back into grace (De paen. 8,6–8). He is presented with the *vestis prior,* the *indumentum Spiritus Sancti,* the *signaculum lavacri* and the *substantia . . . sacramenti* (De pud. 9,8–11).

From a consideration of the controversy with the Montanists it is obvious that the bone of contention (De pud. 3 and 21) was whether the Church possessed the power to forgive guilt before God. Nevertheless, we should try to understand more clearly how Tertullian connects what we have seen to be the two component elements of the one penance with the reconciliation with God and the forgiveness of guilt before God.

From the subjective viewpoint, the penitent pleads with God with his prayer for forgiveness and makes expiation for his sins by his penitential practices. These include the humiliation which he experiences by making his exhomologesis in the Church. It is by making *satisfactio* (De paen. 7,14; 8,9) that the sinner receives divine forgiveness. Quite apart from the fact that, according to Tertullian, grace did not enter into the possibility to make satisfaction, the relationship between subjective penance and the divine forgiveness is clear and understandable.

But how is the act of forgiveness on the Church's part related with the pardon before God? This question evokes two ideas in Tertullian which, superficially, appear irreconcilable. For, at first sight, they are two different theories on how the efficacy of the Church's acts is related with the remission of guilt before God.

The first idea is based on the infallibly efficacious prayer of the Church. When the Church and Christ himself in the Church pray for the sinner, the prayer is sure to be heard (De paen. 10,6 f.). This idea is also found still in De pud. (5; 13; 18,13).[38] This prayer (*facile impetratur semper, quod filius postulat*) is, therefore, not merely an additional support of the sinner's personal prayer which, even with this support, is still not assured of success. Rather, it is connected essentially with the forgiveness of sins, so that this *ad remedium conlaborare* (De paen. 10,5) on the Church's part is necessary. For this reason it should not occur in those cases where the Church knows for certain that God will not forgive (De pud. 19,28). Granted that the necessary conditions on the penitent's part are fulfilled, therefore, this intercessory prayer works automatically, that is, in virtue of its value as the prayer of Christ active in the Church. This theory does full justice to the sacramental aspect of penance; εὐχή, like that of the anointing of the sick in James 5:15, can constitute the sacrament. This idea is only a reflection of the Church's intercession for sinners, as actually practiced, and in its turn it influenced the liturgy of the Church's forgiveness of sins. But this liturgy must have originated from the same basic ideas and thus shows that the theory is not merely Tertullian's private view, but has clear roots in the faith-consciousness of his day. The 'deprecative' form of absolution must not only still be possible but evokes a state of affairs which theology has a positive duty to elaborate, without, however, obscuring what is expressed by the indicative form of absolution. The full Latin liturgy of absolution which even today still combines both formulas is worth maintaining.

But there is in Tertullian yet another idea about the effectiveness of the Church's act for the remission of guilt before God. This is the theory of absolution. Nevertheless, it is only in De pud. that it is discernible as a Catholic teaching. Since, however, Tertullian is not contesting an innovation but attempting to justify his own standpoint, this theory was possibly indeed elaborated in the polemic against the Montanists, but it was already traditional in its essence.[39] It may even have been the more strongly accentuated by Tertullian himself in order to facilitate his polemic, it being easier to attack the emphasized claim to a *potestas*. According to this theory, the Church's act is considered as the forgiveness of sins in the name, and in the place, of God. The Church has a *ius* (21,9), it can *delicta donare* (21), it has a *potestas delicta donandi* (21) and a *delictorum eiusmodi remittendorum potestas* (21). The bishop explains: *ego . . . delicta paenitentia functis dimitto* (1), he has the *potestas solvendi et alligandi* (21) and the *fructus paenitentiae*, the *venia . . . in sua potestate* (3). It is possible that in one or other of the passages mentioned it may only be the right to grant the peace of the Church, the forgiveness of guilt before the Church as such that is intended. But in general it is a question of the forgiveness of guilt before God in the name and in the place of God. This power of binding and loosing is paralleled with the forgiveness of sins, the *solvere alligata retro delicta* which Peter exercised in baptism. The discussion between the Catholics and the Montanists turned around the question as to whether the bishops possess that power which was the original and unique prerogative of the Lord himself and which, according to Tertullian, only the prophets inspired immediately by his Spirit are able to exercise in his name (21). For Tertullian this power belongs so exclusively to God that he puts it on the same level as the ability to perform wonders in God's name (21). It is participation in the *potestas Christi* (22). This view may derive from his polemical stance. Nevertheless, throughout De pud. it is possible to discern a Catholic notion of the forgiveness of sins, according to which the bishop forgives guilt before God by absolution in God's name and as his representative.

It is impossible to distribute these two ideas neatly between Tertullian's two writings. They are not only present in both writings, but they have the same weight in both cases. We can only conclude from this that Tertullian at least did not see a contradiction between the two ideas. We can, however, only surmise how they are inter-related, so long as we confine ourselves to Tertullian's thinking. It is certain that, according to the second view, the Church's declaration, made with authoritative power, refers explicitly immediately to the forgiveness of guilt before God. But this does not necessarily exclude the existence of an intermediary between the act of the Church and the *venia* which, without being explicitly mentioned, binds the two moments together. The second view is correct, especially if there exists between the authoritative act of the Church and the forgiveness of guilt an essential and effective connection which is clear and objective. This connection would be expressed simply by the fact that this act of the Church forgives guilt. On this assumption Tertullian's middle term would be God's 'hearing' of the Church. In so far as, in the final analysis, guilt is forgivable by God alone (only he can restore the lost baptismal grace and definitively re-bestow his purely gratuitous love on man), the act on the Church's part is never something which God needs or which renders his own action supefluous, but is related to God's 'hearing' of the Church's prayer. With regard to man, however, this action of the Church which is heard by God is the word addressed authoritatively to him in God's name.[40] It is this word which achieves forgiveness and gives man assurance of this forgiveness. Thus, in forgiving sins, the Church remains always in dependence upon God and his action. But the merit of the second view is that it does make clear that the Church really can do this in God's name. Both views express the same realities but in different terms. Both views finally make the same point. Thus for Tertullian they must have been connected and complemented each other. Certainly he must have had a more or less clear idea on this subject. In fact as much as, during his Montanist period, he contested the validity of the Church's power and prayer with regard to capital sins, he did not do so earlier, even though the second theory must have been known to him. And even as a Montanist he clearly allowed this power to the bishop in respect of the *leviora delicta* (De pud. 18,18). This would be illogical for a Montanist as such, since according to the fundamental conviction of this movement it is only individual, inspired prophets who are able to forgive sins in God's name (De pud. 21). But for Tertullian, who developed even further this fundamental conviction, it shows that the theory of the bishop's power to forgive sins is no novelty, which he would certainly not have invented in this question. Thus he must have had some idea of how this view could be combined with the other theory of the infallibly efficacious prayer of the Church in Christ for the forgiveness of sins by God alone.

3. *The Inter-Relationship between Both Effects of the Church's Act*

With this 'harmonization' of the views on the way in which the act on the Church's part is related with the forgiveness of guilt before God all the relevant questions are still not yet solved. The Church's act of reconciliation achieves both *pax* with the Church and *venia* before God. But how are the *pax cum ecclesia* and the *venia* before God related with each other?

Obviously *pax* is only to be granted when God is ready to pardon. Tertullian bases his argument on this point: because God does not grant *venia*, neither must the Church give *pax* (De pud. 12). Thus the Church's judgement is only a *praeiudicium* of God's definitive judgement (Apol. 39), since the Church's decision can be erroneous.[41] Moreover, we have already noted that the Church's judgement brings about the remission of guilt before God in association with the penitent's penance and is not a mere external act of church discipline which lifts the excommunication.

Nevertheless, it is precisely this 'power', considered as the authority to reconcile with the Church, that is questioned in De pud. For it is precisely in this work, where Tertullian as Montanist still holds out the absolute possibility of a forgiveness before God in the next life for those guilty of capital sins, that he contests the right of the Church to grant the *pax* of the Church and *communicatio* to such a sinner (3). At the same time, the Catholics take it for granted that this *pax* and *communicatio* include the pardon of sins before God, that is the actual fruit of penance, since they consider that penance without this *pax* is futile. According to the notions at that time, therefore, on the one hand, the *pax* cannot be identified simply with the forgiveness of guilt before God. Otherwise, Tertullian would have no cause to reject the granting of the *pax* while holding out the prospect of a *venia* before God, at least in the next life. On the other hand, both are essentially related in such a way that the *pax* ought not to be considered a mere external formality of church law, since then the Catholics would not be able to hold that without *pax* penance has no effect. In so far as the Church's judgement is considered as *praeiudicium* of God's judgement, the *humana pax* (De pud. 3) must, therefore, be the actual effective cause of reconciliation with God. Only as such does it precede this reconciliation as *praeiudicium,* is distinct from it (as the cause is from the effect) but is nevertheless indissolubly connected with it.

The act of reconciliation performed by the bishop brings about the forgiveness of sins by means of the reconciliation of the sinner with the mystical but visible body of Christ.[42] Only in this way is it possible to understand why what seems to pertain to mere 'church law and discipline', that is 'public penance', is presented as being so inextricably linked with the reality of the sacrament.

But there still remains the further question of how the notion of peace with the Church is to be understood more precisely as the middle point between the act of the Church and the forgiveness of guilt before God. Moreover, the view that the content of the Church's act is, first and foremost, the granting of peace with the community of the Church, has to be related with those two notions concerning the forgiveness of guilt by the Church which we have distinguished and attempted to reconcile. The first question could be answered simply by saying that the peace with the Church is a condition that man's subjective penance will be met by God with the forgiveness of guilt. In this case this peace would be in no way causally related with the forgiveness of guilt. It would be merely the external condition for the possible effectiveness of man's subjective penance, as the unique cause on his side, and for the acceptance of the performed *satisfactio* for forgiveness on God's side. This is Poschmann's solution (p. 345). It commends itself by its clarity and does full justice to Tertullian's stress on subjective penance as the cause of the forgiveness of guilt before God. Nevertheless it neglects other aspects of his overall view. In fact, even when it is a question of the effects of baptism (*the* sacrament), he ascribes the same efficacy (at least in part) to man's subjective action, yet without in any way contesting that baptism itself is the real cause. Indeed, one ought to say rather that he has a too 'materialistic' view of the causality of the baptismal rite.[43] But this does not mean that, according to Tertullian, the subjective acts of the person being baptized are merely the external condition for the effectiveness of baptism, simply because even as a ritual baptism possesses a causal efficacy with regard to baptismal grace. Similarly, with regard to penance, it does not follow that the peace with the Church is merely a condition, just because subjective penance affects the forgiveness of guilt.

What is more, Tertullian ascribes to the Church a *potestas donandi delicta,* an idea which would be meaningless if this activity were a mere precondition for the *donare delicta* which would never be performed by the Church. It seems, therefore, that in Tertullian, where it is a question of the *paenitentia secunda,* the same effects are ascribed to both the subjective and the church factors, with a particular stress on the former. The later theory which attempts to justify both factors as the cause of the effectiveness of penance ought also to be a valid and clear interpretation of Tertullian's teaching. In any case the peace with the Church cannot be construed as a mere external and juridical precondition and presupposition for the forgiveness of guilt. Such a view assumes a too external and juridical notion of the church community which obviously conflicts with Tertullian's own vision.[44] Only if the Church is understood as a purely external organization can belonging to it be considered a mere precondition for the possession of the Spirit which removes guilt. Now for Tertullian the Church is more than a mere confessional organization. It is *vera mater viventium* (De anima 43), the *corpus Christi* (De bapt. 6), so that it is there where the Trinity is (De spect. 25; De bapt. 15; Adv. Marc. III 24). Nevertheless, in his Catholic period Tertullian does not place the Church on the same level as the Spirit itself (as he does almost in De pud. 21), but he considers it at the same time as the *ecclesia quam . . . Apostoli struxerant* (De bapt. 11; cf. De virg. vel. 2: the *una ecclesia* is the unity of the Churches *quas et ipsi Apostoli vel apostolici viri condiderunt*). If the Church is thus considered 'as a physical means of grace, like a secondary source of grace',[45] then Tertullian would hardly view belonging to it as a mere external precondition of grace. The fact that the peace with the Church granted by a church official is no guarantee for fellowship with God by grace does not contradict this notion. Such a possibility of a sacrament being valid but fruitless is verifiable in other instances. And this does not prevent Tertullian from having a very realistic view of the effect of baptism.

The second question is rather more difficult to answer. If insertion into the fellowship of the Church, itself being seen as a means of grace, is to some extent a middle member between the Church's act of the reconciliation of a penitent and the forgiveness of sin before God, how does this idea fit into the thought of an act of the Church as the forgiveness of guilt? Tertullian seems to suggest the second idea which we discussed above well before he expressed the idea of the role of an intermediary. But this idea, with its theory of 'absolution', does not exclude an 'intermediary' between the act of the Church and the remission of guilt, that is, God's hearing of the Church's prayer. In discussing the question of the meaning of the whole Church's intercessory prayer, we have already seen that this ought to be viewed as the expression of a profound reality, that is, of the fact that the Spirit which remits sins is the Spirit of this Church and can be received only in it and from it considered as a whole. Granted all these notions, we can bring all the elements of our question together: the bishop's official act receives the sinner back into the organism of grace that is the Church, and in this way the sinner again becomes a member, so that the Church, as the body of Christ, can concern itself about his salvation. Thus the Church both suffers and prays for his salvation. And by suffering with and praying for the sinner in its Spirit the Church is 'heard by God'. It also allows this

Spirit to take possession of this, its member, once more and in this way reconciles him with God. It does not matter whether these images fit together harmoniously, as long as they show how the individual elements affect the whole reality. Each image represents only a part of this total reality and spotlights only one aspect of the whole event. Taken together, they present a more adequate view of the subject, than when, for the sake of greater clarity, attention is centred on one alone. In so far as it is the actual bearer of the Spirit, the Church is the indispensible mediator of grace. Thus reconciliation with God necessarily presupposes a reconciliation of the sinner with the Church, into which he has to be reincorporated. This is penance considered as reconciliation with the Church. Once he is again newly incorporated, the penitent experiences the Spirit in the Church. He benefits from the participation which the Church has had in his condition by its suffering and intercession. The Church gives him its Spirit, which always remains a grace (even with regard to the Church as a whole), even if it is inalienably its Spirit, in so far as the Church lives indissolubly united with Christ. This is church penance considered as the answered prayer of the church community for the sinner. It is through this prayer that he recovers, as his own possession, the Spirit, the *indumentum Spiritus sancti,* the *signaculum lavacri* (De pud. 9,11), and that his guilt is remitted. This is church penance considered as the absolution of guilt by the Church.

In conclusion, it may still be asked how the penitent's subjective penance is related to this whole procedure. Without a doubt, Tertullian considered the penance of personal satisfaction too exclusively as the work of man alone. But how is this subjective penance supported by the Spirit of God, which is the Spirit of the Church? Tertullian seems to have conceived this aspect of penance too much like the Stoics or the Semi-Pelagians as the work of man himself.[46] Nevertheless, in De paen. 10,6 he does state that Christ himself operates also in the repentant sinner and not only in the community, for whose help he is pleading: *non potest corpus de unius membri vexatione laetum agere . . . in uno et altero ecclesia est, ecclesia vero Christus.*[47] Thus both the Church and Christ live already in the penitent and in his penance. If he seeks grace, returns to the Church and asks for its Spirit, then he is already influenced by the Spirit and considered a member of the Church who is asking for unity with the whole body of the Church and healing from his guilt. Tertullian indicates here that even man's subjective penance, which appears to deserve forgiveness so independently, is to be understood as the work of Christ's body, accomplished by the Spirit. All that remains is for the whole of penance to be seen as one event, both personal and ecclesial, as the activity of man and the act of Church. But this enterprise was accomplished—and even then only for a short time—by Thomas Aquinas.[48]

6

THE PENITENTIAL TEACHING OF CYPRIAN OF CARTHAGE[1]

So much has already been written about the penitential teaching of Cyprian of Carthage[2] that there is hardly any hope of saying something new on the subject in this present study. Nevertheless, even today a detailed and comprehensive treatment of this topic need not be entirely superfluous. There is a whole range of disputed points which it can discuss precisely and by showing their relevance. It can highlight certain forgotten themes (e.g. the question of the penitential liturgy), take a fresh look at questions which have been overlooked and attempt to give a bird's-eye view of the whole of Cyprian's penitential teaching. The scope given to the present study means, however, that no consideration will be allotted to the question which has been treated often and in detail, namely, whether in Cyprian's time, and because of his influence, there was a notable relaxation in the Church's penitential discipline. In the present essay the penitential discipline in Cyprian's time in North Africa and Rome is of less concern than is the penitential liturgy and his corresponding theology.

I. THE EXTERNAL FORM: THE PENITENTIAL LITURGY

Cyprian's writings do not present an essentially different picture of the form of penance from that which is already discernible in Tertullian.[3] It is usually possible to distinguish three stages[4] in the penitential process as a whole: the performance of penance (*paenitentiam agere; delicta expiare*), the 'exhomologesis' (*exhomologesim facere; ad exhomologesim venire*), the reconciliation by the imposition of hands on the part of the bishop (and of the clergy).[5] What appears to be most important is that these three stages always occur in this order.

1. The Performance of Penance

It is easy to understand what is meant by *paenitentiam agere*. It is a matter of works of penance by which the sinner, on his part, attempts to reconcile himself with God. It is like *satisfacere* and *satisfactio,* which consists in prayer, fasting, wearing penitential garb, abstaining from baths, renouncing pleasures, carrying out vigils, sleeping on a hard bed, almsgiving, etc.[6] In so far as this penance is performed at the Church's instigation (cf. De lapsis 32), and to the extent that, of its very nature, it is observable publicly in the life of the Church and is accompanied and supported by the prayer of the Church, this penance is not only a purely subjective, 'private' penance of the sinner, but also a public act of the Church, even if it is considered as the activity of the sinner himself.[7] This also follows from the fact that, with regard both to its necessary duration and its sufficient intensity, this penance is subject to the Church's judgement. During the time of his penance the penitent is naturally excluded from the Eucharist. According to Cyprian this is obviously a direct effect of sin itself and does not require a specific act on the Church's part. In his view those sinners who have not been the subject of a specific act on the Church's part (cf. De lapsis 25 f.) receive the Eucharist unworthily.

2. The Exhomologesis

Cyprian always introduces exhomologesis as the second stage of the whole penitential process. He does indeed recognize a wider meaning of the word which, according to its etymology, signifies simply 'confession' in the widest sense (De test. III 114; De lapsis

31.28). But the usage of the word in these passages makes it clear that it is not a question of the specific, technical sense of the term (*exhomologesis conscientiae; exhomologesim Deo facere*).[8] In its technical sense the word always signifies the second stage of the penitential process, and when he uses it Cyprian means neither the whole process nor an introductory confession in view of penance before the bishop.[9] When, in danger of death, the first stage, that is, the sinner's performance of penance, has perforce to be omitted, either totally or partially, the exhomologesis is obviously the first stage to occur. But this does not change its nature. Consequently, even in this context (Epist. 18,1; 19,2) the word cannot assume another meaning. It is easy to understand from Tertullian what exhomologesis is. According to him exhomologesis means the sinner's performance of penance, in so far as it is carried out publicly in the Church, that is, the 'liturgical' acts. This is because a 'confession' that one had sinned is necessarily connected with these 'liturgical' acts, even if the sins in question are not individually and explicitly made known to the community. Cyprian emphasizes the 'liturgical' character of exhomologesis more than does Tertullian. For him, therefore, exhomologesis is that part of the penitential process which takes place before the community. In every case it occurs immediately before the reconciliation by means of the imposition of hands. A clear idea of this can be gathered from Tertullian: the sinner prays for reconciliation on bended knee before the bishop, the clergy and the community. It is not clear, however, whether this happened frequently during the time of penance or whether it is just a matter of the unrepeatable beginning of the whole rite of reconciliation. The above-mentioned passages (cf. also Epist. 4,4) all give the impression that the exhomologesis occurs immediately before the reconciliation. Also, in the reconciliation of the sick, where the exhomologesis certainly occurs only once (Epist. 18,1; 19,2; 20,3), it is presented in exactly the same way as for the usual performance of penance in the Church. One must assume, therefore, that in fact it took place only at the end of the time of penance or that—to put it more precisely and cautiously—liturgical works of penance and blessings of the penitent during the time of penance were not called exhomologesis. It is possible to prove the existence of such acts before the actual exhomologesis from Tertullian's writings. Even in Cyprian's time they must have existed, at least in so far as the penitent had his special place *in vestibulo ecclesiae,* and thus, because of his place, his dress and his non-participation in the Eucharist during the celebration of the liturgy was known as a penitent.[10]

If, therefore, the exhomologesis in Cyprian does not mean the confession before the bishop, there can still be no doubt (as even Koch[11] admits) that a confession of the sinner before the bishop precedes the introduction to the official performance of penance. In Epist. 55,29 there is a distinction made between *confessio* and exhomologesis. Unless this is a mere tautology, then the *confessio* must be understood as distinct from the exhomologesis, that is, as referring to that confession which is made before the bishop at the introduction of penance. In De lapsis 28 there is explicit mention of an *apud sacerdotes Dei dolenter et simpliciter confiteri.* Even if it is not sure here whether in fact an actual church penance ensued, other cases where there was such a penance must have involved a previous confession. This is evident from the fact that penance had to be done for secret sins[12] and that the *examinare causas singulorum* (Epist. 55,6) and the establishment of the *iustum tempus* for penance (Epist. 17,2; 64,1) was not possible without a confession of the precise guilt.

Of its very nature, therefore, the penitential process had to begin with an actual *confessio* before the bishop. In the case of a sin which was already known, this *confessio* may have been quite informal. But it is no way proven that the exhomologesis before the reconciliation included a detailed confession of guilt, even when this guilt was not publicly known. Nevertheless, at the time of reconciliation the people had to express its opinion and give its agreement (Epist. 64,1), and thus the duration of penance and the completed performance of penance was publicly established at the exhomologesis: *exhomologesis fit inspecta vita eius, qui agit paenitentiam* (Epist. 17,2). It is difficult to see precisely how the fulfilment of the conditions for reconciliation was established at the exhomologesis, whether on the basis of the penitent's own testimony or through the testimonies of others. The procedure may be imagined along the lines of the examinations before baptism, when the catechumen and witnesses are questioned by the bishop and his clergy about the life of the candidate during the time of preparation for baptism.[13]

3. Reconciliation by the Imposition of Hands

The third stage is the reconciliation through the imposition of hands[14] by the bishop. Cyprian is the West's first witness to the fact that this reconciliation, the meaning and effect of which will be discussed later, occurs through an *imposition of hands*. The same rite occurs earlier in Origen (In Levit. hom. 2,4),[15] and the Didascalia Apostolorum (II 18,7; 41,2; 43,1) already in the first half of the third century recognizes such an imposition of hands as self-evident in Syria. Thus it could not have originated in Africa but is considerably older than Cyprian, even if 1 Timothy 5:22 is left out of consideration as a reasonable witness for it.[16] According to Cyprian the bishop and the clergy impose hands.[17] This counts as an imposition of hands *in paenitentiam* (Epist. 15,1, etc.). In the East this is accompanied by an anointing of the sinner.[18] But Cyprian shows no evidence of this for the West and it must have been totally missing there. Also at the time of Cyprian the imposition of hands was naturally accompanied by a prayer, as Tertullian already mentions—although not in close connection with the concluding rite of reconciliation. This prayer is the intercession of the Church for the forgiveness of guilt and for the re-bestowal of the Holy Spirit which was lost through sin and which remits the guilt by its return. The last point becomes still more clear in Cyprian. In the Didascalia Apostolorum (II 41) there is also evidence for the intercession of the whole community on the occasion of the imposition of hands.

A) THE ORIGIN OF THE RITE

What is the origin of the imposition of hands as a rite of reconciliation? This is a relevant question, regardless of whether this gesture was used already in the beginning (1 Tim. 5:22) or only later in reconciliation. It is a question which can be subdivided into two further questions, although historically they may coincide with each other. In the first place, is the imposition of hands intended as Confirmation? And then it should be asked: if it is not to be understood as an actual Confirmation, then what meaning does it have? It could at least be modelled on the administration of Confirmation, or it must have an entirely different origin. The usual imposition of hands in penance (that is, where it is not a matter of the reconciliation of heretics) is generally considered an independent rite which is comprehensible in itself without further explanation. All that is normally asked is whether the imposition of hands in the reconciliation of heretics is identical with the usual reconciliation or with Confirmation. Moreover, the question is posed in this way on the supposition of our modern theological awareness, according to which it is taken for granted that Confirmation cannot be repeated. Thus Confirmation can naturally have no relevance for the (usual) reconciliation of penitents. Apart from this presupposition, however, a simple glance at the rite suggests that the imposition of hands in the reconciliation of heretics cannot be so clearly distinguished from that used in the usual reconciliation of other penitents. At the same time, there exist close relationships between this imposition of hands and that used in Confirmation. The problem posed by these relationships is universally recognized. For these reasons, we consider it methodologically correct to pose our first question.

B) THE IMPOSITION OF HANDS AND CONFIRMATION?

This is the answer to this question:[19] At the time of Cyprian the imposition of hands in penance is not simply the imposition of hands used in Confirmation. These rites are to be distinguished clearly from each other. As proof of this assertion it should be observed first of all that the institution of penance existed long before the middle of the third century, without this reconciliation with the Church as a community of grace being in any way considered the repetition of a sacramental act of Christian initiation. Quite on the contrary, it needs to be underlined that in the early Church baptism and Confirmation are so tightly bound together[20] in the one rite of initiation that it is very difficult to distinguish within this rite two distinct sacraments. In this regard, it can be said that in Paul's baptismal theology (as distinct from that of the Acts of the Apostles),[21] which was stronger in the East than in the West, 'baptism' has the comprehensive meaning of the one Christian initiation which includes together both baptism and the bestowal of the Spirit associated with Confirmation in the modern senses. Now one of the basic principles of the theology of penance, as this is evinced already in Hermas and Tertullian, is that 'baptism', that is, precisely the whole rite of Christian initiation is unrepeatable and once-and-for-all. A later *metanoia* is, therefore, something quite different. Already, for this reason, it is quite unlikely that the conclusion of the Church's penitential process should be conceived as the actual repetition of a part of Christian initiation. Although the second *metanoia* does indeed restore the (partial) loss of the effects of Christian initiation, this penance is, nevertheless, only a substitute for, and an addition to, baptism as a whole. It is, therefore, not a repetition of a part of Christian initiation and was in this sense conceived as a 'second' baptism by Hermas, Tertullian and the Didascalia Apostolorum.

Furthermore, in the very place where, apart from in Cyprian, the imposition of hands is clearly mentioned, namely, in the Didascalia Apostolorum,[22] this penitential rite is indubitably distinguished from Confirmation. Although in this passage Confirmation still appears to be administered by means of a simple imposition of hands without an anointing (II 32,3),[23] the author places the imposition of hands of penance in parallel not with the imposition of hands after baptism[24] but with baptism itself (II 41): *quemadmodum igitur gentilem baptizas ac postea recipis, ita et huic* (the penitent) *manum impones, omnibus pro eo precantibus, ac deinde eum introduces et participem facies ecclesiae, et erit ei in loco baptismi impositio manus; namque aut per impositionem manus aut per baptismum accipiunt participationem Spiritus Sancti.* The bestowal of the Spirit as the effect of both rites (baptism and the penitential imposition of hands) is the same. It is indeed self-evident, then as today, that the forgiveness of sins is achieved through the communication of the Holy Spirit. But what is striking is that *baptism* and the penitential imposition of hands are compared with each other. Certainly it could be said that 'baptism' is a comprehensive notion which also includes the imposition of hands of Confirmation. But if the Didascalia Apostolorum really intended to draw attention to the identity of the imposition of hands of Confirmation with that of reconciliation, then it would surely have underlined the imposition of hands in baptism, just as in II 32,3, for example, it distinguishes baptism from the *impositio manus episcoporum* in the same initiation rite. Indeed, such a stress is all the more to be expected, in that the imposition of hands of confirmation in the Didascalia Apostolorum is not the only imposition of hands by the bishop in the whole initiation rite (there is already an imposition of hands at the anointing before baptism, III 12). If, therefore, one is looking for a close parallel to the penitential imposition of hands in the baptismal rite, it would not be completely impossible to consider the imposition of hands before baptism just as well as the imposition of hands of Confirmation. In fine, therefore, according to the Didascalia Apostolorum, the penitential imposition of hands is a rite which, as a bestowal of the Spirit, takes the place of the whole of baptism and is not the repetition of a particular part of the initiation rite.

Cyprian's own position on this point is somewhat more difficult to ascertain, because he appears to consider the reconciliation of heretics parallel with, indeed a repetition of, the imposition of hands at Confirmation. What needs to be demonstrated first of all, therefore, is that, in his view, the reconciliation of heretics, at least in the practice which he represents, is identical with the usual penitential reconciliation through the imposition of hands. Such a conclusion would still be very important in itself, even if, thereby, our actual problem were not yet solved. The penitential imposition of hands is always administered to reconcile a sinner with the Church, to *admitti ad Ecclesiam* (Epist. 4,4; cf. 16,2), even in cases where there is no question of sins against faith, as, for example, in the case of sins against purity. From the whole theology of the relationship between membership of the Church and the possession of the Spirit, as this is developed by Cyprian in the controversy over the baptism of heretics it is abundantly obvious that, in his view, even in the case of these sins such an imposition of hands signifies the re-bestowal of the Holy Spirit.[25] Tertullian had also already proposed this as an effect of the *paenitentia secunda,* and the Didascalia Apostolorum mentions it explicitly with regard to the imposition of hands for sinners of every category. If, therefore, Cyprian, along with his contemporaries,[26] explains the imposition of hands at the reconciliation of heretics as a re-bestowal of church fellowship and a bestowal of the Spirit, then this, on its own, is neither completely surprising nor a proof that any other imposition of hands is involved than that of the usual penitential reconciliation.

The imposition of hands alone which Pope Stephen I wishes to be applied at every reconciliation of heretics must be done *in paenitentiam.*[27] This pope's denial of a (new) baptism of heretics is based on the fact that the mere imposition of hands in such cases is an ancient *consuetudo* (Epist. 74,1; cf. De rebaptismate 1.6), and this fact is not disputed by his adversaries (Epist. 71,2.3; 73,13.23; 74,2; 75,6; Sent. episc. 30.64.77). Even Cyprian dates his own contrary practice in Africa only from the time of Agrippina (Epist. 71,4; 73,3). This suggests that even in Africa the imposition of hands, which Cyprian himself used for the reconciliation of heretics baptized in the Catholic Church, must have been the rite of reconciliation of all heretics at the beginning of the third century. Pope Stephen's appeal to traditional procedure shows, however, that the principle was not determined by theological considerations but by ancient practice.

c) THE IMPOSITION OF HANDS AND THE RECONCILIATION OF HERETICS

What, therefore, is the origin of this practice, if it is not based on radical theological considerations? The first point which must be made is that certainly those heretics who were baptized in the Catholic Church (and these were obviously the original cases) were reconciled through the imposition of hands. The ancient teaching concerning the unrepeatable character of baptism (as it is found already in Hermas) did not allow any other practice, in the form of a full or partial repetition of the rite of initiation, in their regard. This practice was then maintained and applied, without considerable theological reflection, where it was a question of the reconciliation (readmission and bestowal of the Spirit) of those new heretics who were baptized outside the Church. That is Cyprian's own explanation of this practice in Epist. 71,2, and we have no reason to doubt his word. In reality, therefore, every reconciliation of a heretic must originally, and even for Stephen, have been understood as a normal penitential reconciliation.[28] Thus Stephen's description of it as being performed *in paenitentiam* is, without a doubt, the most exact notion possible. This is confirmed by Cyprian's own description of the imposition of hands for heretics and apostates who were originally Catholics as *in paenitentiam* (Epist. 71,2; Sent. episc. 8; Epist. 15,1; 18,1; 19,2). Since Cyprian recognizes the notion,[29] at least for these sinners, his own terminology evidences both the original conception and Stephen's practice as a penitential imposition of hands. If, however, the reconciliation were originally intended as a new imposition of hands of Confirmation, then this must apply to every case of the penitential imposition of hands. But this is completely out of the question, both because of the awareness of the unity of baptism-Confirmation, on the one hand, and of the unrepeatable character of baptism, on the other. Such a theory has also to reckon with certain serious difficulties. It would render incomprehensible the fact that in the ancient tradition (Hermas-Tertullian-Cyprian) a more considerable role is given to the performance of subjective penance in the remission of sins committed after baptism than in baptism itself with regard to previous faults. This is because in the reconciliation of penance only an essential part of initiation *in remissionem peccatorum* was repeated.

What is more, there can be no doubt that, as far as Stephen I is concerned, the imposition of hands for heretics meant the usual penitential reconciliation. If indeed this were thought of as a renewal of Confirmation,[30] then obviously its characteristics and effect could be described only in terms of the latter, and this only in so far as Confirmation is considered distinct from baptism. Now the principal characteristic and the specific effect of the imposition of hands in penance is in general the *pax cum ecclesia,* the *communicatio.* But it can hardly be maintained that this is also the characteristic hallmark of the imposition of hands in Confirmation, as distinct from baptism in water.

After all this, it still remains to be shown that even in Cyprian no decisive arguments are to be found for the assumption that the meaning of the ancient and traditional imposition of hands in penance is a renewal of Confirmation.

Against the conclusion which we have just reached it might be objected that Cyprian supposes that Stephen, in imposing hands upon heretics, intends to confirm them. There can be no doubt that Cyprian does have this impression. Indeed he expounds Stephen's view (Epist. 73,6) accordingly, as if the imposition of hands offered by him to the heretics were a *manum imponi ut spiritum sanctum consequatur et signetur,*[31] while he himself is of the opinion that, in the reception of heretics, either both, that is, the *baptizari in remissam peccatorum* and the *consequi Spiritum Sanctum* through the imposition of hands should be given or neither.[32] In other words, if he says that the imposition of hands *ad accipiendum Spiritum Sanctum* is insufficient and the baptism must be administered as well (but not instead of the imposition of hands), it is clear that this observation implies the supposition mentioned above (Epist. 72,1). Otherwise, the prescription that *sacramentum utrumque* should be administered to the heretics would be superfluous (Epist. 73,21; Sent. episc. 5; cf. also 16). It also has to be admitted that even the rather clumsy defender of Stephen's position in De rebaptismate (cf., for example, 10.12) considers the imposition of hands for heretics as Confirmation.

But is this interpretation of Stephen's view on the part of his adversaries and indeed his unskillful theological friend the correct one? In other words, did he himself see clearly and consciously in this imposition of hands for heretics that previously valid ritual which belongs to Christian initiation? This question cannot be simplified by the suggestion that Stephen has in mind only the Novatians who had not administered Confirmation in their initiation ceremony. If this were the case, then Confirmation could be prescribed for these heretics with impunity and without the suggestion that a Confirmation actually administered by heretics was invalid (as d'Alès holds).[33] Without any doubt Stephen has in mind heretics in general, and all his adversaries presuppose that these possess an initiation which includes an imposition of hands. Nevertheless, the interpretation of Stephen's view on the part of his adversaries need not be exact in every respect. What is certainly correct is that Stephen presupposes that when the heretic comes to the Church he does not possess the Holy Spirit. It is for this reason that he receives the imposition of hands. Everything else is mere interpretation. As such it may perhaps even be relevant and not contradicted by Stephen himself. But it appears rather as a conclusion from his position than as a presentation of this view itself. Basically, this position consists in maintaining the traditional practice. But this practice does not indicate an imposition of hands in the sense of a new Confirmation. Thus it is really indifferent how Stephen himself would have interpreted this practice, had he been pressed to give a precise theological interpretation of it.

Obviously it is not only as a conclusion from Stephen's practice (cf., for example, Sent. episc. 5; Epist. 69,11; 70,3; 72,1) but also precisely as his own explicit teaching (Epist. 69,10; 74,5; 75,8) that Cyprian propounds that heretics do not possess the Holy Spirit and that they receive it only through the Catholic imposition of hands. This is tantamount to saying that, at least as far as the end-product is concerned, the heretics' imposition of hands is ineffective. Cyprian would not have received this view ready-made from out of the blue, and he is, therefore, undoubtedly correct when he constantly presupposes that the reconciling imposition of hands is, in Stephen's view, a rite *ad accipiendum Spiritum* (Epist. 69,11; 72,1; 73,6; 74.5). But is it thereby proven that Stephen considers the reconciliation of heretics and penitents as an imposition of hands of Confirmation which is either valid for the first time or repeated? This teaching could be just as much the simple expression of Stephen's practice as the mere description of it. Stephen imposes hands on the heretic as on every other sinner because he does not in fact possess the Spirit as a result of his sins and, therefore, must receive it.[34] According to the theology of that time every serious sin entails man's loss of both the *substantia baptismi* and the Holy Spirit. It is understandable, therefore, that the imposition of hands which concludes the sin-remitting penance should be described as *ad accipiendum Spiritum Sanctum*. This designation is justified without any thought of Confirmation and without any clear previous reflection as to how this Spirit-bestowing imposition of hands administered to penitents and heretics is related with that other imposition of hands belonging to baptism. *In paenitentiam* and *ad accipiendum Spiritum Sanctum* are expressions which can indicate the same imposition of hands without thereby referring to Confirmation. Stephen certainly sees in the imposition of hands for penitents and heretics a communication of the Spirit. Nevertheless, Cyprian's interpretation of this view with reference to Confirmation says nothing as to whether Stephen would have agreed with this interpretation or whether he would have proposed another elaborated and clear idea of the communication of the Spirit through the imposition of hands for penitents which would have clearly distinguished it from that of Confirmation.

The critical point of our problem is reached, however, only when, according to the explicit statements of Cyprian and Firmilian, the baptism by heretics is not only held by Stephen to be valid, legitimate, that is, in the modern sense (as already recognized by Augustine), *validum*, but also when he ascribes to it an effect which—to use our terminology—is tantamount to the 'fruitfulness' of baptism. According to the account of his adversaries, baptism by the heretics in Stephen's opinion effects: *gratia Christi, gratia baptismi regeneratio* (*caelestis*) *secundae nativitatis, remissa* (*remissio*) *peccatorum*, an *innovari et sanctificari* (Epist. 73,4.16.17.18.20; 74,5.6.7; 75,8.9.12.14.16.17.18.22.23.25). This account cannot be simply false, since the view which it relates is even expressed—if only briefly—where Stephen is quoted verbatim (Epist. 75,18: *gratia Christi*). On the one hand, therefore, Stephen (contrary to Augustine) acknowledges in the baptism by heretics the production of grace, even if this is not also the possession of the Spirit.[35] On the other hand, he denies to the initiation by heretics the possibility of bestowing the Holy Spirit in such a way that, as it were, it accompanies the heretics when they approach the Catholic Church, since it is only there that it is first bestowed. This position of Stephen may strike us as being somewhat strange, indeed completely illogical. This is certainly how it appears to his adversaries, since their arguments concentrate on the observation that the principle by which he ascribes the production of grace to baptism by heretics ought also to be applied to their imposition of hands. Their contention is that these effects which he ascribes to baptism by heretics are only conceivable if heretics who are about to be baptized or already baptized also receive the Holy Spirit. But this considerable logical difficulty in Stephen's view is not a sufficient reason to dispute it as a fact. In the light of the theology of that time, this view is not as inconceivable as it may appear at first sight, and this on two scores. Firstly, Tertullian (De bapt. 6–8) already conceived the effect of baptism and distinguished it from the effect of the post-baptismal imposition of hands in such a way that it was only the imposition of hands that bestowed the Holy Spirit. Baptism itself, however, has other effects which are all resumed in the *remissio peccatorum* considered as the mere preparation of man for the possession of the Spirit.[36] Stephen was able to follow this line, by ascribing even to the baptism by heretics the effects of baptism understood in this very restricted sense, while denying them the possession of the Spirit and, therefore, the efficacy of their post-baptismal imposition of hands. Moreover, Tertullian already teased out the question of the effectiveness of the baptism of a person who is unrepentant. He tried to answer this question by supposing that the actual administration was effective, but that the effect was immediately lost again (De paen. 6). If Stephen had thought of this case in a similar way he could hold that the baptism by heretics with the imposition of hands was a means of grace, while still allowing the heretics to come to the Church so that they could there receive the Spirit anew by the imposition of hands. If it was not only the interpretation of his adversaries but the actual opinion of Stephen himself that the heretics' imposition of hands was absolutely ineffective in the communication of the Spirit, then the first explanation of his position has the better chance of corresponding to his true opinion. The latter, however, was certainly not very consciously elaborated. In our present context, all that need be said is that Stephen holds the heretics' imposition of hands, as opposed to their baptism, as so absolutely ineffective, that in fact he considers it to be invalid.[37] Thus the following interpretation of his teaching at least becomes probable for his adversaries and for the author of De rebaptismate: the imposition of hands with which, according to Stephen, heretics are received is the imposition of hands of Confirmation. In other words, if one considers an earlier imposition of hands ineffective and invalid, then one is compelled to think that the imposition of hands which is presently being administered is specifically identical with that of the heretics, the validity and effectiveness of which is being contested. Otherwise the imposition of hands of Confirmation would remain denied even to reconciled heretics.

It also has to be admitted that in Stephen's private theology there are very considerable obscurities and even no less important contradictions, of which his opponents take full advantage in their theological arguments. Nevertheless, the content of this theology did not enter into his actual decision on the question which we are discussing. But this does not mean that the considerations of his opponents were always correct, since they were hardly able to make the distinction between a valid and a fruitful administration of the sacraments. As far as Stephen is concerned this fact shows only more clearly that this theological position cannot have been at the origin of the practice which he is defending, but is rather an unfortunate theory invented subsequently to justify an already existing practice. Indeed had it evolved from this theory it would not have succeeded, since without the pre-existing practice it would have been shown to be logically impracticable. This is clear in Cyprian and Firmilian. In other words, by logic alone it would be obvious that one cannot recognize that heretics have the one rite of initiation which is actually effective, while at the same time withholding the same recognition for the other rite of initiation. However, the practice could not have emanated from such a consideration, and heretics would even have had to be received without imposition of hands if this were in fact considered Confirmation. This last observation obliges us not to explain the practice in the same way that Stephen tried to do. Thus, despite the obscure theory of Cyprian's contemporaries, we maintain our own interpretation: the imposition of hands for heretics is the general imposition of hands for penitents. This was used first in the case of apostates who were baptized as Catholics and then, without much theological reflection, was extended to the reconciliation of those who had become Christians outside the Church.

The Church maintained this practice universally and without its being questioned. Thus the consequences which ensued for the validity of the sacraments administered by heretics are legitimate and correct, even though both the first attempt at a theological justification of this practice and its implications were problematical. This penitential imposition of hands is a 'substitute' for baptism, that is, for Christian initiation as a whole, in so far as it restores the original effects of this initiation. Thus it can be described without hesitation as *ad accipiendum Spiritum Sanctum* and is in no way the repetition of just the last part of Christian initiation, that is, Confirmation. Originally, this initiation was practically always considered 'baptism' as a whole, and this was clearly unrepeatable.

It is, however, possible to discern in the middle of the third century the bases of a theological development which will bring about an association between Confirmation and the imposition of hands for heretics. The effects of these will become significant only later. They are of no concern for our present purpose.

Although these inquiries into the theological obscurities of the early Church may appear to be entirely negative, one positive result which they produce needs to be stressed. The fact that at this time the penitential liturgy had developed to such an extent that there was a danger of going beyond the evident ritual parallel and identifying it with a part of the sacramental rite of initiation shows that there must have been a strong awareness of the sacramental character of penance. If the theology at that time considered baptism as a whole to be a sacrament, then this must also have applied to penance and its imposition of hands.[38]

D) THE MEANING OF THE IMPOSITION OF HANDS

We must now turn to the second question mentioned above. If the imposition of hands used at the reconciliation of heretics and penitents is not identifiable with a (first or repeated) rite belonging to Christian initiation, what meaning does it have and why precisely is it used in reconciliation? The first point which must be made in answer to this question is that reconciliation concerns the restoration of those lost interior gifts of grace which the Christian originally received in baptism (considered as a whole). This restoration is fittingly expressed through the imposition of hands, since this gesture always expresses the communication of that which the person imposing the hands possesses, and because the first bestowal of these gifts was symbolized in this way. Now there were several different kinds of imposition of hands. Is, therefore, the imposition of hands in penance to be understood as a parallel to (but not as a repetition of) the imposition of hands in Confirmation, because it bestows the Spirit, or is it to be construed as one (or as the last) imposition of hands of those blessings of penitents which without any doubt at a later date often occurred during the time of penance?

In the latter case it would appear to be very similar to those impositions of hands of exorcism which already in Cyprian's day were applied to catechumens. The first hypothesis seems the more likely. Already in the Didascalia Apostolorum the imposition of hands of reconciliation is presented as a gesture signifying a communication of the Spirit, and thus it is seen in parallel to the bestowal of the Spirit at Confirmation. Even if Cyprian's erroneous interpretation of Stephen's view is rejected, namely, that the latter understands the imposition of hands for heretics simply as Confirmation, this interpretation is hardly conceivable if the imposition of hands in penance were not understood as being similar to Confirmation, that is, as a rite *ad accipiendum Spiritum Sanctum.* Later in the West and even more so in the East there was a strong tendency towards the identification of the imposition of hands for heretics, and partially even that of penitents, with Confirmation. After the Schism this identification became actual and clear for the Greek Church. This development is all the more easily comprehensible if, from the beginning, there was an affinity between both rites, that is, if already originally the imposition of hands of penance was modelled on that of Confirmation.

Nevertheless the second hypothesis mentioned above is not entirely unlikely. At least it must have had some influence on the elaboration of the imposition of hands of penance. The exercises undertaken during the time of penance (fasts, prostrations, exhortations) also show many similarities with elements of the catechumenate. Thus it is not unlikely that a considerable amount of this particular time of preparation served as a model for the organization of the time of penance. At the beginning of the third century, at least in the church order of Hippolytus (Dix, pp. 30–2) frequent impositions of hands used as exorcism for catechumens are already an established part of the catechumenate. In Cyprian such an exorcism is found at least immediately before baptism (Sent. episc. 1.8.37) and similar impositions of hands seem to be attested by him elsewhere (Ad Demetr. 15; Tertullian, Apol. 23). Later in Africa sinners were frequently blessed during the time of penance by impositions of hands (Augustine, Sermo 232,8).[39] Such blessings must be understood as parallel to the repeated impositions of hands during the catechumenate, as indeed Augustine mentions.[40] Thus it is not completely unlikely that the imposition of hands at penance, as we find it in Cyprian and his contemporaries as the conclusion of the time of penance, is either one or perhaps even the last imposition of hands which was considered analogous to the exorcism of the catechumenate. An observation from the viewpoint of the history of the liturgy is relevant here. It is self-evident for Cyprian that in the imposition of hands at penance, given that the other *acta paenitentia* have been carried out, this can be performed by the presbyter, while the imposition of hands by a deacon counts in a case of necessity (Epist. 18,1). In the more 'normal' imposition of hands by the bishop the clergy also takes part (Epist. 17,2). On the other hand, it appears that at this time, at least in the West, Confirmation was reserved absolutely to the bishop, so that it happened that a person could be baptized and die without Confirmation or a person could be baptized by a presbyter and finally confirmed by a bishop.[41] This striking difference seems to indicate that the imposition of hands at penance was seen rather as an exorcism than as a strict parallel to the imposition of hands of Confirmation, reserved exclusively to the bishop, which concluded initiation. An imposition of hands which, in certain circumstances, could be performed even by a deacon must have been considered at that time to have quite a different character from Confirmation, which was so exclusively reserved to the bishop and which was still administered by him even when a priest performed the baptism. The imposition of hands at penance is described as being performed *in paenitentiam;* whereas the exorcism before baptism is aimed at a 'purification' (cf. Hippolytus, Par; Dix, p. 31) which should give the bishop the assurance that the candidate is now truly 'pure'. Even on this score there is an inner connection between both rites. Augustine explains later that the imposition of hands is repeatable since it is nothing more than a prayer over a man. In this context he must have been thinking of the imposition of hands more as an exorcism applied to catechumens and penitents in the time of penance. Since, however, he could hardly have derived this principle from the once-and-for-all imposition of Confirmation and the definitive reconciliation of penitents (De bapt. III 16,21) he must also have seen the concluding imposition of hands for penitents rather in the same category as the other impositions of hands during the time of penance. In any case the use of the imposition of hands for catechumens and sinners during the time of penance shows that already in Cyprian's day it was not necessary to relate the imposition of hands of penitential reconciliation only to Confirmation, but that this gesture was fairly indeterminate, enjoying fluidity and an applicability beyond the communication of the Spirit in Confirmation and Ordination. Its use for penitents and heretics, therefore, does not have to be seen necessarily in the light of Confirmation, although this is not to deny that already in the third century there exist the foundations of the later development.

As will be made clearer below, already at this time personal-subjective penance is stressed in a way which does not make particularly easy its connection with the Church's objective activity in the reconciliation of man with God. Now would such an insistence on the personal-subjective performance in penance have been at all possible if the reconciling imposition of hands had been seen in a line with the bestowal of the Spirit in Christian initiation? Or is this phenomenon not easier to understand when the imposition of hands of penance is taken rather as one of the many impositions of hands in the sense of exorcisms or blessings as they also occur before baptism and which, despite the importance accorded to them, leave the decisive role to the catechumens' subjective conversion? This also explains more satisfactorily why in the case of a hasty granting of *communicatio* by priests in the absence of their bishop, a practice which Cyprian condemns (Epist. 15,1; 17,2), the imposition of hands was omitted. Since in a case of necessity this imposition of hands can be performed even by a priest and a deacon (Epist. 18,1; 19,2) it is difficult to explain why it was omitted if it was considered to be the specific formal rite of reconciliation.[42] This fact is more easily understood if the imposition of hands stands in the last place, along with the exhomologesis, as one act of penance beside others. Just as the *lapsi* were dispensed from the *agere paenitentiam* by these laxists, so they were dispensed from the exorcism which is the priest's support of the exhomologesis. In other words, they were dispensed from the imposition of hands which is conceived more as a part of the humiliating penance than as the formal act of reconciliation. The latter was seen, therefore, rather in the actual granting of communion, albeit expressed in words, and in the participation in the Eucharist.[43] This itself is supported by the symbol of the imposition of hands as *prius* before the *venire ad communicationem* (Epist. 17,2).

A radical solution to our question has been attempted by contesting its presuppositions, namely, that at that time in the West the imposition of hands was the decisive rite of Confirmation.[44] On the assumption that here at that time the anointing was the actual rite of Confirmation a great deal becomes clear. The two questions with which we began this essay are easily answered. The imposition of hands for heretics and indeed for usual penitents does not move at all in the 'dangerous' proximity to actual Confirmation, and the meaning of the imposition of hands in penance can be sought with impunity in another direction without so much as a glance at Confirmation. Nevertheless, such a solution for Africa of the third century and later is impracticable. At this time the episcopal imposition of hands and it alone is the actual rite of Confirmation, and not the anointing. The attempt of Saint-Palais d'Aussac to demonstrate the opposite thesis cannot be recognized as convincing.[45]

A perfectly clear and unified explanation of the imposition of hands in the reconciliation of penitents and heretics in Cyprian's day on the basis of the available material is not possible today, and it probably did not exist even in the third century. This imposition of hands can indeed be sufficiently distinguished from Confirmation, in so far as it cannot be intended as a repetition of Confirmation. But its positive meaning, that is, whether it was considered either as a gesture for the (re-)bestowal of the Spirit or as prayer in the sense of an exorcism, or whether at that time these two functions were not so clearly distinguished—all this cannot be clarified with certainty. It would appear that such a differentiation was unknown at that time. This observation tends to support the argument for the apostolic origin of the imposition of hands in penance. If it were a later, entirely new liturgical creation, and indeed by reflected, conscious analogy with a certain other imposition of hands, then its meaning would have been known as being precisely different from that of other, similar gestures. If, however, the rite of reconciliation is just as old and original as the other impositions of hands, then it is more easily explained that both for us and for the time which we have been studying there appear analogies with all these other impositions of hands. Thus our final word on this subject should be that the dilemma should not be posed in such a way that this imposition of hands of penance should be definitely, clearly and solely explained by one or other of the similar rites.

II. THE THEOLOGY OF PENANCE

1. The Sins of Daily Life and Their Private Remission

As much as Cyprian values the holiness, splendour and power of the man who, being newly born in baptism, is able to do everything through God's gratuitous and immense grace (Ad Donat. 4 f.14 f.), he still knows that the sanctified Christian continually falls into daily faults: *cotidie deesse non potest quod peccetur in conspectu Dei* (De op. et eleem. 18); *sine aliquo conscientiae vulnere esse non possumus* (ibid., 3). This is because we have to fight with the devil, the flesh and the world (De mort. 4–5).[46] According to Cyprian the 'filth of daily sins' must be continually removed, even though he was reasonably clear that the *sanctificatio et vivificatio* of the baptismal grace (which obviously must be protected) is not lost through such sins (De dom. or. 12). If he states *non deesse sanatis* (through baptism) *quaedam postmodum vulnera* (De op. et eleem. 3), this expresses the idea that even the justified person still sins, just as, by sinning, he does not cease to be a person who is sanctified in baptism. Already here in the struggle against sin in general[47] there is a clear distinction between the post-baptismal remission of sins and the *remissa peccatorum* in baptism. Sins committed before baptism are remitted *Christi sanguine et sanctificatione, semel in baptismo,* whereas sins committed after baptism find forgiveness through *assidua et iugis operatio*[48] of man himself (De op. et eleem. 2), therefore by prayer, fasting, almsgiving, etc. (ibid., 5.18, etc.). The *remissa peccatorum* is granted only once in baptism[49] (De op. et eleem. 2). Any sins committed after baptism must be expiated by the sinner himself, so that the ensuing forgiveness, by reason of the sinner's own *operatio,* is not a *remissa* in Cyprian's sense. He is perfectly consistent in the terminology which he uses to describe this distinction between a purely gratuitous forgiveness of the guilt of sins in baptism and the remission of serious and daily sins committed after baptism.[50] This is already abundantly clear from the way in which the notion of *remissa(-io) peccatorum, remittere* is reserved for baptism.[51] The exceptions to this restricted usage are only apparent.[52] The distinction between the forgiveness of sins in baptism and the remission of sins committed after baptism which Cyprian elaborates especially for serious sins also applies, therefore, to other sins committed after baptism.[53] All of these sins must be remitted through the sinner's own penance, since they are not forgiven simply by grace in view of Christ. This general penitential teaching of Cyprian on the necessary performance of penance by the sinner himself for sins committed after baptism already provides the basis for his idea of the remission of those sins which, as opposed to the sins of every day, entail the loss of the grace of baptism. The general difference between the pardon of sins in and after baptism is not obliterated by the fact that a *satisfactio* through *paenitentia* is necessary to obtain *venia* even for the catechumens (Ad. Demetr. 25). That the difference still maintains here is evident from the expectation of salvation *sub ipso licet exitu, sub ipsa morte* on Cyprian's part. This expectation does not apply to post-baptismal penance even on the death-bed (Epist. 55,23).[54] At the same time, it is not as obvious as Poschmann[55] thinks that the penance prescribed before baptism refers merely to the renunciation of previous sins and to the intention to lead a Christian life, considered as a precondition for baptism. This is not stated explicitly in the text, and it harmonizes neither with the notion of *satisfacere* nor with the theology of Tertullian, whom Cyprian must be considered to follow until the contrary is proven. All that can be said is that here is an obscure point in Cyprian which should not be exploited in favour of unwarranted harmonizations. On the one hand, the pure *remissa* that is baptism does indeed presuppose a real penance which is considered as a satisfaction. On the other hand, after baptism a remission of sins is possible only through penance which, as making satisfaction, expiates sins because there is no longer a simple *remissio*. Thus this notion of the post-baptismal forgiveness of sins acquires a certain semi-pelagian nuance,[56] despite the fact that it is based on scriptural expressions concerning the remission of sins through good works. This impression is not cancelled out by the fact that the forgiveness, despite the *satisfactio,* is seen as a free act (*venia*) of the Lord acting as judge, *qui peccata nostra portavit . . . quem Deus tradidit pro peccatis nostris* (De lapsis 17). The fact that the *satisfactio* is itself the work of divine grace remains totally unexpressed and in the background, which explains why Cyprian is very anxious about the adequacy of this *satisfactio* in individual cases.

2. *The Nature of Serious Sin*

Apart from the everyday faults of those who have been justified, there are also, according to Cyprian, sins which in today's terminology have to be styled 'serious'. Although the terminology in Cyprian is not so elaborate, the fact is clear. Cyprian does not call everyday sins *crimen,* but applies this term (along with others) to 'serious' or 'mortal sins'. Certainly in his terminology even daily sins are *peccata* (De dom. or. 22; Test. III 54) and *delicta* (De op. et eleem. 2). The unusual expression *mortale crimen* is, nevertheless, obviously not yet an actual *terminus technicus* for mortal sins, just as in Cyprian there is still wanting an established special expression for daily sins. The expression *peccata* (*delicta*) *minora* is also used in comparison with the more serious sins of a kind which, as the object of church penance, obviously have considerable gravity (Epist, 16,2; 17,2). At the same time, the image of sin as a 'wound' is used for daily sins (De op. et eleem. 3), as well as for the serious sins which are subject to church penance (Epist. 30,3). The same applies to a purely relative category of expressions such as *graviora peccata* (Epist. 64,5). The notion of *peccatum in Deum* (an inheritance from Tertullian) does not concern the distinction which interests us at present and in itself remains vague, since it is used both for sins committed before baptism (Epist. 64,5) and, in practice, for all the faults which later jeopardize salvation in any way at all.[57] This expression, therefore, does not suppose any real counterpart, although Cyprian can explain on one occasion that even such sins *quae non in Deum committuntur* (Epist. 17,2)[58] have to be submitted to church penance. He does this probably to stress the seriousness of the apostates' sin.

Thus the terminology is very unclear, but in reality the distinction is obviously made by Cyprian. While daily sins do not destroy grace,

Cyprian recognizes alongside these faults on account of which God *offensus sedem, quam inhabitat, derelinquat* (De hab. virg. 2). Sinners are such, *de quorum pectoribus excesserit Spiritus Sanctus* (Epist. 66,2). The *lapsi* are dead (Epist. 15,2; 21,2; 33,1; De lapsis 8), they have lost their wedding-garment, they are naked and mortally wounded (Epist. 30,7; De lapsis 30.55), and they carry their own corpse around with them (De lapsis 30). Also the baptized person loses grace when he does not preserve his innocence (Test. III 26). This certainly means interior grace, since according to Epist. 70,2 the baptized person has *in se gratiam Christi* and according to Epist. 64,3 the baptismal grace is the Holy Spirit. But the sinner loses 'the grace of the life-dispensing bath' (De lapsis 24) and even children who were involved in the fall of their parents lose what they had received immediately after their birth (De lapsis 9). Cyprian's expression *mortale crimen* (De bono pat. 14), therefore, must be understood not only as 'sin which brings about the death of hell' but as 'sin which causes the death of the inner life of grace in the Holy Spirit'. Alongside this consideration of sin from the viewpoint of grace there are found in Cyprian obviously more ancient and already traditional viewpoints, that is, the moral and the eschatological, for determining the nature of sin. It is *offensa . . . indignantis Domini* (De lapsis 16.19), an *abicere legem Dei* (De lapsis 21) by which man exposes himself to the present and future judgement of God and to eternal punishment (De lapsis 7,23–6). From both of the last-mentioned viewpoints sin must almost inevitably appear above all as the object of a judgement. This is important because in his theology of the forgiveness of sins Cyprian pays only scant attention to this interior nature of sin, that is, in so far as it concerns grace. Although he knows well that the reconciled sinner receives back the Holy Spirit (Epist. 57,4),[59] he does not exploit any further the theology of the nature of sin as a loss of grace in relation to the forgiveness of sins in the Church. Rather, he considers sin almost exclusively from the moral and eschatological viewpoints. Through his fault the sinner has become God's enemy and must expect a judgement; accordingly, the remission of sin is more of a reconciliation with God and an assurance that one will be able to withstand the judgement and not incur eternal punishment.[60]

Nevertheless, Cyprian does still consider serious sin from an ecclesial viewpoint. Sin 'separates' man from the fellowship of the

Church, from peace with the Church and from the central mystery of the Christian life, the Eucharist. In the case of apostasy from the faith, which in Cyprian's theology and polemic (because of the circumstances of his day) receives special prominence, these effects are obvious. These sins, however, separate the sinner from the Church not only in so far as they are an explicit denial of faith and of the gospel but also because they entail the loss of baptismal grace. And this is a characteristic of all serious sins. Only on this presupposition is it understandable that even the reconciliation of those guilty of sins of impurity is considered an *accepta communicatione ad ecclesiam admitti* (Epist. 4,4). The same is said of the other *minora delicta/peccata* which are obviously not sins against faith (Epist. 16,2; 17,2).[61] Naturally, although those guilty of such sins, unless through their own unrepetance they have broken off all connection with the Church, still have a relationship with it, that is, they have not simply 'left' the Church (Epist. 57,1.3; 65,5), they are, nevertheless, in a true sense separated from it as a community of grace. In Cyprian there are no precise statements about the exact limits and the actual relationship of a sinner's belonging (at *limen Ecclesiae:* Epist. 57,3; 30,6) and not belonging to the church community. Nevertheless, not belonging to the community should not be understood merely as the consequence of excommunication by the bishop,[62] as it was later expressed at the beginning of the penitential process. According to Cyprian this is evident from the automatic and immediate exclusion from the Eucharist, which follows from even secret sins (De lapsis 15.25 f; Epist. 16,2; cf. also Epist. 75,21).[63] There are no further considerations of the question why according to Cyprian every serious sin entails the loss of grace in some sense. But it is easy to see the reason for this from his theology as a whole. The sinner received the Holy Spirit in baptism. Indeed it is the specific theme of the controversy with the heretics that the baptism which bestows the Spirit is valid. By sinning the Christian has lost this Spirit. Now the Church is the only place where this Spirit can be received, since in baptizing it is the mother of the divine life in the faithful. This too is a fundamental principle in the controversy with the heretics. Thus it is self-evident for Cyprian that an offense against the Spirit of the Church is also directed against the Church itself and that this means a separation both from the Spirit and from the Church. For the same reason reconciliation with the Church and reception of the Spirit belong together (Epist. 57,4). Following the view of Hermas, Callistus and the author of the Didascalia Apostolorum the bishop of Carthage also knows that in the Church there is cockle along with wheat (Epist. 54,3–4; 55,25). It would be presumptuous to wish to distinguish the one from the other neatly at the present time. And the Lord's judgement will concern those *quos in ea (Ecclesia) intus invenerit* (Epist. 55,29). This means, however, that in the Church there are people of different moral standings. But this does not lead Cyprian to overlook the fact that sin does entail a change of relationship between the Church and the baptized. As is clear from the controversy with the heretics, his position forced him to understand the 'cockle' in the Church to be those who belonged to it purely formally. This view was not totally superseded later, even by Augustine.

Now which faults have these moral, theological and ecclesial effects of serious sin? In the first place, at least theoretically, the sins of Paul's catalogues of vices which exclude people from the kingdom of God (Gal. 5:19 ff.; 1 Cor. 6:9) are offences *quae mortem pariant* (Test. III 64 f.; Epist. 59,4). Naturally one cannot expect here a more precise consideration of the basic criterion by which these faults are distinguished from daily sins. Cyprian contents himself with passages from Scripture and common sense, everyday moral judgement. The sins which are included in this group are those which are *in concreto* submitted to church penance. This applies primarily obviously to all sins against faith (apostasy), and indeed even in those cases where Cyprian himself is aware that they must be treated very mildly and leniently.[64] This applies even to cases which have remained secret (De lapsis 25.26.27). But still other sins, such as concubinage and illicit living together by those who are unmarried,[65] impurity (Epist. 55,20), adultery, frequentation of brothels, fraud (Epist. 55,26 f; 59,14 f.) etc. are subject to church penance. In general it seems that *idolatria, adulterium* and *fraus* formed a kind of triad for such sins, while murder is not explicitly mentioned (but cf. De bono pat. 14). Among sins against faith were also counted schism and insubordination to church authority (cf., for example, Epist. 59,14.15; 66,9; 69,6.7, etc.). On the one hand, therefore, serious sin and offence subjected to church penance coincide in theory, but, on the other hand, the circle of offences subjected to church penance is so much restricted in practice that it remains relatively small, and therefore the number of penitents is normally not very great.

3. *The Necessity of Personal and Church Penance for Serious Sins*

Before we consider the meaning and effect of the individual 'parts' of penance in Cyprian's view it is necessary to take a look at the necessity and the unity of the whole penitential process. For both sins against faith and for *minora delicta* the bishop of Carthage prescribes the one penance which we have described above. If, instead of allowing the immediate access of the *lapsi* merely on the basis of the letters of martyrs, he prescribes the *legitima paenitentia,* then he bases this mostly on the need for a long-lasting personal penance for sins in order to move God to forgiveness (De lapsis 17). But even this penance is considered as being imposed by the Church. It is performed by the Church in the exhomologesis, controlled by it, supported by its prayer and sacrifice, and concluded by it in the granting of the *pax.* No other possibility of forgiveness is in any way considered. The struggle against the laxists is at the same time a demand for personally hard penance and an exhortation to submit oneself to the exhomologesis and to receive the *communicatio* from the bishop who alone is authorized to give it. Laxism undermines both of these points in the same way (Epist. 15,1; 16,2). The personal penance which Cyprian stresses so much is never in his view merely an individual, private, interior performance which has nothing to do with the Church. This would still not be the case even if, in his view, the concluding rite were only the solemn elaborate end of a personal penance.[66] It is impossible to say today exactly how the laxists justified their practice. It seems, however, to be derived from the understandable desire to participate again in the Eucharist as a complete Christian, from grounds for pardon which could be made applicable to the *lapsi,* from appeal to the intercession of the martyrs and perhaps also with reference to John 20 (cf. De cath. eccl. un. 4).[67] Indeed, even on the part of the laxists penance is considered an indivisible totality, and therefore both its personal side and its ecclesial side are neglected: *ante actam paenitentiam, ante exomologesim . . . te manum ab episcopo . . . impositam* (Epist. 15,1; 16,2; De lapsis 16). For his own part, in order to justify his requirement Cyprian argues that the person who has sinned 'against God' can receive pardon from God alone and must, therefore, merit it by a long penance (De lapsis 17). For us today this would imply simply that the sinner has to perform 'subjective' penance, whereas for Cyprian it entails the necessity of a penance which itself clearly has an ecclesial aspect. He does not consider further, however, how his argument can justifiably cover this point. For him the ecclesial aspect of guilt was so evident that it obviously had to be considered in the remission of guilt. Although the sinner can separate himself from the Church by his own act alone, the new *pax* is the gift of the Church itself. It can, therefore, be granted only by the episcopal representative of this Church who alone can 'bind and loosen' (Epist. 57,1; 33,1) and who alone is *ad tempus iudex vice Christi* (Epist. 59,5). Since this *pax* is necessary for salvation,[68] penance for a sin which separates a person from the Church can reach its goal only when the penitent receives the peace with the Church from the bishop once more. *Nec ad communicationem venire quis possit, nisi prius illi ab episcopo et clero manus fuerit imposita* (Epist. 17,2).[69] Even in this case the general principle: *habere non potest Deum patrem, qui Ecclesiam non habet matrem* (De cath. eccl. un. 6) is valid, since sin denies that God is father and the Church mother (De lapsis 9). Thus both of these aspects demand the one personal-ecclesial penance, and this necessary penance is personal-ecclesial. Moreover, as a support of this view Cyprian appeals to the *scripturae caelestes* (De lapsis 23), the *Domini ac Dei lex* (De lapsis 15), the *Domini praecepta* (De lapsis 18; Epist. 15,1), the gospel (De lapsis 20; Epist. 16,1), the *evangelii lex* (Epist. 15,1). The ecclesial aspect of this evangelical law is not explained in any detail. Cyprian did not even consider this necessary, since he knew that he had both tradition and private relations (Epist. 16,4) on his side.

4. *The Effect of the Personal Act of Penance*

The sinner must, therefore, do personal penance for the faults which he has committed after baptism. As we have seen, when Cyprian considers the remission of sins he views sin almost exclusively from the moral and eschatological viewpoints. God is *graviter offensus* (De lapsis 16), since sin is essentially *in Deum*. Thus the sinner has deserved *aeterna supplicia* (De lapsis 7; Epist. 30,7). In any case, it is only God who can forgive his sin: *solus Deus misereri potest. Veniam peccatis, quae in ipsum commissa sunt, solus potest ille largiri qui peccata nostra portavit* (De lapsis 17).[70] Now God does not forgive the sins committed after baptism in exactly the same way as he does in baptism itself, *quia semel in baptismo remissa peccatorum datur* (De op. et eleem. 2). The sinner cannot expect and hope to receive the forgiveness of sins through the Church and its representatives in the manner of a simple baptismal *remissa*. This is the meaning of the following: *homo Deo maior non potest esse*[71] *nec remittere aut donare indulgentia sua non potest, quod in Dominum delicto graviore commissum est* (De lapsis 17). Thus what Firmilian writes about the activity of the bishops must also contradict Cyprian's view: *non quasi a nobis remissionem peccatorum (lapsi) consequantur, sed ut per nos ad intelligentiam delictorum suorum convertantur et Domino plenius satisfacere cogantur* (Epist. 75,4).[72] The Church cannot simply forgive (*donare*) sins committed after baptism as it does in baptism.[73] God has to be propitiated. And man has to do this himself by his penance. If this applies already to daily sins, it is even more appropriate for serious ones.

This *assidua et iugis operatio* (De op. et eleem. 2) of *satisfactio*[74] in a *longa et plena paenitentia* (De lapsis 16) means a *Dominum promereri* (Epist. 19,1; 26), a *rogare, deprecari Dominum* (De lapsis 16), a *Deum* (*offensam . . . Domini*) *placare* (De lapsis 16,29,35; Epist. 43,2) and thus a *delicta redimere* (De lapsis 35; Epist. 59,13; cf.De habitu virg. 11). The satisfaction that is penance is, therefore, directed towards God in order to change his attitude and it succeeds in this, as it were, by the payment of sins which are conceived as *debita* (De dom. or. 22). This exoneration of guilt lasts a long time and it can also be presented by the image of a long healing process[75] from wounds (Epist. 30,6; 31,6.7; De lapsis 35). And Cyprian is aware of the contrast between this process and the totally different event which occurs in baptism (cf. Epist. 59,13: *gratia quae de baptismi sanctificatione percipitur—paenitentia per quam culpa curatur*). In some circumstances this exoneration of guilt can be continued in the next life (Epist. 55,20). Cyprian already has a place for this purpose, since even the just still seem to wait for the day of judgement and the arrival of the Kingdom of God in 'paradise', in *refrigerium*.[76] The only exception to this are the martyrs who are immediately crowned, united with God and enter into possession of the *regnum caelorum*. In any case Cyprian considers that the payment of 'guilts' through satisfaction in order to propitiate God will be definitively effective only at the general judgement. After the destruction of this world and this age the people of Christ will stand before its judge (De lapsis 17).

Christ will 'examine' (*recensere*) this people and its enemies and pronounce judgement on everyone according to his deserts (Epist. 58,10). As opposed to the martyr who is crowned immediately after his death, the penitent has to wait *ad sententiam Domini* (Epist. 55,20). Although he certainly can hope for forgiveness, especially since he can at this moment count on the great help of the *martyrum merita et opera iustorum* (De lapsis 17), this assurance does not dispense with the actual and definitive decision. The final decision is made in the next life, considered spatially and, above all, temporally (Epist. 57,1), and everything which happens previously (personal penance and reconciliation with the Church) is, by comparison, only an interim (Epist. 55,29) and 'reserves' the sinner and his salvation always to God.[77] Certainly Cyprian knows that even in this life *satisfactio,* after a certain time determined by human standards, can have blotted out the guilt of sin (cf. Epist. 15,4; 56,1 f.),[78] that the penitent in this life already can be a *curatus* (Epist. 55,19) with a *purgata conscientia* (De lapsis 16), who has the Spirit of the Father (Epist. 57,4). Nevertheless, Cyprian always views the final effect of penance eschatologically.[79] Even in the place where he considers a three-year penance sufficient *ad deprecandam clementiam Domini,* he makes this point quite clear when he says: *puto his indulgentiam Domini non defuturam* (Epist. 56,2). Forgiveness is granted eschatologically as the actual goal of penance.[80] But the penitent can count on receiving it. Cyprian evinces no serious doubt about this future forgiveness, provided that full penance is done. Wherever there is any doubt expressed this concerns not God's readiness to forgive but the fulfilment of the conditions prescribed for it on the sinner's part. The frequent mention of a *potest clementer ignoscere* (*misereri*)[81] highlights precisely the future character[82] of the forgiveness together with the possibility that the conditions on man's side may not be fulfilled, but it in no way suggests that God may not be ready to pardon. The penance which Cyprian prescribes is totally orientated to man's position before God's judgement. In God's verdict it is revealed whether his penance, as well as the intercession of the martyrs and the Church, has been completely successful in absolving the guilt of his sin.

This conception is easily derivable from the actual form of the institution of penance. But it also coincides with the long duration of this penance and, in any case, is one of the fundamental views of the

Patristic age, as the distinction between baptism and penance already shows. It is for this reason that we will consider the dogmatic significance of this conception somewhat more closely in order to pinpoint its deficiencies and its advantages. Two points are particularly worthy of note: the notion of sin and its remission as the incurring of punishment and punitive expiation, respectively, and the opposition between the post-baptismal forgiveness of sins and that of baptism.

As has already been shown, a consideration of sin, its effects and its forgiveness from the viewpoint of the theology of grace is not entirely alien to Cyprian. He is also aware of the loss of baptismal grace, its recovery by reconciliation and the parallel between penance as *satisfactio* and baptism. Nevertheless, all of these points are peripheral to his theology, as can be seen particularly from his theology of *satisfactio* and its particular effect. In general on this question the Bishop of Carthage passes over the consideration from the viewpoint of the theology of grace in order to focus on the eschatological judgement. This judgement is seen not as manifestation of the fact that a person has or has not grace, but as a decision on the question whether God is satisfied with the sinner's performance of penance and the co-operation of the Church therein and, for this reason, no longer insists on punishment. Since Poschmann it has often been said that Cyprian does not make a clear distinction between guilt and liability to punishment and, therefore, considers that sin is 'forgiven' only when the *reatus poenae* is totally remitted. This is correct in so far as even in Cyprian there are present only the bases of a consideration of sin and its forgiveness from the viewpoint of the theology of grace. To this extent he does not consider the *reatus poenae* exclusively as the essence of habitual sin. He also recognizes the existence of a profound assurance of salvation even before the guilt of sin is completely 'paid up'.[83] Thus he also provides a basis for the modern distinction between *reatus culpae* and *reatus poenae* as well as for the more recent notion of 'forgiveness' in anticipation of a remission of the punishment due to sin. Nevertheless, all these are no more than bases. Thus, simplifying somewhat, we may still say that for Cyprian habitual sin is liability to punishment and the remission of sin is the elimination of this liability by penance. In addition to what we have said explicitly on the subject, this follows from the way in which Cyprian considers the remission of daily sins to be essentially identical to that of serious sins. In fact De op. et eleem. 2 is concerned primarily with the forgiveness of daily sins.

It would be wrong, however, to concentrate only on the lack of the said distinction in this view. Indeed this defect has a positive significance. Where the distinction between *reatus culpae* and *reatus poenae* is taken too much for granted, the view imposes itself in fact and spontaneously—if perhaps not yet theoretically—that the remission of the *reatus culpae* is brought about as a more or less self-evident sacramental (*ex opere operato*) infusion of grace. The precondition of this infusion, namely, 'sorrow', as opposed to 'penance', is fairly easily attained. This entails that 'doing penance' is inevitably oriented to the remission of the 'punishment' due to sin and loses its meaning for sorrow and for the remission of guilt. And since, after all, once the guilt has been forgiven, the 'punishment' is not a radically existential question (of salvation), the remission of punishment is relegated to a position of second importance. Cyprian's own view, on the contrary, makes it easier for him to 'realize' that true sorrow is penance in action. In fact his theory of sin and the remission of sins presupposes as self-evident and supporting his whole view the idea that genuine sorrow is penance. This is true, however problematical and imperfect this view may be when considered in itself.

It is not surprising that for Cyprian *paenitentia* and *satisfactio*[84] are *termini technici,* while a corresponding notion for 'sorrow' in the modern sense of a mere change of 'attitude' is unknown to him. The only sorrow which he knows is the one which is just as clearly and really effective as was the sin in question. Thus he prescribes a *longa et plena paenitentia*. This theory of sin and the forgiveness of sins is so consonant with his thinking that the bases of a more nuanced view which we discussed above do not show themselves effectively. A further development which would not depart from the basic living principle is possible only if it goes beyond even the generally accepted theory in contemporary theology; and this is a task which one can hardly set for the Bishop of Carthage.

This view is not only an interpretation and a construction which exceeds what is empirically tangible in Cyprian himself. He provides many sufficient indications of the fact that for him genuine sorrow must be just as real an act as the sin which is being expiated, and that assurance of its genuineness and its success before God is given to the extent that it really is an act. One has only to consider the general line of argument followed by Cyprian in De lapsis or in the corresponding letters to realize that for him the refusal to take on a *paenitentia* with a long-lasting *satisfactio* is, in itself, tantamount to a lack of 'sorrow', so the question does not arise at all why one cannot be satisfied with the sorrow of the *lapsi*. A *pax* without previous doing of penance is only a useless appearance (De lapsis 15–16). Not surprisingly (cf. Epist. 55,18), despite the real difficulties involved in a speedy reconciliation, Cyprian knows only the distinction between a *paenitentia plena et iusta* and the *paenitentiae simulatio*.

Once one presupposes that in Cyprian sorrow and doing penance are completely identical, then the postponement of sorrow until the point of death becomes understandable. If there is no *paenitentiam agere* present, the true *dolor delictorum* is also lacking (Epist. 55,23). This notion that 'sorrow', to be really effective, must be realized in the doing of penance is well expressed in Epist. 31,6 by the apparently nonsensical formulation (*paenitentia . . . paenitentiam probat*). Here we read: *sed pudor, sed modestia, sed paenitentia,*[85] *sed disciplina, sed humilitas atque subiectio . . . hoc est quod paenitentiam probat*. Penance as an act is the real proof of penance as an attitude even for the person who is doing this penance himself. There are many other indications which could be adduced in support of this view. Although the psychology which it implies, even when it is applied to a complicated individual case, may appear to be somewhat crude, nevertheless its importance and its practicality immediately become apparent once one asks how genuine 'sorrow' is to be established both by the Church and by the sinner himself. His desire to be at peace with the Church, his regret of having been in a situation in which he 'had' to deny, his fear of God's judgement and his subsequent repudiation of his fall (*secundum quid*) are all possible without excluding the fall itself and, therefore, do not necessarily amount to and express true 'sorrow'. As long as the existential situation, brought about by sin, lasts, how can a person really be sorry for this sin other than by behaving in a contrary manner? If this is a valid argument, then a person can be 'sorry' for a denial of faith only by a renewed confession (Epist. 55,4; 19,2). If a person is not able to produce such a sorrow, he can rectify his unjust act only by an act of penance which shows that the position and attitude which led to his sin have been radically altered for the good. This is because Cyprian is convinced that such sin usually springs from guilty attitudes which are already previously present and come to light in the sin (De lapsis 21/22; Epist. 65,3). Such attitudes are not eradicated by a mere 'regret' of the act alone. If, for instance, the love of material possessions leads to a fall from faith, then one cannot normally be existentially and convincingly sorry for this fault without giving up the corresponding material advantage (cf. De lapsis 35). Behind the 'still imperfect' theory of the remission of sins, which does not distinguish between the punishment due to sin and the guilt of sin, the Bishop of Carthage holds, therefore, an insight which is obscured by the too self-evident distinction between the incurring of guilt and the incurring of punishment, an insight into an existentially realistic psychology of true sorrow and, therefore, of the true nature of guilt itself.

The background of Cyprian's penitential teaching becomes even clearer when it is asked: how does he know that sins committed after baptism have to be remitted in a way different from those committed before baptism? The 'argument from Scripture', according to which good works remit sins (cf. Sir 3:30; Tob 4:10, Luke 11:40), without relating to the baptismal remission in Christ's blood so that there remains only one other object of this remission, namely, sins committed after baptism, is too artificial and complicated to have been the real basis of this teaching. Indeed it is a proof (De op. et eleem. 2; Epist. 55,22) which already presupposes its conclusion.

A reason for Cyprian's view could also be the *semel* of baptism which he mentions in this context. Since, according to tradition (Eph. 4:5; cf. Heb. 6:4),[86] there is only 'one' baptism, and this expression, right from the beginning, means not only the specific unity of every valid baptism but also the fact that it is possible only once for every individual,[87] Cyprian and his predecessors who, as he, taught the difference between the remission of sins before and after baptism, could have concluded that here there was not only an external, ritual difference but a profound, real one. A mere ritual difference would involve that there was simply one pardon of sins.

In connection with the idea of the unrepeatable possibility of 'baptism for the pardon of sins', and based upon it, the teaching of the intrinsic difference of the post-baptismal forgiveness of sins was always a more or less explicit part of the apostolic tradition. Nevertheless, everything is not clear on this point. Like Tertullian, Cyprian also does not make any distinction either between guilt and punishment or between their remission. If in baptism guilt is forgiven and washed away, it must follow necessarily that in baptism the punishment is waived. Moreover, this waiving of the punishment is only another expression for the pardon of guilt, and not something additional to the teaching of the forgiveness of guilt, as it is so considered by us today, and which, therefore, requires its own proof and a special declaration. This is the meaning of the following statement of Tertullian: *exempto scilicet reatu eximitur et poena* (De bapt. 5). It is precisely the possibility of concluding to the pardon of the *poena* from the remission of the *reatus* that shows that both are here the same and, therefore, are remitted at the same time and together. Clement of Alexandria holds the same view (Paed. I 6,26,2). The verbal difference between ἁμαρτία and ἐπιτιμία does not indicate that he is aware of different possibilities for the remission of guilt and punishment, but rather the contrary, since it is presupposed as self-evident that in baptism the ἐπιτιμία is forgiven along with guilt.

The ancient teaching, already traditional before Cyprian, on the complete remission of guilt in the one baptism does not explain how a possible remission of sins after baptism comes about otherwise than in baptism itself. On the contrary, this possibility itself is difficult to account for logically. Nevertheless since it was a firm datum of tradition and, at the same time, baptism was unrepeatable, it was necessary and natural to look in another direction for such a unified remission of guilt and punishment in the case of sins committed after baptism. For this purpose all that could be considered was a *paenitentia plena* which takes away the *reatus culpae* and the *reatus poenae* simultaneously.[88] If this conclusion were the only actual theological reason for the existence of the post-baptismal penitential practice and for the difference between it and the forgiveness of sins in baptism, then it is difficult to see how a pelagian interpretation can be precluded from the assertion that the person who sins after baptism can and must obliterate his faults through his own works without the grace of 'Christ's blood'.[89] In any case, it would seem to make the well-attested intervention on the Church's part unnecessary. The accusation of pelagianism cannot be avoided by maintaining that the works of penance themselves remit 'only' the punishment due to sins, since according to Cyprian it is certainly sin itself that is remitted through the works of penance. It is also of little use, in this regard, to hold that these works of penance are only at all effective by the power of Christ's redeeming grace.[90] Although this point is undoubtedly valid, it actually serves to highlight the opposition between the remission of sins in baptism and in post-baptismal penance. It might be thought, therefore, that it is only in baptism that sins and punishments were forgiven together gratuitously, whereas in penance only the guilt but not the punishment was forgiven in this way. But this would be a distinction alien to Cyprian, and it would not explain how and from what source he knows about these two kinds of forgiveness. If he knew about it from an explicit theoretical tradition, then it is no longer possible to say why Cyprian did not consider the distinction between guilt and punishment more explicitly. Indeed it is only the fact that he did not so consider this question that makes the acceptance of such a tradition thinkable.

We are left, therefore, with the following dilemma: either the explicit tradition mentioned above had the dogmatic meaning that the post-baptismal remission of sins occurs by one's own efforts without the grace of Christ's blood, in which case this theory can simply maintain an opposition between baptism and penance and disregard the distinction between guilt and punishment, or this tradition is simply a matter of a practice in the Church, according to which penance has to be done for sins committed after baptism. The explanation of this practice on the part of Cyprian and those who followed him would then be simply a theologumenon having no dogmatic significance. The first possibility is totally unacceptable for dogmatic reasons and is also historically at least unlikely. According to the second possibility, Cyprian is interpreting a tradition which has already been handed on to him. For its part, this tradition does not appear to have arisen from previous thinking. Nevertheless, the last point must be proven. As far as its theoretical presuppositions are concerned, it must also have been semi-pelagian. But this cannot apply to Cyprian. Moreover, if it is understood in the strict sense of the term, it applies even less to the time before Cyprian. Now if the practice did not emanate from such a theory, then the question remains, where could the difference of treatment of catechumens and those who have sinned after baptism have come from, since every practice has a theoretical background? The reason must have been that a greater doubt is objectively justifiable with regard to the sincerity of a new change of attitude after baptism than with regard to the *metanoia* in baptism. This doubt is shared by both the penitent himself and the Church.

Thus in Cyprian's teaching the question of the distinction between the remission of sins in and after baptism brings out the same insight which had already been in evidence in his way of considering the nature of sin and the remission of sins. Despite a certain obscurity, the specific origin of Cyprian's teaching about the *paenitentia iusta* is his living awareness that only the act of penance is proper sorrow, giving the assurance of the genuine 'attitude' to which God grants his forgiveness. From this it follows almost self-evidently that something different and 'more' is demanded from a sinner who is baptized than from the catechumen. At his conversion to Christianity the latter breaks both from his whole past and from the surrounding pagan world. In the 'baptismal vows' of the *abrenuntiatio* he expresses in the most real and vital way possible an attitude which leaves absolutely nothing to be desired. He 'experiences' his new birth to the divine life in baptism at a depth and an intensity which leaves him in no doubt about the complete forgiveness of his guilt.[91]
The person who sins after baptism, however, has lost all this and has shown by his action that the radical Christian attitude and condition is not alive in him (any more). Thus the mere fact of being a Christian was not an existential proof of a true Christian attitude. He could consider this 'Christian' life, along with its wishes and sentiments, only with a more bitter scepticism. In view of this shattering experience, the question must have arisen concerning what would reassure both himself and the church community that he would struggle to recover that attitude which would make him worthy of the Spirit of God and of peace with God. Not 'sorrow' in feeling and words but only hard action could restore to a worthy man faith in his attitude. This experience, therefore, must have been the simple but continually effective starting-point from which the early Church prescribed, regulated and supervised personal penance, while the tangible forms and obligations of penance (prayer, fasting, penitential garb, etc.) merely continued the penitential practice of the synagogue.[92] For the latter there was no need of a special discovery. They needed only to be filled with new spirit and life and to be energetically prescribed.

Cyprian's theory about this institution, which was already traditional for a long time before him, combines elements which are correct with those which are only provisional and indeed questionable. It is still possible to discern its *Sitz im Leben*. Thus the bishop of Carthage orders the confessors to observe *actum et opera et merita* of the individual penitents in order to discover *quorum paenitentiam satisfactioni proximam conspicitis* (Epist. 15,4). In this way the confessors were able to ascertain not the 'absolution' of guilt before God but only the genuineness of the penitents' sorrow, proven by their deed. But Cyprian is still not satisfied with this. His practice demands less than his teaching, but it still demands a great deal. It is in fact inspired by another conviction than that which he develops in his theory, namely that God forgives the person who is truly sorry and that this sorrow expresses itself in, and is proven by, *paenitentia: paenitentia . . . paenitentiam probat*. In this practice, which is simpler and also clearer than the theory, the *paenitentia* is for Cyprian what makes a sinner into a *reformatum et depositis prioris vitae delictis ad sobrios et bonos mores et ad innocentiae disciplinam poenitentiae dolore correctum* (Epist. 55,23). God is able to forgive the guilt of such a person by his grace. Cyprian also considers those worthy to receive the peace of the Church who, after their fall, have made a new confession, without suffering death for it (Epist. 25). He thinks that such a deed is a clear indication that one *commissi vere et firmiter paenitet et fidei calor praevalet* (Epist. 55,4). Moreover, attention has already been drawn above to the notion of *satisfactio* as an interior healing of the sinner. This need not be understood only as an 'image' of the strictly juridical notion of *satisfactio*. The 'payment of guilts' could just as well be seen as an image drawn from the juridical sphere to describe a *paenitentia* which in deed and truly heals the sinner from the interior consequences of sin in the very depths of his person, including his body. Only after this process is man free from all the 'punishments' of sin. Indeed in the early Church the principal 'works' of penance that were fasting and prayer[93] were frequently and insistently characterized as exorcism. It is the deed and not only the mere 'attitude' that transforms man and expels the 'forces of darkness'. Finally, Greek theology too, beginning with Clement of Alexandria, in its theory conceives the works of penance very clearly as an inner healing of man. Could it not be that this conception has just as much right to our attention as a correct and original explanation of the penitential prescriptions practised in the early Church?

Despite this explanation of the real basis of penitential practice in the early Church, it is still possible to derive from it the teaching which has in fact long since been taken from it, namely, that in the sacrament of penance all the 'punishments' of sin are not necessarily and always forgiven. This constitutes a difference between baptism and penance which naturally can and must be shown in greater detail. Just the experience of an existentially limited intensity of conversion, due to the after-effect of previous guilt, includes, on its own, the persistence of a punishment of sin. Nevertheless, 'punishment' here is not to be understood as only imposed from outside, without an intrinsic relationship to man's moral situation and as a mere extrinsic reality. On this supposition, the real theological problem consists not in the question of why the punishments due to sin[94] can persist, despite sorrow, but rather in the question of why they are totally waived in baptism. This question, however, only presented itself at the periphery of consciousness in the early Church. This is easily explained by the enthusiastic experience of the new birth in baptism on the part of the whole man. In any case, an objective answer to this question can be expected only from a systematic treatment of the subject.

5. *The Effect of Reconciliation by the Church*

A) THE EFFECTIVENESS OF THE CHURCH'S ACT IN PENANCE (APART FROM IN THE ACTUAL RECONCILIATION)

The Church's activity in penance is not confined to the re-bestowal of church fellowship—as we would say today, the 'absolution'. The whole Church with the bishop and the people and, especially, the confessors lend the penitent their support primarily in so far as they share in penance through prayer and the eucharistic offering. Thus the bishop prays daily for the penitents with tears asking for the *plenissima pax* (Epist. 43,6; De lapsis 32) and offers sacrifice for those who have fallen (De lapsis 16).[95] The confessors pray in a similar vein (De lapsis 36). As in Tertullian so also for Cyprian an intercession by the whole church community at the time of the liturgical exhomologesis would have been self-evident; it also gives its consent to the reconciliation (Epist. 64,1). The Bishop of Carthage obviously visualizes all this as a support of the penitent's own *satisfactio*. He even recognizes a *per episcopos et sacerdotes Domini Domino satisfacere* (Epist. 43,3).[96] Since in Cyprian *satisfactio* is clearly distinguished from reconciliation itself, as its necessary prerequisite, it can be achieved only by such a support given to the penitent by intercession, but in no way exclusively *per sacerdotes*. The effect of this intervention, being a wish for divine pardon, is viewed just as eschatologically as the penitent's personal *satisfactio*. It, too, is effective at the judgement (De lapsis 17,36). In so far as the impositions of hands (?) at the exhomologesis are considered an exorcism, they too, by their scope and effect, are a similar support of the sinner's personal satisfaction through penance on the Church's part. This is the best way of understanding two otherwise quite unconnected elements which Cyprian brings together:[97] *purgare conscientiam*[98] *sacrificio et manu sacerdotis* (De lapsis 16). The Bishop of Carthage does not say explicitly how far he considers this aspect of church penance to be necessary for salvation. Nevertheless it is for him an actual part of the one essential church penance, without which there is no reconciliation with God. The ecclesial aspect, therefore, shares in this necessity.[99] But this does not necessarily mean that sacrifice and the prayer of the Church have to be explicitly connected with the individual performance of penance. If this connection does not exist today, this is, therefore, no proof that such an intercession on the Church's part is unnecessary.

Thus this aspect of the penitential process in the early Church should not be neglected as if it were irrelevant for the sacrament, even if it is generally overlooked in modern dogmatic treatises. This aspect implies an awareness of the manner in which the *satisfactio* of the sinner effects grace, an awareness which appears only too briefly in Cyprian's explicit theory. In other words, this aspect supposes a living consciousness of the union between all the members of the Church. Where the Church's intercession is conceived in this way as being more or less necessary, it is completely impossible to experience *satisfactio* as an autonomous extinction of 'guilts' before God by one's own efforts. For Tertullian the intercession of Christ present in the Church, being assured of a hearing, was one of the notions by which he grasped the Church's decisive act in the *paenitentia secunda*. This can no longer be said of Cyprian, since he considered the granting of the *pax* and the *communicatio* alone as the decisive act of the Church. But this does not necessarily mean that the importance which he accords to the Church's intercession is any the less. The Church is an organism which communicates grace. *Spiritu eius* (*Ecclesiae*) *animamur* (De cath. eccl. un. 5) . . . *haec nos Deo servat* (ibid., 6). This organism does not communicate grace as a static reality, however, but continually applies to its members grace and Spirit-dispensing influence through sacrifice and prayer which can never fail it. Sacrifice and prayer belong inalienably to the very nature of the Church. It is for this reason that it is the mother of life who dispenses and grants the Spirit. The bestowal of the Spirit incorporates people into this Church which offers sacrifice, prays and, in so doing, again bestows the Spirit. This intercession precedes the reincorporation into the Church; it refers the sinner to God[100] and as co-operation with the sinner's own penance is indispensable for the success of this penance.

B) THE EFFECT OF THE RECONCILIATION BY THE CHURCH

The decisive act of the Church with regard to the sinner who has separated himself from the Church and thereby lost his right of access to the Eucharist is the readmission.

This reconciliation takes place through (or on the occasion of) the imposition of hands and has an immediately tangible effect in the sphere of the Church. Cyprian speaks of an *in Ecclesiam suscipi* (*recipi*) (Epist. 55,29; 4,4), *ad Ecclesiam redire* (Epist. 4,4; 19,2), of the *ius communicationis* (*communicationem*) *accipere* (Epist. 16,2; 19,2), *ad communicationem venire* (*admitti*) (Epist. 17,2), of the *pax* (Epist. 18,1; 19,2; 20,3; 55,29; 57,1.4), of the *Ecclesiae reconciliari* (Sent. episc. 8,22), of a *pax data et communicatio concessa* (Epist. 66,5). The actual *communicatio* is evident above all in the active participation in the sacrifice and in the legitimate reception of the Eucharist (Epist. 15,1; 16,2.3). The granting of the *pax* is the exclusive prerogative of the bishop[101] (Epist. 15,2; 16,1.3; 17,2; 19,1; 64,1). Only in a case of necessity can the peace of the Church be granted by a simple priest or even by a deacon (Epist. 16,1; 17,2; 18,1; 19,2). The action of the bishop is described as a 'judgement'. He is *iudex ad tempus a Deo datus* (Epist. 66,3), *ad tempus iudex vice Christi* (Epist. 59,5) and in virtue of this office in the Church he judges individual cases even in the case of sinners (Epist. 57,5; 66,5) and passes a *sententia* (Epist. 55,18). It is obvious that, as far as its reference to salvation is concerned, this judgement does not prejudice in any way Christ's last judgement[102] (De lapsis 17; Epist. 55,18.20.29; 58,3), but this does not mean that for Cyprian it is not a true judicial sentence.[103] Thus he has no need to fear any difficulty arising from an opposition between the bishop's judgement and that of Christ, because they do not refer immediately to the same object. The judgement reserved to Christ alone concerns directly the remission of guilt by a *plena satisfactio*. The declaration of the bishop, however, is the new recognition of full church fellowship. Generally the bishop should pronounce this judgement only when he has reason to believe that the *satisfactio plena* has been reached. Nevertheless, Cyprian knows cases where such a judgement on the bishop's part is valid and is to be upheld although full satisfaction has not yet been made (Epist. 64,1; 55,13). A *pax* which is granted after too short a penance or on the sick-bed is recognized as valid, although Cyprian is conscious that under the force of circumstances, even where the official requirements of penance are concerned, he is falling short of the ideal (Epist. 59,16; 55,7). Nevertheless, he does know cases in which the granting of the *pax* is simply void. A *pax* without any penance[104] at all is an *inrita et falsa pax . . . et nihil accipientibus profutura* (De lapsis 15). The same applies where the will is lacking to renounce a sinful decision (Epist. 57,3).[105] Also the *pax* granted by a bishop who does not hold his power legitimately (Epist. 66,5)[106] is invalid, as it is when it is bestowed by *non communicantibus* (Epist. 59,13). A more precise and basic consideration of when a reconciliation is valid[107] is still wanting. The bishop's judicial power which he exercises in the new recognition of full church fellowship is based primarily, apart from a general appeal to the *evangelii vigor* and the *Domini ac Dei lex* (De lapsis 15), on Matthew 16 and 18,[108] that is, on the power of binding and loosing there promised by the Lord (Epist. 57,1). The context in which Cyprian uses this passage shows clearly that he understands the *ligare in terris* as an *Ecclesiam cludere* and the *sovere illic* as a granting of the *communicatio et pax*. The more immediate object of the power of binding and loosing is, therefore, the relationship of men to the Church,[109] but only in so far as the positive relationship is *subsidium* and *pignus* of eternal salvation. That which is bound if this positive relationship is lacking is, as Cyprian makes clear from his free quotation of the Matthew passage, also already *eo ipso* bound in heaven; there is no further possibility of salvation. Nevertheless the person who possesses this *pignus* really receives the possibility of withstanding the future judgement (*solvi possent*).[110]

Apart from his application of the heavenly loosening to the last judgement, Cyprian's interpretation of Matthew 16 and 18 corresponds exactly to the immediate meaning of the biblical words themselves. The direct application of the binding and loosening on earth to the relationship of man to the Church is thoroughly justified.[111] In the letter of the forty-two African bishops to Pope Cornelius the biblical foundation of the institution of penance in the early Church is again in evidence, as it is already in the polemic against the Montanists and indeed with the main emphasis on the ecclesial interpretation.[112] Indeed without this emphasis the concrete form assumed by the celebration of penance, that is, as an exclusion from and readmission into the Church as a fellowship of grace, remains finally unintelligible. In view of the appeal to Matthew it is, at first sight, surprising that Cyprian never has recourse to John 20. He quotes John 20:21 f. only with regard to the general authority of the apostles and bishops and especially with regard to the power to baptize (cf. De cath. eccl. un. 4; Epist. 69,11; 73,7; 75,16). Nevertheless this fact is not particularly significant. For one thing, Matthew 16 is also cited in the same context (De cath. eccl. un. 4; Epist. 75,16), and in Cyprian's view this passage can certainly refer to the bishop's power in penance. Moreover it is easy to understand why the Bishop of Carthage refrains automatically from adducing John 20 in favour of the power of penance. The *remittere peccata* mentioned here is taken by him quite spontaneously and self-evidently as the *remissa peccatorum* in the strict sense. Thus this text is excluded as far as penance is concerned. Applied to penance it would have suggested that the bishops have the same power to forgive post-baptismal sins which Cyprian attributes to them only in baptism. Thus Cyprian confines his use of the text to baptism. His preference for Matthew 16 is probably best explained by the fact that this text brings out more clearly the unity of the episcopate with the one Peter (cf. De cath. eccl. un. 4) than Matthew 18 or John 20. Cyprian considered that this aspect was particularly important, even in the question of penance, when faced with the laxists among his clergy who attempted to reconcile sinners off their own bat and to emancipate themselves from the bishop. It may even be possible to deduce from De cath. eccl. un. 4 that these laxists in the Carthage clergy themselves appealed to John 20, because the *quamvis* . . . seems to suppose a contrary opinion. This must have made use of John 20:21 f.[113] What is more, it is a fact that the schismatics attacked in this writing rebelled against Cyprian because of the question of penance.

This second reason for Cyprian's reserve with regard to John 20 does not contradict the one already mentioned. In fact the laxists had simply readmitted sinners without reference to the bishop or the unity of the bishops in council. This is what Cyprian would call the straightforward *remissa peccatorum*. It is not unlikely that they appealed to John 20 in this sense and that, precisely for this reason, Cyprian did not enlist the aid of this text for his own notion in the question of penance.[114]

The power of binding and loosing promised in Matthew 16 and 18 finds its immediate application in the exclusion of a sinner from the Church and his readmission into it. Moreover, Cyprian considers that this power is exercised not merely 'on the occasion of', that is, 'also' along with the forgiveness of sins. Rather, he sees it, along with the Church's support of the sinner's own *satisfactio,* as the Church's own and direct act in the whole penitential process. There is never any question of another act on the Church's part.[115] The bishop's authoritative act is always the granting of the *pax* and the *communicatio*. All the other effects appear always as essentially and intrinsically connected consequences of the restoration of peace with the Church. Moreover, Cyprian interprets Matthew 16, in so far as this passage mentions an act of the Church, quite naturally in terms of exclusion from and readmission into the Church. Any exposition of Cyprian's view of the salvific effect of the Church's penitential process must, therefore, give explicit attention to this middle role played by the Church. If, and in so far as, he considers the act of the Church to have sacramental effects, that is, to cause grace, these effects flow from the act whereby the sinner is reconciled with the Church.

Now reconciliation with the Church has real effects with regard to grace in the next life. Negatively speaking, the blessing of belonging to the Church, which the unreconciled sinner lacks, is so indispensable for his salvation that without it he is lost. The *perdere pacem* is a *perdere salutem* (Epist. 36, 2). Even a martyr who is *extra Ecclesiam constitutus* and thus *ab unitate atque a caritate divisus* cannot receive the crown through his death (Epist. 55,17). Men who, by following schismatic priests, have fallen away from the Church and died in this situation *extra Ecclesiam sine communicatione et pace perierunt* (Epist. 72,2). Thus full church membership is an absolutely indispensable precondition for a real possibility of salvation. To reject it means a *spei salutis subsidium denegare* (Epist. 57,1), whereas the reconciliation is a *pignus vitae percipere* (Epist. 55,13). Thus the former represents a binding realized also in heaven, while the latter opens up the possibility of a loosening at the last judgement (Epist. 57,1). If a person, through the granting of an invalid peace with the Church, prevents anyone from seeking a valid peace with the Church legitimately, he hinders the *communicatio ad salutem* (De lapsis 16). The person who is not in the Church is already a *semetipso damnatus,* so that there is no longer any need for an actual judgement passed by the Lord (De un. 17). On the other hand, the person who is again readmitted to the Church is enabled with this peace to pass over to the Lord (Epist. 18,1; 20.3). There he comes into judgement and must 'stand in wait for forgiveness' (*ad veniam stare*) (Epist. 55,20). It is an advantage that the Lord is coming to his Church and that he will judge (only) those *quos in ea* (*Ecclesia*) *intus invenerit* (Epist. 55,29). Certainly a *deprecari in die illo* is still necessary, but only the person who is in the Church (Epist. 65,5) is capable of it. As opposed to the martyrs who enter 'immediately' into glory he must still *pendere in die iudicii ad sententiam Domini* (Epist. 55,20), but in the Church he has the firm assurance that when the Lord comes in judgement acknowledging a *paenitentia plena et iusta* he will also ratify as valid the granting of church fellowship (Epist. 55,18). This applies particularly with regard to the completion of the penitent's own penance through the intercession of the Church in its martyrs and priests (De lapsis 36).

The renewal of church fellowship by the bishops is, therefore, of salvific importance for the penitent at least in so far as it provides the indispensable precondition for salvation at the judgement. Since the *satisfactio* is definitively effective only at the judgement, the renewal of church fellowship is just as necessary for salvation as *satisfactio*.[116] This is not only the theology of a bishop but a practical conviction which dictates the behaviour of Christians. If peace with the Church did not have in itself any meaning for salvation, then Christians would hardly have been so bothered about it on the death-bed, when indeed the earthly tangible consequences,[117] such as access to the liturgy, must have been meaningless. But this is not all. The legitimately communicated peace with the Church conveys the possibility of receiving the sacrament of the Lord's body (Epist. 15,1; 16,2; 17,2). Granted the necessity for salvation which Cyprian ascribes to the reception of the Eucharist,[118] the possibility of a non-sacrilegious participation in this sacrament is very important. The unworthiness to receive this sacrament resides primarily in the sin and not only in the excommunication. Nevertheless it is the imposition of hands in penance and not the mere *satisfactio* which belongs to the prerequisites for worthiness to receive the Eucharist, which means that through *satisfactio* and the imposition of hands an interior change is accomplished in the sinner which makes him worthy to receive the Lord's body again. Cyprian does not devote any special considerations to the precise nature of this change in this context. He knows, however, that *Spiritum Sanctum consecutis ad bibendum calicem Domini pervenitur* (Epist. 63,8).[119] Thus his eucharistic thought seems to suggest that the reason for the renewed worthiness to receive the Eucharist consists in the possession of the Spirit which is communicated by the imposition of hands.[120]

In fact for Cyprian the passage between a *manus imposito ad accipiendum Spiritum Sanctum* and a *manus impositio in paenitentiam* is so fluid that he is able to explain the imposition of hands in penance defended by Stephen quite simply as a communication of the Spirit. If these two impositions of hands had been completely distinct for the bishop of Carthage, this misunderstanding would be hardly thinkable. Even independently of our present question the imposition of hands of reconciliation is understood either simply as a gesture of the communication of the Spirit, or at least it stands very close to it conceptually. Finally, the peace with the Church is also considered explicitly as the reason for the new reception of the Spirit: *quomodo potest ad confessionem paratus aut idoneus inveniri, qui non prius pace accepta receperit Spiritum Patris* (Epist. 57,4). Cyprian says this to justify a premature reconciliation in face of the threat of a new persecution. The Spirit is accordingly necessary to undergo martyrdom. It can only be present for a person who has sinned previously, however, if he has received it again *pace accepta*. Thus in this case even a premature communication of the *pax* is justified. Already the knowledge of the connection between *pax* and possession of the Spirit leads to practical consequences, even if this is naturally not their only reason. This knowledge can hardly have originated out of the top of his head. Moreover, this is not the only passage in Cyprian's work where he links explicitly the usual reconciliation of a sinner with the bestowal of the Spirit.[121]

What was concluded for the connection between *pax* and possession of the Spirit in Cyprian, both from the fact that a sinner is again made worthy to receive the Eucharist and from the rite used to effect reconciliation, shows that this connection is not an idea derived from Cyprian by argumentation and by using Epist. 57 as a proof text. Despite the fact that it is rarely attested, it must have been a commonplace for him, as well as not being entirely unknown to the tradition of his day (Hermas, Tertullian, Didascalia). The same idea appears even more clearly in Cyprian's general theology of the Church. What is more striking, however, is the fact that the rebestowal of the Spirit is never placed by Cyprian in relation to *satisfactio*. Given the importance which he ascribes to the latter for the forgiveness of sins, this may be surprising at first sight. This applies particularly where the remission of sins is considered as the bestowal of grace. Nevertheless, upon closer consideration, this observation is seen to be self-evident. This is because for Cyprian the *satisfactio* is the long-lasting payment of the 'guilts' of sin which receives its definitive answer from God's side only with the last judgement. It is not possible to connect any bestowal of the Spirit, considered as an actual and present event, with such a notion as this, as long as it is not broadened or modified. This is also why in Cyprian the communication of the Spirit was too closely linked with an external, temporally fixed ritual (baptism-confirmation).

In our opinion, this observation and its explanation justify us in understanding the statement of Epist. 57,4 clearly in the sense that Cyprian, in speaking of the reception of the Spirit through the *pax accepta,* is really thinking only of the *pax* itself and in no way of the *satisfactio* as the cause of the communication of the Spirit. This maintains, despite his demand for at least a sufficient *satisfactio,* as a precondition of the *pax*. It is not the *satisfactio* which bestows the Spirit[122] but the *pax*. Thus the relationship existing between *satisfactio* and *pax,* as it was explained above, is in fact now reversed. Whereas previously the *pax* was the precondition (*pignus*) for the effectiveness of the *satisfactio* as the cause of the forgiveness of sins at the judgement, now a certain[123] *satisfactio* is required so that the *pax* may effectively bring about the communication of the Spirit. This will have to be borne in mind when we come to discuss the relationship between personal penance and church reconciliation with regard to the unity of their effects.

But perhaps it could still be asked here whether Cyprian saw the communication of the Spirit in the granting of the *pax,* that is, the actual ritual, or in the renewed church membership, considered in its duration, allowed by the bishop's act. The way in which this discussion of the problem appears in Augustine[124] shows that this question should not be peremptorily rejected as too subtle for a Father of the Church. At the same time, no clear answer to it is found in Cyprian. On the one hand, he considers the bishop's possession of the Spirit the indispensable prerequisite for the effectiveness of his administration of baptism and his granting of the *pax* (Epist. 66,5). Thus one could ascribe the principal cause of the communication of the Spirit to the episcopal act of reconciliation as such. On the other hand, it is not completely clear that the penitential imposition of hands, on its own, is anything more than a gesture which supports the sinner's own exhomologesis. This exhomologesis, however, is a part and an indication of his *satisfactio* which is followed less 'formally' by the *pax*. Thus it is not to be simply excluded that it was the full church membership (*in facto esse*) which was considered the actual and immediate principle communicating the Spirit.[125] The restoration of church fellowship through the bishop's authoritative verdict as such, therefore, has an essential salvific importance and brings about effects concerning grace and the communication of the Spirit.

In order to appreciate the precise reason why according to Cyprian the renewed recognition of full church membership has this salvific meaning and is a cause of grace it is necessary to refer to his theology of the Church. *Salus extra Ecclesiam non est* (Epist. 73,21). *Christianus non est, qui in Christi Ecclesia non est* (Epist. 55,24). *Habere non potest Deum patrem, qui Ecclesiam non habet matrem* (De cath. eccl. un. 6). *Ut habere quis possit Deum patrem, habeat ante Ecclesiam matrem* (Epist. 74,7). *Quomodo potest esse eum Christo, qui cum sponsa Christi atque in eius Ecclesia non est?* (Epist. 52,1). *Haec nos Deo servat* (De cath. eccl. un. 6). These statements about the necessity of the Church for salvation cannot be understood merely in terms of an external precondition which simply precedes the actual event by which man is saved. The Church is here seen rather as itself bringing about salvation, and this Church is the actual, historical, tangible Church. Even if we leave Cyprian's theology of baptism out of consideration, this is evident from his view of penance. This view demands the actual granting of peace with the Church, realized through the imposition of hands by the bishop alone, which entails legal and empirically verifiable consequences. This peace with the Church[126] communicates the Holy Spirit to the man to whom it is announced. In the context of the question of penance it is not explained why this is so. The fact of such an efficacy of the peace with the Church with regard to grace follows self-evidently from the view which he holds of the necessity of the Church for salvation. It is for him a self-evident theological axiom which is not disputed even by his adversaries in the controversy over the baptism of heretics. In any case, it follows from Cyprian's theology of the Church[127] that only the Church of the bishops who derive from Peter and are united under him is the 'Church'. As visibly, legally constituted it is the Church of Christ which he 'has prepared through his own blood' (Epist. 72,2). It is his body (Epist. 63,13) and, therefore, bound to him alone and united with him (Epist. 74,6). As this visible Church of Christ, it alone possesses the Spirit[128] and transmits it to the members who belong to it legitimately by baptism. *Spiritu eius animamur* (De cath. eccl. un. 5). This life-giving influence is exercised in the Church, however, not only in the once-and-for-all act of baptism but also through the continuing possession of life by its members who, therefore, must remain always united with it. *Quidquid a matrice discesserit seorsum vivere et spirare non poterit, substantiam salutis amittit* (De. cath. eccl. un. 23). Thus Cyprian's ecclesiology would be violated by the view which sees in church membership a mere juridical precondition that man can withstand God's judgement in the question of his salvation—which salvation, however, he has to achieve by his own efforts. It is only in the Church that man enters into life-giving contact with the Spirit of Christ which, emanating from the Church, continually inspires man. And it is for this reason that the *pax* with the Church is the means by which the Spirit is communicated.

6. *The Unity of Satisfactio and Pax in Their Remitting of Sins*

Does Cyprian's theology shift from the idea of *satisfactio* as man's act which remits sins to that of reconciliation as the act of the Church which conveys the Spirit? Does this mean that there are contradictions or, at least, important inconsistencies in the penitential theology of this Father of the Church? It is certainly difficult to understand logically that *satisfactio* as the remission of sins achieved by the penitent himself is a presupposition of reconciliation,[129] while this reconciliation appears at the same time as a presupposition of the forgiveness of sins by God. Nevertheless this difficulty need not have existed for Cyprian.

Cyprian does not demand a *plena satisfactio* as a prerequisite for reconciliation in every case. At least in those cases where it is not required one and the same *satisfactio* cannot be the presupposition for church reconciliation and for the full forgiveness of guilt at the judgement. Thus the *satisfactio* can only be the condition for the reconciliation which then, in its turn, is required so that full *satisfactio* made on earth or in the next life achieves forgiveness by God. Nevertheless, apart from these cases, even when Cyprian normally demands a *plena satisfactio* as a condition for the *pax* of the Church, he does not actually prescribe the forgiveness of guilt by God as a condition for church reconciliation. If this were the case reconciliation would always arrive too late to have any effect on the forgiveness of guilt. Rather he expects a *satisfactio* which offers the prospect that later at the judgement God will forgive the guilt. For such a future forgiveness the peace with the Church can still have an important meaning. This solution of the difficulty corresponds totally to Cyprian's view, according to which God will answer the *satisfactio* with *venia* definitively only in the future at the judgement. He considers the peace with the Church explicitly as an indispensable prerequisite for this *venia*. For all this, however, the real difficulties in Cyprian's two-sided theology of penance are not yet eliminated. If church reconciliation alone is the cause of the renewed reception of the Spirit, then thereby the remission of sins is achieved, and indeed here and now. But then what is the position of *satisfactio* which will not have this effect until the judgement?

It is fairly easy to answer this particular difficulty in Cyprian's theology of penance in the light of today's common theological distinction between the liability for guilt and the liability for punishment. The forgiveness of guilt itself occurs on the supposition of a certain *satisfactio* ('sorrow') by means of the communication of the Spirit in church reconciliation. This 'forgiveness' is required so that full *satisfactio* (which, according to Cyprian, will be achieved at the last judgement) can usher in the total remission of the punishments due to sin (that is, quite simply the *venia* according to Cyprian). Thus both church reconciliation and personal *satisfactio* count as causes of forgiveness without being relegated to a mere 'precondition' for the remission of sins. Certainly, to regard *satisfactio* as mere 'sorrow' would not correspond to Cyprian's view. On the other hand, to consider the *pax* only a precondition would jeopardize the 'sacrament' as *opus operatum* and would not adequately represent the view of the Bishop of Carthage. But is this suggested solution of the difficulty in this theology of penance one which Cyprian himself could have envisaged?

The distinction between guilt and punishment, remission of guilt and remission of punishment is not so common and familiar for Cyprian, even if it is not totally foreign to him, that one can take it for granted that for him there could arise no serious tension between the remission of sins through *satisfactio* and the remission of sins through reconciliation. What is more, in view of Cyprian's basic tendency, such a solution undermines considerably the importance of the *satisfactio plena*. This *satisfactio plena,* in his view, is in some way decisive for salvation, and there subsists an uncertainty about this salvation so long as there is no assurance that the *satisfactio* has been carried out to a sufficient degree. On the other hand, in this 'solution' salvation is already fundamentally assured through the possession of the Spirit, and in comparison with this the remission of guilt remains a secondary matter. It could also be observed that even in our modern way of thinking the certainty of possession of the Spirit because of reconciliation, granted the subjective and necessarily presupposed disposition of the penitent, always remains questionable and thus allows for that radical uncertainty about salvation which Cyprian stresses. Against this last point, however, it should be remarked that Cyprian, far from emitting any uncertainty about the possession of the Spirit, regards this as a characteristic of the situation in which the sinner finds himself after baptism. In the solution offered, however, this uncertainty would apply just as much to the newly baptized.

We must, therefore, be content with the observation that, as yet, a perfect accord between the different assertions in Cyprian's theology of penance has not been found. It is worth noting, in this regard, that the Bishop of Carthage, despite these tensions in his theory, did not succumb to the temptation simply to sacrifice one of the two aspects. The original, essential importance of reconciliation for the reception of the Spirit and the remission of sins (at least in fact) is underlined just as much as the causal importance of personal activity for the remission of sins and thus, at least in fact, for the reception of the Spirit. Perhaps, on the whole, this theology of penance is even better than the penitential teaching common today. The latter, as opposed to Thomas Aquinas, considers it possible to safeguard the causality of the Church or sacramental activity with regard to the communication of grace and the remission of sins only by relegating the *satisfactio,* considered as 'sorrow', to the mere precondition for the grace of the sacrament of penance. A truly thomistic theology of penance would vindicate Cyprian on this point and show that the full importance of the sacrament as *opus operatum* can be safeguarded without such a depreciation of the *satisfactio*.

Let us then leave Cyprian's theology of penance simply in its own historical position, without trying to force his statements into a synthesis which he himself does not provide. Nevertheless, it is possible to pose a further question: how could Cyprian stop short here psychologically without experiencing the need for a more precise synthesis and without the temptation to sacrifice one of his two basic principles in the theology of penance for the sake of the other? The answer to this question is of some historical importance, since it can show that it is completely unjustifiable to hold an interpretation of Cyprian in which one or other of these basic statements is depreciated. This is precisely what has happened with Galtier on the one hand and H. Koch on the other,[130] as if it were psychologically totally impossible that both statements, being the starting-points for contrary interpretations, could not have originated in Cyprian's mind. Moreover, the answer to our question is relatively simple: possession of the Spirit and freedom from guilt are not so closely connected for Cyprian that every time communication of the Spirit is mentioned he had to think *eo ipso* clearly of the remission of guilt, and *vice versa*. We do this today quite automatically. And indeed Cyprian also recognizes that the Holy Spirit leaves a man on account of serious sin, that is, that sin is a loss of grace.[131] Nevertheless, in his explanation of the remission of sins as such he never exploits explicitly and immediately the notion of the rebestowal of the Holy Spirit. He uses this notion to describe the effect of the *pax* but never directly the nature of the remission of sins. This is less surprising than it may appear today. In the Bible the consequences of sin are considered exclusively from a moral and eschatological viewpoint.[132] The description of the consequences of sin from the point of view of the theology of grace is totally lacking here. Thus in the Bible there can be no explanation of the renewed remission of sins in terms of a rebestowal of grace and of the Spirit. In the second century polemic against the amoral, gnostic notion of grace, the loss of grace through sin had to be stressed. Thus developed the explicit notion of sin as a loss of grace. But naturally this development was not so rapid that this viewpoint predominated immediately over the moral and eschatological approaches. It took even longer for the post-baptismal remission of sins considered as the regaining of grace, under the influence of the idea just mentioned, to become the dominant viewpoint.

It is therefore not surprising if, with regard to the remission of sins, the moral and eschatological viewpoints predominated much longer. Certainly Cyprian, following Tertullian, knew the notion of the *mortale crimen* (De bono pat. 14) as sin which brings about the death of grace. Nevertheless such offences are much less clearly differentiated from other sins by means of the treatment from the viewpoint of grace in Cyprian than they are in Tertullian.[133] The more ancient approach to sin is still prevalent. It is therefore hardly surprising that the consideration of the nature of sin from the viewpoint of grace is not exploited by Cyprian in the theology of the remission of sins. Presumably a consideration of the forgiveness of sins from the point of view of a theology of grace did not emanate exclusively from such a view of sin itself, but developed rather from an ecclesiological reflection: the person who sins separates himself from the Church. This is an idea which was understandable even without a clear consideration of sin from the viewpoint of the theology of grace. The person who returns to the Church receives the Holy Spirit through it as the mediator of grace.

Despite a determination of the nature of sin from the viewpoint of grace in certain cases, at that time the idea was completely unthinkable that the Holy Spirit and the guilt of sin could coexist simultaneously in a man. We could perhaps visualize such a possibility, since for us the possession of the Spirit is justifiably compatible with a venial fault. At that time, however, the clear knowledge of the essential difference between a serious and a venial sin was only beginning to show itself. It would take much longer before it became clearly and commonly accepted. Can we say, therefore, that at that time the possession of the Spirit and the remission of certain sins which were only vaguely distinguished from other 'venial' sins must have been quite self-evidently identical? In fact all that Tertullian, for example, can say when faced with a casually-minded and unrepentant catechumen is that, even if, against all expectation, he receives baptism, he will lose the Spirit again soon afterwards. He does not dare, therefore, to state categorically that unrepentance and possession of the Spirit are always and everywhere incompatible. We have already referred to similar points of obscurity in Pope Stephen. On the other hand, at that time it was perfectly possible to envisage a purification from sin which was followed only later by a communication of the Spirit. This is directly observable in Tertullian. But it is essentially no different in Cyprian. Certainly in his view possession of the Spirit is necessary in order to be able to dispense the pardon of sins in baptism (Epist. 69,10 f.). Nevertheless, for him the purification and sanctification of baptism which forgives sins, on the one hand, and the imposition of hands which communicates the Spirit, on the other, are two 'sacraments' (Epist. 72,1; 73,9.21; 74,5.7; 75,8.18).[134]

Thus the idea of a purification from sins, in so far as it is effective already here on earth, by means of *satisfactio,* allowing for the new communication of the Holy Spirit in reconciliation through the imposition of hands, is not totally out of the question for Cyprian. According to his way of thinking, however, there could be no question that the bestowal of the Spirit would be brought about by penance considered more or less as man's own effort.[135] If, according to the ideas of that time, this activity can purify from sin, then this is only in so far as the purification itself is considered from a moral viewpoint. It cannot communicate the Spirit of God which, according to Cyprian, is given by God through the sacraments of initiation. Given the state of theological reflection at that time, therefore, it is not at all surprising that in Cyprian the theology of the remission of sins and that of the communication of the Spirit went their separate ways. The importance of all this for us is that we are not justified, for the sake of pure logic, in depreciating either Cyprian's theology of *satisfactio* as a cause of the remission of sin and the remission of guilt or his theology of *pax* as the Church's act communicating the Spirit. Cyprian rightly insisted on both aspects, and, differently from us, he still experienced no problem in holding both of the assertions. In so far as this theology, being a reflection of the teaching of the Church at that time, has a claim to lasting relevance, we have the task of grasping the subjective act of man and the act of the Church in their unity in such a way that one causality can be predicated of both acts with regard to the one effect which is both the reception of the Spirit and the remission of sins together. Once this unity of *satisfactio* and the act of the Church has been grasped, and the penitent's role within this unity is seen as being caused by grace, then the semi-pelagian tone of Cyprian's teaching on satisfaction is eliminated.

7. *The Sacramental Nature of Church Penance*

We can resume what has been said above by broaching the question: does Cyprian in his theology of penance bear witness to the existence of a sacrament of penance? That church penance is not called a *sacramentum,*[136] as are baptism, confirmation and Eucharist, is irrelevant, because even these sacraments are not so called for the reason which today justifies this designation. In any event, how important the bishop's power in the granting of reconciliation was for the Bishop of Carthage is evident, for example, from Epist. 66,5. He points to the consequences of Puppian's challenge of his episcopal power with reference to the fact that very many Christians would die *sine spe salutis et pacis*. He explains this fact more precisely by saying that some would not be validly baptized and, therefore, would not receive the Spirit, while others would not be validly reconciled with the community of the Church.[137] Thus baptism and the granting of reconciliation are both fundamental acts on the bishop's part which are decisive for salvation.

The ability to perform these acts rests, according to Cyprian, on an authorization by Christ. It is a matter of an authoritative, indeed judicial, activity of the bishop which is performed by means of a visible sign, that is, by the imposition of hands and prayer. This act is decisive for salvation and thus the sinner is strictly obliged to submit himself to it. It is the cause of effects which concern grace. In today's terminology we would call such an act a sacrament. Although the comprehensive description of reconciliation which we have given still lacks elements which in today's notion of sacrament clearly distinguish the sacrament itself from signs which are associated with it, such as sacramentals, etc., these elements were no more consciously emphasized in the early Church with regard to the other sacraments, for example, in baptism as opposed to the accompanying 'ceremonies', than here in the case of the reconciliation of penance. Cyprian attributes the strictly eschatologically effective removal of sins, as he understands it, to *satisfactio* as its cause. This does not deprive the church reconciliation of its sacramental character since, on the one hand, for Cyprian the effect of this reconciliation as far as grace is concerned does not coincide simply with the remission of sins and, on the other hand, he understands the whole of penance as a unity[138] consisting of *satisfactio* and reconciliation, which parts should never be separated or thought of as being effective separately. The difference between this sacrament and baptism has already been sufficiently emphasized above. In penance there is not a simple *remissa peccatorum* because the reconciliation presupposes a *plena satisfactio* and because the complete sacrament includes this *satisfactio* as an essential element. To this extent, it can be styled, even in Cyprian's sense, as a sacrament of the remission of sins committed after baptism, even if the reconciliation and the *pax,* together with the bestowal of the Spirit which they entail, are not directed towards the immediate and full remission of sin. The sacramental character of this remission is also implicit in the fact that the *satisfactio* itself includes a co-operation on the Church's part.

8. Lasting Consequences after Complete Reconciliation?

In the later history of the Patristic development of penance the penitent still has to observe, even after his reconciliation, prescriptions and obligations which imprint the mark of penance profoundly on his subsequent life. Now did such obligations, which in time made the whole of the ancient penitential practice impracticable, exist already in the third century? In general this question has to be answered in the negative. A probable indication to this effect is the fact that at this time penance itself, at least in principle, lasted a very long time and, even more than later, was determined by the judgement of the individual bishop. The bishop could make it last until he saw that the *plena satisfactio* was reached. Later, however, there were fixed points for reconciliation, which meant that there was a general reconciliation for all those who had done penance up to a particular point of time. It was this state of affairs, rather than that existing at Cyprian's time, which prompted the suggestion that further penitential obligations might be necessary even after the reconciliation. Nevertheless already in Cyprian's time there are indications of the lasting consequences of a church penance or, better, of the fault which led up to this penance. Thus the priest Trofinus, being converted from schism, is received again in Rome only as a layman (*ut laicus communicet*) (Epist. 55,11). The same principle applies to bishops, priests and deacons who have apostasized or become schismatics and wish to do penance. Pope Cornelius, with the agreement of the bishops, already lays down the general principle that penitents, even if they have fallen into sin as lay people, should not be allowed access to the *ordinatio cleri atque sacerdotalis honor* (Epist. 67,6; 72,2). Pope Stephen and other bishops, however, appear to have been somewhat more lenient in their judgement in certain circumstances in the case of bishops who have fallen (cf. Epist. 67,5.9).

As a further 'lasting consequence' it might be mentioned that a person who has once received church reconciliation is not able to do so a second time. Nevertheless this principle is not stated explicitly in Cyprian. It is already present in the Pastor Hermae, however, and is explicitly mentioned by Tertullian as a principle for the African Church. And this is still the case later, for example in Augustine.

Thus it is without a doubt current in the middle of the third century. The fact that Cyprian himself does not mention this principle explicitly allows us to conclude that in everyday practice it did not apply to many cases which demanded his attention.[139] Indeed this principle helps us to understand why Cyprian could make the granting or the refusal of church reconciliation appear more like a disciplinary than a dogmatic question (Epist. 55,21). All the Churches refused reconciliation in this particular case. The Bishop of Carthage could believe, therefore, that a person who refused reconciliation in other cases did not necessarily have to hold a different dogmatic view on the right, authority and obligation of the Church with regard to sinners. In the struggle against Novatianism, however, he recognized that a kind of rigoristic penitential practice could exist which was to be rejected radically for dogmatic reasons. This is because the person who explains the refusal of reconciliation as the refusal of a necessary *pignus vitae,* and at the same time is convinced that the Church could grant this *pignus vitae,* implicitly teaches that the Church is obliged to give this guarantee of salvation, at least in normal cases. Cyprian did not consider how this principle could be reconciled with a refusal, albeit exceptional, of reconciliation to a repentant sinner. This refusal was linked necessarily with the once-and-for-all character of the granting of penance. The notion of a 'substitute' for a sacrament through the *votum sacramenti* was completely unknown to Cyprian. It is only with Augustine that both theoretically and explicitly a possibility of salvation is opened to a sinner who is excluded from a second church reconciliation. This is all the more noteworthy in that Augustine, throughout his whole life, could not bring himself to a clear idea on the possibility of a 'baptism of desire'.

9. *A 'Private' Sacramental Penance in Cyprian?*

A) THE QUESTION AND ITS TREATMENT

It is already difficult to pose precisely the terms of the problem with which we are now concerned at the end of this exposition of Cyprian's theology of penance. In fact, since this question arises again especially in the high Patristic age, a more precise determination of the *status quaestionis* is called for than the situation of Cyprian himself would seem to require. In general the question may be formulated as follows: in the third century is there, beside the 'public', another 'private' but sacramental[140] penance by which the Church forgives sins? This question is not as clear as it may appear at first sight, since, it may be asked, when is a sacramental penance public and when is it private? Thus in order to pose our question more precisely we need to clarify the difference between these two notions. Now this is a difficult task from both the 'liturgical' and the 'historical' viewpoints.

In earlier periods of the study of the early Church's penitential discipline from the point of view of the history of dogma 'excommunication' was regarded as something added to penance itself in the sense of a modern punishment by the Church (cf. on this point J. Grotz). At least in so far as the sinner was also reconciled with the Church, excommunication occurred in many or even in all incidents of the penitential process in the early Church. Nevertheless, according to this approach it always occurred as only accidental to the actual sacramental event. The theory has even been propounded that the sacramental 'absolution' from sin occurred at the beginning of the penitential process so that at the end of it only the excommunication, considered a mere punishment of the Church, was lifted *in foro externo*.[141] On this basis it was easy to establish the difference between public and private penance. A public penance is one which occurs between the introduction and the absolution of an excommunication, this last being considered a punishment of the Church and, therefore, concerned with the *forum externum*. In all other cases penance is 'private'.

This view of the situation is, however, certainly false. In the early Church every serious sin was considered the deprivation of full peace with the Church.[142] Reconciliation restores this peace with the Church, but it was also considered as entailing the effects of grace in the next life, the rebestowal of the Holy Spirit and, in this sense, the removal of guilt. This viewpoint of the early Church makes it impossible, therefore, to distinguish a 'public' church penance from a supposedly sacramental 'private' one by claiming that the one presupposes and revokes an 'excommunication', while the other does not.

In fact even from a modern dogmatic viewpoint it is not possible to establish the distinction in this way. For a very long time there has been an *excommunicatio latae* and one that is *ferendae sententiae* which is not connected with every sin and which does not follow necessarily from it but is appended as a subsequent punishment by the Church for certain sins, in addition to the consequences which sin naturally entails. But this practice does not supersede the view of the early Church. Even modern theology recognizes the fact of the removal of full church fellowship, the deprivation of the unrestricted participation in the visible and invisible blessings of the Church. This deprivation is entailed always and necessarily by serious sin itself and is made good only by sacramental absolution. What we are talking about is the exclusion from the Eucharist.[143] In the penitential practice of the early Church, therefore, excommunication and its removal by the granting of the *pax* is seen in its actual theological essence and precisely not as pertaining to canon law (*iure ecclesiastico*). Moreover, this point is not overlooked in today's practice of 'private' sacramental penance on the occasion of every sacramental absolution of serious sin. Thus the 'excommunication' so understood dogmatically is of no use in establishing the distinction between 'public' and 'private' sacramental penance, as if one could then use this notion historically.

In the third century 'excommunication' always (or almost always) had the effects which followed automatically from serious sin, that is, exclusion from the Eucharist. By his serious sin the sinner placed himself in the 'position of being a penitent' because at that time everyone communicated and placed the highest value on the exercise of this right. Thus the penance in the early Church which is called public by everyone should in fact be styled 'private' in the sense that it does not involve the lifting of an additional, specifically imposed punishment by the Church, that is, the liberation from an 'excommunication' in today's canonical sense. In those days it was more a question of the abolition of the connatural, albeit ecclesial too, effect of sin itself. If, therefore, this idea of excommunication is to serve as any basis at all for the distinction between the two notions under discussion, this can be only with regard to greater or lesser explicitness or solemnity of the excommunication. But how is this to be done?

For 'liturgical' reasons such a distinction is not easy simply by looking at the actual celebration of penance. The penitential practice of the early Church, which is usually called 'public', is in fact public in very many different degrees. At the same time, even today's form of administering this sacrament, which is dubbed 'private', is not entirely devoid of all public aspects. In the 'public' penitential institution of the early Church there may have been occasionally a public individual confession of the sins themselves. But it is false to maintain that such a confession, as distinct from the performance of penance itself, was necessarily or even usually public. Thus the public character of the confession cannot be legitimately considered as a criterion for distinguishing between public and private penance; it is just not always verified in those cases where everyone would speak about 'public' penance. The public character of the performance of penance, however, was so varied and subject to so many different, fluid and vague nuances that such a penance could lack practically all public character, just as today's private penance does. On the other hand, it frequently appeared no different to the consciousness of that time from the normal 'public' penance. If, for example, in Cyprian a sick person was reconciled because of the letter of a martyr, then he received the peace of the Church through the imposition of hands and he kept it when he recovered his health. Thus he appeared practically never publicly in the 'class of penitents', so that on the one hand his penance was very 'private', while on the other hand it was still nothing other than 'public', although adapted to concrete circumstances. Doubtless Cyprian was not aware that he was here granting a special sacramental penance which differed in any way from the normal church penance. If one wishes to call this instance of what is generally called 'public' church penance 'private', this is merely a question of arbitrary terminology.

Nevertheless this way of approaching our question leads easily to the impression that the Fathers of the Church themselves subscribed to two independent forms of church penance. For this reason it is better to avoid such terminology. There are enough examples from the fourth century and afterwards to show that for practical reasons the normal basic model of 'public' penance is taken so much for granted in certain cases that there is no longer even a mention of the word 'public'. And even here it is only a question of practical variations of this normal form of penance which is usually called 'public'. Even today's 'private' penance, however, has a certain public character. A sacrament, considered as a visible rite, is always by this very fact in a certain sense 'public'.

The fact that a person is making a confession and receiving absolution is even today not the object of the secret of confession and can, therefore, be easily known. The external form, such as the times of confession, the confessional in the church, etc. entails this public knowledge, at least as far as the intention to receive the sacrament of penance is concerned. It is perfectly possible to envisage a situation in which at some time and for some reason it was known that venial sins were not to be confessed. In this situation a confession in today's style (without anything otherwise being changed) would make its 'public character' real even with regard to serious sins. In general the penance of the early Church is called public when the penitent was placed in the class of penitents. Similarly there would be a private sacramental penance wherever this enlisting did not take place, irrespective of how this 'private' forgiveness of sins actually occurred. The completion of this penance itself could obviously vary a great deal. Now there certainly were classes of penitents in the early Church. Later Augustine[144] calls them the *proprie paenitentes* who have to submit themselves to the *paenitentia maior et insignior,*[145] the *paenitentia qualis agitur in Ecclesia.*[146] The consequences of belonging to the class of penitents are even fairly easy to describe: exclusion from the Eucharist, obligation to do certain works of penance even publicly, a special place at the celebration of the liturgy and even partial exclusion from it, submission to determined church penitential rituals, for example, impositions of hands, public reconciliation as well as tangible lasting consequences after reconciliation. Without a doubt this *paenitentia,* because of these consequences manifestly public in the Church, was also called *publica.*[147]

But which elements, constituting the public character of this penance, are essential to it and which, in certain circumstances, can be wanting without its ceasing to be 'public'?[148] If explicit excommunication and its abolition do not belong to these essential characteristics, since by these alone a sinner does not necessarily have to appear in the class of penitents (cf. Epist. 4,4), then what is in fact the most important element is excluded. Excommunication and its abolition constitute the most basic organizational principle of 'public' penance in the early Church. Moreover, their absence from the explicit ritual is one of the most conspicuous characteristics of today's private penance. Thus such an exclusion is not logically possible. If, however, the actual entry of the sinner into the class of penitents by his public performance of penance is stressed as being essential to the penitential state in the strict sense, then it is possible to prove the existence of a 'private penance' in the early Church (the reconciliation of heretics, the penance of the sick, the penance of clerics). In this case, this penitential process of the early Church becomes a specific form of penance clearly distinct from public penance. In the mind of the early Church itself, however, it represented only the practical applications of public penance to concrete cases and circumstances. This is clear from certain indications, such as lasting consequences of penance, the unrepeatable character of penance of the sick, etc. Thus the one notion of private penance would embrace different, otherwise unassociated elements which individually suit public penance, such as the ancient, unrepeatable penance of the sick with its lasting consequences and the (supposed) sacramental *correptio* in Augustine or even in our modern private penance.

But for penance to become public must the sinner belong to the class of penitents only *de iure* or also *de facto?* If we consider those cases in which a sinner in fact did not appear as a penitent, as in the reconciliation of a person who is dying, and in which the Fathers of the Church were conscious of conferring the usual penance,[149] it is very difficult, from both the dogmatic and the historical viewpoints, to prove the existence of a specifically private penance. This usual penance was generally 'public' and was deprived of its (greater) public character in the cases mentioned only by force of circumstances. Nevertheless, such a penance which is public juridically can in fact not be public. Moreover, it would be at least very difficult to prove that our modern 'private' penance is not 'public' in this juridical sense. This would be so, even if this notion required certain elements of even a practically public nature which no longer exist in today's penance. In our view it is even more difficult, indeed it is impossible, to prove the existence of such a private penance alongside this public penance, as we understand it, in the early Church. At that time, wherever there is evidence of a sacramental penance there is also the awareness, indeed also the explicit expression, of a reconciliation with the Church. In other words, there is the conviction that the penitent belongs *de iure* to the class of penitents and must be transferred from it into the status of a complete Christian. All this means not that the notion of a 'private' penance becomes theoretically impossible[150] but that it is not met in fact in the early Church. A very clear indication of this, at least as far as the early

Latin Church is concerned, is the awareness that reconciliation is always a reconciliation with the Church. It could be asked, however, what it is that makes a penitent in fact a member of the class of penitents, although it is difficult to find an answer to this question if one refuses to draw arbitrary distinctions which obscure rather than clarify the issue.

Against all these somewhat circumstantial considerations, it may be objected that historically there is no doubt that, at least from the seventh century onwards, when a private penance clearly distinguished from 'public' penance was indisputably accepted, these two notions were clearly distinguished from each other. This distinction between these two notions is, therefore, a historical fact and needs no further verification. It is an undisputable fact. The *paenitentia publica* and the *reconciliatio publice statuta* is clearly mentioned for the first time, in opposition to sacramental private penance, in Theodore's penitential book.[151] From this time onwards, the term *publica* is certainly no longer merely a more precise description of the one penance but a *differentia specifica* distinguishing it from another form of the umbrella notion of church-sacramental penance. On the basis of this clear historical starting-point, it should be easy to maintain convincingly the distinction between these two notions. However, in reality these historical notions are far from clear and definite. On the contrary, they contain confusedly very heterogeneous elements and have undergone considerable changes even since the seventh century. In the *paenitentiale Theodori,* for example, the notion of public penance includes explicitly the fixed day of reconciliation (*coena Domini*), the reconciliation *intra aspidem,* and indeed (normally) by the bishop, the public performance of penance,[152] together with the unrepeatable character of penance and its lasting consequences. On the other hand, it is difficult to say what Theodore understands by a penance which is not public. He does not use the term 'private'.[153] And it is obviously not possible to exclude from this notion all the characteristics of his public penance. His practice of private penance clearly places no value on the secret performance of the duties of penance and it involves a long-lasting exclusion from the Eucharist. Moreover, here also reconciliation is granted only after the performance of penance. In the ninth century even for what was explicitly called 'private' penance reconciliation was normally required on Maundy Thursday;[154] thus even this element could not have belonged specifically to the essence of public penance. In other words, it is clear that the ritual of private penance during the first centuries of its proven existence was normally still very complicated.[155] It involved a fairly large amount of public knowledge. Thus, from the historical point of view, the only characteristic of this new Anglo-Saxon 'private penance', distinguishing it from the ancient 'public' penance, is its lack of the unrepeatable character and the lasting consequences which were present in the ancient penance. But if one wishes to make such a difference the decisive distinguishing mark, is this sufficiently well expressed by the two notions 'public' and 'private'? 'Repeatable' and 'unrepeatable' penance would seem to be sufficient and indeed clearer notions. In any event, it may be asked whether the early Western Church provided a reasonable context in which a clear, concrete case for the notion of 'private' penance could be found. It is difficult to discover the normal practice of such a form of sacramental penance in the early Church. Certainly there is no question of two different forms of penance—the one private, the other public—between which one could make a free choice. It must be said, however, that the uncritical use of these two notions tends to lead almost inevitably to such a view. At least it suggests the idea that in the early Church there was a sacramental private penance which was generally available if and when a once-and-for-all, unrepeatable, 'public' penance was no longer possible. Such an idea, flowing from certain dogmatic assumptions,[156] is really based on the previous desire to prove the existence of private penance in the early Church. If, however, it is readily admitted that such a 'private' penance does not in fact alleviate substantially the dogmatic problem posed by the unrepeatable public penance, then the real use of this vague distinction for the early history of penance becomes very meagre indeed.[157] This applies even if, presupposing the corresponding development of the notion, it is possible to prove the existence of this distinction in the early Church, since the practice of denying a second sacramental penance still subsists, at least in many cases, and even in Augustine, despite his *correptio secreta*. Thus it needs to be asked why some have recourse to these notions as a support for their own theses and are not content to expound them as notions of that time, in their original meaning, and to say what people of that time understood by them.

To take our modern 'private penance' as the historical starting-point is to incur similar difficulties. This approach involves taking our modern penitential practice as the classical normal case of 'private penance' and, on this basis, attempting to determine precisely what is private and what is public penance. The 'private' character of our modern penance is made up of many different elements. The Church's act in this penance represents an ideal case of the mere *forum internum*. There is no explicit, tangible imposition and lifting of an excommunication which is expressed in the rite. The penitential duty which is imposed remains secret and its execution is not done openly. It is generally minimal and is decided by the confessor on the spot. Normally the penitent receives absolution immediately. It remains secret whether a serious sin is involved or not. There are no after-effects of this penance. There is no difference between the treatment of clerics and that of the laity. The sacramental rite is reduced to an absolute minimum. Moreover, this penance is able to be repeated. These are all the elements which make today's form of penance, as opposed to that of the early Church, appear 'private'.

But what, among all these elements, is really essential for a private penance? In fact even today there still exists the exclusion from the Eucharist, that is, excommunication in the sense of the early Church. Whether or not this is expressed in the rite of penance itself makes no difference to the fact. Even in the early Church, given certain circumstances, the public character of the performance could be very little in evidence. Even then reconciliation could be granted immediately. This was done with the awareness that it was only the adaptation of the one usual public penance to special circumstances, which shows that even this form was modelled on the penance of excommunication. In Cyprian the normal public penance has no lasting consequences. A penance could exist in merely desisting from the fault in question, that is, it was possibly minimal and insignificant, and even then reconciliation was considered as the lifting of excommunication, that is, as a shortened public penance. The fact that, in today's confessional practice, a serious fault remains a secret is due purely to the external circumstance that confessions of devotion are common, even though they are not obligatory. But this practice is irrelevant to the nature of penance and its correct celebration. Indeed the same circumstance is perfectly compatible with a public penance. When, towards the end of the early period of the Church's history, it became common for everyone to undertake penance on his death-bed, this penance lost its public defamatory character, even though this penance at the point of death was thoroughly public, as its ritual and its lasting consequences in the event of a subsequent recovery show. Thus a circumstance which is purely external and accidental to both forms of penance can make 'private' penance public, for example, if confessions of devotion were no longer practised. Similarly, a public penance can become private if it is freely undertaken by everyone. In other words, there is only one element in our actual modern private penance which clearly distinguishes it from the penance of the early Church, and which has nothing at all to do with either its 'public character' or its 'private character', and that is the fact that it is repeatable. And this element is best left with its proper name. Thus even on the basis of today's form of 'private penance', it is not possible to arrive at a useful notion of a specifically private penance.

All these considerations lead to the conclusion that, although church penance remains exactly the same in its essence, with regard to the degrees in which it is expressed publicly it is susceptible of an extraordinary number of variations. This variety of degrees and levels in the public character of penance is such that it would be purely arbitrary to dub certain forms of it 'public' and others which evince hardly any differences making them at all or only occasionally less public, on the contrary, 'private'. The Fathers of the Church were well justified, therefore, in calling the whole of church penance simply 'public'.[158] This does not mean that they simply overlooked the practical and perhaps considerable differences in the public character of this penance. If one wishes to describe, in this regard, today's penance in relation to the form of the early Church, one ought to say objectively and clearly: through a whole variety of means and for different reasons the public character of today's penitential process has become considerably restricted. This is better than saying that today public penance has been superseded by private penance. The real difference between the penance of the early Church and that of today, a difference which ought to be called by its proper name, lies in the unrepeatable character of penance in the early Church, as opposed to the repeatable character of today's penance since the early Middle Ages. This is a clear difference, intelligible both conceptually and juridically.

In today's penitential rite the change in relationship between man and the Church is no longer formally expressed and is, for the most part, no longer clearly recognized, even if, in fact, it is undoubtedly objectively present. It is unfortunate and only leads to misunderstandings when the historian of dogma today simply wishes to present the different forms of penance in the early Church as 'public' or 'private'. It would be more correct to describe the many, and not only the two, different forms in which the one penance appears, according to what they have in common and their peculiarities, and thus to determine the precise degree of their public character. This would naturally also involve discussing whether penitential practices with a very limited public character (*correptio secreta,* monastic penance, etc.) could be counted as sacramental-church penance.

If, however, an answer is sought to the badly posed question of whether the Church before the seventh century knew a sacramental 'private' penance besides the 'public' penance, then it must be in the negative. In the West at least, the only penance which was sacramental was the one unrepeatable penance which also reconciled men explicitly with the Church and which, despite the considerably different degrees in its public character in its individual instances, was always experienced as one and the same penance. Talk about a private penance, however, is apt to obscure this basic insight, even if, by drawing attention to certain notions, what it conveys is not necessarily false.

B) A LOOK BACK AT TERTULLIAN

Galtier is of the opinion that in Tertullian[159] there are several 'species' of penance which are essentially different from each other. The one is defended by the Catholics for capital sins but rejected by Tertullian in so far as it concludes with reconciliation. The other concerns the *delicta leviora.* The latter is related to the former as a *castigatio* to *damnatio.* It is a forgiveness by a bishiop for a sin which, although serious, is relatively less so than the capital sins. Thus it must be a church-sacramental penance but it cannot count as a public penance, since the *castigatio* was distinguished from the *damnatio* of public penance and does not include an excommunication.[160]

It is a fact that Tertullian speaks about two species of *paenitentia* (De pud. 2; 3; 4; 18). And the Catholics did have a *paenitentia* for the *delicta leviora.* But the two species are only introduced by Tertullian by his differentiation of penance according to its effect (*discriminatur conditio paenitentiae;* De pud. 2), that is, in so far as the one penance ends with the *venia* of church reconciliation, while the other can never reach this pardon.

But what Galtier has not proven is that the Catholics made an essential distinction between the penance for capital sins and that for the *leviora peccata*. The impression that the penance for *leviora delicta* does not begin with an 'excommunication' (De pud. 7) comes only from the fact that Tertullian in his new theory of sin, with which he attempts to underpin his rigorism, can no longer recognize the *leviora delicta* as serious sins. Thus he accommodates his interpretation of the parables of the lost drachma and the lost sheep to this view by explaining that the sinners whom they intimate are still 'alive', just as the lost sheep and the lost drachma were still in the house, which stands for the Church. This was just his way of providing the theological basis for his opinion that those guilty of capital sins, because they have lost the grace of baptism which was granted only once, cannot be received back into the Church, whereas those sinners with *leviora delicta* are still alive, that is, they have not lost the grace of baptism and, therefore, can be reconciled with the Church.[161]

The *castigatio* is here (De pud. 2) certainly opposed to the *damnatio*. But since, in this passage, the *damnatio* clearly signifies the eternal exclusion from the Church because of a *delictum irremissible,* the *castigatio* cannot mean a species of penance alongside another *paenitentia* among the Catholics which is called *damnatio* and alone entails an actual *poena*. The distinction between *castigatio* and *damnatio* is introduced in the passage by Tertullian only to facilitate the distinction between *remissibilia* and *irremissibilia*. Thus in this context *castigatio* must have the general meaning of 'correction', which is also able to be a characteristic of the public penitential process, at least in Tertullian (De paen. 11,6).[162]

Thus is not to deny that, even among the Catholics, sins were treated differently according to their gravity, in so far as the duration of the penance was concerned. But it is by no means evident that the *leviora delicta,* which they considered as serious sins entailing the loss of grace, were treated differently from capital sins. This explicit difference between sins was also introduced only by Tertullian, but, nevertheless, he also recognizes even for the *leviora delicta* an extra *gregem dari* (De pud. 7). Thus it seems more than unthinkable that such an *excommunicatio* would be imposed only as the beginning of a penance for the *leviora delicta,* whereas it would not be demanded in other cases, so that penance would at one time be 'public' and at another 'private'.

C) VARIATIONS OF THE PENITENTIAL PROCESS IN CYPRIAN

It is certain that penance in Cyprian has a great variety, as far as its duration and its public character are concerned. Thus, for example, an immediate restitution of church fellowship is envisaged for a deacon and a virgin who have lived together but without having had sexual relationship. If the case is more serious than this, however, both partners must perform a *paenitentia plena* (Epist. 4,4). There was a considerable difference between the treatment of the *libellatici* and that of the *sacrificati*. In danger of death even the *sacrificati* receive reconciliation immediately, even if their time of penance has not yet ended. Heretics, too, are reconciled immediately in certain cases (Epist. 55,11; 59,16).

But does this possibility of different forms of penance justify us in speaking about the existence of a private penance alongside public penance? Certainly Cyprian does not distinguish between these two forms verbatim, even if he may have recognized their existence. Moreover, both 'species' of the penitential process have this in common that they both include the granting of the *communicatio,* an *admitti ad Ecclesiam* (Epist. 4,4). This applies even to the milder process. Thus even this process is conceived as being accompanied by a kind of excommunication, even if this is not visibly and tangibly expressed in terms of the obligation to a long penance and a public exhomologesis.

In Epist. 16,2 and 17,2 in fact penance for the *minora delicta (peccata)* is described in the form of a 'public' penance. Obviously these *minora delicta* can only have been presented as light by comparison with actual complete apostasy. Nevertheless these *minora delicta* which are subject to public penance are still described as *non in Deum commisssa* (Epist. 17,2). On the other hand, sins *in Deum* included obviously not only apostasy but also, for example, adultery and fraud (Epist. 55,27), and this certainly not in any vague sense.[163] Rather, it applies to them in the technical sense of Epist. 17,2 since, by the use of this expression, Cyprian shows that, as far as their forgivable character is concerned, apostasy and adultery ought not to be distinguished. If, however, even the lesser sins like adultery and fraud were submitted to 'public' penance[164] it is highly unlikely that there would have existed, besides this form of penance, one which was still essentially different from it. If this were the case, it would be difficult to visualize which sins it would cover.

Obviously the *iustum tempus* for the penance (Epist. 17,2) for certain *minora delicta* could be reduced to the period of time between the sin itself and confession, followed immediately by absolution (Epist. 4,4). Since already the sin alone and not only the official declaration brings about the *excommunicatio* as the separation from the Church, the body of Christ, this period of time can be counted as the duration of the excommunication. This means that those guilty of such sins do not in fact appear among the penitents. Now, as important as this difference may seem to us, from the point of view of the practice of the early Church it was obviously a question only of a differentiation within the one penitential system. And this differentiation has its basis solely in the differing seriousness of the sins subjected to penance. Even in these cases the sinner was considered as having been at first separated from the Church. The prerequisites and the guarantees of his genuine repentance, which were demanded of him before he could be readmitted to the Church, depended upon the seriousness of the sins in question. Thus the penance prescribed must have been very varied in practice. Nevertheless the procedure always followed the same schema, that is, exclusion followed by reconciliation with the Church. There is no indication here that this difference was either conceived or considered as one between a 'public' and a 'private' penance. It is merely a question of variations of the one form of penance. It is, however, correct to say that these differences were very much in evidence in everyday practice.

Finally, it may be asked which 'kind of penance' is involved in De lapsis 28. It is here recounted that zealous Christians make an *exomologesis conscientiae* to God's priests in seeking a remedy for their small wounds. Without having actually fallen, they have nevertheless played with this idea (*quoniam de hoc vel cogitaverunt*). The unusual phrase *exomologesis conscientiae* makes it quite clear that here it is only a question of a private confession before the *sacerdotes Dei*. The meaning of this confession is the unburdening[165] of the anxious conscience (*animi sui pondus exponere*) and the prayer to the priests for a *salutaris medella* (*medellam exquirere*). Nothing more is said in this passage.[166] It is not possible to say, therefore, what the *salutaris medella* comprises. Obviously it was not clear even to the people who were asking exactly how the small guilt was to be healed. Were they, therefore, to learn from the priests precisely what they had to do themselves? The *medellam exquirere* (=inquire about) need not mean more than this. Or should the priests actually give the remedy to them? But, in this case, what did this remedy consist of? One could think of a brief penance of excommunication (cf. Epist. 4,4) or of the offering of the sacrifice for this small guilt. Even the real *lapsi* do not appear to have rejected this (Epist. 15,1; 16,2). Or was it a question of a prayer for the sinner? It is not possible to answer this question. In any case it is not possible to prove, from this text, the existence of a sacramental 'private penance'.[167] Not every priestly intercession is necessarily an actual sacrament. Even today we have a votive mass *pro remissione peccatorum*.

PART FOUR

The Tradition of the East

7

PENITENTIAL TEACHING AND PRACTICE ACCORDING TO THE DIDASCALIA APOSTOLORUM[1]

For a surprisingly long time the penitential teaching and practice of the Didascalia Apostolorum[2] received scant attention as far as the history of the sacrament of penance was concerned. It was occasionally cited in works on this subject. But, apart from E. Schwartz[3] and H. Achelis/J. Fleming,[4] who dedicate two brief pages to the penitential teaching of the Didascalia, it is really only B. Poschmann[5] who has attempted a more detailed treatment of this topic. As the studies of P. Galtier, J. Grotz and H. von Campenhausen[6] show, this has meant that the topic is once more the focal point of studies in the history of dogma. Thus it is obvious that the history of penance can in no way omit the witness of the Didascalia Apostolorum.

This 'Teaching of the Apostles' is a relatively early source for the history of penance and therefore provides valuable information, from the canonical, liturgical and dogmatic points of view, on the teaching and practice of penance in the early Church. It may even transpire that this text is, to a certain extent, unique, when compared with the other witnesses of the first half of the third century. This is because it does not recognize the sole opportunity for the performance of church penance which for many centuries was of profound significance for the history of penance in the whole of the West. These introductory remarks on the history of penance in general should serve to justify a more detailed examination of the teaching and practice of penance according to the Didascalia Apostolorum.

I. THE QUESTION OF PENANCE

According to the latest research the Didascalia Apostolorum[7] was composed in northern Syria certainly in the first half of the third century and possibly even in the first decades of that century. The penitential teaching of this writing is perfectly at home in the setting of the other views on church penance which are known to us from the third century. It is possible, as A. von Harnack and E. Schwartz believe, that, in its present form, it contains statements which are directed against the Novatians. These would naturally have to be considered additions, if the original work is taken to be prior to the Novatian controversy.[8] Nevertheless, this by no means proves that the supposed original work was in any way rigoristic. It is possible to construct an original work of this tendency for the Didascalia Apostolorum only on the false supposition of a radical rigorism which excludes those guilty of mortal sin definitively from the Church and which is in evidence wherever there is a mention of excommunication (when the contrary is not expressly stated). Consequently, every time a condemnation is pronounced as a result of sin, both conversion and the removal of this condemnation must be considered impossible.[9]

It is perfectly possible that even an early edition of the Didascalia underwent anti-Novatianist modifications.[10] These would then have been merely the expression of, and stress on, a point of view which was already present in the original writing. But it is impossible to prove the contrary. On the one hand, the teaching about the practice of excommunication in its many forms is so current throughout the whole of the Didascalia that it is impossible to assume or explain the whole teaching on the questions concerning penance as a later addition—as if originally in every single passage there were only a mention of excommunication with no consideration of the question of what was to happen to repentant excommunicates. On the other hand, there is, in fact, not the slightest trace of an early rigorism in the original writing. Thus it is scarcely possible to detect and to separate the anti-Novatian additions which are eventually present, in order to be in a position to consider the penitential teaching of the supposed original writing purely on its own. The teaching of the Didascalia is, therefore, to be considered as a whole and is to be assessed as a witness for the teaching on penance in Syria about the middle of the third century. It remains legitimate, however, to accept this witness as a whole even for the first half of the third century.

II. THE THEOLOGY OF SIN

The theology of sin in the Didascalia Apostolorum is not very precise. There are naturally different degrees of guilt, all of which do not entail eternal punishment (I 3,3–5). At the same time, sin committed after baptism which deserves the punishment of hell is usually designated simply as sin (e.g., I 3,3; II 7). Only once is there a mention of 'sin unto death' (V 9,5).[11] But this does not include every fault, since everybody sins (II 18,4.6) and is, nevertheless, able to be without 'sins' (in the sense of mortal sins) (II 18,1; II 13,1.3). Mortal sin does not only entail the punishment of hell. It is also the loss of life (I 3,11; 8,18), in so far as it expels the Holy Spirit which was received at baptism (VI 21,1.2.3.4.5.6). A person guilty of such a sin is 'mortally injured' and has an 'incurable' wound (II 63,5; VI 14,10).[12] This (mortal) sin has an ecclesial aspect: on the one hand, through his act the sinner separates himself from the Church (II 4,3; 43,2.3; 56,2),[13] indeed he is no longer a Christian (II 8,3), while, on the other hand, the Church is marred by the sin of such a 'Christian' (II 10,1; VI 14,10).[14]

III. EXCOMMUNICATION

Those guilty of mortal sin must be excommunicated (VI 14,10). Precisely who is affected here is ascertainable more by practical directives than by theoretical explanations. Obviously heretics are included in this group of sinners (VI 14,1). Nevertheless, it is generally stated that the person who has done something 'evil' (*iniquum; mala opera*) (II 8,3.4; II 9,1; 39,5) should be excommunicated. Such bad behaviour includes quarrelsome and slanderous behaviour (II 46,4), the disregarding of the excommunication of another person (III 8,5), false accusation concerning a fault deserving excommunication (II 42,5; 43,1), lying (II 39,5.6), schismatic tendencies (VI 3; 4,3–4), 'confusion, quarrels, calumnies, murmurrings, bickerings, insults, accusations, reproaches and vexations'[15] (II 43,3; cf. 43,2; 32,3).[16]

As is obvious, the circle of sins which call for the penance of excommunication is very wide. There is no mention of a narrowly defined category, along the lines of the 'triad of sins'.[17] If excommunication is simply the most effective pedagogical means which the bishop has, but one which must be applied judiciously and only after the less drastic means of correction has failed (II 41,3–9), then it must be appropriate for all sins which are in any way serious but which do not belong to the 'small imperfections' of the just (II 18,5). Also those people are to be 'avoided' who have become guilty of offenses which occasion conflict with the civil penal law (V 2,I–2). Thus they are also excommunicated officially by the Church.

Not to appear at the celebration of the liturgy was tantamount to the destruction of the 'body of Christ' (II 59,1); thus it could be concluded that those people who habitually absented themselves from the liturgy were officially excluded from the 'body of Christ'. Similarly, the *condemnatio* by the whole community which the person who curses his fellow-Christians incurs (II 32,3) ought also to be considered an excommunication.

In the passage IV 5–8 there is a fairly long consideration of the question of the person from whom the bishop ought not to accept alms. The section ends with the conclusion that nothing ought to be accepted from those who are excommunicated until they once more become full members of the Church (IV 8,3; cf. also 6,9). Thus the sinners who are here rejected as givers of alms must refer not merely to pagans but also to Christians who, through the sins mentioned, have incurred excommunication.

The description of the sins liable for excommunication is, therefore, very vivid: to imprison a person unjustly, to abuse slaves and the poor, sexual offences, misuse of authority on the part of civil rulers, the fabrication of idols, the procuration of false testimony before the court by lawyers and witnesses, fraud in working with precious metal, the falsification of weights and measures, the diluting of wine, predicting the future through dreams, murder, participation in capital punishment, unlawful soldiery, usury, idolatry, theft, etc. This list evinces great similarities with the catalogue of professions and occupations which, according to Hippolytus, exclude a man from the catechumenate.[18] It is, therefore, only logical that such sins should be liable to excommunication. In fact it seems that elsewhere there was less willingness to extend this list than there was in the Didascalia, especially where, as in the West, the possibility of only one penance was the clear norm. According to II 38, it may be assumed that excommunication was generally applied wherever the gradually intensified exhortation of the bishop, according to Matthew 18:15–17, remained ineffective, and that it was basically appropriate (when there was no sign of improvement) wherever the bishop could meaningfully intervene with either exhortation or reprimand.[19] Origen's problem, namely, that even in the absence of improvement one could not excommunicate in all the cases where the evangelical procedure of reprimand was necessary, is not yet found in the Didascalia. It is much quicker in its use of excommunication, and is able to be so because—as we shall see later—it knew nothing of a unique opportunity for reconciliation.

There are various reasons for excommunication: allowing the person guilty of mortal sin to remain in the Church taints it (II 10,1) and constitutes a danger for the morale of Christians (II 10,1.2; 17,4; 43,5); the exclusion, on the other hand, effects a salutary fear in the other Christians (II 17,5; 49,4; 50,4).

The actual carrying out of the exclusion is fairly complicated. It would appear that, in fact, a distinction has to be made between two events which here may be called the real and the liturgical excommunication.[20] The justification for this distinction will appear in the following exposition which attempts to situate the unconnected individual data of the Didascalia in their proper place. This reconstruction is itself justified in so far as it affords an understanding of the individual data and avoids the many superficial repetitions which a continuous reading would inevitably entail. But this procedure is justified above all by the way it inserts the penitential teaching of the Didascalia, especially with regard to its strictness, in the context of the other data known to us from this time.

1. The Real Excommunication

The *real* 'excommunication' has its first step—and this would also have been its original form—in the voluntary withdrawal of the sinner from the liturgical and social life of the community; he does this either because in his new religious and moral situation he no longer places any value on such a participation or because he is aware of the interior and exterior contradiction in his relationship to the Church and therefore avoids the liturgy (II 10,3). All this implies a long self-exclusion from the Church.

It can also happen that, in the case of a less 'tactful' person (*inerubidus:* II 10,4) who, despite his fault, remains undisturbed in the Church, the initiative has to come from the community. After all, the bishop exercises a certain supervision over the behaviour of the Christians entrusted to him (II 6,4; 5,2; 18,7; 20,2–5; 21,2; 37,1–3, etc.). He is supported in this task by the deacons (II 17,2; 28,6; 44,3 f.; 57,6; 58,1), while the co-operation of the laity in this regard (through advice, accusation, etc.), although it was obviously customary, was rather underplayed because in practice it inevitably led to strife and unrest in the community (II 37,2–3; 42,1–6; 47,3). Thus a bishop could exclude a Christian sinner *motu proprio* if he had not separated himself from the church community of his own accord (II 10,4, etc.). Such an exclusion obviously had to have a public character. To begin with, it would often be preceded by an accusation on the part of other members of the community which would demand an impartial, careful and lenient verdict, in order to avoid an unjust excommunication. This care was also required in order that unjust accusations which derived only from personal animosity could be energetically counteracted, even eventually with the excommunication of the accuser (II 42; 43,1; 49,3–4; 48,1–3; 56,2). If in this process it is established that there is an objective reason for an expulsion, then the bishop has to effect the real excommunication: he reprimands the sinner in the assembly of the community and expels him from it (II 10,4–5). This judicial sentence (II 11,2; 6,11) of an unerring bishop (II 6,4) could be accepted by the person who is expelled repentantly and sorrowfully (II 10,5) or even obstinately.[21] Since in the individual case it is in no way established whether and when the sinner would be able to be readmitted into the community of the Church, at this moment a later reconciliation would still be unsure. This is because it is not at all clear either that the excommunication to be imposed would be accepted repentantly by the sinner or that he would in fact reform himself. All that is certain is the general principle that a possibility for reconciliation must be offered to repentant sinners.[22]

It is also obvious that this excommunication was, first and foremost, a matter of church discipline. Indeed, it must have frequently happened that such a real excommunication took place in the sinner's absence, simply because the latter did not appear. The reason for the sinner's voluntary absence, however, need not be his religious indifference. It could very well be the Christian's sorrow and real penitence (II 10,3), making him decide to announce himself in the Church again only when he has actually reformed himself and therefore has eradicated the original cause for the excommunication. Nevertheless, even in such a case as this, for perfectly comprehensible theological[23] and pastoral[24] reasons, the repentant sinner is not simply 'forgiven' his excommunication. This doubtless explains why the real excommunication which was practically nonexistent was compensated liturgically and an attempt was made to prelude the already possible reconciliation with at least a short, more ceremonial period of penance, so that excommunication and reconciliation did not coincide.

It even appears that there is in the Didascalia already that stage in the development of the penitential process[25] at which even the person who had previously been really formally excommunicated was submitted to the subsequent liturgical excommunication just mentioned. But this development will come as no surprise to anyone conversant with the laws of liturgical progress. In any case it is the best explanation of the two to seven weeks of the period of penance mentioned in II 16,2: what is meant there is not the actual time of penance and conversion[26] but a more liturgical-ceremonial interval between the liturgical excommunication and reconciliation which was naturally characterized by prayer, fasting and solitude (II 16,2). Thus this time limit does not prove an exception to the general penitential practice of that century and one must discount Connolly's argument, according to which the Didascalia shows signs of a twofold penitential practice.[27] At the same time, this interpretation of the brief time limit of II 16,2 confirms the existence of two distinct kinds of excommunication in the Didascalia.[28]

2. *The Liturgical Excommunication*

The precise procedure for the *liturgical* excommunication is laid down in II 16,1–2.[29] According to this passage, the bishop summons the repentant sinner first of all into the church assembly; at this point the sinner himself is actually outside the Church, even though he is already repentant, that is, he has already done penance and is still doing it. Thus he is able to be called in and examined concerning his worthiness for readmission to the Church (II 16,2). Now this makes sense only if he has not just fallen into the sin for which he has been expelled from the Church's fellowship. Next the penitent confesses his guilt within the community (II 50,4), begs forgiveness and promises that he will mend his ways (II 16,4). Then he is examined as to whether he has really already done penance (II 50,4a) and is still doing it and therefore whether he basically deserves reconciliation. The bishop admonishes and exhorts the penitent and gives him instructions about the following short penitential period of a few weeks, during which the penitent has to pray, fast and be alone. At the same time the bishop determines the precise length of this penitential period (two to seven weeks), according to the seriousness of the penitent's guilt. After this the sinner is dismissed and is to be considered by every one as an outsider.[30] It would appear that this dismissal is itself expressed by the penitent's being led ceremonially out of the church (by the bishop, deacons or laity ?), since there is a mention of a subsequent return into the church. After the penitent had been thus ostracized, the whole community would (sometimes) have ratified the bishop's sentence.[31] Finally, a general prayer was said for the penitent. With this the act of liturgical excommunication comes to an end. From now on the sinner is 'bound' not only by his own sinful condition (II 21,1; VI 19,3) but also body and soul through the visible act of the official Church, exercising its heavenly power (II 34,4; cf. also II 11,2 with II 10,4–5; 21,1).

The separation of the penitent from the Church during the penitential period just mentioned[32] is, however, only a relative one. If the bishop did not bother about the penitent during these weeks, it is obvious that the salvation of the latter's soul would be seriously jeopardized (II 21,3). Since the bishop is called to bear the burden of other people's sins (II 25,7–9.12), as a mediator between God and men (II 25,7; 26,4; 35,3), so he must look after the penitent and help him in his penance (II 21,2; 40,2): he must visit him, talk to him, trust him and lead him to complete conversion. At the same time the penitent must also take part in the liturgy, even if, like the catechumens, he remains excluded from the celebration of the Eucharist (II 39,6; 40,1; VI 14,1).[33]

3. The Effects of Excommunication

The juridical excommunication, expressed by the bishop, is not a mere measure of the Church's temporal discipline. By this excommunication the sinner is excluded from the Church. But this Church is God's vineyard (I praef.), the living and life-giving mother of the faithful (II 61,4), the bearer of the Holy Spirit (VI 14,7), the body of Christ (II 59,1), outside of which there is no salvation (II 20,5; 21,7.8; 47,3). This means that the person who is legitimately excommunicated is bound body and soul by a heavenly and divine authority (II 34,4), he has lost life and eternal glory and is shameful in men's eyes and guilty before God (II 47,3).

With regard to the effect of an excommunication which was either inflicted or upheld illegitimately, the Didascalia appears to be hesitant in its view. In one passage it stresses that such a measure has no validity before God (II 48,2–3) and works only to the detriment of the salvation of the person who excommunicates illegitimately (II 48,5). On the other hand, it is also stated that an illegitimate excommunication (or the refusal of reconciliation) involves more harm for the person who is excommunicated than is caused by the murder of a just man, since such an excommunication thrusts the person who is expelled from the Church into hell (II 21,7 f.; 56,2). What this second statement certainly shows is how profoundly convinced the author of the Didascalia was of the other-worldly effect which is, in principle, connected with an excommunication.

IV. RECONCILIATION

Provided that they are repentant, all those who have been excommunicated can be reconciled with the Church again, since God forgives all repentant sinners (II 12,1–3; 13,4; 14,1–3; 14,11; 15; 16; 18,1–3.7; 20,2–11; 21; 23; 24, etc.). Even idolatry, murder, adultery and heresy find *τόπος μετανοίας* (II 23,1; 24,3; VI 14,1).[34] The idea that God and the Church could treat the repentant sinner differently, that is, that God could grant forgiveness while the Church still had to refuse reconciliation, is totally unknown to the Didascalia. The one forgiveness necessarily calls for the other. The only unforgivable sin is the obstinate rebellion against God (*ἁμαρτάνειν ἐκ παρατάξεως*) (II 23,2), as well as the obdurate perseverance in heresy or unbelief

(VI 14,2–7), interpreted as a sin against the Holy Spirit—in other words, actual unrepentance.

1. The Rite

As we have already seen, the rite of reconciliation takes place several weeks after the liturgical excommunication. It consists of a reception of the penitent by the bishop before the assembled community (*recipe eum*), the episcopal imposition of hands[35] accompanied by the prayer of the whole community (*tota Ecclesia pro eo orante ei manus impone*), and the reinstatement of the penitent in his previous place in the Church (*ac deinde permitte ut in Ecclesia sit*) (II 18,7),[36] where he is able once more to take part in the celebration of the Eucharist with the community and the bishop.[37]

By analogy with the procedure for baptism, we need to distinguish the actual place of reconciliation from that of the celebration of the liturgy. Otherwise it is not possible to understand the *introducere* (II 41,2) which follows the imposition of hands.

2. The Meaning of the Rite

Now how is this external service of church reconciliation[38] to be understood? The Didascalia is clearly aware of the parallel of this rite with the form of initiation (II 41,2). A part of this parallel is perfectly comprehensible and presents no difficulty at all: after baptism *and* after the penitential imposition of hands, both of which occur outside the actual precincts of the church (however one may visualize this location at the time of the Didascalia), the newly baptized person or the reconciled penitent is introduced into the actual place where the liturgy is celebrated so that he can take part in the subsequent celebration of the Eucharist.[39]

In both cases it is a question of the same event having its basis in the fact that the preceding rite has made the person a fully legitimate participant in the worship of God. This does mean, however, that, in the case of baptism, the *whole* of the rite of initiation, as it was required at this time for access to the celebration of the Eucharist (that is, including today's Confirmation[40]), must have preceded this introduction. Thus, following the parallel just mentioned, the imposition of hands of reconciliation in penance corresponds to baptism and Confirmation. 'Baptism' here means the whole of the rite of sacramental initiation.

But what is the precise import of the parallel in this respect? To begin with, the text states only that the penitent receives the imposition of hands at the place of baptism.[41] Accordingly, the comparison lies in the effect (the communication of the Spirit) despite the difference of the rite itself. In other words, it is important to notice that, according to the precise wording of the expression, the Holy Spirit is not bestowed in the penitential imposition of hands *in the same way* as in baptism.[42] Rather, *at the place of* the baptismal rite an imposition of hands is administered which has the same effect, namely, the bestowal of the Spirit. This is the only way to understand the sentence: *aut per manus impositionem aut per baptismum accipiunt participationem Spiritus Sancti.* Moreover, it should not be forgotten that in the Didascalia the once-and-for-all possibility of baptism[43] is a self-evident principle (VI 12,2). Thus the penitential imposition of hands is not envisaged here as the formal repetition of the rite of initiation or of one of its parts. The parallel—in so far as it is apparent—consists only in an identity of the effect of baptism and the penitential imposition of hands. The Didascalia, as opposed to the Constitutiones Apostolorum,[44] does not stress that baptism also involves an imposition of hands by which the Spirit is communicated. It does not give the slightest hint that the penitential imposition of hands could be a repetition of the imposition of hands in confirmation, considered either materially or formally. Indeed, such a repetition of the imposition of hands in confirmation is rather excluded both by the once-and-for-all possibility of baptism and by the opposition which the Didascalia emphasizes between the two rites. The passage in II 41,2, *Quemadmodum igitur gentilem baptizas ac postea recipis, ita et huic manum impones . . . ac deinde eum introduces . . .*, does not contradict the opposition just mentioned. The *et* here does not stress that the hand is imposed as in baptism. It merely underlines the general parallel between the two rites (baptism and penance) with regard both to a man's access to the liturgy (cf. II 41,1) and to the communication of the Spirit. The *et* requires no other explanation than this parallel (cf. Connolly 104,21).

Obviously there is also an imposition of hands in baptism; but it is incorrect to hold that it is precisely on this point that the Didascalia sees the parallel in question. Otherwise, it would be completely impossible to understand why the baptismal imposition of hands is never mentioned, whereas *baptism* is mentioned three times. Now if the author of the Didascalia already considered the imposition of hands after baptism as an independent part which, as such, does not belong essentially and necessarily to initiation (either because the actual bestowal of the Spirit took place through an anointing as at confirmation or because the imposition of hands had already become to be considered as totally independent from the actual baptism), then he would naturally have been 'free' to adduce this rite as formally identical (as a repetition of 'confirmation') or at least as materially so (as applicable to another purpose) in another place—in the present instance, therefore, with regard to reconciliation. But these assumptions are not verified in the case of the Didascalia, since otherwise it could not be said that *baptism* communicates the Holy Spirit or that it is communicated *in baptism* by the imposition of hands. If, therefore, the imposition of hands after baptism still belongs essentially to the one initiation and is thereby unrepeatable, then the Didascalia could not consider the penitential imposition of hands as a repetition of this post-baptismal imposition of hands.

Nevertheless, the question of the meaning of the penitential imposition of hands is not yet actually answered. If reconciliation was conceived as a parallel to baptism (if only in the sense explained above), then it is possible that the imposition of hands of confirmation after baptism served as a model for a similar rite in reconciliation, simply because in both cases it was a matter of expressing the communication of the Spirit. But is the imposition of hands of confirmation after baptism the only possible model which could have served in the production of the penitential imposition of hands? In fact there is in the Didascalia yet another imposition of hands, associated with an anointing of the head by the bishop (III 12,2–3),[45] an *ungere in manus impositione,* and one which occurs *before* baptism. In accordance with the other data of the history of the liturgy, this anointing must be seen as an exorcism.[46] The connection of anointing and imposition of hands in this instance does not necessarily exclude the possibility of a parallel with the penitential imposition of hands. In fact in Origen also the rite of reconciliation appears to have been connected with an anointing. In any case, later in the East such a connection was common. It is difficult to prove, despite the silence of the text on this point, that this connection could not have been the real background for the teaching of the Didascalia.[47] Nevertheless, it is not possible to prove this assumption positively. In the Didascalia it is the anointing that is clearly emphasized in this exorcism before baptism. Thus it is rather unlikely that an eventual imposition of hands employed in connection with the exorcism before baptism could have been singled out as the model for the penitential imposition of hands.

We are left, therefore, with the imposition of hands after baptism, to which the Didascalia ascribes the communication of the Holy Spirit (II 32,3; 33,1; 33,2; VI 7,2).[48] Here there is no mention of an anointing.[49] Now the penitential imposition of hands is also considered as a communication of the Holy Spirit—and indeed without mention of an anointing. It follows that, in all probability, the Didascalia intends the penitential imposition of hands to be understood as an imitation (not as a formal repetition!) of the imposition of hands of confirmation. In other words: according to the Didascalia, the rite of reconciliation is an imposition of hands because, and in so far as, this is a gesture which bestows the Spirit, and not because it has a healing character (i.e., is an exorcism). Obviously this does not mean that it is only the imposition of hands in confirmation, considered as a rite conferring the Spirit, that was the unique model for the creation of the rite of reconciliation. The mere fact that the imposition of hands as a gesture of the communication of the Spirit is not the prerogative of confirmation[50] makes this impossible. Moreover, this symbol is so old and self-evident and appropriate that it imposes itself wherever it is a question of the bestowal of the Spirit. Nevertheless, after all that has been said above, it is obvious that a parallel was perceived between the imposition of hands of confirmation and the penitential imposition of hands, in so far as both communicate the Holy Spirit. This is not only a simple fact which is stated explicitly in II 41,2. The expression, *per impositionem manus . . . accipiunt* (in penance) *participationem Spiritus Sancti* could always be understood by synecdoche; that is, the imposition of hands is, in itself, a prayer of the bishop which helps the penitent to purify himself from his sins and is, therefore, merely a penitential rite at the conclusion of the penitential process which itself ends with the renewed possession of the Spirit. If, however, our explanation is the correct one, then the imposition of hands is intended precisely as the communication of the Spirit and expresses the fact that this possession of the Spirit is not only the immanent effect of the sinner's own penance but is granted to him by the Church along the lines of initiation.

3. The Theological Meaning of Reconciliation

We must now turn to the theological meaning of reconciliation and its rite. The bishop represents almighty God and, according to Matthew 18:18, has the power to forgive sins (II 18,2). The 'loosing' by virtue of this scriptural text occurs in the remission of sins (*solve per remissionem:* II 18,2). This heavenly and divine authority frees not only the body—as the power of kings would do—but also souls (II 34,4). It is worth noting that in the Didascalia the notions of binding and loosing clearly have the double meaning which they have in the New Testament in Matthew. Thus binding and loosing are to be understood both as the imposition and relaxation of a generally obligatory norm and as the imputation and lifting of an individual state of guilt.[51] The bishop undertakes the lifting of personal guilt 'in God's place' (II 18,2). It is through the bishop that the Redeemer says to the sinner: Your sins are forgiven you (II 20,9), and the bishop grants the ἄφεσις from sins (II 18,1.2.7). Thus this authority of loosing—in so far as there is a question of explicitly stressed moments—is understood as 'binding in heaven', that is, as a direct if, naturally, representative remission of guilt before God, not however as a 'loosing' as the bond of guilt imposed by the Church 'on earth' which has a subsequent heavenly effect. The same conclusion follows from the teaching that the bishop bestows the Spirit in the same way through his imposition of hands in reconciliation as he does in baptism (II 41,2).[52] Here baptism and penance are paralleled not only in their effect (in such a view the sinner's personal penance could still be seen as the decisive moment), but also the bishop's imposition of hands (therefore the act of the Church) is paralleled with baptism, with the result that the urgently demanded penance of the sinner himself appears more like a precondition[53] for the bishop's announcement that the penitent's sins are remitted. This is an anticipation of part of the Scotist theory of penance.[54]

Naturally this does not mean that the ecclesial aspect of penance is simply lacking. Grave guilt entails radically and necessarily the separation from the Church. And the exercise of the power to forgive sins as God's representative is always seen as an act in which the penitent is again reconciled with the Church (II 18,7; 20,4.10–11; 24,2; 33,3; 43,1; IV 8,3; VI 14,1). Nevertheless, this readmission into the Church is seen more as the consequence of the remission of sins and healing through the bishop than as the means of the remission of sins and the communication of the Spirit: *sanans suscipe:* II 42,2.[55] In any case in the Didascalia the authoritative forgiveness of sins is independent of incorporation into the Church as a means of salvation. Thus its sacramental character is more clearly attested here than elsewhere: the parallel with baptism, the teaching on the bishop's representative power to forgive sins in God's name and the idea of the communication of the Spirit as an initiation express with all the clarity desirable not only the sacramental nature of penance as a whole but also that of the bishop's part in the penitential process.

At the same time, there is nothing to indicate that the correction and exhortation of a sinner by the bishop which is private or carried out before two witnesses but which does not include an excommunication has a sacramental character and, therefore, represents a 'private' sacramental penance (II 37,1–3; 38,1–3). In this case it is a question of those doctrinal and educative measures which the bishop as doctor and educator of the faithful ought not to withhold from the sinner even in the penance of excommunication, without, however, in any particular case having a sacramental character in themselves. They are obligations which pertain to the bishop's simple pastoral charge (cf., e.g., II 5,2.3; 20,2; 41,3–8, etc.). The bishop even shares this pedagogical and intercessory activity with the laity, as, for example, widows, who fast together with the penitents (III 8,1–3).

4. *The Repeatable Character of Reconciliation*

Now is this forgiveness of sins by the imposition of hands explained by the Didascalia as a possibility which is presented once and for all or not? It is never clearly stated that it is possible only once. Nevertheless, this alone is not sufficient proof that the author of this work is unaware of such a once-and-for-all possibility. One has only to remember that in Origen's numerous and detailed views on penance it is only once mentioned that this penance is possible only once to realize that the silence of any text on this question can hardly be construed as an adequate argument that this principle was not held in the circle represented by the text in question. Certainly a declaration on this subject should be expected in a book which considers thematically questions of church discipline, especially here, since the detailed considerations of the Didascalia offer sufficient opportunity to discuss such a principle. There is frequent stress on the fact that sins can be forgiven before God and also before the Church, and those who contest such a church reconciliation as impossible are often taken to task. Thus it would have been appropriate at least once to refer to the fact that church reconciliation is possible only once, in order to convince the sinner that he should not count on the Church's unlimited leniency and to demonstrate to the rigorist that his strictness is understood. For these reasons the silence of the Didascalia is surprising, to say the least.

In one passage, however, there is a positive hint of the possibility of a repeated reconciliation. In II 43 there is mention of the treatment of a troublemaker in the community who, by his false accusations against a fellow-Christian before the bishop, causes strife in the community and who even, through his unjust incriminations, causes the bishop to excommunicate the person who is wrongly accused (II 42). Now, for his part, the bishop must react against this miscreant with excommunication (II 43,1). If he subsequently mends his ways and does penance for a certain time (*aliquod tempus*), then he should be readmitted into the Church (II 43,1). If, afterwards, he shows, however, that he is continuing his bad behaviour, then he must be excluded from the church again (II 43,2). This measure is justified on a broad basis and in detail: this sinner brings only harm and shame to the Church as long as he lives in the fellowship of the Church. In reality he is not a member of the Church, even though he appears to belong to it. Just as a doctor amputates superfluous fingers and excises cancer without depriving the body of anything but only effecting its own perfection, so also the bishop must confidently exclude the troublemaker a second time since the Church can only thereby benefit (II 43,2–4). That he cannot be readmitted again after this second excommunication is not explicitly stated, but it is intended.[56] Otherwise, the long justification of the renewed exclusion would not make sense; since it is more than obvious that the repetition of a fault which is the reason for a just excommunication, in view of an explicit promise of reform (II 43,1), is a still more serious reason for an exclusion. The expression, *Cum enim bis ex Ecclesia egressus fuerit, recte abscissus est* (II 43,4), is therefore to be understood in the sense of a permanent exclusion. This does not constitute a contradiction to the penitential principle of the Didascalia, since in this case the sinner is obviously unrepentant and obstinate; that is, the conditions which are always necessary for reconciliation appear to be permanently lacking. Now if this *permanent* exclusion is specifically justified, and this at considerable length and in detail for this particular case, then the author of the Didascalia cannot be aware of a principle which self-evidently, generally and without exception would preclude the readmission of a person who has been excommunicated a second time. Otherwise, he would only have to recall this principle of the *μία μετάνοια*, and the permanent exclusion envisaged here would have a far better justification as an individual example than the one which it has in fact. Thus it must be concluded that the Didascalia does not appear to know the principle of the one *metanoia*.[57]

This observation is by no means as unlikely as it may appear at first sight. Wherever we meet the contrary principle in the second and third centuries it is clearly derived from the Pastor Hermae: in Africa with Tertullian or in the area of Alexandria with Clement and Origen, who both cite Hermas explicitly and even treat him as canonical scripture. The Syrian author of the Didascalia, however, certainly knew nothing of the Latin literature. According to Connolly,[58] neither has he undergone the literary influence of Clement of Alexandria and Origen. Moreover, this applies to a greater extent to all questions of church discipline which are less easily changed than ideas. Although the author of the Didascalia may indeed have known Hermas (according to Connolly),[59] the allusions to him in this writing are, nevertheless, fairly slight.[60] But a knowledge of Hermas still does not mean an acceptance of his penitential principle. If one does not start out from the false supposition that Hermas himself represents an unheard-of innovation from strictness towards leniency, so that the once-and-for-all penance after baptism was already to be considered a concession,[61] then there is no longer any argument to the effect that a greater leniency than that found in Hermas is unlikely as long as it is not demonstrated by the strictest proofs which remove all doubt. The difference between the Didascalia and the Alexandrian tradition from the point of view of the liturgy of penance has already been noted. Thus it is not at all unlikely that this difference applies also to penitential discipline, that is, that the once-and-for-all possibility of penance after baptism is unknown to the Didascalia. Further observations confirm this impression that in fact the Didascalia does not know the one *metanoia*.

Achelis/Flemming (p. 306 f.) remark that there is no trace of the triad of unforgivable sins[62] in Syria according to the Didascalia and the Constitutiones Apostolorum. Although this is correct, this observation must be seen in its proper perspective. The striking point about this fact is not that in the Didascalia there are no unforgiveable sins but that the group of sins which are subject to excommunication is hardly limited in any way and, above all, is less determined than elsewhere. Where, however, the principle of the unrepeatable character of church forgiveness is in force the group of sins which are subject to excommunication must, in practice, be defined as narrowly as possible, if one wishes to avoid falling into insoluble difficulties in all too many cases where the penitential discipline is concerned. In fact it is remarkable that wherever the principle of the once-and-for-all penance is in force there is in practice the tendency to submit to excommunication more or less only the triad of sins and similar offences also punishable by civil law, although in theory there is the awareness that the circle of mortal sins is somewhat wider. All these problems do not burden the Didascalia. It is much freer with excommunication, treating the three capital sins no differently from the essentially lighter offences and, *vice versa,* punishing the latter as capital sins, that is, with excommunication. Given this wide possibility of excommunication, it is difficult to conceive that a relapse after an already completed penance did not occur more frequently than where in practice only the most serious offences were punished with a very lengthy penance of excommunication. In view of the great emphasis on the possibility of forgiveness for repented guilt in the Didascalia, a person who has relapsed with regard to a slight fault can hardly be refused a new reconciliation in principle,[63] provided he has subsequently submitted himself to excommunication.

5. Parallels to the Ban Practice of the Synagogue

The whole of the practice of excommunication in the Didascalia, down to the slightest details and more clearly than elsewhere, has the characteristics of the ban practice of the synagogue, although both the theological background and the purpose of the two institutions remain quite different. Given the spiritual and geographical proximity of the Didascalia to Judaism and its community life[64] (despite its controversy with Judaism) this affinity is not surprising. The parallels[65] between the penitential practice of the Church, as this is presented in the Didascalia, and the synagogal practice of the ban are clear: a consequence of the *nezipha* (reprimand) and the *nidduy* (simple ban) was that the person so punished had to 'withdraw to his own house and in this way manifest his sorrow for what he has done'.[66] Similarly, the bishop prescribes for one who is excommunicated: *ut humiliter secum maneat et oret rogetque in diebus ieiunii.* It is striking that here the co-operation of the community in the penance is not confined, as it is elsewhere, to prayer for the sinner and assent to the reconciliation by the bishop, but is also expressed 'liturgically' in the excommunication itself by a general ceremony of indignation and condemnation on the part of the whole community: *Irascantur ei et iudicium de eo faciant* (II 16,I; similarly II 32,3). This also has an even more impressive parallel in the synagogal ban.[67] The reasons for the exclusion, from the very nature of the case, obviously often vary between the two communities, but even here there are remarkable parallels. For instance, a person who describes his fellow man as 'slave' may be banned.[68] The Christian community 'judges' solemnly the person who insults his brother by calling him 'fool' and *raca* (II 32,3). The verdict of the synagogue in a contention between two Jews which is itself a civil matter may be imposed by the ban.[69] In the Didascalia, too, an actual civil contest between two Christians, in which the bishop is the arbiter, can end with the excommunication of one of the parties.[70] To the principle that the person who bans unjustly himself incurs the ban[71] there corresponds in the Christian context the instruction that anyone who allows another person to be excommunicated because of false accusations before the bishop must be excommunicated (II 42,5; 43,1).[72] It is also noticeable that both in Judaism and in the Didascalia the incidence of exclusions from the community is very great.[73]

These examples, which could be multiplied,[74] are explicable, in part, by the very nature of the matters which they involve, and do not suppose even a mediate dependence on the one side or the other. There are some aspects, however, which are explicable only on the assumption that the practice of the synagogal ban has been applied in its external form to church excommunication, as this is represented in the Didascalia, without many elaborations, since the time of the early Church. Now the ban of the synagogue, either in its simple form (*nidduy, shamta*) or in its accute form (*cherem*), is not possible only once. Even less is it insoluble.[75] Indeed, from the very nature of the case, it could hardly be otherwise. *Every* ban is able to be dissolved, therefore. In view of the affinity of the Didascalia's excommunication practice with these Jewish practices, it is difficult to believe that excommunication could be lifted only once, especially since this excommunication is applied frequently and lightly and leniency is preached with regard to sinners.

What is more, the Constitutiones Apostolorum do not appear to recognize a once-and-for-all granting of reconciliation. In Const. II 40,1 the 'second stumble', which is treated exactly as the first, cannot really mean a second stumble before the first undertaking of penance.[76] Now if the Constitutiones Apostolorum do not know of one *metanoia,* then it is also unlikely that the Didascalia was aware of it.

An *argumentum e silentio* always presents difficulties. Where, however, a practice is not known it cannot be expected that its absence should be explicitly noted. At the same time, it may be expected that in a work of church order or church law such an important principle should be mentioned if in fact it were in force. On the supposition that the principle of the once-and-for-all possibility of church penance was never generally in force in the East, it is possible to explain much more easily why the passage from public church penance to sacramental private penance was able to be achieved in a less striking and a less reflexive way than in the West.

The Didascalia gives us, therefore, an excellent picture of the nature of penance in the Eastern Church in the first half of the third century. There is an elaborate penitential liturgy, a clear consciousness of the sacramental character of public church penance, as well as an application of this penance to practically all the kinds of sin which we today would call 'serious' (at least if we prescind from mere sins of thought). There is no mention of a sacramental private penance without excommunication existing alongside the public church penance of excommunication. In this respect the Didascalia still belongs completely to the earliest period of the history of penance. At the same time, it does not recognize the once-and-for-all character of this church penance of excommunication. It provides, therefore, testimony to the effect that the Western practice, emanating from Hermas, of granting penance only once cannot simply and without proof be presented as the 'more ancient' practice. The parallels with the synagogal practice of the ban also support this. It follows from this, as indeed a close examination of Hermas would also show, that the unrepeatable possibility of penance after baptism in the Western Church represents a canonical measure which was undertaken for pastoral reasons, and that it does not derive from a dogmatic principle. The Didascalia also shows very clearly that the assumption of a linear 'evolutionary' principle for the history of penance, according to which the development proceeds inevitably from a definite strictness towards an ever-increasing leniency, with progressive concessions made to sin, is not justified on historical grounds.

8

THE PENITENTIAL TEACHING OF ORIGEN

With Origen the history of penance enters the realm of theology in the proper sense of this term. He is the first theologian of the Church in the strict sense, that is, one who attempts to organize the data of the transmitted revelation into a powerful 'system'. This necessary and, in the final analysis, inevitable enterprise is undertaken with the explicit intention of making more comprehensible the Word which has been revealed and is transmitted within the Church. Nevertheless, this approach incurs the risk that the structure of the system, together with the basic notions which are used as explanations, may dominate and violate the transmitted doctrine to be believed. A correct appreciation of Origen's teaching on penance presupposes an acquaintance with some of his own fundamental methodological preconceptions. It is for this reason that we begin this study with a brief consideration of his theology as a whole.[1]

I. TEACHING ON PENANCE, THEOLOGY AND THE CHURCH

Origen does not wish to be anything other than a man of the Church. Consequently, what is prescribed by the gospel and taught by the Church are, for him, the inviolable and self-evident norm of the whole of his thinking.[2] Although he offers a more profound explanation and understanding (*gnosis*) of the transmitted teaching of the faith and of the Scriptures which must remain inaccessible to the majority of ordinary Christians, he does not do so by appealing to a secret tradition, after the manner of the Gnostics. Rather, it is here a matter either of a theologico-speculative interpretation of this doctrine to be believed, which doctrine still remains an obligatory norm for this explanation, or of a consideration of questions which were previously open. It can, nevertheless, also be a question of the gradual, ever-ascending search for that inaccessible 'truth' which lies behind, as in its 'parable', the immediate meaning and expression of the doctrine and practice of the faith. This 'truth' does not, however, simply render redundant this more immediate level of truth and reality. On the contrary, it confirms its validity. What is meant, therefore, is an investigation which is possible and permissible for a man only to the extent that he continually purifies himself and approaches the higher reality in love.[3] Naturally, this theology has not always been fortunate enough to maintain, in fact, its connection with its own basis. Nevertheless, its proper fundamental orientation is unmistakeably clear. It is, therefore, usually quite easy to distinguish in this theology the testimony of the tradition of the faith in teaching and practice, on the one hand, from the theologico-systematic explanation of this tradition by Origen, on the other, provided one begins with the basic philosophical and theological notions. According to these principles of Origen, we even can and must rank his testimony of the Church's teaching, in its 'common' formulation for the 'masses', not as of an inferior value but precisely as the continuing norm of his actual theological endeavour. Wherever, therefore, in a particular case Origen's theological explanation does not conform to this norm, as he himself represents it, then one ought to disagree with him in his own name. Moreover, it would be false to recognize in the Church's consciousness of the faith attested by him only that which survives his incidental theological interpretation.

For a correct appreciation of Origen's theological ideas it is vital to bear in mind the specific manifold character which, in his own view, belongs to the general object of theology. Concern about any particular intended realities must consider the *μυστήριον*,[4] which according to a fundamental Platonic notion, in general, and to the idea that the whole of reality is in a condition of becoming, for Origen in particular, is the principal object of theology. The becoming in question consists of a *unique* movement of spirits from God and back to him which has many different stages. Thus, according to Origen, the universe of angels, demons, men, matter and spirit is not merely a collection of disparate things held together by the transcendent creator, but an interiorly interrelated and hierarchically structured reality. Everything—nature and history—is included in this reality and organized by the one Logos which is both the image of the one God and the revelation of the unity to which the world is destined. Every level and degree of reality is, therefore, a shadow, a resemblance and an image of the eventual highest level. Each level refers inevitably to this last where the 'truth' finally lies. This truth is the meaning which is finally intended by all the other levels, their fulfilment, even their 'suppression' in the terminology of Hegel. Naturally the lower level is not, as such, destroyed or radically denied and threatened in this way. On the contrary, it is only by its corresponding higher reality that it is seen in its true light.[5] Thus everything, when seen in its proper order, is the image and likeness of the one Logos. This applies just as much to earthly, external history as it does to the 'phenomenal' character of the interior history of spirits in their free relationship with God. The body acts as the image of the fallen *and* redeemable soul; the Old Testament is the *typos* of the New, and this, in its turn, is the image of the eternal Kingdom in which God will be all in all.[6] Likewise, the Church acquires a sacramental structure in all its aspects: in the preaching of Christ and about Christ, as the Church itself, in the Scriptures, the hierarchy, the liturgy and the actual sacraments.[7] In each case there is an external level, for instance, Jesus' body, the words of the Scriptures, the external institution of a hierarchy, the visible offering, the elements of the Eucharist, baptism in water, etc. All this is the sign, the body, the visible aspect of the corresponding hidden spiritual reality which is present within these things and active through them. The inner truth thus both hides itself and reveals itself at the same time. It is in this way that are revealed the interior union of all men with the Logos, the spiritual meaning of the Scriptures, the interior hierarchy of the Church according to how near men are to God's Logos, the interior sacrifice of Christ himself and of Christians, union with the Logos in the eucharistic meal and the interior purification by baptism in the Spirit.

These two 'levels' of the Church are neither opposed to each other nor are they merely juxtaposed. The external level is the 'bodily' aspect of the interior level, which latter expresses itself and is effective in the former.[8] Corresponding to this external level in the Church is the external hierarchy of bishops, priests and deacons, which Origen recognizes unhesitatingly as a divine institution, so that, in his view, a Church without them would be unthinkable.[9] This hierarchy cannot, therefore, be something which is merely exterior, like the reflection of merit or fault in a pre-corporeal existence.[10] With its inalienable duties, it is the revelation of the truth contained typologically in the historical levitical priesthood. According to Origen, it is, on the one hand, indeed only the reflection of the eternal hierarchy, itself still considered to be in some way 'external', in which Christ himself will be the 'true' bishop in the definitive Kingdom of God. On the other hand, it is the expression of the 'true' interior hierarchy of the faithful.[11] The latter is of particular importance for our present purpose. The grades of this interior hierarchy are measured by the corresponding participation in Christ's offering and in the union with the Logos in obedience towards the Father. The activity of the external officials is valid and legitimate. Origen underlines this explicitly with regard to the offering of sacrifice,[12] along with the authority to teach.[13] Moreover, in any one individual case the interior and the external hierarchy *ought* to coincide. Thus priests and bishops should enter the rank in the interior hierarchy which corresponds to their external dignity.[14] For his part, Origen knows very well that, in his day, this is not very often the case[15] and he frequently laments the fact. At the same time, he recognizes that there are many Christians in the interior hierarchy who are far worthier of a place in the external hierarchy than many actual priests and bishops.[16]

The event of salvation within this Church, as it is accomplished, for instance, in the forgiveness of sins, must therefore be connected necessarily with all these 'levels' of the *mysterion* of the Church.

But did Origen himself see within his own system these relationships to the different levels of reality of the Church, and say as much, at least with regard to the role of the forgiveness of sins committed after baptism? Did he apply these connections and relationships, as they, in his view, existed in general and principally between the external and interior Church, also to the forgiveness of sins? These questions themselves indicate that in this study particular care will be taken to refer the individual assertions of Origen on the forgiveness of sins to the correct level of the reality of the Church and to assess precisely their theological import. These preliminary remarks dictate sufficiently the structure of this explanation of Origen's teaching on penance. Nevertheless, before the objective, church aspect of the forgiveness of sins, we will describe firstly the 'subjective' aspect: the penance of the sinner himself, in so far as he does it under the influence of grace.

II. THE PERSONAL PENANCE OF THE SINNER

1. Sin Committed after Baptism

The Church has never claimed to be an actual sinless community of saints. The letters of Paul make it abundantly clear that a Christian was capable of sinning after baptism and that this frequently happened. The images of the dead branch on the tree of the Church, of the mixture of wheat and chaff on the threshing-floor of the Church, of Noah's ark with its clean and unclean animals—all these are quite frequently applied to the community of the Church in the second and at the beginning of the third century. Nevertheless, it may still be said that it is only with Origen that 'the early Christian dream of God's sinless bride . . . came to an end'.[17] For it is only with him that the harsh reality of everyday Christian life is confronted theologically and reflectively with the knowledge of a holy Church without wrinkle and stain.[18] This point will be considered in greater detail below. In any case the progress in the Church's self-awareness with Origen is evidenced by the fact that the enthusiasm for baptism, even in comparison with Cyprian of Carthage, is remarkably less intense. Without any doubt, Origen fully appreciates the power, the efficacy and the fundamental importance of baptism as the basis of the whole of the spiritual life. And he certainly has not overlooked the once-and-for-all, immediately effective meaning of baptism,[19] which is the foundation of all further progress, in favour of a merely interior, slow and gradual moral-mystical ascent of man towards God. But he knows much more clearly than any of the theologians before him that, more often than not,[20] when baptism is mentioned in the sense just outlined, it is a matter of what it *should* be, rather than of what it in fact is. In his view, the newly baptized often receive 'today' only the *typus tantummodo mysteriorum* without *virtus eorum ac ratio*.[21] If a person perseveres in sin he does not receive the ἄφεσις ἁμαρτιῶν[22] in baptism, and Origen knows that this is only too often the case.[23] Even if baptism is not actually received unworthily, according to Origen it is still only a *beginning,* albeit a fundamental and indispensable one.[24] Even Cyprian still considered that baptism was the sudden and complete change of the whole man, which communicated the Spirit in its fullness and which then only had to be preserved. Origen no longer shares this view.[25] It is by effort and exertion that a baptized person, who was previously ensnared by vices, is able to free himself slowly from his previous habits.[26] Thus man is always a sinner.[27] Compared with the definitive, eschatological purification of the rebirth in Spirit and fire, the purification of baptism is only a 'prelude', 'in a mirror and likeness'.[28] A relapse after baptism is, therefore, only to be expected, without, however, man's being totally deprived of God's mercy.[29] Origen views the sins of the baptized clearly and dispassionately. These sins are numerous and found in Christians of all conditions and classes, beginning with the bishops.[30] What is more, he tries to make sense of this fact and its precise theological nature. We will consider later more closely the change of the relationship of the baptized to the Church which is caused by sin. For the moment we must look at the other aspects of the nature of sin, that is, the sin of baptized Christians. What Origen has in mind are the actual sins of real men with all the degrees of guilt which these sins have within the developed psychological situation of an individual Christian. It is not surprising, therefore, if the obscurity and the complexity of this concrete situation prevents Origen's theology of sin[31] from being expressed in well-known and neat categories. Thus the *formae et modi et numeri peccatorum*[32] are more fluid in his thinking than they are in today's moral theology. His 'distinctions' are frequently more like descriptions and often have no clear theological basis at all.[33] Nevertheless, it is obvious that Origen maintains the distinction which is fundamental for the theology of penance, namely, that between those sins which cause the loss of grace and those which do not have this effect.

A) THE DIFFERENCE BETWEEN SINS

Origen considers, in the first place, that the different seriousness of individual sins[34] is a teaching attested by the Scriptures. This difference, however, is not one merely of degree. This is because many sins destroy the grace of baptism, while others do not have this effect. Thus Origen generally distinguishes, in his terminology, between mortal sins and non-mortal sins: *mortale peccatum,*[35] *peccatum ad mortem,*[36] ἁμάρτημα (ἁμαρτία) πρὸς θάνατον,[37] and, on the other hand, ἁμάρτημα μὴ θανατήφορον (*non ad mortem*),[38] *levis culpa,*[39] *peccatum leve,*[40] *minus peccatum*[41] and *parvum peccatum.*[42]

This opposition is also found figuratively in the distinction between illness and death, expressed by the notions of *vulnus facile* and *insanabilis plaga,*[43] that is, of sin which does harm and that which destroys.[44] On the basis of these notions alone, it is still not clear whether the distinction involved corresponds to today's realities of mortal sin and venial sin. All the same, as we shall see, it is basically a question of the same distinction.

B) LIGHT SINS

Origen frequently considers the *levis culpa* of the ἁμαρτήματα μὴ θανατήφορα as not destructive of grace. The person who has only the ῥύπος of sin which does not lead to death is a τηρήσας τὸ βάπτισμα τοῦ ἁγίου πνεύματος;[45] he counts as one who is burdened by ἁμαρτήματα μὴ θανατήφορα, and as long as he does not prove himself to be unrepentant he remains a brother in the fullest sense of this term and must not be excluded from the Church.[46] It is even quite clear from In Num. hom. 10,1[47] that Origen holds that a certain coexistence of (light) sin and holiness is possible. In this passage he explains at considerable length how one can be a 'saint' (radically and initially) and still at the same time and inevitably a sinner. This 'holiness' consists precisely in the continual ever-renewed striving to purify oneself increasingly from sins. The only person who is not holy is the one who does not make this effort.[48] Now if there are in this sense *sancti iidemque peccatores* (GCS 30:p. 70,16), then there must be sins which do not simply drive the Holy Spirit out of man. Mortal sins are not compatible with the indwelling of God and Christ in a man. This *simul iustus et peccator,* therefore, can refer only to those sins which Origen considers *non ad mortem,* as *culpa levis*. In In Luc. hom. 2 (GCS 35)[49] he suggests that in fact it is perfectly possible for a person who has once been justified not to sin any more. Unless, therefore, one wishes to make Origen crudely contradict himself (cf. In Num. hom. 10,1), then this possibility of not committing further sins must be understood of the avoidance of mortal sins. On the other hand, the inevitable sins (In Num. hom. 10,1) must be construed as ἁμαρτήματα μὴ θανατήφορα. Indeed the distinction as a whole is meaningful and understandable only if light sins can be compatible with the preserved baptismal grace. But this means that they must be venial sins in today's sense. Origen here talks about damages but not about destruction, about injuries but not about mortal wounds.[50]

This agreement between Origen and today's theology on the question of this basic distinction can be brought out even more clearly by another consideration. If these notions are not in fact identical, then Origen could make the difference between mortal and non-mortal sin, between sin which causes damage and sins which kills, intelligible only with regard to its eschatological effects. In this case, mortal sin, as opposed to a non-mortal sin, would be conceivable only as a fault which in fact causes eschatological death and leads to definitive destruction. In other words, it is not possible to find another meaning for the distinction in question in terms of the present state of grace than that of today's theology. Now, even apart from the fact that an exclusively eschatological understanding of this question does not fit into Origen's system—involving, as it does, the definitive salvation of *all men*—such a conception is already precluded because, in his view, even mortal sins can be remitted in this life.[51] Thus the θάνατος which these sins entail can refer only and immediately to the present life of grace, while non-mortal sins precisely do not have *this* effect.

Indeed the condition in which the sinner guilty of such a *culpa levis* remains corresponds to his preservation of baptismal grace. He still lives within the area of the Church's grace. He is still truly a brother.[52] Immediately, and without the need for this connection to be renewed, he is still under the helpful and salvific influence of the Church's fellowship. His brothers, the officials in the Church and in the heavenly groups of angels—which also belong to the interior reality of the Church[53]—can still intercede for and help him. In so far as the Christian, after committing venial sins, still lives within the fellowship of grace that is the Church and only in it and by the grace of the Church, which is constantly made actual in its life and activity, he can achieve the forgiveness of his sins. This is what Origen means when he speaks quite generally of the Christian's being able to have his *peccatum* remitted only by the help of priests and the *meliores*.[54]

C) MORTAL SINS

Now what about mortal sins, those faults which incur death? According to Origen, 'death' is the most common characteristic of sin. It is appropriate, therefore, that our reflection should begin with this notion. We have already seen that by death Origen means the nature or the necessary consequence of the sins in question, that is, a present and not an immediately eschatological reality. Sin causes death at the very moment when it is committed. Now what does such a death through sin mean for Origen? After such a fault the Christian is dead because Jesus, who is life itself, no longer lives in him. Or, expressed against the background of a more actual notion of grace: Jesus 'no longer enters' into the *anima defuncta*.[55] This is because in this soul is preserved neither the Spirit of baptism nor its gifts as these are described in Hebrews 6:4.[56] This man has lost the Holy Spirit, the 'robe', the 'ring' (cf. Luke 15:22) and his sonship[57] and has, as it were, returned to Satan by a miscarriage of the child of the Logos.[58] He is expelled from God's Kingdom,[59] is dead among the dead 'outside'[60] and belongs to the devil.[61] In a certain sense he no longer exists as far as God is concerned.[62] This is what Origen means when he uses the notion of 'dead'.

This spiritual death is often the result of a longer or shorter process leading up to it or of an illness which is considered a mortal wound. Sin is 'incurable', that is, its development cannot be influenced favourably, death cannot be halted.[63] Thus the expressions 'incurable' and mortal sin are almost identical for Origen. Sin is 'incurable', however, because it leads to death, but not because the person guilty of mortal sin cannot be raised again to a new life.[64] Such an idea is to be excluded from any consideration of 'incurable' sin according to Origen.

Mortal sin is not only a loss of grace in the sense of a relegation through a 'relapse into pagan behaviour'[65] to the state prior to baptism. It is a specific loss of grace which is clearly distinct from the pre-baptismal state. The sins of Christians, whom God has loved, are worse than those of pagans and heretics;[66] there are sins against the Holy Spirit which can be committed only by those who possess this Spirit. This presupposes the presence of the Holy Spirit which is communicated to the believer through Christ's death in baptism.[67] Thus, in Origen's view, 'sin against the Holy Spirit' (Matt. 12:31 f.) does not suppose a special obstinacy but is present wherever a Christian ὁ καὶ παρόντος ἀυτοῦ (*sc.* τὸ παρὸν πνεῦμα ἅγιον: GCS 10:p. 408, 24) ἐν τῇ ψυχῇ ἁμαρτάνων.[68] This corresponds to the situation of Hebrews 6:4 ff. The sin against the Holy Spirit is unforgivable, since it is committed in clear opposition to the συμβουλία and σύμπνοια of the ἐνύπαρχον πνεῦμα.[69] It is even its complete 'reversal' since in τὸ τῆς υἱοθεσίας πνεῦμα with every good deed one is continually reborn from God in the Spirit as a son of God with Jesus Christ.[70] The sin against the Holy Spirit cancels this new participation in the life of the Trinity and, therefore, spells death. The person who is guilty of such a sin opposes himself immediately to God, who is present within him, and this in direct contradiction to the inner dynamism of his own state of grace. Thus he stands before the wrath of God and not only in contradiction to his world: *non per ministros retribuet Babyloni Deus, sed ipse retribuet, quod meretur.*[71] Afflicted with the *plaga insanabilis* of mortal sin, man is no longer open to the salvific influence of created reality, the 'servant of God'.[72] Thus he falls completely under the influence of the *sinful* forces in the world. To a certain extent he has become the property of the devil[73] and stands in a kind of spiritual-personal relationship to him;[74] he is 'consecrated'[75] to him, begotten by him[76] and a member of the *corpus peccati,* whose head is the devil himself.[77]

For such a sin against the Holy Spirit there is no *aphesis*:[78] οὐ γίνεται ἄφεσις τῷ εἰς αὐτὸ (τὸ πνεῦμα) ἡμαρτηκότι. The person who offends in this way is a ἀσύγγνωστος.[79] Nevertheless, it is not easy to say precisely what is meant here by the *aphesis* which is no longer possible after mortal sin. It is obvious that on this point Origen is dependent on a traditional teaching which he has received from Hermas through Clement of Alexandria. For his part, he does not appear to sense any need to explain this notion more clearly. He certainly does not mean that mortal sins against the Holy Spirit simply cannot be remitted.[80] This point will be demonstrated later in greater detail. Thus the *aphesis* is not simply identifiable with *every* remission of guilt. But this is only a negative definition of this notion.

What does it mean positively? The answer to this question requires, in its turn, a more precise definition of the specific character of the post-baptismal remission of sins and is, therefore, important for us at this point. Nevertheless, the answer is to be given here only in so far as it does not presuppose the whole teaching of the nature of the remission of sins committed after baptism—a point which will be considered later. Rather, it will be derived provisionally from those texts which themselves speak explicitly and immediately of *aphesis*. In the narrow, technical sense in these texts *aphesis* appears first in connection with baptism, where it is in a special sense unique to Christian initiation. The only conceivable application of this sense to mortal sins committed after baptism would be by way of a possible baptism in blood in martyrdom.[81] But the unique possibility could explain the nature of *aphesis* only *if* there were no longer any possibility of the forgiveness of later sins after baptism. In this case the *aphesis* would simply mean the once-and-for-all forgiveness of sins which was only possible in baptism. But this hypothesis is not verified. Thus the connection of baptism which is possible only once with the *aphesis* allows only one conclusion, which is that the latter is a *special* forgiveness of sins—indeed possible only in baptism. If, however, this special forgiveness differed from other possibilities of forgiveness after baptism *only* by virtue of the sacramental and unique *rite*, then a stress on the once-and-for-all character of the baptismal *aphesis* would be superfluous. A mere warning not to forfeit the grace of such a *once-and-for-all* forgiveness in baptism would be meaningless. Thus the difference between the *aphesis* in baptism and that after baptism cannot refer only to the rite of the sacrament of initiation.

On this question In Joan. II 11 provides further help. Since sin committed after baptism is more serious than the faults committed before baptism it does not receive the same forgiveness as the latter. It is a sin against the Holy Spirit, and only if it were lighter than this would a remission by a συγγνώμη be considered.[82] Even if baptism could be repeated it still does not appear, therefore, to be able to remit sins committed after baptism. The *aphesis can* only apply to sins which are not committed as a conscious contradiction against the dynamism of the Holy Spirit which is given to man in baptism. Thus the impossibility of a renewed *aphesis* does not depend upon the unrepeatable character of sacramental baptism (and the forgiveness which it involves). Neither does it depend, however, on the fact that God does not wish to grant a further *aphesis*. The only criterion here is the intrinsic nature of the guilt to be remitted. The nature of a further possible means for the forgiveness of sin must, therefore, obviously correspond to the intrinsic nature of the sin to be remitted. This is not the case, however, of baptism and the *aphesis* which is granted with it, in regard to the sins committed after baptism. We have already described in some detail the nature of mortal sin committed after baptism. It follows from what we have said that the remission which this sin calls for cannot come about by way of a direct and immediate effect of the Church's usual and normal activity, that is, for Origen the activity of priests, the faithful and angels. This activity of the Church naturally includes sacrifice, prayer, instruction and correction, all of which are effective only in those cases where the sinner has not, through 'death', fallen out of the fellowship of grace itself. In the latter case he must be given up as 'incurable', which means that he can no longer be preserved from death, even by 'God's servants'. At the same time, this idea also implies that *aphesis* for sins which do *not* incur death is, according to De or. 28,9 f., obviously possible by means of prayer and sacrifice.[83] With regard to sins committed after baptism, therefore, *aphesis* would mean that forgiveness of sins which is brought about by the συνεργεῖν[84] of the Church for one of its living members who is still united with it. But it is precisely no longer possible if this living relationship has been disrupted through the death of sin.

This view fits well into Origen's theology of serious and light sins. Nevertheless, it has the disadvantage of dissociating the *aphesis* of baptism from that for sins committed after baptism, despite the similarity of the two ideas. Before baptism the candidate is not yet a member of the Church and, therefore, he is not yet in a position where the 'sin-remitting' activity of the Church can affect him. The most that can be said is that a non-baptized person does not block himself off directly and explicitly from this influence of the Church, as does the person who commits serious sin after baptism.

This discrepancy does not, however, detract from the approach to a solution which we have suggested. The genuine meaning of the formula of once-and-for-all *aphesis* in baptism does not have to coincide completely and in all respects with the notion of *aphesis* which is derivable from Origen's theory of sin committed by a baptized person. In order to do full justice to the technical notion of *aphesis* in Origen's work it is, in any event, necessary to make a further observation. This is that for Origen ἄφεσις is the opposite of κόλασις.[85] By this he means a remission of sins without the suffering of the consequences of sin. The place where this notion appears most clearly is In Jer. hom. 16,5–7.[86] The person who has received the ἄφεσις ἁμαρτημάτων in the bath of regeneration and subsequently, despite the light of faith which he has received (ἐν γνώσει: GCS 6:p. 137,30), backslides into sins must, as opposed to the ἄφεσις of baptism, ἀπολαμβάνειν τὰς ἁμαρτίας (GCS 6:p. 137,18–27). Obviously what are meant here are sins which are not only 'hay' and 'straw' but 'wood' (cf. 1 Cor. 3:11 f.) (138,8 ff., 15 ff.; 138,23 f.) and which bring about the condition envisaged in Hebrews 10:26 f.,[87] in other words, faults which are without any doubt mortal sins. In this passage the ἀπολαμβάνειν τὰς ἁμαρτίας stands in opposition to the ἄφεσις achieved in suffering the punitive fire of God in the next life, a fire which destroys sins and so eradicates the evil in man. It frees from guilt (ἀφανισμὸς τῶν κακῶν: 139,3) and thus prepares the purified but not to be 'burned' 'image and likeness' (138,22) of God in man for the reception of salvation and the rewarding even of those good works done in life. From this text it is clear, therefore, that κόλασις (139,3), as opposed to ἄφεσις, is to be understood as a 'medicinal'[88] punishment for the remission of sins. The *aphesis* in baptism is, accordingly, a forgiveness without the need to suffer the consequences of sins. It is irrelevant that the text here presents the remission by 'punishment' as taking place in the next life. For it will be pointed out later that the contrite penitent is able, already in this life through his penance, to anticipate the purificatory baptism of fire[89] in the next life, through which sins committed after the baptism in water and the Spirit are remitted. That these ideas are based on the esoteric notion of the *apocatastasis*[90] and that there is no distinction made between those who are repentant and those who leave this life in their obstinacy does not affect in any way the fundamental idea of a pure *aphesis* as opposed to a salutary suffering of punishment. Nevertheless this idea is not to be seen as opposed to the refusal of every forgiveness.[91] By way of conclusion it may be stated that, because of their special gravity, there is no longer any *aphesis* for mortal sins committed after baptism. This is because, on the one hand, the rite of baptism can no longer be considered appropriate for their forgiveness, and, on the other hand, they cannot be remitted by the immediate operation of the Church's prayer and sacrifice. Rather, they must be expiated through the undergoing of the punishment which they have deserved. From the very nature of the case, it is obvious that the last aspect is a corollary of the ineffectiveness of the Church's prayer and sacrifice in such cases. This ineffectiveness rests, however, on the nature of mortal sin which excludes from the Church's inner fellowship of grace and causes the spiritual death of the sinner, precisely because man has opposed himself to the Holy Spirit.

D) CONCRETE MORTAL SINS ACCORDING TO ORIGEN

Which sin, according to Origen's view, leads to death and which does not? Origen obviously considers sin not so much in its objectivity as in the way that it occurs in the actual life of the individual with all its unforeseeable circumstances. Thus he states with regard to the question just posed:[92] *Quae autem sunt species peccatorum ad mortem, quae vero non ad mortem, sed ad damnum, non puto facile a quoquam homine posse discerni. Scriptum namque est: delicta quis intelligit?* It is later added that it is possible, nevertheless, to have some idea of these *ex parte aliqua* from the Scriptures (*in evangelio per parabolas*). In fact Origen renounces all attempts to establish any theoretical objective norms for such sins.[93] He simply stands by the statements of the Scriptures and the actual practice of the Church as it occurred in the exercise of the Church's penitential discipline at that time, and thus used a purely human criterion to distinguish between mortal sins which were subject to the penance of the Church and other faults. Thus for him the following are those guilty of mortal sins: *masculorum concubitor, adulter, homicida, mollis, fornicarius, avarus, idolorum cultor,*[94] the person who commits a *blasphemia,*[95] the *maledicus in Deum* and *in proximum* and the other sinners whom Paul names in 1 Corinthians 6:9 f. and excludes from the Kingdom of God.[96] In De or. 28,10 the following are spelt out: *εἰδωλολατρεία, μοιχεία, πορνεία, ἑκούσιος φόνος*.[97] In In Joan. 28,7 the expression of reversion to the *ἐθνικὸς βίος* means a mortal sin[98] which concerns not only falling away from the faith but lapsing into every 'pagen' vice.[99] Thus it is stated that through murder, adultery, theft, perjury, violence, etc., a person becomes the property of the devil,[100] with the obvious implication that these are mortal sins. The cursing of one's parents also seems to be reckoned with these faults.[101] The state of the conscience of the Christian people on this question at that time is particularly well expressed in a passage of In Jer. hom. 20:[102] 'And every one of us [Origen is speaking reproachfully] who has not practised idolatry, who has not committed an act of impurity (would that we were indeed clean in this respect at least!) believes that, on leaving this life, he will be saved.'

On the other hand, according to Origen, the following, by way of example, are not mortal sins: λοιδορία, φυσίωσις, πολυποσία, λόγος ψευδὴς καί ἀργός *aut talis aliqua culpa levis, quae etiam in illis, qui videntur proficere in ecclesia, frequenter inveniuntur.*[103] Otherwise, not a great deal is said about individual venial sins which may be explicitly distinguished from mortal sins.[104]

There is, however, a further question to be considered. Did Origen maintain only the double distinction of sins into mortal sins and non-mortal sins, or did he also make a further essential distinction within the category of mortal sins? By this is not meant a distinction in the vague sense that even the individual mortal sins can differ considerably from each other *pro qualitate vel quantitate.* This is a point which Origen also stresses.[105] It is more a question here of *two* radically different *classes* of mortal sins. In general it appears that such an idea is not demonstrably present in Origen.[106] Indeed, in view of his reserve with regard to the simple distinction between mortal and non-mortal sins, it is hardly to be expected. Nevertheless, one text, namely In Levit. hom. 15,2, does seem to express this idea. The text in question[107] makes the distinction between *culpa mortalis* and *crimen mortale.* At the same time, the *culpa mortalis* is compared with the *sermonis vel morum vitium,* with the *communia quae frequenter incurrimus.*[108] The *crimen mortale,* on the other hand, is put on the same level as the *blasphemia fidei.*[109] This interpretation arises from the way in which the text is actually formulated. Most specialists in the history of penance, therefore, have taken the text in this sense, exactly as it is presented.[110] However, in its present formulation this text does arouse serious doubts. It is indeed stated that through the *culpa mortalis* one sells one's house to the devil,[111] even though on each occasion and even if this should happen repeatedly, a redemption always remains possible. Now, as we have already seen,[112] this idea is not necessarily connected with Origen's idea of *mortal* sin. Moreover, 'house' here seems to be meant in such a sense that it can be applied to every *individual* virtue.[113] Thus one could possess many 'houses', and, given Origen's essential gradation of beatitude,[114] it would be perfectly conceivable to sell one 'house' without totally losing beatitude. This applies even apart from the notion of the *apocatastasis*. Thus the general meaning of the text does not indicate that here it is a question of *culpa mortalis* distinct from a *crimen mortale*. On the contrary, it gives rise to serious doubts about the actual existence of such a distinction in the original Greek text which is lost. As we have seen, this distinction is not found anywhere else in Origen. The *sermonis vitium,* which in our text would count as a *culpa mortalis,* is *not* considered elsewhere as a mortal sin.[115] And is it likely that Origen would in fact compare a *culpa mortalis* with the *communia quae frequenter incurrimus,* when *frequenter inveniuntur* is elsewhere precisely a characteristic of the *culpa levis*?[116] In any case, the sharp distinction between *blasphemia fidei*[117] and another *culpa mortalis* is not made elsewhere, with regard to church penance, either by Origen or by other authors. Once it is considered that according to Origen's theology every *mortal* sin (therefore even a *culpa mortalis*) in itself separates the sinner from the fellowship of the Church, and that the penance of excommunication, which in fact is granted only once, is the appropriate expression of this separation, then it would appear that a remission for an actual *culpa mortalis* without church penance and excommunication *semper . . . et sine intermissione* is excluded. For these and other[118] reasons we consider that the term *mortalis* as the description of the *culpa* in this text should be omitted. It is probably a question of an early dittography, arising from the expression *crimen mortale* in the Greek text or even in Rufinus' Latin translation.[119] Its omission makes the text more intelligible.[120] In any case, this distinction between *culpa mortalis* and *crimen mortale* here is so unique and doubtful that it would hardly be methodologically justifiable to derive from it consequences for Origen's theology of penance which do not fit into the view which he expresses elsewhere.

2. *The Forgivable Character of Sin*

It is not here a question of the possibility which the *Church* has of forgiving mortal sins. Through his own fault alone the sinner has in fact incurred 'excommunication' and normally he is also explicitly charged with a declaration of excommunication on the Church's part. Whether the Church is able to receive him back into its full fellowship after the remission of his sins or how it participates in this supposed remission does not interest us here. Rather it is a question of whether a person guilty of mortal sins can remit his sin before God and indeed in *this* life. According to Origen's eschatology there is no definitive and eternal rejection for a sinner who dies unrepentant. Through the purifying fire of the future age, even in his case, God's love will so conquer the wickedness of created freedom that, in the final analysis, the whole of created freedom will be saved for ever.[121] Thus in this definitive perspective there is no problem whatsoever of the forgiveness of mortal sins for Origen. Everyone is agreed on this point. Origen also tries to withdraw this teaching from the existential reach of the man who is not yet purified, for whom it is obviously a temptation. For this eschatology he appeals to God's essential goodness and establishes his thesis with the application of metaphysical principles. In this way, however, he enters into contradiction with the teaching of the Church, and the question of whether he recognizes the fundamental possibility of the forgiveness of mortal sins in this life becomes even more poignant. If this were the case, then this forgiveness would be limited only by man himself and his refusal, which would be the free rejection of God's offer of forgiveness. To pose the question in this way is not in itself to contradict the teaching of the Church. And it is only this question which is relevant to the history of the controversies about penance and to the Church's theology of penance of that time and today.

Now Origen does not defend any kind of rigorism according to which a divine forgiveness for mortal sins in *this* life would be impossible or even only doubtful. His theology of the freedom of the spiritual creature, of the love of God and of the saving significance of all punishment is already so weighted against a negative answer in this question that it would be astounding if, despite all this, he still came to another conclusion. This conclusion, in fact, flows from his basic metaphysical principles upon which his world-view and his theology are built. Nevertheless, it also has very concrete consequences for the everyday life of the Christian and for the practice of the Church. Even in these views Origen still wishes to be a man of the Church, and thus it is unthinkable that he would have formulated them in opposition to the Church's teaching or that he would not have noticed the contradiction. Thus his answer to our question, despite the fact that some of its presuppositions do not agree with the teaching of the Church, can certainly be regarded as a witness of the tradition of the *Church*. What is more, he felt that in propagating his view he was doing nothing more or less than defending the tradition of the Church against a heretical Gnostic fatalism which, he was convinced, regarded man's ethical stance as the necessary consequence of his particular φύσις.[122]

Neither the notion of an 'incurable' sin nor the denial of the possibility of an *aphesis* for mortal sins committed after baptism has anything whatsoever to do with the challenging of the fact that such sins are forgivable. This means that already the principal arguments for the view that Origen is a witness for an 'early Christian' rigorism are obviated. Rather, he teaches positively the possibility of forgiveness for mortal sins. But it still remains to adduce several indications which stress that in the statements concerned it really is a question of a possibility of forgiveness *in this life*. Since it is obvious that Origen's teaching on penance has not undergone a theological development, a precise chronological ordering and treatment of the relevant witnesses either here or in what follows would contribute nothing. It can, therefore, be omitted.[123]

In In Exod. hom. 6,9 Origen explains that through murder, adultery, perjury, robbery and violence, which he means to be considered as the price paid by the devil, a person becomes the property of Satan, just as he becomes the property of Christ through Christ's blood. He was himself afraid that even some *qui in ecclesia sunt* might in this way have again become the possession of the devil in secret, since he is intent on sowing his weed among the wheat. *Et tamen, si quis forte huismodi pecuniam a diabolo deceptus accepit, non usquequaque desperet: misericors enim est et miserator Dominus et creaturae suae non vult mortem sed ut convertatur et vivat. Poenitendo, flendo, satisfaciendo deleat, quod admissum est. Dicit enim propheta quia, cum conversus ingemueris, salvus eris.*[124] Thus, in Origen's view, actual mortal sins can be remitted through penance and not only by means of the purifying fire in the next life. The 'earth' as it were 'swallows up' by the *mors admissi sceleris* the person guilty of impurity. *Nec tamen penitus desperandum est. Possible namque est ut, si forte resipiscat, qui devoratus est, rursum possit evomi, sicut Jonas.* And since this event is distinguished from the liberation of sinners from the underworld by Jesus Christ, this return and its saving effects must concern something which happens in this life.[125] In In Ps. 36 hom. 1,5[126] the Christian who commits impurity is told: *per exhomologesim . . . revela ea* (the guilt) *Domino et spera in eum, et ipse faciet . . . spera in eum, quod possis ab eo veniam promereri, et ipse faciet. Quid faciet? Sine dubio sanum te faciet*. At the same time, the preacher of this homily expresses the hope that none of his hearers has become guilty of *fornicatio*. Thus Origen seems here to be thinking of a mortal sin. Moreover, there is no indication that the restored health in question is promised only for the next life.

In In Ps. 36 hom. 4,2[127] this instruction is given to a sinner whose fault has separated him from the Church (*quomodo ad Ecclesiam redire?*) and who has forfeited his salvation (*quomodo possum ego salvus fieri . . . iam nulla spes est*): *non iaceat post casum, ne prosternatur, sed exsurgat et emendet culpam, expurget paenitentiae suae satisfactione commissum*. What Origen clearly has in mind here[128] is *fornicatio, impudicitia* and those cases which correspond in some way to Peter's denial or the sin of David with Uriah's wife.[129] The sinner must begin his reform immediately and thus the exhortation is intended as a message of confidence to the simple Christian who knows nothing about the theory of the final salvation of all things. This is abundantly clear from the question quoted above. This exhortation, therefore, must concern an effect which takes place in this life; indeed it concludes with a *redire ad Ecclesiam*. In In Levit. hom. 14,4[130] it is explained why a less grievous sin like taking God's name in vain is treated more seriously in the Old Testament than a greater offence like blasphemy: the punishment of death for the less grievous was, at the same time, its remission, so that this did not require further punishment in the next world.[131] The serious sin, on the other hand, was not expiated by a punishment in this life and *manet illis aeternis ignibus extinguendum* (485,9). According to Origen, Paul was cognisant of this (486,20). And thus the apostle punishes the sinner guilty of impurity in 1 Corinthians 5 'with death', that is, he hands him over to Satan *in interitum carnis* in this life so that his spirit will then be saved in the next world. This spiritual death consists in the *afflictio corporis, quae solet a poenitentibus expendi* (486,26 f.). This leads to the following consequence: *Unde et si nunc quis forte nostrum recordatur in semetipso alicuius peccati conscientiam, se qui se obnoxium novit esse delicto, confugiat ad paenitentiam et spontaneum suscipiat carnis interitum ut expurgatus in praesenti vita spiritus noster mundus et purus pergat ad Christum Dominum nostrum* (486,28–487,3). Thus, according to Origen, the sin of the incestuous person at Corinth can be fully remitted in this life by the *interitus carnis*. Moreover, this sinner is for Origen the biblical type *par excellence* of the one who is subject to church penance. The *interitus carnis* is the *paenitentia,* which consists of the *afflictio carnis quae solet*[132] *a penitentibus expendi.* A similar train of thought is found in detail in In Levit. hom. 11,2.[133] There it is expressly a question of those sins which correspond to Hebrews 10:28 f.,[134] therefore, of *peccata ad mortem.* In the new covenant the punishment for such sins is no longer bodily death, since the bishop ought not to impose such a punishment.[135] Rather, what is now appropriate for the remission of sin is *paenitentia*[136] in so far as this is freely undertaken.[137] If this is not the case, *nobis ultio reponitur in futurum.*[138]

In In Jer. hom. 20,9[139] there appear two sinners who have become guilty of the same offence of impurity. One of these, however, is unrepentant, while the other is conscience-struck and does hard penance, not only for a few days but for a long period of time. Thus in his heart is already burning the purifying fire of judgement. Indeed the more intense this is, the greater must be his trust in God and the more rapidly will he find mercy. Penance in this life is sufficient 'period of punishment' for him, if it lasts as long as in the case of the incestuous person in Corinth. When Paul saw that this person had undergone sufficient affliction he ordered that love should be allowed to take over so that the penitent should not be destroyed by affliction. Origen concludes from this:

> Every one of us examines his own conscience and sees wherein he has sinned; for he must be punished for his sins. He asks God that the fire which was in Jeremiah and then on Simon and Cleophas[140] should also come on him so that he will not be destined for the fire of the next world. For the person who does not undergo fire here, but remorselessly sins again, will be set aside for that fire.

Thus the interior fire of penance remits sin, and indeed even mortal sin, here on earth, exactly as the fire of judgement in the next world.

What Origen says on one occasion, therefore, applies also to mortal sins:

> . . . *Qui audiunt, sciant scriptum esse quia cum conversus ingemueris, tunc salvus eris et scies ubi fueris. Et si dixeris tu peccata tua prior, ego exaudiam te tamquam populum sanctum. Audisti quomodo, etiam si peccator fuisti, tantum si conversus es et desisti a peccato, iam sanctus appellaris? Nihil ergo desperandum est his, qui compunguntur, et convertuntur ad Dominum: non enim superat bonitatem Dei malitia delictorum.*[141]

Mortal sins are remissible in this life, even if after baptism this requires no longer the *aphesis* but the interior fire of penance.[142]

3. *Penance*

A) THE FIRE OF PENANCE

In the following section we will consider more closely the subjective penance of the person guilty of mortal sin. Penance is first and foremost a grace. Now it is obviously impossible to give here even the briefest sketch of the whole of Origen's teaching on grace.[143] Nevertheless, we must have some information about this teaching, even though we shall confine ourselves essentially to those questions which are connected immediately with the teaching on penance. Origen has often been accused of holding a semipelagian, purely external 'synergism' between grace and human freedom. Nevertheless such a description appears too superficial and schematic to be able really to do justice to Origen's basic ideas. In any event, for Origen 'grace' is not merely a divine help given to man to enable him to lead a human, moral life. Man is called to a real participation in the life of the Logos by possessing the Holy Spirit and moving towards the Father. The 'supernatural' character of this possession of the Spirit by which man as an inalienable reflection of the Logos is enabled to share really, ontologically in the life of the Logos by faith, gnosis and love is not developed explicitly. Nevertheless, this does not mean in any way a denial of this supernatural or purely gratuitous character of the divinization of the created spirit. It is only the result of the way Origen considers the created spirit as it actually is. Accordingly, he has no occasion to distinguish this situation explicitly as 'supernatural' from another merely 'purely natural' one. He also takes it for granted that we do not have this life 'from ourselves'. The ability to be modelled on the Logos is increased by the activity of the Holy Spirit and this strengthens the reciprocal activity between human freedom and the divine help. Now if this co-operation is seen, in itself, 'synergetically' and if it is asked which factor of this co-operation has the initiative, then it must not be forgotten that Origen, in face of the gnostic naturalism of his time, had every reason to stress human freedom. It was obviously of prime importance that the inalienable image and existence of the Logos within man's ἡγεμονικόν, being the starting-point for every possibility of salvation and for man's inheritance of salvation, is not to be understood in the sense of mere 'nature'. Today also theology must recognize within man, as he actually is, an aspect of his existence which, on the one hand, is supernatural but, on the other, is an indispensable, real, ontological characteristic of his true nature.[144] It is certain that Origen does not stress very explicitly that the actual decision in favour of the good, as the exercise of free choice with regard to good and evil, is itself still a special grace. But could he see this clearly if, on the one hand, he propounded a radical eschatological optimism, according to which—as he certainly intended it to be understood—all men would be saved and, on the other, he attacked gnosticism, for which freedom is not an inalienable reality in man?

In any case, according to Origen a person guilty of mortal sin has lost the Spirit of grace and is really dead. His rebirth to life is, therefore, above all a work of God himself. This is true, even if Origen in his preaching repeatedly exhorts man as he actually is to penance and conversion, that is, to an activity which he himself must freely undertake and see through. Despite all this, the new beginning of life is always the work of God. Mortal sin, as opposed to that fault which does not incur death, is no longer able to be healed by created power alone.[145] In the case of a *plaga insanabilis,* therefore, the *magnus medicus* himself must intervene;[146] *sacrificia sacerdotum* and the *obsecrationes pontificum* are, in this case, unable to effect a cure, and an improvement through the *scientia divinae legis* is impossible. Thus we read of these sins: *ipsius Domini agere virtutem.*[147] Nevertheless, the Lord has arranged that others should have a special responsibility for loosing the bond of death incurred by the person who commits such a sin against the Holy Spirit. This applies above all to the angels. They play an important rôle in the very first stirrings of the new beginning of the spiritual life. For surely, it is first and foremost always Christ's prayer and command that call the dead from the grave of sin.[148] Nevertheless, as far as the idea of the remission of mortal sin is concerned, there is no further explanation[149] of how the living command, reserved to Christ alone, actually operates in raising men from the death of sin and precisely how it is distinguished from the activity of the other forces, that is, of angels and of the Church, which certainly co-operate in this remission. It is, however, possible to derive a clearer idea of the nature of this divine initiative from Origen's more general views. The most important of these, for our present purpose, is doubtless the assumption that conversion requires a divine impulse, but could subsequently be understood as an act of human freedom. This would correspond to our modern notion of *gratia efficax,* and undoubtedly it ought to be thought of in this way. For if a sinner is to be summoned from the grave by a divine command this is a matter of God's action with regard to a person who is repentant, but not with regard to one who is obdurate. Nevertheless, the effect of this divine action cannot be identified with *gratia efficax* in the sense of modern theology. For Origen does not seem to have conceived the actual *doing* of good, once the free choice between good and evil has been made, as grace. In his view God gives the possibility to do either, and then all the rest is left to the decision of man himself.[150] If, however, this motion on the part of God and Jesus Christ is understood exclusively in the sense of a prevenient grace which makes conversion possible, then this idea, as far as its positive content is concerned, would be perfectly appropriate,[151] even though it would remain fairly formal and undetermined. For we would then immediately have to ask what it is precisely that constitutes this impulse of grace for Origen. The specific character of this revivifying motion on God's part must, therefore, be looked for elsewhere.

According to Origen, the grace which makes conversion possible must reside in the experience of divine judgement on sin. If angels and men desire to preserve the sinner from mortal sin, that is, if they wish to heal him but, nevertheless, have to face the fact that their effort is futile, then there is nothing else that they can do. As opposed to a *parvum peccatum,* which does not entail a judgement which reaches up to heaven, the *crimen* of mortal sin calls for the judgement of God himself, a judgement which corresponds to the seriousness of the fault committed.[152] This judgement consists in a rejection of the sinner on God's part and it can occur in two quite different ways. Either the sinner does not notice it at all, and this is the most dreadful form of God's anger with regard to man,[153] or else the Logos, which is united with his soul and accuses him, gives him a 'synesthesis' of his faults and their punishment. But the latter is already the beginning of blessedness, the first sign that the soul is alive again. On the other hand, to experience no pain at all[154] is the most terrifying experience of all. The person who does not come to judgement has simply lost his salvation. Thus no one should wish to flee from God's 'judgement', even if he had the possibility of doing so.[155] The sinner should even pray for the inner fire of judgement, so that he may become worthy to receive it in his heart.[156] For this fire is, in the final analysis, nothing other than the Logos of the Lord itself.[157]

In order to appreciate this idea properly, it is necessary to bear in mind Origen's teaching on the inalienable existence of the Logos in created spirits.[158] The person who, in this regard, approaches judgement or, more precisely, is already near it, is the one who allows the fire which is within him to achieve its full effect as judgement on his sins.[159] The intrinsic contradiction between the Logos existing radically within the soul and mortal sin is not always experienced. But when this does happen, then the 'burning fire' of God's Logos becomes the fire of judgement in the depths of man's being. It purifies the soul and punishes invisibly and spiritually. But it also illumines and is simultaneously a grace which has been requested and a judgement quite different from the fire which is prepared for the devil.[160] By committing an 'incurable' sin a man has, as it were, done all that he is capable of. And God has allowed him to go into this extreme situation where he is placed in utter darkness and thus in this gloom experiences the meaningless of sin,[161] since the Logos rooted within the soul cannot be completely eradicated by sin. Thus man vegetates in his state of interior confusion which flows from sin, and the experience of this is the effect of God's fire within man.[162] And the sinner's desperate attempt to persevere in his fault is weakened by its *ἀλογία*.[163]

This notion of Origen's of an impulse to conversion has its weak points. Certainly he recognizes that this fire of the interior Logos can even temporarily harden a man *pro ipsis motuum morum qualitatibus*[164] and that God can impose a greater punishment. For a man does not necessarily have to experience the burning and radical opposition of his sin to the permanent presence of the Logos. Moreover, there is always the danger that sin may appear as a necessary phase, as it were, in the process of man's development, provoking, in its turn, dialectically the very judgement which sooner or later effects the cure.[165] It is only when the existence of the Logos within man is considered as purely gratuitous that the judging and healing experience of the radical opposition of sin to it can itself be understood as a grace. But Origen himself is not clear about this gratuitous character.[166] What is more, the *actual* experience of the interior fire, as opposed to the insensibility on the part of a person who is obstinate, must be considered as a special grace. This is something more than is possible merely by reason of the indwelling of the Logos. Only on these conditions would the specifically gratuitous character of the impulse to conversion be fully safeguarded. The notion of just such an impulse is widely accepted today and, from what we have said, gains in both importance and clarity through Origen's thought. This grace is not merely a question of an extrinsic psychological stimulus to a change of attitude, a stimulus which would be connected with its very formal 'supernatural' ('ontological') 'elevation' of this act. Rather, the impulse is determined concretely by the actual situation in which the sinner finds himself. This impulse is the awakening experience within the human being of the burning contradiction which created freedom cannot exclude from its nature, the contradiction between one's personal decision and the inalienable, real, ontological, supernatural orientation towards God which is an indelible mark of human existence. It is at this point, at the very ground of being, that God's fire burns, that God's voice continually calls the sinner from the grave of his sin.

In this view of Origen we meet for the first time a major theology of *attritio*. However, it is not considered here, as it is from Augustine down to the present day, principally as an imperfect act of conversion from sin by reason of its imperfect motive. Rather, Origen considers first and foremost the experience and the recognition of the radical opposition to God on the part of the sinner himself. The conversion from sin follows not only because of the punishment, which is a misfortune for men, but because of the judging holiness of

God, who is a consuming fire. Origen knows very well that, in the final analysis, it is only love that can move created freedom with a definitively free 'necessity'.[167] Nevertheless, quite rightly, he does not see conversion from sin primarily as a free movement of love which, with a freedom of indifference, turns itself towards God. Rather, he considers this movement as a consequence of the experience of God who burns like a fire within man and who, as such, is the first thing to make man aware that he is destitute by virtue of his sin. The first grace of a sinner is not that which represents his highest and final activity, namely love, but the experience and the acceptance of what he actually is: man within whom God's judgement is already burning.

B) THE PENANCE OF THE SINNER

The experience of the fire of judgement at the ground of being does not, however, represent the whole of penance. This fire would only consume sin. According to Origen's thought, however, corporeity as such is already a manifestation of original sin and the means of overcoming it.[168] Thus that which occurs at the very core of a spiritual creature must also be expressed externally and bodily, as reflecting and adumbrating the 'true' realities. But this means that God himself (or the Logos), considered as the real physician who heals mortal sins, is obliged to intervene with burning and cutting in a way which begins in the sinner's heart but extends to include his *whole* reality. Man must not only bear all this passively, but even do it actively by his penance which, in its turn, is influenced and helped by the whole of created reality. The purpose is the *spontaneus interitus carnis,* the destructive overthrow of man's sinful reality as a being of flesh, and this as a free act of his own penance. This is what we must now consider in more detail.[169]

God has many different ways of forgiving sins.[170] The fire burning in man's heart spreads over the whole man.[171] It begins as a punishment of the conscience and a torment of the heart[172] and burns more fiercely than an external fire which torments martyrs.[173] It consists in disgust over the sin which has been committed.[174] Man is completely paralysed by the terror of the interior judgement, he no longer wishes to eat and drink,[175] he weeps with groans coming from his heart.[176] Then this penance becomes active, a *spontaneus carnis interitus*;[177] man himself chooses the *afflictio corporis, quae solet a paenitentibus expendi,* and thus brings about himself the *interitus carnis* which consists in the *afflictio.*[178] To this belong the *abstinentia cotidiana,*[179] the *severitatis austeritas,*[180] in other words, the external works of penance, as they were customary in the *dura et laboriosa paenitentia,*[181] the *πικρὰ ἁμαρτίας μετάνοια.*[182] Because the *interitus carnis* also consists in spontaneity above all, a man can be exhorted to undertake it actively. *Spontaneum suscipiat carnis interitum.*[183] Through this free undertaking the terror caused by God's judgement can really take effect and the *sensus carnalis* or, as it is also called, the *cupiditas carnalis,*[184] can die out. This is the death which, as opposed to the death of sin, is caused by God himself. It is the *laudabilis carnis interitus,* the *mors laudabilis, qua peccato quis moritur,* in which also the *flesh* dies to sin and vices.[185] Viewed from the purely temporal angle, this 'death and becoming' can occur very quickly,[186] although, in comparison with the brief moment of sin, this process can last a very long time.[187] Nevertheless, this whole active penance on the sinner's part is only the willing acceptance and performance of that penance which is imposed upon him by God and by the fact that he is a sinful man. It includes the readiness to suffer purifying afflictions which are laid down by God: sickness of the body, loss of earthly possessions, death of relatives and all those external sufferings which are attributable to God's providence.[188] In addition to all this, it is still necessary to undergo the obligatory *correptiones* of the church community with patience.[189] The supra-terrestrial created spirits, too, take part in this varied penitential suffering in order to change man by his salutary death. The *interitus carnis* of a person guilty of mortal sin is achieved by a 'handing over to Satan', an event which is reflected externally in excommunication by the Church. In any case, the devil takes the place which God has relinquished in the Christian who has committed mortal sin.[190] The devil, however, is not only man's enemy but also ἐκδικητής, and this means God's punishing agent.[191] Thus it is better to experience his 'curse' rather than a 'blessing' in *miseriae et supplicia* and to bear these with patience.[192] This applies even to the inner 'state of confusion' (*σπαράσσεσθαι*) caused by these 'Babylonians'.[193]

According to Origen, even the consequences of sin caused by demons have a salvific meaning. Thus he does not distinguish these from the punishments of sin which have been prescribed for man's salvation by the good angels.[194] This may be due to the fact that in his view all angels, albeit in differing degrees, are fallen.[195] In any case, the good angels also have a role to play in the punishments which are administered to sinners in penance.[196]

Up until now we have considered only the objective penance of the sinner, that is, apart from its ecclesial aspect. In this way we have tried to determine the actual content of the ἀπολαμβάνειν τὰς ἁμαρτίας which, as an alternative to a simple *aphesis*, remits sins after baptism. A proper understanding of Origen's view, however, requires further clarifications.

It is obvious that, according to Origen's way of thinking, punishment has an essentially medicinal character.[197] An exclusively vindictive punishment, which would be merely the expression of the objective value of the moral law, is totally alien to him. He considers the punishment of sin, first and foremost, as the intrinsic and connatural *consequence* of sin, flowing from the very nature of the offence.[198] Such an idea of the punishment of sin does not necessarily imply that this latter must come to an end. Nevertheless these two ideas are linked together by Origen. In fact it would be conceivable that an intrinsic consequence of sin, which should actually facilitate and encourage conversion, in the event does not achieve this aim. It is, after all, possible that a man remains definitively unrepentant for other reasons. Thus this notion of the punishment of sin as an essentially medicinal *consequence* of sin can hardly be rejected on the supposition that it makes the general idea of the *apocatastasis* inevitable. Obviously in the present instance it is a question of punishment only because and in so far as this is a consequence of sin, and not *vice versa*. Moreover, it cannot be said that such a notion *necessarily* includes the denial of an *external* punishment of sin, a position which Jerome actually accused Origen of holding.[199]

In other words, it is perfectly possible to understand a punishment of sin as a consequence which flows necessarily from the nature of sin itself. This would be the clash between the sinner's guilty act and condition—which could even be definitive—and the objectively imposed structure and order of his true reality. In this sense it could be described as an 'external' punishment. Origen is perfectly able to grant this[200] without relinquishing his basic speculative principle that in the religious sphere there are no punishments which could be considered vindictive. The latter would be punishments which are not the intrinsic consequence of guilt and which are imposed by an external cause only as a vindictive reaction to sin. 'Punishment' arises as the consequence of sin from the clash between guilt and the objective ordering of reality which exists for itself and not primarily in view of the punishment of the sinner. Thus this reality *also* reveals the transcendence of the moral order. In this sense one could *also* speak of a 'vindictive' aspect, of *δίκη ἅμα καὶ ἰατρεία*.[201]

This notion of the medicinal nature of the punishment of sin obviously raises several questions which are not answered explicitly by Origen. How, for instance, could such punishments really overcome sin? They can certainly not be understood as the execution of a purely juridical sentence. We will go into this question in more detail below. At the same time, there can be no question here of what one may call an automatically effective self-destruction of evil.[202]

Such a notion would be gnostic and would be in direct contradiction to the concept of freedom which Origen directs against Gnosticism. If, in his view, guilt springs essentially from freedom, it follows that it can be taken away only by freedom. It may appear from many passages in his work that moral evil is taken away simply by the fact that, being suffered by God's longanimity, it leads finally *ad absurdum* or, as non-existent darkness, it is dissolved necessarily by God's light.[203] Thus it would seem that, in the final analysis, in the light of the general teaching of the restoration of all things, the distinction between a punitive consequence of sin which is accepted freely and one which is suffered merely passively is only secondary and provisional. Nevertheless, for Origen man's freedom is an original datum, and thus in his view punishment can have a salvific meaning only if it is undertaken willingly. If, therefore, God's punishment is to have a meaning for man's salvation, it must be able to persuade man to undertake this punishment freely.[204] Even on this supposition, however, it is still not possible to avoid the question of how punishment, considered as the consequence and manifestation of guilt in the flesh, can, by being freely accepted, be so changed as to become a cure for the guilt. In other words, how is it that guilt, which becomes punishment and enters into the instrument of the flesh, is able to be so ambivalent that it can also become the manifestation of, and even an impulsion towards, the free return of the spirit towards God which removes guilt? To answer this question from Origen's thought would presuppose at least a precise treatment of his metaphysics and theology of *σάρξ*. For the 'flesh' means two things: the manifestation of guilt and the means of taking it away.

Such an undertaking, however, in the context of this study would lead us too far astray.

It follows from Origen's view of the nature of punishment that there can be no question of a juridical notion of penance. This penance can be nothing other than the voluntary undertaking of the punishments of sin. Its purpose is man's inner restoration to health, and it ends as soon as this end is reached. In such a way of thinking it is impossible to have the idea of a juridical relationship of guilt between the sinner and God, a state which would be independent of man's moral condition and so would require a punishment which, even after man's complete conversion, would still be in order. If occasionally it does appear that Origen does entertain such an idea,[205] this is only a question of images and comparisons with human relationships which ought not to be exaggerated. This observation is confirmed by another consideration. According to Origen, actions and even sins 'form' men. They do not simply fade into the past in such a way that they can, nevertheless, still be reckoned juridically. Rather, they leave in man a *τύπος* which remains imprinted on his heart,[206] *secundum sui qualitatem agentis mentem imaginantur et formant.*[207] *Notae quaedam et signacula relinquantur* in the depth of the heart.[208] The object of reforming penance is the real, ontological condition of man.[209] Such an idea of the meaning of penance implies that this could not be thought of as the execution of a purely juridical sentence. While in Cyprian 'healing' was used essentially as an image for the endurance of a punishment, in Origen it is precisely the contrary.

With reference to what we have already seen, the observation which we have just made clarifies two points. First, according to Origen, despite his theological reflection on the question, the difference between sins, that is, between mortal sins and non-mortal sins, cannot be as clear-cut as it is for us today. *Every* sin leaves behind its *τύπος*, which has to be remitted by penance, if not always by official church penance. This means that the difference between serious and light sins is also made somewhat unimportant, especially since the remission of the *τύπος* of a mortal sin is always in fact possible, at the very latest by means of the fire of judgement in the next life. This may be a reason why in the early period there are only a few witnesses for mortal sin as a loss of *grace*[210] or, indeed, for non-mortal sins as not radically destroying the grace of baptism.

Second, it is impossible to observe in Origen a clear differentiation between 'guilt' and 'punishment'. For instance, punishment is corporeity, man's inner confusion and division, his contradiction of God, of the inner fire and, especially, of the structure of his given reality. All this, however, is so essentially a consequence of guilt that, according to Origen, the latter is only actually finally remitted when it is destroyed by penance or the fire of the next life. In other words, when the reality through which guilty freedom has operated and expressed itself is transformed by the *interitus carnis*. Thus it is possible to understand why Origen appears to know no other moment for the remission of guilt than the completion of penance itself. Leaving aside the baptismal *aphesis,* the remission of guilt is seen as an event and a process, not as the infusion of grace at a particular moment. Although mortal sin is also considered as a loss of baptismal grace and although certain consequences are derived from this for the prescribed penance, no further account is taken of the specific nature of mortal sin in the question of the nature of forgiveness. As in the case of all other sins, it is here a question of overcoming the *moral* condition which man has acquired through mortal sin. Origen is less explicit about the direct regaining of baptismal grace. Certainly he knows clearly that the Holy Spirit is bestowed in baptism in a way which would not be possible through a mere moral transformation of man's conscience.[211] Nevertheless, he hardly looks at penance from this point of view. Penance achieves forgiveness by man's moral reformation. Obviously the idea of a reacquisition of grace by penance is not radically excluded, for Origen also knows that the Holy Spirit is the cause of men's sanctification.[212] He does not, however, look at penance explicitly[213] from this point of view, even though it is obviously implied in his notion of mortal sin. This is clear from the opposition which he establishes between baptism in the Spirit and baptism by fire,[214] the latter including penance in this life.[215] This penance is seen by Origen more in its opposition to baptism in water and the Spirit than as a new reception of the Spirit. Both baptisms are similar, however, in that they remit sin.[216] In the case of baptism proper this applies *de iure,* at least, if not in fact. But this observation also has a positive aspect, along the lines of Cyprian's theology: once the bestowal of grace is not tied clearly and explicitly to subjective penance it becomes possible to see the bestowal of the Spirit as the effect of the Church's action in the remission of sins. In the case of penance this does not appear to be so. It still remains to be considered, however, whether and how Origen himself thinks along these lines.

All that has just been said raises once more the question of the relationship of personal penance to grace. Here is one way of answering this question: 'He [Christ] brings forgiveness of sins, we receive it in baptism . . . but this forgiveness is confined to those sins which were committed *before* baptism. The sins which we commit later . . . must be expiated by ourselves'.[217] 'The baptized person must obtain for himself the forgiveness of sins committed after baptism'.[218] Such a view is surely correct. If the remission of post-baptismal sins, as opposed to the *aphesis* at initiation consists in the fact that one 'takes it upon oneself' (ἀπολαμβάνειν τὰς ἁμαρτίας) and pursues it and its bitter consequences to the end, then this remission appears not to demand directly the redeeming grace of *Christ* but to be performed by man 'himself'. We have already seen that it is at least *possible* to conceive, even in Origen's system, the beginning of conversion and the experience of the interior fire of judgement as grace. Already the mere fact of this experience means that God has desisted from his great anger, which would otherwise make the sinner insensitive to the fire. The very presence of the fire is itself a grace, since the contradiction implied in sin would not exist at all if God did not preserve the supernatural existence of the Logos within man. It is in this way that he prevents man from remaining imprisoned in his complacent carnal existence as a being of this transitory world.

However, all this does not answer the question posed above. For the actual penance which is required for the *interitus carnis* goes beyond the interior fire of judgement. Now the question is: should this additional element be considered as itself a grace or as the work of man alone? Can such a penance be a grace *Christi* and, in particular, be related with his actual work of redemption on the cross? Indeed, even the interior fire of judgement could be an 'ideal' grace of the Logos, having no connection whatsoever with the salvation which God's incarnate Son obtained on the cross. What makes this difficulty even more acute is the fact that the *interitus carnis* which remits sin is, in fact, to be undertaken for mortal sins outside the community of the Church, so that thereby the sinner may become worthy to share once again in the Church's fellowship of grace.[219] This fact could indicate that penance is to be understood as man's own work. Against such a view, however, it must be stressed that, according to Origen, the *misericors et miserator Dominus* has provided the possibility of a penance for sins committed after baptism, precisely because he did not wish the sinner to die.[220] But does this necessarily mean that the remission of sins through personal penance, which is doubtless necessary, is itself a grace? Certainly Origen recognizes that there are graces which are effective even *before* actual membership of the Church.[221] Thus penance outside the Church with a view to regaining membership with it *need not necessarily* be a work devoid of grace which a man has undertaken on his own initiative. If this were the case, then he would only have finished with sin in so far as he has expiated it completely on his own.

Penance, however, in so far as it is *interitus carnis,* is in fact precisely a participation in the death *Christi*;[222] the renunciation of sins, in so far as it is a conversion, is a crucifixion with the Lord.[223] It is Christ himself who is poor and weak in those who are spiritually weak and poor; with them he suffers in the prison of the world,[224] while the sinner hangs invisibly with him on the cross.[225] The Lamb of God continues to take away the sins of *every* individual until sin has been totally eliminated from the entire world.[226] If, in reality, the mystery of the incarnation and of the death of the Logos consists in the fact that the dominion of the devil and the sinful flesh is overthrown,[227] then penance is a participation in Christ's own destiny. For, in the final analysis, it is his coming in the flesh and especially his death which make possible the experience of the opposition between flesh and spirit[228] and elevate the order of the flesh to that of heaven.[229] Thus the *interitus carnis,* far from being the conquest of sin by man himself, is a part of Christ's continuing destiny in this world. Indeed, it is, in a certain sense, the most important part of this destiny, since it is more essential for him to triumph in us than for himself alone.[230] But this means that penance is a grace. Moreover, it should now appear to the impartial observer that the teaching of the *aphesis* in baptism is even more problematical than the victory over sin by post-baptismal penance. For if every sin leaves its τύπος in man, if especially the whole of man's fleshly existence is an expression of the creature's sinfulness, and if Origen explicitly recognizes that baptism represents not the end but only the beginning of the complete destruction of sin in the flesh,[231] then his notion of the *aphesis* in baptism appears to fit less comfortably into *his* system of *Christian* redemption than his teaching on penance. In other words, the mere remission of the 'punishment' due to sin must inevitably appear as a retention of the medicine which heals, since punishment and the means of healing are materially identical, and thus the healing is not yet complete through baptism alone. It follows that Origen must have accepted the *aphesis* teaching as part of traditional teaching and handed it on without having integrated this idea into his system and experience.[232]

In view of all this, it would be erroneous to wish to explain Origen's notion of *metanoia* solely on the basis of the *aphesis*. It would also be misleading, on the same basis, to understand *metanoia* as an expiation of sin, without grace, by man's autonomous moral effort. Rather, it is a matter of a specifically Christian event, in so far as it is a participation in Christ's redeeming death. This is, however, an event which is possible not only at its onset but also in its final execution only 'in Christ' and, in this sense, must be a grace. Baptism in water and baptism in fire are *sacramenta* in the Lord's hand.[233] *Omnis purificatio peccatorum, etiam haec, quae* (as opposed to baptism, the grace of which is granted only once) *per paenitentiam quaeritur, illius ope indiget, de cuius latere aqua processit et sanguis*.[234]

III. CHURCH PENANCE

1. The Ecclesial Meaning of Penance

So far we have been concerned with the personal penance of the sinner himself. Now we must consider this penance further; that is, in so far as it occurs within the Church and is accompanied and met by the activity of the church community. First of all, however, we must consider an aspect of sin itself which, although we have not previously given it much attention, is very important in the present context. This is the fact that sin itself has an ecclesial aspect. According to Origen, the sinner 'dies' through his mortal sin, in so far as he becomes impervious to the healing influence of the Church which is able to preserve him from death. If, later, we are going to understand Origen's view on the nature of excommunication, we must at this point stress that he considers every sin an immediate contradiction of the Church, in so far as this latter is a holy community and the body of Christ himself. In this church community the illness of sin is by no means the private affair of the individual affected. No one in the Church is able to say: *quid hoc ad me spectat, si alius male agit?* For it is a matter of: *polluitur enim ex uno peccatore . . . plebs universa*. To tolerate sin would be a *universae ecclesiae moliri interitum,* since then God's anger is directed to the whole people.[235] Also just a little leaven corrupts *totam unitatis conspersionem et consensus* in the Church.[236] The person who is guilty of a sin of impurity, for example, offends not only his own body as the temple of God but also the body of the Church. *In omnem ecclesiam videtur delinquere, qui corpus suum maculaverit, quia per unum membrum macula in omne corpus diffunditur.*[237] Because of this effect which the sin of every baptized person has on the church community Origen is fully aware that the Church is a Church of sinners. This is true not only in the sense that sinful humanity, like the prostitute Rahab or the sinful woman in the gospel, is accepted by Christ and saved from sin,[238] but also in the sense that in this world sinfulness is a *permanent* mark of the Church itself. The Lord weeps over the Church as he wept over Jerusalem,[239] and in this world it can never be totally cleansed from sin.[240] At the same time Origen still considers the Church to be holy. This means that there is a kind of dialectic at work in the relationship of the sinner to the Church. On the one hand, the sinner still belongs to the Church, since before excommunication he is still one of its members, at least externally, and is a *νομιζόμενος εἶναι ἀπὸ τῆς ἐκκλησίας*.[241] And this 'reckoned as belonging to the Church' cannot be a mere illusion for the man who, in his earthly experience, is unable to separate the cockle from the wheat, the vessels of mercy from those of anger, the good fish from the bad. The fact is that both are found together in the one Church at this time.[242] If this were not so, the Lord would not be able to weep over her.[243]

On the other hand, the sinner stands in permanent opposition to the holy Church. Thus, even without being excommunicated, he is, because of his sin, already in fact 'outside'.[244] This is why Origen is able occasionally to count as belonging to the Church only the saints and to exclude from its fellowship those who *πιστεύειν νομιζόμενοι* ἐκκλησιαστικοί.[245] It is not possible to resolve this dialectical relationship of the sinner to the Church in Origen's thought[246] simply on the assumption that the sinner is allowed membership of the visibly hierarchical Church but not to the 'spiritual' fellowship of the Church. In any case, it is easy to show[247] that for Origen these two realities are not independent of each other. This point is particularly clear in the question which we are now discussing. It is precisely the connection and the relationship between these two sides of the one Church that explain why the loss of grace through a mortal sin constitutes a contradiction not only against the spiritual interior fellowship of Christians who are with and in the Lord but also against the *visible* Church. It is for this reason that a person guilty of such a sin should, in principle, always be excommunicated, unless this is practically impossible. Mere leniency, however, could not prevent it.[248] Origen could certainly subscribe to the idea that the sinner still remains a member of the visible Church. However, the more this truth was understood undialectically, in the sense that the Christian's relationship to the Church had in no way changed by his sin, the more insignificant excommunication appeared as a measure which was appropriate to every mortal sin. It was felt less and less that membership of the church community was the prerogative of the saint and that, for the sinner, it was a contradiction of his interior condition. Thus exclusion from the fellowship of the Church was considered less and less as an essential part of the penitential process, even though it is still present today in the exclusion from the Eucharist. Because of the way in which excommunication was understood and practised it was inevitable that it should come to be regarded as an additional means of punishment for specific mortal sins. This development originated only with Augustine's polemic against the Donatists and did not begin with Origen. It is necessary to understand this if we are to appreciate properly Origen's insistence on a 'binding', that is, excommunication for mortal sins.

2. *The Church's Saving Action with Regard to the Sinner*

Mortal sin, of its very nature, demands a clarification and an explanation of the relationship in which the sinner stands to the Church. His membership has, in fact, become ambiguous, and thus it is necessary to make it clear that he no longer belongs to the Church 'in truth'. The sinner must, therefore, be excommunicated. Since, however, according to Origen, every consequence and punishment of sin must, in the final analysis, be salvific, even this death must issue in a new life of the spirit.[249] Excommunication is, therefore, the Church's first saving act with regard to the sinner.[250]

Nevertheless, Origen does not appear to recognize a precise technical term for this excommunication.[251] *Tradere in interitum carnis* includes excommunication, since it concerns the actual *paenitentes*. Nevertheless, this is a general concept, since it also includes the *afflictio corporis*.[252] Although κόλασις and *correptio* are expressed most poignantly in excommunication, they still signify any correction of a sinner, even when he is not excluded from the Church on account of a mortal sin.[253] Apart from the question of terminology, the fact of excommunication is expressed quite simply as an expulsion from the Church, and this in both the active and the passive sense. The result in either case is that the sinner is 'outside'.[254] The notion of *ligare* (δέειν) seems to be used by Origen almost in the technical sense as an expression for the excommunication of a sinner. The bishop's power of *binding* is exercised precisely in the act of excommunication and even in those cases where the exclusion can, in principle, be lifted and is intended for only a certain time. Thus binding and loosing are not, at least conceptually, contradictory or mutually exclusive notions but, even supposing the intention to bind really, two successive phases of one dynamic event.[255]

Excommunication is imposed by the bishop. The exclusion from the community is expressed *per episcopi vocem,*[256] *per episcopi sententiam,*[257] *ab episcopo,*[258] *per sacerdotes,*[259] *per eos qui ecclesiae praesident et potestatem habent non solum solvendi sed et ligandi,*[260] with reference to an *apostolica auctoritas*[261] of the *episcopus arguens*.[262] All these expressions reflect the *actual* practice in Origen's day. There is no doubt that the bishops at that time claimed this power for themselves not only in practice but also as their theoretically justified right. Origen himself explicitly attests this fact.[263] Indeed, given the actual position of the bishop in the Church at that time,[264] it is unthinkable that anyone else other than he could have exercised such a right of excluding people from the Church. Nevertheless, it is possible that Origen recognized, at least theoretically, in others than the bishops a power of binding and a right to excommunicate. In any event, it is no argument against the bishops' exclusive right to 'bind' that good Christians 'avoid' those people who, through their influence, could corrupt them but who for some reason or other either cannot be excommunicated or have not in fact been excommunicated.[265] In behaving so, these Christians are merely following the exhortation of 2 Thessalonians 3:6. In any case, it is a private practice of individual Christians which does not alter the official position of a sinner with regard to the Church. It was obviously not at all infrequent that Christians did not want to have anything to do with others whom they considered, rightly or even wrongly, to be a 'scandal' for the Church and for the liturgical assembly in particular.[266] Origen approved of this behaviour of privately avoiding sinners. He held the view that where it was a question of lighter sins for which no actual excommunication was imposed but which were not renounced one could regard those Christians who committed such sins according to Matthew 18 *privately* as 'pagans and public sinners'.[267] This 'binding'[268] is obviously an expression of the sinner's moral situation before God and in no way affects the bishop's exclusive right to bind in the strict sense. The meaning here is quite dfferent from the official exclusion from the Church.

It does seem, however, that according to Origen all the τέλειοι also have, along with Peter, the keys of the Kingdom of heaven, just as they all also have the power mentioned in John 20:22.[269] Thus *omnis fidelis,* who is Peter by virtue of his heavenly profession of faith and a way of life which corresponds to it, has the keys of the Kingdom of heaven not only in so far as he enters into the Kingdom of heaven through the door of his own virtues,[270] but also to the extent that his sentence of binding and loosing with regard to others is the judgement of God 'invested' in him. Obviously this applies only when such a sentence emanates from one who is truly a Peter, a τέλειος.[271] But precisely how are these views of Origen to be understood? Later we will consider more closely his idea of the 'binding' on the part of a perfect spiritual person; this need not concern us at the moment. Where it is a question of a 'binding', it would appear that Origen is not thinking only of the hierarchy. We will examine the actual reason for this later when we consider the question of the 'loosing'. What needs to be said here, however, is that basically, according to Origen's fundamental conception, every external hierarchy, together with its activity, must have corresponding to it necessarily an internal hierarchy within the Church, together with its activity. Nevertheless, Origen is unable to describe this 'binding' concretely. His view on this point remains abstract, unclear and general. If ever he wishes to provide a concrete content for, or a meaningful example of, this idea of the possibility of 'binding' on the part of an authentic Peter or, *vice versa,* the impossibility to do this on the part of those who are not Peter, then he refers to the episcopal power of binding.[272] This shows that in fact in the Church of Origen's day there was no other 'binding' than that which was performed by the bishop. And this is why he could not evoke a concrete example of another kind. But the question needs to be asked: what is the nature of a binding on the part of a spiritual person who is not a bishop? Certainly, within a community led by bishops, there can be no question of a recognized and official excommunication existing alongside that of the bishop, let alone contrary to his will.[273] At the same time, a purely internal binding would be meaningless, since Origen himself never tires of stressing that the sinner is bound before God merely by his deed.[274] It would be possible, however, for a spiritual and charismatic person to 'bind' meaningfully in the sense that, either privately or publicly, he exhorts, warns and rebukes sinners and thus makes them aware of their unconfessed sinful condition. This role of the spiritual person in the Church, which could be even more effective when related to the avoidance of sinners on the part of strict Christians which we have already seen, is perfectly feasible. It would have been very important and, in fact, would have been no different from that played by all the great 'preachers of penance' throughout the history of the Church. It is indeed a role which is indispensable to the constant need of spiritual renewal within the Church, which must always begin with the acknowledgement that it is 'bound' by sin. From the dogmatic point of view such a role is thoroughly compatible with the bishop's exclusive right to the official 'binding'. Thus it can be styled a 'binding' only by analogy.

But all this does not answer fully the questions concerning the authority which is at the origin of excommunication. Does Origen demand as part of the episcopal authority which imposes an excommunication that the bishop himself be a spiritual person? In other words: if a bishop were a sinner would he so lose his power that his excommunication would be invalid? Is Origen in this sense to be understood as a forerunner of Donatism?

In the general introduction to this study the point has already been made that Origen's *general* orientation in ecclesiology is *not* Donatist.[275] But is this still the case with regard to this particular question? What we are doing here is to confine the question of the requirements for the validity of the penitential measures taken by a bishop to the validity of 'binding'. For its part, the 'loosing' of sin and of the sinner is not only the counterpart to 'binding' but includes more than the mere lifting of excommunication. Thus in the case of loosing the situation and the circumstances can be quite different from those in the case of the binding. In the first place, we need to note that Origen recognizes an excommunication which he holds as invalid and illegitimate.[276] We must, however, look more closely at what he means by this. For Origen an excommunication is above all 'invalid' when it does not express clearly and effectively the actual exclusion from the Church which has occurred through sin. But this does not mean that it is not present visibly within the Church, at least as a fact, albeit juridically invalid. Nor does it mean that it should be considered non-existent. This is why, in the case of an unjust excommunication or, for example, deposition from the clerical state, Origen's advice is very simple: bear it patiently.[277] Even when a bishop acts unjustly his external authority is not to be ignored. Even in the case of an invalid sentence, this authority must be respected with patience. In this respect, therefore, according to Origen the bishop's authority with regard to excommunication is not dependent upon the moral rectitude of his behaviour and judgement. It follows that it depends even less upon his personal holiness. Nevertheless, an unjust excommunication can do no harm to the person excommunicated in the internal sphere of grace and salvation. But this is self-evident.

What we have just seen, however, seems to be contradicted by Origen's teaching that only the *holy* are able to 'bind', and this only with a just judgement.[278] In order to resolve the apparent conflict between this view and the previous result of our study we need to examine the *Sitz im Leben* of Origen and his theology. It is obvious that the view which smacks of Donatism has a double origin in his theology. First, Origen wishes to preclude the view that unjust excommunications have a salvific value in God's eyes. His own bitter personal experience is in evidence here. Thus the fact that the bishop must be a τέλειος can be understood as a defence against an *unjust* excommunication. For it is obvious that Origen did not wish to hold that practically all excommunications, even those of people who were really sinners, were null before God simply because the bishops concerned were not τέλειοι.[279] Indeed, the picture which Origen paints of the moral condition of the episcopate of his day hardly gives the impression that he considered the majority of bishops at that time to be perfect spiritual people or even good Christians. Thus the conditions which he lays down for a valid excommunication sound more Donatist than they were intended; they are in fact directed against the religious significance of unjust excommunications.

Second, Origen considers the conditions for binding always in connection with the conditions for 'loosing' and the remission of sin. Given his comprehensive notion of 'loosing', he was able to lay down such conditions without their having to be understood in a Donatist sense. The rigorous application of the same conditions to the binding, however, would lead to false conclusions. In fact Origen was much more concerned with the question of correct loosing than with that of binding.[280] If he strays from the text which he wishes to interpret he considers binding and loosing somewhat unguardedly, carelessly and imprecisely in the same category. It is only if this phenomenon is forced that Origen is made to contradict what we have seen to be his notion of unjust excommunication, as well as to maintain a false opposition to the anti-Donatism which he otherwise holds. When it is seen in its true light, therefore, Origen's view of excommunication is that it is declared by the bishop in so far as he is an official and not because he is a spiritual person.

3. *Excommunication*

A) THE OBJECT OF EXCOMMUNICATION

All mortal sins, whether they are publicly known or secret, *are subject to* excommunication. This basic principle is of the greatest importance for a correct understanding of the institution of penance in Origen. That is why we must consider it in more detail at this point. In the first place, it is obvious that without any doubt the (three) capital sins considered 'irremediably' to lead to death *have to be* bound. For these even the attempt at a remission through 'prayer' without binding is forbidden and ineffective.[281] Apart from these, 'mortal sins' are mentioned as the obligatory object of excommunication. This applies—although with some reservation—even before the sinner, after repeated exhortation, has shown that he is clearly unrepentant.[282] Beyond what we have already seen Origen provides only a little information about the individual sins which are submitted to excommunication. Explicitly named in connection with excommunication are ἀσέλγεια,[283] *incesti scelus,*[284] impurity and blasphemy,[285] but also heresy and offences against the *disciplina ecclesiastica* and the *Evangelii regula.*[286] Otherwise, sins deserving excommunication are hinted at only very vaguely.[287] In general all mortal sins have to be bound, while the mortal sins in question are to be understood in the sense which we have already outlined. What is important, however, is the special stress which Origen puts on the fact that even secret sins have, in principle, to be submitted to excommunication, although it is also obvious to him that many of these sins escape episcopal excommunication since they are not self-evident. The 'sin against God' after baptism (*in fide*) must not, however, be kept secret but is to be made known to 'all' in order that it may be remitted by the *interventus* and the *correptio* of all.[288] If a person should 'remember' later that he has burdened himself with serious guilt, then he must 'of his own accord' undertake the *interitus carnis* (*spontaneum carnis interitum suscipiat*).[289] If public penance is described as an occasion when the sinner *non erubescit sacerdoti Domini indicare peccatum,*[290] this presupposes that, on other occasions, the priest has no knowledge of the guilt in question. Thus public penance did not exist merely for generally known scandals but also for secret sins. In any case, the exhortation to seek the advice of an experienced doctor of souls in order to discern whether a secret sin is a *languor, qui in conventu totius ecclesiae exponi debeat et curari* shows that secret sins were not as a matter of course and without consideration exempt from obligatory public penance. It was a question of deciding in each individual case whether the guilt was so great that a public penance was absolutely necessary, that is, whether it really was a mortal sin.[291] Origen expresses the same exhortation to confess secret sins publicly, despite the fear of humiliation and being despised by others, in another passage of the same homily.[292] Origen's basic ideas also lead to the same conclusion. For if, on the one hand, even secret sin separates a man interiorly from the Church[293] and if, on the other hand, it is *only* the practical impossibility that hinders the community of the Church from imposing of its own accord, as in the case of *peccata manifesta,* excommunication,[294] then this view presupposes that an interior 'excommunication' which exists in God's eyes *should* be expressed in exclusion from the Church. Whenever a sinner earnestly wishes to expiate his own fault this excommunication which he introduces himself and which is, in this sense, the *sponataneus interitus carnis,* must be his first step towards penance.

In the case of the *levis culpa,* however, there is no question of an excommunication.[295] And in those cases where it is not a matter of the spontaneous confession of serious guilt but of an intervention on the Church's part against sins, allowance is made for moderation and leniency in the sentence passed. In these cases excommunication should be applied *sparsam.*[296]

B) EXCOMMUNICATION IN PRACTICE

The bishops exercise a kind of supervision over the Christian life of their communities. They are strictly obliged to ensure, without any respect for persons, that the *ecclesiastica disciplina et Evangelii regula* are correctly observed. They are the guardians of the community, who must follow the example of the Lord and, as the 'eye' of Christ's body, are responsible for the whole Church.[297] This supervision enables the bishop to know the religious and the moral life of every Christian in the community, although he is undoubtedly supported in this matter by the other members of the community.[298] They not only have to admonish the sinner privately but they are also obliged to report him to the Church if he is not showing any sign of improvement. For the same reason they ought not to refuse to appear before the bishop as trustworthy witnesses against a person who is accused of a fault.[299] It is obvious that such a supervision of the way of life of every individual Christian was a difficult task for all those concerned: the bishop, the clergy and the faithful. Thus the clergy were not infrequently afraid of being slandered by the accused. This applied even to bishops, few of whom were saints. The temptation was to appear not strict but lenient. Thus there was a continual risk of turning a blind eye even to offences which were clearly subject to excommunication.[300] Indeed, some sins were explicitly declared to be curable without excommunication,[301] if it were anticipated that there would be a violent opposition from those concerned, who were unwilling either to be corrected or to be deprived of their rights as members of the Church. Given the defamatory nature of excommunication, all this is understandable.[302] If, however, a bishop is conscientious he must take the necessary measures, once it becomes known that a member of his community is guilty of a serious fault. He may become aware of this fault by his own observation, by information from a third party[303] or even by the spontaneous confession of the sinner himself.[304] In these circumstances, the following should happen, at least according to Origen's theory: if it is a question of definite and indisputable mortal sins, such as unnatural impurity, adultery and murder, the sentence of excommunication should be declared clearly and decisively.[305] If the position is not so clear, as is often the case with a spontaneous confession to a doctor of souls, then the director of conscience has to decide whether a penance of excommunication is required.[306] If the sin was made known to the church authorities in any other way, then the sinner should be corrected by the bishop privately, with the possible cooperation of witnesses, or even publicly before the whole community. This official and possibly even public correction could take place quite independently of an excommunication. In fact it (*correptio, confutatio*) occurred more often than excommunication.[307]

If this correction is ineffective and if the sinner perseveres in his fault which is certainly not a *levis culpa,* then he must be excommunicated.[308] Obviously the excommunication was performed before the whole community with a certain official and liturgical solemnity.[309] Thus its defamatory character was obvious.[310] Of its very nature this ceremony would include a repeated *correptio* and if, at this moment, the sinner were repentant he would confess his guilt.[311] At least as far as previously secret sins are concerned, it is very possible that this public confession was not very detailed.[312] The admission that one was guilty of mortal sin was already in itself a *publicare delictum* which was defamatory. Moreover, in fact and in practice there was very little difference between an actual individual public confession of sins and excommunication in the presence[313] of the penitent, who accepted this exclusion from the community. Certainly people were not reflectively aware of this difference, as theoretically important as it may appear to us today. When the guilt was already known publicly before the sinner's confession, the bishop had no need to exercise any reserve in his *correptio*. Origen suggests that such a public confession often found an echo of deep pharisaism in the community of 'good Christians'.[314]

The whole event took place with the active participation of the bishop, who used his discretion to impose the excommunication whenever it appeared *to him* to be appropriate. From the very nature of the case it is obvious that, at least where it was a question of previously secret sins, this act on the bishop's part had to be preceded by a private avowal and confession by the sinner before the bishop. This provided him with the reason for his decision and its execution. We need not concern ourselves here with the question of whether the doctor of souls who, in the case of secret sins, was to be consulted, had always to be, in Origen's theory, a bishop or a priest. In any case, what is confided to him in private confession has also to be brought before the bishop in the form of a personal avowal, at least in the sense that, where a public penance is necessary, it is essential that confession is also made to the bishop.[315]

There are only a few obscure indications in Origen concerning the excommunicated penitent's external condition. As far as those who are truly repentant are concerned, the exclusion would be lifted after some time and the intervening period represented a kind of second catechumenate.[316] Since it had to be a period of hard personal penance,[317] the connection of the penitent with the bishop during it could not be severed entirely. Obviously the penitents had to provide proof of their conversion.[318] At the same time, it does appear that they were excluded from the liturgy itself and not only from the Eucharist. For expressions such as *exire de coetu et congregatione Ecclesiae,*[319] *a conventu Ecclesiae abscindi,*[320] which make a distinction between the Church itself and the meetings of the Church, should be understood as literally as possible. Thus those who are excommunicated are not only juridically ostracized from the fellowship of the Church and from the Eucharist but they are also forbidden to take part in any way in the liturgy of the community. *Ciciuntur ab oratione communi.*[321] Nothing more is said, however, about how the penitents were supervised or how the exclusion from the liturgy was carried out in practice. Nor is it said that this exclusion was really complete.[322]

c) THE THEOLOGICAL MEANING OF EXCOMMUNICATION

According to Origen the separation of a sinner from the Church is not an additional church punishment which the bishop imposes arbitrarily in the case of serious public scandals. Rather, he holds that it flows always and necessarily from the very nature of mortal sin itself. It expresses what mortal sin always brings about and what has already happened in God's eyes: the inner separation from the fellowship of the Church. This means that external participation in the life of the Church has become hypocrisy and must be purified.[323] A Church which did not do this would be corrupt and would itself incur hell together with the sinful and dead member.[324]

We must look more closely, however, at the meaning of this separation from the Church. It is only in this way that we will be able to grasp clearly the salvific meaning of the official lifting of excommunication which we will examine later. Thus the topic which we are now considering has a special importance. By excommunication the sinner is cut off from the *community* of believers,[325] separated from the body of Christ,[326] alienated from his homeland, that is, the Church,[327] and from the people of God,[328] his city which is built of living stones.[329] This separation from church fellowship means, in particular, exclusion from the Eucharist.[330] This gives rise to the situation which we have already described. The sinner finds himself under the dominating power of the devil[331] and is at the same time subject to God's anger,[332] which is no longer mediated by created punitive powers, such as the Church, angels or the law. A close examination of this separation which occurs in excommunication shows clearly that the Church is not seen here merely as an external organization but as a fellowship which is necessary for salvation. Obviously excommunication is an external act of the hierarchical Church, having all the evident consequences of exclusion from the liturgy. Nevertheless, the more important effect of this exclusion from the fellowship which is a source of grace is the loss, at least temporary, of salvation. For the separation from the homeland, from the body of Christ, from the heavenly Jerusalem and, quite simply, from the community means being handed over to darkness and the divine anger. 'How can I achieve complete happiness . . . how can I return to the Church?'[333] Both of these questions have the same meaning for the excommunicated penitent. If Origen stresses the necessity of the Church for salvation, and indeed precisely in the context of the exclusion from it of the one who previously belonged to it,[334] then the Church which he has in mind is the actual Church which, in his view, is always, at one and the same time, an inner fellowship of grace *and* an externally, hierarchically organized Church.[335] The internal detrimental effect which excommunication has on salvation, that is, on the relationship between man and God, is in no way diminished by the fact that Origen ascribes this effect already to mortal sin itself, even when there is no official church excommunication present.[336] *Both* views are correct and the one ought not to be disputed in favour of the other. Origen does not attempt to explain how they are to be reconciled logically. The question is: if a man is already, by reason of his sin, 'outside', that is, outside the inner fellowship of grace, what interior effect in God's eyes can the explicit excommunication still have upon him? But this is to pose, with regard to the particular case of excommunication, the central question of sacramental theology. How can a sacrament have the same effect which is also achieved by the personal act of man himself? In Origen's sacramental theology, and indeed still later in the Church, this question was not experienced as a dilemma[337] which was to be resolved one-sidedly, either in favour of the sacramental sign or in favour of the personal action. However, this does not give us the right simply to evade the question, even with regard to excommunication. Excommunication is 'only' the expression for man's act and, as the τύπος of this act, it brings about what the sinner has done. He has fallen away officially from God's grace, and this is expressed by excommunication. A closer consideration of Origen's teaching of the Church as the community which opposes sin at all its levels,[338] and of the Eucharist which establishes a living contact with the flesh of the Logos and in which God and man are united,[339] would show even more clearly the significance of excommunication as the separation from this community and from the body of Christ.

The further questions concerning excommunication, such as the lifting of it, its consequences, etc., will be answered in what follows, when we consider the further action of the Church which is aimed at the remission of sin.

4. *Reconciliation by the Whole Church*

A) THE DIFFERENT FUNCTIONS WITHIN THE CHURCH COMMUNITY

Scholars are still divided in their interpretation of the texts in Origen's work which are concerned with the question of the positive role of the Church in the remission of mortal sins committed after baptism. At first sight it appears that Origen teaches that the Church has a role in the remission of sins which is the prerogative of the holy bishop in so far as he is spiritual, or even of the lay person, provided that he, too, is spiritual, that is, 'perfect'. It would seem, therefore, that on this point Origen's teaching on penance contradicts his overall and basic anti-Donatist position which recognizes an objective validity and efficacy of the hierarchy and of the sacraments. In order to clarify this important question it is not sufficient merely to consider in general Origen's view of plurality and diversity within the Church. We must also try to see how this aspect of the Church both appears and is effective particularly in the Church's *reconciling* activity. On this point at least Origen himself is clear in principle. Now once this point is established, it becomes methodologically essential, when confronted with the individual statements of Origen on the Church's reconciling activity and their presuppositions, always to ask which level of the Church they refer to. If account is not taken of the precise function within the Church to which these statements refer, then it is hardly possible to avoid serious misunderstandings concerning Origen's teaching on penance. Moreover, at the outset of all our considerations it is vital to observe that Origen does recognize a *sacrament* of penance. This does not mean, however, that this sacrament should be considered in isolation, as it usually is today. To consider it in this way would hardly be helpful. It would in fact be submitting it to the disadvantage of modern sacramental theology which considers the sacraments individually. If it were viewed in this way it would be an event separated from the general life of the Church, which must be a continually reconciling and sanctifying fellowship. It would subsist only by reason of an 'institution' by Jesus Christ and, quite apart from baptism, would be the only expression of the Church's reconciling activity, while in all other cases where sins are forgiven it is man himself who 'alone' brings about the remission of his sins by sorrow and penance. If we today reflect on this commonly accepted understanding of the sacrament of penance, we can see immediately how unsatisfactory it is. The Church offers the sacrifice of the altar for the forgiveness of sins. It prays and does penance. Every conversion of a sinner is in fact supported by the intercession and the expiation of the whole Church, long before the actual 'confession'. The example of the holy members of this community also has a role to play, as well as the call to penance announced by the preachers of the gospel of justice and grace, which the Holy Spirit is constantly giving as a grace to the Church. Every profound *metanoia* of an individual is part of the living experience of the Church. It originates in the Church and, in its turn, affects the Church. For this Church throughout its history is on a continual journey from Adam to Christ. Thus the experience of sin, consisting in its awful sense of loss and separation from God, is a grace for the Church, although this is possible only in Christ, himself deserted by God on the cross, who in this sense too is head of his Church. The remission of sin is complete only when the 'punishments of sin' have been fully changed and destroyed in us.[340] All this is soon clear upon reflection. And yet none of it is found in previous treatises on penance, although that is where it all ought to be. In general the work of Origen, or of a Church Father, is approached with only those questions about the sacrament of penance which relate to penance as it is currently known to us. It is hardly surprising, therefore, if these works are found to contain a detailed treatment of those points which, while being acknowledged as 'also' important, do not come within the ambit of our rather arbitrarily defined dogmatic treatises. Similarly, points which we would consider important are often treated only peripherally and indistinctly by the Church Fathers, while the main point of their discussion is often found elsewhere than where we would expect it to be. If, therefore, any effort is made to integrate the insights of the witnesses of the early Church into the artificial setting of the contents of modern treatises of penance, it is difficult to avoid misunderstandings. Moreover, if these insights are not viewed in a wider context, then the picture of, say, Origen's teaching on penance does not only become incomplete and distorted but it also loses those characteristics which could be so important for developing the teaching on the sacrament of penance today.

At least in his teaching on penance Origen was very much aware of both the Church's manifold nature and its activity in the remission of sins. Something has already been said on this topic.[341] If Christ is both priest and sacrifice in the forgiveness of sins, then for Origen it follows necessarily that the *ministri et sacerdotes ecclesiae secundum imaginem eius, qui sacerdotium ecclesiae dedit* participate in the remission of sins.[342] For the present we need not consider precisely *how* this co-operation takes place or which of its aspects is emphasized in this passage. What is more important is the fact that Origen appears to take it as self-evident that there is a correspondence between the head of the Church and its members in the remission of sins. Thus it is that bishops correspond to angels, because the one Church has two levels—*duplex ecclesia una hominum, altera angelorum*. The correspondence also applies obviously to the various duties.[343] Origen also takes this correspondence for granted in his notion of penance in which both angels and bishops have their part to play.[344] There is not only a correspondence between the exterior and interior hierarchy, in such a sense that the external function does not eliminate or supply for the interior function, or in any way coincide with it. But even *within* the level of the external hierarchy the lower members are dependent on the higher in the remission of sin. Even in the dimension of this visible unity the lower member needs the co-operation of the higher in the forgiveness of every sin.[345] These examples illustrate Origen's basic conviction that the various aspects of the Church which are neither reducible to each other nor mutually exclusive are at work in its activity of reconciliation. But this obviously does not mean that the distinction and demarcation of all the functions of the individual 'levels' of the Church are always clearly made. Rather it is a question of the same activity ascribed both to the external official and to the interior 'perfect'. Thus there is no explicit and clear emphasis on the idea that the official hierarchy possesses a special duty, that is, of officially lifting official excommunication, besides that which it has in common with the 'perfect'. The fact that in this case it would appear that, contrary to the general principle, the duties of the individual groups do not only correspond to each other without competing with each other but even partially overlap and replace each other is due, in the first place, to the very nature of the general principle and, in the second place, to the nature of the sin which has to be remitted. From the point of view of our method, this observation provides an indication of the perspective in which we should treat Origen's teaching in what follows. In other words, should we consider the power of spiritual lay people to lift official excommunication apart from official reconciliation as an exception or even as a usurpation of the prerogative of the official hierarchy, or indeed *vice versa*. It is, therefore, necessary to examine a little more closely this apparent exception to Origen's general basic ecclesiological thought.

In the first place, the overlapping mentioned above is a corollary of the very basic principle which we have explained. In fact, according to Origen the interior and the exterior hierarchy are not to be distinguished in such a way that they simply lie side by side or the one beneath the other without being related. Despite the fact that its own specific acts are fundamentally valid, the exterior hierarchy must be the expression and manifestation of the Church's interior hierarchy. Thus it ought to correspond to the latter *in such a way* that the leaders of the one hierarchy are in fact always the leaders of the other. Ideally, therefore, the one responsible for the duties and functions in the interior hierarchy, that is, the spiritual person, is the depositary of the powers of the exterior hierarchy, and *vice versa*. This ideal agreement, however, is not always realized. Nevertheless, its absence does not deprive the exterior hierarchy as such of its proper character. It is an ideal which should be the object of continual striving.[346] In this regard, it is worth recalling what has been said earlier about the perspective in which Origen regarded the nature of sin. If, in his view, there is not and in fact cannot be a clear distinction between guilt itself and the punishment due to sin,[347] then it follows that, according to him, the remission of sin must necessarily include the overcoming of the whole of man's carnal character. But this does not come about merely through the sacrament of penance as such. Not only could Origen assume this as part of tradition and teach it himself,[348] but it is also evidenced by man's immediate experience of his moral life. Given this concept of sin, it follows that any inquiry about an *ecclesial* means of reconciliation must be directed towards that activity of the Church by which the carnal side of a humanity bound together within the Church is purified and transformed. This activity is nothing other than the redemptive penance undertaken by the saints with and under the direction of Christ their head. This entails, however, that the Church as a whole and in all its dimensions must be opposed to sin as the indispensable instrument of salvation. Thus its interior hierarchy, that is, the ever-increasing holiness of its spiritual members, must exercise a reconciling function. Moreover, in the ideal situation—which really ought to be the 'normal' one—the officials of the exterior hierarchy should play a part in this activity of the interior hierarchy. In other words, they exercise their office properly only when they also reconcile *as spiritual persons*. In any event, the bishop, the priest and the deacon are σύμβολον ἀληθινῶν κατὰ ὀνόματα ταῦτα πραγμάτων in the full sense only in so far as they realize in 'truth' what they represent symbolically in the sacramental sign. This ideal performance of the duty of the interior hierarchy on the part of the bearers of official hierarchical power is a participation in the function which is originally the prerogative of the interior hierarchy. It is only good method, therefore, to take the latter as the starting-point. Thus Origen's recognition of a reconciling function exercised by spiritual persons is not to be considered as an unjustified extension of the episcopal official power to the laity. Quite the contrary. The bishop, in so far as he is himself a spiritual person—which is what he ought to be—participates in a function which belongs originally and inalienably to the saints, each according to his place, within the body of Christ. Nevertheless, in so far as he exercises a specific visible function, the bishop has to have a role in the whole process of reconciliation which is reserved to him and which he does not share with the spiritual person. These requirements are implicit in Origen's notion of the fundamental relationship between 'groups' within the Church. But they must be confirmed by reference to the texts themselves. This applies particularly to the idea that a specifically reconciling function within the Church has its starting-point with the spiritual persons and then becomes the right of the bishops, even if this method does not account for the full episcopal power in the forgiveness of sins. In other words, our methodological principle is to be pursued without prejudice to the specific power which is reserved exclusively to the official church.[349]

B) RECONCILIATION ACHIEVED BY THE CHURCH OF THE SAINTS

The previous considerations have led to the expectation that Origen recognizes a sin-remitting activity on the part of the 'interior' hierarchy, that is, of the Church of the saints. Such an activity, therefore, is exercised not only by the exterior officials of the Church, even though these latter may have a part to play in it. The question which now remains to be asked is *whether* in Origen's view the 'saints' in fact contribute to the remission of sins and whether the *bishops* also do this as 'saints'. Thus we must try to see the precise nature of this activity and what it presupposes in those who exercise it.

It is not only Peter and the other apostles who are the rock on which Christ has built his Church, but πᾶς ὁ χριστοῦ μιμητής, all 'perfect believers' (τέλειοι) have the keys of heaven, that is, the power to bind and to loose. Everyone who has the ἔργον of Peter, that is, not only the traditional faith in Christ but also that which is inspired from above, together with freedom from sin through the virtues which open the individual heavens, is able to loose and forgive in such a way that his activity takes effect also in heaven.[350] The holier a person is, therefore, the greater is his power of loosing.[351] As is obvious from the text taken as a whole—the 'saints' observe the command of fraternal correction laid down in Matthew 18—it is a question of the 'saints' here on earth and of their activity. Certainly it would be a misunderstanding of Origen to see in these 'saints' a narrow and sharply defined caste which is clearly distinguishable from 'ordinary' Christians. *Every* Christian, to the extent of his inspired faith and his particular freedom from sin, must belong to them.[352] The only ones who are excluded are those who are bound by their own sins.[353] In the final analysis, *all* Christians must convert their brothers and heal their sins.[354] In other words, sins have to be remitted *interventu et correptione omnium*.[355] In fact the circle of the Church's reconciling ἅγιοι must be drawn even wider, since both martyrs and angels also belong to the circle of powers which, as the 'interior Church', contribute to the remission of sins.[356] Indeed, although their activity in this regard is naturally, at least partially, different from that of the other saints,[357] they can nevertheless be included with the saints because their activity has its basis in their personal activity and holiness; they are also members of the Church of the saints.

Now this power of the 'saints' includes a whole lot of activities which the 'saints' are able to do. Thus the spiritual person is simply appointed by God himself, as was Jesus the friend of sinners, to live among sinners in order to work for their conversion.[358] Just as Jesus himself, despite his ἀπάθεια, suffered the condition of the poor and the sick,[359] so also the perfect persons weep with those who weep and especially grieve over those who do not wish to do any penance.[360] As compassionate doctors of souls they have the gift of mourning and suffering with sinners, the *disciplina condolendi et compatiendi*.[361] By prayer, fasting and the exercise of virtues they also fight for the rest of the people and for those who are weaker than themselves.[362] They strive for the weak and for sinners against the demonic powers.[363] Their most sublime deed with regard to the reconciliation of their brothers in the Church is the shedding of their blood in martyrdom, in imitation of Christ's sacrificial death: in this way they effectively destroy the power of the demons, they drive away sins and thus redeem at least some.[364] Through their intercessions the spiritual persons intervene for sinners so that they may obtain forgiveness. They may even be asked spontaneously for this intercession.[365] Obviously they will observe above all the gospel precept concerning fraternal correction which is incumbent on all Christians.[366] Since, however, the 'saints' are like Peter and Paul,[367] there applies to them that which is said of Paul, namely, that they, inseparable from the love of Jesus, 'by sacrificing, not by transgressing', wish themselves to be anathema in the place of others in order to gain salvation for their brothers.[368] This *assumere peccatorem et monendo, hortando, docendo, instruendo adducere eum ad poenitentiam, ab errore corrigere, a vitiis emendare et efficere talem, ut ei converso propitius fiat Deus* is explicitly described as a *delicta repropitiare.*[369] The *hostiam iugulare verbo Dei et doctrinae sanae victimas offerre* is called *purgare a peccatis conscientias auditorum,* indeed even *remissionem peccatorum tribuere.*[370] Thus it must be that these means for the forgiveness of sins are in fact tantamount to the power of 'loosing' which in Origen's view is the prerogative of the τέλειοι. There is nothing in Origen's work which warrants another explanation. In other words, he holds that the 'loosing' of sins is an essentially wider and more comprehensive notion than the official lifting of an excommunication imposed by the Church.[371] Thus he does not ascribe to the saints any more than that which is recognized even by contemporary church teaching. What this binding power *necessarily* presupposes, then as today, is holiness and the living, grace-giving union with the holy Church, the body of Christ.[372] Even today any well-balanced teaching on the Church's activity in the remission of sins must take account of this role played by the 'saints' and not concentrate solely on the sacramental powers exercised in the two sacraments which remit sins in the strictest sense. It is obvious that throughout all this consideration of the act of reconciliation Origen has in mind not only mortal sins, at least not primarily, but all sins in general.

Now, since according to this way of thinking even the members of the official hierarchy must be spiritual people, it follows that they possess this power only if and in so far as they are spiritual. Although it is undeniable that Origen recognizes a binding and loosing which is reserved exclusively to the bishop, he still holds that he has a power to remit sins which is his *in so far* as he is a spiritual person and not because he is a bishop.[373] This is because the bishop, as such, *must* also be 'holy'. We have already considered the nature of the bishop's activity in this regard.[374] Now if, on the one hand, the 'saints' effect the forgiveness of sins by their intercession and, on the other hand, the forgiveness of sins is attributable to the bishops who also exercise this role through their 'prayer',[375] then there is surely no reason for the assumption that the episcopal 'prayer' for the remission of sins must be of a radically different kind from that of the other saints. Nevertheless, even prescinding from the fact that the bishops enjoy the power to impose and lift excommunication and thus of binding and loosing, this does not mean that the bishops' power to remit sins has to be identical in all respects with that of the other spiritual people. Already in the case of the *correptio* it is necessary to distinguish between one which is private and one which is official. The latter is without any doubt the prerogative of the clergy.[376]

Origen also recognizes sacrifice as a means of reconciling the sinner. Certainly by 'sacrifice' for sin he often means the interior sacrifice of the contrite heart and the corrective and converting word of God pronounced by the priest.[377] Nevertheless, since he also talks about the *sacrificia sacerdotum,* as distinct from the *obsecrationes* and the *scientia divinae legis,* and since he explicitly ascribes to these a sin-remitting efficacy,[378] there can be no doubt that for Origen the actual liturgical sacrifice of the Eucharist belongs to the spiritual bishops' reconciling activity.[379] Thus there are two points at which the bishop's spiritual power to remit sins is expressed in an exterior official act of the Church. In other passages it is not at all clear what Origen has in mind when he ascribes a reconciling activity to bishops and priests.[380] It could refer to a wide variety of activities: the simple charismatic role, in the strictest sense, played by a spiritual person, the official *correptio* just mentioned, the offering of sacrifice and, finally, that act which we will later have to describe as specifically sacramental, that is, the authoritative loosing from the actual excommunication from the Church imposed by the bishop.

If we wish to describe the whole of the reconciling activity of the Church of the saints theologically we could say: the Church of the saints, being affected by the sin of one of its members, guards its solidarity with this sinful member. It is, therefore, obliged to do what the sinner himself has to do for the remission of his sins. Only he, however, has to actually *ἀπολαμβάνειν τὰς ἁμαρτίας*. He has to face up to the reality of his sinful condition, which is itself the most severe guilt and punishment. At the same time, he must renounce all his apathy with regard to his own condition and allow the immanent fire of judgement to destroy his sin completely in both his interior and his exterior being. But likewise the Church 'takes' this guilt 'on itself'.[381] Having itself become sinful by the sin of its member, it expiates the sin together with the sinner.[382] Everything that the Church does in its saints is only this process of taking sin upon itself in all the various forms which correspond to its manifold nature.

5. *The Official Power of the Church*

A) THE LIFTING OF EXCOMMUNICATION: THE FACT AND THE TERMINOLOGY

According to Origen mortal sins are subject radically and necessarily to church excommunication which is imposed by the bishop. By this excommunication a sinner is handed over to Satan in order to have his sin remitted. Excommunication is essentially able to be lifted and, after suitable penance, it can be reversed in such a way that the sinner is once more reconciled with the Church as a real member. We need not consider for the moment whether such a reconciliation is feasible in all concrete cases. What is certain is the fact: there is a reconciliation in the sense just described. Even after an official *proici* there is for the *egrediens de populo Dei* a *rursum per poenitentiam reverti,*[383] a *προίεσθαι* of those who have been excluded to the *κοινόν* of the Church,[384] an *ad Ecclesiam redire*.[385] Granted that there has been sufficient penance outside the Church, there is a *ἐπανιέναι* and *κοινωνεῖν τῇ ἐκκλησίᾳ*,[386] a *revocare* and *Ecclesiae membris associare,*[387] as happened in the case of the incestuous person in Corinth, a *reconiungere eiectum Ecclesiae*.[388] Now although the lifting of excommunication and the reincorporation of the excommunicated within the visible community of the Church is of a different nature than the reconciling activity of the Church by the saints as described above, and although with the term 'loosing' often, if not mostly, he means precisely this latter activity, he still appears *also* to designate the lifting of excommunication as *solvere*. Certainly 'binding' means first and foremost excommunication. It would be astounding, therefore, if 'loosing' did not *also* mean the exact opposite. Thus if, in one and the same context, Origen speaks of the bishops' *potestas solvendi et ligandi* and if he understands by *potestas ligandi* the power of excluding people from the Church,[389] then one ought to interpret the *potestas solvendi* as the power of reconciling the penitent with the Church. After all we have seen, there is no need to prove that it is the bishop who performs the reconciliation. Nevertheless, this point is not stressed as explicitly as might be expected. But he is certainly the one who imposes the excommunication. Origen maintains that the bishops base their claim to the power of binding and *loosing* on Scripture. Moreover, the bishop has a very prominent role to play elsewhere, for instance, in supervising morals, in hearing the confession, in administering the *correptio,* and he appears—at least in practice—as the most important person in all the other reconciling activity of the Church. Thus there can be no doubt that he is the one who executes the reconciliation of the penitent with the Church. Given the strictly monarchical-episcopal structure of the individual Churches at that time, as is evident also in Origen, and the fact that only the bishop is able to impose an actual excommunication and that on this point there is not the slightest trace in Origen of 'competition' on the part of, say, the confessors or any others, it is obvious that for him it was only the bishop who, both in practice and in theory, has the right to perform such an official reconciliation.

There is one allusion to a *rite* of reconciliation, if we accept that Origen sees in public penance the fulfilment of the instruction laid down in the letter of James 5:14 f.[390] Since in this text there is a mention of an imposition of hands accompanied by prayer, and since both in the West in Cyprian and in the East[391] this is also attested at this time, there can be little doubt that Origen also at least thought of it. For him, therefore, reconciliation takes place by imposition of hands accompanied by prayer. The whole community would be present and praying, thus providing a suitable parallel to the act of excommunication. The fact that the Didascalia Apostolorum attests such a co-operation on the part of the whole community at the reconciliation of penitents[392] would confirm this reconstruction. It remains to be asked, therefore, whether, according to James 5:14 f., Origen and his contemporaries envisaged an anointing which accompanied the imposition of hands. Later in the East it is clear that in some places reconciliation includes an anointing. Leaving aside Origen himself, the first traces of this practice are discernible in Syria about A.D. 300.[393] Thus it is highly likely that Origen also knew of this practice and considered it the 'carrying out' of the passage in James with regard to the reconciliation of penance.[394] The conclusive text from In Lev. hom. 2,4, according to which the reconciling imposition of hands was already in Origen's view accompanied by an anointing, receives a further confirmation from In Lev. hom. 8,11.[395] There is here mention of a *olei imago* in the sense that the penitent, having been purified of his sins, again receives a share in the graces given by the Holy Spirit. Since the reference here is not to the newly baptized but to the man who is to be justified again, because he has fallen into sin after his baptism,[396] the real anointing in question must be the reconciliation of penance.

What is the precise meaning of these ceremonies according to Origen? If we are to answer this question we must first of all recognize that Origen views the period of penance as parallel to the period of the catechumenate, as a kind of intense catechumenate.[397] Thus we can assume that the liturgical forms of the catechumenate and of its conclusion were transferred to the corresponding phases of the period of penance. It is certain that Origen knows of an imposition of hands which has the character of an exorcism.[398] In view of the evidence provided by the church order of Hippolytus and the practice attested in Cyprian, it is probable that such impositions of hands occurred also in the circles known to Origen during the period of the catechumenate and in the immediate preparation for baptism. The most obvious meaning of these impositions is as exorcisms or gestures of prayer, since they were formally distinguished from the authoritative granting of new access to church fellowship. In fact they form part of that intercessory reconciling activity which we have already described as the duty of bishops. Such an imposition of hands would be preceded by others during the period of penance and would only attract special attention if in fact it coincided with the end of this period and with reconciliation. At the same time, Origen also recognizes the imposition of hands as a rite for the bestowal of the

Spirit after baptism.[399] Similarly in the Didascalia Apostolorum[400] and in Firmilian of Caesarea, Origen's pupil,[401] the imposition of hands is a gesture for the bestowal of the Spirit. Likewise in In Lev. hom. 8,11[402] the reconciliation, more precisely, the rite of reconciliation, because it includes an anointing, ought to be seen as a communication of the Spirit. Thus it is more likely that the imposition of hands with an anointing is not intended—at least, not primarily—as an exorcism but as a sign of the bestowal of the Spirit. This means that in a certain sense the rite of reconciliation should be considered a liturgical parallel to the rite of confirmation, on which it appears to be modelled. This does not entail, however, that Origen must have considered this rite a formal repetition of confirmation. Such a view is precluded by the fact that, on the one hand, confirmation is still too much bound up with initiation while, on the other hand, the once-and-for-all character of this initiation in baptism is explicitly stressed.

B) THE EXTENT OF THE CHURCH'S POWER OF RECONCILIATION

The question which we must now ask is: can the bishop receive back into church fellowship *all* sinners who are genuinely repentant and after a sufficient period of penance? Or are certain sins *eo ipso* excluded from such a gracious act? As we have already seen, Origen does not know any mortal sins which cannot be forgiven by *God* himself. Thus in this life, and quite independently of the theory of the *apocatastasis,* all faults can be forgiven by God by means of penance. This means that Origen would hardly be likely to restrict the Church's power of reconciliation. In his view the relationship of man to God ought to be reflected in man's relationship to the Church of God. The person who is separated from God has not only fallen foul of the Church interiorly and invisibly but must also be visibly separated from the Church *per sententiam episcopi.* If, therefore, *all* sins are able to be forgiven in God's eyes, then it would be a crass contradiction in Origen's thinking if he did not allow *all* those sinners who are reconciled with God the possibility of also being reconciled again with the Church by the word of the bishop. Such a contradiction is tenable only on the basis of firm proof from the texts of Origen himself. Now such proof is not forthcoming. The only text which could support it with any degree of probability is De or .28. We will consider this text presently. All the other texts which are adduced on this question concern not the forgiveness of sins by the Church but God's forgiveness, and these have already been considered. Moreover, Origen has no reason to introduce a further essential distinction into his notion of mortal sin. And it is only such a distinction which could make it possible to treat a particular class of mortal sins, as for example the three 'capital sins', in a different way from that provided for the other mortal sins. Thus if Origen submits mortal sins to church penance without making such a differentiation, and if this penance ends in a reconciliation with the Church, then he must have *all* mortal sins in mind, that is, *every* person guilty of mortal sin who is repentant is able to return to the Church. And this is in fact the case. According to Contra Celsum III 51,[403] a late work, the Church excludes sinners who have committed fornication or some other ἄτοπον, from its fellowship and allows them back only after a long period of penance. With this observation Origen is attempting to counter Celsus' accusation and to stress how strict Christian morality really is. Given this perspective, he would surely have stressed the fact if there had been any sins which totally and radically were excluded from such a reinstatement. But he does not know of any such sins. A similar universal and unrestrictive expression about the reconciliation of those guilty of mortal sins with the Church is found in In Ezech. hom. 3,8:[404] *iuste autem proicitur, qui digna facit abiectione, ut auferatur a populo Dei et eradicetur ab eo et tradatur Satanae. Et in praesenti quidem potest quis egrediens de populo Dei rursum paenitentiam reverti.* Since this particular possibility of a return is opposed to a return in the next life,[405] there can hardly be any sins *in praesenti* which exclude people from the Church totally and permanently. If there were, then the view expressed in this passage would be groundless. Further, such expressions about the possibility of those guilty of mortal sins being reconciled without any restrictive conditions are found frequently elsewhere in Origen.[406] Thus in practice he declares explicitly that the Church is able to forgive almost all those sins which, because of their seriousness, would seem to warrant a definitive exclusion: impurity to the extent of incest,[407] blasphemy[408] and sins against faith.[409]

There remains, however, the view expressed in De or. 28. Does this agree with Origen's overall teaching on the Church's ability to forgive *all* mortal sins? As far as our present purpose is concerned, this text simply says the following: bishops should not presume to forgive on their own, through their own sacrifice and prayer, 'against the Lord', idolatry, prostitution, adultery, voluntary homicide and other serious sins which are 'incurable mortal sins'. Rather such sins ought to be 'retained', since the bishop should 'remit' (ἀφιέναι) only what God also forgives. This is all that this frequently-quoted text actually provides on our subject. From it we may take two main points: if it implies that every church forgiveness is excluded for the sins in question, then, all other things being equal, a *divine* forgiveness is also excluded, since the latter is the condition of the former.[410] In this case, Origen would be denying the ability not only of the Church but also of *God* to forgive *all* mortal sins.[411] We have already seen, however, that such a horrifying rigorism is totally alien to Origen's writings. Moreover, since this text does not exclude every kind of divine forgiveness[412] for all mortal sins, it follows that it is not possible to contest every form of church reconciliation in these cases.

In the second place, the interpretation of this text just outlined would completely deprive the Church's institution of penance, ending as it does with reconciliation, of this object and indeed would render it redundant. For the text withdraws *every* 'serious' case, *every* mortal sin from such a power of prayer enjoyed by priests. Thus if this power is identical with that power which is the basis of the official penance of church excommunication and reconciliation, then it must be asked whether such an institution would still have any object at all. In this case, Origen would be denying the very justification of such an institution, whereas in fact it is obvious that in this text he is only concerned about the misuse which 'some' are making of it.[413] In view of the fact that Origen is a man of the Church, he can hardly be credited with the rejection of such a long-standing institution of the Church. For all his radicalism, not even Tertullian dared to do that. Perhaps, then, Origen assigned only light and daily sins to the penance of excommunication. This idea is in direct contradiction to his own statements.[414] Moreover, it would again lead to consequences which are impossible in practice. How, for example, can all sins which are not 'serious' be made the necessary object of a penance of excommunication, in the expectation that such a rule will be taken seriously in practice? These considerations alone lead to the conclusion that in this text the power to forgive sins by means of prayer and sacrifice, which Origen is here restricting, can hardly be the power of church penance of excommunication and the power to forgive sins which is exercised within it. In the light of all that we have said earlier, it is not difficult to see what is meant positively by this power to forgive sins by means of prayer and sacrifice. It is the sin-remitting activity of the Church of the saints, undertaken principally but by no means exclusively by the bishops as spiritual persons and even outside any process of excommunication. It is the Church's support of the penitent by prayer, sacrifice, exhortation, correction, penitential practices, etc., even by sharing in the burden of sin. It is an activity which has always been practised and must continue to be in the community of the saints. In other words, this is what Origen is saying here: mortal sins cannot be remitted *solely* by *this* reconciling activity. Rather they must be 'retained', that is, subjected to excommunication. In this case, the bishop should not simply *ad gratiam iudicare,*[415] that is, bypass excommunication and attempt to apply to incurable sins that medicine which is effective only for sins which have not caused spiritual death, namely, prayer and sacrifice alone. In this passage Origen does not say explicitly that the prescribed penance of excommunication will end with a reconciliation, provided that the sinner is repentant. But this is self-evident for him and indeed precisely in respect of the sins referred to in De or. 28. If he were not to take this obvious principle for granted even in this passage, then he would be contesting the fact that any penance of excommunication, imposed for any mortal sin whatsoever, could end with a church reconciliation. De or., therefore, denies the possibility of a remission of mortal sins by 'prayer' alone, but not the possibility of pardon by means of the 'death' of the penance of excommunication.[416]

What it is contesting is reconciliation by 'sacrifice' alone, but not reconciliation through μετάνοια τελεία.[417] Even when, according to 1 Corinthians 2:25 and 1 John 5:16,[418] both 'sacrifice' and 'prayer' are useless, the *anima contribulata* and the *spiritus humilitatis* are still effective.[419] Indeed the very reasoning of De or. includes the idea that the 'servant' alone cannot heal a mortal sin. This requires the intervention of God, which itself must be expressed by the sinner being excluded from the Church and surrendered to Satan for the destruction of his flesh.[420] This *interitus carnis* brings about the man's salvation and he is subsequently reconciled with the Church. As opposed to this 'taking of sin upon oneself' by the penance of excommunication, any attempt to remit mortal sins by prayer and sacrifice alone would be to presume that an *aphesis* by God and the Church (in the technical sense of this term in Origen)[421] were possible for these sins. But such an *aphesis* for these sins does not exist in God's eyes. Thus the Church should not have the presumption to wish to grant it. In other words, in no way does De or. 28 exclude a power of reconciliation in respect of those who have been excommunicated. What is disputed here is the possibility of remitting serious sins solely through the bishop's prayer. Moreover, this prayer is not the prayer which is operative in the reconciliation of excommunicates. Origen is not saying anything different, therefore, from what he maintains elsewhere when he contests the possibility that incurable sins can be remitted by the prayer of the bishop alone. The person guilty of mortal sin must be excommunicated. His sin must be 'retained'. The text does not say that after sufficient penance he ought not to be 'loosened', but it does exclude this both logically and in fact. Otherwise there would be no penance of excommunication ending in reconciliation for mortal sins. And this would stand in contradiction to the whole of Origen's teaching on penance. For he recognizes for every person guilty of mortal sin both forgiveness before God and reincorporation into the Church. Thus De or. 28 is perfectly comprehensible within the general framework of Origen's teaching on penance, without giving rise to any kind of rigorism. Even in this passage the possibility of reconciliation for those who are excommunicated is not restricted. What is restricted, however, is the range of the charismatic remission of sins, and this in favour of the penance of excommunication.

All this leads to yet another conclusion which, although it does not belong strictly to the present context, may be considered briefly. The bishop's priestly prayer for the forgiveness of sins which is effective outside the penance of excommunication, that is, not with regard to mortal sins, should be understood in today's sense as the sacramental absolution from venial sins outside public penance. Indeed it is 'only' the prayer of the saints for sinners, which the bishop has to offer primarily as a spiritual person, but which is not his official prerogative. It is rather an ἐξουσία which he shares basically with every saint who is filled with the Spirit. This is because the whole Church of the saints can and must συνεργεῖν[422] along with the sinner who is doing penance.

c) THE CONCLUSION OF RECONCILIATION

We now need to raise the question of the duration of the penance of excommunication. From what we have already seen, it is to be expected that the duration of the period of penance varied in length according to the different cases. The criterion for mesuring the length of the period of penance was not only the objective and subjective seriousness of a sin as such but also the extent to which this period provided evidence to the leaders of the community and to the community at large of the sinner's sincere, serious and effective intention to mend his ways.[423]

Thus the length of the period of penance necessarily differed from case to case. The excommunication could even be imposed by the bishop himself acting against the will of the member of the community in question. The situation could arise, therefore, in which such a sinner obstinately, and despite the excommunication, was unwilling to eliminate the cause which occasioned it. He consequently remained banned by the Church until he later changed his attitude and the excommunication itself, after being a predominantly disciplinary measure, became an actual part of the institution of penance. With this came the prospect of a proximate lifting of the excommunication.[424] This could also account for the varied duration of excommunication. We cannot tell how long the period of penance lasted in the majority of cases. What is clear is that penance lasted longer than the catechumenate. This point is stressed explicitly.[425] Such a comparison is meaningful, however, only if the two periods belong, more or less, to the same 'order of importance'. At the same time, it should be borne in mind that Origen, as Hippolytus,[426] envisages a catechumenate lasting several years. This means that the penance of excommunication could easily last several years, so that a penance of more than three years would not have been considered abnormal. Nevertheless, the possibility of a substantial reduction of the amount of penance required would not have been discounted,[427] if there were evidence of particular zeal and real conversion. Without feeling himself to be out of step with the penitential practice of his day, Origen is able to make capital out of the fact that, in the brief time-lapse between the two letters to the Corinthians, the incestuous person was both excommunicated and reconciled again with the Church.[428] Nevertheless, it would appear that Origen detects a special zeal for penance operating in this case; thus it would be wrong to conclude that in the circles known to him the penance of excommunication usually lasted only a few weeks. This would contradict his own testimony to the effect that the period of penance must be longer than the period of the catechumenate.[429] At the same time, he stresses that the period of penance should be measured with moderation and that, in the determination of its duration, the case of the incestuous person in Corinth is typical.[430] In any event Origen does not evince any notion of a life-long penance.

6. *The Meaning of Excommunication*

A) THE LASTING CONSEQUENCES OF EXCOMMUNICATION

Reconciliation does not mark the end of all the consequences of excommunication. What we have seen in Cyprian is also found in Origen. Above all, the reconciled person remains a Christian of diminished rights, since he is permanently excluded from holding ecclesiastical office.[431] Naturally this would concern, in the first place, those penitents who were simple Christians when they had fallen into sin and had done penance. Subsequently they were barred from ecclesiastical offices. Nevertheless, at the same time both in the East and in the West those sinners who, previously, had held ecclesiastical office were treated in the same way.[432] The question which can be asked, however, is whether every kind of excommunication imposed on a bishop or a priest was in fact experienced and considered as an excommunication of penitents and, accordingly, entailed this lasting consequence even after it was lifted.

Yet another consequence which remained permanently after reconciliation was the impossibility of a second church penance: *in gravioribus enim criminibus semel tantum poenitentiae conceditur locus.*[433] The principle of the unrepeatable character of church penance of excommunication was clearly received from Hermas and Clemens and was practised in Origen's day. It is presented as being self-evident and not needing further justification. Moreover, Origen does not appear to have seen any problem in reconciling this principle of church discipline with his theological principle that God always accepts genuine penance. It may be that cases of this kind did not occur frequently enough to necessitate theological reflection. Or perhaps the principle was quietly and discretely simply not applied in all its rigour to such cases. Nevertheless, given the salvific importance attributed to the Church in the theology of that time, it is doubtful whether any would then have ventured the theory which is found later in Augustine,[434] namely, that a Christian who has fallen back into sin again could receive salvation even without church reconciliation, provided that he did penance.

B) THE THEOLOGICAL MEANING OF OFFICIAL CHURCH RECONCILIATION

We have now reached the decisive point in our discussion of Origen's teaching on penance. For all that the remission of sin, even quite independently of excommunication and its being lifted, was not only a matter of what happened within the private individual but was also achieved by the co-operation of the Church of the saints, it remains a fact that this involvement of the whole body in the guilt of one of its members should not be styled 'sacramental' in today's sense of this term.[435] Apart from the case of the reconciliation of a person who is excommunicated, the texts of Origen provide evidence only for an ecclesial but not for an ecclesial-sacramental remission of sins. Can, therefore, the official reconciliation of an excommunicate be considered as a sacramental act? It has already been sufficiently proven that this act was performed by the hierarchical Church with the awareness that it has been empowered to do so by Christ. But this does not entitle us to call it sacramental. Our question can be answered only when a further question is settled: does Origen ascribe to this act a meaning which goes beyond that of a purely church disciplinary measure? This obviously also implies the question of how such an assumed transcendent meaning of the act of reconciliation fits into the whole celebration of penance and how it is related to the reconciling activity within this celebration of both the sinner himself and the Church of the saints. It is only by keeping these questions in mind that we will avoid the danger of ascribing to reconciliation a meaning which it does not have in Origen's view. He provides very little information either explicitly or thematically on this problem. Thus we will find an answer to our question partly by paying careful attention to significant motifs and indications in other areas of his teaching.

In considering the theological significance of excommunication, we have made it sufficiently clear that reconciliation with the Church is not purely a matter of discipline. If the Church is the necessary means of grace and salvation, and this precisely in so far as it is a visible community of salvation, then it follows that reconciliation, considered as a readmission, must have a decisive meaning for salvation.[436] If the excommunicated person, by virtue of his legitimate exclusion, is 'handed over to Satan' and thus stands outside the possibility of salvation—even if, in Origen's view, this 'being outside' still has a mysterious salvific meaning—then everything depends on the return to the homeland and to the people of God, and on the reincorporation into the unity of Christ's body. How can man be saved? How can he return to the Church? For Origen these questions are two sides of the same coin.[437] Here we have a parallel to what we have already seen with regard to excommunication: the saving significance of official reconciliation as readmission into the fellowship of the Church which is necessary for salvation is not undermined by the fact that this official act only achieves officially what must have already taken place 'interiorly' somehow by the conversion of the sinner himself. This corresponds to the fact that the sinner is already 'outside' the fellowship of grace before he is exteriorly and officially excommunicated. In fact in the present instance the position is even clearer. If, according to Origen, the person guilty of mortal sin, who is already 'outside' in God's eyes, must also be unconditionally and necessarily excommunicated, and if it would be presumption on the part of those in authority and even worse presumption on the part of the sinner himself to attempt to bypass this phase by relying on the interior reconciliatory power of the Church (its prayer), then it follows that a person guilty of mortal sin cannot be genuinely repentant if he does not have recourse to the penance of excommunication. He cannot return to the church interiorly, therefore, without being prepared to submit himself to exterior excommunication. But if *this* is necessary, then the same applies to its official lifting by the Church, that is, to the reconciliation by the bishop.

This is also what happens at baptism. Origen makes it abundantly clear that before baptism a person must dissociate himself interiorly from sin. In so doing, however, it is far from Origen's mind to cast doubt on the necessity, the efficacy and the saving significance of visible sacramental baptism.[438] Both the interior and the exterior act have the same aim, but we shall have to consider more closely, with the help of Origen himself, precisely *how* they are interrelated. The point which needs to be made for the moment is that Origen considers reconciliation an indispensable, visible reincorporation into the interior fellowship of grace which is necessary for salvation. This obviously means that, in his view, it already has a transcendent effect and should in this sense be described as 'sacramental'. In later terminology it would represent *at least* 'the necessary condition', without which any further activity on the part of the penitent or of the Church would be useless, since the penitent would remain outside the community which was necessary for salvation. Thus according to the Scholastic theory reconciliation would have at least a *causalitas dispositiva*. The *dispositio exigens formam* which was acquired by it was not an *ornatus animae,* as it was called up until Thomas Aquinas' commentary on the Sentences, but the fully effective membership of the body of Christ who communicates his Spirit and his salvation to all his fully legitimate members. Nevertheless, this distinction need not prevent us from seeing a genuine sacramental causality in this way of conceiving the effect of reconciliation. The fully legitimate membership of the Church of grace would be the *res et sacramentum* of complete salvation and, as such, the immediate effect of the official church reconciliation.

But does this translation of Origen's teaching into more recent categories not betray his original thinking? Does it not ascribe to reconciliation an effect which, according to Origen, is really the result of the sinner's personal penance, albeit supported by the cooperation of the Church of the saints? This objection raises the question of the relationship between reconciliation and the other reconciling activities. It is obvious that Origen himself did not experience any more difficulty on this point than he did with regard to the relationship between the personal purification from sin as a preparation for baptism and the forgiveness of sins through the sacramental act of baptism. Today we do not find it very easy to envisage a purification from sin which is not purely and simply identical with the communication of the Holy Spirit. But Origen did not experience this difficulty. Thus he was able to ascribe that purification from sins to the personal preparation for baptism[439] and to consider the communication of the Holy Spirit as an effect of the sacrament.[440] We can, therefore, say that according to Origen, despite all the penance performed during the time of the catechumenate and the purification from sins which is gained thereby, it is only the incorporation into the Church by baptism that communicates the Holy Spirit. The principle, *si desit eis gratia Spiritus, nec membra esse Christi corporis possunt,*[441] can therefore be reversed: it is only by being a member of Christ's body in the full sense that a person can also posses the Holy Spirit. In view of the fact that Origen conceives the period of penance of excommunicates as a kind of second catechumenate and reconciliation as a *reconiungere membris Ecclesiae,* there is no reason why this idea should not be applied to penance. It is by reconciliation that the purified penitent is reincorporated into the fellowship of the Church and so recovers the Holy Spirit which he had lost. We have already seen[442] that Origen considers personal penance less as an acquisition of the Holy Spirit than as a moral purging of the interior state of sin, in other words, as a destruction of the 'flesh'. This fits into what we have just said.

Moreover, the *interitus carnis,* Origen's comprehensive key expression for the personal penance of the excommunicate, also corresponds very precisely to the 'death' which according to In Rom. V, 8 the catechumens have to undergo before receiving the Spirit in baptism. In this connection, it should not be forgotten either that the imposition of hands in reconciliation appears to be considered as a gesture for the communication of the Spirit. Origen obviously gives great prominence to personal penance, and this interpretation of its relationship to reconciliation does not diminish its importance. For, according to Origen, reconciliation always presupposes excommunication. It is this excommunication that occasions that which is most fundamental: conversion. The sinner is shaken out of the insensitivity of his sinfulness by grace and experiences the interior fire of judgement which burns for his salvation. This fire is the Logos itself. It is in this way that sin reaches its furthest limit and so actually becomes a means of redemption. The actual reversal in man's development is, therefore, the work of God alone and occurs before the intervention of the Church with its reconciliation.[443]

The conclusion which we have just reached somewhat indirectly is confirmed by the text In Lev.hom. 8,11.[444] It has already been shown that this text concerns penance for sins committed after baptism.[445] Here there is a clear distinction made within penance between a *purgatio* (*purificatio*) from sins, on the one hand, and a receiving of the *donum gratiae,* a replenishment by the Holy Spirit, a reacquisition of the 'robe' and the 'ring', that is, sonship, on the other hand. The purification is achieved by conversion from sin, by a gradual process, through which the sinner by his own effort, but also supported by the priest, abolishes sin and continually eradicates the consequences of sin. In other words, it occurs by 'subjective penance'.[446] The communication of the Spirit, however, *per olei imaginem designatur.* Even if it is considered uncertain that Origen knew of a liturgical anointing which was associated with the well-attested imposition of hands, the clear distinction between purification from sins and reception of the Spirit must imply a distinction also in the *causes* of these two events—just as there is in baptism and the preparation for it. Once this is granted, then the only possible cause of the reception of the Spirit is the rite of reconciliation. If the text is allowed its most obvious meaning,[447] that is, if the *olei imago* is taken in the sense of a real anointing which accompanies the imposition of hands, then it expresses immediately what is meant: the purification from sins *datur per illa omnia quae superius diximus* (that is, through the progressive destruction of sin by means of the *poenitudinem gerere* (415,6), the *deponere peccata* (414,10), etc. But the communication of the Spirit occurs in the act of reconciliation by the *olei imago.*[448]

The only objection that could be levelled against this view is that it follows the lines of current modern sacramental theology in ascribing one effect to man's personal act and the other to the sacramental act of the Church. In other words, it overlooks the fact that, in Origen's view, the visible act of the Church, in so far as it is effective, is the *typus ecclesiis traditus,*[449] that is, the manifestation of that which is accomplished in the depths of man's being as an encounter between God and man. Accordingly, for this objection there would be no act of the Church having an effect which 'otherwise' would not happen and which occurs *after* that which man has done previously with God's grace alone.

Against this it must be stressed that for Origen excommunication and reconciliation are two phases of one simple event. They both have the same aim. Excommunication is not merely a vindictive punishment which is to be lifted as quickly as possible, even in view of penance. It is rather a τύπος of the fact that the person guilty of mortal sin is now in *the* situation of grace in which alone he can be cured, that is, in the immediate grace of God's own judgement. After the failure of the Church's created saving powers the sin is pronounced 'incurable' and, by excommunication, the sinner is handed over to the judgement of God who is his physician. Thus excommunication and reconciliation *together* 'cover' visibly in the Church as a *τύπος* the one event which happens in fact. The sinner who recognizes the 'truth' of his sin, that is, his 'being outside', is redeemed. But it is precisely because this 'outside' is itself also included in the grace of Christ in virtue of his death that the sinner returns as he does, sharing in that death by his own *interitus carnis*.

It is only *within* the one event, which, as a *whole,* has an ecclesial *and* an interior aspect and occurs with these two aspects interacting inseparably that the relationship which we have stressed between an individual moment of the ecclesial dimension and an individual moment of the interior dimension is understood and justified.[450]

To complete our view on this question we need to make two further points. The sinner's personal interior penance and even the reconciling activity of the Church of the saints are both visible within the Church, even though they are carried out as an event of the 'interior' Church in virtue of the Spirit of its holiness. Thus even the sinner's personal penance occurs publicly in the Church, since it is an exhomologesis which is under church supervision and, in certain circumstances, may even be enforced officially. The reconciling activity of the Church of the saints is visible in the exhortation of fellow Christians and of the bishop as well as in the offering of sacrifice by priests.

c) A SYSTEMATIC SURVEY

Moreover, although the beginning of penance, consisting of the immediate, divinely inspired awareness of the interior fire of judgement, and its end, consisting of the direct reception of the Holy Spirit, are both essential for the person guilty of mortal sin and his penance, this does not mean that a mediation of created sanctifying powers, acting in all their human and ecclesial dimensions, is in any way excluded. In fact God's immediate act of conversion leads man back into this reality of the created sanctifying powers and subjects him to their influence. Christ honours the 'angel of the Church', who has to lead the sinner to full health and who, therefore, like the good Samaritan, brings the sinner back into the inn of the Church.[451] God hands the sinner over to the 'angel of penance'.[452] We have already seen that even the devil, to whom the person guilty of mortal sin is 'handed over', has, in Origen's system, a positive role in penance which he carries out unwillingly as God's agent. Thus the process of penance as a *whole* is visible as a reality of the Church in all its phases. It takes place in all the dimensions of created reality in the ambit of the visible, hierarchical Church, just as it does in the Church considered as an interior community of grace and in the depths of man's personal freedom, that is, at the point where man is in direct contact with God. The process comprises three phases which do not necessarily succeed each other chronologically. It begins with insensitivity and the immediacy of God which is experienced within it as a radical judgement; it passes into and through the medium of the created punitive and, thereby, healing reality of the Church and of man's flesh; it ends with the immediate awareness of God, this time experienced as radical love in the reception of the Holy Spirit. If we distinguish in this way the dimensions and the development of the penitential process and represent it schematically we obtain a record of all its aspects in the schema produced on page 318 which is designed to illustrate both the complexity and the unity of Origen's view of the penance of Christians.

This schema ought to be fully comprehensible, for the most part,[453] in the light of what we have already seen. This applies even to most of the connections between the individual elements of the penitential process. The following considerations are intended to facilitate a further understanding, particularly concerning the sacramental nature and efficacy of the process.

The first striking aspect of this schema is that the three dimensions of the penitential process which it distinguishes obviously evince a relationship with what later theology will call *sacramentum—res et sacramentum—res sacramenti*. This relationship becomes clear immediately *res et sacramentum* is understood in its most meaningful and objective sense and not as a formal, abstract, juridical or ontological concept. This notion really means an inner relationship of the recipient of the sacrament to the Church.[454] It is brought about by the sacramental sign. It is specific to each individual sacrament, and through it a special grace is communicated. On this view the *sacramentum* is the visible event in the dimension of the official Church (of the *potestas ordinis*), the *res et sacramentum* is the relationship of man to the Church as the means of grace, signified and

		Direction of the Progress of the Penitential Process		
		God alone in grace as *judgment* ▶	the created powers as the grace of reconciliation ▶	◀ (again) God alone in grace as *salvation*
The Dimensions of the Penitential Process	The Exterior Official Church	official church excommunication as the image of the explusion into the 'outside' that is God's judgment ▼	public penance and official *correptio,* sacrifice of the Church, 'prayer' ▶ ▼	◀ official reconciliation (*reverti ad Ecclesiam*) ▼
	The Interior Church of the Saints	▲ the interior separation from the Church as a means of grace ▼	the interior reconciling activity of the Church of the saints by means of the co-redemptive 'assumption' of the sinner's guilt ▼	full participation in the Church as the means of grace (*reconiungi corpori Christi et membris Ecclesiae*) ▼
	Man as Spirit and Flesh	the experience of God as the interior fire of judgment ▶	*interitus carnis ut spiritus salvus fiat* ▶	reception of the Holy Spirit

effected by the *sacramentum,* and finally the *res sacramenti* is the grace of the Church which accrues to man as a result of this relationship and which effects his whole activity and being. The relationship between the three notions of later theology and the three dimensions of the penitential process which are discernible in Origen should now be quite clear. The events or effects which we have just outlined in fact are each produced by one of the three dimensions. The peculiarity of Origen's view consists solely in the fact that the sacramental event (*sacramentum*) and its immediate (*res et sacramentum*) and mediated (*res sacramenti*) effect itself have three stages in each of these dimensions. They are to be considered, therefore, as a dynamic process and not merely as static entities. It is only when each dimension is seen in relation to the others that its full significance can be assessed precisely.

The three stages which are discernible in the schema with regard to the direction and the succession of the development in the penitential process could obviously be put in a different order. Origen's thought would probably not be violated if the second and third stages were transposed. For the handing over of the penitent to the saving powers of the interior Church can also be understood as the *consequence* (as well as the presupposition) of a change of an intimate awareness of God as anger and judgement to an awareness of him as love. In this sense God would deliver to the Church the person who is already saved. The awareness of his judgement is already a grace for him, so that the first and the third stages of the schema are practically only two aspects of one and the same act by which God transforms man. Such a transposition is not made unfeasible by the fact that in the dimension of the visible and official Church public penance and the official *correptio* obviously and clearly take place *before* church reconciliation. For it should not be forgotten that the reconciling activity of the Church, both as official and as holy, like the interior work of penance, the *interitus carnis,* which ends only with actual death, continues beyond reconciliation, even if somewhat less explicitly than previously. The Church's teaching about penance, the sacrifice on its altars, its prayer, the interior expiation of the saints, the offering of the martyrs and the death of the elderly—all these are permanent features of the Church which exercise a saving influence on the sinner. Thus reconciliation, in so far as it is a readmission to the Church, may very easily be considered as an incorporation into this Spirit-permeated, reconciling and *active* medium of grace that is the Church. The Church bestows the Spirit on the new and the renewed member not only through its being but also through its permanent life.

This clarifies a point which previously was probably left vague and, when expressed, did not appear to correspond very well to Origen's own thinking. Reconciliation bestows the Spirit. Provided that this is correctly understood, it is what Origen means. In this view reconciliation confers the Spirit in so far as it means the incorporation into the static and active medium of grace that is the inner Church of the saints. In other words, this middle term in Origen's system must not be overlooked. Origen is so insistent that the personal possession of the Spirit is an indispensable condition in everyone who, by prayer, exhortation, etc., contributes to the reconciliation of others, that it is unthinkable that he should renounce this principle *completely* where it is a question of the bestowal of the Spirit by official reconciliation. It can certainly be applied here without the implication of Donatism. We have already established that Origen does not lean in this direction in the case of the other sacraments, and this would also contradict his view on the teaching of penance. The person who is reconciling does not transmit *his* Spirit of grace but reincorporates the penitent legitimately into the visible Church. But, in so doing, he places the penitent within that medium of grace which as a whole possesses this Spirit perpetually and inalienably and, therefore, communicates it to all those who legitimately belong to it. Thus the Church achieves in them that victory of the Spirit over the mortal flesh which is the condition for the personal possession of the gift of the Holy Spirit. There is every indication, therefore, that Origen's view of the effects of church reconciliation is already similar to that which will be held later by Augustine.[455] Accordingly, reconciliation does not simply transmit the Spirit from the person who is reconciling, as the Donatists would have it, or even from God to the penitent through the instrumentality of the person reconciling, after the fashion of the usual way of explaining sacramental causality. Rather it communicates the Spirit in so far as it incorporates the penitent into the community which already possesses this Spirit, namely, the Church. And this happens irrespective of whether the person reconciling possesses this Spirit personally or not. Nevertheless, the person who claims the right to take part in the Church's reconciling activity must also possess this Spirit himself. The person who is not holy, therefore, communicates the Spirit only when and in so far as he incorporates the penitent into the permanently holy body of Christ. If this body were ever to be deprived of the Spirit—which of course is absolutely impossible—then the sacrament would be ineffective. The fact that the interior personal state of the individual dispensing the sacrament is irrelevant to the effect of the sacrament should not lead to the conclusion that the posession of the Spirit by the Church of the saints is also irrelevant to the power of its sacraments. The reconciling activity of the Church of the saints is only the necessary expression of its holy reality. Thus this activity is the indispensable condition of the effective communication of the Spirit by official reconciliation. Consequently, the individual phases which are discernible in the process of penance suppose each other and are *interdependent* to such an extent that, in the final analysis, one of them cannot be isolated from the others and stand in relation to them completely and independently as an efficient cause to its external effect. The individual phases are supported by the whole and it is only within this whole that it is possible to ascribe to one phase a 'causal' relationship with regard to another. Obviously all this throws some light on Origen's notion of the causality of the sacramental sign.

The schema also illustrates the fact that, according to Origen, what happens visibly in the sphere of the official Church is not only the tangible embodiment of the *Church's* activity, having an effect in the depth of man's soul, but also the expression of man's interior journey of conversion. This man meets God in his fire of judgement burning immediately within him. He is, therefore, 'outside' the Church and begins again to allow himself to be influenced by the saving grace of Christ's body. It is for this reason that he does penance publicly and then receives the Holy Spirit by dying in penance. He is then once more in the fellowship of the Church. For Origen the sacramental sign is the embodiment of the act of God *and* the act of man as they occur within the Church. Later Thomas Aquinas will say that the 'acts of the penitent' are the interior constitutive elements (*materia*) of the sacramental event. We have something similar in Origen, although without the notion of hylomorphism. Moreover, the sacramental sign is so organically articulated in the penitential institution of the early Church that *everything* is clearly at the same time the expression of the act of God and the act of man. This made it impossible for Origen to ascribe a part of the visible sacramental event exclusively to man's interior act and another part exclusively to God's act.

All these considerations justify us in treating the whole external event of penance, from excommunication up to reconciliation, as the expression of that which is happening in the interior reality of the

Church and within the personal depths of the man who is converting himself. Considered as the unity of the visible activity of the hierarchical Church and of the public activity and suffering of the penitent within the Church, this event is what Origen calls σύμβολον, τύπος,[456] in the case of baptism. This applies to what happens interiorly and we have here perhaps some more light thrown on the *way* in which Origen envisages the efficacy of the sacrament. It is no longer a question here of showing that with regard to the sacramental event in general or to penance in particular this event is the *effective* sign of the interior event of grace. This has also been already treated elsewhere.[457] What we wish to consider at the moment is how to define more precisely the *way* in which the visible event is effective. Now, according to Origen, all the phases of the penitential process in its different dimensions are so interdependent that the interior and exterior aspects should be considered to be related to each other reciprocally as cause and effect. This is the only way of doing justice to Origen's own testimony. It is possible that the notion of τύπος (σύμβολον) will help us to answer the question of how such a relationship of *reciprocal* dependence of the individual phases in the one process can be conceived. However, this relationship should not be depreciated by making the σύμβολον a mere subsequent and, ultimately, unimportant reflection of an event which exists independently in itself. At the same time, it ought not to be exaggerated in the sense that it can no longer be considered the expression and consequence, that is, the 'manifestation' of the interior aspect. On one occasion Origen[458] calls the bodily gesture of prayer σύμβολον and εἰκών of the free interior attitude of prayer[459] which is visible in the body and so impresses on it an 'image' of the ἰδιώματα of the soul. Indeed, in general for Origen what is perceived by the senses is essentially only a sign and an image of what is true and real.[460] But the relationship between the body and the soul is the most simple and the most intelligible case illustrating what A. von Harnack says on the subject of the 'symbol' of the ancients:

> We today understand by symbol a thing which is not what it signifies; at that time symbol was understood as a thing which in some way was what it signified; at the same time, according to that previous way of thinking, the true heavenly reality always lay in or behind the manifestation, without coinciding with it completely on earth.[461]

The scholastic theory of the relationship between the soul and the body still provides us today with perhaps the best access for our thinking habits to an understanding of the ancient notion of *σύμβολον*. Origen himself justifies such an approach, since he holds that the corporeal is a *σύμβολον* of the psychic. Now if the corporeal is understood not merely as the juxtaposed expression of a spiritual reality which is itself independent of this expression, but rather as a manifestation in which the spiritual, even though it is distinct from the manifestation, *must* be expressed in order to be *itself,* then it is possible to understand how the interior and the exterior aspects are related to each other in the symbol of the sacrament. The symbol is the expression of grace in the mystery, in the sense that this grace is expressed only there and depends upon it, in the same way that the symbol depends upon the grace. The 'incarnation' is the way in which the grace becomes present. By being given a body it is given existence. According to Origen the sacrament-image is not, as in modern sacramental theology, 'image' because it is effective, or even 'image and effective', but it is precisely 'effective as image' or 'effective, because it is image'. Grace is produced and is present because and in so far as it is embodied within its symbol, just as there are spiritual attitudes which are only present if they are realized by the bodily gesture which they themselves produce. Thus the *σύμβολον* of the sacrament is a cause by being the image of that which is caused.[462] This is not the place to give a more precise definition and explanation of this *σύμβολον* which is simultaneously cause and effect of the reality signified. We believe, however, that with it we have reached to some extent Origen's notion of *σύμβολον* in relation to the sacramental event, and that we may apply it to the process of penance. If we wish to understand Origen's view of the way that the visible aspect of this process is effective, then we must accept that this whole process is a unity of the act of God and the act of man within the Church. By his penance man exposes himself to God's judgement which is grace and manifests this visibly in the Church. This act is only effective in so far as it is simultaneously a consequence and a cause, that is, an image which renders the reality present in expressing it. But similarly God also reveals the saving act of his judgement within the Church. This is evident in the word of binding and loosing expressed by the Church. It is in this way, and only in this way, that God's grace is really present. The Church's word of judgement and of pardon is, therefore, also simultaneously the consequence and the cause of the same creative word of God which is here and now expressed in the depths of the sinner who is to receive grace.[463]

7. *Penance as a Sacrament*

A) CHURCH PENANCE AS A SACRAMENT

We are now in a position to raise the question of the sacramentality of church penance, even though we have previously already used the terms 'sacrament' and 'sacramental' unhesitatingly to describe what we have found in Origen's work. In fact all has already been said on this subject. According to Origen penance leads to an interior pardon for man by the reception of the Holy Spirit. This process is also visible in the dimension of the official-hierarchical Church. This visible aspect is, on the one hand, necessary, since Origen clearly sees the need for the penance of excommunication in the case of mortal sins, and, on the other hand, it is prescribed by the hierarchical Church in virtue of an explicit authorization by Jesus Christ with reference to John 20 and Matthew 16.[464] Now where the visible aspect of a grace-giving process is so necessary that this process cannot exist without it—and it is only in this way that it can be thought of meaningfully as necessary—and where the power to establish this visible aspect is given by Christ himself, there we have, in today's terminology, a sacrament. The question of precisely *how* the causal relationship between the sacramental sign and the grace signified by it is to be considered in no way alters the fact that there is a sacrament. Even if *this* further question, when viewed in the light of a later and possibly theologically necessary solution, was not answered very exactly by a previous theologian, this does not justify the conclusion that this theologian either denied or overlooked the existence of the sacrament.[465] Origen knew of a *sacrament* of penance.

At the same time, this sacramental process is still firmly embedded in the general reconciling activity of the Church. Origen does not only recognize *alongside* the penance of excommunication other forms of the Church's reconciling activity which, incidentally, he overlooks less willingly than generally happens today. He also implicates the reconciling activity of the Church of saints *within* the sacramental process itself. According to the most probable interpretation of his views, the repentant sinner is reincorporated into the mystical body by reconciliation in such a way that he thereby receives the Holy Spirit. In view of these considerations, it can hardly be reckoned a deficiency if sacramental church penance rather than being totally isolated remains organically connected with the whole life of the Church which is constantly renewing its holiness by penance.

B) 'PRIVATE' SACRAMENTAL PENANCE IN ORIGEN?

Is there, according to Origen, in addition to the penance of excommunication, yet another remission of sins which would be sacramental in the modern sense, that is, a 'private', 'secret' absolution from sins by the priests? Since we have already answered this question in essence, all that is required here is a summary. There is no evidence of a real sacramental 'private penance' in Origen.[466] Certainly, even in his view, the Church, in the person of its official representatives, supports the effort of the sinner, even when it is a matter of the remission of sins which are not subject to the penance of excommunication as mortal sins. Thus he refers to private exhortations, corrections, intercessory prayers, sacrifices, pastoral counselling, etc., on the part of priests. It could even be said that Origen considers such a support to be necessary and, therefore, as obligatory for the laity.[467] Nevertheless, this is not sufficient proof that this obligatory measure taken by the official Church was a sacrament in the strict sense, that is, as distinct from liturgical prayer, from the Church's supervision of morals and from the eucharistic sacrifice in general. It has already been shown that De or. 28 contains nothing more than this.[468]

In Lev. hom. 15,2[469] presents no more of an argument in favour of a sacramental private penance. Obviously Origen also recognizes the existence of mortal sins which in fact do not entail excommunication. This does not, however, warrant the conclusion that these sins *ought* not to be remitted by a public church penance. But even if it were accepted that this false conclusion[470] were in fact correct, it would still have to be demonstrated that such sins could be remitted not only with the help of the Church but by a specifically sacramental means, that is, private penance, which is distinct from the other aids which the Church offers for reconciliation. The private confession before the physician of souls,[471] who does not consider that a public penance is necessary, does not in itself represent a private performance of penance. For, even supposing that this doctor of souls was normally a priest, it should not be forgotten that according to Origen, at least in theory, every spiritual person possesses the power to loosen, in the sense which we explained earlier. Thus it is hardly possible to decide in the cases in question whether Origen is thinking of priests as such or of a spiritual person, who is in fact either a priest or a lay person.

Moreover, no further precision is given on the role of the physician of souls in the case of non-mortal sins. It needs to be proven specifically that this role is other than the Church's usual reconciling rôle, which we have seen to exist alongside the penance of excommunication and which is not sacramental in today's sense. This cannot be presupposed. It is methodologically false to understand the remission of sins by the Church in any form as a 'private' sacramental absolution provided it is done by the Church and does not involve a lifting of excommunication. This is because, according to Origen, a third possibility is conceivable. This is not to be considered sacramental, however, since it is open to every spiritual person. And even if it were reserved to the priest, it could only represent those powers which cannot be identified with the actual power to perform the sacrament of penance.

The only possible inkling of a private sacramental penance in Origen is found in De or. 28, which presupposes that the priest is able to remit at least certain sins without excommunication by his 'prayer', and in so doing he acts in the awareness of the power mentioned in John 20. In this case there is an objective sacrament, irrespective of whether the priest is explicitly aware or not of the sacramental character of his action, say, in parallel to baptism or to the reconciliation of an excommunicate. In fact he intends to exercise the sacramental power conferred in John 20 and thus his 'prayer' for forgiveness is more than a mere prayer of intercession. This theological deduction, however, comes up against a whole series of difficulties.

Does the appeal to John 20, when the sins for which the power of remission is being sought are not mortal sins, represent a special biblical basis? Is the binding and loosing in this text, when applied to such 'light' sins, to be understood any differently from what lies within the capability of a spiritual lay person? Is it to be supposed that, when and wherever such a 'prayer' occurs, the other preconditions, especially confession, necessary for the dispensing of a sacrament, are fulfilled? If this 'prayer' is construed as sacramental, it must be admitted at the same time that Origen in the same text and elsewhere allows it efficacy only if the priest is a spiritual person. There is a hint of Donatism here which tends to speak against the sacramental view of this 'prayer' and suggests that it is the intercession of a friend of God, for whom it is decisive that, as an intecessor, he is an ἐμπνευσθείς, who is 'known by his fruits'.[472] Origen does not display any Donatist tendencies elsewhere in his sacramental teaching or in his teaching on penance. It is, therefore, methodologically correct not to assume such tendencies in this passage, so long as the 'prayer' of the priests in De or. 28 can be interpreted as other than sacramental. This is obviously possible and is not excluded by the appeal to John 20:23. If this passage really does refer to a specific act of the Church, other than the accompaniment of the personal penance of every Christian, then one could expect that this would also be mentioned in In Lev. hom. 2,4,[473] where Origen takes the opportunity to enumerate as comprehensively as possible the many different ways in which sins may be remitted. In this passage, apart from baptism, martyrdom and public church penance, there is mention only of the subjective performance of penance. Finally, it is difficult to see for which category of sins such a private sacramental penance would be appropriate. The attempt to prove in Origen a third group of serious sins between mortal sins which are subject to public church penance and venial sins must be considered futile. Even secret mortal sins are subject to public church penance. Today, our own practical daily experience, contrary to theory and liturgical ceremony, knows of only a sacramental intervention of the Church for the remission of sins. This is why we tend to think that every form of the remission of sins which is clearly attested in Origen is to be interpreted as sacramental. But there is no real basis for this interpretation. In any case, Origen considers 'prayer' for the forgiveness of sins to be so much a part of the priest's other activity for the remission of sins (*monendo, docendo, instruendo*[474]—*per sacrificia sacerdotum et obsecrationes pontificum . . . per scientiam divinae legis*)[475] that he hardly appears to be aware of a special power which is not already implied in the rest of the priest's activity. He considers, rather, that these other priestly functions (moral correction, prayer, sacrifice, teaching), with their corresponding power, are also able to remit sins.

In the reconciliation after an excommunication we have a function which is clearly reserved exclusively to the bishop, even though in its effect it is related with the activity which the whole Church exercises in the remission of sins. The only proper sacrament discernible in Origen is the penance of excommunication. Apart from this, there are indeed acts of the hierarchical Church which are directed towards the forgiveness of sins, but these cannot be called sacramental in today's sense.

NOTES

CHAPTER ONE: THE HISTORY OF PENANCE

1. Cf. the following comprehensive articles by the author. They are partially repetitive. They also contain references to further literature:

'Busse, christl.' in: König, F., *Religions-Wissenschaftliches Wörterbuch—Die Grundbegriffe* (Freiburg/Br. 1956), pp. 142–44.

'Das katholische Verstandnis von Sünde und Sündenvergebung im Neuen Testament und in der Busspraxis der alten Kirche' in: *Die Sündenvergebung in der Kirche* (Evgl. Akademie, Bad Boll—Akademie der Diözese, Rottenburg, 1958), pp. 33–50.

'Bussdisziplin, altkirchliche', pp. 805–15; 'Busse', pp. 815–18; 'Bussakrament', p. 826, in: LThK vol. II (Freiburg/Br. 1958).

'Die Busse' in: *Kirche und Sakramente* (QD 10) (Freiburg/Br. 1960), pp. 83–5.

'Penance' in: *Sacramentum Mundi* 4 (New York/London 1969), pp. 385–99.

'Pastoraltheologie des Busssacramentes' in: *Handbuch der Pastoraltheologie* vol. IV (Freiburg/Br. 1969), pp. 128–44 (this article includes references to the author's treatment of systematic and practical questions concerning penance which are not considered in the present volume).

'Penance' and 'Penance, Sacrament of' in Rahner/Vorgrimler, *Dictionary of Theology*, 2nd edn (New York 1981 [= *Concise Theological Dictionary*, London]), pp. 370–75.

2. Cf. Matt. 6:1–18; 9:15; Mark 9:29.
3. Cf. DS 1525–6; 1551–4.
4. This is particularly clear in 1 Cor. 5:3–5 and 2 Cor. 2:5–11, even if the traditional exegesis of these passages is not correct. These passages also suggest a re-examination of the conclusion reached by H. Thyen in his work: *Studien zur Sündenvergebung im Neuen Testament und Seinen Alttestamentlichen und jüdischen Voraussetzungen*.
5. Cf. 2 Cor. 5:18 ff.
6. Cf. Acts 2:38; Rom. 6; 1 Cor. 6:11.
7. Cf. Matt. 26:28; 1 Cor. 11:26.
8. Cf. Matt. 6:12.
9. Cf. Matt. 6:1–18; 9:15; Mark 9:29.
10. Cf. 1 John 5:16.
11. Cf. Matt. 18:15.
12. Cf. 2 Thess. 3:14.
13. Cf. 1 Tim. 5:20.

14. Cf. DS 1670. The council takes great care to formulate that Jesus instituted the sacrament *praecipue* by this saying.

15. Cf. 1 QS VI 24–VII 25 in: J. Maier, *Die Texte vom Toten Meer,* 2 vols. (Munich/Basel 1960), vol. i, pp. 34–6.

16. Naturally a thorough justification of the Church's power to forgive sins should not lose sight of the notion which the early Church had of Jesus' own power to forgive sins, as well as of the way in which he applied it. This notion of the early Church is particularly evident in Matt. 9:8, especially by comparison with Mark 2:12. In the present context, however, we must content ourselves with the simple reference to this vital connection.

17. Cf. Strack-Billerbeck I 741–4.

18. Jesus understands his power as a superior 'binding' force (Mark 3:27) which overcomes Satan by 'loosening' his bonds (1 John 3:8); cf. Luke 11:20 etc. He communicates a similar *ἐξουσία* to the disciples (Matt. 10:1). Paul also understands the ban in this way (cf. 1 Cor. 5:5; 2 Cor. 2:11; 1 Tim. 1:20).

19. Cf. Matt. 18:17 and 1 Cor. 5:3 f.

20. Similarly only the Son of Man has the power on earth really to forgive sins, even though only God is able to do this in fact; Mark 2:11–12 etc.

21. The person who is outside, that is, is not yet baptized, is not judged, that is, he does not have the ban imposed upon him; cf. 1 Cor. 5:9–13.

22. Cf. DS 3807–8.

23. The letter of Clement of Rome to the Church in Corinth, however, represents an important hinge-document (cf. 51.3 and 52.1). In the edn of the letter in the collection *Sources Chrétiennes,* p. 50, A. Jaubert says: 'Il semble que Clément n'ait eu qu'à puiser dans une mine toute préparée', by which she means the Jewish background, which she considers under the heading 'Courants pénitentiels'. On p. 51 she says: 'On pourrait à l'aide de ces passages reconstituer les textes et les exhortations qui servaient à une cérémonie pénitentielle dans la communauté chrétienne et l'on pourrait y joindre les passages qui ont pour thème la remonstrance au pécher.' These observations are important for an understanding of Hermas, since he too, according to the generally accepted view, is writing in Rome. This means that even if he were not already acquainted with the text of the letter of Clement, he must certainly have known the tradition which gave rise to this letter.

24. Cf. Hermas, Sim. VIII 11.3; IX 21.3 f.; Mand. IV 1; Vis. III 7.6; Sim. IX 14,2 etc.

25. Mand. IV 1.8; 3.6.

26. From Tertullian, De paen. 7.11 up to can.11 of the third synod of Toledo, A.D. 589.

27. Clement of Alex., Strom. II 13,57,1; Origen, Lev. 15,2.

28. Sim. VIII 11; Mand. IV 1.8; 3.1–7 etc.

29. Ignatius of Antioch; Dionysius of Corinth; Polycarp; Justin; Irenaeus; Clement of Alex.; etc.

30. For Africa cf. Cyprian, Ep. 55,21; for Spain: the synod of Elvira and still in A.D. 380 the synod of Saragossa; see DS 212.

31. The council of Nicaea; DS 129. See also DS 212 and 236.

32. Irenaeus, Adv.haer. III 4.3.

33. Tertullian, De paen. 12.9.

34. Not yet John 20; see Tertullian, De pud. 21.9.

35. Cf. D 43.

36. Cf. the texts in Mansi I, 921–34, as well as the results of more recent textual-critical investigations of these questions.

37. Hippol., Phil. IX 12.

38. Cf. G. Dix, *The Treatise on the Apostolic Tradition of St. Hippolytus of Rome* (London 1937), p. 5 (new edn 1972).
39. Cf. Origen, In Ps. 37 hom. 2,6.
40. Cf. the synod of Ancyra (A.D. 314), of Elvira and Toledo (A.D. 400), Siricius, Ep. 1, 3.6.
41. Cf. Didascalia Apost. II 16,2.
42. Herm.Mand. IV 3.3 f.; Tertullian, De paen. 7.10; Origen, Ex. 6.9.
43. This is the meaning of Origen, De or. 28.
44. Tertullian, De paen. 10–12.
45. Cyprian, Ep. 66.5; 55.17; 72.2; Origen, Ios. 3.5; In Ps. 36,2.4.
46. Cyprian, Ep. 57.4; cf. Ep. 15.1; 16.2; 17.2; Origen, Lev. 8.11; Didasc. Apost. II 41.2.
47. Cyprian, Ep. 17.2; 43.3.
48. Tertullian, De paen. 10.6.
49. Tertullian, De pud. 21.
50. Tertullian, De paen. 8; De pud. 9.
51. Cyprian, Ep. 16.2; 17.2; 4.4; Origen, Lev. 14.2.
52. It is only in this way that a full readmission to the Church can be realized, so that all the stages of penance are variations of the penance of excommunication.
53. B. Poschmann, *Busse und Letzte Ölung* (HDG IV/3), p. 55.
54. Innocent I, Ep. 1.7; Leo I, Sermo 45; 49.3.
55. Cf. Augustine, Ep. 82.8,11.
56. Thus, for example, heretics who were not actually guilty of heresy were reconciled immediately; the same applied to those who were seriously ill.
57. Cf. Jerome, Ep. 80.9; Ambrose, De paen. 2; Augustine, Ep. 153,3,7; Siricius, Ep. 1.5.
58. It is possible that at the point of death even the *viatecum* was administered, although without *reconciliatio absolutissima*; cf. for example Siricius, Ep. 1,5,6; Innocent I, Ep. 6.2; Leo I, Ep. 108.4; 167.13.
59. Cf. Caesarius of Arles, Sermo 258.2; Avitus, Ep. 18; and others.
60. For example, the council of Agde (A.D. 506) can. 15; the third council of Orleans (A.D. 538) can. 24.
61. Cf. Siricius, Ep. 1,14.18; Basilius, Ep. 188 can. 3; Leo I, Ep. 167 inquis. 2.
62. Cf. the council of Arles (A.D. 314) can. 8 (=DS 127); Siricius, Ep. 5.8; Augustine, Ep. 185.10; Leo I, Ep. 167 inquis. 19.
63. Cf. DS 127, together with DS 183 and 216.
64. For example Ambrose, De paen. I 8.36; Pacian, Ep. 3.7; Jerome, In or. III 12.
65. Even in Augustine the remission of guilt is attributed explicitly to the action of the Church; cf. Sermo 96,6; In Io. tract. 49.24.
66. Coelestin I, Ep. 4.2; Innocent I, Ep. 3.2; Augustine, Ep. 228.2; and others.
67. Cf. below where it will be a question of the 'absolutions'; see DS 308–9; it is very clear in Augustine.
68. Augustine, Sermo 99.9; In Io. tract. 124.7; De civ.Dei XX 9.2; Sermo 71,23.37.
69. Jerome, In Mt. III 16.19; Consultationes Zachaei et Apollonii n. 18; Gregory the Great, In ev.hom. II 26.6.
70. Synod of Barcelona (A.D. 541) can. 9; Isidore of Seville, De eccl. off. II 17.6.
71. Cf. Isidore of Seville in: PL 81.30–3.
72. Felix III, Ep. 13; cf. J. Grotz, pp. 1–10.
73. Cf. for example, Avitus of Vienne, Ep. 15 and 16.
74. Thus the synod of Gerunda (A.D. 517) can. 9; the fourth synod of Toledo (A.D. 633) can. 54.
75. Cf. the Paenitentiale Theodori I 13.

76. This is first attested by the synod of Châlons (between A.D. 639 and 654) can. 8; this point is, however, contested by C. Vogel (cf. 'Bussbücher' in: LThK 2, 802–5).

77. *Liber de poenitentiarum mensura taxanda* (end of 6th cent.) in: *S. Columbani opera,* ed. G. S. M. Walker (Dublin 1957); cf. J. Hennig, 'Kolumban' in: LThK 6,403 f.

78. PL 180,886; cf. B. Geyer, 'Die Siebzahl der Sakramente in ihrer historischen Entwicklung' in: ThGl 10 (1918), pp. 325–48; see especially p. 329.

79. *Sententiae* PL 186,910.

80. Mansi XXII 1110, 1173 ff., XXIII 396 f., 448.

81. P. Anciaux, *La théologie du sacrament de pénitence au XIIe siècle* (Louvain 1949), pp. 31–6, 164–274, 392–490.

82. Can. 88; Mansi XIV 99.

83. Cf. PL 140, 1011 and Gratian, De paen. I c. 90.

84. Provided, however, that there is present the *votum sacramenti*; cf. Anselm, PL 158, 662; Bruno of Segni, PL 165,137; Abelard, PL 178,664 f.; Roland Bandinelli, according to: A. Gietl, *Die Sentezen Rolands* (Freiburg/Br. 1891), p. 248; the circle of the Victorines, PL 176, 565.

85. Anselm, PL 158, 662; Abelard, PL 178, 664 f.; Peter Lombard, IV Sent. d. 17 c. 1; William of Auxerre, cf. V. Heynck, in: FStud 36 (1954), pp. 47–57 f.; Alexander of Hales, cf. P. Schmoll, *Die Busslehre der Frühscholastik* (Munich 1909), pp. 146–50; Albert the Great, cf. ibid., pp. 133 f.

86. This was the view held by the Victorines.

87. Cf. Hugh of St Victor, PL 176,564.

88. Cf. Richard of St Victor, PL 196,1165; Praepositinus, cf. Schmoll (Anm.85), pp. 83–8.

89. The precise evidence for this is provided by V. Heynck, 'Zur Busslehre des hl. Bonaventura' in: FStud 36 (1954), pp. 1–81.

90. Thus already Guido of Orchelles, William of Auxerre, Alexander of Hales, William of Melitona, Bonaventure and Albert the Great.

91. This is already the effect of the power of the keys, working in advance; thus Albert the Great, as opposed to Alexander of Hales and Bonaventure.

92. At the time in question, this teaching was practically universally accepted; cf. Peter Lombard, IV Sent.d. 22 q. 2a. I sol. 3.

93. This is what Thomas Aquinas, in his youth and with regard to his general sacramental teaching, saw and taught as the immediate, dispositive effect, that is, the *res et sacramentum.*

94. On the special question of Thomas Aquinas' teaching on penance, cf.: R. M. Schultes, *Reue und Busse* (Paderborn 1906); P. de Vooght, 'La justification dans le sacrement de pénitence d'apres saint Thomas d'Aquin' in: EThL 5 (1918), pp. 225–56; id., 'À propos de la causalité du sacrement de pénitence. Théologie thomiste et théologie tout court' in: EThL 7(1930), pp. 663–75; R.Marine, 'La reviviscenza dei meriti secondo la dottrina del dottore Angelico' in: Gr 13 (1932), pp. 75–108; H. Bouillard, *Conversion et grâce chez saint Thomas d'Aquin* (Paris 1944); G. N. Rus, *De munere sacramenti paenitentiae in aedificando corpore Christi ad mentem S.Thomae* (Rome 1944); M. Flick, *L'attimo della giustificazione secondo S.Tomaso* (Rome 1947); Ch.R. Meyer, *The Thomistic Concept of Justifying Contrition* (Mundelein 1949); P. de Letter, 'Thomistic Theology of Sacramental Forgiveness' in: Bijdragen 13 (1952), pp. 401–9.

95. It occurred first as 'exhomologesis'.

96. It appears as the title of a specific writing: *confessio sacramentalis* in Peter of Blois; cf. PL 207,1077–92.

97. It was justified, for example, with reference to the OT or by appeal to Jas. 5. In some canonists, however, as the *Glossa ordinaria* on Gratian and Nicholas de Tudes-

chis, the obligation to confess is derived only from the law of the Church; cf. on this point P. Anciaux, *La théologie du sacrement de pénitence au XIIe siècle* (louvain 1949).

98. Cf. P. Anciaux (n.97); A. Landgraf, 'Sünde und Trennung von der Kirche in der Frühscholastik' in: Scholastik 5 (1930), pp. 210–47.

99. According to him the indicative part of the formula of absolution has precisely *this* effect.

100. Cf. Thomas Aquinas, IV Sent. d. 16 p. 1 a. 2; q. 5 dubium.

101. Cf. WA I 539.

102. Vatican II, *Lumen Gentium* (Dogmatic Constitution on the Church) II; cf. A. Grillmeier's commentary on the passage in: 'Das Zweite Vatikanische Konzil I' (LThK) (Freiburg/Br. 1966), pp. 187–8.

103. For the details, see the following essays themselves. For the moment, we shall content ourselves with the observations which we consider essential for an appreciation of the orientation of our own work.

104. Of special importance in this regard are G. Bardy, H. von Campenhausen, P. Galtier, to mention but a few alongside B. Poschmann and the important work of J. Grotz. For the details of the relevant literature, see the bibliography.

105. Even today this book, which appeared in 1940 in Bonn, is still considered a standard work, offering a most useful introduction to our subject.

106. With regard to Hermas, R. Joly has recently propounded yet another view which does not involve the complete rejection of the 'penance jubilee' theory. If we understand his justification of his position aright, then it is really the mere number of proponents of this view, considered quantitatively, that has forced him to his own compromise. It is our contention that an examination of the context in which Hermas wrote, together with the traditions with which he could have been connected in his Roman milieu, ought to decide the question clearly today. In any event, the proposed compromise is hardly convincing.

107. Cf. on this point Poschmann, p. 12, where the peace with the Church 'effects' peace with God and coincides with it 'in fact', if not also 'formally'; or p. 485, where the *pax cum ecclesia* is rejected as 'efficient cause' and accepted only as the 'presupposition or condition' of divine forgiveness. This dogmatic formulation is not very felicitous.

108. We have in mind here such questions as: in what sense is the person guilty of mortal sin outside the Church; what part does (the ancient penance of) excommunication play in this regard; how is the ordering of the different effects of church reconciliation to be construed logically?

109. Cf. on this point chap. 2 in this volume, 'Sin as Loss of Grace in Early Church Literature'.

110. B. Poschmann, *Der Ablass im Licht der Bussgeschichte* (Theophaneia 4) (Bonn 1948).

111. B. Poschmann, 'Busse and Letzte Olung' (HDG IV,3) (Freiburg/Br. 1951).

112. Cf. ZKTh 71 (1949), pp. 481–90.

113. The person who should be named directly in this regard is rather M. de la Taille, who has shown courageously that the early Church's notion of penance is more justifiable than today's and is in accordance with the teaching of Trent on penance. H. de Lubac, M. Schmaus and others have made similar contributions.

114. Cf. V. Heynck, 'Zur Busslehre des hl. Bonaventura' in: FSt 36 (1954), pp. 1–81.

115. Cf. our reviews of P. Galtier, *De Paenitentia*; E. F. Latko, 'Origen's Concept of Penance' in: ZKTh 72 (1950), pp. 116–18; and of C. Vogel, 'La discipline penitentielle en Gaule' in: ZKTh 76 (1954), p. 498; etc.

116. H. Karpp, *Die Busse. Quellen zur Entstehung des altkirchlichen Busswesens* (Traditio Christiana I) (Zurich 1969).

117. Pastoral practice and pastoral psychology give rise to a whole range of questions which suggest the need for new forms of penance. In this connection we could mention other questions, concerning authority, freedom, sociological conditions, which are discernible outside the religious sphere, for instance, even in criminal law. All these questions are directly relevant in the field of education. These few observations must suffice to show—contrary to what might be a first impression—the various dimensions which our question has today.

CHAPTER TWO: SIN AS LOSS OF GRACE IN EARLY CHURCH LITERATURE

1. This essay, although revised, appeared first in: ZKTh 60 (1936), pp. 471–510. This explains both the rudimentary nature of the theme and the elementary way in which it is developed. If it were tackled afresh today it is obvious that all the published works which have appeared in the meantime on the relevant exegetical, textual critical and hermeneutical questions would have to be considered. It was, however, that original approach, in the form which we have preserved, that instigated and, to a certain extent, determined the author's studies on the history of penance which are collected together in this volume. It ought, therefore, to serve principally both as a clarification of the question in hand and as an announcement of our main theme, and this precisely in the form in which it affected both historically and in fact the subsequent studies. Thus the author is perfectly aware that this essay, if undertaken in today's circumstances, would have quite a different appearance. For the same reason, the reader of all these present studies must bear in mind their original historical context.

2. After an intense, but only brief, interest in questions concerning the history of penance in the 40s and the beginning of the 50s—an interest which, however, was unable to make any special impact on theology in general—studies on this theme have become rare in recent years. Even these generally concern the pastoral aspect and do not allow much weight to the systematic-dogmatic side. This observation alone, therefore, provides some justification for the history of dogma today. Mention should be made, however, of the specialist works of B. Poschmann, *Paenitentia secunda* (Bonn 1940); id., *Busse und Letzte Ölung* (HDG IV,3) (Freiburg/Br 1951); J. Grotz, *Die Entwicklung des Busstufenwesens in der vornicänischen Kirche* (Freiburg/Br. 1955); G. Teichtweier, *Die Sündenlehre des Origenes* (Regensburg 1958); C. Vogel, *Le pécheur et la pénitence dans l'Eglise ancienne* (Paris 1966).

3. Cf. on this point: S. Schiffini, *Tractatus de gratia divina* (Freiburg/Br. 1901), n.342; G. Lahousse, *De gratia divina* (Brugge 1902), n.326 ff.; C.Mazzella, *De gratia Christi* (Rome 1905), n.1102 f.,1112 f.; Chr. Pesch, *Praelectiones dogmaticae* V (Freiburg/Br. 1916), n.372 f.; id., *Compendium theologiae dogmaticae* III (Freiburg/Br. 1941–2), n.319; J. M. Herve, *Manuale theol. dogm.* (Paris 1925) II, n.65; B. Beraza, *De gratia Christi* (Bilbao 1929), n.951; H. Lange, *De gratia* (Freiburg/Br. 1929), n.467, 471; H. Lennerz, *De gratia redemptoris* (Rome 1934), p. 260; H. Rondet, *Gratia Christi* (Paris 1948); L. Lercher, *Instit. theol. dogm.* III (Innsbruck 1951), n.644; M. Schmaus, *Kath. Dogmatik* III/2 (Munich 1951), pp. 234–9; J. Pohle/J. Gummersbach, *Lehrbuch der Dogmatik* II (Paderborn 1956), p. 783 f.; J. Brinktrine, *Die Lehre von der Gnade* (Paderborn 1957), p. 208 f.; L. Ott, *Grundriss der kathol. Dogmatik* (Freiburg/Br. 1957), p. 318 f.; A. A. Tanquerey, *Synop-*

sis theologiae dogmaticae II (Paris/Rome 1959), n.171; F. Diekamp/K. Jüssen, *Kath. Dogmatik* (Münster 1959), p. 564 f.; H. Lais, *Dogmatik* I (Kevelaer 1965), p. 236.

Of its very nature, the question which we are considering does not concern a specifically Catholic problem. It is all the more surprising, therefore, that the corresponding manuals on the Protestant side normally do not even touch on the question. It is only exceptionally, and even then in a rudimentary form, that some information is found, as in W. Elert, *Der christliche Glaube* (Berlin 1940), p. 592 ff. [*Das Problem der Perseveranz* (*in der Rechtifertigungsgnade*)]; W. Trillhaas, *Dogmatik* (Berlin 1962), pp. 197, 203 f.

In any event, in all these studies the earliest development of the teaching of the loss of grace through sin, as this is evinced in very sparse indications, is completely overlooked. Nevertheless, these indications may very well represent notions such as those which H. Thyen attempts to derive and prove in *Studien zur Sündenvergebung im Neuen Testament und seinen altestamentlichen und jüdischen Voraussetzungen* (Göttingen 1970).

4. Cf. the recurrence of the following key words. *Judgement:* Matt. 10:15; 11:22,24; 12:36,41 ff.; 16:27; 24:30 f.; 25:31,32, etc.; Luke 10:14; 11:31; 20:47; John 5:22,27,29; 12:48. *Eternal damnation:* Matt. 3:10,12; 5:29 f.; 8:12; 10:28; 13:30,41 f.,50; 18:8 f.; 22:13; 23:33; 24:51; 25:30,41,46; Mark 9:43,47,48; Luke 3:17; 13:28; 16:22 ff.; John 15:6.

5. *Judgement.* In Paul: Acts 17:31; Rom. 2:5 ff.; 2:16; 14:10; 1 Cor. 3:13; 4:5; 2 Cor. 5:10; 2 Thess. 2:12; 2 Tim. 4:1. In Heb. 6:2; 9:27; 10:27,30 f. In James 2:13; 5:12. In Jude 15. In Peter: Acts 10:42; 1 Pet. 4:5; 2 Pet. 2:3,9. In John: 1 John 2:28; 4:17; Rev. 11:18; 20:12,13. *Eternal damnation.* 1 Thess. 5:3; 2 Thess. 1:9; Heb. 10:27; Jas. 4:12; 2 Pet. 2:3 ff.,17; Jude 7:13; Rev. 14:11; 19:3; 20:10,14 f.; 21:8; 22:15.

6. 1 Cor. 6:9 f.; Gal. 5:19–21; Eph. 5:5; Col. 3:5–6 (the ὀργή is God's final judgement as in Rom. 2:5; Rev. 6:17; etc.); similarly Rev. 21:8.

7. 1 Cor. 6:9. This passage represents the classical biblical reference for our question in the textbooks.

8. Cf. R. Cornely, *Commentarius in epist. ad Romanos* (Paris 1896), p. 599 f. This interpretation is generally supported by exegetes, even if the precise meaning is variously interpreted in the different commentaries. Cf. J. Sickenberger, *Die beiden Briefe des heiligen Paulus an die Korinther und sein Brief an die Römer* (Hl.Schrift.NT V) (Bonn 1921), p. 238, where the passage is interpreted far too rapidly in the sense of Catholic dogma; M. J. Lagrange, *Saint Paul Epître aux Romains* (Paris 1922), p. 281 f.; O. Holtzmann, *Das Neue Testament* II (Giessen 1926), p. 663; O. Kuss, *Die Briefe an die Römer, Korinther und Galater* (RNT6) (Regensburg 1940), p. 92; A. Nygren, *Der Römerbrief* (Göttingen 1954), p. 287; O. Michel, *Der Brief an die Römer* (Meyers Kom. 4) (Göttingen 1957), p. 246, where particular attention is given to the meaning of 'standing' and 'falling'; J. Huby/S. Lyonnet, *Saint Paul* (VS 10) (Paris 1957), p. 397; F. J. Leenhardt, *L'Epître de saint Paul aux Romains* (Neuchâtel/Paris 1957), p. 163 f. P. Althaus, *Der Brief an die Römer* (NTD III) (Göttingen 1958), p. 105.

9. Cf. R. Cornely, p. 605, together with the other authors mentioned in n.8. J. Sickenberger actually draws the conclusion.

10. For what follows, cf. especially H. Conzelmann, χάρις D. *Neues Testament,* in ThW IX, pp. 381–93 (Stuttgart 1971).

11. χάρις is here synonymous with καταλλαγή in 5:19 and δικαιοσύνη in 5:21. Thus it has a wider meaning.

12. This is the meaning of καταργέω; for this cf. F. Zorell, *Lexicon Graecum Novi Testamenti* (Paris 1931), p. 682.

13. Cf. F. Zorell, ibid., p. 997. W. Bauer, *Griechisch-deutsches Wörterbuch zu den*

Schriften des NT und der ubrigen urchristlichen Literatur (Berlin 1958), p. 1232; W. Michaelis, *παραπίπτω*, in: ThW, VI, pp. 170–3 (Stuttgart 1959).

14. That is, enlightenment by the Holy Spirit, the tasting of the heavenly gifts, participation in the Spirit, etc.

15. The correct meaning of *ἀδύνατον* is thus obvious: it is a matter of the moral impossibility of changing, through the preaching of an apostle, a person who has completely fallen away from the faith. It is not, therefore, a matter of the impossibility of a new acquisition of interior sanctifying grace.

16. If this were the case, then *ἀδύνατον ἀνακαινίζεσθαι* would be expected here.

17. Cf. W. Estius (1542–1613), *Commentarii in omnes Divi Pauli epistolas* (Douai 1614–16 and finally Paris 1892) on the passage and the edn of the NT by J. Th. A. Crampon (1826–94) (Tournai 1885).

18. Cf. F. Zorell, p. 449; W. Bauer, p. 535; G. Bertram, *ὕβρις*, etc. in: ThW VIII, pp. 295–307.

19. This person is, however, given to us by the grace of the Father and lives in us as in his temple.

20. Cf. F. Zorell, p. 1383; W. Bauer, p. 1679; U. Wilckens, *ὕστερος*, etc., in: ThW VIII, pp. 590–600.

21. This is how it is understood by J. E. Belser, *Die Epistel des hl. Jakobus* (Freiburg/Br. 1909), p. 60, and M. Meinertz/W. Vrede, *Die katholischen Briefe* (Bonn 1932), p. 23 f.

22. Cf. F. Zorell, p. 578; W. Bauer, pp. 693–5; R. Bultmann, *θάνατος*, etc., in: ThW III, pp. 7–25.

23. The eschatological meaning is brought out very clearly especially in the commentaries of J. Knabenbauer, *Comment. in Evang. sec. Joan.* (Paris 1906), p. 313 and F. Tillmann, *Das Johannesevangelium* (Bonn 1931), p. 185, while R. Cornely, p. 366, stresses the ethical aspect of the passage in Rom. 7. For the meaning of 'death' in John 8:51 cf. also R. Bultmann, *Das Evangelium des Johannes* (Meyers Kom. II) (Göttingen 1952), p. 246, who remains, however, strangely hesitant, and A. Schlatter, *Der Evangelist Johannes* (Stuttgart 1948), p. 218, who refers to Luke 2:26 and Ps. 89:49 with regard to the 'not to see death'. A. Wikenhauser, *Das Evangelium nach Johannes* (RNT 4) defends an eschatological meaning of the passage. The interpretation of the passage in the letter to the Romans which is prevalent today appears to owe its origin to Protestant thinking and considerations about the law (gospel). Because justification was the focal point of all the discussion, whenever death was considered the accent was placed on the nature of sin as death *before* justification. Hardly any attention was paid to sin as a possibility or as a fact or to the way its nature was affected by justification *after* justification (by faith and baptism), and this despite the formula *simul iustus et peccator*. The different approaches which we are considering here do not, however, have much relevance to sin in this sense. Cf. O. Kuss, *Der Römerbrief* II (Regensburg 1959), pp. 444–48, 450 and H. Thyen, loc. cit.

24. Cf. R. Cornely, p. 366: *mortem obii vita innocentiae iustitiaeque privatus*.

25. Cf. F. Zorell, p. 1416; W. Bauer, p. 1713; G. Bertram, *φρήν*, etc., in: ThW IX, pp. 216–31 (Stuttgart 1970).

26. R. Cornely, *Comment. in Epist. ad Corinth. alteram* (Paris 1892), p. 205.

27. Cf. M. Meinertz/W. Vrede, *Die katholischen Briefe* (Bonn 1932), p. 177.

28. Cf. L. Fonck, *Die Parabeln des Herrn* (Innsbruck 1909), p. 911, and J. Jeremias, *Die Gleichnisse Jesu* (Göttingen 1956), pp. 113–16.

29. Cf. L. Fonck, p. 418, but see also J. Jeremias, pp. 154–7, who explains the meaning of the parable in terms of justification.

30. F. Zorell, p. 864, and R. Cornely, *Comment. in priorem Epist. ad Corinth.* (Paris 1890), p. 93, together with W. Bauer, p. 1055 f. and O. Michel, *νάος*, in: ThW IV pp. 884–95 (esp. p. 892) (Stuttgart 1942).

31. This rejection is here expressed by a gnomic aorist.

32. Barn. 4,7.8 (Th. Klauser, Doctrina duodec.ap.—Barn.ep. [Flor.Patr.I], Bonn 1940, p. 36 no. 34). Cf. also the new edn in the series 'Sources Chrétiennes': *Epître de Barnabé* (SC 172), ed. P. Prigent/R. A. Kraft (Paris 1971) with a comprehensive introduction (pp. 9–70).

33. Polycarp 2,11,2 (Fischer, Munich 1956, p. 260 f. nos. 17–19). For the 'Apostolic Fathers' we are using the edn of J. A. Fischer. The reader is also referred, however, to the edn in the series 'Sources Chrétiennes': *Clément de Rome, Epître aux Corinthiens* (SC 167), ed. A. Jaubert (Paris 1971). Particularly valuable in this edn are the comprehensive introduction (pp. 13–96), where, in particular, the question of 'Courants pénitentiels?' (pp. 50–2) in Judaism is considered, and the glossary (pp. 231–74).

34. Ign.ad Smyrn. 9,1 (Fischer, p. 212 f. nos. 1–4); cf. Ign.ad Rom. 7,1 (Fischer, pp. 188–91 nos. 19 f. and nos. 1 f.); Ign.ad Philad. 6,2 (Fischer, p. 198 f. nos. 5–8); Polycarp 2,7,1 (Fischer, pp. 256–9 nos. 18–21 and no. 1).

35. 1 Clem. 2,3 (Fischer, p. 26 f. nos. 7–10); 36,6 (Fischer, p. 70 f. nos. 15 f.); 48,1 (Fischer, p. 84 f. nos. 19–22).

36. 1 Clem. 30,6 (Fischer, p. 62 f. nos. 3 f.); 35,6 (Fischer, p. 68 f. nos. 9–11).

37. 1 Clem. 30,8 (Fischer, p. 63 f. nos. 6–8).

38. 1 Clem. 14,2 (Fischer, pp. 40–3 no. 28 and nos. 1–3); 47,7 (Fischer, p. 84 f. nos. 15–18); 59,1 (Fischer, p. 98 f. nos. 9 f.).

39. Ign.ad Trall. 8,2 (Fischer, p. 176 f. nos. 18–20); 1 Clem. 46,8 (Fischer, pp. 82–5 nos. 28 f. and no. 1).

40. Polycarp 2,5,1 (Fischer, p. 254 f. nos. 4 f.).

41. 1 Clem. 3,4 (Fischer, pp. 26–9 no. 25 and nos. 1–6).

42. Didache 1,1 (Th. Klauser, Doctrina duodec. ap.—Barn. ep. [Flor. Patr.I], Bonn 1940, p. 14 nos. 5–7); 2,4 (ibid., p. 16 nos. 10–12); 5,1 (ibid., p. 20 nos. 1–10); Barn. 5,4 (ibid., p. 38 nos. 31–6); 19,7.8 (ibid., pp. 14–31).

43. Barn. 10,5 (Klauser, op. cit., p. 50 nos. 25–34); 1 Clem. 9,1 (Fischer, p. 36 f. nos. 6–9); Ign.ad Magn. 5,1 (Fischer, p. 164 f. nos. 8 f.). cf. Ign. ad Trall. 6,2 (Fischer, p. 176 f. nos. 5–7); 11,1 (Fischer, p. 178 f. nos. 8–10); Ign. ad Smyrn. 7,1 (Fischer, pp. 208–11 nos. 16–19 and nos. 1 f.).

44. Barn. 19,10 (Klauser, op. cit., pp. 66 f. nos. 36 f. and nos. 1–6); 1 Clem. 13,2 (Fischer, p. 40 f. nos. 17–21); 21,1 (ibid., p. 52 f. nos. 6–8); 28,1 (ibid., p. 60 f. nos. 4–6); Polycarp 2,6,2 (Fischer, p. 256 f. nos. 9–12).

45. Barn. 4,1 ff. (Klauser, op. cit., p. 35 nos. 13 ff.); Didache 16,1 ff. (ibid., pp. 29 f. nos. 23 ff.).

46. Barn. 4,12 (Klauser, op. cit., p. 37 nos. 26–31).

47. Barn. 21,1 (Klauser, op. cit., p. 68 nos. 18–25).

48. 1 Clem. 51,3,4 (Fischer, p. 88 f. nos. 13–16); Ign. ad Eph. 16,2 (Fischer, p. 154 f. nos. 15–18).

49. Ign. ad Eph. 16,1 (Fischer, p. 154 f. nos. 14 f.); Ign. ad Philad. 3,3 (ibid., p. 196 f. nos. 6–8); Polycarp 2,5,3 (ibid., pp. 254–7 nos. 13–17 and nos. 1 f.); cf. also Barn. 4,13 (Klauser, op. cit., p. 37 f. nos. 33 f. and nos. 1 f.). With regard to Ign. ad Eph. 16,1, Fischer remarks (p. 155, no.71): 1 Cor. 6:9 f.; (see also Matt. 24:4; Mark 13:5; Luke 21:8; 1 Cor. 15:33; Gal. 6:7; in effect the formula μὴ πλανᾶσθε was also current in diatribe: A. Vögtle, *Die Tugend- und Lasterkataloge im Neuen Testament* (Münster 1936), p. 123. See also Eph. 5:5. Those who ruin houses are firstly those who destroy family life, that is, adulterers who, for example in Lev. 20:10 (cf. John 8:5), are threatened with death, and then (v. 2b), in a figurative sense, the adherents of sects. The same applies to Polycarp 2,11,2 (Fischer, p. 261 n.128).

50. Klauser, op. cit., p. 29 nos. 23 f.

51. Fischer, p. 96 f., nos. 13 f.

52. Fischer, p. 146 f., nos. 3–6.
53. Ign. ad Magn. 10,1 (Fischer, p. 168 f. no. 7).
54. Ign. ad Magn. 10,2 (Fischer, p. 168 f. no. 9).
55. Ign. ad Magn. 11 (Fischer, p. 168 f. no. 19); cf. the use of this expression in 1 Tim. 1:1 and see Col. 1:27.
56. Ign. ad Philad. 3,2 (Fischer, p. 196 f. no. 5).
57. Ign. ad Smyrn. 5,2 (Fischer, p. 208 f. no. 5). See Fischer's n.34: the person who does not confess Christ as *σαρκοφόρος* is himself a *νεκροφόρος*: just as he lacks true faith, so he is bereft of true life and of any claim to a blessed resurrection; cf. Sm 2.
58. Ign. ad Trall. 6,2 (Fischer, p. 176 f. no. 6).
59. Ign. ad Smyrn. 7,1 (Fischer, pp. 208–11 no. 19). Cf. John 4:10; 2 Cor. 9:15.
60. Ign.ad Polycarpem 5,2 (Fischer, p. 220 f. no. 6).
61. Ibid.
62. Fischer, p. 160 f. no. 1. On this point see Fischer's note 98: the *φάρμακον ἀθανασίας* or *ἀντίδοτος ἀθανασίας* was an elixir which Isis was supposed to have discovered. Certainly the notion of an antidote to death played a role in both the magic and the mystery cults and in the Jewish tradition; cf. R. Bultmann, *ἀθανασία*, in: ThW III, 24; Th. Schäfer, *Antidotum* in: RAC I, pp. 457–61.
63. Fischer, p. 178 f. nos. 8–10.
64. Fischer, p. 198 f. no. 23.
65. Cf. the introductory remarks to III above: 'The Apostolic Fathers'.
66. 2 Clem. 6,9 (K. Bihlmeyer, *Die Apostolischen Väter* [Tübingen 1924], p. 74 nos. 5 ff.).
67. 2 Clem. 7,6 (ibid., p. 74 nos. 19–21).
68. 2 Clem. 8,6 (ibid., p. 75 no. 4 f.).
69. Cf. M. Whittaker, *Die Apostolischen Väter* I. *Der Hirt des Hermas,* Sim. VIII 6 (GCS 48) (Berlin 1956), p. 71 nos. 17 f.
70. GCS 48:p. 89 f. no. 31 and nos. 1–6.
71. Sim. VIII 6,3 (GCS 48:p. 71 nos. 17 ff.).
72. Sim. IX 16,2–7 (GCS 48:p. 89 f. nos. 28–31 and nos. 1–18).
73. Sim. VIII 6,3 (GCS 48:p. 71 no. 19).
74. GCS 48:p. 91 nos. 4–12.
75. Sim. V 6,5 (GCS 48:p. 57 nos. 17–19); Sim. V 7,2 (GCS 48:p. 58 nos. 8 f.).
76. Mand. X 2,1 (GCS 48:p. 38 nos. 26 f.).
77. Mand. X 2,5 (GCS 48:p. 39 no. 9).
78. Mand. X 2,6 (GCS 48:p. 39 nos. 10–12).
79. Cf. especially Mand. V 1,1–4 (GCS 48:p. 29 nos. 5–16); Mand. X 2,6 (GCS 48:p. 39 nos. 10–12); Mand. XI 2.3.9.13.14 (the application of this notion to true and false prophets) (GCS 48:p. 40 f. nos. 6–14; nos. 3–8; 17–25).
80. Mand. III 4 (GCS 48:p. 25 nos. 10–14).
81. Mand. X 2,2.4 (GCS 48:p. 38 f. nos. 27 ff. and nos. 5–8).
82. Mand. III 4 (GCS 48:p. 25 nos. 10–13).
83. Vis. III 11,2 (GCS 48:p. 17 nos. 20–3).
84. Sim. VIII 6,3 (GCS 48:p. 71 nos. 15–21); Sim. IX 14,3 (GCS 48:p. 88 nos. 13–17).
85. Sim. IX 32,2 (GCS 48:p. 103 nos. 1–4).
86. Sim. IX 32,3,4 (GCS 48:p. 103 nos. 4–14). Cf. also Sim. VIII 2,4 (GCS 48:p. 67 nos. 18–20): *δοὺς αὐτοῖς ἱματισμὸν λευκὸν καὶ σφραγῖδα.*
87. Ibid. (GCS 48:p. 103 nos. 11–14). [This is the passage in Whittaker's edn: *unde si tu de vestimento tristis efficeris et rixaris quia non integrum recipis, quid putas dominum esse facturum, qui tibi spiritum dedit integrum, et tu illud totum ita inutile fecisti, ut domino suo in usu esse non possit, quia usus ipsius spiritus a te inutilis esses coepit et corruptus?*]

88. Vis. II 2,7 (GCS 48:p. 6 nos. 10–13).
89. Mand. IV 1,2 (GCS 48:p. 26 no. 3).
90. Sim. IX 14,3 (GCS 48:p. 88 no. 17).
91. Cf. for example F. X. Funk, *Patres Apostolici* I (Tübingen 1901), pp. lii, cxxx.
92. Cf. F. Mitzka, 'Gnosticismus und Gnadenlehre' in: ZKTh 51 (1927), pp. 60–4.
93. 2 Clem. 8,6–9,5 (K. Bihlmeyer, *Die Apostolischen Väter* (Tübingen 1924), p. 75 nos. 3–12; Hermas, Sim. V 6–7 (GCS 48:p. 57 f. nos. 5–25 and nos. 1–16).
94. Obviously the notion is not only found in the Gnostics. It is already found in Paul (2 Cor. 1:22; Eph. 1:13; cf. also Rev. 7:3). Nevertheless, its use in the NT could hardly account for the surprisingly frequent occurrence of the notion in the Gnostic writings. It occurs 20 times, for instance, in the (Gnostic) Acts of Thomas (cf. DThC II,1 col.205); in the Pistis Sophia c. 86, c. 91 and often elsewhere (W. Till, *Koptisch-Gnostische Schriften* I [Berliner-Akademie Ausgabe] originally ed. C. Schmidt (Berlin 1959), p. 127 no. 18 and p. 134 no. 27; cf. the glossary (ibid. p. 396); in the first book of Jeu c. 33 and often elsewhere (W. Till, p. 290 no. 3; cf. the glossary); for a general survey of its meaning and use see G. Fitzner, *σφραγίς*, etc., in: ThW VII, pp. 939–54 (esp. p. 952 ff.) (Stuttgart 1964). For its use among the Church Fathers cf. the following witnesses: Clemens Alex., Ecl. proph. etc. (O. Stählin, *Clemens Alexandrinus* III [GCS 9^3,17] (Leipzig 1909) 140,19; 188,18; 185,12); see O. Stählin, *Clemens Alexandrinus* IV—Register [GCS 39] (Leipzig 1936) 737; Excerpta ex Theodoto 80,3 (Fr.Sagnard, *Clement d'Alexandrie: Extraits de Theodote* [SC 23] reprinted Paris 1970, p. 204 f. no. 1); 83 (SC 23:p. 208 f. no. 2); 86,2 (SC 23:p. 210 f. nos. 6–9). Hippolytus, Philosophumena V 10,2 (P. Wendland [GCS 26] (Leipzig 1916)103 no. 18). Hippolytus calls this work *κατὰ πασῶν αἱρέσεων ἐλέγκος* = Refutatio omnium haeresium; for the external in the Gnostics cf. Irenaeus, Adv.haer. I 20,4 (W. Harvey [Cambridge 1857; reprinted 1949] I 210) (I 25,6 [PG 7, 685]); Epiphanius, Haer. I 27,5,9 (K. Holl [GCS 25; 31; 37] (Leipzig 1915/33) 308 nos. 3 ff.).
95. Cf. A. d'Alès, *L'édit de Calliste* (Paris 1914), p. 52: *le deuxième siècle ne nous a légué aucun document plus considérable pour l'histoire de la pénitence, que le Pasteur d'Hermas.* Apart from M. Whittaker's edn in the GCS, which we are generally using here, we refer the reader to the revised and extended edn in the series 'Sources Chrétiennes' 53 bis: R. Joly, *Hermas—Le Pasteur* (Paris 1968).
96. See the detailed historical studies on the penitential teaching of Hermas, Irenaeus of Lyons and especially Tertullian in this volume. In the present essay these individual authors are considered principally from the viewpoint of the loss of grace; the other studies in this volume attempt rather to summarize the whole penitential teaching of these individual authors and so to determine their place in the development of the nature of church penance.
97. Irenaeus, Adv. haer. V 9,3 (Ad. Rousseau, et al. [SC 153] (Paris 1969), pp. 114–17 nos. 58–61).
98. Irenaeus, Adv.haer. V 9,4 (SC 153:p. 120 nos. 89f.).
99. Irenaeus, Adv. haer. V 8,3 (SC 153:p. 104 nos. 86–9).
100. Irenaeus, Adv.haer. IV praef. 4 (Ad. Rousseau et al. [SC 100] (Paris 1965), p. 388 no. 48).
101. Ibid., p. 388 nos. 59 f.
102. The same idea is often found elsewhere in Irenaeus. Evil men *ἀπέστησαν ἀπὸ τῆς τοῦ θεοῦ χάριτος* (II 54; W. Harvey, I 308; II 33,5 PG 7,834). The 'perfect' are those *qui et Spiritum semper perseverantem habent Dei et animas et corpora sine querela servaverint* (V 6,I SC 153:p. 80 f. nos. 52–5). The most perfect expression of Catholic teaching on grace in this respect is found in Adv. haer. I 1,12 (W. Harvey I 57) (I 6,4 [PG 7,509]: *ἡμᾶς* (the Catholics) *μέν γὰρ ἐν χρήσει τὴν χάριν λαμβάνειν λέγουσιν* (the Gnostics) *διὸ καὶ ἀφαιρεθήσεσθαι αὐτῆς*; *αὐτοὺς* (the Gnostics) *δὲ ἰδιόκτητον ἄνωθεν . . . συγκατεληλυθυῖαν ἔχειν τὴν χάριν καὶ διὰ τοῦτο*

προστεϑήσεσϑαι ἀυτοῖς. This statement reflects both the Gnostics' view of the Catholics' notion of grace and their own view. Its meaning is best rendered as follows: 'According to us Catholics, say the Gnostics, grace is received as a loan, but according to them (the Gnostics) it is received from above as a personal gift and, therefore, it can only increase.' The contrast 'according to us . . . according to them (in our view . . . in their view)' is demanded by the overall meaning of the sentence, since the whole passage transmits the notion of the Gnostics. According to them, Catholics (the psychics) do not receive 'grace' in the same way as do the 'pneumatic' Gnostics. Otherwise they would already have the right of access to the pleroma, which is not the case, since the 'psychic' Catholics lead a good life (cf. Irenaeus, Adv.haer. I 1,12 [W. Harvey, I 59]; I 6,4[PG 7,152]). Thus this statement of the Gnostics cannot ascribe the possession of 'grace' to the Catholics. It formulates the Catholic view of the nature of grace in opposition to the Gnostic notion. But it does provide us with a poignant formulation of the Catholic notion of grace in the words of the Gnostics. The Gnostics themselves obviously considered that their own view was superior to that of the Catholics: grace is not an inalienable possession; it can be taken away from a man if he does not lead a moral life which corresponds to the rules propounded by the one who dispenses this grace.

103. On Irenaeus' penitential teaching cf. DThC VII, 2 col. 2496; A. d'Alès, 'La Discipline pénitentielle au IIe siècle en dehors d'Hermas' in: RSR 4 (1913), pp. 201–22; B. Poschmann, *Paenitentia secunda* (Bonn 1940), pp. 211–29; J. I. Hochban, 'St. Irenaeus on the Atonement' in: ThSt 7 (1946), pp. 525–57; H. Holstein, 'L'Exhomologèse dans l'"Adversus haereses" de S. Irénée' in: RSR 35 (1948), pp. 282–8; cf. the author's 'The Post-baptismal Forgiveness of Sins in the Regula Fidei of Irenaeus' in the present volume. In Adv.haer. IV 27,4(SC 100:p. 748 f. nos. 159 f.) it is stated: *iniusti et idolatres et fornicatores vitam perdiderunt*. This very probably refers also to those who are already baptized. Thus the 'life' in this text should be understood as the life of grace. The remaining texts in Irenaeus have nothing more to say about the question of penance in so far as it concerns us here. Adv.haer. IV 40,1 (SC 100:p. 974 f.) and V 11,1 (SC 153:pp. 132–7) do not draw any distinction between baptized and unbaptized penitents; the distinction is between the baptized and the unrepentant who postpone baptism.

104. This argument should not, however, be considered either the first or the most important one for Tertullian's teaching on penance. There are several other factors which gave rise to this teaching. The principal reason for his false teaching on penance must be seen in both his practical rigorism and his exaggerated idealism. His montanist view of the Church also played a role at this point. Nevertheless, his speculation on the subject of the loss of grace must also have exercised considerable influence on the development of this penitential teaching. Certainly he would have wanted to corroborate the already established teaching on the unforgivable nature of the capital sins with any supporting arguments.

105. Tertullian maintained that only God could forgive capital sins, either in the next life or already here through montanist prophets by a special impulse of the Holy Spirit. This does not contradict our explanation of his thought. The forgiveness which is impossible is that through an act of the hierarchical Church, that is, of a bishop, such as is the case in baptism as the Church's sacramental application of Christ's redemption. It is only this possibility which, according to Tertullian, would jeopardize the definitive nature of baptism, which alone can give sacramental grace.

106. Cf. the texts of the Church Fathers which stress emphatically the uniqueness of baptism in J. Stufler, 'Die Verschiedenen Wirkungen der Taufe und Busse bei Tertullian' in: ZKTh 31 (1907), pp. 372–6.

107. Cf. J. Stufler, ibid.

108. Tertullian himself gives the reason why all sins are not *peccata ad mortem*. We are so often tempted and we sin so often *ut, si nulla sit venia istorum* (of daily sins), *nemini salus competat*. De pud. 19 (CSL 20) 265,20 f.

109. For Tertullian's teaching on capital sins cf. A. d'Alès, *L'édit de Calliste* (Paris, 1914), p. 197 ff. The indeterminateness of capital sins, with regard to both their number and their nature, only shows that the teaching was invented as a compensation for the previous error.

110. Tertullian, De cultu fem. II,1 (CSL 70) 71,8.11–12. The text here runs: *templum dei simus, inlato in nos et consecrato spiritu sancto* . . . and: *ne deus ille qui inhabitat inquinatam sedem offensus derelinquat*. This terminology is found already in the Shepherd of Hermas. For instance, in Mand. X 2,5 we read: μὴ θλῖβε (corresponding to Tertullian's *offensus*) τὸ πνεῦμα τὸ ἅγιον τὸ ἐν σοὶ κατοικοῦν μήποτε . . . ἀποστῇ ἀπὸ σοῦ (GCS 48:p. 39 nos. 9 f). There are similar reminiscences of Hermas when we read in Tertullian's De spect. 15 (CSL 20:p. 16 nos. 21–4): *deus praecepit spiritum sanctum, utpote pro naturae suae bono tenerum et delicatum, tranquillitate et lenitate et quiete et pace tractare, non furore, non bile, non ira, non dolore inquietare*. Cf. Hermas, Mand. V 1,3 (GCS 48:p. 29 nos. 11, 14 f.) the πνεῦμα ἅγιον is τρυφερόν (*tener*) and, therefore, lives only in the person who is μακρόθυμος. It retires when ὀξυχολία enters into a man's heart. Another parallel to this is Tertullian, De or. 12 (CSL 20:p. 188 nos. 12–17). The στενοχωρεῖσθαι in Hermas, Mand. V 1,3 (GCS 48:p. 29, 11) corresponds to the *angi* of the Holy Spirit in De pat. 15 (CSL 47:p. 23 no. 17).

111. De pat. 15 (CSL 47:p. 22 no 21 and p. 23 nos. 12 ff.).

112. Ad mart. 1,3 (CCHL I) 3 nos. 15 f.

113. Cf. also De cultu fem. II,2 (CSL 70:p. 73 no. 9).

114. Adv. Marc. I 28 (CSL 47:p. 329 f. no. 29 and nos. 1,2 f., 4 f.,7).

115. De Anima I (CSL 20:p. 299 nos. 21 f.); De bapt. 6/7 (CSL 20:p. 206 f.). According to Tertullian the communication of the Spirit occurs only through confirmation which is conferred together with baptism. This is a point which we need not consider further here, especially since Tertullian himself makes this distinction in other passages; cf. Adv. Marc. IV 17 (CSL 47:p. 474 no. 21).

116. De carn. resur. 8 (CSL 47:p. 37 no. 3).

117. De fuga in persec. 10,2 (CCHL II:p. 1147 nos. 16 f.); Adv.Marc.III 12 (CSL 47:p. 393 no. 1).

118. De carne Christi 4 (CSL 70:p. 197 no. 31); De carn. resur. 47 (CSL 47:p. 96 no. 28).

119. De carne Christi 17 (CSL 70:p. 232 no. 11); De bapt. I (CSL 20:p. 201 no. 13); De exhort. cast. 1,4 (CCHL II:p. 1015 nos. 17 f.).

120. De bapt. 5 (CSL 20:p. 206 nos. 10–14); De paen. 2,3 (CCHL I:p. 322 nos. 8–14); de anima 41 (CSL 20:p. 368 f. no. 30 and nos. 1–3).

121. De paen. 2,6 (CCHL I:p. 323 no. 30).

122. De paen. 6,13 (CCHL 1:p. 331 nos. 49 f.). Cf. ibid., p. 331 nos. 48 f. (6,12): *quis autem promittit permansurum et quod tribuerit invitus?*

123. De paen. 7,11 (CCHL I:p. 334 no. 40). Tertullian does not seem to have been very clear on the question of whether a person who did not undertake a serious conversion before baptism would really receive the grace of baptism. He contents himself with the observation that such a 'baptized' person is at least in danger of losing this grace again.

124. De pud. 7 (CSL 20:p. 233 nos. 4 f.). Tertullian says of heretics, *de vivis mortuos faciunt*, in De praescr.haer. 30,17 (CCHL I:p. 212 no. 47).

125. De pud. 2 (CSL 20:p. 224 nos. 6–11).

126. De pud. 9 (CSL 20:p. 236 nos. 27 ff.).

127. De pud. 9 (CSL 20:p. 237 nos. 8 f. and p. 236 nos. 28 f.).
128. De pud. 9 (CSL 20:p. 237 no. 12; p. 236 no. 30).
129. De pud. 16 (CSL 20:p. 253 no. 27; p. 254 no. 1).
130. De pud. 22 (CSL 20:p. 273 no. 22).
131. De pud. 9 (CSL 20:p. 238 nos. 3 f.).
132. De pud. 9 (CSL 20:p. 236 nos. 27 ff.; p. 237 no. 8).
133. Cf. for example Adv.Marc. II 2 (CSL 47:p. 335 nos. 19–27); II 6 (CSL 47:p. 341 nos. 13–22); II 8 (CSL 47:p. 345 nos. 8–13); De bapt. 5 (CSL 20:p. 206 nos. 11–14); De spect. 2 (CSL 20:p. 3 nos. 20 f.; p. 4 nos. 11–14); De pat. 5 (CSL 47:p. 7 no. 1); De cultu fem. I 1,2 (CCHL I:p. 343 no. 19); De anima 16 (CSL 20:p. 321 nos. 21–23); 41 (CSL 20:p. 368,18–369,7); De carn. resur. 26 (CSL 47:p. 63 nos. 11–24).
134. De paen. 8,6 (CCHL 1:p. 335 nos. 21–32).
135. De spect. 24 (CSL 20:p. 24 no. 17).
136. Hermas, Sim. VIII 6,3 (GCS 48:p. 71 no. 18).
137. De pud. 5 (CSL 20:p. 227 nos. 18 f.).
138. De pud. 7 (CSL 20:p. 232 no. 15; p. 233 no. 7).
139. De pud. 13 (CSL 20:p. 246 nos. 2 f.: *baptismate amisso*).
140. De pud. 19 (CSL 20:p. 265 nos. 7 f.).
141. De pud. 14 (CSL 20:p. 248 no. 18; p. 249 no. 16).
142. De pud. 2 (CSL 20:p. 224 nos. 6–16); 19 (CSL 20:p. 265 no. 29; p. 266 no. 7).
143. De pud. 16 (CSL 20:p. 253 nos. 1 f.).
144. De pud. 18 (CSL 20:p. 261 no. 26).
145. De pud. 7 (CSL 20:p. 232 nos. 19 ff.; p. 233 nos. 3 f.). In De pud. 19 (CSL 20:p. 265 nos. 15–21) Tertullian mentions yet another group of *delicta non ad mortem,* namely the *delicta cotidianae incursionis.* It should be noted that, in Tertullian's Catholic period, taking part in *spectacula* was considered *rescindere signaculum* (De spect. 24 [CSL 20:p. 24 no. 17]). In his montanist period, however, such a sinner is a *vivens adhuc peccator,* who sins *non moriendo sed errando* and thus is reckoned as *salvus* (De pud. 7 [CSL 20:p. 232 nos. 19,20 f.; p. 233 no. 3]). This laxity on the part of a rigorist Tertullian is comprehensible only on the assumption which we have already explained: if such sinners were also in Tertullian's later view dead and completely devoid of baptismal grace, then logically he would have to deny them any possibility of having their sins forgiven. In order to avoid this conclusion he maintains that these sins are not mortal.
146. De pud. 16 (CSL 20:p. 255 nos. 27 f.); 12 (CSL 20:p. 241 nos. 21 f.).
147. De pud. 14 (CSL 20:p. 249 no. 20): *nihil de transacto praecavetur, sed de adhuc salvo.* With sheer consistency Tertullian considers that only those guilty of capital sins are outside the Church, while all other sinners are still in it. Cf. De pud. 7 (CSL 20:p. 233 nos. 17 f.): *intra domum dei ecclesiam licet esse aliqua delicta;* in the case of capital sins, however, *statim homo de ecclesia expellitur* (ibid., nos. 23 f.). The man guilty of a capital sin no longer has the *solacium navis ecclesiae* (ibid., p. 245 nos. 20 f.); he belongs to those *extra ecclesiam proiectis* (ibid., no. 25).
148. De pud. 9 (CSL 20:p. 237 nos. 5 f. and for the explanation in brackets ibid., p. 236 nos. 28 f.).
149. Ibid., p. 237 nos. 5–7.
150. De pud. 18 (CSL 20:p. 261 nos. 14 f.).
151. Ibid.; cf. also De pud. 17 (CSL 20:p. 257 nos. 3–6); 9 (ibid., p. 237 nos. 9 f.): *rursus illi mactabitur Christus.*
152. Tertullian leaves open the further possibility of forgiveness by God himself, either in the next life or through the mediation of some prophets specially inspired for the particular task. This element of indecisiveness does not, however, affect the argument put forward. The latter concerns only the exclusion of every certainly

effective *ex opere operato* means which is administered after the manner of baptism by the *ecclesia numerus episcoporum* (De pud. 21 [CSL 20:p. 271 nos. 9 f.]). In effect Tertullian seems to have considered the pardon by God in the next life as a last, undetermined hope, of which there was no certainty.

153. De pud. 9 (CSL 20:p. 238 nos. 25–7). If baptism in blood is the only sure means of forgiveness for those guilty of capital sins, then the *omnis substantia* (of baptism) cannot be destroyed by those sins which can be forgiven without martyrdom.

154. De pud. 22 (CSL 20:p. 272 nos. 23–5).

155. De pat. 13 (CSL 47:p. 21 no. 4); Scorp. 6,9 (CSL 20:p. 158 nos. 3–10); De bapt. 16 (CSL 20:p. 214 no. 14); Apolog. 50,13.15 f. (CCHL I:p. 171 nos. 60 f.67–70).

156. De bapt. 15 (CSL 20:p. 214 nos. 7 f.).

157. De bapt. 16 (CSL 20:p. 214 nos. 22 f.).

158. Cf. F. X. Funk, 'Das Indulgenzedikt des Papstes Kallistus' in: ThQ 88 (1906), pp. 543, 554 f.

159. Cf. A. d'Alès, *L'édit de Calliste* (Paris 1914), p. 154 ff.

160. De pud. 12 (CSL 20:p. 242 nos. 25–7).

161. Cf. J. Stufler, 'Die verschiedenen Wirkungen der Taufe und Busse nach Tertullian' in: ZKTh 31 (1907), pp. 372–6; with regard to De bapt. 15 (CSL 20:p. 214 nos. 7 f.).

162. Cf. for example Hippolytus, Philosophumena IV 41,2 (GCS 26:p. 172 nos. 21 ff.); 42,1 (ibid., p. 173 nos. 13 f.); IX 15,1 (ibid., p. 253 nos. 10 ff.); IX 13 (ibid., p. 251 nos. 22 ff.). On the work of Hippolytus cf. n.94 above.

163. De pud. 18 (CSL 20:p. 261 nos. 25 f.); 21 (ibid., p. 270 nos. 30–2).

164. The sins for which, therefore, public penance is appropriate are those mentioned in De paen. There appears to be no reason to see here a reference to private church penance. Authors who think that there is are: A. d'Alès, *L'édit de Calliste* (Paris 1941), p. 437, and P. Galtier, *L'église et la rémission des péchés aux premiers siècles* (Paris 1932), p. 272 ff. The sins which Tertullian, even in his montanist period, allows to be submitted to the institution of penance are serious ones, both objectively and in so far as previous practice is concerned. It should be assumed, therefore, that they are submitted to public penance, even if Tertullian presents them as *leviora delicta* by comparison with capital sins. Tertullian himself does not seem to have averted to the fact that since such sins have become 'venial' in his theology they no longer require church penance. Similarly he did not see that, in the light of his own opinions, there was no longer an essential difference between the *leviora delicta* and the *delicta cotidianae incursionis*. Tertullian would have been decidedly aware of these contradictions in his theory only if, before him, the difference between serious and venial sins had already been explained reflexively with regard to their effect on grace. But there is no indication that this was the case.

165. Thus, for example, Augustine attacked the notion that only capital sins were serious sins; cf. De fide et operibus 19 n.34 (J. Zycha, S.Aur.Augustini . . . [CSL 41] 79 f. nos. 15–23 and nos. 1 f.); Speculum 29 (Fr. Weihrich, S.Aur.Augustini . . . [CSL 12] 199 f. nos. 25–9 and nos. 1–4). He appears, however, to have held in practice this view which he rejected in theory; cf. K. Adam, *Die kirchliche Sundenvergebung nach dem hl. Augustin* (Paderborn 1917), p. 27. Caesarius of Arles draws a distinction between *capitalia crimina* and *minuta peccata*. The latter include not only gossip in the church but also *iuramenta, periuria, maledicta, sordidae cogitationes, voluptuosa delectatio aurium*; cf. Sermo 64,2 (G. Morin, S.Caes.Arel.Sermo I [CCHL 103] p. 264 nos. 3–8); the group of the *capitalia*, however, includes more than the three well-known major sins; cf. Sermo 179 (G. Morin, S.Caes.Arel.Serm. II [CCHL 104] p. 684 nos. 29–32). Gregory of Nyssa, Epist. can. 7,6 (PG 45, 232 f.),

deplores the fact that there is traditionally no church penance applicable to certain sins, even though he holds that these faults are serious. But in general they must have been considered otherwise. Basil, De iud.Dei 7 (PG31,669) appears to take a similar practice and theory for granted, while deploring it. At that time the institution of penance was obviously still administered as *paenitentia publica* in the form which it had previously. The only sins which were considered with certainty to destroy grace were capital sins. Then in Augustine's day there was an ever-increasing general awareness of the much wider circle of serious sins. This had to give rise to certain difficulties, since church penance in its previous form was not applicable to this enlarged circle of sins. However, the form of the traditional institution of penance was not to be altered so easily and so quickly. Thus the idea arose gradually that certain serious sins could be remitted in the same way as venial sins. All that this required was the sinner's personal penance without the mediation of the Church (cf. K. Adam, *Die kirchliche Sündenvergebung nach dem hl.Augustin* (Paderborn 1917), p. 20 f.; K. Jüssen, *Die dogmatischen Anschauungen des Hesychius von Jerusalem* II (Münster 1934), pp. 97 ff., 103 ff.). The criterion for deciding which sins are to be submitted to church penance and which sins are to be expiated by personal penance cannot be found, therefore, in the way these sins deprive men of grace or leave grace intact. It became necessary to introduce into penance at this point another way of distinguishing sins (sins of deed/sins of thought; public, notorious sins/secret sins; etc.).

166. Cf. A. d'Alès, *L'édit de Calliste* (Paris 1914), p. 208 ff.

167. For this he takes as his basis the decalogue, the decree of the Council of Jerusalem, the sentence passed on the incestuous person in 1 Cor. and similar texts.

168. In De pud. 5 three capital sins are mentioned: *idolatria, moechia* and *homicidium,* cf. De pud. 12 (CSL 20:p. 226 f.; ibid., p. 242 nos. 4 f.); in De pud. 19 (ibid., p. 265 nos. 23 f.) it is a question of *homicidium, idolatria, fraus negatio, blasphemia, utique et moechia et fornicatio et si qua alia violatio templi dei*; Adv.Marc. IV 9 (CSL 47:p. 441 nos. 28 f.; p. 442 no. 1) names seven capital sins. Cf. A. d'Alès, *L'édit de Calliste* (Paris 1914), p. 205 ff.

169. The expression 'mortal sin' must have been drawn from 1 John 5:16. Thus already in Tertullian, besides *delictum ad mortem* (De pud. 2 [CSL 20:p. 224 no. 10] and De pud. 19 [ibid., p. 266 no. 2]), is also found the expression *mortalia delicta* (cf. De pud. 19 [ibid., p. 266 nos. 8 f.]). Corresponding to this, Cyprian also has the notion *mortale crimen* (De bono pat. 14 [CSL 3,1:p. 407 no. 21]). In Origen we find ἁμαρτήματα μὴ θανατηφόρα (In Matth. XIII n.30 [GCS 38:p. 264 no. 16]) and in translations of his works *crimen mortale, culpa mortalis* (In Lev.hom. XII n.3 [GCS 29:p. 489 nos. 13 f.]) and *mortale peccatum* (ibid., p. 460 nos. 1,5). The same expression is then also found in Pacian, Epist. 3 ad Sympronianum (PL 13,1063).

170. De pud. 19 (CSL 20:p. 266 nos. 8 f.).

171. This notion of the *delicta mortalia* in Tertullian is disputed by other authors who hold that Tertullian considered the *delicta leviora* to be mortal sins in today's sense. Thus for example B. I. Döllinger, *Hippolytus und Kallistus* (Regensburg 1853), p. 137; B. Poschmann, *Die Sichtbarkeit der Kirche nach der Lehre des hl.Cyprian* (Paderborn 1908), p. 143; P. Galtier, *L'église et la rémission des péchés aux premiers siècles* (Paris 1932), p. 272 n.5. Certainly it is possible to conclude from Tertullian that, according to the Catholics also, the *leviora delicta* were the object of church penance, that is, that they were necessarily treated as serious sins (cf. P. Galtier, p. 273 f.; A. d'Alès, p. 437). Nevertheless, it is not correct to conclude that Tertullian, in his own theory, considered such faults as mortal sins in our sense. Those guilty of such sins are styled 'lost' (cf. De pud. 7 [CSL 20:p. 232 nos. 20 f.]), although the context demands that the term is used here in a wide sense. According to Tertullian, the parables of the lost sheep and the lost drachma can be applied to Christians who have

sinned. It is in this sense that a person guilty of such a sin is 'lost'. The precise nature of this 'being lost' needs to be underlined particularly in relation to these parables: *Licet enim perisse dicatur, erit et de perditionis genere retractare* (cf. De pud. 7 [CSL 20:p. 232 nos. 17 f.]). It is here a question of an erring, not of a destruction (*quia et ovis non moriendo, sed errando et drachma non interiendo, sed latitando perierunt*; ibid., nos. 19–20). 'In this sense it could be said (finally) that what is "lost" is (actually) still safe' = *ita licet dici perisse, quod salvum est*; ibid., nos. 20 f. The following *perit igitur* must, therefore be placed in quotation marks if full justice is to be given to this meaning. It is only this that enables Tertullian to say immediately afterwards of such a sinner that he is not lost (in the strict sense), provided that he does not refuse penance (*quod potest recuperari, non perit, nisi foris perseveraverit;* ibid., p. 233, nos. 2 f.). The sinner is still *vivens adhuc peccator,* as opposed to the person guilty of capital sin who dies immediately after his deed. Tertullian deduces from these different conditions ('being lost' in the wide sense and actual death) the fact that the respective sins are forgivable or unforgivable. Thus these notions cannot simply be other expressions for the forgivable or unforgivable character of the sins concerned. Rather they explain the fact that the one sinner has preserved the fundamental grace of baptism, while the other has lost it. In other words, it is a question here of venial sins, on the one hand, and of mortal sins in today's sense, on the other. The expression *extra gregem datus* (ibid., p. 232 no. 26) can, therefore, only be understood as a reminiscence of Tertullian's Catholic period. It no longer fits in with the new notion of the *delicta leviora.* Nevertheless, Tertullian has to hold on to this idea because the penance which was considered necessary for such sins at that time included such an excommunication. At the same time, Tertullian's new notion of the *delicta leviora* entailed logically that there are *delicta mediocria intra domum dei ibidem delitescentia mox ibidem et reperta* (ibid., p. 233 nos. 17 ff.). In clear contrast to this, it is said of the person guilty of a capital sin: *statim homo de ecclesia expellitur nec illic manet.* This phrase *nec illic manet* (ibid., p. 233 no. 24), following the *expellitur,* makes sense only if Tertullian wishes to stress the contrast with the sinner who, despite his sin, remains within the Church.

172. We are here leaving aside Hippolytus and Clement of Alexandria. Hippolytus reprimanded pope Callistus for not deposing bishops even when they have sinned 'mortally' (cf. Philosophumena IX 12, 22 [GCS 26:p. 249 nos. 21 ff.; cf. n.94]). What Hippolytus understood precisely by such sins is difficult to say. Already Döllinger, p. 136 f., could only surmise. Mortal sins, for Hippolytus too, must have been identifiable with *delicta irremissibilia,* but it is not at all clear precisely which sins these were or whether he considered them mortal sins only in today's sense. In one passage he enumerates the three well-known capital sins (cf. Fragm. zu den Proverbien XXI [GCS 1:p. 163 f.]). But it is not clear whether this is intended as an exhaustive list of the capital sins. Even Tertullian frequently mentions these three, although he recognizes others. What Clement of Alexandria contributes to our question corresponds to what we have found in the Shepherd of Hermas. Without any doubt, in the question of penance Clement of Alexandria depends entirely on Hermas (cf. A. d'Alès, p. 74 ff.). He clearly expresses the loss of grace through sin. At the same time, he does not give us a clear answer on the question of the difference between sins with regard to their effect on grace. The sinner passes his own death sentence (cf. Quis dives salvetur 39,2 [GCS 17:p. 185 no. 18]); he is left for dead by the Logos and the Holy Spirit, since that which is holy ought not to be sullied. The sinner, however, offends God, who dwells within him, and defiles the Logos (Paed. II 10,100, 1 [GCS 12:p. 217 nos. 9 ff.]; cf. Paed. II 10,100,4 [GCS 12:p. 217 nos. 20 ff.]). Thus the sinner has died, as far as God is concerned (Quis dives salvetur 42,9 [GCS 17:p. 189 nos. 16 ff.]); he is already dead to God (Paed. III 11,81,1 [GCS 12:p. 280 nos. 31 ff.]); the image of God is no longer in

his soul (Paed. III 2,4–5,1 [GCS 12:p. 237 ff.]). Thus conversion is a real rebirth, a second baptism (Quis dives salvetur 42,14 [GCS 17:p. 190 no. 11]); a true παλιγγενεσία ζωῆς (Strom. II 23,147,2 [GCS 15:p. 193 no. 26]); once sin has been set aside God can once more take up his residence in man (Quis dives salvetur 39,2 [GCS 17:p. 185 nos. 18 f.]). Clement recognizes the variety of sins (cf. for example Strom. II 15,62,1 ff. [GCS 15:p. 146 ff.]); he quotes 1 John 5:6 (ibid., II 15,66,4 f. [GCS 15:p. 148 nos. 20 ff.]). Nevertheless, he does not examine the differentiation of sins according to their effect on grace.

173. De habitu virginum 2 (CSL 3,1:p. 188 nos. 23–5).

174. Epist. 15,2 (CSL 3,2:p. 514 nos. 16 f.); Epist. 21,1 (from Celerinus; CSL 3,2:p. 530 no. 17); Epist. 33,1 (CSL 3,2:p. 566 nos. 18 ff.); De lapsis 8 (CSL 3,1:p. 242 f. no. 14 and no. 1).

175. Epist. 30,7 (CSL 3,2:p. 555 no. 5); De lapsis 30 (CSL 3,1:p. 259 no. 16); 35 (CSL 3,1:p. 262 no. 26).

176. De lapsis 30 (CSL 3,1:p. 259 no. 24).

177. Test. III 27 (CSL 3,1:p. 141 nos. 17 f.).

178. Epist. 70,2 (CSL 3,2:p. 768 no. 15).

179. Epist. 64,3 (CSL 3,2:p. 719 nos. 6–9).

180. De lapsis 24 (CSL 3,1:p. 254 nos. 20 f.).

181. De lapsis 9 (CSL 3,1:p. 243 nos. 10 f.).

182. De bono pat. 14 (CSL 3,1:p. 407 no. 21).

183. Test. III 28 (CSL 3,1:p. 142 nos. 6 f.); in the case of Cyprian, however, these sins are not actually unforgiveable. Cf. A. d'Alès, p. 312 ff.

184. Test. III 54 (CSL 3,1:p. 156 no. 5).

185. De dom. orat. 12 (CSL 3,1:p. 175 nos. 4 f.).

186. De op. et eleem. 3 (CSL 3,1:p. 375 no. 3).

187. De dom. orat. 22 (CSL 3,1:p. 283 no. 19).

188. De op. et eleem. 2 (CSL 3,1:p. 374 nos. 17 f., 24).

189. In Lev.hom. XII, 3 (GCS 29:p. 460 nos. 1–7).

190. In Jer.hom. II,2–3 (GCS 6:p. 19). This idea is derived from the context. Origen considers the person who preserves the baptism of the Holy Spirit (τηρεῖν τὸ βάπτισμα τοῦ ἁγίου πνεύματος: ibid., [GCS 6:p. 19 no. 22]) fortunate, as opposed to the person guilty of mortal sin.

191. In Lev. hom. XI,2 (GCS 29:p. 452 nos. 8 f.).

192. In Lev. hom. VIII,11 (GCS 29:p. 417 nos. 12 ff.).

193. On the question of the different classes of sins in Origen cf. 'The Penitential Teaching of Origen' in this volume.

194. In any case the ἁμαρτήματα μή θανατηφόρα, which Origen mentions in Matth. XIII,30 (GCS 6:p. 264 nos. 16 ff.) are not considered as destroying the state of grace.

195. Didascalia Apost. IV,21,1.2.4.5.6. (F. X. Funk, *Didaskalia et Constitutiones Apostolorum* I [Paderborn 1905], p. 368 nos. 12 f., p. 370 nos. 3 f., 20 f.; p. 372 nos. 1f., 13 ff.

196. Didascalia Apost. II 41,2 (F. X. Funk, p. 130 nos. 1–5).

CHAPTER THREE: THE PENITENTIAL TEACHING OF THE SHEPHERD OF HERMAS

1. This essay, which is here presented in a revised form, appeared originally in ZKTh 77 (1955), pp. 385–431.

2. J. Stufler, 'Die Bussdisziplin der abendländischen Kirche bis Kallistus' in:

ZKTh 31(1909), pp. 433–73; Vanbeck, 'La Pénitence dans le Pasteur d'Hermas' in: RHLR nouv.série 2 (1911), pp. 389–403; A. d'Alès, *L'édit de Calliste* (Paris 1914), pp. 52–113 (with references to previous literature); H. Koch, *Die Bussfrist des Pastor Hermä* (Festgabe A. v. Harnack) (Tübingen 1921), pp. 173–82; C. D. Watkins, *A History of Penance* I (London 1920), pp. 47–72; M. Dibelius, *Der Hirt des Hermas* (Handbuch zum NT, Ergänzungsband) (Tübingen 1925); A. d'Alès, *De sacramento paenitentiae* (Paris 1926), pp. 17–21; J. Hoh, *Die kirchliche Busse im zweiten Jahrhundert* (Breslau 1932), pp. 10–34; L. Kogler, *Busssakrament und Ablass* (Linz 1931); J. Lebreton, 'Le développement des institutions ecclésiastiques à la fin du IIe et au début du IIIe siècle, in: RSR 24 (1934), pp. 124–64; E. Amann, 'La pénitence dans le "pasteur" d'Hermas' in: DThC XII/1 (Paris 1933), pp. 759–63; B. Poschmann, *Paenitentia secunda* (Bonn 1940), pp. 134–205; P. Galtier, *De paenitentia* (Rome 1950), n.238–45; S. Prete, 'Cristianesimo antico e riforma ortodossa. Note intorno al "Pastore" di Erma (II.Sec.): Convivium', Raccolta nuova 1950, pp. 114–28; P. Galtier, *Aux origines du sacrement de la Pénitence* (Rome 1951), pp. 132–44; J. Grotz, *Die Entwicklung des Bussstufenwesens in der vornicänischen Kirche* (Freiburg 1955), pp. 13–70; R. Joly, 'La doctrine pénitentielle du Pasteur d'Hermas' in: RHR 147 (1955), pp. 32–49; id., *Hermas le Pasteur*, SC 53 bis (Paris 1968), pp. 22–30; W. Doskocil, *Der Bann in der Urkirche* (NThSt Kan. Abt. vol. 11) (Munich 1958), pp. 160–91; S.Giet, *Hermas et les Pasteurs. Les trois auteurs du Pasteur d'Hermas* (Paris 1963), pp. 123–34, 174–8, 189–94, 230–4; C. Vogel, *Le pécheur et la pénitence dans l'église ancienne* (Paris 1966), pp. 16–18, 62–6; K. Baus, *Von der Urgemeinde zur frühchristlichen Grosskirche* (HdKG I) (Freiburg 1962), pp. 364–6, 166 f.

3. B. Poschmann, *Paenitentia secunda. Die kirchliche Busse im ältesten Christentum bis Cyprian und Origenes* (Bonn 1940). Ch. 3: 'Die Busslehre des Hermas', pp. 134–205.

4. J. Grotz, *Die Entwicklung des Bussstufenwesens in der vornicänischen Kirche* (Freiburg/Br. 1955). Part One: 'Die Busslehre des Hermas', pp. 11–70.

5. We are obviously unable to avoid repeating a great deal of what has already been said by others (especially by Poschmann). Nevertheless, we consider it more appropriate to give a synthetic view of the whole of Hermas' penitential teaching than merely to criticize and supplement the conclusions of others. The latter approach may render some service to the specialist, but it would inevitably remain incomprehensible to the reader who lacks the necessary background.

6. Cf. for example Galtier's thesis 17, *De paenitentia* (Rome 1950), n. 270, p. 224: '*Cum constet mentem fuisse Ecclesiae antiquae remissionem peccati haberi in "reconciliatione" post peractam paenitentiam publicam, dicendum omnino videtur eam "reconciliationem" fuisse sacramentalem nec ei praemissam esse de iure privatam peccati absolutionem.*' Thus even those who, like Galtier, defend the existence of private penance in the early Church acknowledge that in the case of public penance reconciliation with the Church is also sacramental absolution. Neither Galtier nor Poschmann separate these two realities temporally. This is in no way altered by the fact that Galtier, in his thesis, is only contesting the view according to which sacramental absolution *precedes* the lifting of excommunication. Grotz holds that the opposite order is the one which is historically verifiable.

7. Cf. H. Windisch, *Taufe und Sünde im ältesten Christentum bis auf Origenes* (Tübingen 1908).

8. The remark of C. Chartier, 'L'excommunication ecclésiastique d'après les écrits de Tertullian' in: Antonianum 10 (1935), pp. 301–344, 499–536 (cf. esp.334), that there were in the early Church several forms of excommunication which ought not to be confused is quite correct. However, this fact, which is recognized both by Poschmann and by myself (cf. Grotz p. 438), does not have the significance which it is often given. What Chartier calls 'partial' excommunication ought not to be minimized

and made into a non-literal excommunication. In the view of the early Church this is where the decisive theological point lies. We may regret that this alienation of the sinner (of every sinner!) from the Eucharist and, therefore, from fellowship with the Church is not expressed more felicitously than with the notion of 'excommunication', and that the corresponding penance is consequently described as 'penance of excommunication', that is, with words which almost inevitably today conjure up the idea of procedures of modern canon law. Nevertheless, this difficulty of terminology ought not to obscure the fact that not only did these 'excommunications' exist in the early Church, but also they represented a decisive aspect of the very notion of penance. They were an element which explained so many other aspects of penance (especially with regard to its public nature) and which, therefore, was found in one form or another in every penance of the early Church.

9. On this question cf. Poschmann, pp. 136–40, and especially R. Joly, pp. 11–21, together with his bibliography (pp. 69–74). More recent French publications on the Shepherd of Hermas express a general reserve and disagreement with regard to the results of researches published in German (thus R. Joly, p. 25; S. Giet, p. 125), without, however, providing either detailed reasons or preferable opinions. In his work mentioned above S. Giet attempts to conclude from the threefold division of the whole of Hermas's composite work to the existence of three different authors. It must be said, with J. A. Fischer (cf. ThRv 61 [1965], p. 308), however, that the deriving of three different authors, simply from what are certainly in the main three distinct parts, does not appear to be justified (cf. on this point also R. Joly, pp. 12 f.; 16 ff.; 140 f.; E. Peterson, *Frühkirche, Judentum und Gnosis* [Freiburg 1959], p. 272; J. A. Fischer, p. 307 f.). One 'author' (who could have sketched the writing at different periods) or a final redactor could have easily composed the whole work from material belonging to different traditions and from drafts of various stages of edition. Also in a work of this period we should not expect to find highly differentiated and precise theological terminology, even if this does not mean that it evinces a naive mentality. Differences of terminology and the clear notion of the differences of doctrine which they presuppose can serve only in a very limited way here as an indication of different authors, since at that time doctrinal disputes and their solution were generally expressed in another form.

10. A review of the state and the history of the text is given in the introduction to Whittaker's edn, *Die Apostolischen Väter* I. *Der Hirt des Hermas* (GCS 48) (Berlin 1956) IX–XX. The work itself is composed in the style of an allegory and belongs to the category of apocalypse. For this reason alone, it is obvious that to explain this work historically, indeed to interpret it at all, is a difficult task.

11. Thus for example S. Giet; J. Daniélou, *Théologie du Judéo-Christianisme* (Tournai 1958), p. 48 f. Cf. also R. Joly, p. 14 f.

12. Origen, Eusebius and Rufinus know nothing of this tradition. S.Giet proposes Pius I's brother, whose name is unknown, as the author of at most the nine parables (p. 288), while he ascribes to 'Hermas' the four visions (which, according to his three-author hypothesis represent the 'first book'), since they evince a Latin and at times a clearly Roman environment as the milieu of composition.

13. Cf. J. Daniélou, pp. 43–9; see also E. Peterson, pp. 254–309.

14. On this question cf. R. van Deemter, *Der Hirt des Hermas—Apokalypse oder Allegorie?* (Delft 1929); A. V. Ström, *Der Hirt des Hermas. Allegorie oder Wirklichkeit* (Leipzig-Uppsala 1936). Deemter and Ström reject the thesis of a purely literary fiction. Others, on the contrary, for instance D. van den Eynde, *Les normes de l'enseignement chrétien dans la littérature patristique des trois premiers siècles* (Paris 1933) p. 89 f., and G. Bardy, *La Théologie de l'Eglise de saint Clement à saint Irénée* (Paris 1945) p. 117 f., think that it is a literary fiction, at least as far as Hermas'

personal relationships are concerned. R. Joly (pp. 17–21) also inclines towards this view. S. Giet leaves open the possibility of *'un cadre biographique'* at least for the visions.

15. These texts have recently been presented in a carefully prepared edn: H. Karpp (ed.), *Die Busse. Quellen z. Entstehung d. altkirchl. Busswesens* (Zurich 1969) (Traditio Christiana, vol. 1); see the general introduction and bibliography. In the interpretation of the individual 'penitential' texts and in the analysis of the texts a special place must be afforded within the work as a whole to the first four visions. If S. Giet's thesis of three authors is correct, then a greater independence must be assumed for the ninth parable. Nevertheless, the generally accepted view today is that *one* author established the eventual form of the work, albeit with the use of several traditions.

16. For further references to the authors named, see in Poschmann, p. 134 f.

17. The Catholic historians of dogma among those mentioned modify this thesis with regard to the extent of the supposed penitential rigorism and on the question of whether this rigorism concerns only the practice of church reconciliation or includes other areas.

18. This means that a great deal of the obscurity in the Shepherd of Hermas is to be construed not simply as a literary elaboration of a more original part, but in relation to the context and the concrete situation of that time. On this assumption, the final redactor would have had to avoid writing too concretely and too clearly to a given situation. Both the obscure style and the literary form were, therefore, understandable as a 'defence-mechanism', which allows a great freedom in the interpretation of what is actually meant. The composition and structure of the work evince different levels, traditions and stages of redaction. It is, therefore, also probable that, in the course of composition, new addressees and changed circumstances had to be considered and that, consequently, the attempt was made to harmonize historical necessities with 'pastoral astuteness'.

19. Cf. Sim. VI 2,3; VIII 6,4; 8,2; IX 19,1.3; 26,3.5; cf. also Vis. I 4,2; III 7,2.

20. In Sim. IX 26,6b it is stated clearly that penance is possible even for those who have previously fallen away from the faith. It may be that this is an allusion to a specific church practice following a persecution. Cf. R. Joly, p. 27 f.

21. It is immaterial whether, with Dibelius (p. 586) and Grotz (p. 27), we read *ποτέ* in Sim. VII 4 or follow the traditional text *πάντως* (or *παντελῶς*). In any case Hermas's children are promised full forgiveness, provided that they do penance in the prescribed way; for then their hearts are 'clean from every wicked deed'. Any element of uncertainty or the hypothetical in such cases consists (apart from the gravity of the sins in question) in the question of whether penance is really done conscientiously and completely but not in any doubt of whether, given such a penance, complete forgiveness will be really granted. The fact that Hermas' children are doing complete penance is evidenced by their undergoing the trial imposed by God and still continuing, and not only by their good intention, to do penance which is taken for granted and is described as 'wholehearted' penance. If, without any justification in the text, the *πάντως* is corrected to a *ποτέ* this can only signify uncertainty with regard to the conditions and consequently with regard to divine forgiveness. For it is certainly complete healing that is promised (*παντώς*, here being connected with the total purification of the heart, must mean not 'certainly' but 'completely'). To translate this word by 'certainly' or 'surely' is to create a contradiction, in so far as the forgiveness, the uncertainty of which has been stressed, is now certain once the condition for it has been fulfilled (cf. Grotz). If, therefore, certain sinners have proven that their conversion is genuine (such would be excommunicates, according to Grotz), then it is no longer possible to speak of the uncertainty of healing in their regard. Moreover, this

text speaks explicitly only of forgiveness by God. The question of how the Church should behave towards such a genuine and tested excommunicate is not considered at all. In the case of a complete pardon by God, however, a complete forgiveness on the part of the Church also ought to be presumed, in principle. The idea that the Church, for its part, should not grant forgiveness, despite God's pardon, was introduced first by Tertullian and was opposed by the Catholics who showed that the notion was nonsensical. For reasons other than those of Tertullian, this view later played a considerable role, for example, with Augustine, in respect of the many recidivists after the first penance. Because at that time already church law prescribed that penance could only be granted once, the bishop of Hippo did not know any other way of helping such people who had fallen but were again repentant. The *τινα* healing promised in Sim. VII 4 (ibid., 65.2) should not to be given too much weight, since it is immediately explained and modified by the following *πάντως*.

22. Cf. J. Grotz, pp. 21, 36 f.

23. Galtier, *De paenitentia,* n.233, p. 162, n.1, believes that there is a chiliastic notion in this disputed text. L. Atzberger, *Geschichte der christlichen Eschatologie innerhalb der vornicänischen Zeit* (Freiburg/Br. 1896), p. 89 f., contests that Hermas was a chiliast.

24. Cf. R. Joly, p. 92, n. 2.

25. For further details on this point cf. Dibelius, pp. 447, 453, 511 ff., and Poschmann, p. 146. In the first four visions, which have a special place in the whole work, the deadline for the possibility of doing penance appears to be immediately imminent. Thus the summons to penance in expectation of the imminent end of the world is the urgent *leitmotif* of these visions (cf. S. Giet, p. 123 ff.). In the *mandata* and *similitudines* we already meet a comparative 'diluted eschatology'. The end of the world is delayed, and this affects the doctrine of penance: the building of the tower is immediately interrupted (Sim. IX 5,2; 14,2) in order to postpone the Parousia (cf. R. Joly).

26. In Hippolytus' Paradosis (17,Dix p. 28), which codifies the traditional Christian practice in about A.D. 220, a period of three years is envisaged for the catechumenate. Although such a long period may not yet have been customary in Hermas' circle (Justin, for instance, does not yet appear to be cognisant of such fixed periods), it is reasonable to assume, granted Hermas' picture of the general state of the Church, that is, as being considerably diminished in its original idealism, that already at this time (as later at the time of Hippolytus) great care was taken in the admission of neophytes and quite long probationary periods were imposed.

27. On this point cf. P. Galtier, *Aux origines du sacrament de la Pénitence,* p. 132, n.34, together with R. Joly's criticism of d'Alès and Poschmann in *La doctrine pénitentielle du Pasteur d'Hermas,* p. 41 ff.; id., *Hermas le Pasteur,* pp. 24 f. and 158 ff.

28. On the identification of these 'teachers' cf. Poschmann, p. 165, and P. Galtier, op. cit., together with R. Joly. G. Bardy prefers to see them as a particular group and connects them with the teachers reprimanded in Sim. VIII 6,5 and IX 19,2 f.; 22,14; cf. G. Bardy, 'Les écoles Romaines au second siècle' in: RHE 28(1932), pp. 501–32 (on Hermas see pp. 503–6). Nevertheless, the praise in Mand. IV and the reprimand in Sim. VIII/IX hardly refer to the same group of teachers, even though they all spread erroneous theories on penance.

29. A. d'Alès, *L'édit de Calliste,* pp. 73–8, has proven quite convincingly against Zahn, Funk, Rauschen and Watkins that this call does not mean a 'jubilee of penance', which Hermas supposedly announced, but that it is to be understood of baptism. This point is generally no longer disputed today; but cf. R. Joly (SC 53b) p. 25. The 'call' is also baptism elsewhere in Hermas (cf. Sim. VIII 1,1; IX 14,5), and in

Sim. VIII 11,1 the 'mission' of the angel of penance is explicitly distinguished from the 'call' by God's son. Thus it cannot be deduced from Mand. IV 3,3.4.6 that it is only after Hermas' preaching of penance that those who are already Christians have a single possibility of penance. Rather it was there from the time of their baptism. Clement of Alexandria also understands this 'call' as baptism (cf. Strom II 13,56 f.).

30. If it were merely a question of God's will to forgive being limited, then Hermas need only have said: from now on or after the *paenitentia secunda* God will no longer forgive, even though a person does penance. However, he always says: there is no further forgiveness, because either penance is not done or is not possible.

31. These conditions are especially clear in the first four visions, above all in Vis. II 2.

32. Cf. S. Giet, p. 192, and P. Aubin, *Le problème de la 'conversion'* (*Théologie historique* I) (Paris 1963), p. 85 ff., together with J. Hoh, p. 14 ff.

33. Thus *2 Clement* 8,6 states: 'Keep the flesh pure and the seal unsullied, so that we may receive eternal life.' This life is, accordingly, attainable only if the baptismal seal has never been lost. But even *2 Clement* recognizes a post-baptismal penance (cf. Poschmann, *Paenitentia secunda,* pp. 124 ff.). In Dial. 44 *Justin* says that the unique hope is to continue to live without sins after the ἄφεσις in baptism. Nevertheless, he also holds that every repentant person receives forgiveness from God (cf. Poschmann, p. 209 f.). *Origen* declares: outside baptism there is no ἄφεσις of sins (Exhort. ad mart. 30), yet he does not dispute the fact that even the most serious sins can be remitted by a subsequent penance. (On this point cf. chap. 8 in this volume, 'The Penitential Teaching of Origen'.) In another context, in In Jerem. hom. XX 19,4, Origen develops a whole theory of the salvific aspect of error (for example in the ethics of marriage). These ideas are relevant here since this theory includes the error over the extent of God's mercy. In his Catholic period, when he taught the possibility of a remission of even the most serious sins, *Tertullian* tells the catechumens quite simply: *semel delicta diluuntur, quia ea iterari non oportet* (De bapt. 15). Indeed in cap. 18 he uses this as the basis for his principle that baptism should not be received too early. Nevertheless, he speaks to Christians only very reluctantly about a post-baptismal penance: *Nihil iam de paenitentia noverint, nihil eius requirant. Piget secundae, immo iam ultimae spei subtexere mentionem, ne tractantes de residuo auxilio paenitendi spatium adhuc delinquendi demonstrare videamur* (De paenit. 7,1–6). *Pacian* preaches to his neophytes: *semel liberamur . . . tenete quod accepistis* (De sancto bapt. 7), and yet he is one of the most outspoken opponents of novatianist rigorism. In Epist. I n.5 he develops explicitly a theory about the pedagogical value of silence with regard to a second possibility of penance as far as neophytes are concerned: *sed nos hanc indulgentiam Dei nostri miseris, non beatis, nec ante peccatum, sed post peccata detegimus; nec sanis medicinam, sed male habentibus nuntiamus.* (Cf. also his description of the capital sins, which is obviously intended in the first place to give the impression that such sins are unforgivable, while—as is clear from what follows—he only wishes to invite those guilty of such sins to undertake public church penance: Paraenesis de paenitentia 4–5. *Chrysostom,* In Hebr. hom. 31 n.2 speaks of Paul's pedagogical silence in the letter to the Hebrews in connection with a further possibility of penance. *Jerome* says of baptism: *solum potest peccata dimittere* (In Isaiam I 1 v.16; PL 24,35). Although this may have been intended as an opposition to the Jewish rites of purification, it still shows how naturally an author could stress the uniqueness of baptism with regard to the forgiveness of sins without being a novatianist. Even for *Augustine* church penance after baptism is something which in fact ought not to occur in the life of a Christian, something on which one should not count: Epist. 265,2; Sermo 352 cap.3 n.8.

34. As we have frequently observed, the expectation of the end of the world in

Hermas is found above all in the visions. But it then appears to recur gradually in the *mandata* right through to the *similitudines*. Cf. S. Giet, pp. 190, 229 f.

35. We say 'if', for it is by no means certain that ὑπὸ χεῖρα ἁμαρτάνειν means 'to sin continually, repeatedly'. Ὑπὸ χεῖρα is not witnessed elsewhere in the sense of 'continually', 'repeatedly'. In Hermas the expression is found in Vis. III 10,7; V 5; Mand. IV 3,6. In the ancient Latin translations it is rendered by *confestim* or *subinde*. But *confestim* does not mean 'continually'. And if—as is perfectly possible—*subinde* is construed in the same sense, then the ancient translations provide no proof for the sense which we have suggested. *Subinde* does usually mean 'often', but this meaning is not compelling. What is more, it would still have to be shown that the translation really understood the Greek text correctly. *Dibelius'* explanation (p. 478) of the possible evolution of ὑπὸ χεῖρα from its use attested by the papyri to the sense which we suggest here is enlightening only if this suggested sense is already taken for granted. In fact the meanings in the papyri are far from clear. The meaning of ὑπὸ χεῖρα just mentioned for Vis. III and V is not proven with certainty from the context. Certainly it makes sense there, but the question remains whether this sense is the correct one. Yet another meaning, such as *sans gêne* would suit these passages. The Latin *sub manu* (which is another possible translation of the Greek) does not mean 'continually'. In other words, we have no proof that the ὑπὸ χεῖρα in Mand. IV 3,6 is not intended as the opposite of the preceding ὑπὸ τοῦ διαβόλου, which was already the view of Windisch (p. 364). Accordingly, Hermas would have in mind the sin of obduracy, for which there was no prospect of true sorrow. At most this sin could be accompanied by the semblance of 'penance' but allowed for no doing of 'wholehearted' penance. In so far as Hermas (as Clement of Alexandria will do so explicitly later, Strom. II 13,57.4) recognizes in a relapse after penance just such an act of malice, an interpretation of Mand. IV 3,6 as a sin of obduracy would amount in fact to the same meaning. Cf. Poschmann, p. 165 n.1.

36. Obviously Tertullian, in his Montanist period, had to leave some hope of forgiveness by God even to the sinner to whom he refused church reconciliation. In fact he did this much more clearly than did Hermas. Thus the way was prepared for the Catholic presentation of the tenet that recidivist sinners can still be forgiven by God, even if the Church denies them a second reconciliation.

37. Augustine, Epist. 153,7 attempts to justify the once and for all character of church reconciliation, quite independently of doubt concerning the sinner's disposition and of the doubt of God's forgiveness to which this gives rise: *ne medicina vilis minus utilis esset aegrotis, quae tanto magis salubris, quanto minus contemptibilis fuerit.*

38. J. Grotz (p. 20) considers that the men who are described in Vis. III 2,7c are 'recidivists'. But this is difficult to prove. These people are near the Church and have not, as the 'alienated', broken off all relationship with the Church (cf. Vis. III 2,9). They may also have had the opportunity of penance, but it is not possible to prove that they were recidivists in the strict sense, that is, that they had fallen again into their old sins after having completed their penance and received church reconciliation. They could just as well be hypocrites who, despite their (exterior) faith, remain full of wickedness, who after their baptism have never really led a Christian life or have reverted to a non-Christian way of life, although exteriorly they remain united with the community, and who finally have remained irresponsive to exhortations and attempts to bring about their conversion. Similarly it is easy to see those who are supposed as possible (but not as actual) recidivists in Sim. VIII 6,2 as those who have sinned after baptism, but not after a post-baptismal completed penance.

39. This lack of examples is, therefore, not a proof that, before Hermas, church penance with excommunication did not exist.

40. Cf. R. Joly, p. 161 nn.4–7.
41. Cf. S. Giet, p. 194.
42. In the first four visions the Church appears above all as pre-existent and as a spiritual reality. In parables IX (which is strongly Christological) and X it is presented at a later stage of development and less spiritualized. In the *mandata* and the first eight *similitudines* it is scarcely mentioned explicitly. On the Church in Hermas and its role in his view of penance, cf.: R. Joly, pp. 28–30, 34–41; S. Giet, pp. 108–21, 169–73, 228 f.; C. Vogel, p. 18, together with W. Doskocil, pp. 169–77.
43. In Sim. III 3 it is stated: 'Just as in winter trees which have lost their leaves resemble one another, making it impossible to know which are withered and which have vitality, so in this world the righteous are not distinguishable from sinners but all resemble one another.' According to this idea, the tower is not simply to be identified with the earthly Church, since in the tower sinners and the righteous are separated, which is precisely not possible in the case of the earthly Church. We could put this more precisely: in the tower sinners and the righteous *are made* separate, in a way which clearly underlines the relationship between these two groups. This analogy also shows, however, that the idea of an earthly Church which is a pure community of saints is totally alien to Hermas. But why should he be so opposed to the reconciliation of a repentant sinner with this Church, if in this world it is never possible to distinguish sinners clearly from the righteous?
44. The justification for the Church's 'old age' in Vis. III 11,2 is derived from the presentation in Vis. II 4,1 and is developed further.
45. W. Doskocil, pp. 160–93, considers the close connection between excommunication and penance in the Shepherd of Hermas.
46. In this question we should obviously not have in mind our modern church life, where one 'attends church anywhere', without in any way affecting practically the rest of the individual's personal and social relationships. Rather we should conjure up the life of a community such as is presented to us, for instance, in Hippolytus' Paradosis. In this context the idea of a secular 'boycott' without an ecclesial significance is impossible (cf. J. Hoh, p. 18 f.). If 'concubinage' (in the ancient sense) and certain professions were punished by excommunication, and if a catechumen (even according to Justin) was not allowed to take part in the actual liturgy, then the cessation of married life inevitably signified an excommunication by the Church as well, however this may be envisaged as having taken place. In this regard, it is worth bearing in mind that for several decades before Hippolytus community life was even more narrow and more strict.
47. Cf. W. Doskocil, p. 174 ff. (especially the summarizing remarks on p. 177). The word 'excommunication' in the sense of a church disciplinary measure or of the early Christian ban is observable for the first time about the beginning of the 5th century in the synod of Carthage (A.D. 390) (cf. Mansi III, 695, c.8); cf. E. Valton, 'Excommunication' in: DThC V,2 (Paris 1913), p. 1735 f.
48. Hermas never appeals to a specific legislative act on the Church's part by which certain sins are punished by excommunication. In his view the excommunication is demanded immediately by the very nature of the sin itself. The question of Hermas' principle of the exclusion of sinners, which is not a positive canonical prescription, cannot be solved simply with reference to the obstinacy of the sinner. That would only raise the further question of why the Church excludes the obstinate sinner without a positive prescription. If the answer is that such a state of sin is incompatible with membership of the Church in the full sense (even though there is no sin against faith itself, and the sinner concerned, according to today's teaching, remains a member of the Church), then the principle is implicitly justified. The man who has excluded himself from grace violates his own membership of the Church,

which is the holy Church of the Holy Spirit. Thus with all the Fathers of the Church it must be said: wherever there is serious sin, there is necessarily this kind of excommunication. This means: every penance for such sins is penance of excommunication (and this still applies even today,since it is only reconciliation that restores the right to celebrate the Eucharist).

49. On this point, cf. A. Gommenginger, 'Bedeutet die Exkommunikation Verlust der Kirchengliedschaft' in: ZKTh 73 (1951), pp. 1–71, and K. Mörsdorf, 'Exkommunikation' in: HThG I (Munich 1962), pp. 375–82.

50. In this context it should be remembered that Paul has the same catalogue of vices for sins which exclude a person from the kingdom of God and for sinners who should be 'avoided' by the community or the bishop (Gal. 5:19–23; 1 Cor. 6:9 f.; Eph. 5:3–9; Col. 3:5–9; cf. Rom. 13:12 f.). Paul, therefore, recognizes a norm for banning which presupposes that every mortal sin in today's sense is 'deserving of excommunication' (in the ancient sense). S. Wipping, 'Die Tugend- und Lasterkataloge im NT' (ZNW, BH 25) (Berlin 1959), p. 115 ff.

51. Already in the ancient ban from the synagogue there were cases in which the actual relatives of the sinner were not obliged to avoid him, while he had to be avoided by others.

52. Cf. S. Giet, p. 157.

53. This is the opinion of K. Adam, 'Die abendländische Kirchenbusse im Ausgang des christlichen Altertums' in: ThQ 110 (1929), pp. 1–66 (for Hermas cf. p. 26). He finds evidence only of an inner church (but sacramental) penance for all offences. J. Hoh also recognizes only an inner church penance, but he does not appear to consider it sacramental.

54. It is possible that such sinners have also experienced correction and exhortation by the pastors of the Church in a 'preaching of penance'. But this alone can hardly be the exercise of that power of the keys which is conferred on the Church in Matt. 16 and 18. This would be difficult to prove, particularly with regard to the sacramental character of this function. Hermas himself must have performed a voluntary but church penance for his own sins of thought (according to Grotz, p. 50 f.). According to the principles enunciated by Hermas (Mand. IV 1,1 f.) this would be possible (Vis. I 2,3 f.). Although he distinguishes sins of thought from those which, as deed, 'bring death', he may, granted his dynamic notion of the struggle between different spirits for man's heart, have been of the opinion that such a sin of thought deprived a person of the seal of baptism because it expelled the Holy Spirit. Nevertheless, this assumption is not easily confirmed. For this to be the case, it would first of all have to be shown that the *μεγάλη ἁμαρτία* in Mand. IV 1,1 coincides with our notion of mortal sin. When there is a mention of death in the context of sins of thought (Vis. I 1,8), this could be understood as the consequence of such sins, in so far as they lead to action. In any event, it need not necessarily be a question of the inner aspect of the sin of thought as such as opposed to the deed. Moreover, it would still have to be shown that Hermas' personal penance (Sim. IX 10,6–11,8, in so far as penance really is involved here) was *ecclesial* in the strict sense. Obviously it could be stressed that Hermas' nightly meeting with the virtues, as his eating of God's word, occurs on the forecourt before the tower, therefore, on the place of the stones which are to be dressed, that is, of the penitents. Before such vague allegories are interpreted so widely it should be noted that the place before the tower is introduced as being perfectly purified (Sim. IX). Hermas precisely is not handed over to the pastor of penance, but he sequesters himself to play with the virtues (Sim. IX 10,6 f.). Hermas does not belong to the stones which have to be dressed for penance (Grotz, p. 50), but it is precisely this symbol of the stones which can be inserted into the tower only when they are dressed which refers to the penance which is imposed on sinners

(Grotz, pp. 48–50). One can hardly recognize in this scene, therefore, a symbol of the fact that Hermas has undertaken a voluntary church penance on account of his sins. The fact that Hermas has spiritually 'rejuvenated' himself by the practice of the virtues, prayer and reading the Scripture is not only a part, but the whole, of the explanation of this symbol.

55. Cf. for example Augustine, Sermo 98,5 593–4: in some circumstances sins of thought were considered mortal and, therefore, remitted *intus inter latebras conscientiae tamquam inter domesticos parietes.* Even if here there may have been a private sacramental penance in the sense of K. Adam (as opposed to Poschmann), this text still affords proof that the recognition of a mortal sin by the Fathers does not allow us to conclude that they knew of a private sacramental penance, since in the instance given there is no question of penance of excommunication. In fact these mortal sins of thought are certainly in Augustine's view remitted only by subjective penance. If, therefore, much earlier Hermas acknowledged sins of thought, which are mortal sins, and if he demanded penance for them, this does not prove that he was thinking of a sacramental penance.

56. Cf. for example Sim. VIII 7,3: to dwell in the tower and to dwell in the walls are clearly distinguished. In this regard it should be noted that to be inserted into the external part of the tower is, according to Hermas, a particularly honourable position. The 'walls', therefore, cannot signify the external part of the tower: Sim. IX 7,5; 8,2.4.5.6; 9,3.

57. Cf. R. Joly, pp. 29 and 40 f.; S. Giet, p. 116.

58. The argument against the identification of the place of penitents with the 'first walls' (cf. Grotz, p. 44 f.) disappears once it is realized that even the access to officially controlled penance presupposed a certain repentance (just as in the case of the catechumenate), even though the actual penance still remained to be done. Thus penance can be both the condition of access to the 'first walls' and then that which is imposed there. Furthermore, it is not surprising that access is gained to the penance of the place of penance by penance and that through (a greater and more intense) penance it is possible to arrive not only in these first walls but also in the tower (cf. the interpretation of Sim. VIII 6,6 by Grotz, p. 45).

59. Sim. VIII 7,3; 8,3 must be understood in this sense, since the distinction between those who come into the tower and those who arrive only at the walls would hardly have much meaning if in fact this second group also came into the tower.

60. There is lacking, however, a clear proof of this, since the fact that here Hermas is thinking more of interior penance is not a convincing proof. In this respect, it should be noted that Sim. VIII 7,5 allows for the fact that a person who has re-entered the tower could still leave it again. This could hardly apply to the Church of the next life.

61. It is worth noting here that according to Grotz not every refusal to undertake the obligation of penance makes excommunication definitive (cf. Grotz, p. 32). Provisionally obstinate sinners have the same possibility of penance as those who are converted immediately after their sin.

62. R. Joly, p. 29, sees also in Maximus (Vis. II 3,4) a person who was at one time a *lapsus* but who was reincorporated into the community.

63. Thus for example H. Koch and J. Hoh.

64. According to Irenaeus' text the 'correction due to his false teaching' must have taken place often during the period of Cerdron's penance; this shows that he must have alternated between appearing in the community as a penitent, on the one hand, and spreading his false teaching, on the other. Quite correctly Poschmann says: 'In this case our passage attests that heretics were not only admitted to penance, but even after a relapse they ought to be readmitted' (op. cit., p. 221). This opinion, which is

shared not only by d'Alès but also by H. Koch (in ZNW 9 [1908], p. 38), should be maintained, despite the protestation of Köhne (in ThGl 35 [1943], p. 33). Kohne himself admits that Cerdon performed exhomologesis, that is, appeared in the liturgy as a penitent, several times. Now the ποτὲ ἐλεγχόμενος, translated as 'now to be corrected', is placed in strict parallel to the 'now appearing as a false teacher' and 'now appearing as a penitent', and so it is eliminated by the ἀφιστάμενος, the definitive exclusion from the community. It is to be concluded from this text that it was often the case that Cerdon, during the period of his penance (that is, at that period when he appeared repeatedly as a penitent at the celebration of the liturgy) continued to spread his false teaching, and that he was alerted to the fact that these two kinds of behaviour were incompatible. Cerdon probably did not accept this, since he obviously wished to belong to the main community and attempted to achieve this through his penance, and at the same time he tried to remain in his esoteric circle. On this supposition (without which it is impossible to understand Cerdon's behaviour) it is easy to see that he does not attach much importance to the secrecy of his circle and that, consequently, it was always possible to recognize the formation of his gnostic, esoteric group.

65. Cf. above for further details on this point.

66. Only in J. Grotz's work is it stressed that the central form of penance had nothing to do with a penance of excommunication. In contrast, previous historians of dogma, for example K. Adam and P. Galtier, had allowed only a modest and insignificant, peripheral existence to a 'penance without excommunication'.

67. In this connection we might at least raise the question, which will still remain to be considered, of whether behind the possible two-tiered church ban in Hermas there is a double ban which is already discernible not only in the practice of the synagogue but also in the New Testament and in the apostolic communities: the simple ban and the (solemn) ban accompanied by a curse. If this were the case, it would make it clearer that in Hermas also the first level in any case involves a real excommunication and that, at the same time, the ban accompanied by a curse in the New Testament and, therefore, the intense form in Hermas do not imply that the sin of the person banned is unforgivable. For the simple ban cf. Rom. 16:17; 1 Cor. 5:9 ff.; 2 Cor. 2:6; 13:2; 2 Tim. 3:5; Tit. 3:10; 2 Thess. 3:6 ff.; Rev. 2:2. For the solemn ban accompanied by a curse cf.: Acts 5:1–11; 8:18–24; 1 Cor. 5:1–5; Gal. 1:8 f.

CHAPTER FOUR: THE POST-BAPTISMAL FORGIVENESS OF SINS IN THE REGULA FIDEI OF IRENAEUS

1. The present study is a revised and extended version of an original one which appeared in ZKTh 70 (1948), pp. 450–5. The basic text of the Regula Fidei can also be found in (PG 7) I 10,1 cols. 550 f. On our theme cf. in general J. Hoh, *Die kirchliche Busse im zweiten Jahrhundert* (Breslau 1932), pp. 89–103; B. Poschmann, *Paenitentia secunda* (Bonn 1940), pp. 211–29; H. Holstein, 'L'Exhomologèse dans l'Adversus haereses de saint Irénée' in: RSR 35 (1948), pp. 282–8. There is a comprehensive bibliography in B. Altaner/A. Stuiber, *Patrologie* (Freiburg/Br. 1966), pp. 118–25.

2. Cf. H. Windisch, *Taufe und Sünde im ältesten Christentum bis auf Origenes* (Tübingen 1908), p. 404.

3. Cf. H. Koch, 'Die Sündenvergebung bei Irenäus' in: ZNW 9 (1908), pp. 36–46.

4. Cf. G. N. Bonwetsch, *Die Theologie des Irenäus* (Gütersloh 1925), p. 131 f.

5. Cf. the remarks of F. Feuardent, reprinted in the 2nd vol. A. Stieren's edn of Irenaeus (Leipzig 1848), p. 613.

6. His remarks are reported by W. Harvey I 91.

7. J. Stufler, 'Die Bussdisziplin der abendländischen Kirche bis Kallistus' in: ZKTh 31 (1907), pp. 433–73; J. Stufler, 'Die Sündenvergebung bei Irenaus' in: ZKTh 32 (1908), pp. 488–97.

8. A. d'Alès, *L'édit de Calliste* (Paris 1914), p. 123.

9. J. Hoh, p. 93.

10. B. Poschmann, p. 220, n.2.

11. Our translation changes the opening clause, which—in the original—depends upon the previous sentence, into an independent sentence.

12. Since this group is determined syntactically by the final phrase τῶν ἀνθρώπων as well as by the initial unique article (as is the case with the group of wicked angels) it is obvious that these four adjectives refer only to men.

13. The four descriptions of this group are also bound together as a unity by the unique initial article. Thus the following phrase τοῖς (μέν)—τοῖς δέ must refer to this whole group of descriptions as a unity and cannot be understood merely as a differentiation within the last description.

14. The adjectives (or participles) used here: δίκαιοι, ὅσιοι, τετηρηκότες and διαμεμενηκότες would, at least in an absolute form, have been unusual as a precise description of angels. In some circumstances, 'holy' could refer to angels (cf. for example 1 Thess. 3:13), even when the term is used absolutely. But this hardly applies to the expressions used here.

15. The precise point at issue here should be kept in mind: it is not a question of the actual legitimacy or the possibility of deriving from biblical expressions or those found in the early Church the fact that even the good angels will be judged in some sense of the last day, but only of whether the expressions of such a notion, which is quite possible in itself, were at that time part and parcel of the current view about the future judgement of the world, and this to the extent that they could be expected to figure here in this brief confession of faith, even though there is nothing in the text itself which would demand such an interpretation.

16. Cf. for example Matt. 16:27; 25:31; Luke 9:26; 12:8 f.; 1 Thess. 3:13; 2 Thess. 1:7. On this point see ThW I 83. Jewish theology at the time of the New Testament knows the same idea: the good angels accompany God at the judgement and are the executors of his sentence on men and demons, but they are not judged themselves. Cf. Strack-Billerbeck, *Kommentar zum NT aus Talmud und Midrasch* I, pp. 672, 973 f.; P. Volz, *Die Eschatologie der jüdischen Gemeinde im neutestamentlichen Zeitalter* (Tübingen 1934), pp. 276 f., 303 f., 316. The only text which constitutes an exception to this general view and perspective is Henoch, pp. 61,6 ff., where the Son of Man appears to judge *all* angels and men. But it should be pointed out that, first, it is unique in the whole of the relevant literature and, second, it is not consistent with the New Testament perspective. Above all, this unique occurrence hardly affords sufficient explanation of such a perspective in a short confession like the Regula Fidei. The most that can be said is that in 1 Cor. 6:3 it could be presupposed that in the end all angels (even the good) will be judged and that consequently such a perspective could have been familiar to Irenaeus. All that need be said on this point at present is that it seems more reasonable today to understand this text too, following Sickenberger, B. Weiss, Lietzmann, Förster (cf. Foerster, W. in ThW II 18) and H. D. Wendland, NTD III (Göttingen 1965) (but contrary to Cornely, Allo and others) as referring to the judgement of the fallen angels. The decisive factor for this question, however, must be that all of the Greek and most of the Latin Church Fathers (beginning with Tertullian, who was the first Latin author to interpret this text which is not found in Irenaeus) understood this passage as referring only to the judgement of fallen angels. It is, therefore, highly unlikely that Irenaeus would have been familiar with the idea of a judgement of the good angels on the basis of this Pauline passage. A further observa-

tion confirms this conclusion: the confession of the future judgement by the returning Lord is usually modified in a 'regula fidei' or in the confessions in general by the statement that it will be a judgement of living and dead men, but never a judgement of angels. Only very exceptionally are those to be judged further distinguished into good and bad (as in Irenaeus). Although this distinction is found in the traditional formulations of the 'regula fidei' which are closest to Irenaeus, it is abundantly clear that here it is only a question of good and bad men: Tertullian, De praescr.haer. 13 (CSL 70:p. 18,14–17), and Origen, Peri archon, I, 5 (PG 11) 118. Moreover, the idea of a judgement of the good angels is not found elsewhere in Irenaeus. In fact this idea seems to be totally alien to the whole of early Christian literature, which is remarkable, in view of the fact that the teaching of a final judgement of the demons appears to have been generally widespread. Cf. L. Atzberger, *Geschichte der christlichen Eschatologie innerhalb der vornicänischen Zeit* (Freiburg 1896). An isolated passage in the fragment of Hippolytus Adv.Graecos 3 (PG 10, 801 A) contains a remark which could refer to a judgement of the good angels. Origen's idea, however, that the guardian angels of men would have to render an account of their activity at the judgement (In Luc.hom. 13 [GCS 35] 92) is so incidental that it cannot be considered relevant to our question. In fact this idea seems to have been introduced by Hermas, Sim. IX 31,6 (GCS 48:p. 100,13–17).

17. Cf. 2 Pet. 2:4; Jude 6. That the fallen angels, despite their previous condemnation, will be finally and definitively condemned only at the last judgement is a view which is very familiar to Jewish theology; cf. Strack-Billerbeck III, p. 783 f. The earlier Church Fathers already witness to the fact that the wicked angels are among those who will be judged in the end. Cf. Atzberger, pp. 107, 160, 162, 282, 330, 412, 598 n.3. This idea is found in Irenaeus not only in our passage; cf. Adv.haer. I 10,3; V 26,2; III 23,3; IV 40,1; Epideixis 85 etc. Irenaeus is fond of quoting explicitly the passage of Matt. 25:41; he understands it in the sense that the fire is still to be prepared even for the devil. Nevertheless, this in no way implies the idea of a judgement of the good angels. For, in the case of the future judgement of the wicked angels, Irenaeus makes certain presuppositions which are not relevant in the case of the good angels: thus, in his opinion, the wicked angels share in the fate of the imperfect world (cf. IV 16,2). Cf. on this point D. Petavius, *Dogmatica theologica, De Angelis lib. III cap.4*; R. Massuet, *Sancti Irenaei episcopi Lugdunensis et martyris detectionis et eversionis falso cognominatae agnitionis, seu contra haereses libri quinque . . .* (Paris 1710) Diss. III art. 8, and A. Stieren (edn of Irenaeus) (Leipzig 1848) II 341 f. In Irenaeus himself, Adv.haer. V 26,2. Otherwise, Irenaeus generally speaks only about the judgement of men; cf. Adv.haer. II 22,2; III 4,2; 5,3; IV 22,2; 33,13; V 27,1; Epid. 69.

18. Matt. 16:27; Mark 8:38; Luke 9:26; Jude 8; 2 Pet. 2:10; Cf. ThW II 255 and I 81 ff.

19. However Irenaeus may have envisaged the nature of angels (cf. on this R. Massuet, Diss III), they are certainly not *σάρξ* (Adv.haer. III 20,4) but, of their very nature, as opposed to the flesh, immortal (V 4,1; 7,1; 13,3).

20. Cf. ThW I 480 f.

21. Adv.haer. IV 20,2.

22. Hermas, Mand. IV 3,3 f. (GCS 48:p. 28,3–11); 1,8 (ibid., p. 26,16–20); cf. R. Joly, *Hermas-Le Pasteur* (SC 53b) (Paris 1958, 1968), p. 159 f., and the introduction, pp. 22–30 ('Thèse intermédiaire', p. 24); cf. chap. 3 in this volume, 'The Penitential Teaching of the Shepherd of Hermas'.

23. According to Adv.haer. I 6,3, the Gnostics maintain that they have grace as an inalienable personal possession (*ἰδιόκτητος*). On this, cf. chap. 2 in this volume, 'Sin as Loss of Grace in Early Church Literature'.

24. The apologetic tendency explains why it is that, in the description of the men who come before the judgement, no attention is paid to humanity before Christ. Irenaeus obviously knows that even these men, in so far as they have lived virtuously before Christ's arrival, are saved and that, consequently, in the history of salvation (Adv.haer. IV 22,2) there have 'from the beginning' been men who would withstand the judgement. But there can be no question of these men here. For if it were a question of the whole of mankind, including the generations before Christ, then it would be saved as a whole and not only partially by *μετάνοια*. In fact Irenaeus recognizes that in Adam all men have lost the Spirit, which is necessary for salvation (Adv.haer. V 16,3 etc.; cf. R. Massuet, n.115) and that, consequently, even the 'righteous' of the Old Covenant have to receive the forgiveness of their sins through Christ (Adv.haer. IV 27,2 etc.).

25. Such unqualified statements are found frequently in Irenaeus. Cf. B. Poschmann, p. 218 ff.

26. For the juridical notion of *κυροῦν*, which is used when a community grants its 'love' once more to a person who has been excommunicated, cf. ThW III 1098 f.:love is 'granted officially'.

27. Translator's note: the text which we have used here is the American Reprint of the Edinburgh Edn, published by The Christian Literature Publishing Co., Buffalo 1887.

28. Translator's note: the translation which we present here is that of J. P. Smith, *St. Irenaeus, Proof of the Apostolic Preaching* (*Ancient Christian Writers,* no.16) (Westminster, Md/London 1952).

CHAPTER FIVE:
TERTULLIAN'S THEOLOGY OF PENANCE

1. The essay which is presented here in a revised and extended form appeared originally in *Abhandlungen über Theologie und Kirche* (Festschrift K. Adam), ed. M. Reding (Düsseldorf 1952), pp. 139–67. On the same theme cf. B. Poschmann, *Paenitentia secunda* (Bonn 1940), pp. 283–348; id., *Busse und Letzte Ölung* (HDG IV,3) (Freiburg/Br. 1951), pp. 20–7. For general considerations see also M. Spanneut, *Tertullien et les premiers moralistes africains* (Gembloux/Paris 1969), as well as the detailed study of J. Moingt, *Théologie trinitaire de Tertullien* (4 vols.) (Paris 1966–9). In recent years Tertullian's thought has attracted great interest in ecclesiology (and in this context it has given rise to information and considerations on penitential discipline): cf. E. Altendorf, *Einheit und Heiligkeit der Kirche* (Berlin 1932); W. Simonis, *Ecclesia visibilis et invisibilis* (Frankfurt/M. 1970); U. Wickert, *Sacramentum Unitatis* (Berlin/New York 1971); R. F. Evans, *One and Holy* (London 1972).

2. Cf. the works mentioned above. There can be no question here of repeating the results of these studies. Our intention is rather to re-examine independently Tertullian's expressed views themselves and so, hopefully, obtain both more satisfactory
Ecclesia visibilis et invisibilis (Frankfurt/M.1970); U. Wickert, *Sacramentum Unitatis*
out will be to uncover in Tertullian's theology of penance principles which are hardly present in today's systematic theology but which could very well be of great importance for the teaching on penance.

3. B. Poschmann, p. 283 ff., lists all the important literature up to 1940. Later works which should be mentioned are: P. Galtier, 'Comment on écarte la pénitence privée' in: Gr 22 (1940), pp. 183–202 (esp. 188–93); J. Köhne, 'Zur Frage der Busse im christlichen Altertum' in: ThGl 35 (1943), pp. 26–36; E. Dekkers, *Tertullianus en de*

geschiednis der liturgie (Brussels/Amsterdam 1947), pp. 217–30; G. H. Joyce, 'Private Penance in the Early Church' in: JThS 42 (1941), pp. 18–42 (on R. C. Mortimer, *The Origins of Private Penance* [Oxford 1939]); C. B. Daly, 'The Sacrament of Penance in Tertullian' in: IER 69 (1947), pp. 693–707, 815–21; 70 (1948), pp. 731–46, 832–48; H. von Campenhausen, *Kirchliches Amt und geistliche Vollmacht in den ersten drei Jahrhunderten* (Tübingen 1963), pp. 243–61; K. Baus, *Von der Urgemeinde zur frühchristlichen Grosskirche* (HdKG I) (Freiburg/Br. 1962). pp. 367–73; B. Altaner/A. Stuiber, *Patrologie* (Freiburg/Br. 1966), pp. 162 ff.; J. Quasten, *Patrology* II (Utrecht 1953), pp. 332–5; J. Grotz, *Die Entwicklung des Busstufenwesens in der vornicänischen Kirche* (Freiburg/Br. 1955), pp. 343–70.

4. On this cf. chap. 2 in this volume, 'Sin as Loss of Grace in Early Church Literature.'

5. Even today this is not possible. Loss of grace is indeed the essence of mortal sin, but it is still not the precise criterion for the distinction between mortal and venial sins.

6. This means in practice apostasy, murder and fornication. On this cf. J. Grotz, pp. 356–64.

7. Edns of the text: E. Preuschen (Tübingen 1910) and P. de Labriolle (Paris 1906). The text which we are using here is that in the relevant volume of the *Corpus scriptorum latinorum* (CSL), published in Vienna.

8. Cf. De spect. 8.

9. Cf. De bapt. 4; De spect. 3,20.

10. Nevertheless, this is, as such, a logical contradiction of the Montanist view that these sins are not in fact mortal sins.

11. Cf. De pud. 18,18.

12. Even in De pud., however, as in De pud. 19,25, further sins are added to these: *fraus, negatio, blasphemia . . . et si qua alia violatio templi Dei;* similarly Adv. Marc. IV 9.

13. Cf. also De or. 7: *exomologesis est petitio veniae, quia qui petit veniam delictum confitetur.*

14. This obviously played a role, and not only later. For the penitent begs the clergy and the community not only to intercede for him but also to grant him the *pax* (De pud. 1; 3; 13). At that time all this certainly meant more than a mere liturgical ceremony. Whether it bore fruit sooner or later depended, therefore, on the impression which the penitent actually made upon the community.

15. This is to be understood as an enforced excommunication, in the case of sinners whose faults had become known without their own confession and who were, nevertheless, not prepared to undertake church penance. The only course of action was to exclude such sinners.

16. This is particularly clear in Cyprian; cf. De lapsis 28. Even the mere thought of an offence is confessed *apud sacerdotes Dei dolenter et simpliciter*. Whether an actual church penance is imposed for these *prava et modica vulnera* may remain an open question. There is only mention of a *exomologesis conscientiae* before the bishop. It remains unclear whether subsequently such people either willingly or compulsorily undertake public penance. It is even less certain that the *salutaris medela* which the bishop may recommend outside the actual church penance includes a sacramental penance. In any event, Tertullian indicates that in the case of secret sins confession before the bishop was the first step towards penance.

17. On this cf. B. Poschmann, *Die abendländische Kirchenbusse im Ausgang des christlichen Altertums* (Munich 1928), pp. 11–16. The reader will find here further literature on the question of the public confession of sins in the early Church.

18. In certain circumstances, such a sinner would already have tried also to obtain

the intercession of an imprisoned confessor (Ad mart. 1,6; De pud. 22,1). Such a 'pre-penance' can be supposed in the background to De paen. 10,1: the sinner is repentant, but he repeatedly postpones the *publicatio sui*.

19. Such a private 'pre-penance' is clear in the Didascalia Apostolorum. On this cf. 'Penitential Teaching and Practice According to the Didascalia Apostolorum' in this volume.

20. Cf. K. Baus, p. 370. On this question cf. also the details in 'The Penitential Teaching of the Shepherd of Hermas' in this volume.

21. On this cf. De pud. 3;5; De paen. 7, 10: *in vestibulo* is a second penance which is still to be opened as a door; De pud. 4: the Montanist will no longer grant access even to the threshold (*limen*) of the Church in the case of unnatural impurity, as opposed to natural impurity. But this obviously presupposes that, according to the Catholics, there are two stages of church penance.

22. It could also be that this introductory rite was performed only at the conclusion of the period of penance, that is, as the actual beginning of the exhomologesis, which then ended with the reconciliation. At least De pud. 13, 7 gives the impression that reconciliation follows immediately upon this introductory rite and the exhomologesis (*inducens-indulgens*), unless, that is, Tertullian is here combining rhetorically two acts which are in fact quite distinct. In this case, it could be assumed that the repeated exhomologesis took place during the long period of penance *foris* and *in vestibulo*. Nevertheless, it is by no means clear what is meant by the *vestibulum*, from which the penitent is led into the church (or its interior): is it an area in front of the church or a place at the entrance to the church? Accordingly, the exhomologesis *in vestibulo* (De paen. 7, 10) would be identical either with the prayer to be readmitted into the church (cf. De pud. 5; 3) or with the rite within the church (De pud. 13; 18). In any case the two phases in the exhomologesis must be distinguished; all that remains obscure is which lasts the longer, that is, whether the first is only an introductory rite or the latter is only a concluding rite and, accordingly, the other has the meaning of the exhomologesis of the long period of penance.

23. Epist. 15,1; 16,2; 17,2; 18,1; 19,2; 20,3; 71,2; De lapsis 16; Sent.episcop. 8.22.

24. Thus in Origen and in the Didascalia Apostolorum still in the 3rd cent.

25. At least this difference is not very striking, although between De paen. and De pud. Tertullian changed over to Montanism.

26. For further details cf. B. Poschmann, pp. 293–300.

27. Correspondingly, the actual rite of public penance (*presbyteris advolvi, caris Dei adgeniculari, omnibus fratribus legationes deprecationis suae iniungere:* De paen. 9,4) is likewise no longer granted to those guilty of capital sins (De pud. 13), although such a penance, which, therefore, would not end in church forgiveness could no longer affect God's unique prerogative to forgive sins, once he has certainly allowed those guilty of capital sins to appear before the Church as penitents (De pud. 3,5).

28. *Hane episcopatus formam apostoli providentius condidereunt* (De fuga 13,6). In the Catholic churches there is an *ordo episcoporum ita per successionem ab initio decurrens* (De praescr. haer. 32). The question here is not whether Tertullian has done full justice to the nature of the episcopate in his ecclesiology. He does, however, testify to the existence in his time of an episcopate which had the final decision in all church questions and practice. Obedience to the bishop's teaching distinguishes Catholics from heretics (De praescr. haer. 42), the *summus sacerdos* has the right to baptize all others *non tamen sine episcopi auctoritate* (De bapt. 17). He also prepares the body and blood of the Lord and distributes them to the faithful (De idol. 7; De cor. 3); he lays down the rules for fasting (De ieiunio 13). Even the Montanists still maintain that excommunication resides *in praesidentis officio* (De

pud. 14). Tertullian draws a sharp distinction between priests and the laity; the priest is *servus maioris loci* (De fuga 11,1) as opposed to the lay person, the *servus minoris loci* (De ieiunio 13).

29. This is still the case in Tertullian's Montanist period, when he could hardly have had an interest in stressing the role of the bishop (De pud. 14). He leaves to the bishop *disciplinae solius officia* (De pud. 21,6). Cf. also Adv.Praxean 1, where the bishop of Rome refuses the *litterae pacis* to the Montanist communities in Asia and Phrygia.

30. Also here what is important is only the fact and not the theological justification which Tertullian gives of this *ius* of the *summus sacerdos*.

31. De pud. 1; 13; 21. At the same time, the bishop of Carthage is otherwise constantly singled out and attacked as an adversary.

32. On Origen cf. 'The Penitential Teaching of Origen' in this volume. On Augustine cf. B. Poschmann, 'Die kirchliche Vermittlung der Sündenvergebung nach Augustin' in ZKTh 45 (1921), pp. 208–28; 405–32; 497–526 (esp. 413–20).

33. Thus it becomes the Spirit of the Church, which it was not previously, so that there was not yet an actual sacrament in the New Testament sense.

34. Naturally there are in general more practically important reasons for this form in the case of the sacrament of penance than in the case of the Eucharist.

35. Cf. De paen. 2,6. A man must be purified already before baptism. This penance before baptism is a *satisfacere* (De paen. 5,9; De pud. 9). It is *pretium* for the *merces* of the baptismal grace (De paen. 6,4); it is *compensatio* for the remission of the punishment due to sin (ibid.). Despite Poschmann's claim (p. 288 n. 1), Galtier, *L'église et la rémission des péchés* (Paris 1932), p. 51 f., was right on this point. The penance which Tertullian demanded before baptism may certainly be identical in some respects with the renunciation of sin and the exercise of Christian virtue (De paen. 6,1), and to this extent it is essentially less in evidence than penance for sins after baptism. This difference may be explained simply by the fact that for Tertullian the sins of a baptized Christian are by far the more serious (De paen. 7,12). Nevertheless, the effect of penance before baptism on sins and their punishment is described in such a way that it is difficult to consider it as a mere condition for the remission of sins which occurs at baptism, and only at baptism. Indeed, in De paen. 2,6 the relationship seems to be presented in such a way that it is the penance that remits the sins, while baptism subsequently admits the Holy Spirit into the soul which has already been purified for its dwelling. Similarly in De bapt. 6: the *ablutio delictorum* is granted through faith, and thus the way is opened for the *superventurus Spiritus sanctus*. According to De bapt. 13 baptism appears almost as a mere form and *external covering* of faith, legally prescribed in the New Testament period. It is really faith that effects salvation, even if this is no longer without its legal form in which it must be professed. Likewise in De paen. 6,17: the neophytes must come to baptism *corde iam loti*. This idea contradicts the affirmation of De paen. 6,9, in so far as there the unrepentant neophyte receives through baptism (if this happens to be administered to him) not only the Holy Spirit (which is conceivable in view of an obscure idea of the relationship between freedom from sin and possession of the Spirit) but also the *abolitio delictorum*. All this only shows that in Tertullian baptism does not evince a clear relationship between the subjective and the sacramental factors, and that it would be fatuous to attempt to clarify this obscurity at any cost. It is possible to discern a Montanistic way of thinking in this 'subjectivism' (cf. K. Adam, *Der Kirchenbegriff Tertullians* [Paderborn 1907], pp. 111 ff., 219 ff.). But, in the final analysis, such ideas have their origin in the biblical and Catholic understanding that the sacrament does not replace or supplement man's interior act which he makes in faith and penance, but that both—each in its own dimension—can and must contribute to the

proper relationship between man and God in grace. This is not to deny that Tertullian expresses the teaching which was already at least intimated before him by Hermas and later clearly attested that in the *paenitentia secunda* subjective penance plays a more important role than in baptism. It appears also in a somewhat exaggerated form in De pud. 10 to be contradicted by Tertullian. But this difference is not so great and clear as totally to obscure the sacramental nature of the *paenitentia secunda* as opposed to baptism, as if, in Tertullian's view, the latter were only an *opus operatum*, while the former were only an *opus operantis*. In both cases the effect of grace is ascribed freely now to the one, now to the other of the two concurrent factors, in the case of baptism more often and more explicitly to the sacramental aspect, in the *paenitentia secunda* more to the subjective aspect. Later theology will have the task of uniting both aspects in such a way that they both make their full contribution, while, at the same time, preserving the traditional distinction between baptism and post-baptismal penance.

Finally, in the historical interpretation of the penitential teaching of this time (for example in Cyprian too) we have to reckon, more than we have previously done, with the fact that remission of sin through penance and re-acquisition of the Spirit were not, for the theology of that time, so obviously one and the same event, but could be understood as two distinct and temporally separate events. If, in these circumstances, the remission of sins occurs through subjective penance (alone), this does not mean that the communication of the Spirit as such cannot be envisaged, even according to this theology, as being made through the imposition of hands at reconciliation or through the baptism of water. Cf., with regard to Origen, the corresponding essay in this volume.

36. Cf. K. Adam, *Der Kirchenbegriff Tertullians* (Paderborn 1907).

37. De cultu feminarum II,1; De pat. 15; Ad mart. 1; De paen. 6,12 f.; 7,11; De pud. 9; 22, etc.

38. The members of the community are often implored, as in De paen., to join in an intercession. The Christ who is presented as *exorator patris* in De pud. 19 is doubtless meant to be the one who is praying to the Father through the Church. Thus if he does not pray in the case of certain sins (De pud. 19), neither can the Church pray for the sinners in question (De pud. 19; 2). But if the Church-Christ prays (cf. De paen. 10,6), then the prayer is heard.

39. The bishop preaches on the occasion of the reconciliation of penitents (cf. De pud. 13). This would provide the opportunity not only for a repudiation of those who contest penance but also to provoke reflection upon what has just happened. Given this, why was more attention given to the parable of the lost sheep (De pud. 13) than to Matt. 16:18 (De pud. 21)? Neither of these texts says anything explicitly about the extent of the possibility of the forgiveness of sins by the Church. Thus Matt. 16:18 could hardly be adduced simply in view of this question. In fact a decision on the extent of possible sins which could be remitted by church penance need not necessarily be reached in the Catholic sense only by stressing the *potestas donandi delicta* (the Catholics could just as easily have said: the Church can and ought to pray in the case of all sins). Thus it is not easy to see why this theory of absolution had its origin only in the Montanist controversy. Much less is it possible to hold, with Poschmann (p. 345), that Tertullian invented this theory 'in order to be able to challenge more effectively this "power" claimed by the officials of the Church'. Indeed, the Catholics themselves often appealed to Matt. 16. If they say, according to De pud. 21: *sed habet potestatem ecclesia delicta donandi*, and Tertullian 'expects' this objection 'as self-evident' (Poschmann), this objection being formulated precisely in the terms of the second theory, then Tertullian cannot be the inventor of this theory. He would have found it easier to contest the forgivable character of sins of impurity if he had not had

to contend with this theory. Nevertheless, granted that it already existed and, therefore, had to be contested, it is quite possible that he, for his part, presented it in a very much accentuated form, so that he could contest it the more easily. Poschmann considers that this *potestas* is conceivable only if it coincides directly with forgiveness by God, which as such is possible only in a prophet who is immediately inspired by God. Accordingly, the whole notion must originate in Tertullian's spiritual view of the Church. But the power in question need not necessarily be viewed in this way; Tertullian's explanation could be a polemical artifice on his part. This does not mean, however, that the Catholics, for their part, did not claim that they could forgive sins 'in the name' or 'in the power' of God.

40. God has in fact promised the Church that he will hear it.

41. Cf. the analogy with baptism according to De paen. 6,10.

42. Following de la Taille and Xiberta, this view is still defended in modern theology by B. Poschmann, 'Die innere Structur des Busssakraments' in: MThZ 1 (1950) no. 3, pp. 12–31.

43. Cf. De bapt. 4: *supervenit enim statim spiritus de coelis et aquis superest sanctificans eas de semetipso et ita sanctificatae vim sanctificandi combibunt.*

44. Cf. K. Adam, *Der Kirchenbegriff Tertullians* (Paderborn 1907), pp. 88–95; J. C. Plumpe, *Mater Ecclesia. An Inquiry into the Church as Mother in Early Christianity* (Washington 1943), pp. 45–62.

45. Cf. K. Adam, p. 89.

46. This is still the case with Cyprian, whereas with Origen it is different. In Origen subjective penance appears to be the expression of the grace of the interior, purifying fire of judgement. Cf. the author's relevant essay in this volume.

47. Hans v. Campenhausen, p. 249 n. 2, interprets this passage differently, referring the *in uno et altero* to the members of the community who have 'remained holy'. But he does not justify this interpretation.

48. According to Thomas the acts of the penitent are an interior part of the essential matter of the sacrament itself. Indeed, for him they are the more self-evident part, so that all that he has actually to prove is that the priestly absolution as such contributes effectively to the remission of sins. On the whole, even where Thomistic terminology is maintained, the Scotist view has prevailed: the action of the penitent is still only a precondition and no longer an essential part of the sacrament.

CHAPTER SIX: THE PENITENTIAL TEACHING OF CYPRIAN OF CARTHAGE

1. The original form of this revised essay appeared in ZKTh 74 (1952), pp. 257–76, 381–438.

2. A list of the most important works up to 1940 will be found in B. Poschmann, *Paenitentia Secunda* (Bonn 1940), p. 369. Poschmann himself (pp. 368–424) provides the most precise presentation of the history of the penitential question during the persecution of Decius and in Cyprian's theology of penance up to that time. Later works: J. Köhne, 'Zur Frage der Busse im christlichen Altertum' in: ThGl 35 (1943), pp. 26–36; G. H. Joyce, 'Private Penance in the Early Church' in: JThS 42 (1941), pp. 18–42 (for Tertullian, Cyprian, Origen); J. H. Taylor, 'St. Cyprian and the Reconciliation of Apostates' in: ThSt 3 (1942), pp. 27–46; F. de Saint-Palais d'Aussac, *La réconciliation des hérétiques dans l'Eglise latine* (Paris 1943); J. Grotz, *Die Entwicklung des Bussstufenwesens in der vornicänischen Kirche* (Freiburg/Br. 1955), pp. 73–171; S. Hübner, 'Kirchenbusse und Excommunication bei Cyprian' in: ZKTh 84

(1962), pp. 49–84, 171–215; B. Altaner/A. Stuiber, *Patrologie* (Freiburg/Br. 1966), p. 180; K. Baus, *Von der Urgemeinde zur frühchristliche Grosskirche* (HdKG I) (Freiburg/Br. 1962), pp. 373–6; J. Quasten, *Patrology* II (Utrecht 1953), pp. 380–1; H. von Campenhausen, *Kirchliches Amt und geistliche Vollmacht in den ersten drei Jahrhunderten* (Tübingen 1963), pp. 310–18.

3. Cf. 'Tertullian's Theology of Penance' in this volume.

4. These stages are to be understood differently from those which J. Grotz describes with the expression 'stages of penance'. In his study J. Grotz draws a distinction between a purely canonical stage prior to the actual church penance, the so-called penance of satisfaction, which was to be performed outside the community of the Church, and the actual sacramental penance ('exhomologesis'), the 'actual church penance', which was to be performed essentially within the community. Between the two Grotz inserts the place of the *communicatio,* which is not the conclusion of church penance but the prerequisite for its beginning in the proper sense. Thus, according to Grotz, the *communicatio* is quite different from the *pax* which was granted only at the end of the penitential process. This thesis is contested above all by S. Hübner, who gives a precise analysis of the basic ideas in Cyprian's theology of penance.

5. Cf. Epist. 15,1; 16,2; 17,2; 59,13; De lapsis 16.

6. Cf. De lapsis 24.30.35 etc.

7. This is not made sufficiently clear in J. Grotz, p. 73 ff. On this cf. S. Hübner, p. 71 ff.

8. It is precisely this strict, technical sense of 'exhomologesis' that J. Grotz ought to have considered. Nevertheless, he derives (p. 132 ff.) his understanding only from the interpretation of this notion in the wide, general sense, as it is found in B. Poschmann and others.

9. Contrary to the view of J. Grotz, according to which the original meaning of 'exhomologesis', 'confession', must have been that of today's confession. It is then only gradually that this notion developed to become church penance in the strict sense.

10. Cf. also Epist. 30,8, where in the case of Rome a *professa frequenter . . . detestatio factorum* is presupposed in the penitent. This must refer to the time prior to his illness.

11. H. Koch, *Cyprianische Untersuchungen* (Bonn 1926), p. 280.

12. According to Epist. 4,4 and De lapsis 28, a secret sin of thought, by which a person toyed with the idea of renouncing his faith, was not necessarily exempted from church penance.

13. Sponsors are already attested in Tertullian and certainly do not pertain primarily to the baptism of infants (cf. De bapt. 18). In any event, before Cyprian in the Paradosis of Hippolytus there is clear evidence of the custom that a Christian had to verify that the neophyte had led a life according to the principles of Christianity during the time of his catechumenate. Cf. E. Dick, 'Das Pateninstitut im altchristlichen Katechumenat' in: ZKTh 63 (1939), pp. 1–49. In view of Cyprian's demand that the confessors should carefully examine penitents with regard to the kind and gravity of their guilt, their seriousness to do penance, the length of their penance, etc. before recommending them to the bishop for reconciliation (Epist. 15,3), it is probable that competent witnesses like the confessors were employed at the exhomologesis to ascertain that the penance had actually been done (cf. Epist. 26). This would be analogous with the questioning of witnesses from the clergy and the people about the worthiness of a candidate for ordination (Epist. 38,1).

14. The designation of the imposition of the hand as a 'rite of reconciliation' ought in no way to predetermine its meaning. It merely expresses the fact that after this last

penitential act the penitent is once more allowed access to the Eucharist as a complete Christian. It is not yet decided whether the imposition of the hand is only the last penitential act or the solemn juridical granting of the *pax*. The *manus impositio* always had to be performed by the imposition of the right hand, since *manus* is always used in the singular. Cf. for example B. J. Bohm, *Die Handauflegung im Urchristentum* (Leipzig 1911), pp. 82, n.1; 87, n.; 98 f. J. A. Jungmann, *Die lateinischen Bussriten* (Innsbruck 1932), p. 36.

15. Origen here inserts into the passage of Jas. 5:14 the phrase *imponant ei manus* and appears to refer the text not to the anointing of the sick but to the previously clearly described penance. Cf. J. Coppens, *L'imposition des mains* (Paris 1925), p. 41 f. Cf. also the relevant details in the essay in this volume on Origen's penitential teaching.

16. Cf. P. Galtier, *Aux origines du sacrement de la pénitence* (Rome 1951), pp. 95–106.

17. Cf. Epist. 15,1; 16,2; 17,2; 18,1; 19,2; 20,3; 71,2; De lapsis 16; Sent. episc. 8.22.

18. Cf. J. Coppens, p. 377.

19. Further literature on this question: P. Galtier, 'Absolution ou Confirmation? La réconciliation des hérétiques' in: RSR 5 (1914), pp. 201–35, 339–94 (on Cyprian: 342–51), 507–44. P. Galtier, 'Imposition des mains' in: DThC VII (Paris 1923), pp. 1397–408; A. d'Alès, *La théologie de S. Cyprien* (Paris 1922), pp. 237–48; J. Coppens, *L'imposition des mains* (Paris 1922), pp. 374–92; F. de Saint-Palais d'Aussac, *La réconciliation des hérétiques dans l'Eglise latine* (Paris 1943). Galtier and Coppens contain numerous references to previous literature.

20. This connection, however, must have been much clearer in the East than in the West.

21. On these differences in the theology of Christian initiation between Paul and the Acts of the Apostles, which represented the starting-point for the difference in the theology of Confirmation between the East and the West, cf.: P. Galtier, 'La consignation à Carthage et à Rome' in: RSR 2 (1911), pp. 350–83; id., 'La consignation dans les églises d'Occident' in: RHE 13 (1912), pp. 257–301; id., 'Onction et confirmation' in: RHE 13 (1912), pp. 467–76; id., 'Imposition des mains' in: DThC VII (Paris 1923), pp. 1319–24; 1343–93; P. de Puniet, 'La liturgie baptismale en Gaule avant Charlemagne' in: RQH 28 (1902), pp. 382–423; id., 'Onction et confirmation' in: RHE 13 (1912), pp. 450–66; id., 'Confirmation' in: DACL III, pp. 2515–43; C. Ruch, 'Confirmation dans la sainte Ecriture' in: DThC III (Paris 1908), pp. 975–1026; G. Bareille, 'Confirmation d'après les Pères grecs et latins' in: DThC III (Paris 1908), pp. 1026–58; J. Coppens, *L'imposition des mains* (Paris 1925); J. B. Umberg, *Die Schriftlehre vom Sakrament der Firmung* (Freiburg/Br. 1920); J. B. Jugie, *Theologia dogmatica christianorum orientalium* III (Paris 1930), pp. 126–44; B. Welte, *Die postbaptismale Salbung* (Freiburg/Br. 1939); H. Elfers, *Die Kirchenordnung Hippolyts von Rom* (Paderborn 1938), pp. 101–60; id., 'Gehört die Salbung mit Chrisma im ältesten abendländischen Initiationsritus zur Taufe oder zur Firmung?' in: ThGl 34 (1942), pp. 334–41; D. van den Eynde, 'Notes sur les rites postbaptisnaux dans les églises d'occident' in: Antonianum 14 (1939), pp. 257–76; E. Dekkers, *Tertullianus en de geschiednis der liturgie* (Brussels/Amsterdam 1947), pp. 197–205.

22. Which originates in the first half of the third century; on the date, cf. P. Galtier, *Aux origines du sacrement de pénitence* (Rome 1951), pp. 189–221.

23. The anointing with the imposition of hands of III 12 is a pre-baptismal anointing; on this cf. 'Penitential Teaching and Practice According to the Didascalia Apostolorum' in this volume.

24. Which would be expected if it were considered a second Confirmation.

25. The person who receives the *pax* receives the Holy Spirit; cf. Epist. 57,4: *pace*

recepta recipere Spiritum Patris. This statement was made in respect of a reconciled sinner.

26. For instance, Pope Stephen, the author of De rebaptismate, and the bishops of the synod held on the subject on the controversy over the baptism of heretics on 1 September A.D. 256.

27. Cyprian, Epist. 74,1.2.3.

28. This means a reconciliation as it was practised in the case of a validly baptized and confirmed person. Thus it cannot be understood as a new Confirmation, since at that early time the rite of initiation was considered to be unrepeatable.

29. Cyprian himself does not know of a mere reconciling imposition of hands for those baptized outside the Church. Thus he can have no term to designate it.

30. This cannot be excluded in principle, since in the early Church there is no explicit statement that the imposition of hands at Confirmation, considered in itself, cannot be repeated. Such a statement is still not found in Augustine. Augustine's frequently quoted word, from his Contra litteras Petiliani Donatistae II 104.239, is not a witness for the unrepeatable character of Confirmation, since the *sacramentum chrismatis* mentioned here is the post-baptismal anointing which is not identical with Confirmation as the communication of the Spirit by a mere imposition of hands. On this cf. W. Roetzer, *Des heiligen Augustinus Schriften als litugie-geschichtliche Quelle* (Munich 1930), p. 172 f. Similarly H. Elfers, *Die Kirchenordnung Hippolyts von Rom* (Paderborn 1938), pp. 115–18, as opposed to J. Coppens, *L'imposition des mains* (Paris 1925), pp. 297–303.

31. In Cyprian the term *signari/signaculum* is a typical expression for Confirmation; cf. Epist. 73,9.

32. It still remains to be shown that Pope Stephen attributed the *remissa peccatorum* to baptism administered by heretics.

33. A. d'Alès, *La théologie de saint Cyprien* (Paris 1922), p. 246 f.

34. Obviously we cannot expect him to provide a precise and profound explanation of why the sinner or the heretic does not possess the Spirit. He is only concerned with the simple fact that it is a question of a heretic or a sinner.

35. In his opinion heretics receive the Spirit only through the penitential imposition of hands.

36. This idea of Tertullian is discernible, for example, in Cyprian too in this baptismal controversy, when he says, or his opponents present him implicitly as saying, that in baptism, as distinct from the imposition of hands, there is a forgiveness of sins, a sanctification and a spiritual renewal, by which a man is *ad accipiendum spiritum idoneus factus* (Epist. 74,5; cf. also Epist. 74,7), that is, through the following imposition of hands.

37. Even in the case of baptism he does not distinguish between an effective and a merely valid administration, but considers it to be effective because it is valid.

38. Obviously this is not to deny that in the third century there was simultaneously a trend of thought which, taken on its own, deviated from a sacramental view of the institution of penance.

39. Cf. J. A. Jungmann, *Die lateinischen Bussriten* (Innsbruck 1932), pp. 12 f., 34 f., 298 ff.

40. Augustinus, De peccat.mer. et rem. 2,26; De fide et oper. 9; Sermo 227.

41. Cf. Cyprian, Epist. 73,9; De rebaptismate 4; Council of Elvira, can. 38 and 77; DS 120 and 121; Hippolytus, Paradosis (Dix, p. 38).

42. In Epist. 16,2 and likewise in Sent.episc. 8 and 22 there is indeed mention of a *per manus impositionem . . . ius communicationis accipere*. Nevertheless, it is questionable whether Cyprian wishes to state here that the imposition of hands as such designates the formal act of absolution. In De lapsis 16 the *manus sacerdotis*, like the

sacrificium, is a means for the *pugare conscientiam.* Would the imposition of hands be designated by the *terminus technicus manus impositio in paenitentiam* (Epist. 15,1; 18,1; 19,2; 20,3; 71.1.2.3; Sent.episc. 8), if this were understood as the formal gesture of reconciliation? This does not appear as obvious as it is often thought. Moreover, full justice is not rendered to the *per* if the imposition of hands is viewed as a part of the whole rite of exhomologesis, that is, as an indispensable and sufficient condition of the access which itself occurs subsequently *via facti* without further formalities.

43. In Dionysius of Alexandria, also about the middle of the third century, reconciliation was not necessarily connected with the imposition of hands. It could also come about *via facti* through simple access to the eucharistic community (Eus.Hist. Eccl. VI 42,5.6; 44,2–6). Cf. B. Poschmann, pp. 275–9.

44. It is in this direction that Saint-Palais d'Aussac looks for a solution to the problem. We cannot here enter into an actual critical appraisal of his attempt, since we must confine our attention to Cyprian's time. Saint-Palais, however, includes the whole of the Latin Patristic literature in his research. What is more, such a discussion belongs necessarily to the study of Confirmation in the early Church from the viewpoint of the history of dogma, and thus goes beyond the bounds of a work on the history of penance. This is the decisive point: in Africa during the third century the actual rite of Confirmation is the episcopal imposition of hands and not an anointing. The literature which Saint-Palais d'Aussac did or could not use is sufficient evidence for this: H. Elfers, *Die Kirchenordnung Hippolyts von Rom* (Paderborn 1938), pp. 101–27, according to which even in Augustine's day the imposition of hands is still clearly the actual rite of Confirmation; H. Elfers, 'Gehört die Salbung mit Chrisma im ältesten abendländischen Initiationsritus zur Taufe oder zur Firmung?' in: ThGl 34 (1942), pp. 334–41; E. Dekkers, *Tertullianus en de geschiednis der liturgie* (Brussels/Amsterdam 1947), pp. 197–204. Cf. also W. Roetzer, *Des heilgen Augustinus Schriften als liturgie-geschichtliche Quelle* (Munich 1930), p. 171 ff.

45. F. Saint-Palais d'Aussac, *La réconciliation des hérétiques dans l'Eglise latine* (Paris 1943).

46. Further evidence in Cyprian: *cottidie delinquimus* (De dom.or. 12); *instruitur et docetur peccare se cottidie, dum cottidie pro peccatis iubetur orare* (De dom.or. 22); cf. also Test. III 54.

47. In his general exhortation on the subject of the remission of sins, De op. et eleem., Cyprian does not understand sin as serious in today's sense.

48. The *operatio,* that is, the simple good 'work' as opposed to the 'words' of prayer, is, strictly speaking, a *terminus technicus* in Tertullian for fasting which is accompanied and supported by prayer. Cf. Tertullian, De or. 18; De ieiunio 4.8.9.13; on this see J. Schümmer, *Die altchristliche Fastenpraxis* (Münster 1933), pp. 78, 174, 224 n.82, 225. By *operatio* (*opera, operari*) Cyprian appears to understand principally almsgiving. Cf. De or. 32: fasting and almsgiving; De lapsis 35: *largiter fiat operatio* and the other passages (CSL 3,3; 440–1). Shortly after Cyprian the Church organized, on a great scale as it were, private penance for daily sins by means of fasting and prayer: the forty days' period of fasting. Originally, this was not an actual preparation for Easter and thus ought not to be confused with the more ancient Passover fast, even if it was placed in the period before Easter and before the actual Passover fast. With the fourth century the observation of Quadragesima becomes established as a penitential fast for all Christians. Thus when later actual church penance draws on this practice, this is fully in keeping with the earlier sense of this penitential fast for all Christians. Cf. Schümmer, op. cit., pp. 201–3. Obviously already in the second and third centuries there were individual ecclesiastical fast days, more or less obligatory, which represented the early Church's 'confessions of devotion'. It was in this way that the Church took care of the *iugis et assidua operatio* of the private penance for

the daily sins of Christians. Such occasions would be the partial fasts of the stations, the Friday fasts, fasting on Saturday.

49. The *semel* (De op. et eleem. 2) can be referred not only to the *in baptismo* but must also apply to the *remissa peccatorum.* In other words it is intended as a fundamental contrast to *iugis operatio* and, therefore, should be rendered by 'only once'. Now stress on the once-and-for-all character of the actual baptismal rite would be out of place in this context. What is meaningful here, however, is the insistence that there is only one, single *remissa,* that is, a once and for all, gratuitous and complete forgiveness of sins, granted independently of personal penance. After this there is only a personal expiation of sins by means of the *iugis operatio.* This is clear from the fact that in the same context the necessity of a personal penance for sins committed after baptism is called for and inculcated and the scriptural texts cited (Prov. 16:6 = 15:27; Sir. 3:30) are referred to this penance and not to baptism.

50. As opposed to J. Grotz, who (p. 102 ff.) says that Cyprian designates the forgiveness of sins both in baptism and in penance as *remissio.* (For more details on the terminology involved see n.52.)

51. The relevant text is in A. d'Alès, *L'édit de Calliste* (Paris 1914), pp. 233–4. *Remissa(-io)* is applied to baptism about thirty times.

52. Epist. 59,16 (*remitto omnia*) does not belong to our present discussion. It is here a question of the 'permission' of the access of all men to church penance and of the fixing and curtailing of the periods of penance. It is, therefore, not a question of the 'remission' of sins as such. The *delictis remittendis* (ibid.) is, accordingly, to be understood in the same context. In De lapsis 18 a *remissio peccatorum* with *praepopera festinatio,* that is, without the demand for and the observance of a long period of penance on the sinner's part, is rejected twice. Thus it is doubtful whether the remission of sins which Cyprian promises to those who perform this penance can still be styled *remissa.* The text itself does not provide an answer to this question; and in the light of Cyprian's usual terminology it should be answered in the negative. The same applies to Epist. 27,3, where Cyprian says that an imprudent martyr is demanding for his clients a *pacem dari et peccata dimitti,* and this precisely without their having to do church penance. Here too it is doubtful whether the granting of the *pax* after a full church penance would be described as a *remissa.* In this case, the question is to be answered in the negative not only from Cyprian's general terminology but also by a consideration of the context of the text itself. In fact in the martyrs' letters of freedom all that is found is the request for the *pacem dare;* this is always demanded in the *libelli* (Epist. 19,2; 22,2; 23; 26; 27,3; 35). If Cyprian, interpreting this, inserts a *peccata dimitti,* this is only to emphasize the abuse of such a *libelli pacis.* For such a request refers to a *peccata dimitti* which is possible only in baptism. It includes necessarily a remission of sins without penance, as this occurs in baptism. Thus Cyprian implies that the remission of sins which he still considers possible is not a simple *dimitti,* is not a *remissa.* That is why he opposes the request of the martyr Paul to baptism. Only as a request for a *remissa* could it be said logically to occur *in Pauli nomine,* because it does not happen in the name of Christ, who achieves a full *remissa* only in baptism. It is obvious that such a *remissa* does not occur either by the sinner's personal penance. Thus the contrast with baptism is not only in the sense underlined by P. Galtier, *L'église et la rémission des péchés aux premiers siècles* (Paris 1932), p. 38 f. In Epist. 21,3 there is a mention of a *remittere peccatum* through the martyrs. Here, however, it is a question of their intercession in the next life, that is, at the last judgement (De lapsis 17). Thus this passage is not relevant to the question of a *remittere* in this life. The only text remaining then is De lapsis 29: *satisfactio et remissio facta per sacerdotes.* It will be shown later that the *per sacerdotes Dei* refers also to *satisfactio.* Thus this passage concerns only a post-baptismal *remissio* which

occurs essentially on the basis of the *satisfactio*. With this clear stress that here we have a restricted meaning of a term which is generally used in another sense, Cyprian was able to use the notion of *remissio* once without being afraid of causing a misunderstanding about the specific and strict sense of this term. J. Grotz does not enter into considerations of this kind. For example (p. 106 ff.) he does not see any essential difference between the forgiveness of sins in baptism and that of church penance. On this cf. S. Hübner, pp. 201–5.

53. If it is a fact that Cyprian uses and can only use the notion of *remissa* (*-io; remittere*) in the sense of the actual forgiveness of sins only in the case of baptism, then this negative conclusion also has a positive aspect. Cyprian certainly recognizes a forgiveness of sins committed after baptism. If this forgiveness in his view is not a *remissa* then it must be distinguished from the *remissa* only in the way that Cyprian himself repeatedly stresses: the post-baptismal forgiveness is granted only to the *assidua et iugis operatio* (De op. et eleem. 2), the *longa et continua satisfactio* (Epist. 43,2). This is what makes it different from the forgiveness of sins in baptism. Thus if Cyprian (Firmilian) refuses to admit that a bishop can grant a *remissio* (*remittere*) of sins committed after baptism (Epist. 75,4; De lapsis 17), what is meant and rejected is the *remissa* without a *longa continua satisfactio*.

54. Neither does Cyprian grant reconciliation on the death-bed to everyone who asks for it; cf. Epist. 30,8 and Epist. 18,1.

55. Cf. ThRv 32 (1933), pp. 259–67 (esp. 262).

56. H. Koch, *Cyprianische Untersuchungen* (Bonn 1926), p. 275, sees in the principle that sin is remitted only when the punishment incurred has been fully carried out an influence of Stoicism on Cyprian. This is probably not totally unjustified, since it is a Stoic notion that punishment should not be remitted but carried out (cf. the evidence in H. Koch, p. 274). Nevertheless, it must be borne in mind that in the case of a forgiveness of the *aeterna supplicia* (De lapsis 7) by God there can be no question of a full performance of penance. Moreover, Cyprian speaks here about God's 'mercy' as a necessary condition of the *venia*, which directly contradicts the Stoic principle *neminem misericordem esse nisi stultum et levem* (Cicero, Pro Murena 29,61). Nevertheless, it is not clear in the Bishop of Carthage that Christian penance itself, which expiates the punishments of sin, is actually a grace of God, and this in the sense that a simple 'remission' of 'punishment' (in the sense of a mere cancellation) would be no greater grace and, consequently, no more complete a *venia*.

57. Also the misuse of temporal goods (De hab. virg. 11), deceit and fornication are sins against God (Epist. 55,27). *Moechia* is a more serious sin than that of the *libellaticus* (Epist. 55,26). Also insubordination with regard to the authority of the Church is apparently considered by Cyprian a sin against God, as his hesitation concerning the forgiveness of this sin shows (Epist. 66,9). The author of De aleatoribus (*c.* A.D. 300) also considers fornication a *delictum in Deum* (De aleator. 10). In practice it is not possible to distinguish between sins against God and other faults, nor is this seriously envisaged. What is stressed is the seriousness of the sin and not how it differs essentially from other sins.

58. It is not legitimate to deduce from this distinction that there is an objective difference in the penitential process, as if Cyprian would have known that he could forgive authoritatively sins *non in Deum* differently from offences *in Deum* (contrary to B. Poschmann, p. 422). If the penitential process was completely identical and even the *iustum tempus* of penance was prescribed for the *delicta quae non in Deum committuntur,* if included among the sins remitted in this way there is, for example, *moechia,* which elsewhere is characterized as *in Deum* and is comparatively more serious than the sins of certain *lapsi,* then it can hardly be supposed that Cyprian was convinced that he remitted these sins 'of his own authority'. Epist. 17,2 (see also

Epist. 59,1) describes some offences as *non in Deum* only by comparison with other sins, in the terms of an *argumentum ad hominem*. This is to show that the *lapsi*, more than any others, must do church penance. This argument is valid, even without the distinction in question (cf. Epist. 16,2). De lapsis 17 speaks about *peccata in Deum commissa* only to show that God alone can forgive them because (not: in so far as) they have been committed 'against God'. Both the notion and the use to which it is put in the argument preserve their meaning, even if there are no other sins besides those committed *in Deum*. What is more, there is no mention here either of another means of forgiveness nor of sins *non in Deum*.

59. If penance brings about a return to 'life', then this must certainly be understood from the point of view of grace and not only from the moral and eschatological viewpoints (Epist. 55,22). The return to life is seen as analogous to the liberation from death in baptism.

60. *Venia*, with the sense of 'remission', is a very frequent expression in Cyprian. It means essentially 'remission of punishment', as Seneca had already defined it: *venia est poenae meritae remissio* (De clem. II 7,1). Hosius (Teubner 1914), p. 250.

61. Contrary to J. Grotz, p. 106 f. There the 'exhomologesis' is only an act by which the Church pronounces its sacramental word of forgiveness, through which God forgives all guilt. The exhomologesis does not, however, have the role of readmitting the sinner to the community of the Church.

62. This would be logically impossible for Cyprian, since he rejects the notion of a baptism which is valid but fruitless from the point of view of grace.

63. It could be said in the first place that Cyprian condemns the reception of the Eucharist after an unrepented sin as sacrilegious. Nevertheless, in the whole of his polemic against the presumption of the *lapsi* he presupposes as the only obvious 'sorrow' that which as church penance is finally confirmed by the *pax* and *communicatio*. Thus the sin which is not yet forgiven by the Church excludes from the Eucharist. Without *pax* with the Church, a person is, according to 1 Cor. 11:27, *eo ipso* unworthy of the Eucharist. This is Cyprian's basic and enduring idea. It applies explicitly also to sins which remain secret. This exclusion must derive, therefore, not from an official excommunication (*ferendae sententiae*) but only from the sin itself. It would be purely arbitrary to postulate here as it were the implicit remission of a general merely church excommunication *latae sententiae*. For Cyprian it is the law *iuris divini* that normally only the sinner who has been absolved by the Church should approach the Eucharist.

64. Cf. Epist. 55,14: the situation of the *libellatici*; Epist. 55,13; De lapsis 13: different cases of *sacrificati*; Epist. 52,2: Novatian is worse than a *sacrificatus*; De lapsis 25: the secret 'sin' of an infant; Epist. 55,26: a *moechus* is worse than a *libellaticus*.

65. This applies particularly to virgins consecrated to God; cf. Epist. 4,4.

66. This point is clearly stressed in recent publications; cf. K. Baus, p. 375; J. Quasten, p. 380 f.; H. von Campenausen, p. 310 f.

67. Cf. in this chapter under II 5,b: 'The Effect of the Reconciliation by the Church'.

68. Actual membership of the Church is so necessary for salvation that even a martyr who is an unreconciled *lapsus coronari in morte non poterit* (Epist. 55,17). This rigoristic viewpoint necessarily rejects the notion that baptism of desire and 'perfect contrition' are sufficient for salvation, even in a case of necessity. It is not clear how it is compatible with the possibility which Cyprian himself proclaims, namely, that even a person who is exteriorly separated from the Church *cor tamen . . . semper in Ecclesia fuit* (Epist. 49,2). The contention of A. d'Alès, *La théologie de S. Cyprien* (Paris 1922), that Cyprian recognized a baptism of desire is, however, incorrect. Although he is familiar with a baptism of blood for catechumens (Epist.

73,22), the only evidence for a baptism of desire is Epist. 73,23, where he dares not refuse salvation to heretics who are *simpliciter admissi in Ecclesia* without baptism, since they, contrary to his principle, have not been (re-)baptized. Similarly Firmilian, Epist. 75,21. But this is only a reluctant concession to practice which does not give rise to considerations of principle. He makes this concession, because otherwise the loss of salvation for such heretics by birth, who had been simply reconciled without baptism, would represent a very 'existential' argument against his own teaching in the controversy over the baptism of heretics.

69. Contrary to J. Grotz, p. 156 ff., who makes a clear distinction between *communicatio* and *pax,* with regard both to their exterior position in the penitential process and their effects. In this view *communicatio* is a purely canonical act which introduces the 'actual church penance' (the exhomologesis). *Pax,* on the other hand, is a purely gratuitous interior event bringing about the forgiveness of sins at the conclusion of the whole penitential process. For details on this point see S.Hübner, pp. 195–201. This is obviously not to deny that the Church's rite of *pax* communicates the Spirit. However, it remains an act of the Church; cf. the further details on this point in this essay.

70. This statement is not made in itself and directly of God's behaviour as opposed to his action in baptism. *Quae in ipsum commissa sunt* in this context can be very well translated: 'because (not: in so far as—somewhat in contrast to other sins) they are directed against God'. It should not be inferred from this statement, therefore, that there are other actual sins which are to be forgiven either by the Church or by man more or less on their own authority, either in baptism, since they were committed before baptism, or afterwards, and this because they were not committed *in Deum.* All that this statement wishes to show is that a forgiveness of God is necessary for these sins. This leads to the idea that man must do something to obtain this pardon. This is the purpose of Cyprian's reasoning in De lapsis. Obviously this enterprise presupposes that there is no longer a *remissa peccatorum* as in baptism. But, once this is granted, it is clear that man must propitiate God only through his own *satisfactio* if he wishes, despite the *semel* applying to baptism, to obtain forgiveness for his further sins.

71. For the meaning of this expression, cf. Epist. 54,3: *esse non potest maior domino suo servus;* and yet that is precisely what the servant wished to be when he wanted to separate carefully the wheat from the cockle in the Church. Thus laxity can be presumption just as much as rigorism.

72. At least the negative part of this statement agrees entirely with De lapsis 17, etc. The view that the positive part must describe fully and adequately the priestly activity would give too much importance to the text. For, leaving aside the activity of reconciliation as such, as it is attested by Cyprian, there is, in any case, no mention in the positive part of the statement of the priestly intercession for the penitents by prayer and sacrifice. Yet this figures explicitly and frequently in Cyprian. With regard to De lapsis 17, etc., P. Galtier, *L'église et la rémission des péchés* (Paris 1932), p. 43 ff.; and in RHE 30 (1934), p. 532 ff., goes too far when he wishes to relate the text to general synodal regulations concerning penance, according to which obviously not every individual sinner received the forgiveness of his sins through bishops.

73. In Epist. 73,7, for example, the subject of the *remissam peccatorum dare* at baptism is explicitly the Church in its *praepositi.* This is confirmed by the explanation in Epist. 75,4

74. *Satisfactio* (*satisfacere*) is undoubtedly the most characteristic notion which Cyprian uses to describe this operation. Alongside and after *paenitentia* it appears most frequently and describes in the best way possible the activity of the penitent and its effect. The actual requirements of *satisfactio* are comprehensively enumerated in

De lapsis 35. For the recurrence of the word, cf. CSL 3,1: 227,11; 247,9; 248,1; 249,25; 258,16.19.22; 260,2.7.25; 262,7.8; 263,27; 264,6; CSL 3,2: 516,11; 518,15; 567,2; 592,4.18; 594,16; 597,1; 631,22,24; 632,5; 644,16; 646,4.10.11; 680,7.18; 681,15; 683,2.8; 686,11.21.24; 688,9; 717,10.14; 722,1; 725,13; 733,20; 812,28. Apart from making amends, that is, actual works of penance, *satisfactio* can also mean the result of these efforts. Cf. Epist. 15,4: *paenitentia satisfactioni proxima,* that is, a penance which has almost obtained reconciliation with God, so that the intercession of the martyrs is now really able to supply the rest.

75. At least in Epist. 30,3; 31.6.7 this image shows that penance was not experienced merely as the removal of a punishment which had been imposed juridically from without, and that it cannot be expected to end without an interior healing and a restoration of complete moral health. This is an indication, therefore, that at that time satisfaction cannot have been the only and comprehensive means of removing guilt. In fact the two letters quoted are not both by Cyprian himself. The same image with the same conceptual background is found also in Tertullian, De paen. 7,13; Didascalia Apostolorum II 41,3–9.

76. Cf. A. d'Alès, *La théologie de S.Cyprien* (Paris 1922), pp. 33–5. Nevertheless, this explanation of Cyprian's eschatology is not very clear, either terminologically or objectively. The question needs to be investigated afresh. Cyprian seems to distinguish between paradise and *regnum coelorum,* between the immediate fate of the martyrs and that of the rest of the righteous. But in Ad Fortunatum 13 even the martyr is offered only the prospect of paradise.

77. This *domino reservari* which is stated with regard to the repentant and reconciled sinner (Epist. 55,29; 55,19) means, on the one hand, the refusal of a *praeiudicare Domino* (Epist. 55,18) on the question of whether he will find the sinner's penance *plena et iusta* or revoke the *sententia servorum.* On the other hand, the phrase has the nuance of 'preservation' and 'protection'. The repentant and reconciled sinner is 'protected' by his penance and the community of grace that is the Church both from a further fall and from the condemning judgement of God. For this use of the term, cf. Epist. 55,22: . . . *Dei . . . punientis ut corrigat et cum correxerit reservantis*; Test. III 57: *fidelem emendari et reservari* (cf. further the biblical passages quoted as an explanation of the meaning: *morti non tradere, misericordiam non avertere, emundare.* Similarly De op. et eleem. I.

78. At least in the ideal case reconciliation presupposes the conviction that the penance done has satisfied divine justice, that is, that the *paenitentia* can even be *plena* (De lapsis 16; Epist. 55,18). Nevertheless, in practice almost all cases of reconciliation, at least where the *lapsi* are concerned, arise out of other considerations which always militate to some extent against this principle. Illness, the *necessitas temporum,* the threat of another persecution, etc. mostly play a role. Practically the only case in which Cyprian sees evidence for the complete performance of penance is that of an erstwhile *lapsus* who becomes a martyr or even a confessor (cf. De lapsis 13; 36; Epist. 19,2; 24–5; 55,4.7; 60,2). The unique cautious exception is the case in Epist. 56,1–3.

79. Contrary to J. Grotz, p. 106 ff. According to him, Cyprian holds that the forgiveness of sins takes place not only at the last judgement but immediately at reconciliation. Merely from the point of view of the language which Cyprian uses, this position does not appear to be tenable, cf. n.77, as well as S. Hübner, p. 206.

80. Moreover, the *paenitentiae fructus* is always the peace with the Church (Epist. 55,29).

81. Thus this word occurs five times in De lapsis 36; it is found once in Epist. 57,1. In De lapsis 17 *potest* has a present sense.

82. This is clearly expressed in Epist. 57,1. When it is stated there: . . . *et legem*

dederit ut ligata in terris et in coelis ligata essent, solvi autem possent, quae hic prius in Ecclesia solverentur, it is not a question of an *'audacieuse atténuation du texte biblique'*, cf. Capelle in: RThAM 7 (1935), p. 233. Since it must necessarily have been done consciously, it can hardly be ascribed to Cyprian without a precise proof. Rather it is here a question of a formulation which Cyprian was unable to avoid, since he introduces an element of time in the biblical statement (*prius—illic*). Thus he can hardly write: *ut . . . solverentur autem, quae . . . in Ecclesia solverentur.* What he wants to say is that the heavenly loosing will occur at the future judgement. The *possent* is only a substitute for the future tense which does not exist. Cf. *habere* with the infinitive as a substitute for the future in Cyprian: CSL 3,3:429; Bardenhewer II 457. For *posse* with the infinitive, particularly in the passive, as a circumlocution of the future passive in Latin, cf. Stolz-Schmalz, *Lateinische Grammatik,* newly rev. by M. Leumann and J. B. Hofmann (Munich 1928), p. 557, with examples and further bibliography. The last chapter of De lapsis obviously wishes to end on an optimistic note (. . . *nec solam iam Dei veniam merebitur sed coronam*). Thus, with its five-fold *potest* it surely wishes to inculcate not uncertainty of the divine forgiveness but its real possibility. This meaning is clearly underlined by reference to the biblical passages Isa. 30:15; Ezek. 33:11; Joel 2:13. That Cyprian reckons on a certain forgiveness in the next life, provided the necessary conditions have been fulfilled, as opposed to Tertullian as a Montanist, is clear, for example, from Epist. 16,2: . . . *possunt agentes paenitentiam veram Deo qua patri et misericordi . . . satisfacere . . . erigere se possunt.* It is certain that there are confessors who have already expiated their fault throughout their life and have become free from *omne delictum* because of their confession. But this is not obvious from the theological viewpoint (Epist. 25). Cyprian's protest against the premature reconciliation of the priest Victor *antequam paenitentiam plenam egisset et Domino . . . satisfecisset* (Epist. 64,1) obviously presupposes an actual *paenitentia plena* which satisfies God. The statement of De lapsis 18: *ante est ut sciamus illos* (*lapsos*) *de Domino impetrasse quod postulant, tunc facere quod* (*martyres*) *mandant,* presupposes a point of time when the request of the confessors that the *lapsi* should be granted peace with the Church is fulfilled. But this means that they have previously received this peace from God in forgiveness. This is not contradicted by the view that it is only at the last judgement that it will be clearly decided whether all this is really valid. Before this judgement there can be only a moral certainty whether the penance is adequate. In any event God's fundamental readiness to forgive is here taken for granted. This is demonstrated in Epist. 55,22–3: *quod utique ad paenitentiam Dominus non hortaretur, nisi quia paenitentibus indulgentiam pollicetur . . . nec iram paenitentibus . . . sed veniam magis et indulgentiam pollicetur.*

83. This will be shown more clearly when we consider the meaning of church reconciliation.

84. In his view the remission of sin is attached absolutely to the remission of the punishment due to sin, which is quite different from our modern view.

85. The variant *patientia* of the Codex Baluzianus and several older editions before Hartel must, in view of the witness of the other codices, be considered an error.

86. Cf. Melito, Fragm. 12 (Otto IX 418); Hermas, Mand. IV 3,1; Tertullian, De bapt. 15; De paen. 7,10; De pud. 18,15; Clemens Alex., Paedag. I 6,29,5—30,1; Hippolyt, Philosoph. VI 41,2 f.; Origen, Exhort. ad mart. 30; Didasc. Apost. VI,12,2. As is generally known, the ἓν βάπτισμα εἰς ἄφεσιν τῶν ἁμαρτιῶν is explicitly confessed later in the Eastern symbols (cf. Hahn, *Bibliothek der Symbole,* pp. 130, 134, 135, 137, 138, 146, 153, 165, 166). For Cyprian, cf. Epist. 63,8: *baptisma . . . semel . . . sumitur nec rursus iteratur.*

87. In Tertullian, De bapt. 15 both of these aspects of the one baptism are men-

tioned together, to enable him to deduce from this unity both the fact that heretics are unable to baptize and the fact that baptism itself cannot be repeated.

88. J. Grotz appears to be simply unaware of this explanation. Cf. S. Hübner, p. 74.

89. Obviously Cyprian does make statements about the necessity of grace for all good actions. *Dei est, inquam, Dei omne quod possumus* (Ad Donat. 4). *Nemo suis viribus fortis est* (De dom.or.14). *Tantum nos posse, quantum credimus* (Test. III, 42). These statements, however, are not applied to the theology of *satisfactio*.

90. Obviously both the OT and the NT say that good works remit sins. But this evidence, which Bossuet already used in Cyprian's defence, is not relevant. For in the Bible these statements are not used to establish the contrast between the two different methods of remission which Cyprian has in mind. In other words, in the Bible it remains debatable whether or not good works remit sins precisely because and in so far as they are an appropriation and effect of Christ's grace, that is, of redemption which is granted gratuitously.

91. For this experience of regeneration, cf. Cyprian's composition Ad Donat. 3–4. It is a question of the experience which the regenerated man has of the power given by God. He overcomes immediately the old, radical addiction to sin which seemed to him previously to be invincible. Because of the experience of this heavenly, God-given vitality he knows already that one day he will stand justified before God. But what is the effect of a further sin after such an experience? This question spotlights what *paenitentia* is in its living source: it is the attempt of a man striving relentlessly for his salvation to restore himself slowly to that original state.

92. Cf. J. Schümmer, *Die altchristliche Fastenpraxis* (Münster 1933), pp. 184–7. It is worth noting that already in the synagogue good works were demanded of a person who had been banned. Thus this is to be understood as a self-evident and traditional practice and not as something which was newly developed from a theory of penitential practice for those who were excluded from the Church. The subsequent theory explains the practice correctly and it turns out, in agreement with the whole of Christian teaching, to be logically and genuinely Christian.

93. Cf. Matt. 17:21; Mark 9:29; Tertullian, De ieiunio 8; Excerpta ex Theodoto 83.84; more in J. Schümmer, *Die altchristliche Fastenpraxis* (Münster 1933), pp. 175 f., 215 f.; F. J. Dölger, *Der Exorzismus im altchristlichen Taufritual* (Paderborn 1909), pp. 80–6; J. Behm, νῆστις etc. in:ThW IV (Stuttgart 1942), pp. 925–35 (esp. 927,930: *der apotropäische Charakter des Fastens im im Heidentum und Judentum*).

94. The punishments due to sin are understood here as the interior consequences of the punishment which are not necessarily taken away *eo ipso* by a change of attitude which is sufficient for salvation.

95. An *offerre pro illis,* that is, the *lapsi* who are not yet actually reconciled, an *offerre nomine eorum* is indeed just as unlawful as the granting of the Eucharist (Epist. 15,1; 16,2; 17,22; 34,1). But what is meant here is obviously an offering of the Eucharist for the *lapsi* who, because of the provision of their gifts for the offering (cf. Epist. 34,1; 65,3), claim this as their right as full Christians, or their own celebration of 'private masses' for themselves in small circles (cf. Epist. 63,16; 57,3; 5,2). Cf. J. A. Jungmann, *Missarum Sollemnia* I (Vienna, 1952), pp. 274, 280. This does not mean, therefore, that the bishop cannot offer the sacrifice for the conversion of sinners as a help to their *satisfactio,* as *purgare conscientiam sacrificio . . . sacerdotis* (De lapsis 16). J. Grotz, p. 82, simply identifies *offerre* with *purgare,* whereas *purgare* is the precondition of *offerre*. On this cf. S. Hübner, p. 66.

96. Accordingly, in the phrase of De lapsis 29: *satisfactio et remissio facta per sacerdotes,* the *per sacerdotes* can refer perfectly well to the *satisfactio*. Thus it becomes clearer how Cyprian envisages the *remissio* as being brought about *per*

sacerdotes without his having to deviate from his usual strict notion of *remissio*. If, in his view, *remissio* means the complete remission of sin, including the punishment which this involves, and if, after baptism, this is attainable only by a *plena satisfactio*, then it is only really possible in so far as the priests contribute their support to the *satisfactio*. It is impossible to derive from De lapsis 29 the notion of a *remissio* through the absolution of the priest as distinct from the *satisfactio*.

97. The sacrifice and the imposition of hands occurred at the same time and the same place, in so far as the imposition of hands was probably performed during the celebration of the Eucharist. But Cyprian does not intimate at which precise stage of the liturgy it occurs. The order (*sacrificio—manus*) suggests an imposition of hands towards the end of the mass, as was later the case in Augustine and the Gallican liturgy. Cf. J. A. Jungmann, *Die lateinischen Bussriten* (Innsbruck 1932), pp. 167,300 ff.

98. The *purgare* does not have only a juridical sense, as Capelle, in RThAM 7 (1935), p. 230 f., remarks appositely. Nevertheless, it is impossible to prove that Cyprian regarded the purification of the conscience as a consequence of the imposition of hands precisely in so far as the latter is the act of reconciliation. It is more prudent and more correct to ascribe this effect to the imposition of hands and the sacrifice only in so far as they are the support of the penitent's own *satisfactio*.

99. On the necessity of the unanimous prayer of the whole Church for the forgiveness of guilt, cf. also De dom. or. 8.

100. Every *spiritualis oratio* presupposes the Spirit which Christ sends. De dom. or. I.

101. This is already evident from the fact that normally the imposition of hands by the bishop is required. Cf. the details in the first part of this essay.

102. We will return to this point later.

103. Thus the observation of Capelle, in RThAM 7 (1935), p. 225, goes too far: *Cyprien répudie donc clairement l'idée que la réconciliation puisse se faire par un jugement de l'Eglise*. Once it is granted that for Cyprian reconciliation occurs in the first place with the Church, then it can be said that it is based on a *sententia*, a *statutum* (Epist. 55,18) or an *examinatio* (Epist. 66,5). How could the *ius communicationis* (Epist. 16,2) be granted otherwise?

104. In view of what has been said earlier, it is obvious that Cyprian makes no distinction here between 'contrition' and the works of penance. The absence of the works of penance is, at least according to De lapsis, evidence of the lack of contrition, since the intention to have sin remitted (our 'contrition') is for Cyprian the intention to settle the *debitum*, that is, to do penance.

105. This is how this passage should be interpreted theologically. A *non proeliaturus lapsus* is one who has not the slightest intention of avoiding to deny his faith on every occasion in the future. Nevertheless, this does not mean that the *proeliaturus* is only the person who in fact confesses his faith in the blood of martyrdom. There is no evidence that Cyprian had this idea. If a *non proeliaturus* gains the *pax* on false pretences, *se ipsum fallit et decipit*. Thus Cyprian must have considered such a *pax* objectively invalid. In fact this must also have been the case (Epist. 55,18) when a sinner *paenitentiae simulatione deluserit* the bishop.

106. For Cyprian this is the immediate consequence of the bishop's sinfulness. Both baptism and penance are invalid (Epist. 66,5), if a person 'has ceased to be a bishop' (Epist. 66,4) because of acts which are dubbed *incesta, impia, nefanda* (Epist. 66,7). Cyprian's 'donatist' presuppositions are clearly in evidence here. But this notion also shows how necessary the *pax* must be for salvation and how it communicates the Spirit if it can be granted only by a person who himself possesses the Spirit.

107. Cyprian considers the *inrita pax* of De lapsis 15 to be such for several reasons

which vary considerably: the absence of the performance of penance, the irregular granting of reconciliation by the bishop, the omission of the exhomologesis (Epist. 15 etc.). What is the most decisive element is not considered. Cyprian stresses most the absence of the performance of penance, and in De lapsis exclusively so.

108. It is not a question of a verbatim quotation. Thus it is not clear whether the bishops, with their paraphrase (. . . *legem dederit ut ligata in terris et in caelis ligata essent, solvi autem possent illic quae prius in Ecclesia solverentur* [Epist. 57,1]), are thinking of either Matt. 16 or Matt. 18. Cyprian never quotes Matt. 18 elsewhere (cf. D. J. Chapman, in RBén. 27 [1910], p. 449). Thus the reference to Matt. 16 is the more probable here.

109. The *spei salutaris subsidium* which is mentioned only in this context is again membership of the Church, in so far as this has a salvific significance. *Pignus vitae in data pace percipiunt* (Epist. 55,13). The possession of the *pax* is the *pignus vitae,* the *spei salutaris subsidium.* It is worth noting that the letter, deviating from Matt., modifies the loosing with the phrase *in Ecclesia* in the place of *in terris.* In the case of the binding, however, it preserves the *in terris.* Thus the loosing has a special connection with the Church. Certainly in Epist. 73,9 (cf. also Sent.episc. 48) there is the unique mention of a *peccata solvere* which occurs in baptism. Here, therefore, the immediate object of the *solvere* is the guilt as such. But this is mentioned only once here in connection with baptism and it cannot be applied to penance. For the *solvere* must be understood of a *remissa* which, according to Cyprian, does not exist in penance. On the other hand, the *solvere* in Epist. 57,1 should be explained in the light of its own context. And this requires an ecclesial interpretation.

110. Cf. the relevant details given above.

111. This could be demonstrated by a more precise exegesis of the Matthean texts.

112. Cf. 'Tertullian's Theology of Penance' in this volume.

113. This would obviously presuppose that this biblical passage already figured in the recension B of De unitate (enumeration according to Battifol) in A.D. 251 and that it was not introduced by Cyprian only in A.D. 255–6 after the subsidence of the polemic against the laxists. D. van den Eynde believes the latter to be the case, because the biblical quotations added to recension B are not to be found previously in Cyprian. Cf. D. van den Eynde, 'La double édition du "De unitate" de S. Cyprien' in: RHE 29 (1933), pp. 5–24.

114. On this, cf. H. Bruders, Matt. 16:19; 18:18 and John 20:22,23 in 'Frühchristlicher Auslegung: Afrika bis 251' in: ZKTh 35 (1911), pp. 79–111.

115. If there is a mention of a *venia* which is granted immediately by the Church (Epist. 31,6; 72,2; cf. De lapsis 35), this can be understood perfectly well of the peace with the Church, since it is precisely the latter which is demanded vehemently by the *lapsi* as their right (De lapsis 35).

116. At this point of our analysis of Cyprian's teaching on penance we are in a position to make yet another distinction: at the judgement *satisfactio* is the cause of the *venia,* but fellowship with the Church is its indispensable prerequisite. Nevertheless, this would be too neat and too clear a formula which does less than justice to Cyprian's idea. If it is true that *satisfactio,* especially in De lapsis, appears as a moral cause of the *venia,* it is still too hasty to conclude that the *pax* could count only as a precondition for the *venia.*

117. The mere naming of a cleric as the executor of a will had the effect of excluding the dying person from sacrifice and prayer for the peace of his soul (Epist. 1,2). This was doubtless the case with an unreconciled sinner, who was known as such. In this case (differently from that in which it is a question of a person who was recognized as a *frater*) the punishment is due to the fact that a sinner is no longer a member of the Church in the full sense and, therefore, being dead, has even less of a

right to *communicatio* with the Church's saving benefits than he had during his lifetime (Epist. 15,1; 16,2; 17,2).

118. Cf., for example, Test. III 25 (John 6:53) and 26: a person must be *baptizatus* if he is to attain the Kingdom of God. In view of the quotation of John 6:35 baptism here includes implicitly communion which was granted for the first time at initiation (Epist. 63,8). Good works had still to be added to baptism and the Eucharist. What is more, Cyprian testifies to the practice of giving communion to infants (De lapsis 25). He could not be surprised, therefore, by any objection against the idea of the necessity of the Eucharist for salvation which might arise from another practice. The Eucharist affords salvation to the person who receives it worthily (De lapsis 26), and it is indispensable for the successful endurance of martyrdom (Epsit. 58,1.9; 57,2.4).

119. Cyprian is here thinking primarily of baptism, although he does recognize that sin which renders a person unworthy of the Eucharist also deprives him of the Spirit. Thus it cannot be far from his mind that the reason for a renewed worthiness after a sin must be a repossession of the Spirit.

120. This possession of the Spirit is nowhere placed in an immediate causal relationship with *satisfactio* as such.

121. The teaching of Pope Stephen may also be relevant here. He understands the imposition of hands for heretics as an imposition of hands of penance, and still states explicitly that it communicates the Spirit. But Stephen is very obscure on this matter. Cyprian does not acknowledge this imposition of hands for heretics and, moreover, he interprets it as Confirmation.

122. How little Cyprian considers linking the reacquisition of the Spirit with *satisfactio* as such is clear from Epist. 25: even after they have been purified from their crime and their fault by means of their confession, the *lapsi* are still *sub diabolo quasi prostrati* until they have been granted the *pax,* even though they have a right to this *pax*. Cyprian could not have said this if he knew that they were already in possession of the Spirit through *satisfactio* alone; in his view Spirit and the grace of baptism, on the one hand, and the exclusion of the devil from within man, on the other, coincide exactly (Epist. 69,15–16).

123. Cyprian knows of an effective *pax* even in those cases where the *satisfactio* is not yet recognized as *plena*.

124. Cf. B. Poschmann, 'Die kirchliche Vermittlung der Sündenvergebung nach Augustinus' in: ZKTh 45 (1921), pp. 208–28, 405–32, 497–526 (esp. 413 ff.). In the case of Augustine this way of posing the question obviously arises from the anti-Donatistic situation: where does the Spirit come from if, in this perspective, the bishop cannot bestow it because although he dispenses the sacraments validly he does so without possessing the Spirit himself?

125. Cf. the details in n.69.

126. The sacramental ('instrumental') causality of reconciliation becomes much clearer in the case of the effect of baptism which is brought about by the water sanctified through the priest's word (Sent. episc. 18). It is effective in the case of infants (Epist. 64,5). *Neque enim Spiritus sine aqua separatim operari potest neque aqua sine Spiritu* (Sent. episc. 5). Cyprian's whole teaching of the *remissa peccatorum* without personal *satisfactio* in baptism points in the same direction; similarly the fact that he does not recognize a 'Baptism of desire', since in his view the baptism of blood is not to be interpreted as baptism of desire. If, therefore, Cyprian is familiar with the idea of a sacrament as *opus operatum,* then the notion that the *pax* causes the possession of the Spirit cannot be discounted as being alien to him.

127. Cf., for example, C. A. Kneller, 'Sacramentum unitatis (Zu Cyprians Schrift an Donatus)' in: ZKTh 40 (1916), pp. 676–703; A. d'Alès, *La théologie de S.Cyprien* (Paris 1922); H. Koch, *Cathedra Petri: neue Untersuchungen über die Anfänge der Primatslehre* (Giessen 1930); B. Poschmann, *Ecclesia principalis. Ein kritischer*

Beitrag zur Frage des Primats dei Cyprian (Breslau 1933); E. Mersch, *Le corps mystique du Christ* II (Paris 1936), pp. 15–34; E. Altendorf, *Einheit und Heiligkeit der Kirche: Untersuchungen zur Entwicklung der altchristlichen Kirchenbegriffe im Abendland von Tertullian bis zu den antidonatistischen Schriften Augustins,* Arbeiten zur Kirchengeschichte 20 (Berlin 1932), pp. 44–116, cf. RHE 29 (1933), p. 1049; J. Zeiller, 'La conception de l'Eglise aux quatre premiers siècles' in: RHE 29 (1933), pp. 571–85, 827–48; M. Bévenot, 'Episcopat et Primat chez Cyprien' in: EThL 42 (1966), pp. 176–95; C. B. Daly, *Absolution and Satisfaction in St. Cyprian's Theology of Penance,* Studia Patr. II. TU 64 (Berlin 1957); M. Jourgon, *Cyprien de Carthage* (Paris 1957); G. Klein, 'Die hermeneutische Struktur des Kirchengedankens bei Cyprian' in: ZKG 68 (1957), pp. 48–68; R. Hardowirgono, 'S. Cypriaan: Het Heil in de Kerk' in: *Bijdragen* 19 (1958), pp. 1–21,137–61; J. Colson, *L'évêque, lien d'unité et de charité chez Saint Cyprien de Carthage* (Paris 1961); K. Delahaye, *Ecclesia Mater chez les Pères des trois premiers siècles* (Paris 1964); A. Demoustier, 'L'ontologie de l'Eglise selon Cyprien' in: RSR 52 (1964), pp. 554–8; W. Simonis, *Ecclesia visibilis et invisibilis* (Frankfurt 1970); U. Wickert, *Sacramentum Unitatis* (Berlin/New York 1971).

128. The whole of Cyprian's argument in the question of the baptism of heretics flows from this axiom. Cf., for example, Sent. episc. 34: *sola possideat gratiam Christi et veritatem.*

129. The *pax* is *fructus paenitentiae* (Epist. 55,17,29).

130. Koch maintains that according to Cyprian the remission of sins (implicitly = the acquisition of grace) is the work of the *satisfactio.* Thus penance cannot be a sacrament, since then the sacramental sign would communicate grace. According to Galtier (De paenitentia, n.150) it is reconciliation which communicates the Spirit (implicity=the remission of sins). Thus *satisfactio* for the guilt, leaving aside the question of the mere 'punishments' of sins, can be only a precondition; and thus penance involves a real sacrament.

131. Cf. the previous considerations on 'the nature of serious sin'.

132. For the different approaches possible, cf. 'Sin as Loss of Grace in Early Church Literature' in this volume.

133. Thus it is mentioned in De op. et eleem. 2 that we can be *post gratiam baptismi sordidati,* and yet *denuo* purified by the *iugis operatio* which, as opposed to baptism, bestows God's forgiveness *rursus.* This thought continues without any interruption in the third chapter and becomes an exhortation for us to heal our sins in this way, since no one is without sin.

134. Cyprian never ascribes a communication of the Spirit to baptism, as distinct from the imposition of hands after baptism. If, for example in Epist. 74,4.5, he stresses the co-operation of the Spirit in baptism itself, it is obvious that, unless he is contradicting himself, he is referring only to the active co-operation of the Spirit on the side both of the person who is administering the baptism and of the water (cf. Epist. 75,9; Sent.episc. 5). In any event this cannot mean a communication of the Spirit to the neophyte. How far it is possible for us to deduce logically such a communication of the Spirit at baptism from the effects which Cyprian ascribes to baptism is quite a different question.

135. When Tertullian in his Montanist period wishes to praise fasting, he says on one occasion (De ieiunio 8) that through fasting the Holy Spirit *inducitur,* just as the wicked spirit is expelled. Nevertheless, according to De bapt. 6.8; De paen. 6,17, in comparison with 2,6, for Tertullian too personal penance and purification from sins are only a preparation and a prerequisite for the communication of the Spirit in the sacrament. In other words, they are not the immediate cause of the communication of the Spirit itself.

136. Cf. J. de Ghellinck, *Pour l'histoire du mot 'Sacramentum'* I (Louvain/Paris

1924) (J. B. Poukens, pp. 153–220). Poukens (p. 215 f.) considers that it is not certain in which of the many senses *sacramentum* is intended when Cyprian uses this term to designate baptism. confirmation and the Eucharist. Thus it is clear how unimportant this designation is for reconciliation. In Epist. 74,4, for instance, Cyprian accuses Pope Stephen of deriving the *disciplina ad celebranda sacramenta* from the heretics, since these sacramenta, according to Stephen's own testimony, were celebrated at the reception of 'heretics' only by an imposition of hands. According to Cyprian this meant that the behaviour of Christians was being dictated by anti-Christians. In view of all this, it is not totally unlikely that Cyprian gave the name of sacrament to the imposition of hands at baptism.

137. In my opinion (as opposed to B. Xiberta, *Clavis Ecclesiae* [Rome 1922], p. 41) Cyprian does not make an essential distinction here between baptism and the reconciliation of penance. He describes both by stressing their immediate effects (*Spiritus Sancti gratia—communicatio*). It is obvious, however, that in the disputed passage the second and third *ne*-clauses (CSL 3:p. 730 nos. 16 and 17) provide a more precise justification for the first *ne*-clause (no. 13). What this says is why many would die without hope of salvation, if Cyprian were not a legitimate bishop. That is why Cyprian links baptism with reconciliation in respect of their importance for salvation. This does not detract from the stress on the difference between baptism and *satisfactio* which is found in other passages, since *satisfactio* means something different from *pax et communicatio*. The latter can easily be seen as a parallel to baptism. Nevertheless, the 'parallelism' between baptism and penance (De op. et eleem. 2; Epist. 55,22), which in fact underline the difference between the two, should not be made into an argument for the sacramental nature of penance.

138. Cyprian does not consider in any detail either how this unity is to be envisaged more precisely or how it comes about.

139. Cf. S. Hübner, p. 50, n.8.

140. On the supposition, that is, that private penance can be shown to be sacramental. Every one agrees that there was a private penance in the Church Fathers in the sense that the sinner remitted his own light sins through his own penitential efforts or at least without an actual intervention of the Church which acted as a sacrament.

141. The following specialists in the history of penance defend this theory: F. Frank, *Die Bussdisziplin der Kirche* (Mainz 1867), p. 811 ff.; F. Probst, *Sakramente und Sakramentalien in den drei ersten christlichen Jahrhunderten* (Tübingen 1872), p. 368 f.; H. J. Schmitz, *Die Bussbücher und die Bussdisziplin der Kirche* I (Mainz 1883), p. 28 f.; II (Düsseldorf 1898), p. 75 f.; J. Stufler, 'Die Sündenvergebung bei Origenes' in: ZKTh 31 (1907), pp. 193–228 (cf. 207); id., 'Einige Bemerkungen zur Busslehre Cyprians' in: ZKTh 33 (1909), pp. 232–47 (cf. 245). The dogmatic theologians followed this theory almost unanimously for a long time. Cf., for example, D. Palmieri, *De paenitentia* (Prati 1896), p. 508 ff.; H. Hurter, *Compendium theol.dogm.* III (Innsbruck 1903), p. 498 (n.501) nota; Ch. Pesch, *Praelect. dogm.* VII (Freiburg/Br. 1920), p. 138 ff. (n.263 ff.). In this context we should also mention J. Grotz. He posits the existence of a purely canonical stage of penance, in the form of an exclusion and a readmission, before the actual sacramental church penance. But he, too, separates the two very carefully. For the discussion of this view, cf. the essay 'The Penitential Teaching of the Shepherd of Hermas' in this volume.

142. The only difficulty against this view for the period which we are considering comes from Tertullian. We will consider it below.

143. This applies at least where this exclusion is considered as *iuris divini*.

144. Epist. 265,7; Sermo 352,3,8; De fide et oper. 26,48.

145. Augustine, Epist. 151,9.

146. Augustine, Sermo 392,3.

147. Thus in Ambrose, De paenit. II 10: *paenitentia quae publice agitur*; De obitu Theod. 34; Council of Toledo (A.D. 400) can.2 (Mansi III 999); Paulinus, Vita S. Ambrosii n.24; Augustine, Sermo 392,3; Rufinus, Hist. eccl. 2 (II), 18; Leo the Great, Epist. 167. Penance was called *publica* both because of its notoreity and also by contrast with the private performance of penance for daily sins, but not as opposed to a private sacramental penance. Augustine's *corripere in secreto* (Sermo 82,8,11) does not alter this picture. See the evidence for this in Poschmann.

148. If in a community today all the participants were obliged to communicate, then the person who is excluded from the Eucharist by serious sin would in fact become a 'public' sinner. But this reception of the sacrament of penance would still remain private.

149. Cyprian makes this clear by the way he formulates the nature of such a reconciliation of the sick. It has precisely the same form as the usual reconciliation. Moreover, later, when the sinner had recovered his health, he had the same obligations as after a normal 'public' penance.

150. At least this is not the case if the rite of reconciliation in public penance requires an explicit mention of reconciliation with the Church.

151. Cf. Paenitentiale Theodori I 12; Wasserschleben, p. 197.

152. This is the meaning of the statement: *reconciliatio ideo in hac provincia publice statuta non est, quia et publica paenitentia non est.* Since the *paenitentia* is distinguished from the *reconciliatio,* it must refer to the performance of penance.

153. As a fixed term, *privata paenitentia* appears, for example, besides *publica paenitentia* in the ordo paenitentiae *Praemonere debet* of the Fulda manuscript (Fulda II) from the tenth century (cf. Schmitz II 57; Jungmann, *Die lateinischen Bussriten* [Innsbruck 1932], p. 176 ff.), while in the earlier manuscripts of this instruction (Fulda I: cf. Jungmann, p. 178; the Pontifical of Poitiers: cf. Morinus App. 55; Ps.-Alcuin, De div.off. 13) the difference is not so pronounced. The term is also missing in the inscription of the penitential ordines of the ninth century from Fulda (cf. B. Opfermann, 'Zwei unveröffentlichte Fuldaer Bussordines des 9.Jh' in: ThGl 36 [1944], pp. 47–51).

154. Cf. J. A. Jungmann, *Die lateinischen Bussriten* (Innsbruck 1932), p. 270 f.

155. Confession and absolution were separated; the absolution was granted only after the completion of the penitential duties; finally reconciliation was performed by the bishop; the penitential rites were very complicated, including long and numerous prayers, kneeling before the altar, certain bodily postures, etc.

156. The view that the Church could not deny reconciliation to a repentant sinner, even in particular cases, and that, therefore, there must have been a 'private' reconciliation if the public one could not take place is such an assumption.

157. P. Galtier recognizes this, *De paenitentia* (Paris 1931) th. XVII, n.307–11.

158. This penance is called 'public' only by contrast with the purely subjective, independent performance of penance for daily sins, without a sacramental mediation of the Church, but not as opposed to another kind of sacramental remission of sins by the Church. This point needs to be repeatedly stressed.

159. P. Galtier, *L'église et la rémission des péchés* (Paris 1932), pp. 273–82, and id. 'A propos de la pénitence primitive: Méthodes et conclusions' in: RHE 30 (1934), pp. 517–57, 797–846 (esp. 809–12), connects Tertullian with Cyprian in the question of private penance. In Tertullian we meet for the first time *'une rémission du péché distincte de celle qui s'obtient par la voie de la pénitence publique'* (p. 809).

160. Nevertheless, P. Galtier (RHE 30), p. 811, concedes: *il peut même lui* (*au coupable*) *arriver d'être mis pour un temps a l'écart du tropeau.* But how does this measure differ from an excommunication?

161. On this point, cf. 'Sin as Loss of Grace in Early Church Literature' in this volume.

162. To claim that the list in Apol. 39, *exhortationes, castigationes et censura divina,* represents only clearly distinct *termini technici* is to force the meaning of the text. Cf. P. Galtier, loc. cit. (RHE 30), p. 812. If this were the case, *castigatio,* as opposed to *censura divina,* could never mean in Tertullian the excommunication which he mentions, by way of conclusion, in similar contexts. From De pud., however, it is clear that, in a possible new terminology, *damnatio* = excommunication without the prospect of a reconciliation. Accordingly, *castigatio* could here mean every punishment by the Church which does not preclude this prospect. But Galtier has not proven that in De pud., granted Tertullian's Montanistic presuppositions, the *castigatio* cannot refer to an excommunication which is removable and that the *leviora delicta* were punished without such an excommunication. This excommunication would always be a mild *castigatio* by comparison with the definitive exclusion (=*damnatio*). At the same time, in itself *castigatio* (*castigare*) can also mean a hard punishment (cf. *Thesaurus linguae latinae* III, p. 530 ff.). Cf. also B. Poschmann, in: ThRv 32 (1933), pp. 257–72 (cf. 264); id., *Paenitentia secunda* (Bonn 1940), pp. 309, 306 ff.; C. M. Chartier, 'La discipline pénitentielle d'après les écrits de saint Cyprien' in: Antonianum 14 (1939), pp. 17–42 (cf. 20 n.1).

163. As is the opinion of P. Galtier, *L'Eglise et la rémission des péchés* (Paris 1932), p. 288.

164. This means a penance of excommunication.

165. As *deponere, exponere* also in Cyprian means 'to liberate oneself from something' (cf. the passages: CSL 3,3:425). Since, however, the *medella* for guilt as such must be sought and applied, this expression can mean only the psychological unburdening of the conscience through the confession of secret guilt, and not convey the idea of the remission of objective guilt. Contrary to P. Galtier, *L'Eglise et la rémission des péchés* (Paris 1932), p. 295.

166. The following sentences (cf. CSL 3,1: 258,2) resume the general exhortation addressed to actual *libellatici,* begun in cap.27.

167. Cf. S. Hübner, p. 183 ff., esp. 185.

CHAPTER SEVEN: PENITENTIAL TEACHING AND PRACTICE ACCORDING TO THE DIDASCALIA APOSTOLORUM

1. The first version of this revised essay appeared in ZKTh 72 (1950), pp. 257–81. The edn of the Didascalia generally quoted in this essay is that of F. X. Funk (cf. n.2).

2. For the literature on *penitential teaching* in the Didascalia Apostolorum, cf. E. Schwartz, *Bussstufen und Katechumenatsklassen* (Strassburg 1911), pp. 16–20; H. Achelis/J. Flemming, *Die Syrische Didaskalia* (TU 25,2: Leipzig 1904), pp. 298–307; R. H. Connolly, *Didascalia Apostolorum* (Oxford 1929), pp. liv–lvi; P. Galtier, *L'église et la rémission des péchés aux premiers siècles* (Paris 1932), pp. 191 f., 353 f., id., *Aux origines du sacrement de la pénitence* (Rome 1951), pp. 157–221; E. Amann, 'Pénitence', in: DThC XII/I (Paris 1933), p. 790; B. Poschmann, *Paenitentia secunda* (Bonn 1940), pp. 476–8; J. Janini Cuesta, 'La penitencia medicinal desde la Didascalia Apostolorum a S. Gregorio de Nisa' in: RET 7 (1947), pp. 337–62; J. Grotz, *Die Entwicklung des Bussstufenwesens in der vornicänischen Kirche* (Freiburg 1955), pp. 371–91; H. von Campenhausen, *Kirchliches Amt und geistliche Vollmacht in den ersten drei Jahrhunderten* (Tübingen 1963); K. Baus, *Von der Urgemeinde zur frühchristlichen Grosskirche* (HdKG I) (Freiburg 1962), pp. 384–6. Edns of the text:

F. X. Funk, *Didascalia et Constitutiones Apostolorum* I (Paderborn 1905). E. Tidner was responsible for a new edn of the traditional Latin version of the Didascalia, which comprises a little more than a third of the whole work: *Didascaliae apostolorum, Canonum ecclesiastricorum, Traditionis apostolicae versiones latinae* (TU 75: Berlin 1963).

3. E. Schwartz, *Bussstufen und Katechumenatsklassen* (Strassburg 1911).

4. H. Achelis/J. Flemming, *Die Syrische Didaskalia* (*Die altesten Quellen des orientalischen Kirchenrechts* II) (TU 25,2: Leipzig 1904).

5. B. Poschmann, *Paenitentia secunda: Die kirchliche Busse im ältesten Christentum bis Cyprian und Origenes* (Bonn 1940).

6. P. Galtier, *L'église et la rémission des péchés aux premiers siècles* (Paris 1932), and *Aux origines du sacrement de la pénitence* (Rome 1951); J. Grotz, *Die Entwicklung des Bussstufenwesens in der vornicänischen Kirche* (Freiburg 1955); H. von Campenhausen, *Kirchliches Amt und geistliche Vollmacht in den ersten drei Jahrhunderten* (Tübingen 1963).

7. Cf. J. Quasten, *Patrology* II (Utrecht/Antwerp 1953), pp. 147–52; A. Stuiber, *Patrologie* (Freiburg/Br. 1966), p. 84 f.

8. Recent research inclines to the view that the supposed anti-Novatianist elements are not absolutely demonstrable for the work itself. In every instance they could be explained as later additions. Cf. P. Galtier, p. 189 ff.; H. von Campenhausen, p. 269.

9. These are the only reasons which E. Schwartz and R. H. Connolly (who finally remains undecided) adduce. This way of stressing the bishop's power of binding by omitting all explicit mention of his power of loosing is clearly evidenced in Origen at about the same time. Cf. the relevant study of Origen's teaching on penance in this volume. Even when the power of loosing is mentioned, it is not intended simply as the counterpart to the binding, since it can be exercised without a binding (although this is obviously not permissible in the case of mortal sins). Thus it is not surprising that only the power of binding is mentioned (II 11,2) if the intention is to impress upon the bishop his obligation with regard to those guilty of mortal sins. As is the case with Origen in De oratione 28, the primary aim is to emphasize both the need for excommunication and the bishop's duty not simply to leave such a sinner in the Church (II 9/10).

10. This is not absolutely certain. In fact the actual opponents of the lenient treatment of sinners (II 14,3.10.12; 15,1; 18.6) seem to be rather zealous, strict and somewhat misanthropic lay people in the communities of the bishops addressed. Even without supposing a theoretical Novatianism, it is possible to understand such 'zealous Christians' who were pressing for discipline and order in the community and thus wished to alienate once and for all those persons who were responsible for scandals. So long as the institution of penance for the forgiveness of sins was identified materially with a disciplinary procedure within a small community, such difficulties and demands were bound to arise from everyday practice. In that situation there were always people who refused to associate either in the liturgy or in civil life (which were very closely related, in any case) with men of questionable life-style. To that extent, the danger of Novatianism was already present, even without (theoretical) Novatianism. Achelis/Flemming (p. 302 n.1) dispute that the opponents of the Didascalia where penance is concerned are Novatians.

11. The *adversus Deum peccare* in II 56,2 is to be understood in the fullest sense, as 'sin against God' was understood elsewhere at this time. Cf. II 31,3: *delinquere in Deum omnipotentem.*

12. The Didascalia clearly states that, provided there is sorrow, all sins can be forgiven. Thus the incurable mortal sin mentioned here is to be understood as it is in

Origen: a sin which has induced the death of grace and has thus showed itself to be previously incurable, that is, it cannot be prevented from causing the death of the soul. Cf. on this point the essay on 'The Penitential Teaching of Origen' in this volume. Cf. also J. Grotz, pp. 378–81.

13. This applies to everyone who disturbs the peace of the Church.

14. In II 14,3.9.13 the point is made in polemic against rigorism in penance that the sinner does not defile the Church. This could refer to the repentant, converted sinner who has returned to the fellowship of the Church. However, it is then stated that not even Judas could harm the Church, were he to take part in its worship. Such inconsistencies arise in the heat of polemic. The fact remains that the Church has to remove such sinners if it is to stay undefiled (VI 14,10). Only when it is physically or morally impossible to apply this principle, when a man is unable to discern clearly the ultimate dispositions of another and where it is a question of a repentant sinner, is it correct to say that, according to the view of the Didascalia, the Church is like Noah's ark (II 14,9) and that, in the Church, the sin of the one member does not harm another (II 14,10.13).

15. This tr. is taken from H. Achelis/J. Flemming, p. 58, 6–8.

16. Cf. J. Grotz, pp. 375–78.

17. These are generally understood to be apostasy, fornication and murder. On this point, cf. J. Grotz, pp. 347, 356–64.

18. Cf. Hippolytus (Dix, pp. 24–8). Didascalia II 39,5–6 shows that the author was aware of the parallel between the treatment of catechumens and that of sinners.

19. Cf. J. Grotz, p. 383 f.

20. J. Grotz's arguments in favour of two radically distinct institutions of penance appear to be inconclusive. Cf. our discussion of his basic ideas in our essay 'The Penitential Teaching of the Shepherd of Hermas' in this volume.

21. The deacon posted at the church entrance (II 57,6) also had to ward off obstinate excommunicates who believed that they were excluded unjustly. There were also people who were not excommunicated because the bishop, on account of his own life-style, could not confront them with the necessary authority, or who had acquired the bishop's indulgence by presents and alms (II 9; IV 8,3). In other words, people were not always prepared to undergo an excommunication willingly and repentantly.

22. The passage II 10,4–5, as opposed to II 16,1–2, refers to this real, official and publicly valid excommunication. This distinction between the real and the liturgical excommunication becomes clear in II 43,1, where a false accuser is excluded from the Church. After some time he is summoned again and has to promise—obviously in the way described in II 16,1–2—that he will do penance during the period which is then imposed upon him (II 16,2). He is admonished (II 16,2; 43,1), and thus begins his period of penance in the strict liturgical sense. When these weeks are up (II 16,2; 43,1) he receives reconciliation by the imposition of hands. The same structure of the penitential process is found in II 50,4: first the sinner is judged and excluded; he has to do penance, that is, he must really be converted. Then he comes to the bishop and prays for readmission, while confessing his guilt and promising to do further penance, that is, the still outstanding liturgical penance which begins with the liturgical exclusion (II 16,2) and which already determines when the readmission will take place. The same procedure is found in II 13,4; *iudica eum* (the sinner) *primum severe* (the real excommunication) *et deinde* (that is, after the real penance) *suscipe eum cum benignitate et misericordia* (at the liturgical excommunication at which it is already decided in practice that the future reconciliation will take place after a couple of weeks), *si promiserit se paenitentiam acturum esse* (a promise which he must have already made previously in order to be admitted to the present rite and which the

penitent is only too pleased to repeat at this stage) *et increpa eum, ange eum* (the official reprimand and exhortation of the liturgical excommunication), *persuade ei ac succurre ei* (the bishop's co-operation in the sinner's penance during the coming liturgical period).

23. At least previously, the sinner was out of right relationship with the Church. This situation must be expressed visibly, since there can hardly be an actual sacramentally visible 'loosing' if there has not been previously a corresponding 'binding'.

24. This could have appeared as preferential treatment to those who had, as it were, been surprised by a spontaneous excommunication on the bishop's part.

25. Cf. II 43,1; 50,4.

26. We have no more precise information about this particular period. Apparently at this time there were no fixed penitential duties in the circle of the Didascalia. In II 43,1 there is mention only of *aliquod tempus*. II 50,4 demands that such a period should last until the sinner has done penance, that is, until (II 16,2) it is possible to establish by examination that he deserves to be readmitted. In these circumstances the length of the penitential period must have varied considerably. Given the general leniency found in the Didascalia and the reasonable demands which the bishop made in determining the period of penance to suit each individual case, this period could not have been generally more than a couple of years, at the most.

27. Cf. R. H. Connolly, pp. lv–lvi.

28. It is not surprising that the real excommunication could fall into disuse sooner than the liturgical excommunication. The latter was, for theological reasons, in a certain sense necessary for the introduction of the reconciliation process. The real excommunication could hardly serve this purpose, since it did not, as such, establish that the reconciliation had in fact already begun. Thus the real excommunication could fall into disuse wherever, on the one hand, its real significance as an actual exclusion from the community was diminished by the fact that the sinner willingly avoided the community and undertook his own conversion, and, on the other hand, the theological-sacramental emphasis (which had originally been placed on it) shifted more and more to a liturgical-ceremonial rite of excommunication. Thus it is possible to see here clearly for the first time that a separation is gradually taking place between excommunication considered as a measure of church discipline and as a punishment, on the one hand, and excommunication considered as an introduction to a sacramental process of reconciliation, on the other. The ultimate practical reason for such a separation, which is given already by Tertullian, Cyprian and others, is that not every necessary excommunication can reckon on the repentance of those concerned. Where this is not the case, then it necessarily deteriorates into a mere church punishment. On the distinction between the two penitential periods and the establishment of the length of the liturgical period of penance, cf. also J. Schümmer, *Die altchristliche Fastenpraxis mit besonderer Berücksichgung der Schriften Tertullians* (Münster 1933), pp. 195–9.

29. This means that II 16,1 is considered as a summary of what is repeated somewhat clumsily (from the literary viewpoint) in II 16,2, that is, after the author has interrupted himself with his theological consideration of why we should pray for sinners in the community (cf. F. X. Funk, p. 60,14–16). This is certainly the simplest way of understanding these two verses. Nevertheless, it is not totally excluded that 16,1 refers to the real excommunication, while 16,2 refers to the liturgical excommunication. This interpretation would make no substantial difference to our view. J. Grotz (p. 388 f.) naturally explains the period of liturgical excommunication, according to his basic thesis, as a church penance which is imposed after the lifting of excommunication or even without a previous excommunication. Nevertheless, it

must be granted even with regard to this full church penance (in Grotz's terminology), that the penitents, although no longer *eiecti,* are still *segregati,* that is, they do not yet stand again in *communio* in the strict sense (J. Grotz, p. 389 f.) and therefore cannot take part in the actual liturgy. These penitents are, therefore, 'excluded' or excommunicated, unless excommunication is taken in the purely arbitrary sense of a situation in which the person excommunicated has absolutely no relationship with the Church and can take no part whatsoever in the liturgy (of the Word).

30. This means that subsequently the excommunicated person should be avoided, which was not possible in the previous period of real excommunication in some circumstances, for example, when the penitent withdrew himself discretely from the community. Even alms for the support of the poor were not accepted from him (IV 8,3); since the care of the poor was essentially the duty of the bishop and of the Church, such an attitude is understandable. Otherwise, almsgiving is generally treated as a means of penance (III 8,3). The penitent would give alms in order to be assured of the prayers of others in respect of his own sins (IV 7,1–3; 8,1–2).

31. This need not be meaningless and superfluous, since, after the penitent's expulsion everything depended on his being avoided in practice by the members of the community. The penitent has 'to remain humbly on his own' and so publicly confess his guilt. But this also demands a corresponding behaviour on the part of the rest of the faithful. Such a general agreement with the bishop's excommunication appears to be intended also in II 32,3.

32. This obviously applies also, in certain circumstances, to the period of real excommunication; especially since the following statements cannot be applied with certainty to penance either before or after the liturgical excommunication.

33. The *permitti in Ecclesia,* as it applies to repentant heretics, refers to the liturgy of the Word, whereas obstinate heretics are excluded from both the liturgy of the Word and the liturgy of prayer (*neque per verbum neque per orationem communicare*). The repentant sinner was allowed access to the liturgy of the Word before the actual liturgical excommunication. This is evident both from the reason given for this access and from the fact that the relevant passages in the Didascalia do not apply absolutely only to the period of liturgical penance.

34. Cf. K. Baus, p. 384.

35. Presumably this was also accompanied by a prayer on the bishop's part.

36. These instructions are not to be understood abstractly and juridically. The individual aspects follow each other in temporal and succession and are, therefore, rules for the liturgical ceremony. The clearly distinguished classes of Christians had their fixed places in the Church. The deacons had to ensure that these places were respected and, occasionally, to show visiting strangers to their proper places (II 57,2–58,6). Since this was also the duty of the deacons on other occasions (II 57,7.9; 58,5), it is easy to imagine that after the imposition of hands and at the bishop's command the deacon leads the penitent to his previous place in the community which he has not been able to occupy during his period of penance because of his exclusion from the liturgy. II 41,2 also contains the real distinction between the *manum imponere pro eo precantibus* and the *deinde introducere et participem facere ecclesiae.* In the corresponding place of the Constitutiones Apostolorum (II 41,2; F. X. Funk, p. 131,8) the *introducere* is explicitly interpreted as a 'leading back to his previous place (νομή)'.

37. The latter is obviously intended, once the *communicare* is distinguished from the *recipere* (II 38,4).

38. On the imposition of hands, cf. also II 43,1. It is obvious that the bishop took this opportunity to express his joy over this event in an address: *gratanter autem paenitentes suscipite gratulantes* (II 15,3).

39. Cf. II 41,2: *Quemadmodum gentilem baptizas ac postea recipis, ita et huic manum impones ac deinde introduces et participem facies ecclesiae*. Cf. also II 41,1: *ad orationem eum* (the penitent who is reconciled) *admitte sicut gentilem* (after baptism).

40. Thus it is here simply presupposed that 'Confirmation', according to the Didascalia too, is a part of the rite of initiation.

41. The Constitutiones Apostolorum have preserved this sentence verbatim: *καὶ ἔσται αὐτῷ ἀντὶ τοῦ λούσματος ἡ χειροθεσία* (II 41,2; F. X. Funk, p. 131, 8 f.). This needs to be underlined here, since the following sentence no longer agrees textually with the Didascalia but stresses that in baptism also the Spirit is bestowed by the imposition of hands. In the Didascalia, however, the text continues: 'Since the Holy Spirit is received either through baptism or through the imposition of hands'. Even granted that 'baptism' here includes an imposition of hands, the difference between the two events is clear both in form and in content.

42. This can be deduced from the text of the Constitutiones Apostolorum mentioned in the previous note; and perhaps this idea is even intended there. If this were the case, however, it would entail a contradiction to the first sentence (*καὶ ἔσται* . . .) which the author himself does not appear to have noticed.

43. Thus the imposition of hands of Confirmation is still an inseparable aspect of the single rite of initiation that is 'baptism'. In II 32,3 it is the *χειροθεσία* of the bishop which communicates the Spirit 'in baptism'. In VI 21,1 it is simply stated that we receive the Holy Spirit 'through baptism'. 'Baptism' here, therefore, is a comprehensive notion which embraces the imposition of hands of Confirmation.

44. The re-wording of the text of the Didascalia in the Constitutiones Apostolorum is an indication that in the Eastern Church the process had already begun which leads to an increasingly stronger identification of the reconciliation of heretics (penitents) with Confirmation. In fact it may be asked whether, in both cases, it is not a question of the same imposition of hands (considered either materially or formally), so that the imposition of hands at penance would be the repetition of the imposition of hands at Confirmation. A further witness to the same development at the same time (the end of the fourth century) is the inauthentic can. 7 of the Council of Constantinople (A.D. 381). According to this, it appears that the validly baptized heretic is reconciled by Confirmation (the sealing with *myron* accompanied by the Eastern formula of Confirmation); cf. C. J. Hefele, *Conciliengeschichte* II (Freiburg 1875), pp. 26–8; H. Elfers, *Die Kirchenordnung Hippolyts von Rom* (Paderborn 1938), p. 132 f.

45. For the explanation of this difficult text, cf. H. Elfers, p. 143 f.

46. Nevertheless, this rite is placed on the same level as the anointing of the king and the priest in the Old Testament. But this is probably only to explain that, in the case of women, the bishop could be satisfied with an anointing of the head. For parallels to this anointing-imposition of hands as an exorcism in preparation for the act of baptism proper, cf. in Clemens of Alex., Excerpta ex Theodoto 83–4 (GCS 17:132, 15–23) [should number 20 here not be read as *ἐπιθέσεις χ.*, instead of the conjecture *ἐπάρσεις χειρῶν*?]; The Acts of Thomas 157 (Hennecke, Neutest. Apokryphen 287; Lipsius/Bonnet II 2,266 f.); Hippolytus, Paradosis (Dix, pp. 30–2); Cyprian, Sent. episc. 1; 8; 37 (CSL 3,1: 436; 441; 450); Cyprian, Epist. 69,15. These parallel passages from the same period attest clearly the exorcism character of the anointing-imposition of hands or the simple imposition of hands before baptism and thus show how the imposition of hands in the Didascalia is to be understood. Nevertheless, it should not be overlooked that this anointing before baptism is not followed by any further anointing. This point has been demonstrated by R. H. Connolly, *Didascalia Apostolorum* (Oxford 1929), p. xlix f. n.8 with reference to 'The Liturgical Homilies of Narsai' (Cambridge, 'Texts and Studies' VIII/I, 1909), p.

xlvii ff. and on the Syr. tr. in general xlii–xlix. In the Syrian Church a (first) communication of the Holy Spirit was already attributed to this anointing, as Connolly illustrates with a whole succession of Syriac texts. Subsequently in the consciousness of that time the anointing as an exorcism and as a rite of the Communication of the Spirit were more or less fused together. Cf. also the texts of J. Coppens, *L'imposition des mains et les rites connexes* (Wetteren 1925), p. 281 n.6. Moreover, the Didascalia also knows of an imposition of hands with prayer as an exorcism which, with the permission of the bishop or the deacon, may be performed even by widows (III 8,1–3). This practice is known at the same time also by Ps.-Clement (De virginitate I 12 [F. X. Funk, *Patres Apost.* II², p. 11]) and even previously by Tertullian (De praescript. haeret. 41).

47. In penance the bishop is considered a 'physician' who has to heal the wounds of sin (II 20,10–11; 41,3–9). The notion of a healing anointing which acts as an exorcism cannot be far removed from this idea. Nevertheless, Origen's witness reflects a usage in the circle of the Alexandrian Church, making a conclusion for the Didascalia difficult. Moreover, the rite of reconciliation, differing according to different regions, must have corresponded to the development of the rite of initiation. In fact the anointing of Confirmation acquired precedence over the imposition of hands of Confirmation in the Alexandrian Church well before this happened in the Syrian Church. Thus the anointing at reconciliation also must have gained acceptance later in Syria than it did in the Alexandrian area.

48. In the chronological list of II 33,2 the expression *Spiritu Sancto replere* follows the expression *per aquam regenerare*. This indicates that the communication of the Spirit by an imposition of hands (II 32,3) cannot occur through that imposition of hands (III 12,2–3) which takes place before baptism. Rather a second imposition of hands is to be assumed after the baptism of water, even though nothing is mentioned about this in III 12,2–3. In fact what is the role of the deaconesses in the rite of initiation? They complete the anointing of the head before baptism with an anointing of the whole body, but they have nothing more to do with imposition of hands after baptism. This would explain why, in this context, the first imposition of hands is mentioned but not the second.

49. As generally in the Syrian Church, as opposed to the Alexandrian Church, the anointing at Confirmation was lacking for a long time. Cf. H. Elfers, pp. 141–7; J. Coppens, p. 330 ff.

50. The bishop was also consecrated by the imposition of hands; cf. II 2,3.

51. For the first notion, cf. I 6,7–9; II 5,4; VI 16,6; 17,6 (binding as the imposition of a law); I 6,10; II 34,7; 35,1; VI 16,1; 12,11; 17,1 (loosing as the abrogation of a law); II 21,1; VI 19,3 (binding as a self-induced state of guilt); II 11,2; 34,4 (imposition and lifting of exclusion from the Church having a heavenly effect); II 18,2–3; 20,10; 33,2 (loosing as the forgiveness of guilt in baptism or penance). On this, cf. V. Brandner, '"Binden und Lösen" in der altsyrischen Kirche' in: *Katholik* 95, 1 (1916), pp. 220–32, 287–304 (for the Didascalia 225–7, 287–9). This ἐξουσία τοῦ λύειν (Const.Apost. II 18,3 [F. X. Funk, p. 65,26] corresponding to Didascalia II 18,3) is now in the Didascalia simply a *solvere per remissionem* as God's representative (II 18,2; Connolly, p. 55,6 f.: loose by forgiveness). The loosing of the guilt here implicitly dispenses with the intermediary of reconciliation with the Church; (at least as far as the explicit meaning of the text is concerned) it means directly forgiving guilt in God's name. Through the bishop the redeemer says to sinners: your sins are forgiven (II 20,9). Thus reception into the Church appears rather as a consequence of the redeeming forgiveness of sins than as its cause. This is also clear from the unhesitating use of the notion of ἄφεσις for the forgiveness of sins after baptism by the bishop without any inkling of the narrower and stricter use which it normally has

with regard to baptism alone, in the Pastor of Hermas, in African theology from Tertullian to Cyprian, in Clement of Alexandria, in Origen and in Firmilian. Cf. II 18,1–2; 18,7; 20,9, as well as II 13,1; 16,2.3; 18,5; 23,2; 26,2. The most that can be said is that in V 9,1–6 something of the earlier use of this notion in the sense of a completely gratuitous forgiveness of guilt is discernible. But here also it is stated that in martyrdom sins are 'covered'—which is elsewhere an effect of the old ἄφεσις in baptism. For Origen, however, 'to cover' was rather a notion which expressed an opposition to the ἄφεσις of baptism and martyrdom.

52. Obviously before this, even in Cyprian, reconciliation and the communication of the Spirit were related causally. Nevertheless, this view was then more clearly counterbalanced by the teaching that the forgiveness was not simply as in baptism but the mere effect of the hard μετάνοια on the part of the penitent himself.

53. Penance is only the cause and the proof of the fact that the penitent is 'worthy' to receive the ἄφεσις: II 16,2 (cf. II 16,3). Elsewhere, too, subjective penance appears repeatedly as a condition of forgiveness and readmission to the Church; cf., for example, II 18,7; 13,4; 24,2; 38,4; 39,6; 41,1; 43,1; 50,4. In itself this is not surprising, since penance is always and everywhere a condition of reconciliation with God and the Church. But in the Didascalia subjective penance as a cause of the remission of sins is emphasized less than elsewhere in the third century. Even the *sanare, vivificare* and *sublevare* happens through the bishop and the ἄφεσις conferred by him (II 18,7; 24,2; 33,3).

54. On this, cf.: N. Krautwig, *Die Grundlagen der Busslehre des J. Duns Scotus* (Freiburg 1938); W. Dettloff, *Die Lehre von der acceptatio divina des Johannes Duns Scotus mit besonderer Berucksichtigung der Rechtfertigungslehre* (Werle 1954), pp. 203–31.

55. This interior sequence of aspects is clearly reflected in the course of the penitential liturgy: the imposition of hands which communicates the Spirit precedes the *introducere et participem facere Ecclesiae* (II 41,2). Thus whereas in Cyprian (Epist. 57,4) the person who receives the Spirit of the Father is the one who has been granted peace with the Church (cf. 'The Penitential Teaching of Cyprian of Carthage' in this volume), here the reverse is the case: it is the person who has received the Spirit who re-enters the *participatio Ecclesiae*. Obviously it should not be overlooked that the Church is aware of being *susceptorium Sancti Spiritus* (VI 14,7), which comes near to saying that it is precisely the incorporation into this Church that grants a share in its Spirit. The faithful live in the living and life-giving mother (II 61,4). In II 33,3 the 'readmission' is placed before the 'coming alive'. Nevertheless, this could mean, as in II 13,5, admission to the official liturgical penance occurring in the liturgical excommunication, which precedes the restoration to life through reconciliation and the actual incorporation into the Church.

56. As F. X. Funk, I 134 (n. on II 43,2–4), also stresses. Similarly H. Achelis/J. Flemming, p. 302.

57. J. Grotz, arguing from the case of the false accuser, makes the generalization that reconciliation after an excommunication was possible only once: 'it was not repeatable' (p. 385). But in a note (p. 385 n.9) he states: 'Obviously this does not justify us in believing that it is non-repeatable as a matter of rigid principle.' Since no further justification is offered, it is reasonable to hold that—outside the sphere of influence of the Alexandrian Church—a once-and-for-all penance did not exist in the East. This affords the simplest explanation of why in the East there was nowhere a controversy over the abolition of such a principle: it simply had never existed.

58. Cf. R. H. Connolly, Didascalia Apostolorum (Oxford 1929), p. lxxxiii.

59. Cf. R. H. Connolly, p. lxxix.

60. F. X. Funk, p. 220, notes with a question mark IV 3,2 as a reference to Hermas,

Mand. II 5. This also appears to Connolly to be the best evidence, as he stresses in his index (p. 278).

61. A concession which could only have been introduced on the authority of Hermas and, therefore, only through the recognition of the notion of the once-and-for-all character of penance.

62. On this, cf. n.17.

63. This does not exclude that reconciliation would be refused in those cases where it was believed that the sinner was incorrigible.

64. The anonymous author of the Didascalia displays a detailed knowledge of Jewish teaching and practices. He calls the Jews explicitly 'brothers' (V 14,23). On this, cf. L. Goppelt, *Christentum und Judentum im ersten und zweiten Jahhundert* (Gütersloh 1954), p. 205 ff.; W. Bauer, *Rechtglaübigkeit und Ketzerei in ältesten Christentum* (*Beiträge zur histor. Theologie* 10) (Tübingen 1964), pp. 253 f., 256–60. *Kirche und Synagogue: Handbuch zur Geschichte von Christen und Juden,* vol. i, ed. K. H. Rengstorf and S. von Kortzfleisch (Stuttgart 1968), p. 69 ff.

65. 'Parallel' does not mean an immediate dependence of the practice in the Didascalia upon the custom of the ban in the synagogue. Prescinding from the general oriental background, this phenomenon can be explained as the preservation in a conservative setting of a practice received originally from early Christianity. It is merely one more instance of the relationship which is known to have existed between the synagogue and the Christian Church, especially in the field of the liturgy. Cf., for example, A. Baumstark, *Vom geschichtlichen Werden der Liturgie* (Freiburg 1923), pp. 13–21; id., *Liturgie comparée* (Chevetogne o.J. [1940]) pp. 11, 87 f., 114 f., 137, 175; M. Simon, *Verus Israel: Etudes sur les relations entre chrétiens et juifs dans l'Empire romain* (Paris 1942).

66. Cf. Strack/Billerbeck, IV 1, pp. 293, 304. Since (ibid.) a funeral rite was prescribed for the person who was banned, he would surely have to fast during the time of his withdrawal. This does not mean, however, that he was excluded from visiting the temple, any more than the excommunicates were refused participation in the liturgy of the Word.

67. Cf. Strack/Billerbeck, IV 1, pp. 302, 327: 'In the act of banning the banned person should be cursed, castigated, struck, have his hair torn out, be entreated, bound, tied and even forced into a narrowly confined area' (p. 302). 'Both the simple ban and the solemn ban were expressed with curses' (p. 327).

68. Cf. Strack/Billerbeck, IV 1, p. 310.

69. Strack/Billerbeck, IV 1, pp. 298, 310.

70. II 47, 1–2 is to be construed in the following way: on the Monday the bishop should try to make a decision in a lawsuit between two Christians in such a way that neither party opposes the bishop's verdict but that both guard the peace with one another. Otherwise (which appears to be the logical corollary), it can inevitably happen that 'the sentence of condemnation of the earthly tribunal' must be passed by the bishop on one 'who is nevertheless a brother'. This sentence is passed only if one of the parties opposes the bishop's verdict and does not comply with it during the course of the week. Thus what is meant can only be excommunication and not a verdict in civil law. For the notion of the 'earthly tribunal' cf., for example, Strack/Billerbeck, I, p. 742, the rabbinical distinction between a 'lower' and an 'upper tribunal'. The latter confirms the ban of the latter 'on earth'.

71. Cf. Strack/Billerbeck, IV 1, p. 313.

72. For understandable reasons, the Didascalia seems to evade the question of what ought to happen to a bishop who excommunicates unjustly. Here he is threatened only with the consequences of his behaviour in the next life (II 43,5 etc.).

73. Cf. above under 3: Excommunication. Apart from the 24 reasons officially

recognized in about the middle of the third century, Strack/Billerbeck, IV I, pp. 309–13, lists eight others (cf. ibid., pp. 313–18).

74. Cf. the obligation of others to avoid a person who has been banned: Strack/Billerbeck, IV 1, pp. 304, 328; Didascalia III 8,5; the ban because of the profanation of a feast day: Strack/Billerbeck, IV 1, p. 311; Didascalia II 59,1; the question of whether the gifts of a person who has been banned should be accepted: Strack/Billerbeck, IV 1, p. 305; Didascalia, IV 5,1–8,3; III 8,3.

75. Strack/Billerbeck, IV 1, p. 320: 'Every simple ban can be loosed. Although this principle is nowhere explicitly stated, it is self-evidently implied in all the prescriptions concerning the lifting of the ban.' P. 328: 'The assumption, which is still held by Schurer, that the *cherem* was not able to be dissolved . . . is to be totally rejected. The *Shulchan Arukh* takes completely for granted that the *cherem* can be dissolved.'

76. F. X. Funk, I, p. 128 n.1, also emphasizes this, even though he wishes to exclude a repeated granting of penance for capital sins. But the assumption that there is such an essential distinction within the penance of excommunication is a purely arbitrary one. Wherever a second reconciliation was refused, this refusal must have affected all those who simply had to undertake a penance of excommunication.

CHAPTER EIGHT: THE PENITENTIAL TEACHING OF ORIGEN

1. The present, thoroughly revised study appeared in its original form in a French tr., under the title 'La doctrine d'Origène sur la Pénitence' in: RSR 37 (1950), pp. 47–97, 252–86, 422–56. In 1964 it appeared unchanged in Italian in the vol.: K. Rahner, *La penitenza della Chiesa* (Rome), pp. 707–876. It appears in German here for the first time. For the abundant literature on Origen's teaching on penance, cf. the general bibliography in the present vol. and H. Crouzel, *Bibliographie critique d'Origène* (*Instrumenta Patristica* VIII) (The Hague 1971).

2. De princ. I praef. 2 (GCS 22: 8,18–20.25–8); Matt XII 6 (GCS 40) 77, 26–29; Matt XII 13 (GCS 40) 94,26–32; Lc 16 (GCS 35) 109, 15–20; Jos 7,6 (GCS 30) 334,11–15; Num 9,1 (GCS 30) 54,20–25; Lev 7,4 (GCS 29) 383,7–9. Cf. G. Bardy, 'La règle de foi d'Origène' in: RSR 9 (1919), pp. 162–96; D. van den Eynde, *Les normes de l'enseignement chrétien dans la littérature patristique des trois premiers siècles* (Gembloux/Paris 1933), pp. 227–34; G. Bardy, *La théologie de l'Eglise de S. Irénée au concile de Nicée* (Paris 1947), pp. 128–65; R. Cadiou, *La jeunesse d'Origène* (Paris 1935), pp. 164–7, 267 ff., 383, *et passim*; H. Crouzel, *Origène et la 'connaissance mystique'* (Brussel/Paris 1961).

3. This question cannot be considered in detail here; but cf. J. Lebreton, 'Le désaccord de la foi populaire et de la théologie savante dans l'Eglise chrétienne de IIIe siècle' in: RHE 19 (1923), pp. 481–506; ibid., 20 (1924), pp. 5–37; J. Lebreton, 'Les degrés de la connaissance religieuse d'après Origène' in: RSR 12 (1922), pp. 265–96; D. van den Eynde, *Les normes de l'enseignement chrétien dans la littérature patristique des trois premiers siècles* (Gembloux/Paris 1933), pp. 152–6, 230–3; H. U. von Balthasar, 'Le Mystérion d'Origène' in: RSR 26 (1936), pp. 513–62 and 27 (1937), pp. 38–64.

4. Cf. on this H. U. von Balthasar, 'Le Mysterion . . .', and H. Crouzel, 'Origène . . .', pp. 25–209. This structure represents both the object of theology and the mode of knowledge which is most appropriate to this object. However, Origen does not expound it in terms of abstract principles. He generally assumes it when considering

particular questions and applies it unconsciously. In what follows no attempt is made to demonstrate this structure. The general reference to the conclusions of von Balthasar and Crouzel seems to be sufficient for our present purposes. Cf. also J. Daniélou, *Origène* (Paris 1948), as well as *Origenes, Gesit und Feuer—Ein Aufbau aus seinen Schriften* by H. U. von Balthasar (Salzburg 1951), pp. 11–43 (Introduction).

5. This is evident from Origen's teaching on the transformation of the body, as distinct from its destruction.

6. Cf. 1 Cor. 15:28.

7. On this, cf. the author's systematic considerations under the title 'Was ist ein Sakrament?' in: *Schriften zur Theologie* X (Einsiedeln-Zurich-Cologne 1972), pp. 377–91.

8. On this, cf. Origen's teaching on baptism according to H. U. von Balthasar, 'Le Mystérion . . . ', pp. 54–8.

9. In Ezech. hom. 8,1 (GCS 33) 402, 5–8. Cf. A. von Harnack, *Der kirchengeschichtliche Ertrag der exegetischen Arbeiten des Origenes* I (TU 42,3) (Leipzig 1918), p. 129 f. It is obvious that Origen considers the bishop's teaching office more important than his other duties (cf. Cant. III [GCS 33] 189, 6–11). He sees the priest and the bishop as *didaskalos,* and he himself had to be ordained priest in order to be able to teach legitimately. This emphasis which stresses the teaching office before the other duties of the hierarchy does not, however, change in any way its usual structure, as Origen also recognizes. Cf. D. van den Eynde, p. 233 f.; J. Daniélou, p. 57 f.

10. Cf. Ad Rom. IX, 2 (PG 14) 1213.

11. In Matt. X 15 (GCS 40) 18,24–19,3; ibid., XIV, 22(GCS 40,2) 336,20–337,7: the exterior hierarchy, divided into three levels, is σύμβολον of the realities mentioned after it; In Luc. hom. 13 (GCS 35) 91,22–5: every Church has a visible bishop, who is νοητός. On this, cf. H. U. von Balthasar, p. 45 ff.

12. In Lev. hom. 6,6 (GCS 29) 367,25–368,7; H. U. von Balthasar, p. 49 f. The section Ad Rom. IX,42 (PG 14) concerns not the Eucharist but the blessings for ordinary meals and the sanctification which they afford if they are made in the right spirit (as opposed to G. Bardy, p. 141). The 'exception' to this principle will be considered below in detail in connection with the power to forgive sins.

13. This is not to dispute the fact that Origen, as distinct from Tertullian, for example, did not elaborate very clear *criteria* for deciding between what was important and unimportant in church teaching and, consequently, in the obligations which emanate from this teaching. Cf. D. van den Eynde, p. 230. Since, however, even the Scriptures had to be interpreted according to the tradition of the Church and the rôle of judging the heretics falls to the bishops (cf. Origen, In Num.hom. 9,1 [GCS 30] 54, 20–9), there can be no doubt that Origen recognized a fundamental teaching authority (at least a negative one). This is connected with the office, but not with the bishop's personal holiness. Nevertheless, this does not mean that in certain aspects of positive teaching personal holiness was not considered a necessary prerequisite. This was all the more important in that, according to Origen, even an unjust decision on the Church's part is to be borne humbly and patiently (cf. In Ezech. hom. 10,1 [GCS 33] 417, 15–17). In his view, there is no earthly court of appeal against the Church.

14. In Lev. hom. 6,3 (GCS 29) 362,23–363,15; ibid., 6,6 (cf. n.13).

15. Cf. A. von Harnack, p. 129 ff.; J. Daniélou, p. 56 f.

16. In Num. hom. 2,1 (GCS 30) 9,22–7.

17. Cf. *Origen, Geist und Feuer,* p. 28 (introduction by H. U. von Balthasar).

18. Cf. In Jos. hom. 21,1 (GCS 30) 428–429,14; In Jer. hom. 15,3 (GCS 6) 127, 25–7; In Num. hom. 10,1 (GCS 30) 68–71; In Gen. hom. 2,3 (GCS 29) 31,10–14.

19. Cf. H. Rahner, 'Taufe und geistliches Leben bei Origenes' in: ZAM 7 (1932), pp. 205–322 (against the one-sidedness of Völker); J. Daniélou, pp. 65–74; H. U. von Balthasar, pp. 54–8.

20. Origen never thought of a renewal or a repetition of baptism. He made the distinction between baptism *secundum typum Ecclesiae traditum* (Ad Rom. V,8 [PG 14] 1038–40) and the interior dying with Christ by the reception of the Spirit without thereby considering the baptism in water a mere meaningless formality. This would be a contradiction of his basic notion of the relationship between *τύπος* and the interior reality (cf. H. U. von Balthasar, p. 56). Thus his notion corresponds to today's distinction between a 'fruitful' and a (merely) 'valid' baptism. The fact that he makes this distinction so clearly—Tertullian, for instance, still did not have the courage to do so—shows how the situation has changed.

21. Ad Rom. V, 8 (PG 14) 1040.

22. In Luc. hom. 21 (GCS 35) 140,1–7; In Num. hom. 3,1 (GCS 30)14,1–6.

23. In Luc. hom. 22 (GCS 35) 145,25–30; cf. J. Daniélou, p. 67 f.

24. Cf. H. Rahner, p. 214 ff.

25. The transformation does not take place *ad subitum*: Ad Rom. VI, 10 (PG 14) 1092; In Cant. II (GCS 33) 171,13–17.

26. Contra Celsum III, 65 (GCS 2) 259,2–7 [SC 136,150,18 ff.]; cf. In Jos. hom. 6,1 (GCS 30) 321,21–322,6; In Lev. hom. 8,7 (GCS 29) 405,11–14.

27. Ad Rom. II, 14 (PG 14) 918; In Num. hom. 10,1 (GCS 30) 68–71; In Jos. hom. 21,2 (GCS 30) 431,11–14; Contra Celsum III 69 (GCS 2) 262,13–15 [SC 136, 158, 35–40]; In Joan. XX 26/27 (GCS 10) 362,20–2; 363, 30–4. On the question whether the 'perfect' can reach impeccability, cf. the dissertation of P. D. Huet (1630–1721) (PG 17) 955 ff. Cf. also: W. Völker, *Das Vollkommenheitsideal des Orgenes* (Tübingen 1931), pp. 162–8 (with further references to the previous literature); A. Lieske, *Die Theologie der Logosmystik bei Origenes* (Münster 1938), p. 90 ff.

28. In Matt. tom. XX 23 (GCS 40) 416,32–417,5.

29. In Ezech. hom. 6,7 (GCS 33) 385, 13–19.

30. Cf. the material in A. von Harnack, I 65 ff.; II 114 ff., 129 ff.

31. On the whole question, cf. the thorough study of G. Teichtweier, *Die Sündenlehre des Origenes* (Regensburg 1958), which we will have occasion to refer to again.

32. In Ezech. hom. 5,1 (GCS 33) 372,21.

33. Thus, for example, sin as *θάνατος-ἀσθένεια-ζημία*: In Joan. XIX 13–14 (GCS 10) 312,22–313,15; the distinction between *ἁμαρτία-ῥύπος* which, in the case of *ῥύπος* can range from a morally light blemish to a pollution of the whole body: In Luc. hom. 14 (GCS 35) 96,20–98,10; In Jer. hom. 2,2 (GCS 6) 18,26–19,8; he also asks himself whether sins which, in themselves, are not 'mortal' but which, because there is no repentance, lead to a justifiable ban on the Church's part (therefore become mortal sins): In Matt. tom. XIII 30 (GCS 40) 264,6–25; 266,7–21; 268,12–25; the only criterion which he recognizes for an essential distinction between sins is simply whether the sinner is ready to do penance or not: In Num. hom. 10,1 (GCS 30) 68–71; the three-fold distinction between sins (according to 1 Cor. 3:12) which, according to their gravity, are like wood, grass or straw: In Lev. hom. 14,3 (GCS 29) 482, 10–19 and *passim*. Weakness, illness, somnolence: In Matt. tom. X 24 (GCS 33,19–30; the five-fold relationship to mortal sin: In Matt. tom. XII 35 (GCS 40) 149,18–33; *impius, infirmus, peccator*: Ad Rom. IV 11 (PG 14) 999; *peccata pingua—tenuia—subtilia*: In Luc. hom. 35 (GCS 35) 214,22–215,4. In addition there is the division into sins of deed, word and thought: In Cant. IV (GCS 33) 239,31–240, 1; In Ex. hom. 6,3 (GCS 29)194, 18 f.; ibid., 3,3 (GCS 29) 166,15 f.; In Lev. hom. 9,7 (GCS 29) 430,2–10; In Is. hom. 4,3 (GCS 33) 261,14 f. (This division is taken from Philo.) On the divisions of sins, cf. further in G. Techtweier, ch. 5; 'Die Arten der Sünde, pp. 210–81, and W. Capitaine, *De Ethica Origenis* (Münster 1898), p. 163 ff.

34. In Ezech. hom. 9,2 (GCS 33) 408, 16–24. It is interesting that Origen refuses to accept the idea that sexual faults are the most serious sins.

35. In Lev. hom. 12,3 (GCS 29) 460,1.

36. In Lev. hom. 11,2 (GCS 29) 452,7; In Matt. tom. XIII 30 (GCS 40) 262.14 f.; In Ex. hom. 10,3 (GCS 29) 249, 20; In Lev. hom. 4,5 (GCS 29) 322,11 f.; Fragm. ad libr. X Strom. (PG II) 103; In Lev. hom. 8,7 (GCS 29) 405,15 f.; ibid., 5,4 (GCS 29) 341,17.

37. De or. 28,10 (GCS 3) 381,16 f.; In Joan. XXVIII 6 (GCS 10) 396,33; ibid., XIX 23 (GCS 10) 325,11; In Jer. hom. 2,2 (GCS 6) 19,2.

38. In Matt. tom. XIII 30 (GCS 40) 264, 14–16; In Ex. hom. 10,3 (GCS 29) 249,22 f.

39. In Jos. hom. 7,6 (GCS 30) 334,3; In Matt. tom. XIII 30 (GCS 40) 264, 26. It is obvious that here *levis culpa* is meant as the opposite of mortal sin.

40. In Lev. hom. 15,2 f. (GCS 29) 481,13; 482,14.

41. In Jer. hom. 2,6 (GCS 33) 296,3; ψιλὸν ἁμάρτημα: Fragm. on 1 Cor. 3:14 (PG 17) 40.

42. In Jer. hom. 2,12 (GCS 33) 302, 15–18. It is debatable, however, whether this distinction is entirely exclusive. Certainly any proof which pretends to demonstrate a further differentiation within mortal sin itself is subject to serious doubts, especially if the text In Lev. hom. 15,2 is taken as the only decisive indication of this assumption. Here, as we will reiterate below when we consider this text more closely, it is advisable to exercise a certain amount of reserve from the viewpoint of literary criticism. Cf. n.106.

43. In Jer. hom. 2,6 (GCS 33) 295,24.29.

44. In Ex. hom. 10,3 (GCS 29) 249,17–19. In the three-fold distinction: θάνατος-ἀσθένεια-ζημία of In Joan. XIX 13–14 (GCS 10) 312,22–313,4 the two last members correspond to the *damnum* of In Ex. hom. 10,3.

45. In Jer. hom. 2,3 (GCS 6) 19,22. The expression evokes the terminology of Hermas (Sim. VIII 6,3) (GCS 48: p. 71,18–21). Cf. also 2 Clement 6,9; 7,6; 8,5. For the notion of keeping with regard to baptism in Origen, cf. In Luc. hom. 24 (GCS 35) 158,23–6: *habere priorum* (as opposed to the eschatological baptism in fire) *baptismatum* (in water and the Spirit); *aquae et Spiritus lavacra servare*.

46. In Matt. tom. XIII 30 (GCS 40) 262 ff.: only the person who commits the *grandia* (263,14), that is, mortal sins, is an ἀδελφὸς ὀνομαζόμενος (263,14), so that even in the case of a person who perseveres obstinately in a non-mortal sin, it has to be left to God to decide whether he still belongs truly to the Church (268,20–5). The *levis culpa* does not deserve the Church's ban: In Jos. hom. 7,6 (GCS 30) 334,2–5 (at least if there is present a firm purpose of amendment). Origen could not have said this if he were thinking of a guilt which was only relatively light but which still destroys the grace of baptism. For, in his view, such an act in itself separates a person objectively from the Church. A person guilty of a sin of impurity (in Origen's view a *peccatum mortale*: cf. In Matt. Tom. XIII 30 (GCS 40) 262,13–26) is already, by that very fact, separated from the Church and, consequently, should also be officially excommunicated, in so far as this is possible: Fragm. in Jer. 48 (GCS 6) 222,10–14. Similarly In Lev. hom. 14,2 (GCS 29)479,22–6, where *peccatum* means a mortal sin. As we have shown, not every sin separates a person from the Church, but in this instance Origen is thinking of those sins mentioned in 1 Cor. 6:9 f. (GCS 29) 481, 5–10; In Jud. hom. 2,5 (GCS 30) 478, 22–479,10, where likewise the simple *peccatum* is to be understood of mortal sin, because it is described as an abandonment on God's part, ibid. (GCS 30) 479,18–23. As we have already seen, Origen does not consider that this happens in the case of every sin. It is, however, a part of his description of mortal sins as opposed to other faults; we will return to this point later. In Jer. hom. 15,5 (GCS 6) 127,26 (when we fall we are only still νομιζόμενοι εἶναι ἀπὸ τῆς ἐκκλησίας).

47. Cf. (GCS 30) 68–71. For a similar emphasis on sinfulness in general even in the case of the saints, cf. In Is. hom. 3,2 (GCS 33) 255,12–14; In Num. hom. 6,3 (GCS 30) 32–5.

48. Obviously Origen is not thinking here of mortal sins. Since he does not recognize the person guilty of a mortal sin as being any longer a brother, he could hardly count him as a 'saint'. The many examples adduced from Paul (cf. ibid. [GCS 30] 69,14–18 and 70,6–16), which are elsewhere counted by Origen, without any doubt, as mortal sins, obviously only serve to show that the Christian ought not to consider himself automatically immune from sin. They do not imply that the Christian, in spite of these sins, can still be a saint at the same time. This is all the more true in that Origen always sees in mortal sin that lack of a genuine purpose of amendment which is incompatible with holiness. What is more, Origen considers that, in the case of mortal sins, exhortation to amendment within the Church without excommunication is futile: In Matt. tom. XIII 30 (GCS 40) 263,4–12.

49. Cf. ibid. (GCS 35) 13,5–20,4.

50. Although according to In Is. hom. 3,2 (GCS 33)255,12 and In Num. hom. 6,3 (GCS 30) 32–5 *every* sin (*peccat enim omnis homo*: ibid. [GCS 30] 255,12) appears to exclude the continuing presence of the Spirit, this ought to be understood, in the context, as referring to the *full* presence of the Spirit, with *all* his gifts as well as his *actual* influence on man's questionable acts. Origen even excludes such a presence in respect of the conjugal act which he, nevertheless, in the same context explains as being free from sin (ibid. [GCS 30] 35,16). All this indicates that Origen has a more actualistic notion of the indwelling of the Spirit than either we are accustomed to or, indeed, he himself presupposes when he speaks about the preservation of baptism, etc. Nevertheless this actualistic view ought not to blur the essential distinction which Origen consistently draws between mortal and non-mortal sins. At the same time, this particular view of the relationship between the Spirit and man should be kept in mind in the prudent interpretation of In Lev. hom. 15,2 (GCS 29) 487–9. If it is there stated that with every actual sin (*communia, quae frequenter incurrimus*: ibid. [GCS 29] 489,20 f.) a person 'sells' his or her 'heavenly house', then, once the exegetical basis for these ideas is taken into consideration, nothing more is being said here than in the texts mentioned above. The passage of In Lev. hom. will be considered more closely below.

51. In Lev. hom. 15,2 (GCS 29) 489,19–22; In Joan. XXVII 6 (GCS 10) 396,32–6; Fragm. ad libr. X Strom. (PG II) 103; In Ezech. hom. 3,8 (GCS 33) 357,32–358,1; In Jer. hom. 20,9 (GCS 6) 191 f. Cf. below for a more precise consideration.

52. Cf. n.48 above.

53. Corresponding to Origen's view of the intrinsic unity of punishment and means of salvation, this activity, too, is to be understood as simultaneously both a punishment and a means of salvation. In contrast to the reaction to a *plaga insanabilis,* however, it does not come immediately from God himself. The *vulnera facilia* of the *minora peccata* are punished and healed by God's 'servants': In Jer. hom. 2,6 (GCS 33) 295,17–20; In Ex. hom. 4,8 (GCS 29)181,26–182,5 contains a similar idea. We are unable to pursue further this profound idea: in the case of venial sins, where man remains connected with the totality of all the means of grace, or is still open to it, this totality still works salvifically in all its dimensions and dynamism for the perfection of man's life of grace: the angels: In Jer. hom. 2,6 (GCS 33) 295,15–18; instruction and correction by the brethren (especially the τέλειοι): In Lev. hom. 3,2 (GCS 29) 302,2–6; In Matt. tom. XIII 30 (GCS 40) 268,15–21; ibid., XII 11 (GCS 40) 86,24–31; De or. 14,6 (GCS 3) 333,11–16; In Num. hom. 10,1 (GCS 30) 68,4, etc.; the intercession of the blessed martyrs and saints: In Num. hom. 10,2 (GCS 30)71,25–72,2; De or. 11,2 (GCS 3) 322,14–18; the activity of the priests of the Church, by which they correct, participate in penance and offer sacrifice: In Matt. tom. XVI 8 (GCS 40) 496,21–8; In Jos. hom. 7,6 (GCS 30) 332,22–333,5; In Lev. hom. 5,3 (GCS 29) 339,11–17; ibid., 5,4 (GCS 29) 342,9–15; ibid., 13,3 (GCS 29) 471,25–7; etc.; the punishing effects of guilt

in the world through suffering, illness, etc.: In Joan. VI 58 (GCS 10)166,23–167,5; In Num. hom. 8,1 (GCS 30) 51,10–24; In Ps. 37,5 (PG 12) 1385, etc.

54. In Num. hom. 10,1 (GCS 30) 68,4–13. This passage evinces the two-fold level of the Church's mediation in the healing of sins: through *meliores* and *sacerdotes*.

55. In Lev. hom. 12,3 (GCS 29) 459,20–460,7.

56. In Luc. hom. 24 (GCS 35) 158,23 ff.; In Joan. XXVIII 7 (GCS 10) 397,29–34.

57. In Lev. hom. 8,11 (GCS 29) 417,12–18; In Joan. XXVIII 15 (GCS 10) 408,11–16; In Lev. hom. 4,3 (GCS 29) 318,18–23.

58. In Ex. hom. 10,4 (GCS 29) 250,20–6.

59. In Lev. hom. 14,2 (GCS 29) 481,3–11. It is worth noting that the sin mentioned here as 'against God' is, according to In Lev. hom. 4,5 (GCS 29) 322,8–11, identical with the *peccatum ad mortem*.

60. In Joan. XXVIII 7 (GCS 10) 397,29–34; 398,3–5.

61. In Ex. hom. 6,9 (GCS 29) 200,15–20; In Ezech. hom. 12,3 (GCS 33) 435,23–436,2.

62. In Jer. fragm. 71 (GCS 6) 232, 26 f.; In Joan. XXVIII 6 (GCS 10) 396, 28: *νεκρὸς τῷ θεῷ*.

63. Cf. In Joan. XIX 13 (GCS 10) 312,22–313,16, where it is clear that mortal sin is considered 'incurable' because and in so far as the 'illness' cannot be treated by the physician (Christ and his assistants) in such a way as to prevent death. At the same time there are diseases and weaknesses which are certainly 'curable' and thus do not entail death. Contrary to Poschmann, p. 473 f., the notion of mortal sin is not used here in the sense of 'sin' which, because of definitive voluntary unrepentance, leads in fact to eternal death. Even according to Poschmann (op. cit. p. 435 f.) this would not correspond to Origen's use of the term elsewhere. It fits neither the context here nor the application of the notion in his commentary on John XXVIII 6 (GCS 10) 396, 33 f. The allusion to the night into which the soul enters (cf. Luc. 12,20; In Joan. XIX 12 [GCS 10] 312,20) is no proof of Poschmann's interpretation. It is not clear from Origen's allegory that by this night he means physical death which sin makes definitive. The prognosis on the part of the physician Christ that the illness will end in death refers to the fact that the illness of the 'Jews' will end in death. This illness was already at a critical stage, although it had not yet led to actual death of the soul. But this will occur because the Jews did not *wish* to be healed (In Joan. XIX 11 [GCS 10] 311,13–14; In Jer. hom. 2,12 [GCS 33] 302,2: *irremediabilis nolentisque curari*). The expression *ἁμαρτία ἀνίατος* is found already in Hermas, Mand V 2,4 (GCS 48:31,4); likewise also: Didascalia apost. VI 14,10; cf. Const. Apost. II, 37,2; 41,7; VI, 18,10; Ps.-Cypr., De sing. cler. 6 (CSL 3,3; 179,18); Ps.-Cypr., De aleatoribus 5 (CSL 3,3: 97,18); Cyprian, epist. 30,7 (of Novatian); Cyprian, De lapsis 15 (*letalis plaga*); the synodal documents of the council of Antioch of A.D. 269 (see in Eusebius, Hist. Eccl. VII 30,12 [GCS 9,2: 710,25]). In all these texts there is nowhere a mention of the fact that a person who has 'died' of an 'incurable' sin cannot be revived. The contrary is either presupposed or expressed (cf. H. Koch, *Cyprianische Untersuchungen* [Bonn 1926], p. 441 f.; P. Galtier, *L'Eglise et la rémission des péchés aux premiers siècles* [Paris 1932], p. 191 ff.). For the identification of the *ἀνίατα τῶν ἁμαρτημάτων* with the *ἁμαρτία πρός θανάτον* and *εἰς κύριον* in Origen, cf. De or. 28,8–10 (GCS 3) 380,12; 381,10 f. and 15 f. For the idea that a terminal illness cannot be halted by angels, etc., cf. In Jer. hom. 2,6 (GCS 33) 295,24–296,2; ibid., 2,12 (GCS 33) 300–2; In Lev. hom. 8,5 (GCS 209) 402, 15–18; In Jos. hom. 7,6 (GCS 30) 334,2–7; In Ps. 37,1 (PG 12) 1372.

64. In Joan. XXVIII 6 (GCS 10) 396,32–4.

65. In Joan. XXVIII 7 (GCS 10) 397,34.

66. In Ezech. hom. 10,2 (GCS 33) 419,1–7. Cf. Ad Rom. IV 12 (PG 14) 1002; In Ezech. hom. 5,3 (GCS 33) 374,1–26.

67. Cf. the long researches in In Joan. XXVIII 15–20 (GCS 10) 408–15; esp. 15 (ibid., 408, 4–409,3). On the basis of these ideas Origen is easily able, for instance, to forgive Peter's denial; the sin of a Christian is greater and more serious because he has already received the *spiritus gratiae* (Heb. 10:29: In Matt. ser. 114 (GCS 40) 236,29–239,32.

68. In Joan. XXVIII 15 (GCS 10) 408,25.

69. In Joan. II 11 (GCS 10) 66,10–17.

70. In Jer. hom. 9,4 (GCS 6) 70,12–27. On this cf. A. Lieske, p. 157. On the whole section of reflections on sin, cf. also G. Teichtweier, who nevertheless recognizes only the presence of the legal-ethical viewpoint. He thus opposes a consideration of the consequences of sin from the viewpoint of grace, and this by appealing to the lack of an adequate distinction between nature and grace (loc. cit. p. 134). In general and as a matter of principle, the first point which must be made in this regard is that from the very nature of the case there is already an inner connection between the individual consequences of sins, making the isolation of any one approach inappropriate. Teichtweier, following his own presuppositions, understands 'death' as the consequence of sin uniquely as the expression of the intensity of the lapse into sin; that is, in this case the sinner stands in an irreducible opposition to God, the source of life (p. 141 f.). This means, however, that both the Church as a community of grace and consequently the theological significance of reconciliation are overlooked.

71. In Jer. hom. 2,6 (GCS 33) 295,10 f. Cf. In Ps. 37 hom. 1,1 (PG 12) 1372: there are sins which can no longer be punished by the law, the bishop or the angel of penance but only by God himself.

72. In Jer. hom. 2,6 (GCS 33) 295,20–2; In Lev. hom. 4,4 (GCS 29) 319,23–320,7; In Jer. hom. 13,1 (GCS 6)102,28–103,3.

73. Cf. n.61 above.

74. In Matt. tom. XII 4 (GCS 40) 75,3–5; ibid. XI 6 (GCS 40) 44,8–10; In Jer. hom. 9,4 (GCS 6) 70,3–11.

75. In Num. hom. 20,3 (GCS 30) 193,9–29.

76. In dependence upon John 8:44 and 1 John 3:8: In Joan. XX 10 (GCS 10) 339,26–30; ibid., XX 13 (GCS 10) 343,19–23; 344,10–14. The fact of being engendered by the devil appears here to be more the presupposition of, and reason for, the (new) sin than its consequence.

77. Ad Rom. V 9 (PG 14) 1046.

78. In Joan. II 11 (GCS 10) 66,11; ibid., XXVIII 15 (GCS 10) 408,18–21; Exhort. ad mart. 30 (GCS 2) 26,20–4; In Matt. series 114 (GCS 40) 239,5–20; In Jer. hom. 16,5 (GCS 6) 137,21–3; In Lev. hom. 2,4 (GCS 29) 295,18–20.

79. In Matt.ser. 114 (GCS 40) 238,8. In Joan. II 11 (GCS 10) 66,13 συγγνώμη is synonymous with ἄφεσις; cf. ibid. (GCS 10) 66,6.9.11.

80. That such sins can in fact be remitted is abundantly obvious from the texts just mentioned and from their context. In Exhort. ad mart. 30 Origen mentions simply without any qualification ἁμαρτήματα which can be granted an ἄφεοις through baptism and martyrdom. In the abstract—and this may indeed be the case elsewhere—it is conceivable that ἁμαρτήματα designates *only* mortal sins; cf. n. 33 above. In the present context, however, this is unlikely. For if this were the case, would Origen take it so easily for granted that the friends—Ambrose and Protoctetus—whom he is exhorting, together with their companions who are threatened, do in fact need to remit mortal sins? If, however, ἁμαρτήματα here refers to all sins, including those which are not mortal, then ἄφεσις cannot mean the remission of sins at all. For no one disputes that according to Origen at least non-mortal sins can be remitted apart from baptism and martyrdom. Moreover, this does not necessarily mean an ἄφεσις, although it could do if 'ἄφεοις were to have this comprehensive meaning. Just before the passage In Joan. XXVIII 15 there is ibid., XXVIII 7 (GCS 10) 397,15–19, that is,

the text which contains the resurrection of Lazarus. This resurrection provides a symbol of the restoration to life of the person who is guilty of mortal sin, that is, who has sinned in the sense of Heb. 6:4 f. and has reverted to a pagan way of life. In Matt. ser. 114 it is stated that sinners who behave according to Heb. 10:29 no longer have hope of a *remissio* either in this world or the next. But Origen adds immediately that such a sinner ought *not* to say: *peccata nostra in nobis sunt et quomodo vivemus*. For God says: *vivo, quoniam nolo mortem peccatoris sicut paenitentiam* (Ezek. 33,10 f.), and he knows which penalties he inflicts *super denegantes et paenitentes,* as opposed to the *denegantes et non paenitentes* (cf. In Matt. ser. 114 [GCS 38] 239,23–8). It is, therefore, clearly presupposed that penance is always effective, even though *remissio* is no longer possible. In In Lev. hom. 2,4 he has his audience saying: *apud nos una tantummodo est venia peccatorum, quae per lavacri gratiam in initiis datur; nulla post haec peccanti misericordia nec venia ulla conceditur*. This is merely the principle which had been in force since Hermas. It refers to mortal sins, since it is these, above all, that are remitted in baptism. But it never occurred to any one to deny that a forgiveness for non-mortal sins was possible. It is obvious that Origen, in his answer, does not intend to dispute this ancient principle—once it has been correctly understood—especially since he himself enunciates it just as unhesitatingly elsewhere. Now if, in order to prove that, despite this principle, Christians are not worse off than Jews, he enumerates seven *remissiones,* then it follows that at least one of these must refer to mortal sins. Otherwise he would only have evaded the objection. Thus the *septima remissio* of public penance is placed at the end of the list as the climax and decisive argument (cf. In Lev. hom. 2,4 [GCS 29] 296,17–22). Likewise, the *remissio* of In Lev. hom. 15,2 (GCS 29) 488,23 f., according to the context (cf. ibid., 489,19 f.), also includes the remission of mortal sins by means of the once-and-for-all public penance. As could be shown from the actual context, this *remissio* in Lev.hom. 2,4 refers to mortal sins not only *de facto* but also absolutely *de iure*. It is a *remissio peccatorum*. The single *venia*—whether in the Greek it is ἄφεσις, συγγνώμη or another word that is behind it is irrelevant, since these expressions can have the same meaning; elsewhere Origen conveys its sense with ἄφεσις—does not exclude a *remissio* in a wider sense. According to In Lev. hom. 2,4 (GCS 29) 296,17, it is *dura et laboriosa*. Thus in this passage ἄφεοις is not used in the strict sense of a simple remission of sins. The only text which does not admit of a clear interpretation on this question in function of its context is In Joan. II 11. Nevertheless, in this work the fact that mortal sin against the Spirit is able to be overcome is so clearly expressed that it would be absurd to interpret this passage differently from the other texts or—as, for instance, G. Rauschen, *Eucharistie und Busssakrament* (Freiburg 1908), p. 179, does—to assume that Origen changes his opinion in the same work. Moreover, if In Joan. II was composed substantially earlier (after A.D. 220) than, for example, In Joan. XXVIII 15 (after A.D. 233), then both texts say the same thing. For just before In Joan. XXVIII 15 occurs the section In Joan. XXVIII 7: the teaching on the restoration to life of the person guilty of mortal sin. Thus there is no reason why In Joan. can and must be interpreted differently from the other texts. That the contrary of ἄφεσις is not unforgiveness but another kind of remission of sins is obvious from Selecta in Ps. 31,1 (PG 12)1301: ἀφίενται μὲν αἱ ἀνομίαι διά τοῦ ἁγίου βαπτίσματος, καλύπτονται δὲ αἱ ἁμαρτίαι διὰ τῆς πικρᾶς ἁμαρτίας μετανοίας. Even though the formulation of this sentence may derive more from Evagrius than immediately from Origen (cf. H. U. von Balthasar, 'Die Hiera des Evagrius' in: ZKTh 63 [1939], pp. 86–106), it nevertheless resumes faithfully Origen's idea of the difference between ἄφεσις and the notion which is actually opposed to it. It is also possible to think that the sentence is a summary from *Didymus*, Expos. in Ps. 31,3 (PG 39)1320. But even in this case, we have an idea which is peculiar to Origen: on the one hand, ἄφεσισ, συγγνώμη in baptism for sins committed *before* the law; on the other hand, no ἄφεσις but an ἐπικάλυψις of sins, in virtue of μετάνοια for offences committed after baptism. For the origin of this formula in Origen, cf. Ad Rom. II 11 (PG 14) 872: *quorum remissae sunt iniquitates per baptismi gratiam vel quorum tecta sunt per paenitentiam peccata*. We will have to consider the text In Jer.hom. 16,5 more closely later. It is evident, therefore, that ἄφεσις and every kind of remission of sins are *not* absolutely identical. Certainly ἄφεσις can have a narrow technical sense, and does so necessarily in several passages. Nevertheless, this obviously does not mean that in other passages it cannot have a wider non-technical sense and then means, quite simply, any kind of 'forgiveness of sins'. This is the case in De or. 28,5 (GCS 3) 378,5 f.; ibid., 31,3 (GCS 3) 396,23; ibid., 33,1 (GCS3) 401,21; In Is.hom. 6,2 (GCS 33) 270,29; 271,5; In Lev. hom. 5,3 (GCS 29) 339,13 f. compared with 340,1 f.; Exhort.ad mart. 30 (GCS2) 27,5; In Matt.tom. XII 14 (GCS 40) 99,5; In Num.hom. 10,1 (GCS 30) 68,9.11; in Lev.hom. 2,4 (GCS 29) 295,26–296,22. In the last passage the contrast between the technical and the more general use of the notion is very clear: *una tantummodo venia peccatorum* (ibid., 295,18)—many *remissiones* (ibid., 295,26). It is also clear, therefore, that the technical usage is traditional: Origen makes his audience raise the lament over the *una venia peccatorum* as a self-evident axiom.

81. Cf., for example, Exhort.ad mart. 30 (GCS 2) 26,20–4. Very often baptism and the remission of sins are simply mentioned together without it being at all evident from the texts that the remission in question is an effect which is proper to baptism. Thus, for example, in Cant. III (GCS 33) 226,16 f.; In Lev.hom. 8,3 (GCS 29) 398,11 f.; ibid., 8,7 (GCS 29) 405,11 f.; In Jos.hom. 15,7 (GCS 30) 393,11 f.; In Luc.hom. 14 (GCS 35) 98,13; ibid., 21 (GCS 35) 139,1–3.18 f.; 140,3.

82. Cf. In Joan. II 11 (GCS 10) 66,13–15.

83. Cf. De or. 28,9 f. (GCS 3) 380,25; 381.5.10.15.

84. Cf. ibid., 381,8.

85. In Joan. fragm. 12 (GCS 10) 494,10: it is through the ἄφεσις, which here obviously refers to baptism, that the punishment imposed for sin according to the law is lifted. Origen's notion of κόλασις must be completely disassociated from any idea of a purely vindictive punishment, such as would contribute nothing to the actual remission of guilt. Such a notion does not exist in Origen's thinking. In his view punishment is always destructive of guilt (at least in so far as it is considered in itself). Thus where ἄφεσις occurs, as opposed to κόλασις, it is a question of a remission of guilt which is not brought about by the expiatory suffering of the punishments due to sin. ἄφεσις is, therefore, the remission of sin without punishment which, nevertheless, obviously allows of a forgiveness precisely through the suffering of such punishment.

86. Cf. In Jer.hom. 16,5–7 (GCS 6) 137–9.

87. This passage states explicitly that sins such as those mentioned in Heb.10:26 f. can be remitted through undergoing punishment. This also clarifies how In Jer. hom. 13,2 (GCS 6) 103,15–104,18 should be understood. This text is repeatedly adduced as a proof that, according to Origen, mortal sins are unforgivable. It is here stated, with regard to the sins of Heb. 10:29 and 6:4 ff., that the sinful Jerusalem, that is, the soul which, after baptism, has relapsed into sin and become unbelieving, cannot count on forbearance, pity and prayer for reconciliation, not even that of Jesus himself. However, this need not mean any more than what is said of the same sins in In Jer. hom. 16,55 ff., namely that such sins can be remitted only by undertaking the punishment which is appropriate to them.

88. Cf., for example, παιδεύων πόνος: In Jer.hom. 12,3 (GCS 6) 91,5.

89. The same idea of a purifying and not merely vindictive baptism of fire for sins committed after baptism figures in: In Jer. hom. 2,2 f. (GCS 6) 17–20. (It is said

explicitly, cf. ibid., 19,3; 18,28 f.: with regard to mortal sins, as opposed to ῥύπος sins, that the sins which are remitted in the fire of judgement are mortal sins.) In Luc.hom. 24 (GCS 35) 158; In Is.hom. 4,5–6 (GCS 33) 262; In Lev.hom. 9,8 (GCS 29) 432,17–27; In Ex. hom. 13,4 (GCS 29) 275,18–23; In Ezech.hom. 1,3 (GCS 33) 324,7–27; Ennarr. in Job 20,25 (PG 17)76.

90. Cf., for example, Comm. in Gen.tom. III 7(PG 12) 68; in Matt. tom. XV 11 (GCS 40) 379,20–380,6; Contra Celsum VI 26 (GCS 3) 96,11–17.

91. It is entirely another question whether this forgiveness of guilt in baptism is entirely compatible with Origen's notion of the salvific meaning of suffering, which latter both emanates from guilt and finally destroys it (thus not to be punished signifies God's most intense anger: In Jer.hom. 2,5 [GCS 33] 294,21–5; In Ex.hom. 8, 5 [GCS 29] 230,8–13, etc.) or with the teaching that bad habits, etc. (which are also in Origen's view the punishments for previous sins) are not yet remitted by baptism. What is clear is that Origen feels himself bound by the Church's teaching of a single ἄφεσις in baptism, and when he considers or evaluates it he understands it in the traditional way of a forgiveness which abrogates punishment.

92. In Ex.hom. 10,3 (GCS 29) 249,21–3.

93. He is obviously clearly aware of the different degrees of subjective imputability which sin can involve. Cf., for example, In Lev.hom. 14,3 (GCS 29) 482,28–483,1: sins *non ex corde, non voto et animo iniquo*; Ad Rom. V 11 (PG 14)999; ibid., II 1 (PG 14) 871 f.; In Num.hom. 28,2 (GCS 30) 282,26–283,9. Cf. E. R. Redepenning, *Origenes. Eine Darstellung seines Lebens und seiner Lehre* (Bonn 1841–6; rep. Aalen 1966) II, p. 424.

94. In Matt.tom. XIII 30 (GCS 40) 262,15–20; 263,17–26 (with reference to 1 Cor. 5:II); 264,3–5 are also listed: φόνος, φαρμακία, παιδοφθορία ἤ τι τῶν τηλικούτων.

95. In Lev.hom. 15,2 (GCS 29) 489,14. Cf. Fragm. 48 in Jer. (GCS 6) 222,13.

96. In Lev.hom. 14,2 (GCS 29) 481,5–14. It is here a question of the deliberate and habitual tendency to blaspheme.

97. Cf. De or. 28 (GCS 3) 381,14; 380,23. Origen does not have in mind here a fixed group of three, since he adds: ἤ τινος ἄλλου χαλεπωτέρου πταίσματος (ibid., 380,28–318,1).

98. Cf. In Joan. XXVIII 7 (GCS 10) 397,34.

99. Cf. In Joan. XXVIII 6 (GCS 10) 396,33 f.

100. In Ex.hom. 6,9 (GCS 29) 200,16–201,5. For adultery as a mortal sin, cf.: Fragm. ad lib. X Strom. (PG 11)103; for fornication: Contra Celsum III 51 (GCS 2) 247,23.

101. In Lev.hom. 11,3 (GCS 29) 452,28–453,3. In general those offences which, in the Old Testament, were punished by death Origen considers, according to the New Testament, to be mortal sins which are subject to church penance *in interitum carnis*; cf. In Lev.hom. 11,2 (GCS 29) 451,1–13. It is obvious that Origen still recognizes here the traditional distinction between *peccatum in Deum* and *non in Deum* (*in hominem*). De or. 28,9 (GCS 3) 381,9–11; 28,3 (GCS 3) 376,25–7; In Lev.hom. 8,10 (GCS 29) 408,5; ibid., 4,5 (GCS 29) 322,9–11; In Num.hom. 10,1 (GCS 30) 68,10–12; In Ezech.hom. 5,4 (GCS 33) 375,25–8; Exhort.ad mart. 17 (GCS 2)16,19–23. But the content of the notion is just as vague as it is elsewhere. In In Lev.hom. 4,5 'sin against God' is identified with 'mortal sin'. For this reason alone, therefore, 'sin against God' does not mean simply sin against faith. In In Lev.hom. 14,2 (GCS 29) 481 it is stressed that both the *maledicus in proximum* and the *maledicus in Deum* are excluded from the kingdom of God.

102. Cf. In Jer.hom. 20 (GCS 6)181,13–19.

103. In Matt.tom. XIII (GCS 40)264,21–9.

104. It is not clear, for example, whether or not Origen (In Lev.hom. 9,9 [GCS 29]

437,29–438,3) regards as mortal sins the frequenting of the circus, the races and the gladiatorial games, which were considered sins in themselves.

105. In Lev.hom. 14,3 (GCS 29) 482,19 f., etc.

106. G. Teichtweier maintains that there is a further subdivision of mortal sin. To do so he proceeds from the different terminology which Origen uses to designate sins. According to this, he holds, more than a mere two-fold distinction is required. Teichtweier sees a confirmation of this assumption in the parallel with the Montanist Tertullian's teaching on sin which implies a three-fold distinction. Cf. op. cit., pp. 237–9. The distinction between mortal sins and non-mortal sins is obviously upheld throughout Origen, as Teichtweier also observes, op. cit., p. 237. But then, in order to justify the further sub-distinction of mortal sins, Teichtweier appeals to what is, for him, the indispensable evidence of the text In Lev.hom. He does so, however, without discussing the literary-critical problem which this passage presents. This is all the more surprising in that in an earlier work, *Das Sein des Menschen: Ein Beitrag zur Anthropologie des Origenes* (Diss.Tübingen 1951), p. 28, he voiced deep doubts about Rufinus' translation. A. von Harnack, *Der kirchengeschichtliche Ertrag der exegetischen Arbeiten des Origenes* I (TU 42,3) (Leipzig 1918), pp. 78–87, and II (TU 42,4) (Leipzig 1919), pp. 126–9, had already expressed certain reservations about the tradition represented by Rufinus. J. Grotz, *Die Entwicklung des Bussstufenwesens in der vornicänischen Kirche* (Freiburg 1955), p. 176, agrees with this, without, however, applying these doubts to the text In Lev.hom. 15,2. With regard to this text in particular, Teichtweier comes to the conclusion that, in all probability, it transmits faithfully Origen's basic teaching (cf. *Das Sein des Menschen,* p. 22). Nevertheless, the disputable nature of the text must be kept in mind. J. Grotz interprets the alleged distinction between *culpa mortalis* and *crimen mortale* in such a way that by the *culpae mortales* he understands mortal sins which are not subject to the punishment of excommunication. This provides him with his proof for the difference which he holds between a repeatable penance without excommunication and a non-repeatable penance with excommunication (cf. p. 289). We have paid particular attention to Grotz's basic thesis in the essay on the penitential theology of the Shepherd of Hermas.

107. Cf. In Lev.hom. 15,2 (GCS 29) 489,13–15.

108. Ibid., 489,15.20–2.

109. Ibid., 489,13–15.

110. Cf., for example, P. Galtier, *L'église et la rémission,* p. 268 ff. He prefers to make this *culpa mortalis* the object of the sacramental absolution without excommunication. Cf. B. Poschmann, p. 346, who accepts the text as it stands, without, however, accepting Galtier's conclusions. For further details about the interpretation of this text, cf. E. T. Latko, *Origen's Concept of Penance* (Quebec 1949), p. 115 f. Cf. also J. Grotz, p. 248 f., and G. Teichtweier, *Die Sündenlehre,* p. 258.

111. Origen interprets typologically the prescriptions of the old law (Lev. 25: 29 ff.) concerning the possibility of buying back a house which has been sold, according as it is *in urbibus muratis* or *in vico* or is a *domus levitae vel sacerdotis*.

112. Cf. esp. nn.50, 63 and 80 above.

113. Cf. In Lev.hom. 15 (GCS 29) 488,11 (*simplicitas* is the house of Jacob; *timor Dei* that of the *obstetrices*).

114. Cf., for example, In Jos.hom. 10,1–3 (GCS 30) 357–61; In Lev.hom. 14,3 (GCS 29) 481,22–484,7; In Luc.hom. 17 (GCS 35) 121. Cf. L. Atzberger, *Geschichte der christlichen Eschatologie innerhalb der vornicänischen Zeit* (Freiburg 1896), pp. 395–8; C. Bigg, *The Christian Platonists of Alexandria* (Oxford 1913), p. 279 f.

115. Cf. esp. nn.33 and 48 above.

116. Certainly Origen is not worried about describing the sinful state of the com-

munity in dismal terms, so long as he is speaking in *general* and *simply* about sins. But when it is a question of mortal sins in the strict sense, then he becomes much more circumspect and no longer takes it simply for granted that practically all his hearers are sinners in this sense. For then he states: *vereor, ne etiam aliquos de his, qui in ecclesia sunt, aliquos de adstantibus, dum nescimus . . .* : In Ex.hom. 6,9 (GCS 29) 204,5–7. Does this notion fit in with the idea that *communia quae frequenter* (we all !) *incurrimus* could be mortal sins ? Cf. similarly in Ps. 36 hom. 1,5 (PG 12) 1328: *si quis vestrum, licet non optem esse in loco conventu talem aliquem* (a fornicator) . . .

117. According to the context (the house in the town which can be bought back only once = *fides quae muro ecclesiastici et apostolici dogmatis cincta est*) only the *blasphemia fidei* is considered a *crimen mortale,* although there are also *culpae mortales* present.

118. For instance, are *crimen* and *culpa* in fact such clearly distinct notions for Origen and his translators that this distinction remains even after the addition of the *mortale/-lis*? In Num.hom. 1,1 (GCS 30) 69,18 there is a mention of the *crimen inflationis,* which is, however, only a venial sin. In Lev.hom. 5,4 (GCS 29) 341,6–9 Origen stresses that the Bible generally does not distinguish between *peccatum* and *delictum*. If ever a distinction is made, then *delictum* means the lighter sin.

119. According to an oral remark, B. Kotting (Münster) also holds the *mortalis* here as not corresponding to Origen's way of thinking, and he recommends that it should be omitted. In his view, it is Rufinus who has introduced the notion of a *culpa mortalis,* which should not be considered as a mortal sin.

120. The text becomes more comprehensible and clearer, because beween *culpa* and *crimen* there is obviously an opposition intended. On the one hand, however, this is hardly expressed in the mere notions of *culpa* and *crimen,* while, on the other hand, it is completely cancelled out if both of these notions are qualified by the same adjective, *mortalis*. It is possible that Rufinus himself had a hand in this deterioration of the text, since, on his own testimony, he translated the homilies on Leviticus very freely (cf. Rufinus, Peroratio in explanat.Origenis super Epist.Pauli ad Romanos [PG 14]1293). Already E. R. Redepenning, II 51 f. n.5 omitted the *mortalis* after culpa and, in so doing, referred both to A. Anrauld and C. de la Rue (cf. [PG 12] 559 n.26). Arnauld's idea, *De frequenti communione liber* (Lovanii 1674), pp. 198–200, that *culpa moralis* should be read in the place of *culpa mortalis,* is supported by In Num.hom. 10,1 (GCS 30) 70,6 f., where a distinction is drawn between *delicta moralia* and *fidei crimen*. Arnauld's conjecture is, therefore, not arbitrary, as D. Petau, *De poenitentia publica et praeparatione ad communionem* lib. VI cap. 9 (Paris 1867), pp. 360–2, maintains. Moreover, Petau's arguments against Arnauld on this matter are too *a priori*. O. D. Watkins, *A History of Penance* I (London 1920), p. 138, is likewise of the opinion that the original text has been altered by the translation. W. A. Baehrens, the editor of GCS 29; 30; 33, does not record in the apparatus of his edition the four MSS. in which C. de la Rue claims to have observed the absence of the *mortalis* after *culpa* (cf. [PG 12] 559 n.26). Neither does he mention this absence in several manuscripts in his *Überlieferung und Textgeschichte der lateinisch erhaltenen Origeneshomilien zum Alten Testament* (TU 42,1) (Leipzig 1916). If, however, the observation of C. dela Rue was correct, then it must have been a question of later MSS.—de la Rue himself refers to this fact—which were not considered for Bahrens' text. Nevertheless, it is still possible to recognize in this omission a critical correction of the text on the part of later copyists.

121. Cf. E. R. Redepenning, II, pp. 444–51; L. Atzberger, pp. 387–418; J. Daniélou, pp. 271–83. We believe that H. U. von Balthasar is right when he says (*Origenes, Geist und Feuer,* loc. cit., Introduction, pp. 33 and 544) that it is contrary to Origen's view that the world's process recommences, once, after several aeons, it is completed and God has become all in all, since this teaching, according to Origen,

figured among those which were philosophically debatable (this is how Contra Celsum VIII 72 [(GCS 3)] 289,9 f. is to be explained) and not among those which are to be held. Cf. Ad Rom. V 10 (PG 14) 1052 f.; ibid., VII 12 (PG 14) 1134; Fragm. of the commentary on Romans in J. A. Cramer, *Catenae Graecorum Patrum in Novum Testamentum*, 8 vols. (Oxford 1838–44), vol. iv, pp. 155–7. See further literature on this question in W. Völker, p. 29 n.2.

122. Cf., for example, In Jer.hom. 2,12 (GCS 33) 300,15–19.

123. We will consider later the only objection which may be levelled against this view and which is derived from De or. 28. This is because it concerns rather the power of the Church. It has already been shown above that the notion of 'incurable' sin which also occurs here does not, in itself, mean that the sin in question is unforgivable.

124. Cf. In Ex.hom. 6,9 (GCS 29) 200 f. The passage quoted is found ibid., 201,13–16. I consider it excessive to wish to derive from this text a clearly defined 'juridical notion of sin and its expiation' (cf. Poschmann, p. 432). The notion of selling is dictated by the scriptural passage. The image of 'payment' is not applied to penance itself. *Satisfacere* for sins occurs here, but also elsewhere in Latin translations (In Num.hom. 9,3 [GCS 30] 57,28: *satisfacere pro delictis*; In Num.hom. 9,8 [GCS 30] 66,16: *paenitentiae tempus et satisfactionis locus*; In Ps. 36 hom. 4,2 [PG 12] 1353: *satisfacere Domino*; *poenitentiae satisfactio*); it is difficult to say, however, which Greek word originally corresponded to this Latin term, since it is not clear either that it was always the same Greek notion or that Rufinus, in transmitting such a term, was not paraphrasing. In the translation of Gregory of Nazianzus' Oratio apologetica, Rufinus, the translator of Origen's Homilies, translates the notions ὑπεραπολογεῖσθαι, ἀπολογία, πρεσβεία with *satisfacere*, *satisfactio* (cf. A. Deneffe, 'Das Wort satisfactio' in: ZKTh 43 (1919), pp. 158–75; for Rufinus see p. 162). Nor is it important what Rufinus himself understood by the notion of *satisfacere*. It need not have expressed anything more than 'to ask', 'to request', etc. In any case, for Origen *satisfactio* is in fact punishment which is voluntarily undertaken. This punishment, however, in Origen's view flows connaturally from sin as its intrinsic consequence and has, as its essential function, the interior healing of sin. In a certain sense it overcomes sin and eliminates it. Thus it is obvious that Origen does not have a juridical notion of the relationship between guilt and punishment (penance), although he may use juridical metaphors to clarify this relationship.

125. In Ex.hom. 6,6 (GCS 29) 197,11–198,5. The quotation is found ibid., 197,28 f.

126. In Ps. 36 hom. 1,5 (PG 12) 1328.

127. Ibid., 4,2 (PG 12) 1351–4.

128. Ibid., (PG 12) 1353 C.

129. Ibid., (PG 12) 1351 D.

130. In Lev.hom. 14,4 (GCS 29) 484–87.

131. Origen applies this principle to Ananias and Saphira: In Matt. tom. XV 15 (GCS 40) 393. Even here (393,5–8) there is a mention of the ἀπολαμβάνειν τὸ ἡμαρτημένον which represents the opposite of ἄφεσις. Because the avaricious couple were in fact believers, they were judged 'to conceive sin' ἐνθαῦτα, that is, in this life and thus to be purified through bodily death.

132. Origen clearly has in mind here quite definite traditional penitential practices, namely the obligations of actual church penance.

133. In Lev.hom. 11,2 (GCS 29) 449–52.

134. Ibid., 450,20–6.

135. Ibid., 451,4–7.

136. Ibid., 452,1.25 f.

137. Ibid., 452,1–4.

138. Ibid., 452,20 f. At the end it is said of such a person guilty of mortal sin: *Quod et si aliquis est qui forte praeventus est in huiuscemodi peccatis, . . . ad auxilium confugiat paenitentiae, ut si semel admisit, secundo non faciat, aut, si et secundo iam aut etiam tertio praeventus est, ultra non addat.* This refers to a repeated lapse before the first (and unique) church penance, without any mention at all of whether this penance itself is possible more than once. It is certain that the logic of Origen's thought demands that a sinner who had relapsed even after the once-and-for-all church penance (In Lev.hom. 15,2 [GCS 29] 489,19 f.) is still able to be saved before God. Nevertheless, Origen does not mention such a case explicitly. In any event, it is obvious that, for the reasons given earlier, even in his circles, such a case must not have occurred very often.

139. In Jer.hom. 20,9 (GCS 6) 191,16–192,15.

140. Origen is thinking of Luke 24:32. The 'was not our heart burning' is also adduced in a similar context. Cf. In Ex.hom. 4,8 (GCS 29) 180,23: *ignis paenitentiae* is this burning of Luke24:32; In Exh.hom. 7,8 (GCS 29) 216,23–9; In Ex.hom. 13,4 (GCS 29) 275,16–23.

141. In Lev.hom. 9,8 (GCS 29) 435,5–11.

142. Further evidence to this effect will be offered in the following context.

143. Cf. Fr. Wörter, *Die christliche Lehre über das Verhältnis von Gnade und Freiheit von den apostolischen Zeiten bis auf Augustinus* (Freiburg 1856), pp. 201–81; G. Capitaine, *De Origenis ethica* (Münster 1898); p. 104 ff.; C. Bigg, p. 245; W. Völker, p. 38 ff.; H. Rahner, pp. 205–23; H. U. von Balthasar, *Le Mystérion,* p. 42 n.9; H. Rondet, *Gratia Christi: Essai d'histoire du dogme et de théologie dogmatique* (Paris 1948), pp. 84–6; A. Lieske, *passim.* Völker contains references to earlier literature on the question. Other works which might be usefully consulted: K. H. Schelkle, 'Erwählung und Freiheit in Römerbrief nach der Auslegung der Väter' in: ThQ 131 (1951), pp. 17–31, 189–207; and E. Maurial, *Origenis de libertate arbitrii doctrina* (Montpellier 1856). In the following considerations we shall use the material from Origen's work which has been made available through these studies.

144. How otherwise could the loss of the *visio beatifica* be experienced existentially *as* a loss? In the case of Origen, it should also be considered that, at least in one perspective—that of the two-tiered Platonism of a natural, physical and human world, on the one hand, and of the spiritual, divine world on the other—he can and must recognize the natural virtues of 'pagans' (cf. H. U. von Balthasar, p. 42 n.9; G. Capitaine, p. 106 n. 1). Nevertheless, he must not, thereby, dispute the absolute necessity and importance for salvation of the virtues given spiritually by God. This implies the distinction between the natural and the supernatural orders (cf. also G. Capitaine, p. 49), while at the same time precluding absolutely a crude *synergismus* between God and man on the same level.

145. This obviously does not exclude that, in the overall process of the healing of the person guilty of mortal sin, these powers are again effective, once the new creative impulse from the side of God/Christ has occurred. Thus the texts which stress the latter point represent only an apparent contradiction of this basic principle.

146. In Jer.hom. 2,6 (GCS 33) 295,24–296,9. The fact that here the activity of the great Physician himself, as opposed to that of his *ministri,* is seen principally as a punitive retribution does not dissolve Origen's viewpoint of the material identity of vindictive and medicinal punishment, from which he considers the matter here. Even in the case of *retributio* it is a question of an activity of the *Physician*.

147. Cf. in Ex.hom. 4,8 (GCS 29)181,26–182,5. Cf. also In Ex.hom. 4,3 (GCS 29) 173,30–174,1. It is not absolutely certain from the text alone that Origen is here thinking clearly about the mortal sins of a baptized Christian or of his interior impenitence. But even this text is clear in the light of De or. 28. For there, too, it is a question

of explaining that the healing of mortal sins is impossible for a baptized person only by the prayer and sacrifice of priests.

148. In Joan. XXVIII 7 f. (GCS 10) 397–9.

149. Actual penance by means of the sin-remitting suffering of the punishments due to sin, which is Origen's more precise theme, already does not strictly belong any more to the activity which is reserved exclusively to God.

150. De princip. III 1,20 (GCS 22) 234,5–235,8. Origen does not appear to have relinquished this position essentially, although he also stresses that a help of grace on God's part is necessary for salvation. Without it man is unable to do anything good, and thus true salvation absolutely needs this help. It is not stated explicitly that the actual acceptance of the possibility offered by God is itself a grace. Even In Matt. tom. X 19 (GCS 40) 25,11–26,28 and In Lev.hom. 16,7 (GCS 29) 505 seem to say nothing on this point (contrary to H. U. von Balthasar, p. 42 n.9). Here, too, there is only a mention of the necessary help of grace which obviously achieves its effect. This grace could be construed as prevenient, but even then, according to Origen, it is explicitly no more than the grace which *facilitates* conversion, as, for example, in De princip. III 2,4 (GCS 22) 251,12–19. In any event, it is a question of the granting of ἱκανότης; cf. In Joan. VI 36 (GCS 10) 145,1–12.

151. Cf. the texts quoted in n.150.

152. In Jer.hom. 2,12 (GCS 33) 302.

153. Cf., for example, In Jer.hom. 2,5 (GCS 33) 294,23: *magna ira est a Deo tormenta non perpeti*; In Luc.hom. 10 (GCS 35) 73,3–7: we are 'anaesthetized' against the domination of the spiritual enemies; In Jer.hom. 6,2 (GCS 6) 48–50: a long consideration of the two kinds of sinners; there are those who die so quickly that they no longer feel their inner condition and punishment, and there are those who still feel these things; In Ex.hom. 8,5 (GCS 29) 230,8: *hoc est terribile, hoc est extremum, cum iam non corripimur pro peccatis*; In Ps. 37 hom. 1,3 (PG 12) 1376.

154. In Jer.hom. 6,2 (GCS 6) 48,26–32; 49,15–22. Insensitivity is a kind of demonic possession and madness: In Num.hom. 8 (GCS 30)52,13–16.

155. Ad Rom. II 2 (PG 14) 874.

156. In Jer.hom. 20,9 (GCS 6) 191,16; 192,11–15.

157. Ibid., 190,14; In Ex.hom. 7,6 (GCS 29) 213,14–16; In Ps. 37 hom, 1,1 (PG 12) 1372 C/D.

158. Cf. the texts in A. Lieske, pp. 109–14.

159. In Jos.hom. 4,3 (GCS 30) 311,18–22. It is here that the famous agraphon is quoted: *qui approximant mihi, approximant igni*. The same quotation is found also in In Jer.hom. 3,3 (GCS 33) 312, 25 f. in this form: *qui iuxta me est, iuxta ignem est*; likewise Didymus, In Ps. 88,8 (PG 39) 1488.

160. Cf. also In Is.hom. 4,5 f. (GCS 33) 262; in Job 20,25 (PG 17) 76; In Ezech. hom.1,3 (GCS 33) 324,7–13; In Lev.hom. 9,8 (GCS 29) 432,17–27; In Ex.hom. 13,4 (GCS 29) 275,18–23.

161. Cf. In Matt.tom. XVII 24 (GCS 40) 651; De or. 29,13 (GCS 3) 388,6–12.

162. In Ezech.hom. 8,4 (GCS 33) 422,5 f.:sin—*nervos animae succidit*; In Ezech.hom. 5,1 (GCS 33) 371,18–372,5: the fiery sword of the interior judgement, which itself cuts in two; Fragm. In Osee (PG 13) 828 C: the interior disintegration of the sinner who falls out of unity.

163. In Luc.hom. 17 (GCS 35) 115,2–5 [Greek fragment].

164. In Cant.hom. II (GCS 33) 128,10–14.

165. Cf., for example, De princip. III 1,7–15 (GCS 22) 204–23; In Num.hom. 14,2 (GCS 30)121–5; In Matt.tom. XIII 23 (GCS 40) 242,18–243,13; De or. 6,5 (GCS 3) 315: Paul; J. Daniélou, p. 277 f.

166. Obviously this indwelling of the Logos is that of the *personal* logos of God,

that is, of Christ the Logos (cf. A. Lieske, p. 110 ff.). As such a personal relationship, it is perfectly able to be considered from the viewpoint of *grace*. Origen also often stresses that the actual function of the *hegemonikon* in directing man towards the divine requires the help of God's grace. Cf. A. Lieske, pp. 107–109. Moreover, it ought not to be overlooked that the inalienable character of the indwelling of the Logos is not an argument against its purely gratuitous character.

167. Ad Rom. V 10 (PG 14) 1052 f.

168. Cf., for example, De princip. I 8,1 (GCS 22) 94–7, etc.; J. Daniélou, pp. 207–17; H. U. von Balthasar, pp. 535–8.

169. For the moment, we are not considering the church aspect of this penance.

170. In Joan. VI 58 (GCS 10) 167,2–5; In Ezech. hom. 3,8 (GCS 33) 356,20–9.

171. In Jer.hom. 20,8 (GCS 6) 190, 33–191,3.

172. Ibid., 20.9 (GCS 6) 191,19.

173. Ibid., 20,8 (GCS 6) 190,29–32; In Joan. XIII 23 (GCS 10) 247,1–6.

174. De or. 29,13 (GCS 3) 388,9. This *κορεσθῆναι* is the counterpart of the *κόρος τῆς θείας ἀγύπης*, which is the essence of original sin; cf. De princip. II 8 (GCS 22) 159,7.

175. In Jer.hom. 20,9 (GCS 6) 191,25.

176. In Ex.hom. 6,9 (GCS 29) 201,15; In Jer.hom. 20,9 (GCS 6) 191,28. With tears also: Selecta in Ps. 115 (PG 12)1577 D; In Lev. hom. 2,4 (GCS 29) 296,18 f.; ibid., 15,2 (GCS 29) 488,26.

177. In Lev. hom. 14,4 (GCS 29) 487,1.

178. Ibid., (GCS 29) 486,26 f.

179. In Ps. 37 hom. 1,2 (PG 12) 1376.

180. Ad Rom. VI 6 (PG 14) 1069.

181. In Lev. hom. 2,4 (GCS 29) 296,17.

182. Selecta in Ps. 13,1 (PG 12) 1301.

183. In Lev. hom. 14,4 (GCS 29) 487,1.

184. In Ps. 37 hom. 1,2 (PG 12) 1375.

185. Ad Rom.praef. (PG 14) 834; ibid., VI 6(PG 14) 1068.

186. Ibid., praef. (PG 14) 834. Origen himself remarks that this *interitus carnis* of the incestuous person in Corinth occurs in the brief period of time between the two letters to the Corinthians.

187. In Ezech.hom. 10,3 (GCS 33) 421,13–19; In Num.hom. 8,1 (GCS 30) 51,15–24.

188. In Ps. 37 hom. 2,5 (PG 12) 1385 (one of the most moving penitential prayers of the early Church); In Lev. hom. 14,2 (GCS 29) 486,1–8.

189. In Ps. 37 hom. 1,1 (PG 12) 1370 f.

190. In Jud.hom. 2,5 (GCS 30) 478,21–3; 479,11–18.

191. In Jer. hom. 19,14 (GCS 6) 71,4; Contra Celsum VIII 33 (GCS 3) 249,1–4; In Num.hom. 13,7 (GCS 30) (117; cf. J. Daniélou, p. 239.

192. In Ezech. hom. 12,3 (GCS 33) 436,23–5; 437,7–13. On the question of the demons as the causes of plagues on Earth, see E. R. Redepenning, II, p. 355.

193. In Jer. hom. 1,4 (GCS 6) 3,18.

194. Cf. in Jer.hom. 2,6 (GCS 33) 295,17–20; Origen believes that non-mortal sins can be healed by the punishment on the part of either good or bad angels.

195. Cf., for example, De princip. I 7,4 f. (GCS 22) 89–94; ibid., I 8,1 (GCS 22) 94–8; E. R. Redepenning, II, pp. 112 ff., 348 ff.

196. In Ps. 37 hom. 1,1 (PG 12) 1372, with reference to the Shepherd of Hermas.

197. In Jer.hom. 20,1 (GCS 6) 176,15–177,9; In Ezech.hom. 1,2 (GCS 33) 321,10–12: *si non esset utile conversioni peccantium adhibere tormenta peccantibus, nunquam misericors et benignus Deus poenis sclera puniret*. This idea is found already in

Plutarch. Cf. J. Daniélou, p. 98 f., who on this point sees a particularly clear influence of 'middle Platonism' on Origen.

198. Cf. Ad Rom. II 6 (PG 14) 883; De princip. II 10,4–8 (GCS 22) 177–183. In here explaining the punishments in the next life as the effect of sin, Origen remains consistent, since a punishment which derived only from God's anger and was in no way (also) an effect of sin could only make the illness worse and would not be medicinal. It follows from this, therefore, that the punishment ceases automatically once the interior conversion has been completed: cf. Ad Rom. II 1 (PG 14) 873.

199. Comm. in Ep. ad Eph. III 5 (PL 26) 522: *nec extrinsecus adhibenda tormenta*; Apol. adv. Rufinum II 7 (PL 23) 429; Ep. ad Avitum (PL 22) 1065.

200. Illnesses, temptations of the devil, the πῦρ καθάρσιον of the end of the world (cf., on this point, L. Atzberger, p. 407), etc.

201. Thus Contra Celsum V 15 (GCS 3)16,7 f. with regard to the πῦρ καθάρσιον of the end of the world.

202. K. Rahner, 'Gnosis' in: LThK 4 (1960), pp. 1019–21; H. Rahner, 'Gnostizismus, christlicher' in: LThK 4 (1960), pp. 1028–30.

203. Cf., for example, In Joan. II 27 (GCS 10) 84,20–6; In Joan. fragm. 3 (GCS 10) 386, 29–387,19; De princip. III 4,3 (GCS 22) 267,28–268,15; In Joan. fragm. 41 (GCS 10) 516; De princip. III 1,12.13.17 (GCS 22) 214–18; 225 ff.; J. Daniélou, p. 277 ff.

204. Cf. In Jer.hom. 20,2 (GCS 6) 178,20–5; De princip. I 2,10 (GCS 22) 44,1–11.

205. Cf., for example, In Luc.hom. 35 (GCS 35) 212–15.

206. In Jer.hom. 16,10 (GCS 6) 142,5–9.

207. Ad Rom. II 1 (PG 14) 873.

208. Ad Rom. II 10 (PG 14) 894; De princip. II 10,4 (GCS 22) 178,5 f.

209. Ad Rom. II 1 (PG 14) 873. The fact that these τύποι reappear at the judgement as enduring realities need not be seen as a contradiction: the whole of man's spiritual past can, on the one hand, be really, ontologically and physically 'resumed' in his present, while on the other hand being essentially marked by later decisions (for example, to do penance). Thus penance 'marks' the past rather than 'extinguishes' it.

210. On this point, cf. 'Sin as Loss of Grace in Early Church Literature' in this volume.

211. In In Lev.hom. 6,2 (GCS 29) 361,7–11 the moral conversion through personal effort as a condition of effective penance is clearly distinguished from the reception of the *gratia Sancti Spiritus* through baptism. The same distinction between μετανοεῖν and ἄφεσις ἁμαρτιῶν is found in In Luc.hom. 21 (GCS 35)139,1–5; 140,1–4. G. Teichtweier, p. 290, also rightly places a great deal of weight on the distinction between ἄφεσις and μετάνοια. He says: 'Ἄφεσις and μετάνοια or ἐξομολόγησις are, therefore, different ways of forgiving sins.' This is contrary to J. Grotz, pp. 257–60, where this distinction is explicitly rejected, since even forgiveness of sins by the Church consists exclusively of ἄφεσις, that is, of the forgiveness by the prayer of the priest, independently of the sinner's personal act of penance. Accordingly, only in serious cases is this 'actual penance' preceded by an excommunication (p. 260; cf. on this point ibid., p. 259: 'The *remissio* means precisely remission without any personal activity'). For the specific effect of baptism, cf. In Joan. VI 33 (GCS 10) 142,23–143,1. For the interpretation of this text, cf. H. U. von Balthasar, *Le Mystérion*, p. 55 f. Although the centurion Cornelius received the Spirit even before his baptism (In Num.hom. 3,1 [GCS 30] 14,6–11; ibid., 11,3 [GCS 30] 81,13), nevertheless, as a matter of principle, the penance and the conversion of the catechumen is a mere precondition for the reception of the Spirit which is bestowed in baptism. Thus, although the virtuous life of pagans deserves a reward by God in the next world, only a baptized person can enter into the actual kingdom of God: Ad Rom. II 7 (PG 14) 888. Before baptism, a person can already believe in Christ and invoke him, but it is only in

baptism that he receives the Spirit and becomes a living member of the Church: Ad. Rom. VIII 5 (PG 14)1166 f. For the reception of the Spirit in baptism, cf. also: In Ezech.hom. 6,5 (GCS 33) 383,15 f.; In Luc.hom. 26 (GCS 35) 165,8–16; De princip. II 10,7 (GCS 22) 181,5–9.

212. Cf. A. Lieske, pp. 141–46.

213. The following passages, however, could be invoked: In Num.hom. 6,3 (GCS 30) 32,22 ff.: *requiescit enim Spiritus sanctus . . . in his, qui purificant animas suas a peccato*; In Jos.hom. 3,2 (GCS 30) 303,17–23: the aim of all *paenitentia et conversio* is *sancti Spiritus gratia*, which is not said only with regard to baptismal conversion; In Lev. hom. 8,11 (GCS 29) 417,12–18: *non solum purgationem consequi possit is, qui convertitur a peccato, sed et Spiritu sancto repleri, quo et recipere priorem stolam et anulum possit et per omnia reconciliatus Patri in locum Filii reparari*. Nevertheless, it is important to note that in these texts the purification from sins and the reception of the Spirit are not necessarily envisaged simply as two aspects of one and the same event. These texts are perfectly comprehensible if the purification from sins is seen as the necessary precondition for the reception of the Spirit, which itself can depend upon causes other than the penitent's mere moral striving after his own purification.

214. In Jer.hom. 2,3 (GCS 6)19,9–15; In Luc.hom. 24 (GCS 35)158. Cf. H. U. von Balthasar, *Le Mystérion*, p. 56 ff.; C. M. Edsman, *Le baptême de feu* (Uppsala 1940), pp. 1–15 (Edsman makes too much of a differentiation within a notion which, in Origen's view, is ultimately unified.)

215. In Jer.hom. 20,8 f. (GCS 6)190–2.

216. A basis for the notion that penance = a new reception of the Spirit is provided by the teaching that, according to Paul, the *interitus carnis* occurs for the recovery of the *πνεῦμα*. Since, however, this recovered *πνεῦμα* is the personal spirit of the sinner himself (cf., for example, In Lev.hom. 14,4 [GCS 29] 487,2: *spiritus noster mundus et purus*; In Ezech.hom. 12,3 (GCS 33) 437,4 f.: *spiritus traditi*; ibid., 437,16: *spiritus eius*), and yet for Origen the *ψυχή* and the *νοῦς* are man's *πνευμα*, in so far as man's spiritual principle possesses the *πνεῦμα* of God, included implicitly in the recovery of the *πνεῦμα* by the *interitus carnis* is its interior restoration to grace. On the notion of *πνεῦμα*, cf. Ad Rom. II 10 (PG 14) 893; In Joan. XXXII 18(GCS 10) 455, 17–22; De princip. II 8,2–3 (GCS 22) 154,18–15,12; E. R. Redepenning, II, p. 369 f.; G. Bardy in: DThC XI 1534 f.; A. Lieske, p. 143 n.56.

217. E. R. Redepenning, II, p. 25. As a proof for this opinion he refers to Ad Rom. III 8 f. (PG 14), although here it is a matter of the redemption through Christ in general. Cf. Contra Celsum III 62 (GCS 2) 256: here also it is a question only of the need which all men have of salvation; In Lev.hom. 2,4 (GCS 29) 295,18–296,22 (the passage which we have already considered on the once-and-for-all *remissio* in baptism and the six other possibilities for the remission of sins); Ad Rom. II 1 (PG 14) 872: the difference between the *remissio* in baptism and the *tegere peccata* through *paenitentia*. The strength of the proof, therefore, consists only in the difference between baptismal *ἄφεσις* and personal penance which remits sin. The question remains, therefore, whether or not this penance can still be grace.

218. E. R. Redepenning, II, p. 424, with a reference to p.25. Poschmann also appears to be of essentially the same opinion; cf. his study, p. 432: 'Thus, in its effect, penance appears as a counterpart to Christ's blood: while the latter redeems us from the Devil—in baptism—through penance it is the sinner himself who must provide his own ransom.'

219. We will discuss this point in more detail below.

220. Thus also B. Poschmann, p. 432. In Ex.hom. 6,9 (GCS 29) 201,18 f. Certainly no more on the subject of God's mercy can be derived from this passage. Thus Poschmann's view appears to be exaggerated: 'Certainly he (the sinner) would not be capable of doing this (providind the ransom) on his own; he has only the *misericors et*

misserator Dominus to thank if his penance has that result' (p. 432). If it were a grace *to undertake* the penance imposed, then without a doubt the remission obtained through it would also be a grace. But such a juridical conclusion has no place in Origen's view of penance (being an inner healing by the destruction of sin). But is every possibility to do penance itself already grace? The same applies to In Lev.hom. 15,2 (GCS 29) 488,23, where it is a question of the *pietas et clementia legislatoris* which allows us to redeem the house of heaven which has been sold to the Devil.

221. Cf. H. U. von Balthasar, *Le Mystérion,* p. 42 ff. The principal passages quoted are Selecta in Ps. 47,9 (PG 12) 1440 in connection with In Joan. XX 20 (GCS 10) 351,33–352,35 and In Cant. III (GCS 33) 215 f.; Ad Rom. V 8 (PG 14) 1166; In Matt. ser. 63 f. (GCS 38) 145,10–151,18.

222. Ad Rom. V 7 (PG 14) 1335 ff.: *si ergo commonitus quis morte Christi, qui pro impiis mortuus est, poeniteat in his omnibus et velut pessimum regem regnantem in sua carne depellat alienumque se ab eius desideriis faciat ac praeceptis, iste vere per mortem Christi peccato mortuus esse dicitur.* There is no reason for wishing to understand this only of baptismal penance. Cf. Fragm. in I Ep. ad Thess. (PG 14)1300: *in Christo autem mortui, qui plena ad Deum mente conversi sunt*; In Num. hom. 12,3 (GCS 30)102,23–103,9.

223. In Matt.tom. XII 24 (GCS 40) 122–5. Such expressions in Origen are to be understood very realistically. Christ is and suffers in the members of the Church as the soul in the body. Cf. also In Matt. ser. 73 (GCS 38)172,18–174,23.

224. In Matt. ser. 72 (GCS 38) 168–70. Granted the fact that in Origen's system of thought there is finally no separation between the Church and the world (cf. H. U. von Balthasar, *Le Mystérion,* pp. 42–5), there need be no contradiction in the fact that the penitent guilty of mortal sin, on the one hand, is still outside the Church, while, on the other hand, in his situation and in his act of penance he is united with Christ.

225. In Jos.hom. 8,3 (GCS 30) 338,5–339,3: the well-known passage of the 'double cross', on which hang both Christ and the devil, but also man himself as both holy and sinner.

226. In Joan. I 32 (GCS 10) 42,3–7.

227. Cf. J. Daniélou, p. 264 ff.

228. In Jer.hom. 11,1 (GCS 6) 79,20–80,5.

229. In Lev.hom. 1,4 (GCS 29) 286,20–287,3.

230. In Num.hom. 7,6 (GCS 30) 48,6–12.

231. Cf. above under nn. 80 and 91.

232. In this context it is worth noting that Origen ascribes to Martyrdom a greater purifying role than to baptism. In Jud. hom. 7,2 (GCS 30) 507,16–508,18. In his view martyrdom is both baptism and the highest form of penance in one.

233. In Ezech.hom. 5,1 (GCS 33) 372,7–12.

234. In Lev.hom. 8,10 (GCS 29) 411,7–9.

235. In Jos.hom. 7,6 (GCS 30) 332,21–334,20.

236. In Matt.ser. 89 (GCS 38) 205,1 f.

237. In Jos.hom. 5,6 (GCS 30) 320,8–13.

238. Cf., for example, In Matt.tom. XII 4 (GCS 40) 75,7–15; In Jos.hom. 3,4 f. (GCS 30) 304–7.

239. Fragm. in 1 Cor. (J. A. Cramer, *Catenae Graecorum Patrum,* V 11); In Jos.hom. 21,1 (GCS 30) 427,12–429,14; Selecta in Ps. 73,3 (PG 12) 1529 C/D; In Jer.hom. 15,3 (GCS 6) 127,25–30; In Luc. hom. 38 (GCS 35) 223,5–9; 224,11; In Matt.tom. XVI 21 (GCS 40) 546,7–549,21; In Luc.hom. 2 (GCS 35) 14: the sin of the ἐκκλησιαστικός which stains the Church obviously occurs in the Church and is not envisaged as existing prior to baptism. It is considered as being repeatedly remitted; In Jer.fragm. 31 (GCS 6) 215,1–17; In Matt.ser. 35 (GCS 38) 68,4–9.

240. In Jos.hom. 21,1 (GCS 30) 428,15–18.

241. In Jer.hom. 15,3 (GCS 6) 127,26.

242. In Jer. fragm. 31 (GCS 6) 215,7–11; In Ezech.hom. 1,11 (GCS 33) 334,30–335,23; In Gen.hom. 2,3 (GCS 29) 30,17–31,12.

243. Cf. above under n.239.

244. In Lev.hom. 14,2 (GCS 29) 479,22–4; In Jer. fragm. 48 (GCS 6) 222,16 f.; cf. also In Jud.hom. 2,5 (GCS 30) 479,6–10; In Lev.hom. 12,6 (GCS 29) 465,1–4.

245. In Matt.tom. XII 11 f. (GCS 40) 88 ff. Cf. also In Matt.tom. XIII 30 (GCS 40) 263,13: ἀδελφὸς ὀνομαζόμενος, who in reality is not a brother.

246. Origen clearly experienced this dialectic. In Lev.hom. 14,2 (GCS 29) 479,27–480,2 he says: *Qui . . . inter nos est et peccat, ex una quidem parte, qua Deo credit* (at least through his external membership) *Israeliticae videtur originis; ex ea parte, qua peccat, de Aegyptio genus ducit*.

247. Cf. H. U. von Balthasar, *Le Mysterion,* p. 40 ff.; A. Lieske, p. 84 ff.

248. In Lev.hom. 14,2 (GCS 29) 479,18–26 these three 'separations' are clearly distinguishable: separation from the spiritual aspect of the Church:*exire a via iustitiae . . . a lege Dei*; contradiction to the visible fellowship of the Church, even before the official church excommunication: *per ipsum peccatum . . . quamvis intret* (*peccator*) *ecclesiam, eiectum esse et segregatum a consortio et unanimitate fidelium*; separation by excommunication: *abici per episcopi sententiam*.

249. In Lev.hom. 144 (GCS 29) 486,23–8; In Num.hom. 19,3 (GCS 30) 183,2–4.

250. It is necessary to say a word here about J. Grotz's fundamentally different understanding of excommunication; cf. also the thorough discussion of his view in the essay contained in this volume: 'The Penitential Teaching of the Shepherd of Hermas'. According to Grotz, excommunication is first and foremost a disciplinary measure of the Church with regard to specific offences. To this extent, therefore, excommunication is purely and simply an accidental element of the Church's penitential procedure, which is effective within the *communio* (cf. pp. 280, 292). As a consequence of historical development, it became taken for granted that sacramental church penance, that is, the *paenitentia secunda,* in the case of mortal sin in the strict sense (which Grotz distinguishes from mortal sins in the wide sense by means of a juridical criterion) can be supplemented by the disciplinary element of excommunication (pp. 299–307). All this, however, amounts to an unjustifiable introduction of today's canonical understanding of excommunication into the penitential theology of the early Church. Above all, the assumption that the *communio* continues while exclusion from the Eucharist is imposed is incompatible with the ecclesiology of the Church Fathers. At the same time, Grotz grants that *communio* in the full sense contains the right to the Eucharist (p. 264) and that exclusion from the Eucharist is included in excommunication (p. 263).

This fundamental position gives rise to a separation between *communio* and *pax cum Ecclesia*. The ecclesiological aspect of reconciliation with the Church becomes a disciplinary action which is effective only in certain cases, while the supernatural effect of the forgiveness of sins is ascribed only to reconciliation with God. According to this view, the readmission into the Church, in so far as it is a purely canonical event, has no sacramental effect whatsoever. This assumption, however, is in open contradiction to the theology of the early Church which teaches the saving significance both of the church community and of membership of it.

Cf. on this point S. Hübner, 'Kirchenbusse und Exkommunikation bei Cyprian' in: ZKTh 84 (1962), pp. 49–84, 171–215.

251. In one passage the Latin tr. has: *propter peccata . . . excommunicare*; cf. In Matt. ser. 14 (GCS 38) 27,32.

252. Cf. Ad Rom.praef. (PG 14)834. In our view, however, it is particularly important that the *tradere in interitum carnis* (*in manus Zabuli,* etc.), at least when this

action does not take place only before God in secret, includes an *a corpore Christi separari, a pelli de ecclesia* by the priests: cf. In Jud.hom. 2,5 (GCS 30) 478,18–479,10; In Ezech.hom. 3,8 (GCS 33) 357,30–2.

253. Cf. In Matt.tom. XIII 30 (GCS 40) 261–8; In Lev. hom. 3,2 (GCS 29) 302; In Jos.hom. 7,6 (GCS 30) 333,24–334,5; In Ps. 37 hom. 1,1 (PG 12) 1370 ff.

254. For example, *ἀπελαύνειν του κοινοῦ*: Contra Celsum III 51 (GCS 2) 247,18; *ἐκβάλλειν*: In Jer.fragm. 48 (GCS 6) 222,16; In Jer. hom. 12,5 (GCS 6) 92,17; Ibid., 14,14 (GCS 6) 120,12 f.; ibid., 7,3 (GCS 6) 54,2; *expellere de ecclesia*: In Matt.tom. XIII 30 (GCS 40) 262, 20–6; In Jos.hom. 7,6 (GCS 30) 333,6; ibid., 21,1 (GCS 30) 429,1; *abscindere a conventu ecclesiae*: In Ps. 37 hom. 1,1 (PG 12) 1371; In Jos.hom. 7,6 (GCS 30) 334,4; *de ecclesia pellere*: In Jud.hom. 2,5 (GCS 30) 479,3 f.; *foras mittere*: In Lev.hom. 14,3 (GCS 29) 483,12; *eicere, proicere*: Ad Rom.praef. (PG 14) 834; In Ps. 37 hom. 1,1 (PG 12) 1371 A; In Ezech.hom. 3,8 (GCS 33) 357,30; *a corpore Christi separare*: In Jud.hom. 2,5 (GCS 30) 478,27; *πόρρω εἶναι τῆς ἐκκλησίας*: In Joan. XXVIII 4 (GCS 10) 393,27; *foris esse et segregatus a conventu fidelium*: In Lev.hom. 14,2 (GCS 29) 479,25 f. *abici a conventu bonorum et segregari a coetu castrisque sanctorum*: In Lev.hom. 8,10 (GCS 29) 408,18 f.

255. Cf., for example, In Matt. tom. XIII 31 (GCS 40) 269,3–5; In Jud.hom. 2,5 (GCS 30) 478,23–479,1. Here we are not considering De or. In the passages mentioned, however, it is obvious that *ligare* is identical with excommunication. We have already shown that the *interitus carnis* included in excommunication is, at least in principle, not thought of as a permanent condition, but actually effects the forgiveness of sins. It can, in principle, end with readmission into the Church, as is explicitly stated: Ad Rom.praef. (PG 14) 834: the *interitus carnis* achieves for the incestuous person in Corinth a *Ecclesiae membris associare,* even though he was *eiectus*; Contra Celsum III 51 (GCS 2) 248,2–5: those who have been ejected are again allowed access to the Church; In Ps. 37 hom. 1,1 (PG 12) 1371: *Paulus eiectum reconiungit ecclesiae*; In Ezech. hom. 3,8 (GCS 33) 357,32–358,1; *et in praesenti quidem potest quis egrediens de populo Dei rursum per paenitentiam reverti.* It is clear from this general principle that the case of the incestuous person in Corinth is seen by Origen not as a single case of exclusively apostolic authority but as a typical example of general church practice. Thus the notion of binding does not exclude a subsequent reconciliation with the Church. On the other hand, the notion of 'loosing' does *not,* in itself, necessarily imply a previous 'binding' on the Church's part (excommunication). For Origen gives us to understand that, at least occasionally, even in the case of mortal sins which have been brought to the bishops' attention, the attempt was made *ad gratiam iudicare,* without excommunication, therefore, obviously not merely to tolerate the sin (according to Origen's own witness, this often happened: In Jos.hom. 7,6 [GCS 30] 332,22–6), but also to forgive it (In Lev.hom. 12,6 [GCS 29] 465,1–5). The same conclusion is apparent from In Matt.tom. XIII 30 (GCS 40) 262,10–263,12, where Origen discusses (if only to reject) the opinion of others that it is necessary for a person guilty of mortal sin only *expelli de ecclesia* if after his deed and despite exhortation he refuses to mend his ways; otherwise it is possible *statim eum dicere lucrifactum* (ibid. [GCS 40] 262,20 f.). At least the attempt, therefore, to 'loosen' was actually made, even if it is held by Origen to be ineffective in the case of mortal sins. Moreover, it is clear from In Matt.tom. XIII 31 (GCS 40) 269,11–18 that Origen himself recognizes the notion of a *λύειν* of sin (by exhortation, correction, etc.) without its being preceded by an excommunication, although also only in the case of non-mortal sins. It remains clear, therefore, that 'binding' on the Church's part means excommunication, but not a definitive excommunication, at least not necessarily. 'Loosing' is a liberation from sin, but one which does not necessarily have to be preceded by an explicit binding on the Church's part.

256. In Lev.hom. 14,3 (GCS 29) 483,8.

257. In Lev.hom. 14,2 (GCS 29) 479,23. The exclusion is a *iudicium eorum qui praesunt ecclesiae*: In Lev.hom. 14,3 (GCS 29) 483,9 f.

258. In Lev.hom. 12,6 (GCS 29) 465,2.

259. In Jud.hom. 2,5 (GCS 30) 479,3.

260. Ibid., (GCS 30) 478,25.

261. Ibid., (GCS 30) 478,21.

262. In Ps. 37,1 (PG 12)1371 B.

263. Cf. In Matt.tom. XII 14 (GCS 40)98,28–99,13: the bishops claim the power of binding and loosing by appealing to Matt.16. Origen recognizes this claim (cf. ibid. [GCS 40]99,7), even if only on certain conditions, to which we will return. De or. 28,8–10: the *τινες* (cf. [GCS 3]381,12), whom Origen here reproaches for exceeding their powers, are described as successors of the apostles (ibid. [GCS 3]381,1), who have received their Spirit (ibid. [GCS 3] 380,8), who lay claim to a *ἱερατικὴ ἀξία* (ibid. [GCS 3] 381,12 f.). Since Origen also recognizes a certain kind of power of binding and loosing in other depositories of the Spirit, his polemic here against *exceeding* this power can, in reality, only apply to the bishops. In no way could it apply, in this context, to all Christians merely because they belong externally to the Church. The bishops' claim is attested in the present text. Moreover, in other places too, Origen, while recognizing the bishops' fundamental power, inveighs against its practical use; cf. A. von Harnack (TU 42,3), pp. 69 ff., 73 ff., (TU 42,4)129 ff. Apart from the bishops, it is just possible to think of the confessors, as they appear in Tertullian and Cyprian with their claims. There is, however, no trace elsewhere in Origen of such claims on the part of the *confessores*. It is possible to conclude from In Ezech.hom. 4,8 (GCS 33) 368,31–369,3 that occasionally even Origen placed too much trust in the intercession of martyrs. This, however, has nothing to do with the claims of the martyrs themselves. With regard to the efficacy of the *death* of martyrs for the forgiveness of sins, cf. also: In Num.hom. 10,2 (GCS 30) 71,25–72,16. Accordingly, De or. must also concern bishops. This also implies that, for the justification of their power with regard to penance, they appealed not only to Matt.16 but also to John 20. Cf. De or. 28 (GCS 3) 380,5–15.

264. Cf. Harnack's detailed considerations in the passages mentioned in n.263.

265. In In Jos.hom. 21,2 (GCS 30) 430,17–20 this state of affairs is clearly discernible.

266. Cf. In Ezech.hom. 1,11 (GCS 33) 335,15–18; In Ps. 37 hom. 2,4 (PG 12) 1384C; ibid., 2,1 (PG 12)1381B. This practice on the part of 'good' Christians could also be an obstacle for those who wished to undertake public penance, since such a penitent would then be 'cut off'.

267. This is certainly the meaning of In Matt.tom. XIII 30 (GCS 40) 264,6–268,25. The emphasis is on the exhortation: *you*—if not the official Church—can treat the sinner as a pagan and public sinner (ibid. [GCS 40] 268,15); thus the *nos* (ibid. (GCS 40) 260,20) refers not to the official Church but to those who have in fact exhorted the sinner in vain. Poschmann (p. 443) misunderstands the meaning when he sees even in this case an official excommunication about which there is only a doubt whether it is also valid in God's eyes. This practice of private avoidance seems to be recommended also in the Epistola Clementis ad Jacobum n.18 (PG 2) 53B, when a bishop is unable, for whatever reasons, to perform an excommunication officially, even though he would clearly wish to do so.

268. This is what In Matt.tom. XIII 31 (GCS 40) 269,3–270,6 calls the attitude of individual Christians towards an unrepentant fellow-Christian who is not excommunicated.

269. In Matt.tom. XII 10 f. (GCS 40) 84–8. The quotation from John 20 figures ibid. (GCS 40) 87,16–22.

270. In Matt.tom. XII 14 (GCS 40) 96,5–97,9.
271. In Matt.tom. XII 14 (GCS 40) 98,5–100,26.
272. In Matt.tom. XII 14 (GCS 40) 98,28–100,26.
273. This was already excluded by the clearly episcopal structure of the Church at that time. Moreover, Origen himself complains that there are people in the Church who ought to be excommunicated and in whose regard the bishops are neglecting their duty (In Jos.hom. 7,6 [GCS 30] 332,21–333,3). This reproach makes sense, however, only if the bishops are in fact the only persons who have the power to excommunicate. Origen also says explicitly that *episcopi, presbyteri* and *diaconi* are those *qui iudicant eos, qui intus sunt,* and that the judgement of souls has been entrusted to the *Ecclesiarum iudicibus*: Ad Rom. II 2 (PG 14) 873; In Jud.hom. 3,3 (GCS 30) 484,2–4.
274. In Lev.hom. 14,2 (GCS 29) 479,22–6; In Jer.fragm. 48 (GCS 6) 222,16 f.; In Lev.hom. 12,6 (GCS 29) 465,1–4; ibid., 14,3 (GCS 29) 483,6–8; In Jud.hom. 2,5 (GCS 30) 479,6–10.
275. Cf. the details above in the introduction to part III: 'Church Penance'.
276. In Lev.hom. 14,3 (GCS 29) 483,8–14: if the bishop's *iudicium* is not *rectum,* because there is no mortal sin, then there arises a situation which is not distinctly and clearly specified by Origen: the person judged is in some way *draussen* (*depellitur et foras mittitur*). This is, however, only 'appearance' (*videtur expulsus*), and he is in fact still inside the Church (*intus est*). These two simultaneous statements can be justified only by saying that the actual exclusion from the community (the liturgy, the Eucharist), which, given the circumstances at that time, could not in practice be lifted from the person judged unjustly (except in the case of schism, etc.), since it was simply the material effect of excommunication, is only an appearance, in so far as this fact is not really the expression of the man's inner separation from the Church's community of grace. Obviously the texts of Origen do not allow us to answer the question whether this is a matter merely of a simple fact or of a fact *juridically* valid *in foro externo.*
277. In Ezech.hom. 10,1 (GCS 33) 417,12–418,10. It is worth noting the *sive digne, sive indigne* (ibid. [GCS 33] 417,21) as well as the *boni* (ibid. [GCS 33] 418,3). If the details concentrate more on the deposition of the cleric than on the excommunication, the latter is always included, since it is explicitly mentioned at the beginning of the passage (*a populo Dei separari*: ibid. [GCS 33] 417,13 f.).
278. In Matt.tom. XII 14 (GCS 40) 98,5–100,26; cf. De or. 28,8 (GCS 3) 380,7–15.
279. He also stresses that the holy Christian must be subject to, and obey, the less holy bishop, just as Jesus behaved towards his step-father Joseph: In Luc. hom. 20 (GCS 35)133,17–134,6. It is clear here that, according to Origen, the inner hierarchy of the Church, based on holiness, does not have to be transferred purely and simply also into the Church's external hierarchy.
280. Cf., on this point, De or. 28 (GCS 3) 375–81.
281. De or. 28,10 (GCS 3) 381,12–16: here the following are explicitly named as mortal sins which have to be bound and retained: *εἰδωλολατρεία, μοιχεία, ποινεία.* Cf. De or. 28,9 (GCS 3) 380,28 which names *ἑκούσιος φόνος* as belonging to the same group. This is not a question of a narrow triad of such sins, since with murder and adultery is also compared *ἄλλο χαλεπώτερον πταῖσμα* (ibid., 380 f.). Adultery and fornication are, of their very nature, not always 'public' and remain mostly unknown. Thus these three capital sins should not simply be identified with public sins.
282. In Matt. tom. XIII 30 (GCS 40) 262,10–263,6. He presents as examples of those guilty of mortal sin: *masculorum concubitor* (certainly usually secret), *adulter, homicida, mollis.* The reservation (*cum qui taliter sentit, non arbitror ad utilitatem communem ista sentire*) concerns the negative reply to the question whether a person should be 'ejected' only after repeated warning. At the same time, if it is said in this context that excommunication ought not to be *actually* imposed for light sins, such as

often occur even among good Christians (ibid., 264,20–9), even after a warning and a relapse (ibid., 265,4–10; 266,14–21; 268,13–25), this concerns sins which are clearly light ones. In Origen's view, this does obviously not exclude the possibility of sins which are serious both subjectively and objectively precisely because the sinner has not repented after repeated warning and so must be excommunicated. In his opinion, there can also be sins which demand excommunication only after a private and public warning: In Jos.hom. 7,6 (GCS 30) 334,3–7. The text In Lev.hom. 14,2 (GCS 29) 479,20–2: *postmodum cum confutatus fuerit pro peccato, exit etiam de coetu et congregatione sanctorum,* on the other hand, obviously concerns the case where a secret sin, or at least one which was at first unknown to the bishop, was committed, but which has already caused an interior separation from the Church (cf. ibid., 479,19 f.), so that the exclusion on the part of the Church has to take place as soon as the fact is known by the bishop—be this by the confession of the sinner himself or in any other way. For this case, cf. also In Jud.hom. 2,5 (GCS 30) 479,2–6.

283. Contra Celsum III 51(GCS 2) 247,23.

284. Ad Rom.praef. (PG 14) 834.

285. In Jer.fragm. 48 (GCS 6) 222,10.14.

286. In Jos.hom. 7,6 f. (GCS 30) 334,13 f.; 335,9–13; In Lev.hom. 14,2 (GCS 29) 480,8–11.

287. In Ps. 37 hom. 1,1 (PG 12) 1370: *gravissime delinquere*; In Ezech. hom. 3,8 (GCS 33) 357,31: *digna abiectione,* etc.

288. In Lev.hom. 8,10 (GCS 29) 408,3–8. The *omnibus publicentur* need not, in itself, mean any more than the fact that the penitent is undertaking public penance by which he becomes known as having committed a mortal sin. It does not say that he makes a detailed confession of the way in which he has precisely become guilty.

289. In Lev.hom. 14,4 (GCS 29) 486,28–492,3. It is really a question of public penance: *quae solet a poenitentibus expendi* (ibid., 486,27) with reference to the person guilty of incest in Corinth (ibid., 486,20–3). On the other hand, it is not certain that In Lev.hom. 3,4 (GCS 29) 308 concerns anything more than the confession of sins before God, by which the devil's role as accuser at the judgement is anticipated. Similarly, this is all that is involved in In Ps. 36 hom. 1,5 (PG 12) 1328. Although the *tradere carnem in interitum* (In Lev.hom. 3,4 [GCS 29] 308,15) is mentioned, it is difficult to think that Origen would consider sins *in sermone solo vel etiam intra cogitationem secreta* as the object of public penance. Cf., for example, in Lev.hom. 12,6 (GCS 29) 465,7–9, where sins of thought are distinguished as a 'blemish' from sins of deed which make a man exteriorly or interiorly an *abiectus.* It ought not to be overlooked that the *interitus carnis* also includes works of penance. Thus it can mean only these, even if they are not done precisely within the official, public penance of the Church.

290. In Lev.hom. 2,4 (GCS 29) 296,19–21.

291. In Ps. 37 hom. 2,6 (PG 12) 1386. This interpretation of the passage appears to me to be the only one possible. Cf., on this point, B. Poschmann, p. 449 ff. The question to be decided by the physician of souls is whether the sin *has* to be expiated publicly. This text does not say that the all-important and decisive viewpoint for making this decision is the eventual edification of the community. In fact A. Vanbeck, 'La pénitence dans Origène' in: RHLR, NF 3 (1912), pp. 544–57; 4 (1913), pp. 115–29; ibid., p. 557, would like to derive from this text the idea that only offences causing scandal require a public penance. On this point it must be said, however, that it is here precisely a question of secret offences which, as such, cannot give rise to scandal. Nevertheless, it is perfectly possible that they must be subjected to public penance. Also, it seems to me that nothing more is demanded of public confession than that which is inevitably involved in public penance. Given the small number of sins which

were subject to public penance and which was even smaller in practice than in Origen's theory, penance also required a relatively precise public confession, even if an individual confession was not made before all the faithful. Obviously this may have happened sometimes out of penitential fervour. On the other hand, the previous confession before the physician of souls had necessarily to be detailed, because it had to be decided whether there was present an actual mortal sin to be submitted to public penance. Apart from this decision, however, the examination of conscience, which Origen recommends in any case in the same context, requires a more precise expression. To conclude to the necessity of a detailed confession of sins before the community either by the sinner himself or by the bishop in the process of correcting the sinner, by reason of the difference between the expressions *languorem exponere* (= before the community) and *causam languoris exponere* (= before the physician of souls) appears to force the words unduly. And would the confession of secret sins be as 'edifying' as it is supposed to be? A detailed *correptio* in the case of a public scandal can have such an effect along with reconciliation. It is very doubtful, however, whether it would have this effect in the case of a painful revelation of secret sins.

292. In Ps. 37 hom. 2,1 (PG 12) 1380 f. The text makes sense only on the supposition that without such a confession the sin *cannot* be healed. For, if this were not the case, why should the sinner take upon himself the social disgrace, described in such vivid colours, in order to undertake the exhomologesis (the word occurs here twice) for his secret sins (*crimina nullo . . . arguente*)?

293. Cf. above under n.244.

294. In Jos.hom. 21,1 (GCS 30) 428,15–429,14. It is always supposed that the Church *must* always be actually free from sinful 'Jebusites' and that everything must be done at least to come near to this state: *eos saltem eiciamus, quos possumus.* Origen could not speak in this way if it were accepted as a matter of principle that secret mortal sins are in no way considered the object of excommunication. The same supposition lies behind In Jer.fragm. 48 (GCS 6) 256,17–29. If it is explained that even the secret sinner is actually separated from the Church, and at the same time it is said that the person cast out of 'Jerusalem' is able to return there only if he does penance outside for a considerable period of time, then this obviously applies to secret sins as well.

295. In Jos.hom. 7,6 (GCS 30) 334,4 f.

296. In Matt.tom. XVI 8 (GCS 40) 496,21–9.

297. In Jos.hom. 7,6 (GCS 30) 332,21–334,20.

298. In Jos.hom. 7,6 (GCS 30) 333,12 f. The 'morals police' which had to supervise the catechumens (cf. Contra Celsum III 51 [GCS 2] 247,13 f.) remain effective in some form or other even after the catechumenate (cf. ibid., 247,15–16).

299. In Lev.hom. 3,2 (GCS 29) 302,15–30; In Jos.hom. 21,1 (GCS 30) 429,6–8.

300. In Jos.hom. 7,6 (GCS 30) 332,22–333,7.

301. De or. 28,10 (GCS 3) 381,12–18; In Lev.hom. 12,6 (GCS 29) 465,3: *ad gratiam iudicare*.

302. In Ps. 37 hom. 1,1 (PG 12) 1370 f.; In Ezech.hom. 10,1 (GCS 33) 417,13–20; In Jer.hom. 14,1 (GCS 6) 120.

303. In this case the correctness of this information must be established by a regular procedure. Ad Rom. II 10 (PG 14) 894A.

304. Cf., on this point, the considerations in n.291.

305. In Matt.tom. XIII 30 (GCS 40) 263,4. Given the reserve with which Origen presents this principle in theory, it is questionable whether this always happened in practice, especially in the case of adultery, which the bishop could know about only by the sinner's personal confession. Because it was practically impossible to apply the

theory, it became customary in this case *ad gratiam iudicare*. This also provided the justification for that practice which, because it was applied too widely and was perhaps even based on a false premiss, is attacked by Origen in De or. 28. In In Jos.hom. 7,6 (GCS 30) 332,21–334,20 also it seems to be supposed that the *fornicans* too (ibid., 333,11) in certain circumstances is excommunicated only if he persists after having been warned and reprimanded (ibid., 333,3–7). It should not be forgotten that to determine precisely what is serious sin both objectively and subjectively was, and is, not an easy business. Given the severity of the penitential procedure at that time, the church authorities were forced unwillingly in practice to impose excommunication only where it was also the thorough conviction of the community which participated in this procedure that it was clearly a question of mortal sins. This is possibly what gave rise to the *consuetudo* in this question that, in practice, only those were excommunicated *qui manifesti sunt in magnis delictis* (cf. in Matt.ser. 89 [GCS 38] 204,31), *qui manifeste et evidenter criminosi sunt* (cf. In Jos.hom. 21,1 [GCS 30] 428,21–429,1). In making this assessment of the practice, we should not overlook the fact that there was also at that time the clear theoretical awareness that there could also be secret sins which kill the sinner and render him excommunicated in God's eyes, and that he had to undertake penance of excommunication of his own initiative.

306. In Ps. 37 hom. 2,6 (PG 12) 1386.

307. In Matt.tom. XVI 8 (GCS 40) 496,13–17.22 ff.; In Jos.hom. 7,6 (GCS 30) 334,3–5; In Lev.hom. 3,2 (GCS 29) 302,18–25; In Ps. 37 hom. 1,1 (PG 12) 1371 f. In this passage priests and deacons are explicitly presented along with the bishops as 'those who correct'.

308. In Jos.hom. 7,6 (GCS 30) 334,2–7.

309. Cf. In Jos.hom. 7,6 (GCS 30) 334,14 f.: *in uno consensu ecclesia universa conspirans*; *interventus et correptio omnium* (In Lev. hom. 8,10 [GCS 29] 408,7) doubtless refers to the same activity, since *interventus et correptio* are thought of as following the public confession of guilt.

310. In Ezech.hom. 10,1 (GCS 33) 417,13 f.

311. In Lev.hom. 8,10 (GCS 29) 408,6 f.: 'sins against God' *omnibus publicentur;* In Ps. 37 hom. 2,1 (PG 12) 1381 f.: *procedat in medium et ipse sui accusator existat . . . ego ipse mei accusator efficior . . . ipse me arguo, ipse me confuto* (says the sinner); ibid., 2,6 (PG 12) 1386: *languorem in conventu totius ecclesiae exponere*. Cf. also Selecta in Ps. 56,10 (PG 12) 1472; in Jer. hom. 20,8 (GCS 6) 189,19–23. These instructions should be understood as realistically as possible. The confession really takes place before the assembled community: *coram hominibus* and with the *iracundia episcopi arguentis* In Ps. 37 hom. 1,1 (PG 12) 1371.

312. Ad Rom. VI 9 (PG 14)1090 refers to Daniel's exhomologesis *in ieiuniis et cilicio et cinere* and thus to his general confession of sins (Dan. 9:5 f.). It is explicitly noted, however, that in the Bible no sins are ascribed to Daniel, because he is a saint, differently from the case of David. Origen is able, therefore, to envisage a penitential exhomologesis which does not involve a precise, detailed confession. Besides the exhomologesis before God or men (cf. In Ps. 36 hom. 1,5 [PG 12] 1328B; In Ps. 37 hom. 2,1 [PG 12] 1381C) Origen seems to know of a still broader notion of exhomologesis: cf. Selecta in Ps. 135,2 (PG 12) 1653–6.

313. Unrepentant sinners, who had become known as such through those who supervised the morals of the community, were indeed excommunicated, even though they had totally withdrawn themselves from the public act of excommunication and the life of the Church.

314. In Ps. 37 hom. 2,1 (PG 12) 1381: *exprobrant . . . confitentem et notant vel irrident*.

315. In Ps. 37 hom. 2,6 (PG 12) 1386. Similarly In Luc.hom. 17 (GCS 35) 119,1–8. That the physician of souls to be asked first is always the bishop seems to be excluded

by the fact that, if this were the case, then the *choice* recommended by Origen would be impossible. If, however, the non-episcopal (priestly or non-priestly) physician of souls were to decide that the penance of excommunication was necessary, then this would have to be made in dependence upon the bishop. This would make a private confession before the bishop inevitable. This is what is meant by the statement: *non erubescit sacerdoti Domini indicare peccatum* (In Lev.hom. 2,4 [GCS 29] 296,20). This is a necessary part of public penance. Moreover, it should not be forgotten that non-priestly, experienced physicians of souls were just as rare in those days as they are nowadays. Thus in the vast majority of cases the confession of sins which Origen recommends to be made before fellow-Christians *qui possunt mederi vulneribus nostris atque peccatis* (In Luc.hom. 17 (GCS) 119,3–5) was made before priests, even though in theory it could be made before others, provided it was not a matter of the immediate undertaking of the penance of excommunication. B. Poschmann, p. 449 n.3, is correct when he sees in the private consultation of the bishop with a view to making this confession a reason why Origen considers this practice to be the fulfilment of Jas. 5:14.

316. Cf. Contra Celsum III 51 (GCS 2) 247,1–248,5.

317. Cf. the texts referred to above in nn.170–96.

318. Contra Celsum III 51 (GCS 2) 247,1–248,5.

319. In Lev.hom. 14,2 (GCS 29) 479,20–2.

320. In Ps. 37 hom. 1,1 (PG 12) 1371.

321. In Matt.ser. 89 (GCS 38) 204,31 f. This happens *propter honorem orationis* (ibid., 205,8 f.). This exclusion obviously does not necessarily mean that penitents should not attend the liturgy at all. Cf. Origen's remark in In Ps. 37 hom. 1,1 (PG 12) 1371. It can quite simply mean that the penitents were present in a special place outside the rest of the assembled community. At this time there were already churches built according to such rules; cf. In Jos.hom. 2,1 (GCS 30) 296,20. This custom would, therefore, correspond to the later πρόσκλαυσις, as it is discernible, for instance, in Gregory the Wonderworker. In the texts quoted, however, the emphasis could lie simply on the *oratio,* so that all that is being said is that the penitent ought to take part in the service of reading and the preaching of God's word but not in the service of prayer. This distinction is found later in the Eastern penitential practice. Origen also certainly is acquainted with this order of the liturgy: cf. Fragm. In 1 Cor. (J. A. Cramer, *Catenae Graecorum Patrum,* V, p. 69).

322. To have a clearer idea of the supervision of the morals of the community, it would be useful to consult the Didascalia Apostolorum—a work which is close both in time and in place of origin to Origen. On its penitential teaching, cf. the essay 'Penitential Teaching and Practice According to the Didascalia Apostolorum' in this volume.

323. For further details, cf. above n.248.

324. Cf. In Jos.hom. 7,6 (GCS) 334,16–18: . . . *quam mecum ire in gehennam.* If exclusion from the Eucharist is considered to be *iuris divini,* then even for today's dogmatic theology every mortal sin still involves an inner separation from the fellowship of the Church's grace, which manifests itself in the sacramental—*visible* dimension (and is, therefore, a kind of *excommunicatio latae sententiae*).

325. In Lev.hom. 14,2 (GCS 29) 479,20–2.

326. In Jud.hom. 2,5 (GCS 30) 475,25.

327. In Ps. 37 hom. 1,6 (PG 12) 1380.

328. In Ezech.hom. 3,8 (GCS 33) 365,30; ibid., 10,1 (GCS 33) 417,13.

329. In Jer.fragm. 48 (GCS 6) 222,8 f.

330. In Ps. 37 hom. 2,6 (PG 12) 1386D–1387; In Joan. XXVIII 4 (GCS 10) 393,25–30.

331. In Jud.hom. 2,5 (GCS 30) 479,2; In Jer.fragm. 48 (GCS 6) 222,9–14.

332. In Ps. 37 hom. 1,1 (PG 12) 1372.

333. In Ps. 36 hom. 4,2 (PG 12) 1353.

334. In Jos. hom. 3,5 (GCS 30) 307,8–10: *nemo ergo sibi persuadeat, nemo semetipsum decipiat: extra hanc domum, id est extra ecclesiam nemo salvatur; si quis foras exierit, mortis suae ipse fit reus.* Cf. In Jer.hom. 5,16 (GCS 6) 45,30–46,2.

335. Cf., for example, the ideas mentioned above in nn.116 and 248.

336. Cf. above under nn. 248 and 250.

337. Cf. H. U. von Balthasar, *Le Mystérion,* pp. 552 n.1; 49–51; 53–62. The 'exception' which is here made with respect to penance in Origen's general sacramental teaching does not exist in reality. For further details, cf. below.

338. Cf., for example, In Ezech.hom. 9,1 (GCS 33) 405,13–406,9; In I Reg.hom. 1,4 (GCS 33) 5–7; Frag. 1 Cor. (J. A. Cramer, *Catenae Graecorum Patrum,* V, p. 182).

339. In Lev.hom. 4,8 (GCS 29) 327,3–27; In Joan. VI 33 (GCS 10) 142; on this point, cf. H. U. von Balthasar, *Le Mystérion,* pp. 39 f., 55 f.; Contra Celsum III 28 (GCS 2) 226,6–18. Moreover, on his eucharistic teaching, see C. Bigg, pp. 264–7, E. R. Redepenning, II, p. 438 ff.; G. Bardy in: DTh XI, 2c 1558 ff.; J. F. De Groot, *Conspectus historiae dogmatum* (2 vols., Rome 1931), vol. i, p. 200 ff.; H. U. von Balthasar, *Le Mystérion,* pp. 548–53, 59 ff.

340. The Church's reconciling activity, which we are discussing in this section, need not necessarily always take place temporally between the excommunication and its lifting. This obviously cannot be the case, since this activity is certainly effective even where there is no question of penance of excommunication. We will return to the question of the relationship between this activity of the Church and the lifting of excommunication when we come to the detailed discussion of the latter. It is far too peremptory to consider those 'punishments' which remain after the remission of 'guilt' simply as a 'sentence of punishment' consisting only in God's 'decree'. The picture changes, however, once we ask what it is in objective, existential reality on *our* part that corresponds to this decree of God: guilt and punishment move closer together. Our 'fleshly condition', the Godless aspect of our un-enlightened being, with all its consequences, is the remaining expression of our guilt and its punishment, even after forgiveness. In the final analysis, therefore, punishment is really reducible to guilt and is its expression. As such, it is something which ought not to be. The remission of the punishments due to sin, therefore, is a theme not only of the teaching on indulgences but must be included in the considerations on penance as a genuine part of the teaching on the *forgiveness of sins*.

341. Cf. above the texts and details in connection with nn. 270–4.

342. In Lev.hom. 5,3 (GCS 29) 338,10–13; 339,11–14.

343. Cf., for example, In Luc.hom. 12 (GCS 35) 84–7; ibid., 13 (GCS 35) 91,20–5; ibid., 23 (GCS 35) 156,25 f.; ibid., 35 (GCS 35) 208,19–22. It is immaterial whether all the speculations on angels are correct (an individul guardian angel for each community; angels which do not exercise their 'episcopal office' properly, etc.). All that matters is that, according to Origen, in the one Church angel and bishop are 'bishop' in their own way. They do not compete with one another.

344. Cf. In Ps. 37 hom. 1,1 (PG 12) 1371 f. All that we need to observe here is the natural way in which Origen transfers the idea of the *correptio* by bishops (priests and deacons) to a corresponding *correptio* by angels. In view of his general notion that there is only a relative difference between angels and spiritual persons, the angels, in the exercise of their rôle, have essentially the same status in the Church as perfect spiritual persons. This implies that the respective roles of the bishop and the spiritual person are no more mutually exclusive than those of the 'visible bishop' and the invisible angel-bishop. Indeed Origen's system as a whole would suggest that the contrary is the case.

345. In Num.hom. 10,1 (GCS 30) 68,4–12:

> *qui meliores sunt, inferiorum semper culpas et peccata suscipiunt . . . Israelita si peccet, id est laicus, ipse suum non potest auferre peccatum, sed requirit levitam, indiget sacerdote, immo . . . pontifice opus est, ut peccatorum remissionem possit accipere. Sacerdos autem, si delinquat aut pontifex, ipse suum potest purgare peccatum, si tamen non peccet in Deum; de huiusmodi enim peccatis non facile remissionem aliquam videmus in legis litteris designari.*

Despite the Old Testament terminology, all this refers to the men and the hierarchy of the New Covenant (cf. In Ps. 37 hom. 1,1 [PG 12] 1372). Since there is also a mention of the sins of bishops and priests, it must be a question of offences committed after baptism, although not only of mortal sins. The special difficulty which the remission of the mortal sins of bishops presents to Origen resides in the fact that, in their case, the penance of excommunication meant the permanent exclusion from office (Contra Celsum III 51 [GCS 2] 247,1–248,5) or that, at that time, a cleric was simply not allowed access to public penance. From the context and considering In Ps. 37 hom. 1,1 (PG 12)1372, where the three groups of the hierarchy (deacons, priests, bishops) co-operate in the reconciliation of men, we can see that, in this passage too, it is these three groups of officials, and not three grades of holiness, that are meant. Consequently here (at least principally) *meliores* is not to be understood as the counterpart of *inferiores* in the sense of moral qualities or spiritual prerogatives. It is a question of grades of offices, from the laity to the bishop. Their reconciling activity must be sought, therefore, on this level of hierarchically ordered and visible sacramentality. In practice, this may be defined as supervision and official reprimand, including the penance of excommunication (In Ps. 37 hom. 1,1, etc.), the offering of sacrifice and the administration of the Eucharist (Contra Celsum VIII 33 [GCS 3] 249,5: the Eucharist as 'healing'; in Num.hom. 16,9 [GCS 30] 152,4–5: we drink *sacramentorum ritu* the blood of him who was wounded for our sins; In Ex.hom. 4,8 [GCS 29] 182,1; De or. 28,9 [GCS 3] 381,4–6). For further details, cf. H. U. von Balthasar, *Le Mystérion*: the Eucharist as the manifestation of Christ's eternal reconciling sacrifice. In every case, therefore, the right of the different officials in the Church is recognized. The lay person, regardless of whether he is spiritual (or whether other lay persons supporting him are also such) cannot dispense with the higher grades of the hierarchy, while these, on their respective levels, have no need of those who are under them, since they, for instance, offer sacrifice. For further examples, cf. below: the martyrs and their death, the saints in this world, etc.

346. Cf., on this point, H. U. von Balthasar, *Le Mystérion*, p. 49 f.

347. Cf. above under n.340.

348. Both aspects are in fact implicit in his teaching on the difference between the baptismal ἄφεσις and the *poenitentia dura et laboriosa*.

349. Cf., on this point, H. von Campenhausen, *Kirchliches Amt und geistliche Vollmacht in den ersten drei Jahrhunderten* (Tübingen 1963), pp. 262–91; also G. Teichtweier, pp. 339–40; J. Grotz, pp. 206–229.

350. Cf. In Matt. tom. XII 10–14 (GCS 84–100; esp. ibid., 84,24–86,5; 88,6–13; 96,6–15; 98,6–28). The question of the power of binding, which is here being considered somewhat vaguely together with the question of the power of loosing, has already been discussed in some detail above. In the present passage the power of loosing is described as ἐξουσία (ibid., 98,6). The Christians who possess it are called, in addition to *Petrus*, τέλειοι (ibid., 86,7 f.24), ἅγιοι (ibid., 88,31), *homines spirituales* (ibid., 88,20), *fideles* (ibid., 96,7), imitators of Christ (ibid., 86,1 f.;88,16) and *stabiles in fide* (ibid., 85,20). The content of their power is described only very vaguely: binding and loosing (*passim*), to open heaven in such a way that the one loosed is free

(ibid., 98,22–4), to obtain ἄφεσις in heaven (ibid., 87,16–22; 99,5). In fact all that is said is that the saints have the effective power of reconciliation. How and by what means this power is exercised is not specified. It would be methodologically false to press the images (that of judging, etc.) which are contained in the text which is itself to be interpreted. We must look for an answer to this question elsewhere in Origen. It would be purely arbitrary to attempt to explain this power of reconciliation simply by the notion which we today recognize as the official priestly power of the sacrament of penance for the forgiveness of sins. The same ἐξουσία as in Matt. tom. XII is also ascribed to the ἅγιοι in De or. 14,6 (GCS 3) 333,12. 14–16.

351. In addition to the text already cited (esp. ibid., 96,15–97,27: every individual virtue is its own door to heaven and its own heaven; all together constitute the whole kingdom of heaven), cf. In Matt. tom. XIII 31 (GCS 40) 269,28–271,9.

352. This follows from the principle already mentioned concerning a power of reconciliation *increasing* with the degree of virtues.

353. In Matt.tom. XII 14 (GCS 40) 99,12–22 (Latin text).

354. In Luc.hom. 34 (GCS 35) 205,7–14.

355. In Lev. hom. 8,10 (GCS 29) 408,7. Although this refers specifically only to sins subject to public penance, it still applies analogously to all sins.

356. We have already mentioned several times angels and their activity in the forgiveness of sins. Cf. under n.344. In fact after his own resurrection the person guilty of mortal sin is delivered by God and Christ to the angels of his respective Church (In Luc.hom. 34 [GCS 35] 204,24). They then have to 'loosen' the remaining fetters of his sins (In Joan. XXVIII 8 [GCS 10] 399,21–4). For the case of martyrs, cf. Exhort. ad mart. 30 (GCS 2) 26,28–27,5; In Num.hom. 10,2 (GCS 30) 71,18–72,27.

357. As will be shown below, the reconciling activity of the saints occurs on two levels: first, through their interior proximity to God by prayer, sorrow, suffering, struggling with the demons, etc.; second—although still by reason of their personal holiness and precisely not strictly as officials—in the visible Church through exhortation, teaching, etc., including the visible sacrifice of the altar, in the case of priests.

358. Selecta in Ps. 27,3 (PG 12) 1285–8.

359. In Matt.tom. X 23 (GCS 40) 33,3 f. Cf. W. Völker, p. 171.

360. Selecta in Ps. 60,3 (PG 12) 1480 f.; Selecta in Threnos I (PG 13) 608C; 629C.

361. In Ps. 37 hom. 2,6 (PG 12) 1386; Ad Rom. IX 15 (PG 14) 1221 f.

362. In Num.hom. 25,4 (GCS 30) 238,4–14.

363. Cf. the texts in W. Völker, p. 175 f.

364. Cf. the references in W.Völker, p. 176 f. According to Origen there is also a martyrdom of every day: In Ps. 118,157; cf. in J. B. Pitra, *Analecta sacra Spicilegio Solesmensi parata,* 8 vols. (Paris 1876–83), vol. iii, p. 307 f.

365. De or. 14,6 (GCS 3) 333,11–16. After all that has been said previously on the subject of the 'saints', there should be no doubt that here they do not only forgive any guilt incurred against themselves, but 'make us worthy (passively) to participate in the power which has been given to them to forgive guilt (in *God's* eyes)'. This applies despite De or. 28,8 (GCS 3) 380,5, where there is mention of an ἐξουσία to forgive precisely guilt incurred against the person who is forgiving.

366. Cf. above under n.299.

367. De or. 14,6 (GCS 3) 333,14 f. See further texts placing them in parallel with the apostles in W. Volker, p. 186.

368. Ad Rom. VII (PG 14) 1139 A/B.

369. In Lev.hom. 5,4 (GCS 29) 342,11–15.

370. In Lev.hom. 5,3 (GCS 29) 339,11–14; 340.1 f. Both of these passages in fact refer to the bishop. The fact, however, that the *tribuere remissionem peccatorum* and the *purgare conscientias* are explained in such a way that they can refer also to

spiritual persons and only express what Origen certainly ascribes also to spiritual persons shows, on the other hand, that it is precisely this influence, by means of exhortation, pleading, prayer, etc. that we must bear in mind when we consider the power to forgive sins which is ascribed to them. Whether the bishops' power to forgive sins is totally *identified* with this spiritual activity of the saints (which Origen obviously asks also of bishops), or whether they have a still wider function to play in this question, which is their sole prerogative, is a point which remains to be considered.

371. It could still be said, however, that if the 'binding' does indeed *include* the lifting of excommunication (and, in view of In Matt.tom. XII 10–14 and tom. XIII 30, there can be no doubt that it does), then spiritual persons must *also* possess even this power to reincorporate penitents into the Church through the loosing of excommunication, since they can certainly 'loose'. Nevertheless, this would be a form of argumentation which rests upon Origen's obscure terminology and certainly is not in line with his true thinking. We have already shown that it cannot be seriously doubted that, in Origen's view, real excommunication is the prerogative of the bishops. If this is the case, then it follows that only they can *really* loose it.

372. Cf. In Matt.tom. XII 14 (GCS 40) 98,28–99,22 etc.

373. In Matt.tom. XII 14 (GCS 40) 99,11–22. According to the whole section, this precise power of loosing belongs also to the spiritual person who is not a member of the official hierarchy. The bishop's holiness, therefore, is presented not only as the mere condition of the effectiveness of his official power but as itself the real cause of and reason for the effectiveness of this loosing.

374. Cf. in Lev.hom. 5,3–4, loc. cit.

375. Cf. in Ex.hom. 4,8 (GCS 29)182,1 f.: we are purified from sins (other than mortal sins) *per obsecrationes pontificum*. This purification is placed on the same level as the purification *per scientiam divinae legis* and is distinguished from the liberation from mortal sins which requires the immediate intervention of God. It from this that the purifying prayer of priests is not to be thought of as sacramental in the strict sense, since Origen holds that the *scientia legis* is certainly an apanage of spiritual persons who do not hold an office (cf. W. Völker, p. 169 ff.). He does, however, recognize in principle a prayer which remits sins. Accordingly, the remission of sins by the bishops through mere 'prayer' is to be understood as that which Origen admits in De or. 28,10 for sins, with the exception of mortal sins. Certainly the bishops lay claim to this prayer clearly in virtue of their ἱερατικὴ ἀξία (cf. [GCS 3] 382,12 f.). They attribute to their 'prayer' for sins a special efficacy deriving from their episcopal status and which is not given to others. This may refer especially to liturgical prayer. Nevertheless, this is still no argument in favour of a real, essential difference (both objectively and according to Origen's view). Objectively this 'priestly' prayer could still be understood as 'sacramental' in the modern sense. It need not be taken as the formula of an actual sacrament. As far as Origen himself is concerned, he does not look for the explanation of the effectiveness of this prayer in the priestly status. All that he is concerned to do is to dispute the effectiveness of prayer alone for mortal sins in particular. Since he seems in this passage to concede such a power of prayer for the forgiveness of sins only to *spiritual* bishops (cf. ibid., 380,8–15; 381,4), it would seem all the more appropriate to understand this power in such a way that, along the lines of In Matt.tom. XII 14, it belongs to the bishop *because* he is spiritual.

376. In Matt.tom. XIII 30 (GCS 40) 262,16–26; 264,9–12; In Lev.hom. 3,2 (GCS 29) 302; In Jos.hom. 7,6 (GCS 30) 333,3–7. In the last passage it is also clear that the bishops themselves could, in the first instance, undertake a quite private *correptio* of the sinner (obviously in the appropriate cases), before they proceed to an official *correptio*. In the first instance they behave precisely as any spiritual person and every

good Christian who likewise has a responsibility *secrete convenire* (ibid., 333,4) as a physician.

377. In Lev.hom. 5,3 f. (GCS 29) 337,28: *contribulati spiritus hostia*; ibid., 340,1: *hostia verbi Dei et doctrinae sanae victima*; ibid., 342,22 f.: *offerre pro peccatis, id est a via peccati convertere peccatores*.

378. In Ex.hom. 4,8 (GCS 29) 182,1. Here, likewise, it is not a question of *sacrificia sacerdotum* for mortal sins.

379. There is no reason why the sacrifices offered for specific groups of sins in De or. 28,9 (GCS 3) 381,4–6 cannot refer to the actual liturgical sacrifice, with the same proviso as was made with regard to the text mentioned in the previous note. We might even, with A. von Harnack (TU 42,3) 79, read In Lev.hom. 3,6 (GCS 29) 310,19–21.26–30 as showing that at that time already the question had arisen of how a poor person without money could come to such a sacrifice.

380. Thus, for example, In Num. hom. 10,1 (GCS 30) 71,7–9: *qui sancti sunt, pro peccatis poenitudinem gerunt, vulnera sua sentiunt, intelligunt lapsus, requirunt sacerdotem, sanitatem deposcunt, purificationem per pontificem quaerunt*. Or In Ps. 37 hom. 1,1 (PG 12) 1369: *omnes, qui post Apostolos in Ecclesia positit sunt, quibusque curandorum vulnerum disciplina commissa est, quos voluit Deus in Ecclesia sua esse medicos animarum*. Such formulations are obviously very general and comprehensive and it would be unjustifiable to think that they refer only to the bishop's strict sacramental activity.

381. In Lev.hom. 5,3 (GCS 29) 339,12 f. The *peccata accipere* in imitation of Jesus is said here of the *sacerdotes Ecclesiae*. In Num.hom. 10,1 (GCS 30) 68,4: *meliores . . . inferiorum semper culpas et peccata suscipiunt*.

382. Cf. also Selecta in Ps. 29,3 (PG 12) 1292D. 1293A; the Church, which feels itself in solidarity with sinners; In Num.hom. 10,2 (GCS 30) 71,15: Christ with the apostles and martyrs *sumit peccata sanctorum*; In Lev.hom. 7,1 f. (GCS 29) 373–80: the solidarity of the whole Church with Christ in heaven and on earth in the reconciliation of all men.

383. In Ezech.hom. 3,8 (GCS 33) 357,30–358,1.

384. Contra Celsum III 51 (GCS 2) 248,3.

385. In Ps. 36 hom. 4,2 (PG 12) 1353. Origen's stress on both the possibility and the effectiveness of penance in this passage shows that the question raised by the doubting sinner: *Quomodo ad Ecclesiam redire* must be answered basically in the affirmative.

386. In Jer.frag. 48 (GCS 6) 222,16,21.

387. Ad Rom.praef. (PG 14) 834.

388. In Ps. 37 hom. 1,1 (PG 12) 1371. This is also said of the incestuous person in Corinth, the type of a repentant sinner.

389. In Jud.hom, 2,5 (GCS 30) 478,23–479,1. It would, however, be false to understand the 'loosing' in such cases exclusively of the lifting of excommunication. According to Origen, 'loosing' in the case of bishops who are really what they ought to be is a wider notion. In In Matt.tom. XII 14 (GCS 40) also this notion retains its indeterminate character, which obviously does not exclude the lifting of excommunication but also includes much more than the bishop has as a spiritual person. In Matt.hom. XIII 31 (GCS 40) 269,11–18, for example, shows that, in Origen's view, there is a 'loosing' by means of a simple once-and-for-all *νουθεσία*, therefore without excommunication.

390. In Lev.hom. 2,4 (GCS 29) 296,17–297,3. Both *in quo et impletur illud, quod Jacobus Apostolus dicit* (ibid., 296, 22 f.) and the fact that this forgiveness of sins according to James is not counted as a new (eighth) possibility makes it clear that Origen wishes to relate this text to the seventh possibility of forgiveness in his list, that is, to *dura et laboriosa per poenitentiam remissio peccatorum* (ibid., 296,17 f.)

and not to the sacrament of the anointing of the sick. This explains why Origen transforms the words 'they should pray over him', in the text of James, into 'they must impose hands upon him', thus clearly modelling the text on the liturgy of reconciliation. The only question that can be asked is whether, in Origen's circle, *all* the elements listed in Jas. 5:14 f. (imposition of hands by the *presbyteri Ecclesiae*, anointing, 'prayer of faith') occurred as aspects of the forgiveness of sins or whether Origen regarded the text as sufficiently 'fulfilled', even if, for example, at that time an anointing was not yet customary. Cf. J. Coppens, *L'imposition des mains* (Wetteren/Paris 1925), pp. 41 f., 374 ff.

391. Cf. Didascalia Apost. II 18,7 (F. X. Funk, *Didascalia et Constitutiones Apostolorum* I [Paderborn 1905], p. 66); ibid., II 41,2 (F. X. Funk, p. 130): ibid., II 43,1 (F. X. Funk, p. 134).

392. Cf. the texts mentioned in the previous note.

393. Thus, for example, in Aphraates, Demostr. XXIII 3 (Patr. Syr. Pars I vol. ii [Paris 1907] 10). For further witnesses, cf. F. Dölger, *Der Exorzismus im altchristlichen Taufritual* (Paderborn 1909), pp. 148–51; J. Coppens, pp. 377–9.

394. Origen also seems to know of a post-baptismal anointing; baptism occurs, that is, *in aquis istis visibilibus et in chrismate visibili*: Ad Rom. V 8 (PG 14) 1058. Cf. also In Lev. hom. 6,5 (GCS 29) 367,11: *unctio chrismatis*. The parallel with baptism, which is already a characteristic of the penitential process, is further confirmed by a parallel anointing.

395. Cf. ibid. (GCS 29) 417,12–18.

396. H. Elfers, *Die Kirchenordnung Hippolyts von Rom* (Paderborn 1938), p. 137, appears to understand the text as referring to confirmation. Nevertheless, the sinner, with whose progressive and gradual purification the whole homily of n.5 is concerned, is obviously already a Christian and no longer a catechumen. In the whole section, beginning from n.5, it is always a question of the contrast between the *sanctus* (*iustus, mundus*) and the *peccator* (ibid. [GCS 29] 393,22; 408,18 f.; 413,3; 412,21). It is never there a question of the contrast between pagan (catechumen) and Christian. The six kinds of leprosy-sins which are considered are all applied to sin which was committed *after* baptism (ibid. [GCS 29] 404,1–5; 405,11–17; 406,5–11; 407,12–21; 408,6) and which is to be submitted to public penance, because it is 'against God' (ibid. [GCS 29] 408,5) and 'mortal' (ibid. [GCS 29] 405,16; 408,6–8). In the description of the purification of such a sinner (ibid. [GCS 29]) the misunderstanding that it is a question of a new baptism, because there is a mention of 'living water' (ibid. [GCS 29] 411,6–9), is explicitly rejected. In contrast to baptism, it is more a question of a *purificatio peccatorum . . . quae per poenitentiam quaeritur* (ibid. [GCS 29] 411,7 f.; cf. also 414,5). Then in n.11 of the homily the gradation of this purification is considered (ibid. [GCS 29] 411,16–417). The expression 'to wash', found in the biblical text cited, recurs frequently, but it is never applied to baptism (ibid. [GCS 29] 413,15–18). The readmission into the *castra* (ibid. [GCS 29] 413,19; 414,16; 416,9) is intended as the counterpart to the exclusion from the camp, that is, the excommunication of the Christian sinner (ibid. [GCS 29] 408,17–20). It is then stated of *these* gradually purified sinners:

> *sic ergo conversis a peccato purificatio per illa omnia datur, quae superius diximus* (that is, this gradual purification), *donum autem gratiae spiritus per olei imaginem designatur, ut non solum purgationem consequi possit is, qui convertitur a peccato, sed et Spiritu sancto repleri, quo et recipere priorem stolam et anulum possit et per omnia reconciliatus Patri in locum Filii reparari.*

It is thus clearly a question of the penance of a Christian after baptism. Certainly the term 'oil' also occurs in the biblical text being interpreted. It is perfectly possible that the communication of the Spirit is 'signified' by the 'oil' as a simple metaphor and not through a real anointing. Thus G. Teichtweier has rejected the assumption of a real anointing on the grounds that all that can be discerned in the overall context is an allegorical interpretation of the Old Testament purification ceremonies. According to the text Selecta in Ez. XVI (PG 13) 812, Teichtweier understands 'oil' exclusively as a symbol which signifies the communication of the Spirit (cf. G. Teichtweier, p. 326). An anointing at reconciliation is, however, attested for the East at this time, and In Lev.hom. 2,4 suggests that Origen is familiar with it. Thus it is justifiable to think here of a real liturgical anointing with oil, through which the gift of God's grace is meaningfully signified. In Origen *imago* does not necessarily mean 'metaphor', figurative speech. It can quite simply mean a real symbolic event: *τύπος*. Thus no objection against our interpretation can be derived from the use of this term.

397. Contra Celsum III 51 (GCS 2) 247 f.

398. In Jos.hom. 24,1 (GCS 30) 448 f.

399. Cf. De princip. I 3,7 (GCS 22) 58,20 f. Cf., on this point, J. Coppens, p. 289.

400. Didascalia Apostolorum VI 7,2 (F. X. Funk, p. 316); II 41,2 (ibid., p. 130). In these texts it is precisely a question of the imposition of hands at the reconciliation of penance. Cf. ibid., II 33,1 f. (ibid., pp. 114–16): the 'hand' of the bishop is precisely that which fills the faithful with the Holy Spirit.

401. Cyprian ep. 75,7 f.18 (CSL 3,2:815.822). On the dependence of Firmilian on Origen: Eusebius, Hist.eccl. VI,27 (GCS 9,2) 580, 16–21.

402. Cf. above under n. 396.

403. Cf. ibid. (GCS 2) 247–8.

404. Ibid. (GCS 33) 357,30–358,1.

405. Ibid. (GCS 33) 358,1–7.

406. Cf. In Lev.hom. 8,10 (GCS 29) 408,3–8: the sin 'against God' obtains *venia* by means of *interventus omnium,* provided it is publicly 'confessed' and subjected to church penance. Origen could not speak in this vein if this *venia* did not also include that of the Church. In Jer.fragm. 48 (GCS 6) 222,7–223,6 simply mentions the sinner who, after doing penance for a sufficient period of time, is again received into the fellowship of the Church. The allusion to 1 Cor. 5:5 and 1 Tim. 1:20 shows that these sinners also include those guilty of incest and blasphemy. In Lev. hom. 14,4 (GCS 29) 486,20–487,3 says, in the context of and with regard to *public* church penance, that through it our spirit is purified in *praesenti vita*. Now to claim that public penance is the cause of an effect obtainable in this life would not make sense unless it were possible for this process to come to an end, that is, without the reconciliation of the sinner with the Church.

407. Ad Rom.praef. (PG 14) 834; In Ps. 37 hom. 1,1 (PG 12)1370 f.: the incestuous person in Corinth is here presented as the typical case of both exclusion from the Church and penance.

408. In Jer.fragm. 48 (GCS 6) 222,12–22, in so far as the case of *βλασφημεῖν* in 1 Tim. 1:20 is considered susceptible of church reconciliation.

409. In Lev.hom. 15,2 (GCS 29)489,19 f.: the *graviora crimina* also include the *blasphemia fidei, quae muro ecclesiastici et apostolici dogmatis cincta est* (ibid., 489,14 f.). The *locus poenitentiae* is granted to these offences, even if only once. The stress on this once-and-for-all character of penance makes sense only if the possibility of penance was really offered: a penance, however, which does not terminate in this life cannot be granted once and refused a second time.

410. The successor of the apostles, being a spiritual person, *ἀφιήσιν ἃ ἐὰν ἀφῇ ὁ ϑεός*: De or. 28,8 (GCS 3) 380,12.

411. The following sins are beyond the reach of the spiritual bishops' power of prayer: *τὰ ἀνίατα* (De or, 28,8 [GCS 3] 380,12); *μοιχία ἑκούσιος φόνος ἄλλο*

καλεπώτερον πταῖσμα (ibid., 380,28 f.); εἰδωλολατρεία, μοιχία, πορνεία (ibid., 381,14); ἁμαρτία πρὸς θάνατον (ibid., 381,17).

412. It should be remembered that in Origen ἀφιέναι, ἄφεσις does not necessarily mean every kind of forgiveness of sin.

413. De or. 28,10 (GCS 3) 381,12. This fact also shows that it is not essential in the discussion of our question to arrange the writings of Origen chronologically. If he recognizes the institution of penance as a whole, as it must already have existed *with* a church reconciliation at least several decades before Contra Celsum III 51, then he must know of a church reconciliation after the penance of excommunication already when he is composing the De oratione. He does not challenge this institution, even though he repudiates the abuse which 'some' make of it. If, however, in De or. he had contested the Church's ability to forgive any sins at all, then he would have opposed this institution. G. Teichtweier, p. 290, holds a similar view. J. Grotz, p. 260, however, considers this passage, where Origen is concerned with the abuse of the ἄφεσις for serious sins, precisely as a confirmation of a power of absolution which can precede an excommunication and be completely separated from it. It is only in this priestly absolution that 'the real sacramental penance' is performed, and this as a kind of *opus operatum* without the sinner's co-operation by penance; cf. p. 255.

414. It is impossible to be excommunicated for a *levis culpa*: In Jos.hom. 7,6 (GCS 30) 334,2 f.; however, a *levis culpa* is only that which remains after the ambit of that which is here outside the bishops' power of prayer alone is considered. In fact the latter is exactly identical with what was earlier established as the object of excommunication, that is, as serious sin. The same conclusion follows from In Lev.hom. 15.2 (GCS 29) 489,20 f.: the *communia quae frequenter incurrimus* do not belong to the object of the penance which is granted once and for all.

415. In Lev.hom. 12,6 (GCS 29) 265,3.

416. In Lev.hom. 11,2 (GCS 29) 452 f.; ibid., 14,4 (GCS 29) 484–7.

417. Fragm.in 1 Reg. 3,14 (PG 17): only 'simple' sins of 'ignorance' can be forgiven by 'sacrifice', the rest only δι' ἔργων καὶ μετανοίας τελείας. It is a question of the story of Heli which in De or. 28,9 is also one of the biblical examples used to illustrate the principles developed here. The ἐν ἀγνοίᾳ καὶ ψιλὰ πλημμελήματα of 17,40, which can be remitted by sacrifice, correspond well to the ἀκούσια πλημμελήματα of De or. (cf. ibid. [GCS 3] 380,27), which can be expiated by 'sacrifice' alone. To the sins by which 'God himself is affronted' correspond in De or. the 'sins against the Lord' (cf. ibid. [GCS 3] 381,10 f.). These parallels show that the fragment is in the spirit of Origen. Thus it is a commentary on De or.: the rejection of prayer and sacrifice is not a denial of the efficacy of the τελεία μετάνοια. Prayer and sacrifice alone can, therefore, be ineffective, and the sin can still be forgiven. G. Teichtweier, p. 292, lays particular emphasis on the need for the sinner's personal performance of penance, in the sense of a μετάνοια. In his view, 'the decisive factor in a post-baptismal remission of serious offences is precisely the sinner's personal performance of penance and not the priest's prayer of forgiveness.' Cf. also ibid., p. 308 ff., and esp. p. 319, where the official absolution by the organs of the Church does not play too preponderant a role.

418. This text is adduced in De or. 28,9 as a proof the principle being defended.

419. In Lev.hom. 4,5 (GCS 29) 322 f.

420. Cf. above under the nn.61, 73, 324 and 331, together with the relevant details.

421. That Origen knew of this traditional ἄφεσις-notion at the time of De or. is evident from the contemporary work Exhort. ad mart. 30 (GCS 2) 26,20 ff. Although he disputes that the ἄφεσις is possible outside baptism and martyrdom, he still assumes that sins can be forgiven, in so far as martyrs, through their vocation, mediate to others (ibid. [GCS 2] 27,5) an ἄφεσις in the wider sense (as θεραπεία: ibid. [GCS

2] 26,29). Obviously this happens under the usual conditions which are precisely underlined in De or.

422. Cf. further details above under nn.350 and 351, together with the relevant text.

423. Cf. Contra Celsum III 51 (GCS 2) 248,1–3: the conversion must be made clearly visible, that is, the penitent should be readmitted only when he has proven that he has mended his ways by a visible way of life. This obviously required a longer or shorter period of time, according to the particular case.

424. This could also be at least part of the *Sitz im Leben* of the later clear distinction between two stages of penance (cf. Didascalia Apost. II 16,1.2; Dionysius, fragm. ep. ad Canonem [see J. B. Pitra, *Iuris ecclesiastici Graecorum historia et monumenta* (Rome 1864–8) I 545]; Gregorius Thaumat., Ep. can. [J. B. Pitra, 1562 ff.]). In the first instance, the sinner is either moved by his own guilty conscience or forced by the bishop's ban (cf. Didascalia Apost. II 10,3–5; 16,1) to keep away for a fairly long time from the life of the community, that is, at least from the actual liturgy, until he has re-established his moral relationships and until he can be sure that the dust has settled over the scandal which he has caused. Only then will he have truly sought reconciliation. Before he receives it, however, a further short period of penance in the strict sense is required (Didascalia Apost. II 16,2). A further period is inevitably needed for the verification of the penitent's conversion, the questioning of witnesses on the subject, etc. The other part of this *Sitz im Leben* must obviously have been a similarly graduated time of preparation in the catechumenate. This 'gradation' is what J. Grotz means by 'stages of penance'. According to him, we must make both in Origen and in all his predecessors in the theology of penance a distinction between excommunication as a stage prior to actual church penance and the much more frequently applied 'real' sacramental church penance without excommunication. 'Excommunication' is imposed only in quite serious cases, where the sinner is obstinate, and in itself has 'nothing to do' with church penance and the forgiveness of sins (J. Grotz, p. 281 f.). In his view, real penance is that which 'has essentially the same characteristics as Cyprian's exhomologesis' (ibid., p. 307). The difference between the two stages is that the unrepeatable excommunication is imposed only in particularly serious cases, whereas the repeatable church penance without excommunication is often performed alone (ibid., p. 248,2 f.).

425. Contra Celsum III 51 (GCS 2) 248,2 f.

426. Traditio Apostolica 17,1 (G. Dix, *The Treatise on the Apostolic Tradition of St Hippolytus of Rome* [London 1937], p. 28). Although here a catechumenate of three years is required, the author adds immediately that if the catechumen is very zealous he can be received more quickly, since it is not time but behaviour that counts.

427. Especially since it was obviously necessary to overcome strong resistance against public penance on the part of Christians and in general there was a tendency to be too lenient rather than too strict. Moreover, the question always had to be decided whether in fact a public church penance had to be imposed or not: De or. 28,10 (GCS 3) 381, 12–22; In Jos. hom. 7,6 (GCS 30) 332–4; In Ps. 37 hom. 1,1 (PG 12) 137 ff.; In Ezech.hom. 10,1 (GCS 33) 416–18; In Jer.hom. 14,14 (GCS 6) 120,4–14. Cf. on this point Jerome's translation (PG 13) 422. In Jer.hom. 12,5 (GCS 6) 92,10 ff.

428. Ad Rom.praef. (PG 14) 834.

429. The fact that in the Didascalia Apost. II 16,2 (F. X. Funk, p. 60) there is a question of a period of penance lasting only a few weeks can hardly be used as an objection against this point. For it must be assumed, following E. Schawartz, *Bussstufen und Katechumenatsklassen,* (Strassburg 1911), p. 19 ff., and B. Poschmann, p. 477, that this length of time refers only to penance in the strict sense of the word, by which the penitent is tested after his prayer to be reconciled with the Church to see whether he is really converted. Naturally this conversion must already have taken

place previously. At the *beginning* of this second stage, the penitent is examined to see 'whether he is worthy to be received into the Church'. The proof of this worthiness must, therefore, already be present and is not merely to be produced in the next few weeks of real penance. Cf. also In Jer. hom. 12,5 (GCS 6) 92,12 f., where it is emphasized that reconciliation ought not to take place too quickly lest the whole Church suffer harm.

430. In Jer.hom. 20,9 (GCS 6) 192,3–10; In Joan. XXVIII 4 (GCS 10) 393,7–14.

431. Contra Celsum III 51 (GCS 2) 248,3–5.

432. In fact the principle applied was that the higher a person's rank in the Church is, the harder he is to be punished: In Ezech.hom. 5,4 (GCS 33) 375,2–9. Although this refers in the first place to the punishments of the next life, it also applied within the Church itself—at least in theory. On this point, cf. G. May, 'Bemerkungen zu der Frage der Diffamation und der Irregularität der öffentlichen Büsser' in: MThZ 12 (1961), pp. 252–68.

433. In Lev.hom. 15,2 (GCS 29) 489,19 f. This does not concern the possibility to repeat penance; cf. In Lev.hom. 11,2 (GCS 29) 452,21–5. It is here a question of penance after a repeated sin, which ought not to be a reason for finally abandoning penance.

434. Augustine, Ep. 153,7 (PL33) 655 f.

435. This is also the view of G. Teichtweier, p. 325.

436. J. Grotz, pp. 304–6, sees in In Joan. XXVIII 7 (GCS 10) 397 f. a proof for his own view that the granting of the *communio* and sacramental reconciliation are not one and the same thing. In fact he understands readmission into the fellowship of the Church as an exclusively canonical measure. In view of Grotz's interpretation of the allegory of Lazarus, it must be asked how a granting of the *communio* can be understood if there is still exclusion from the Eucharist. Grotz must grant that such a granting of *communio* does not mean full integration into the community of the Church. At the same time, the text suggests the continuation of an excommunication, in so far as the description of the Christian summoned out of the grave is not compatible with one who shares in the fellowship of the Church. This is evident from the following: '. . . he is still wearing the bonds of death of his earlier sins and a band round his eyes, and he does not see, nor can he go anywhere or do anything because of the bonds of death, until Jesus orders those who can untie him to let him go' (ibid. [GCS 10] 397). 'There the person who follows Jesus can see how such a person does indeed come out because of Jesus' call but is still bound with the cords of his sin and tied by them; because of his sorrow and his listening to Jesus' voice he does indeed live, but he is still bound hands and feet with the bonds of the grave, the shackles of death, because he is not yet delivered from the chains of sin nor free to do anything properly' (ibid. [GCS 10] 397–8). 'And because death still dwells in him, he is not only bound hands and feet but also blindfolded' (ibid. [GCS 10] 397–8). For the tr. of the texts, cf. also H. Karpp, *Die Busse: Quellen zur Entstehung des altkirchlichen Busswesens* (Zürich 1969), pp. 235–9. According to this text, therefore, by Jesus' call the sinner becomes aware of the helplessness of his separation from the community of the Church's grace and reveals his readiness to return. Even after his summons from the grave the sinner is still bound and does not yet enjoy the freedom to realize his return on his part. Grotz, however, considers that at this point the *communio* is already given, although he does so in function of an external, juridical notion of the Church which does not consider its interior effect on grace. This, however, contradicts Origen's ecclesiology. He calls the immediate effect of the 'loosing' man's freedom which allows him to attain fellowship with Christ. This is realized in the participation in the Eucharist.

437. In Ps.hom. 2,4 (PG 12) 1353.

438. Cf. H. U. von Balthasar, *Le Mystérion,* pp. 54–6.

439. Cf., for example, In Luc.hom. 21 (GCS 35)139 f.: it could here be a question simply of giving up sin, without any reference to an actual purification from previous sins. Nevertheless, the thinking seems to be moving in that direction. In Luc. hom. 22 (GCS 35)145 f.: here the idea is somewhat clearer; the catechumens must no longer be a *generatio viperarum,* when they come to baptism. Ad Rom. V 8 (PG 14)1037–41. Here the idea is clear: the catechumen must be already dead to sin, the old man must be already dead and must discard all impurity, if he wishes to be buried with Christ in the new grave of baptism and receive the Spirit. Cf. also Contra Celsum III 59 f. (GCS 2) 254 f. This conception must have presented few difficulties for Origen, since he unconsciously recognized that even the unbaptized were capable of supernatural virtues. Cf. H. U. von Balthasar, *Le Mystérion,* p. 42 ff.

440. Cf. Ad Rom.; this teaching receives its clearest expression in the fragment of Origen which Athanasius has transmitted to us; cf. Ep. IV ad Serapionem n.10 (PG 26) 649–52: the Son is already at work in the catechumens, but the Holy Spirit only in those who have received him through the gift of baptism. This notion lies at the basis of the idea that only the baptized can commit sins against the Holy Spirit. Cf. above nn.65–71 and the corresponding text. Accordingly, John's baptism is already 'purifying' but does not fill converts with the Holy Spirit, as does Jesus' baptism; cf. In Joan. VI 32 (GCS 10) 141,22–7. Cf. H. Rahner, pp. 208–14.

441. Ad Rom. IX 2 (PG 14)1215.

441. Cf. above under nn. 89, 198, 211, 213 and 316, together with the corresponding considerations.

443. This is obviously the case in today's theology too. It is necessary for God to have touched man's heart with his grace before he can produce the 'sorrow' which is essential for the sacrament and its effect. This is self-evident. Nevertheless, our treatises on the sacrament of penance sometimes give the impression not so much of denying this truth as of forgetting it. They take it so much for granted that they usually give a very scant theological reflection on this purely divine beginning of man's conversion.

444. Cf. ibid. (GCS 29) 417,12–18.

445. This still applies, even if the real liturgical anointing with oil at reconciliation is not accepted as proven.

446. The *profectus quidam purgationum* (In Lev.hom. 8 [GCS 29] 412,4) bring it about that gradually the person arrives *ad summam puritatis* (ibid., 412,6). These purifications consist, for instance, in the renunciation of all sins and all their harmful consequences, in thoughts, words and deeds (ibid., 412,18–413,2; 41,16), in the renunciation of *arrogantia* (ibid., 414,12), in the positive conversion to God through virtue (ibid., 415,6 ff.), in the production of new virtues (ibid., 415,11 ff.). After these purifications (cf. the three-fold *post*: ibid., 417,4.) the Spirit is communicated.

447. It should not be overlooked that Origen applies the text Jas. 5:14 f. to penance and, in so doing, introduces into it an imposition of hands. This is understandable only if a real imposition of hands did occur in penance. Thus, it is also unlikely that the anointing with oil which is likewise mentioned in Jas. 5 did not figure in the rite of reconciliation. If this were not the case, there would be no reason why Origen thought of referring this text to reconciliation at all. After all, he is the one who introduces the imposition of hands into the text. Thus he must have discovered another indication in the text which suggested to him that here James was thinking of a remission of sins apart from that granted during a real illness. Now such an indication could only be the anointing with oil, since this was also used in the reconciliation of penitents. That Origen in Lev.hom. 8,11 (GCS 29) 416,1–417,1 understands the application of the oil 'mystically' is not an argument against the actual use of real oil in reconciliation, but means only the quest for the higher 'truth' contained in the real symbols of the liturgy.

448. G. Teichtweier, p. 326, rejects this decisively, since 'according to the whole context of this passage . . . it is all only an allegorical interpretation of the Old Testament purification ceremonies'. The passages which he adduces, however, esp. Selecta in Ez. XVI (PG 13) 812, do not contradict the observations made above.

449. Cf. Ad Rom. V 8 (PG 14) 1038.

450. This general theological observation alone renders questionable the dividing of the event of penance into a purely canonical excommunication, on the one hand, and a sacramental, 'real' penance, on the other (cf. J. Grotz).

451. In Luc.hom. 34 (GCS 35) 204,14–26.

452. In Ps. 37 hom. 1,1 (PG 12) 1372. It should not be forgotten that this activity of the created heavenly powers is also the 'truth' of the τύπος which happens in the Church, where the bishop, the angel's earthly counterpart, has an analogous rôle in the education of penitents.

453. For the sake of the clarity and simplicity of the schema, we have attempted to express here Origen's notion that the whole penitential event is also an 'image' of the eschatological purification of man, who must endure the future fire of judgement. This 'prospective' tendency of every sacramental event towards an eschatological truth should not be overlooked. Cf. H. U. von Balthasar, *Le Mystérion,* p. 56 ff. What is here said concerning baptism also applies to penance: *ego puto quod et post resurrectionem ex mortuis indigeamus sacramento eluente nos atque purgante*: In Luc.hom. 14 (GCS 35) 99,8–12; cf. In Matt.tom. XV 23 (GCS 40) 416–18. In fact, according to In Jer.hom. 20,8–9 (GCS 6) 190–2, the penitential fire of this life is an anticipation of the eschatological fire which will purify man definitively.

454. Cf., for example, M. de la Taille, *Mysterium fidei 3* (Paris 1931), p. 581, where this relationship of *res et sacramentum* to the Church, especially in penance, is already fairly clear. It is certainly evident in Augustine's teaching on the Eucharist: the Eucharist is also essentially *sacramentum communionis ad Ecclesiam,* and it is perfectly comprehensible to present this most profound unity with Christ's mystical body as the *res et sacramentum* of the Eucharist.

455. Cf., for example, B. Poschmann, 'Die kirchliche Vermittlung der Sündenvergebung nach Augustin' in: ZKTh 45 (1921), pp. 208–28; 405–32; 497–526.

456. Cf., for example, In Joan. VI 33 (GCS 10) 142,28; Contra Celsum III 51 (GCS2) 247,10; In Jer.hom. 19,13 (GCS 6) 169,22 f.; Ad Rom. V 8 (PG 14) 1038; σύμβολον, πύπος are here distinguished from the καθάρσιον ψυχῆς, the δύναμις of the event or—as we can also say with Origen—from the ἀληθινὰ κατὰ τὰ ὀνόματα ταῦτα (which designate the symbol) πράγματα. In Matt.tom. XVI 22 (GCS 40) 338,10–13: it is here said of what is the interior 'truth', the signified reality of the officials of the hierarchy. Obviously this does not mean that τύπος and σύμβολον (which are also often used elsewhere as synonyms by Origen) *only* or even principally have this meaning of sacramental sign and image (which is fulfilled by the reality signified). Mostly these words have the meaning which today's theological terminology still knows by the word 'type'.

457. Cf. H. U. von Balthasar, *Le Mystérion,* p. 55.

458. The drawing of this parallel (the body as σύμβολον of the soul) seems justified, because Origen himself in his teaching on the sacraments speaks about an 'embodiment' of the power of grace: In Joan. VI 33 (GCS 10)142,26: σωματικῶς γίνεσθαι.

459. De or. 31,2 f (GCS 3) 396,12 f.; 396,23 f. On this parallel between the spiritual and bodily expression (*signum*): In Num. hom. 2,2 (GCS 30)10–12.

460. Cf. H. U. von Balthasar, *Le Mystérion,* p. 517 f.

461. A. von Harnack, *Lehrbuch der Dogmengeschichte* I (Tübingen 1931), p. 476. On this Platonic-early Christian notion of image, cf. A. Lieske, p. 212 ff., and the literature which he cites; G. Söhngen, *Symbol und Wirklicheit im Kultmysterium*

(Bonn 1940), p. 55 ff., points out that such a notion could also find an application in today's theology.

462. In Scholastic terminology, we must say: the sacramental sign should not be considered as the efficient cause of something which is completely different from itself, but belongs to that category of causality which is difficult to define, lying, as it does, between efficient and formal-material causality. Accordingly, the sign is itself only in so far as (exactly like a *forma*) it is at work in its *formandum* and *formatum*. Thus, on the one hand, the *actus* of this *formatio* is different from the sign, and, on the other hand, the sign would not be itself if it did not establish this *actus*.

463. Although both grace and judgement should be manifested exteriorly in order to exist, Origen knows that they can also exist without having their normal manifestation always and in every case. According to Origen, it is possible for a person to be 'outside' in God's eyes, while still appearing to be in the Church. With regard to the grace of baptism (therefore giving a positive case), he stresses that, in certain circumstances, it is able to exist without the sacrament, that is, without its exterior manifestation: In Num. hom. 3,1 (GCS 30) 14,1–17. Nevertheless, this does not alter the principle that, according to Origen, 'in this lower, visible world, to which we now belong, every interior reality must be manifested exteriorly' (E. R. Redepenning, II, p. 421 f.). How the 'exception' is reconcilable with this principle presents a problem even for theology today, when, on the one hand, it maintains the *necessitas medii* of the sacrament, while, on the other hand, it grants that it is possible to be justified by the mere *votum sacramenti*. Simply because Origen recognizes that in certain circumstances the reality can exist without its full manifestation does not mean that he considers the *σύμβολον* in the sacramental event to be only a subsequent sign having no importance for the reality signified, any more than the teaching that purely 'interior' faith and love effects justification allows us to accuse modern theology of denying the necessity of the sacramental sign.

464. Cf. De or. 28,9.10 (GCS 3) 380,16–19; 381,12 f.; In Matt. tom. XII 14 (GCS 40) 98,28–99,9. It should be noted that Origen explicitly attests that the episcopate make its appeal for this power to these texts. Thus this power refers explicitly to the penance of excommunication. It is, therefore, immaterial that Origen himself understands the binding and loosing also, although not exclusively, in a sense which refers to the reconciling activity carried out by others than the official hierarchical Church.

465. We have already seen that in those places where Origen's view of the causality of the sacrament is obscure, there are also difficulties which even modern theology has to discuss.

466. The idea of a sacramental 'private penance' in Origen is also rejected by G. Teichtweier, p. 322, as well as by B. Altaner/A. Stuiber, *Patrologie* (Freiburg 1966), p. 207. Even J. Grotz, p. 299, would wish to avoid the misunderstanding which might arise as a consequence of his interpretation of Origen's theology of penance, namely the assumption of a private penance. Thus he stresses that excommunication and penance without excommunication are not two completely independent kinds of penance—which would allow the conclusion that sacramental penance without excommunication is a kind of private penance—but that excommunication is 'only a preliminary stage for real church penance'.

467. On the reasonable assumption that In Num.hom. 10,1 (GCS 30) 48,4–9 really is concerned also with non-mortal sins. Only subsequently, in the question of how the priest, as opposed to the lay person, remits his sins is the distinction drawn between ordinary sins and mortal sins (ibid., 68,10–12). Nevertheless, upon closer analysis, this text shows how Origen thinks of the reconciliation of the lay person by the priest in the case of non-mortal sins: it is done through the same priestly functions by which the priest *ipse suum potest purgare peccatum* (ibid., 68,10). It is a question, therefore,

of functions by which the priest can reconcile himself, but which are refused to the lay person because he cannot exercise these functions. If it were here a question of sacramental absolution, then both priest and lay person would be in the same position, since no priest can absolve himself any more than a lay person. It must, therefore, be a question of functions which the priest as such can exercise in general—and in his own favour. These are easy to name: the knowledge of truth, in which the official διδάσκαλος is not dependent upon others as the lay person is, the official liturgical prayer of the Church for reconciliation, in which the priest is able to include himself and the liturgical sacrifice. Thus it is obvious why Origen disputes the possibility of a reconciliation of oneself only in the case of *mortal* sins (ibid., 68,10–12). In this case, according to Origen's system, the priest, too, is the mere object of the Church's hierarchical activity. This assumes, however, that there is not a sacramental absolution outside the penance for mortal sins. The same applies to texts like In Num.hom. 10,1 (GCS 10) 71,3–12. The *requirere sacerdotem,* the *peccatum suum per pontificem curare* certainly includes here the remission of mortal sin, for otherwise the result would be an *in peccatis suis mori* (ibid., 71,7). In the case of *other* sins this need mean nothing more than the disciplinary, admonitory and liturgical support of the penitent by the Church, without this support being an actual sacrament.

468. Cf. above under n.421, together with the relevant text.

469. Cf. ibid. (GCS 29) 489,11–22 and above under nn.107–11, together with the relevant text. Even apart from the question of whether here *culpa mortalis* is really to be read as opposed to *crimen mortale,* it is not in any case mentioned at all that the *communia, quae frequenter incurrimus* and *sine intermissione redimuntur* are remitted by means of a specifically sacramental act of the Church. Otherwise it would have to be assumed that at that time confession occurred extraordinarily frequently (*sine intermissione,* for example, the *sermonis vitia* [ibid., 489,15], etc.). This, however, is a very unlikely notion.

470. We have already seen that, according to Origen, even secret mortal sins are, as a matter of principle, subject to public church penance. Such a sinner must likewise 'do outside the Church, for a sufficient period of time, what he has to do': In Jer.fragm. 48 (GCS 6) 222,14–16.

471. In Ps. 37 hom. 2,6 (PG 12) 1386.

472. Cf. De or. 28,8 (GCS 3) 380,8 f.

473. Cf. ibid. (GCS 29) 295, 26–297,3.

474. Cf. In Lev.hom. 5,4 (GCS 29) 342,12 f.

475. Cf. In Ex.hom. 4,8 (GCS 29) 182,1–5. The fact that the *obsecrationes* of the bishops are listed here under other means for the remission of sins of a more therapeutic kind and that all together are opposed to the remission of mortal sins (*difficiliora,* which require God's own intervention: ibid., 182,4 f.) shows that Origen himself sees in these *obsecrationes* a contrast with church penance. He hardly means, therefore, that the mere 'prayer' of the priest for the remission of sins is a special sacramental event.

BIBLIOGRAPHY

LIST OF EDITIONS OF TEXTS

1. The Apostolic Fathers

Bihlmeyer	Bihlmeyer, K., *Die Apostolischen Väter,* vol. I. Tübingen 1924; 2nd edn 1956. Based on: Funk, F. X., *Patres Apotolici* 1–2. Tübingen 1901.
Fischer	Fischer, J. A., *Die Apostoliscen Väter.* Munich 1956.
SC 167	Jaubert, A., *Clément de Rome. Epître aux Corinthiens.* Paris 1971.
GCS 48	Whittaker, M., *Die Apostolischen Väter,* vol. I: *Der Hirt des Hermas.* Berlin 1956.
SC 53 bis	Joly, R., *Hermas. Le Pasteur.* Paris 1968.

2. Irenaeus of Lyon

Harvey	Harvey, W. Wigan, *Sancti Irenaei episcopi Lugdunensis libros quinque adversus hareses* (Adv. haer.), 2 vols. Cambridge 1857.
PG 7	Migne, J.-P., *Patrolgia Graeca,* vol. VII: *Sancti Irenaei,* ed. D. R. Massuet. Paris 1857.
TU 31,1	Ter-Mekerttschian, K., and Ter-Minassiantz, E., *Des heiligen Irenäus Schrift zum Erweise der Apostolischen Verkündigung.* Leipzig 1907.

3. Tertullian

CSL 20	Reifferscheid, A., and Wissowa, G., eds., *Qu. S.F. Tertulliani Opera* I (De spectaculis; De idololatria; Ad nationes; De

testimonio animae; Scorpiace; De oratione; De baptismo; De pudicitia; De ieiunio adversus psychicos; De anima). Vienna 1890.

CSL 69 — Hoppe, H., ed., *Qu. S.F. Tertulliani Opera* II/1 (Apologeticum). Vienna 1939.

CSL 70 — Kroymann, A., ed., *Qu. S.F. Tertulliani Opera* II/2 (De praescriptione haereticorum; De cultu feminarum; Ad uxorem; De exhortatione castitatis; De corona; De carne Christi; Adversus Judaeos). Vienna 1942.

CSL 47 — Kroymann, A., ed., *Qu. S.F. Tertulliani Opera* III (De patientia; De carnis resurrectione; Adversus Hermogenem; Adversus Valentinianos; Adversus omnes haereses; Adversus Praxean; Adversus Marcionem). Vienna 1906.

CSL 76 — Bulhart, V., and Borleffs, P., eds., *Qu. S.F. Tertulliani Opera* IV (Ad martyras; Ad Scapulam; De fuga; De monogamia; De virginiabus velandis; De pallio; [Borleffs =] De paenitentia). Vienna 1957.

4. Cyprian of Carthage

CSL 3,1 — Hartel, G., ed., *S. Th. C. Cypriani Opera omnia* (Ad Donatum; Quod idola Dii non sint; Ad Quirinum [Testimoniorum libri tres]; De habitu virginum; De catholicae ecclesiae unitate; De lapsis; De dominica oratione; De mortalitate; Ad Fortunatum [De exhortatione martyrii]; Ad Demetrianum; De opere et eleemosynis; De bono patientiae; De zelo et livore; Sententiae episcoporum numero LXXXVII). Vienna 1868.

CSL 3,2 — Hartel, G., ed., *S. Th. C. Cypriani Opera omnia* (Epistulae). Vienna 1871.

CSL 3,3 — Hartel, G., ed., *S. Th. C. Cypriani Opera omnia* (Appendix scriptorum quae C. Cypriani nomen ferunt: De spectaculis; De bono pudicitiae; De laude martyrii; Ad Novatianum; De rebaptismate; De aleatoribus; De montibus Sina et Sion; Ad Vigilium episcopum de Judaica incredulitate; Adversus Judaeos; Orationes; De duodecim abusivis saeculi; De singularitate clericorum; De duplici martyrio; De pascha computus; Epistulae; Carmina).

5. Didascalia Apostolorum

TU 25,2 — Achelis, H., and Flemming, J., eds., *Die Syrische Didaskalia*. Leipzig 1904.

Funk, F. X. — *Didascalia et Constitutiones Apostolicorum*, vol. I. Paderborn 1905.

Connolly, R. H. — *Didascalia Apostolorum. The Syriac Version Translated and Accompanied by the Verona Latin Fragments*. Oxford 1929.

TU 75 — Tidner, E., ed., *Didascaliae apostolorum, Canonum ecclesiasticorum, Traditionis apostolicae versiones latinae*. Berlin 1963.

6. *Origen*

GCS 2 — P. Koetschau, ed., *Origenes* I (Die Schrift vom Martyrium; Buch I–IV gegen Celsus). Leipzig 1899 (new edn in preparation).

GCS 3 — Koetschau, P., ed., *Origenes* II (Buch V–VIII gegen Celsus; Die Schrift vom Gebet). Leipzig 1899 (new edn in preparation).

GCS 6 — Klostermann, E., ed., *Origenes* III (Jeremiahomilien; Klageliederkommentar; Erklärung der Samuel- und Königsbücher). Leipzig 1901.

GCS 10 — Preuschen, E., ed., *Origenes* IV (Der Johanneskommentar). Leipzig 1903 (new edn in preparation).

GCS 22 — Koetschau, P., ed., *Origenes* V (De principiis). Leipzig 1913.

GCS 29 — Baehrens, W. A., ed., *Origenes* VI (Homilien zum Hexateuch in Rufins Ubersetzung I: Die Homilien zu Genesis, Exodus und Leviticus). Leipzig 1920 (new edn in preparation).

GCS 30 — Baehrens, W. A., ed., *Origenes* VII (Homilien zum Hexateuch in Rufins Ubersetzung II: Die Homilien zu Numeri, Josua und Judices). Leipzig 1921 (new edn in preparation).

GCS 33 — Baehrens, W. A., ed., *Origenes* VIII (Homilien zu Samuel I, zum Hohenlied und zu den Propheten, Kommentar zum Hohenlied in Rufins und Hieronymus' Ubersetzung). Leipzig 1925 (new edn in preparation).

GCS 35 — Rauer, M., ed., *Origenes* IX (Homilien zu Lukas in der Ubersetzung des Hieronumus und der griechischen Reste der Homilien und des Lukas-Kommentars). Leipzig 1930 (2nd edn Berlin, as GCS 49).

GCS 40 — Klostermann, E., and Benz, E., eds., *Origenes* X (Matthäuserklärung I: Die griechisch erhaltenen Tomoi). Leipzig 1935.

GCS 38 — Klostermann, E., and Benz, E., eds., *Origenes* XI (Matthäuserklärung II: Die lateinische Ubersetzung der Commentariorum series). Leipzig 1933.

GCS 41/1 — Klostermann, E., and Benz, E., eds., *Origenes* XII/1 (Matthäuserklärung: Fragmente und Indices). Leipzig 1941.

GCS 41/2 — Klostermann, E., and Früchtel, L., eds., *Origenes* XII/2 (Matthäuserklärung: Fragmente und Indices). Berlin 1955.

7. Other Texts Used (apart from PG and PL)

GCS 12	Stählin, O., ed., *Clemens Alexandrinus* I (Protrepticus und Paedagogus). Leipzig 1909; 3rd edn Berlin 1972.
GCS 17	Stählin, O., ed., *Clemens Alexandrinus* III (Stromata VII–VIII; Excerpta ex Theodoto; Eclogae propheticae; Quis dives salvetur; Fragmente). Leipzig 1909.
CSL 73	Faller, O., ed., *S. Ambrosii Opera* VII (Expl. symboli; De sacramentis; De mysteriis; De paenitentia; De excessu fratris; De obitu Valentiniani; De obitu Theodosii). Vienna 1955.

LIST OF LITERATURE CITED AND OF FURTHER LITERATURE

Achelis, H., and Flemming, J., *Die Syrische Didaskalia* (TU 25,2). Leipzig 1904.

Adam, K., *Der Kirchenbegriff Tertullians*. Paderborn 1907. *Das sogenannte Bußedikt des Papstes Kallistus*. Munich 1917. *Die kirchliche Sündenvergebung nach dem hl. Augustin*. Paderborn 1917. 'Die geheime Kirchenbuße im Ausgang des christlichen Altertums. Kritische Bemerkungen zu Poschmanns Untersuchung' (ThQ 110, 1929).

Akinian, P. N., 'Cyprianus: Buβe (armenisch)' (*Handes Amsorya, Monatsschrift für armenische Philologie,* Vienna 1961). Not consulted.

Alès, A. d', *La théologie de Tertullien*. Paris 1905. 'La discipline pénitentielle au IIe siècle en dehors d'Hermas' (RSR 2, 1911). 'La discipline pénitentielle au IIe siècle en dehors d'Hermas' (RSR 4, 1913). *L'édit de Calliste*. Paris 1914. *La théologie de S. Cyprien*. Paris 1922.

Altaner, B., and Stuiber, A., *Patrologie*. Freiburg/Br. 1966.

Altendorf, E., *Einheit und Heiligkeit der Kirche. Untersuchungen zur Entwicklung der altchristlichen Kirchenbegriffe im Abendland von Tertullian bis zu den antidonatistischen Schriften Augustins,* Berlin 1932.

Althaus, P., *Der Brief an die Römer* (NTD 6). Göttingen 1958.

Amann, E., 'La pénitence primitive' (DThC XII/1, Paris 1933).

Anciaux, P., 'Histoire de la discipline pénitentielle' in *Problèmes du Confesseur,* Paris 1963; reprinted from *Pénitence et Pénitences,* Brügge 1953. *Das Sakrament der Buße. Geschichte, Wesen und Form der kirchlichen Buße*. Mainz 1961. (Original title: *Het Sacrament der Boetvaardigheid*.)

(Anonymus), 'Die Lehre des Origenes über die Buβe' (*Katholik* 45/I, 1865).

Atzberger, L., *Geschichte der christlichen Eschatologie innerhalb der vornicänischen Zeit*. Freiburg/Br. 1896.

Aubin, P., *Le problème de la 'conversion'*. Paris 1963.

Baehrens, W. A., *Überlieferung und Textgeschichte der lateinisch erhaltenen Origeneshomilien zum Alten Testament* (TU 42,1). Leipzig 1916.

Balthasar, H. U. von, 'Le Mystérion d'Origène' (RSR 26, 1936; 27, 1937). 'Die Hiera des Evagrius' (ZKTh 63, 1939). *Origenes. Geist und Feuer—Ein Aufbau aus seinen Schriften.* Salzburg 1951.

Bardenhewer, O., *Geschichte der altchristlichen Literatur,* 4 vols. Freiburg/Br. 1913–24.

Bardy, G., 'La règle de foi d'Origène' (RSR 9, 1919). *Origène* (*Les Moralistes chrétiens*). Paris 1931. 'Origène' (DThC XI/2, Paris 1932). *La théologie de l'Eglise de saint Clément à saint Irénée.* Paris 1945. *La théologie de l'Eglise de saint Irénée au concile de Nicée.* Paris 1947. 'Les idées morales d'Origène' (MSR 13, 1956).

Bareille, G., 'Confirmation d'après les Pères grecs et latins' (DThC III, Paris 1908).

Batiffol, P., *Etudes d'histoire et de théologie positive.* Paris 1926.

Bauer, W., *Griechisch-deutsches Wörterbuch zu den Schriften des NT und der übrigen urchristlichen Literatur.* Berlin 1958. *Rechtgläubigkeit und Ketzerei im ältesten Christentum.* Tübingen 1964.

Baumeister, A., *Die Ethik des Pastor Hermae.* Freiburg/Br. 1912.

Baumstark, A., *Vom geschichtlichen Werden der Liturgie.* Freiburg/Br. 1923. *Liturgie comparée.* Chevetogne o.J. 1940.

Baus, K., *Von der Urgemeinde zur frühchristlichen Großkirche* (HdKG1), Freiburg/Br. 1962.

Beaucamp, P., 'Un évêque du IIIe siècle aux prises avec les pécheurs: son activité apostolique' (BLE 69, 1949).

Behm, J., 'κυρόω etc.' (ThW III, Stuttgart 1938). 'νῆστις etc.' (ThW IV, Stuttgart 1942).

Belser, J. E., *Die Epistel des hl.Jakobus,* Freiburg/Br. 1909.

Bertram, G., 'ὕβρις' (ThW VIII, Stuttgart 1969). 'φρήν' (ThW IX, Stuttgart 1970).

Bettencourt, S., *Doctrina ascetica Origenis.* Rome 1945.

Bettenson, H., *The Early Christian Fathers* (*Texts*). London/New York 1956.

Bévenot, M., 'The Sacrament of Penance and St. Cyprian's De Lapsis' (ThSt 16, 1955). 'Episcopat et Primat chez Cyprien' (EThL 42, 1966).

Bigg, C., *The Christian Platonists of Alexandria.* Oxford 1913.

Billerbeck, P., see Strack, H. L.

Billicsich, F., *Das Problem des Übels in der Philosophie des Abendlandes.* Vienna 1952.

Blötzer, J., 'Die geheime Sünde in der altchristlichen Bußdisziplin' (ZKTh 11, 1887).

Bohm, J., *Die Handauflegung im Urchristentum.* Leipzig 1911.

Bonwetsch, G. N., *Die Theologie des Irenäus.* Gütersloh 1925.

Boudinhon, M., 'La missa poenitentium dans l'ancienne discipline d'Occident' (RHLR 7, 1902).

Brandner, V., '"Binden und Lösen" in der altsyrischen Kirche' (*Katholik* 95/I, 1916).

Brewer, H., 'Die kirchliche Privatbuße im christlichen Altertum' (ZKTh 45, 1921).

Brinktrine, J., *Die Lehre von der Gnade.* Paderborn 1957.

Bruders, H., 'Mt 16,19; 18,18 und Jo 20,22.23 in frühchristlicher Auslegung. Afrika bis 251' (ZKTh 35, 1911).

Bultmann, R., 'θάνατος' (ThW III, Stuttgart 1938). *Das Evangelium des Johannes* (Meyers Kom. 2). Göttingen 1952.

Cadiou, R., *La jeunesse d'Origène*. Paris 1935.
Campenhausen, H. von, *Kirchliches Amt und geistliche Vollmacht in den ersten drei Jahrhunderten*. Tübingen 1963.
Capelle, B., 'L'absolution sacerdotale chez S. Cyprien' (RThAM 7, 1935).
Capitaine, G., *De ethica Origenis*. Münster 1898.
Carra de Vaux Saint-Cyr, M.-B., 'Le Sacrement de Pénitence' (LV 13, 1964).
Cavallera, F., 'La doctrine de la pénitence au IIIe siècle' (BLE 30, 1929; 31, 1930). 'A propos de l'histoire du sacrement de pénitence' (BLE 24, 1923).
Chartier, C. M., 'L'excommunication ecclésiastique d'après les écrits de Tertullien' (*Antonianum* 10, 1935). 'La discipline pénitentielle d'après les écrits de saint Cyprien' (*Antonianum* 14, 1939).
Clark, K. W., 'The Sins of Hermas' in *Early Christian Origins. Studies in Honour of H. R. Willoughby*. Chicago, 1961.
Clerc, J. Le, *Parrhasiana, ou Pensées diverses sur des matières de critique d'histoire, de morale ou de politique*. Amsterdam 1699, 1701.
Colson, J., *L'évêque, lien d'unité et de charité chez saint Cyprien de Carthage*. Paris 1961.
Conzelmann, H., 'χάρις' (ThW IX, Stuttgart 1971).
Coppens, J., *L'imposition des mains*. Wetterers/Paris 1925.
Cornely, R., *Commentarius in epistolam ad Romanos*. Paris 1896.
Coruzel, H., *Théologie de l'Image de Dieu chez Origène*. Paris 1956. 'Notes critiques sur Origène' (BLE, 59, 1958). *Origène et la 'connaissance mystique'*. Brussels/Paris 1961. *Virginité et Mariage selon Origène*. Bruges/Paris 1963. *Bibliographie critique d'Origène* (Instrumenta Patristica VIII). The Hague 1971.
Cuesta Gonzales, F. de La, 'La penitencia en "El Pastor" de Hermas' (*Studium legionense* 4, León 1963).
Daillé, J. (Dallaeus, J.), *De sacramentali sive auriculari Latinorum confessione disputatio*. Ghent 1661.
Daly, C. B., 'The Sacrament of Penance in Tertullian' (IER 69, 1947; 70, 1948). *Absolution and Satisfaction in St. Cyprian's Theology of Penance* (TU 64; Studía Patrístíca II). Berlin 1957.
Daniélou, J., *Origène*. Paris 1948. *Théologie du Judéo-Christianisme*. Tournai 1958.
Deemter, R. van, *Der Hirt des Hermas—Apokalypse oder Allegoire?* Delft 1929.
Dekkers, E., *Tertullianus en de geschiedenis der liturgie*. Brussels/Amsterdam 1947.
Delahaye, K., *Ecclesia mater chez les Pères des trois premiers siècles*. Paris 1964.
Delling, G., 'ἀρχή' (ThW I, Stuttgart 1933).
Demoustier, A., 'L'ontologie de l'Eglise selon Cyprien' (RSR 52, 1964).
Deneffe, A., 'Das Wort satisfactio' (ZKTh 43, 1919).
Dettloff, W., *Die Lehre von der acceptatio divina des Johannes Duns Scotus mit besonderer Berücksichtigung der Rechtfertigungslehre* Werl 1954.
Dibelius, M., *Der Hirt des Hermas* (Hdb NT, Erg. Bd.). Tübingen 1925.
Dick, E., 'Das Pateninstitut im altchristlichen Katechumenat' (ZKTh 63, 1939).
Diekamp, F., and Jüssen, K., *Katholische Dogmatik*. Münster 1959.
Dölger, F. J., *Der Exorzismus im altchristlichen Taufritual*. Paderborn 1909.
Döllinger, J. I., *Hippolytus und Kallistus, oder die römische Kirche in der ersten Hälfte des dritten Jahrhunderts*. Regensburg 1853.
Doskocil, W., *Der Bann in der Urkirche* (NTSt, Kan.Abt.11). Munich 1958.

D'Ercole, G., *Penitenza canonico-sacramentale dalle origini alla pace constantiniana* (*Communio* 4). Rome 1963.

Edsman, C. M., *Le baptême de feu*. Uppsala 1940.

Elert, W., *Der christliche Glaube*. Berlin 1940.

Elfers, H., *Die Kirchenordnung Hippolyts von Rom*. Paderborn 1938. 'Gehört die Salbung mit Chrisma im ältesten abendländischen Initiationsritus zu Taufe oder zur Firmung?' (ThGl 34, 1942).

Esser, G., *Die Bußschriften Tertullians De paenitentia und De pudicitia und das Indulgenzedikt des Papstes Kallistus*. Bonner Universitätsprogramm 1905. 'Nochmals das Indulgenzedikt des Papstes Kallistus und die Bußschriften Tertullians' (*Katholik* 87, 1907; 88, 1908).

Estius, W., *Commentarii in omnes Divi Pauli epistolas*. Douai 1614–16; finally Paris 1892.

Evans, R. F., *One and Holy. The Church in Latin Patristic Thought*. London 1972.

Eynde, D. van den, *Les normes de l'enseignement chrétien dans la littérature patristique des trois premiers siècles*. Paris 1933. 'La double édition du "De unitate" de S. Cyprien' (RHE 29, 1933). 'Notes sur les rites postbaptismaux dans les églises d'occident' (*Antonianum* 1, 1939).

Fechtrup, B., 'Über die Grundsätze, welche die Kirche in den ersten Jahrhunderten bei Zulassung zur Buße für die schweren Sünden und bei Erteilung der Lossprechung von denselben befolgte' (ThQ 54, 1872).

Fermaud, U., *Exposition critique des opinions d'Origène*. Strasbourg 1859.

Fischer, J. A., Rezension zu St. Giet (ThRv 61, 1965).

Flemming, J., see Achelis, H.

Foerster, W., 'δαίμων' (ThW II, Stuttgart 1935).

Fonck, L., *Die Parabeln des Herrn*. Innsbruck 1909.

Frank, F., *Die Bußdisziplin der Kirche*. Mainz 1867.

Freppel, C. E., *Origène*, 2 vols. Paris 1868.

Friedrich, G., see Kittel, G.

Funk, F. X., 'Das Indulgenzedikt des Papstes Kallistus' (ThQ 88, 1906). *Zur altchristlichen Bußdisziplin* (Kirchengeschichtl. Abhandl. und Unters. 1). Paderborn 1897.

Galtier, P., 'La consignation à Carthage et à Rome' (RSR 2, 1911). 'La consignation dans les églises d'occident' (RHE 13, 1912). 'Onction et confirmation' (RHE 13, 1912). 'Absolution ou Confirmation? La réconciliation des hérétiques' (RSR 5, 1914). 'Imposition des mains' (DThC VII, Paris 1923). 'La rémission des péchés moindres dans l'Eglise du troisième au cinquième siècle' (RSR 13, 1923; cf. *L'église et la rémission* [1932], pp. 264–72). "Les péchés "incurables" d'Origène' (Gr 10, 1929; cf. *L'église et la rémission* [1932], pp. 184–213). *L'église et la rémission des péchés aux premiers siècles*. Paris 1932. 'A propos de la pénitence primitive. Méthodes et conclusions' (RHE 30, 1934). 'Comment on écarte la pénitence privée' (Gr 22, 1940). *De paenitentia*. Rome 1950. *Aux origines du sacrament de la pénitence*. Rome 1951.

Garcia, Z., 'El perdon de los pecados en la primitiva Iglesia: La doctrina de Origenes' (RF 26, 1910).

Gaudemet, J., 'Note sur les formes anciennes de l'excommunication' (RevSR 23, 1949).

Ghellinck, J. de, *Pour l'histoire du mot 'Sacramentum'* I (Spicileg. sacr. Lovan. 3). Louvain/Paris 1924.

Giet, S., *L'Apocalypse d'Hermas et la pénitence* (TU 78; Studia Patristica III). Berlin 1961. *Hermas et les Pasteurs. Les trois auteurs du Pasteur d'Hermas.* Paris 1963.

Goetz, C., *Die Bußlehre Cyprians.* Königsberg 1895.

Gommenginger, A., 'Bedeutet die Exkommunikation Verlust der Kirchengliedschaft?'' (ZKTh 73, 1951).

Goppelt, L., *Christentum und Judentum im ersten und zweiten Jahrhundert.* Gütersloh 1954.

Green, W. M., 'Initium omnis peccati superbia: Augustine on Pride as the First Sin' (U. Calif. Class. 13, 1949).

Groot, J. F. De, *Conspectus historiae dogmatum,* 2 vols. Rome 1931.

Grotz, J., *Die Entwicklung des Bußstufenwesens in der vornicänischen Kirche.* Freiburg/Br. 1955.

Gummersbach, J., see Pohle, J.

Hagemann, H., *Die römische Kirche und ihr Einfluß auf Disciplin und Dogma in den ersten drei Jahrhunderten.* Freiburg/Br. 1864.

Hahn, A., *Bibliothek der Symbole und Glaubensregeln der Alten Kirche.* Breslau 1897.

Hall, S. G., *Repentance in I Clement* (TU 93; Studia Patristica VIII). Berlin 1966.

Hamel, A., *Kirche bei Hippolyt von Rom.* Gütersloh 1951.

Hardowirgono, R., 'S. Cypriaan: Het Heil in de Kerk' (*Bijdragen* 19, 1958).

Harnack, A. von, *Der kirchengeschichtliche Ertrag der exegetischen Arbeiten des Origenes* I (TU 42,3). Leipzig 1918. *Der kirchengeschichtliche Ertrag der exegetischen Arbeiten des Origenes* II (TU 42,4). Leipzig 1919. *Lehrbuch der Dogmengeschichte,* 3 vols. Tübingen 1931.

Haslehurst, R. S. T., *Some Account of the Penitential Discipline of the Early Church in the First Four Centuries.* London 1921.

Hausherr, I., *De doctrina spirituali christianorum orientalium quaestiones et scripta.* Rome 1933.

Hefele, C. J., *Conciliengeschichte* II. Freiburg/Br. 1875.

Heilmann, A., and Kraft, H., *Texte der Kirchenväter,* 4 vols. Munich 1963–4.

Henrion, M. R. A., and Verwort, A., *Histoire Ecclésiastique depuis la création jusqu'au pontificat de Pie IX.* Paris 1857.

Hervé, J. M., *Manuale theologiae dogmaticae.* Paris 1925.

Hochban, J. I., 'St. Irenaeus on the Atonement' (ThSt 7, 1946).

Hoh, J., *Die kirchliche Buße im zweiten Jahrhundert.* Breslau 1932.

Holl, K., *Enthusiasmus und Bußgewalt beim griechischen Mönchtum.* Leipzig 1898.

Holstein, H., 'L'Exhomologèse dans l'"Adversus haereses" de Saint Irénée' (RSR 35, 1948).

Holtzmann, O., *Das Neue Testament* II. Gießen 1926.

Huby, J., and Lyonnet, S., *Saint Paul* (VS 10), Paris 1957.

Hübner, S., 'Kirchenbuße und Exkommunikation bei Cyprian' (ZKTh 84, 1962).

Huet, P. D., *Origeniana* (ed. Delarue IV). Paris 1759.

Huhn, J., *Ursprung und Wesen des Bösen und der Sünde nach der Lehre des Kirchenvaters Ambrosius.* Paderborn 1933.

Hurter, H., *Compendium theologiae dogmaticae* III. Innsbruck 1903.
Janini Cuesta, J., 'La penitencia medicinal desde la Didascalia Apostolorum a S. Gregorio de Nisa' (RET 7, 1947).
Jeremias, J., *Die Gleichnisse Jesu.* Göttingen 1956.
Joly, R., 'La doctrine pénitentielle du Pasteur d'Hermas' (RHR 147, 1955). *Hermas le Pasteur* (SC 53b; introduction). Paris 1968.
Jourgon, M., *Cyprien de Carthage.* Paris 1957.
Joyce, G. H., 'Private Penance in the Early Church' (JThS 42, 1941).
Jüssen, K., *Die dogmatischen Anschauungen des Hesychius von Jerusalem.* Münster 1934. see Diekamp, F.
Jugie, J. B., *Theologia dogmatica christianorum orientalium* III. Paris 1930.
Jungmann, J. A., *Die lateinischen Bußriten.* Innsbruck 1932. *Missarum Sollemnia* I. Vienna 1952.
Karpp, H., *Die Buße. Quellen zur Entstehung des altkirchlichen Bußwesens* (Traditio christiana 1). Zürich 1969.
Kirk, K. E., *The Vision of God.* London 1932.
Kirsch, P. A., *Zur Geschichte der katholischen Beichte.* Würzburg 1902. 'Die Behandlung der crimina capitalia in der morgenländischen Kirche im Unterschied zur abendländischen' (AkathKR 84, 1904).
Kittel, G., and Friedrich, G., *Theologisches Wörterbuch zum Neuen Testament* (ThW). Stuttgart 1933 ff.
Kittel, G., 'ἄγγελος' (ThW I, Stuttgart 1933). 'δόξα' (ThW II, Stuttgart 1935).
Klee, H., *Die Beichte, eine historisch-kritische Untersuchung.* Frankfurt/M. 1828.
Klein, G., 'Die hermeneutische Struktur des Kirchengedankens bei Cyprian' (ZKG 68, 1957).
Knabenbauer, J., *Commentarium in Evangelium secundum Joannem.* Paris 1906.
Kneller, C. A., 'Sacramentum unitatis (Zu Cyprians Schrift an Donatus)' (ZKTh 40, 1916).
Koch, Hal, *Pronoia und Paideusis. Studien über Origenes und sein Verhältnis zum Platonismus.* Berlin/Leipzig 1932.
Koch, Hugo. 'Die Sündenvergebung bei Irenäus' (ZNW 9, 1908). *Die Bußfrist des Pastor Hermä* (Festgabe A. von Harnack). Tübingen 1921. *Cyprianische Untersuchungen.* Bonn 1926. *Cathedra Petri. Neue Untersuchungen über die Anfänge der Primatslehre.* Gießen 1930.
Köhne, J., 'Die Bußdauer auf Grund der Briefe Cyprians' (ThGl 29, 1937). 'Zur Frage der Buße im christlichen Altertum' (ThGl 35, 1943).
Kogler, L., *Bußsakrament und Ablaß* Linz 1931.
Kortzfleisch, S. von, see Rengstorf, K. H.
Kraft, H., see Heilmann, A.
Krautwig, N., *Die Grundlagen der Bußlehre des J. Duns Scotus.* Freiburg/Br. 1938.
Kurtscheid, B., *Das Beichtsiegel.* Freiburg/Br. 1912.
Kuß, O., *Die Briefe an die Römer, Korinther und Galater* (RNT 6). Regensburg 1940. *Der Römerbrief* II. Regensburg 1959.
Lagrange, M. J., *Saint Paul Epître aux Romains.* Paris 1922.
Lahousse, G., *De gratia divina.* Bruges 1902.
Lais, H., *Dogmatik* I. Kevelaer 1965.

Lange, H., *De gratia*. Freiburg/Br. 1929.

Langstadt, E., *Tertullian's Doctrine of Sin and the Power of Absolution in "de pudicitia"* (TU 64; Studia Patristica II). Berlin 1957.

la Taille, M. de, *Mysterium fidei 3*. Paris 1931.

Latko, E., *Origen's Concept of Penance*. Quebec 1949.

Lebreton, J., 'Les degrés de la connaissance religieuse d'après Origène' (RSR 12, 1922). 'Le désaccord de la foi populaire et de la théologie savante dans l'Eglise chrétienne du IIIe siècle' (RHE 19, 1923; 20, 1924). 'Le développement des institutions ecclésiastiques à la fin du IIe siècle et au début du IIIe siècle' (RSR 24, 1934).

Leenhardt, F. J., *L'Epître de saint Paul aux Romains*. Neuchâtel/Paris 1957.

Lennerz, H., *De gratia redemptoris*. Rome 1934.

Lercher, L., *Institutiones theologiae dogmaticae* III. Innsbruck 1951.

Lieske, A., *Die Theologie der Logosmystik bei Origenes*. Münster 1938.

Ludwig, A., 'Die Bußstationen in der abendländischen Kirche' (AkathKR 83, 1903).

Lumper, G., *Historia theologico-critica de vita, scriptis atque doctrina sanctorum Patrum*, 13 vols. Augustae Vindelicorum 1783–99.

Lyonnet, S., see Huby, J.

Maréchal, B., *Concordance des saints Pères de l'Eglise*, 2 vols. Paris 1739.

Massuet, R., *Sancti Irenaei episcopi Lugdunensis et martyris detectionis et eversionis falso cognominatae agnitionis, seu contra haereses libri quinque*. Paris 1710.

Maurial, E., *Origenis de libertate arbitrii doctrina*. Montpellier 1856.

May, G., 'Bemerkungen zu der Frage der Diffamation und der Irregularität der öffentlichen Büßer' (MThZ 12, 1961).

Mazzella, C., *De gratia Christi*. Rome 1905.

Meinertz, M., and Vrede, W., *Die katholischen Briefe*. Bonn 1932.

Mersch, E., *Le corps mystique du Christ II*. Paris 1936.

Michaelis, W., 'παραπίπτω' (ThW VI, Stuttgart 1959).

Michel, O., 'νάος' (ThW IV, Stuttgart 1942). *Der Brief an die Römer* (Meyers Kom. 4). Göttingen 1957.

Mitzka, F., 'Gnostizismus und Gnadenlehre' (ZKTh 51, 1927).

Möhler, J. A., *Patrologie oder christliche Geschichte*. Regensburg 1840.

Mörsdorf, K., 'Exkommunikation' (HThG I, München 1962).

Morinus, J., *Commentarius historicus de disciplina in administratione sacramenti Paenitentiae*. Antwerpiae 1682.

Mortimer, R. C., *The Origins of Private Penance in the Western Church*. Oxford 1939.

Müller, K., 'Bußinstitutionen in Karthago unter Cyprian' (ZKG 16, 1896).

Münscher, W., *Handbuch der christlichen Dogmengeschichte*. Cassel 1832.

Navickas, J. C., *The Doctrine of St. Cyprian on the Sacraments*. Würzburg 1924.

Nygren, A., *Der Römerbrief*. Göttingen 1954.

O'Donnell, M. J., *Penance in the Early Church*. Dublin 1908.

O'Hagan, A. P. *The Great Tribulation to Come in the Pastor of Hermas* (TU 79; Studia Patristica IV). Berlin 1961.

Opfermann, B., 'Zwei unveröffentlichte Fuldaer Bußordines des 9. Jahrhunderts' (ThGl 36, 1944).

Ott, L., *Grundriß der katholischen Dogmatik*. Freiburg/Br. 1957.

Palmieri, D., *De paenitentia*. Prati 1896.

Permaneder, Fr M., *Bibliotheca Patristica,* 3 vols. Landshut 1841–2.

Pesch, C., *Praelectiones dogmaticae* V. Freiburg/Br. 1916. *Compendium theologiae dogmaticae* III. Freiburg/Br. 1941–2.

Petavius, D., *Dogmata theologica,* 6 vols. Venice 1745 ff. (8 vols. Paris 1865–7). *De poenitentia publica et praeparatione ad communionem, lib. IV*. Paris 1867 (*De la pénitence publique,* Paris 1644).

Peterson, E., *Frühkirche, Judentum und Gnosis.* Freiburg/Br. 1959.

Pitra, J. B., *Juris ecclesiastici Graecorum historia et monumenta.* Rome 1864–8. *Analecta sacra Spicilegio Solesmensi parata,* 8 vols. Paris 1876–83.

Plumpe, J. C., *Mater Ecclesia. An Inquiry into the Concept of the Church as a Mother in Early Christianity.* Washington 1943.

Pohle, J., and Gummersbach, J., *Lehrbuch der Dogmatik* II. Paderborn 1956.

Poschmann, B., *Die Sichtbarkeit der Kirche nach der Lehre des hl. Cyprian.* Paderborn 1908. *Die Sündenvergebung bei Origenes.* Braunsberg 1912 (reproduced in *Paenitentia secunda,* 1940). 'Die kirchliche Vermittlung der Sündenvergebung nach Augustinus' (ZKTh 45, 1921). *Die abendländische Kirchenbuße im Ausgang des christlichen Altertums.* Munich 1928. *Ecclesia principalis. Ein kritischer Beitrag zur Frage des Primats bei Cyprian.* Breslau 1933. Review of (Theophaneia—Beitr. z. Religions- u. Kirchengeschichte des Altertums, ed. F. J. Dölger and T. Klauser, vol. I). Galtier, P., *L'église et la rémission des péchés* (ThRv 32, 1933). *Paenitentia secunda. Die kirchliche Buße im ältesten Christentum bis Cyprian und Origenes* (*Theophaneia—Beitr. z. Religious- u. Kirchengeschichte des Altertums,* see F. J. Dölger and T. Klauser, vol. i). Bonn 1940. 'Die innere Struktur des Bußsakraments' (MThZ 1, 1950). *Buße und Letzte Ölung* (HDG IV, 3). Freiburg/Br. 1951.

Poukens, J. B., *Saint Cyprien et ses contemporains,* see Ghellinck, J. de.

Pressensé, E., *Histoire des trois premiers siècles de l'Eglise ancienne.* Paris 1869.

Prete, S., 'Cristianesimo antico e riforma ortodossa. Note intorno al Pastore di Erma (II. Sec.)' (*Convivium,* 1950).

Probst, F., *Sakramente und Sakramentalien in den drei ersten christlichen Jahrhunderten.* Tübingen 1872.

Puniet, P. de, 'La liturgie baptismale en Gaule avant Charlemagne' (RQH 28, 1902). 'Onction et confirmation' (RHE 13, 1912). 'Confirmation' (DACL III, Paris 1914).

Quasten, J., *Patrology,* 3 vols. Utrecht 1950–60.

Rager, J., *Die Lehre von der Sündenvergebung bei Origenes: Eine dogmengeschichtliche Untersuchung.* Diss. Freiburg/Br. 1917.

Rahner, H., 'Taufe und geistliches Leben bei Origenes' (ZAM 7, 1932). 'Gnostizismus, christlicher' (LThK 4, 1960).

Rahner, K., 'Gnosis' (LThK 4, 1960).

Rauschen, G., *Eucharistie und Bußsakrament in den ersten sechs Jahrhunderten der Kirche.* Freiburg/Br. 1908.

Redepenning, E. B., *Origenes. Eine Darstellung seines Lebens und seiner Lehre.* Bonn, 1841–6 (Reprint Aalen 1966).

Rengstorf, K. H., and Kortzfleisch, S. von, *Kirche und Synagoge. Handbuch zur Geschichte von Christen und Juden* I. Stuttgart 1968.

Roetzer, W., *Des heiligen Augustinus Schriften als liturgiegeschichtliche Quelle.* Munich 1930.

Rolffs, E., *Urkunden aus dem antimontanistischen Kampfe des Abendlandes* (TU 12,4). Leipzig 1895.

Rondet, H., *Gratia Christi*, Paris 1948. 'Aux origines de la théologie du péché' (NRTh 79, 1957).

Ruch, C., 'Confirmation dans la sainte Ecriture' (DThC III, Paris 1908).

Rüthy, A. E., 'Zur neutestamentlichen Begründung des Bußsakramentes' (IKZ 44, 1954).

Saint-Palais d'Aussac, F. de, *La réconciliation des hérétiques dans l'Eglise latine*. Paris 1943.

Schäfer, K. T. 'Antidotum' (RAC I, Stuttgart 1950).

Schanz, P., 'Die Absolutionsgewalt in der alten Kirche' (ThQ 79, 1897).

Schelkle, K. H., 'Erwählung und Freiheit im Römerbrief nach der Auslegung der Väter (ThQ 131, 1951).

Schiffini, S., *Tractatus de gratia divina*. Freiburg/Br. 1901.

Schlatter, A., *Der Evangelist Johannes*. Stuttgart 1948.

Schmaus, M., *Katholische Dogmatik* III/2. Munich 1951.

Schmitz, H. J., *Die Bußbücher und die Bußdisziplin der Kirche* I. Mainz 1883. II, Düsseldorf 1898.

Schümmer, J., *Die altchristliche Fastenpraxis mit besonderer Berücksichtigung der Schriften Tertullians*. Münster 1933.

Schwane, J., *Dogmengeschichte der vornizänischen Zeit*. Münster 1862.

Schwartz, E., *Bußstufen und Katechumenatsklassen*. Straßburg 1911.

Seeberg, R., *Lehrbuch der Dogmengeschichte*. Leipzig 1895.

Sickenberger, J., *Die beiden Briefe des heiligen Paulus an die Korinther und sein Brief an die Römer*. Bonn 1921.

Simon, M., *Verus Israel. Etudes sur les relations entre chrétiens et juifs dans l'Empire romain*. Paris 1942.

Simonis, W., *Ecclesia visibilis et invisibilis*. Frankfurt/M. 1970.

Söhngen, G., *Symbol und Wirklichkeit im Kultmysterium*. Bonn 1940.

Spanneut, M., *Tertullien et les premiers moralistes africains*. Gembloux/Paris 1969.

Steitz, G. E., 'Die Bußdisciplin der morgenländischen Kirche in den ersten Jahrhunderten' (*Jahrbuch f. dt. Theologie* (Gotha) 8 1863).

Strack, H. L., and Billerbeck, P., *Kommentar zum NT aus Talmud und Midrasch*. Munich 1922–56.

Ström, A. V., *Der Hirt des Hermas. Allegorie oder Wirklichkeit*. Leipzig/Uppsala 1936.

Stufler, J., 'Die Sündenvergebung bei Origenes' (ZKTh 31, 1907). 'Die verschiedenen Wirkungen der Taufe und Buße bei Tertullian' (ZKTh 31, 1907). 'Die Bußdisziplin der abendländischen Kirche bis Kallistus' (ZKTh 31, 1907). 'Die Sündenvergebung bei Irenänus' (ZKTh 32, 1908). 'Einige Bemerkungen zur Bußlehre Cyprians' (ZKTh 33, 1909). 'Öffentliche und geheime Buße bei Origenes' (ZKTh 37, 1913).

Stuiber, A., see Altaner, B.

Tanghe, D. A., 'L'Eucharistie pour la rémission des péchés' (*Irénikon* 34, 1961).

Tanquerey, A. A., *Synopsis theologiae dogmaticae* II. Paris/Rome 1959.

Taylor, J. H. 'St. Cyprian and the Reconciliation of Apostates' (ThSt 3, 1942).

Teichtweier, G., *Das Sein des Menschen. Ein Beitrag zur Anthropologie des Origenes*. Diss. Tübingen 1951. *Die Sündenlehre des Origenes*. Regensburg 1958.

Telfer, W. *The Forgiveness of Sins.* London 1959; Philadelphia 1960.

Thyen, H., *Studien zur Sündenvergebung im Neuen Testament und Seinen alttestamentlichen und jüdischen Voraussetzungen* (Forschungen zur Religion u. Literatur des Alten u. Neuen Testaments H. 96). Göttingen 1970.

Tillmann, F., *Das Johannesevangelium.* Bonn 1931.

Tricalet, P. J., *Bibliothèque portative des Pères de l'Eglise,* 9 vols. Paris 1758–63.

Trillhaas, W., *Dogmatik.* Berlin 1962.

Umberg, J. B., *Die Schriftlehre vom Sakrament der Firmung.* Freiburg/Br. 1920.

Vacandard, E., *La pénitence publique dans l'Eglise primitive.* Paris 1903.

Valton, E., 'Excommunication' (DThC V/2, Paris 1912).

Vanbeck, A. (pseudonym for J. Turmel), 'La Pénitence dans le Pasteur d'Hermas' (RHLR, m.s. 2, 1911). 'La pénitence dans Origène' (RHLR, m.s. 3, 1912; 4, 1913).

Verde, F. M., 'Il problema del male da Plutarco a S. Agostino' (*Sapienza* 11, 1958).

Verwort, A., see Henrion, M. R. A.

Vincenzi, L., *In S. Gregorii Nysseni et Origenis scripta et doctrinam* . . . Rome 1864.

Vögtle, A., *Die Tugend- und Lasterkataloge im Neuen Testament.* Münster 1936.

Völker, W., *Das Volkommenheitsideal des Origenes.* Tübingen 1931.

Vogel, C., *Le pécheur et la pénitence dans l'Eglise ancienne* (texts). Paris 1966.

Volz, P., *Die Eschatologie der jüdischen Gemeinde im neutestamentlichen Zeitalter.* Tübingen 1934.

Vorgrimler, H., 'Matthieu 16, 18s et le sacrement de pénitence' in *L'Homme devant Dieu* (Mélanges offerts au Père Henri de Lubac) I, Paris 1963.

Vrede, W., see Meinertz, M.

Watkins, O. D., *A History of Penance* I, London 1920.

Welte, B., *Die postbaptismale Salbung.* Freiburg/Br. 1939.

Wendland, H. D., *Der Brief an die Römer* (NTD 3). Götttingen 1958.

Wickert, U., *Sacramentum Unitatis.* Berlin/New York 1971.

Wikenhauser, A., *Das Evangelium nach Johannes* (RNT 4). Regensburg 1957.

Wilckens, U., 'ὕστερος' (ThW VIII, Stuttgart 1969).

Windisch, H., *Taufe und Sünde im ältesten Christentum bis auf Origenes.* Tübingen 1908.

Wipping, S., *Die Tugend- und Lasterkataloge im NT* (ZNW, BH 25). Berlin 1959.

Wörter, F., *Die christliche Lehre über das Verhältnis von Gnade und Freiheit von den apostolischen Zeiten bis auf Augustinus.* Freiburg/Br. 1856.

Xiberta, B., *Clavis Ecclesiae.* Rome 1922. 'La Doctrina de Origenes (sobre el Sacramento de la Penitencia)' (*Reseña Eclesiastica* 18, 1926).

Young, F. W., *The Shepherd of Hermas. A Study of his Concept of Repentance.* Diss. Duke University 1946. (Not consulted.)

Zezschwitz, C. A. G., 'Die Privatbeichte in der morgenländischen Kirche' (*Zeitschrift f. Protestantismus und Kirche* (Erlangen, m.s. 43, 1862).

Zorell, F., *Lexicon Graecum Novi Testamenti.* Paris 1931.

INDEX

Absolution, 13–16, 20–21, 135, 141, 144–45, 150
  sacramental, 210
Achelis, H., 225, 242
Adam, K., 65
Agrippina, 159
Alès, A. de', 19, 66, 115, 162
Alger of Lüttich, 15
Amann, E., 65
Aphesis, 76–78, 255–58, 263, 266, 273, 276–79, 308
Apocatastasis, 258, 261, 273, 304
Apostasy, 67–68, 175–76
Aquinas, Thomas, 15–17, 22, 151, 202, 313, 321
Attritio, 16, 270
Augustine, Saint, 82, 126, 139, 163, 168, 176, 198, 207–8, 213, 215, 270, 281, 311, 320
Auricular confession, 13
Authentic existence, 4

Ban, the synagogal, 243–45
Baptism, 4–7, 9, 11–12, 23–25, 27, 34, 38–39, 42–43, 45–47, 49–50, 52, 70–71, 135–36, 235–37
  and *aphesis,* 256–58
  and Confirmation, 157
  by heretics, 163–64
  of heretics, 159–60
  and imposition of hands, 158, 166
  Origen's notion of, 250–51
  and remission of sin, 171–72, 184–87
  see also Forgiveness, Grace, Penance
Baptism of blood, 43, 48–49, 68, 256
Baptism of fire, 258
Baptism of desire, 208
Barnabas, Letter of, 35–36
Batiffol, P., 65
Bishop, 131, 133–35, 138–39
  and confession, 154–55
  and Confirmation, 168
  and excommunication, 282, 284–86, 302
  and imposition of hands, 156
  power of, 192–93, 300
  and reconciliation, 206
Bonaventure, 15–17
Bonwetsch, G. N., 114
Burchard of Worms, 15

Callistus, Pope, 10, 176
Campenhausen, H. von, 225
Connolly, R. H., 231, 241
Capital sins, 9, 11–12, 44, 47–48, 50–51, 65–66, 68, 127, 129–30, 146–47, 218–19, 242, 287, 305
Carthage, synod of, 10
Cerdon, 9, 107
Chalon-sur-Saône, synod of, 15
Christian initiation, 157–58, 162, 166, 169

Church, 7–13
and forgiveness, 139–40, 179
and guilt, 15
interior hierarchy of, 297
and mortal sin, 261–62
prayer of, 143–44, 146, 150
and reconciliation, 20, 142, 147–49, 157, 191, 194, 293–96, 298–99, 301
relationship of to sinner, 61–62, 110
and salvation, 199
and sin, 6, 24, 129, 175, 280
teaching of Hermas on, 85–86, 89–90, 95, 108–9
Church penance, 13–14, 17, 19, 21, 89, 92–93, 95–98, 100–101, 104, 106, 109, 111–12, 118, 126–33, 137–38, 141–42, 150, 155, 173, 176, 190, 205, 207, 211, 261
Clement, First Letter of, 35–36
Clement, Second Letter of, 35, 39–40
Clement of Alexandria, 78, 82, 109, 185, 188, 241, 255
Clement of Rome, 64
Columban, penetential of, 14
Concupiscence, 4
Confession, 14–15, 17, 130, 153–55, 211–12
Confirmation, 10, 156–63, 165–70, 234–35
Constitutiones Apostolorum, 235, 242, 244
Contrition, 16
Conversion
see Metanoia
Cornelius, Pope, 193, 207
Correptio secreta, 12
Cyprian of Carthage, 10, 19, 41, 52, 59, 62, 109, 112, 115, 126, 132, 134, 152–63, 165, 167–90, 192–94, 196–208, 211, 216, 220, 250–51, 275–76, 302–3, 310

De la Taille, M., 17
De Lubac, H., 17
Death, 35–36, 40
and sin, 24–25, 27, 31, 254, 259, 272
Dibelius, M., 65
Didache, 35–36
Didascalia Apostolorum, 53, 109, 156, 158–59, 167, 176, 197, 225–27, 229, 231, 233–37, 239–45, 302, 304
Donaldson, J., 119–20
Donatism, 61, 281, 285–86, 320, 327
Duns Scotus, J., 16

Eschatology, 262
Esser, G., 19
Estius, W., 30
Eucharist, 5, 8, 10–11, 37, 61–62, 110, 140, 153, 155, 170, 175, 177, 191, 196–97, 210, 212, 216, 234, 281, 290–91
Excommunication, 10, 12, 58–59, 61–64, 87–88, 90–98, 101–5, 109–13, 129, 131–33, 135–36, 141, 209–10, 212, 216, 228–29, 242–44, 261, 280–92, 301–2, 312, 314
effect of, 233
liturgical, 232, 234
penance of, 306–10, 315–16
real, 230–31
Exhomologesis, 130, 132–34, 136–37, 141–43, 153–55, 169, 177, 189–90, 198, 220
Exorcism, 168, 170

Firmilian of Caesarea, 163, 165, 179, 304
Fischer, J. A., 106
Fleming, J., 225, 242
Forgiveness, 15–16, 19, 21, 68, 143, 147
see also Sin
Fortunatus, 41
Freedom, 266–68, 274
Funk, F. X., 65

Galtier, P., 19, 60, 66, 202, 218–19, 225
Gnostic
see Gnosticism
Gnosticism, 40–43, 118, 247, 267, 274
Grace, 3–4, 6, 8, 16, 24–25, 27–31, 33, 36–41
loss of, 42–48, 50, 52–53
Origen's teaching on, 266, 268, 276, 278
and personal penance, 277
Gratian, Decree of, 15
Grotz, J., vii, 22, 58–64, 69, 87–97, 101–5, 108–11, 209, 225
Guilt, 5, 21, 145–49, 185–86, 201, 274, 276

Harnack, A. von, 18, 65, 226, 322
Harvey, W. Wigan, 119
Hegel, G. W. F., 248
Hermas, Shepherd of, 8–9, 19, 31, 35, 38–41, 45–56, 57–61, 63–112, 117, 157–58, 160, 176, 197, 207, 241–42, 245, 255
Hippolytus, 10, 41, 100, 128, 167, 229, 303, 309
Hoh, J., 65, 94, 97, 115
Holy Spirit
  see Spirit
Huge of St.-Cher, 15
Hus, Jan, 17, 61
Hylomorphism, 321

Ignatius of Antioch, Letters of, 35–37, 106
Imposition of hands, 153, 156–70, 190–91, 196, 199, 234–37, 303–4
Indulgences, 20–21
Irenaeus of Lyon, 41–42, 45, 107, 114–115, 117–19

Jerome, Saint, 273
John, Gospel of, 6, 8, 193–94, 283, 326–27
Joly, R., 66
Judaism, 28, 243
Judgement, 25, 27, 32, 34–35, 116–18, 181, 193, 201, 269, 271–72, 277
Justification, 4
Justin Martyr, 100

Karpp, H., 22
Koch, H., 19, 65, 114, 202
Kolasis, 282

Law, 28–29
Lent, 11
Leo the Great, 132
Logos, 248, 254, 266–67, 269–71, 277–78
Luther, Martin, 17

Matthew, Gospel of, 6–9, 19, 63, 134, 192–94, 229, 238, 283, 298
Maximus, 83–84
Metanoia, 4, 10, 30, 41, 64, 67, 74–79, 83, 106, 112, 117–18, 157–58, 187, 241–43, 279, 294

Montanism, 9, 42, 45, 47, 52, 125, 134, 137–38, 143–45, 193
  see also Tertullian
Montanist
  see Montanism
Mortal sin
  see Sin
Muratorian Canon, 65
Mysterion, 247, 249

New Testament, 5–7, 23, 27, 31–32, 34–35, 37, 63, 109–10, 238
  notion of sin in, 24
Nicea, Council of, 12, 59
Novatian
  see Novatianism
Novatianism, 9, 10, 12, 41, 162, 208, 226

Old Testament, 34, 38, 63, 248, 264
Origen, 44, 53, 59, 109, 115, 131, 139, 156, 229, 236, 241, 246–48, 269–71
  and activity of saints, 298–99
  and Church, 249–50, 293–97
  and ecclesial aspect of sin, 279–80
  and excommunication, 281–92, 301–2, 309–10, 312, 315
  and human freedom, 267–68
  and reconciliation, 300, 303–8, 311, 313–14, 320
  and relationship of grace and penance, 277–78
  and sacrament of penance, 324–28
  and sacramental sign, 321, 323
  and sin, 251–55, 258–66, 272–75
  and stages of the penitential process, 317–19, 322
Original sin, 40, 271

Paenitentia interior, 16
Paenitentia publica, 12, 19–20
Paenitentia secunda, 136–38, 143, 148, 159, 190
Paenitentia solemnis, 15
Penance, 3–6, 38–39, 41
  and baptism, 135–36
  and confession, 17
  of the dying, 14
  effects of, 141–42, 180
  of excommunication, 10, 12–13, 62–64, 87–88, 92–96, 109–11, 113

and forgiveness, 138
and grace, 266
and history of dogma, 18–22
and imposition of hands, 156–57, 167–69, 196
and judgement, 271
juridical, 275
obligation of, 207
and participation in Christ, 278
personal-ecclesial, 177–78
post-baptismal, 114–15
practice of, 132–33
and reconciliation, 150, 134, 143
and remission of sin, 172, 263
repeatability of, 217
sacrament of, 205–6, 293–94, 324–28
sacramental, 11, 15, 59, 209–13, 215, 218
and sorrow, 182–83
and satisfaction, 179, 201–2
stages of, 153–54
teaching of Hermas on, 65–66, 68–76, 97, 100
teaching of Tertullian on, 42–44, 46, 49–50
unrepeatable character of, 79–82
see also Church penance

Personal penance, 11, 279, 314
Pius I, Pope, 65
Pleroma, 40
Pneuma, 31, 40
Polycarp, Letter of, 35
Poschmann, B., vii, 17, 19–22, 57, 59, 66, 84, 90, 106, 108, 115, 117, 127, 148, 172, 181, 225
Private penance, 21, 58–60, 132, 209–18, 220–21
Public penance, 13, 21, 58–60, 92, 131, 147, 209–18, 220–21, 287
Puech, H.-Ch, 65
Punishment, 21, 32, 185–86, 201, 274–76

Rahner, K., 59
Rauschen, G., 65
Reconciliation, 5, 7–11, 13, 17, 21, 62, 106–8, 110, 134–36, 138–39, 141, 146–47, 149–50, 153–70, 190–91, 194, 200, 206–9, 219, 240, 296–99, 303–6, 308, 310, 312–13, 315–16, 319–20
rite of, 234, 236, 238, 302

Reformation, 17
Regula Fidei, 114–15, 118–19
Res et sacramentum, 16, 19, 21, 317, 319
Rigorism, 41, 44, 128, 226, 262
See also Montanism, Tertullian
Ripelius, Hugo, 17
Roberts, A., 119–20
Rome, synod of, 10
Rufinus, 261

Sacrament, effect of, 15–17
Sacramental sign, 16
Saint-Palais d'Aussac, 170
Salvation, 4, 8–9, 31, 199, 264
Sanctifying grace, 23
see also Grace
Satisfactio, 182–83, 188, 190, 194–95, 197–98, 200–6
Schmaus, M., 17
Schwartz, E., 65, 225–26
Second baptism, 43, 48, 68, 158
Second penance, 74
Seeberg, R., 65
Semi-Pelagians, 150
Simon Magister, 15
Sin, 3–4, 6–8
and the Apostolic Fathers, 35–40, 42
basic distinction of in Origen, 252–53
confession of, 131
consequences of, 26, 41
and death, 31–32
ecclesial, 280–81
eschatological notion of, 25
and excommunication, 61, 228, 291
forgiveness of, 72–74, 78–79, 81
habitual, 23
juridical-ethical, 24
mortal, 10, 46, 50, 52–53, 128–29, 173–76, 227, 254, 259–69, 276, 287
and the New Testament, 27–30, 33–34
post-baptismal, 77, 172
and punishment, 273–75
and reconciliation, 305
remission of, 20, 75, 171, 184, 203, 258
teaching of Hermas on, 67–68
teaching of Tertullian on, 43
unforgiveable, 47–48, 51, 127

Smith, J. P., 120
Sorrow, 3–4, 15–16, 182–83, 201–2

Spirit, 25, 30, 39, 45–46, 52–53, 150, 156, 158–59, 162–64, 167, 197–200, 236–37, 266–67, 276, 294, 314
  sin against the, 234, 255–56
Stephen I, Pope, 159–65, 167, 196, 204, 207
Stoics, 150
Stufler, J., 19, 66, 115
Subjective penance, 11, 13, 21, 98, 141–43, 148, 151, 153, 160, 169, 177, 266, 276
Symbolon, 322–23
Synergism, 266

Tertullian, 6, 9, 17, 19, 41–53, 68, 82, 100, 107–9, 125–31, 133–50, 152, 154, 156–58, 160, 164, 172, 185, 189–90, 197, 203–4, 207, 218–19, 241
Toledo, synod of, 13
Trent, Council of, 6, 17
Trofinus, 207

Vatican, Second Council of, 17, 21
Venial sin
  see Sin

William of Auvergne, 15
William of Melitona, 15
Windisch, H., 61, 65, 114
Wycliffe, John, 17, 61

Xiberta, B., 17, 19